THE SOCIAL PSYCHOLOGY
OF MORALITY

THE SOCIAL PSYCHOLOGY OF MORALITY

Exploring the Causes of Good and Evil

Edited by Mario Mikulincer and Phillip R. Shaver

American Psychological Association • Washington, DC

Published by
American Psychological Association
750 First Street, NE
Washington, DC 20002
www.apa.org

To order
APA Order Department
P.O. Box 92984
Washington, DC 20090-2984
Tel: (800) 374-2721; Direct: (202) 336-5510
Fax: (202) 336-5502; TDD/TTY: (202) 336-6123
Online: www.apa.org/pubs/books
E-mail: order@apa.org

In the U.K., Europe, Africa, and the Middle East, copies may be ordered from
American Psychological Association
3 Henrietta Street
Covent Garden, London
WC2E 8LU England

Typeset in Goudy by Circle Graphics, Inc., Columbia, MD

Printer: Maple-Vail Books, York, PA
Cover Designer: Mercury Publishing Services, Rockville, MD

The opinions and statements published are the responsibility of the authors, and such opinions and statements do not necessarily represent the policies of the American Psychological Association.

Library of Congress Cataloging-in-Publication Data

The social psychology of morality : exploring the causes of good and evil / edited by Mario Mikulincer and Phillip R. Shaver.
     p. cm.
  Includes bibliographical references.
  ISBN-13: 978-1-4338-1011-4
  ISBN-10: 1-4338-1011-5
  1. Ethics. 2. Social psychology. I. Mikulincer, Mario. II. Shaver, Phillip R.
  BJ45.S635 2011
  155.2'5—dc23
                              2011019722

British Library Cataloguing-in-Publication Data

A CIP record is available from the British Library.

Printed in the United States of America
First Edition

DOI: 10.1037/13091-000

THE HERZLIYA SERIES ON PERSONALITY
AND SOCIAL PSYCHOLOGY

Mario Mikulincer and Phillip R. Shaver, Series Editors

Series Titles

Prosocial Motives, Emotions, and Behavior: The Better Angels of Our Nature
Edited by Mario Mikulincer and Phillip R. Shaver

Human Aggression and Violence: Causes, Manifestations, and Consequences
Edited by Phillip R. Shaver and Mario Mikulincer

The Social Psychology of Morality: Exploring the Causes of Good and Evil
Edited by Mario Mikulincer and Phillip R. Shaver

CONTENTS

CONTRIBUTORS

Avi Assor, PhD, Department of Educational Psychology, School of Education, Ben-Gurion University, Beer-Sheva, Israel

Shahar Ayal, PhD, School of Psychology, Interdisciplinary Center Herzliya, Herzliya, Israel

Brock Bastian, PhD, Department of Psychology, University of Queensland, Brisbane, Australia

Roy F. Baumeister, PhD, Department of Psychology, Florida State University, Tallahassee

Paul Bloom, PhD, Department of Psychology, Yale University, New Haven, CT

Fiery Cushman, PhD, Department of Psychology, Harvard University, Boston, MA

Peter H. Ditto, PhD, Department of Psychology, University of California, Irvine

Guy Doron, PhD, School of Psychology, Interdisciplinary Center Herzliya, Herzliya, Israel

William L. Dunlop, MA, Department of Psychology, University of British Columbia, Vancouver, Canada

Tal Eyal, PhD, Department of Psychology, Ben-Gurion University of the Negev, Beer-Sheva, Israel

Jeremy A. Frimer, MA, Department of Psychology, University of British Columbia, Vancouver, Canada

Francesca Gino, PhD, Harvard Business School, Harvard University, Boston, MA

Jesse Graham, PhD, Department of Psychology, University of Virginia, Charlottesville

Kurt Gray, PhD, Department of Psychology, University of Maryland, College Park

Joshua Greene, PhD, Department of Psychology, Harvard University, Boston, MA

Jonathan Haidt, PhD, Department of Psychology, University of Virginia, Charlottesville

Nick Haslam, PhD, School of Behavioral Science, University of Melbourne, Melbourne, Australia

Gilad Hirschberger, PhD, School of Psychology, Interdisciplinary Center Herzliya, Herzliya, Israel

Ronnie Janoff-Bulman, PhD, Department of Psychology, University of Massachusetts at Amherst

Michael Kyrios, PhD, Faculty of Life and Social Sciences, Swinburne University of Technology, Melbourne, Australia

Simon Laham, PhD, Department of Psychology, University of Melbourne, Melbourne, Australia

Nira Liberman, PhD, Department of Psychology, Tel-Aviv University, Tel-Aviv, Israel

Brittany Liu, MA, Department of Psychology, University of California, Irvine

Stephen Loughnan, PhD, Department of Psychology, University of Kent, Canterbury, England

Anna Merritt, MA, Department of Psychology, Stanford University, Stanford, CA

Mario Mikulincer, PhD, School of Psychology, Interdisciplinary Center Herzliya, Herzliya, Israel

Benoît Monin, PhD, Department of Psychology, Stanford University, Stanford, CA

Laurie Anne Pearlman, PhD, Independent Practice, Holyoke, MA

David A. Pizarro, PhD, Department of Psychology, Cornell University, Ithaca, NY

Tom Pyszczynski, PhD, Department of Psychology, University of Colorado at Colorado Springs

Sonia Roccas, PhD, Department of Education and Psychology, The Open University of Israel, Raanana, Israel

Lilach Sagiv, PhD, School of Business, The Hebrew University of Jerusalem, Jerusalem, Israel

Dar Sar-El, PhD, School of Psychology, Interdisciplinary Center Herzliya, Herzliya, Israel

Phillip R. Shaver, PhD, Department of Psychology, University of California, Davis

Linda J. Skitka, PhD, Department of Psychology, University of Illinois at Chicago

Ervin Staub, PhD, Department of Psychology, University of Massachusetts at Amherst

Noga Sverdlik, PhD, Department of Education and Psychology, The Open University of Israel, Raanana, Israel, and School of Psychology, Interdisciplinary Center Herzliya, Herzliya, Israel

David Tannenbaum, MA, Department of Psychology, University of California, Irvine

Lawrence J. Walker, PhD, Department of Psychology, University of British Columbia, Vancouver, Canada

Daniel M. Wegner, PhD, Department of Psychology, Harvard University, Cambridge, MA

ACKNOWLEDGMENTS

We are grateful to everyone who made the preparation of this book enjoyable and successful. We thank all of the chapter authors—an amazing group of scholars and warm human beings who care about both science and the betterment of humanity. We also thank Professor Uriel Reichmann, president of the Interdisciplinary Center Herzliya, who provided financial and staff support for an annual series of conferences on Personality and Social Psychology. We thank the staff of the Interdisciplinary Center Herzliya—Keren Mifano, Tammy Berger, Shulli Sardes, and Tsachi Ein-Dor—who handled all of the arrangements for the conference, dealt effectively with many on-site details, and coped masterfully with the inevitable glitches and minicrises. We also thank Maureen Adams, senior acquisitions editor at APA Books, for seeing the value of this book and the conference series from which it originated and for being a generous, thoughtful, and supportive friend during this book's preparation. Finally, we thank the anonymous reviewers for their useful comments and staff members at APA Books for their careful copyediting, indexing, design, and production of the finished product.

THE SOCIAL PSYCHOLOGY
OF MORALITY

INTRODUCTION

MARIO MIKULINCER AND PHILLIP R. SHAVER

Human beings are, and always have been, deeply concerned with good and evil, right and wrong, and innocence and guilt, as we know from the oldest written records; the annals of philosophy, religion, and literature; and our own daily struggles. It's impossible to peer into one's own "heart" or to look outward at the social and political world, as brought home daily by the mass media, without immediately sensing that some things are right, sometimes even heroically virtuous, and some are terribly wrong, sometimes to the point of being evil, no matter how that troublesome term is defined. It's also obvious that people often disagree about which actions are good and which are evil. "Our" good is sometimes "their" evil, although often, if we set aside our personal and ideological investments and defenses, we notice that there is considerable agreement across individuals, cultures, and religions about the fundamentals.

In the previous two volumes of the Herzliya Series on Personality and Social Psychology, we focused, first, on prosocial motives, emotions, and behavior (Mikulincer & Shaver, 2009) and then on aggression, violence, and their effects (Shaver & Mikulincer, 2010). Authors of chapters in those two volumes provided solid, convincing, scholarly evidence that both kindness and cruelty

3

have evolutionary and genetic roots and that both are affected by experiences, situations, and cultural norms and ideologies. In this, the third volume in the series, we examine ways in which people make decisions about what is right and what is wrong—what is good and what is evil—and how these decisions are influenced by internal psychological and external social and cultural forces. In the process of examining various aspects of morality, we address several questions: What are the foundations of virtuous and evil behavior? Where do moral rules and standards come from? How does "conscience" work? Are there measurable individual differences in conscience and moral character? Are there domains in which morality shades over into psychopathology, or domains in which psychopathology erodes or eclipses morality? What accounts for evil behavior? What causes people to defend themselves and condemn others when moral issues are raised or debated, despite the existence of fairly universal standards of moral behavior and universal feelings of revulsion in response to moral hypocrisy? Is moral judgment mainly a matter of cognition and rules or of feelings and "the gut"? How do people become involved in, and then try to justify, everything from lying and cheating to genocide? How can morality be clarified and encouraged?

These are ancient questions, perhaps never to be fully answered. Yet they arise daily in everyone's lives and are discussed constantly and endlessly in families, in the media, in classrooms, in legislatures, at the United Nations, and in diverse religious communities. In this volume, we consider the discoveries of a contemporary group of psychological researchers who are probing diverse issues related to morality and immorality. Much creative thinking and brilliant research have occurred in recent years in an effort to answer age-old questions about morality and moral heroism, on the one hand, and destructive behavior and the rationalization of evil, on the other. Top researchers in this vibrant scientific field generously agreed to contribute to this book after lecturing on their work and engaging in intense discussions of it at the Interdisciplinary Center Herzliya in Israel. As a group, these contributions represent many of the newest and most exciting approaches to the study of moral psychology and its relation to prosocial and antisocial behavior.

PSYCHOLOGICAL APPROACHES

Morality was considered first in the social sciences by sociologists such as Emile Durkheim (who lived from 1858 to 1917). They were concerned with how religious and moral systems organize and constrain individuals' behavior. Their work was motivated by a concern that modern industrial societies might weaken the hold of traditional moral and religious systems on individuals and contribute to a plague of crime, anomie, and suicide. Within psychology, a more individualistic science, theorizing about morality was dominated by cognitive–rationalistic approaches that emphasized the importance of moral reasoning and reflection as well as general cognitive capabilities (e.g., John Piaget's work from the 1920s to the 1960s). These approaches, with roots extending back to Immanuel Kant's rationalistic theory of ethics, downplayed emotions, intuitions, and internal and interpersonal conflicts as well as unconscious, irrational mental forces. They seemed to advocate a form of moral education that would lead, ideally, to everyone becoming a thoughtful judge.

The most influential psychologist who endorsed the rationalistic approach to morality was Lawrence Kohlberg, who wrote in 1971 that

> the moral force in personality is cognitive. Affective forces are involved in moral decisions, but affect is neither moral nor immoral. When the affective arousal is channeled into moral directions, it is moral; when it is not so channeled, it is not. The moral channeling mechanisms themselves are cognitive. (pp. 230–231)

Eventually, although the cognitive–rationalistic approach to morality continued to be influential, it was challenged, first by Carol Gilligan (1982), who worked with Kohlberg but began to notice that women and girls were more likely than men and boys to include in their moral judgments not just ideas about justice but also feelings of "care." More recently, in a revolutionary article, Haidt (2001), coauthor of the opening chapter in this volume, highlighted four issues that a cognitive approach to morality cannot handle. First, although some moral judgments are based on conscious reasoning, reflection, and deliberation, others are made rapidly and automatically without conscious reasoning (Chapter 2, this volume). Second, the cognitive approach to morality portrays moral judgment as a truth-seeking process (both Piaget and Kohlberg tended to view children and adults as amateur scientists as well as logicians), which makes it difficult to explain why, in many cases, people behave more like lawyers defending a client than like objective, disinterested judges. Moral actors are often affected by what Kunda (1990) called "motivated reasoning" (e.g., Chapters 3 and 5, this volume). Third, a cognitive approach to morality assumes that conscious reasoning precedes judgment and behavior, but there is considerable evidence that moral reasoning is often post hoc—an attempt to explain and justify intuitive judgments and moral or immoral actions (Chapters 11, 20, and 21, this volume). Fourth, the cognitive approach has difficulty explaining why moral judgments and actions often covary more directly with moral emotions (e.g., sympathy, empathy, disgust, guilt) than with conscious reasoning (Chapter 1, this volume).

The cognitive approach to morality also has trouble explaining why moral judgments and choices are based not only on issues such as harm, rights, justice, and fairness but also on considerations of loyalty, authority, and purity (Chapter 1, this volume). Moreover, recent research shows

- that moral judgments and actions are present even in the first year of life, before language and rationality have developed very far (Chapter 4, this volume);
- that emotion regulation and self-regulation influence moral judgments (Chapters 7, 14, and 18, this volume);
- that conscious reasoning and reflection are often used to justify or obfuscate dishonest behavior, moral hypocrisy, and moral inconsistency (Chapters 8 and 9, this volume);
- that what we might expect to be morally irrelevant motivational and cognitive processes in fact influence moral judgments and behavior (Chapters 10, 12, and 13, this volume);
- that moral judgments and decisions are often interpersonal, being influenced by other people's moral intuitions and actions (Chapter 6, this volume); and
- that moral reasoning can be distorted by psychopathology and may sometimes contribute to it (Chapters 16 and 17, this volume).

These limitations of the cognitive–rationalistic approach to moral psychology have inspired a new generation of social psychologists to begin to map unexplored regions of moral psychology, especially those having to do with emotions and emotion regulation, unconscious processes, evolutionary forces, intra- and interpersonal processes, egotistical motives and defenses, existential and social concerns, and group dynamics. These psychologists do not deny the importance of conscious reasoning and cognitive capabilities in some moral reasoning, but just as Tversky and Kahneman (1974) successfully challenged the "rational man" assumption in economics, the new generation of morality researchers are challenging the "rational person" model of moral judgments and decisions.

The conceptual ferment in the contemporary social psychology of morality is well portrayed in the present volume. Its chapters deal with basic biological and psychological processes that underlie moral choices and lead to both virtuous and despicable behavior. We hope and believe that these creative researchers' ideas and findings will inspire readers, including scholars and students, to enter this field and explore all aspects of morality, including good and evil behavior.

ORGANIZATION

The book is organized into six parts. The first, "Basic Issues and Controversies," includes six chapters dealing with conceptions of good and evil; moral reasoning and intuitions; moral universals and development; two approaches—deontological and consequentialist—to conceptualizing and explaining moral behavior; the formation of moral character; and the social nature of many moral judgments and actions. The second section of the book, "Motivational and Cognitive Processes," includes six chapters concerning basic psychological mechanisms involved in immoral behavior, moral hypocrisy, moral self-regulation, dehumanization, and moral values. The third section, "Developmental, Personality, and Clinical Aspects," includes five chapters on self-determination and attachment theories as they apply to morality, character development and moral trajectories, and the involvement of morality in psychological disorders such as obsessive–compulsive disorder, as well as psychotherapy with traumatized individuals who might be considered the victims of evil. The fourth section, "Good and Evil: Morality, Conflict, and Violence," includes four chapters that deal with societal aspects of good and evil and implications of morality for broader social, cultural, and political issues such as violence, intergroup conflict, and genocide. The fifth and final section of the book, "Synthesis," is an integrative commentary on the issues and approaches covered in the previous chapters.

The authors generously took time out of their busy schedules to fly to Israel, deliver fascinating lectures, participate in extensive discussions following each lecture, and return home to turn their lectures and discussion notes into this book. The meeting at which the talks were presented was cohosted by the two of us, and we worked with the chapter authors to make the book as provocative, engaging, coherent, and accessible as possible so that it can be read and digested by researchers, educators, students, and the literate public. Readers of the book from the fields of personality, social, and clinical psychology; the close relationships field; developmental psychology; neuroscience; and political psychology will gain a deeper and broader understanding of morality and its social and psychological effects. They will also learn useful methods for studying morality and promising psychological and social interventions to reduce immoral behavior, which at times reaches levels that almost anyone would consider evil.

REFERENCES

Gilligan, C. (1982). *In a different voice. Psychological theory and women's development.* Cambridge, MA: Harvard University Press.

Haidt, J. (2001). The emotional dog and its rational tail: A social intuitionist approach to moral judgment. *Psychological Review, 108,* 814–834. doi:10.1037/0033-295X.108.4.814

Kunda, Z. (1990). The case for motivated reasoning. *Psychological Bulletin, 108,* 480–498. doi:10.1037/0033-2909.108.3.480

Mikulincer, M., & Shaver, P. R. (Eds.). (2009). *Prosocial motives, emotions, and behavior: The better angels of our nature.* Washington, DC: American Psychological Association.

Shaver, P. R., & Mikulincer, M. (Eds.). (2010). *Human aggression and violence: Causes, manifestations, and consequences.* Washington, DC: American Psychological Association.

Tversky, A., & Kahneman, D. (1974). Judgment under uncertainty: Heuristics and biases. *Science, 185,* 1124–1131. doi:10.1126/science.185.4157.1124

I

BASIC ISSUES
AND CONTROVERSIES

1

SACRED VALUES AND EVIL ADVERSARIES: A MORAL FOUNDATIONS APPROACH

JESSE GRAHAM AND JONATHAN HAIDT

At the age of 87, several years after he had stopped writing, Isaiah Berlin responded to an invitation from a Chinese professor to summarize his ideas for publication in China. He produced an extraordinary essay that defended moral pluralism and warned against its enemy, *moral monism* (or *moral absolutism*), which he defined as the thesis that "to all true questions there must be one true answer and one only, all the other answers being false." He then wrote,

> Most revolutionaries believe, covertly or overtly, that in order to create the ideal world eggs must be broken, otherwise one cannot obtain the omelette. Eggs are certainly broken—never more violently or ubiquitously than in our times—but the omelette is far to seek, it recedes into an infinite distance. That is one of the corollaries of unbridled monism, as I call it—some call it fanaticism, but monism is at the root of every extremism. (Berlin, 1998, p. 14)

In this chapter, we build upon Berlin's idea[1] and argue that the elevation or sacralization of a moral principle or symbol is a major cause of evil. This idea has been developed quite ably by others in recent years (see Chapter 20, this volume, on "idealistic evil"; Glover, 1999, on tribalism; and Skitka & Mullen, 2002, and Chapter 19, this volume, on the "dark side" of moral convictions). We hope to add to these analyses of morality and evil by offering a map of moral space that may be helpful in explaining why so many different principles and objects can become sacred, along with an account of how sacredness permits and motivates different patterns of evil behavior.

We begin by defining our key terms—sacredness and morality. We then introduce moral foundations theory as a way of broadening and mapping the moral domain and thereby identifying diverse kinds of sacred objects. In the third section, we show how this moral foundations approach can also broaden our view of evil, and we offer a definition of evil based on group-level perceptions of threats to sacralized objects. In the fourth section, we take a qualitative approach to sacredness, showing how two diametrically opposed moralities can both lead to idealistic violence. In the fifth section, we introduce the Moral Foundations Sacredness Scale, a simple instrument that can be used to measure the degree to which people sacralize each of the five foundations of morality. We conclude by considering unanswered questions about which foundational values are most likely to lead to idealistic violence.

SACREDNESS AND MORALITY

Evidence for totemism, animal worship, and other protoreligious practices goes back tens of thousands of years; even *Homo neanderthalensis* may have treated some objects as sacred (Solecki, 1975). Human beings have been engaged in religious practices for so long, with such intensity, and so ubiquitously that many researchers now believe that religion is an evolutionary adaptation (e.g., Wilson, 2002), even if belief in gods may have originally emerged as a by-product of other cognitive capacities (Atran & Norenzayan, 2004; Boyer, 2003; Kirkpatrick, 1999). But as we have argued elsewhere (Graham & Haidt, 2010), the social psychology of religion should not focus on belief in gods; it should focus on the group-binding and society-constituting effects of ritual practice and other religious behaviors. Whether one believes that God is a delusion, a reality, or an adaptation, it is hard to deny that human behav-

---

[1]We note that Berlin's use of the word *monism* did not refer to the elevation of a single moral principle but rather to the belief that there is a single correct truth, which might involve several moral principles. Nonetheless, as we argue, when any moral principles are sacralized, the result may be the kind of certainty, self-righteousness, and even willingness to "break eggs" in pursuit of those moral principles that Berlin warned about.

ior now includes a rather strong tendency to invest objects, people, places, days, colors, words, and shapes with extraordinary importance that is in no way justified by practical or utilitarian considerations (Eliade, 1959). The psychology of sacredness may (or may not) have coevolved with belief in gods, but it is now a very general aspect of human nature. We believe that sacredness is crucial for understanding morality, including fully secular moralities.

The academic study of sacredness is roughly a century old, and most of the major treatments of it have emphasized the radical discontinuity between sacredness and the concerns of ordinary life. Nisbet (1966/1993) summarized the sociological use of the word: "The sacred includes the mores, the nonrational, the religious and ritualistic ways of behavior that are valued beyond whatever utility they possess" (p. 6). The first major treatment of sacredness came from Emile Durkheim (1915/1965), who argued that the distinction between sacred and profane (i.e., ordinary, practical) is among the most fundamental and generative aspects of human cognition. It is generative because sacredness is always a collective representation serving collective functions. Shared emotions and practices related to sacred things bind people together into cults, churches, and communities. Sacredness does not require a God. Flags, national holidays, and other markers of collective solidarity are sacred in the same way—and serve the same group-binding function—as crosses and holy days.

A few years later, Rudolph Otto (1917/1958) wrote about *das Heilige* (from the Greek *heilos*, translated as "sacred" or "holy") as something that could in different instances be mysterious, awe inspiring, or terrifying but that above all was "wholly other," a category completely separate from ordinary life. Following Otto, Eliade (1959) explored the psychological and phenomenological aspects of sacredness, but he also followed Durkheim in emphasizing its social functions. People want to live in a sacralized cosmos, he said, and they work together to create dense webs of shared meanings that valorize their land, their traditions, and their place at the center of the cosmos. Eliade noted that Western modernity was a historical aberration in having created the first fully desacralized, profane world. But he also noted that sacredness cannot be entirely removed from people's lives. When deprived of shared sacred objects, people still invest certain dates, objects, and places with a kind of sacred importance—for example, things related to the first time one fell in love or traveled abroad:

> Even for the most frankly nonreligious man, all these places still retain an exceptional, a unique quality; they are the "holy places" of his private universe, as if it were in such spots that he had received the revelation of a reality *other* than that in which he participates through his ordinary daily life. (Eliade, 1959, p. 24)

Psychologists have operationalized sacredness in ways that are consistent with these earlier approaches. Tetlock, Kristel, Elson, Green, and Lerner (2000) concentrated on the absolute separation from the profane, defining *sacred values* as "any value that a moral community explicitly or implicitly treats as possessing infinite or transcendental significance that precludes comparisons, trade-offs, or indeed any other mingling with bounded or secular values" (p. 853). They found that when participants were asked to resolve dilemmas in which sacred values (i.e., human life) could be traded off for a profane value (i.e., money), they often felt tainted and immoral, and they sometimes refused to make trade-offs at all. Ritov and Baron (1999) examined *protected* values—defined as "those that people think should not be traded off" (p. 79)—and found that when such values are activated, people are more likely to show the omission bias and become less utilitarian (see also Baron & Spranca, 1997).

We draw from these treatments of sacredness to offer this definition, tailored for use in moral psychology: *Sacredness* refers to the human tendency to invest people, places, times, and ideas with importance far beyond the utility they possess. Trade-offs or compromises involving what is sacralized are resisted or refused. In prototypical cases, these investments tie individuals to larger groups with shared identities and ennobling projects, and so trade-offs or compromises are felt to be acts of betrayal, even in nonprototypical cases in which no group is implicated.

This definition of sacredness complements our definition of morality. Because we have emphasized the diversity of moral content across cultures, we have avoided definitions of the moral domain that list specific principles or virtues (e.g., Turiel's [1983] stipulation that morality involves matters of "justice, rights, and welfare" exclusively, and all else is social convention or personal preference). Rather, we have taken a social-functionalist approach (Keltner & Haidt, 1999) and defined moral systems by what they do: *Moral systems* are interlocking sets of values, virtues, norms, practices, identities, institutions, technologies, and evolved psychological mechanisms that work together to suppress or regulate selfishness and make coordinated social life possible (adapted from Haidt, 2008).

Considering these two definitions together, the relevance of sacredness for moral psychology should be apparent. The human ability to live peacefully and cooperatively in large groups of nonkin is one of the greatest puzzles in the social sciences, particularly for those who take an evolutionary perspective (Darwin, 1871/1998; Henrich & Henrich, 2007: Richerson & Boyd, 2005). The existence and resilience of human moral systems require an explanation. If the "evolved psychological mechanisms" that are part of moral systems include a psychology of sacredness, then the puzzle is much easier to solve[2] than

---

[2] Of course, this move just pushes the evolutionary puzzle back one step: How did human beings evolve a psychology of sacredness that made them fail to pursue their individual self-interest? We believe that this question is perfectly answered by theories of multilevel selection in which genes are passed on as individuals compete with individuals and as groups compete with groups (see Haidt & Kesebir, 2010; Wilson, 2002).

if human beings are modeled as fully profane—that is, as rational agents in pursuit of self-interest, broadly construed. In the next section, we present our theory of morality (Haidt & Graham, 2007) as augmented by greater attention to questions of sacredness.

MORALITY IS CONSTRUCTED ON FIVE FOUNDATIONS

Moral foundations theory was first proposed by two cultural psychologists who noticed convergences between anthropological descriptions of morality and evolutionary theories of human sociality. For example, anthropological accounts of reciprocal gift giving as a means of forging relationships (Malinowski, 1922) bore obvious similarities to evolutionary discussions of "reciprocal altruism" (Trivers, 1971). Haidt and Joseph (2004) drew on several existing accounts of moral variation (especially that of Shweder, Much, Mahapatra, & Park, 1997) to propose that there are five innate psychological "foundations" upon which cultures construct widely divergent moral systems: harm/care, fairness/reciprocity, ingroup/loyalty, authority/respect, and purity/sanctity. Graham, Haidt, and Nosek (2009) developed several ways to measure endorsement of these five foundations (e.g., the Moral Foundations Questionnaire), and found a pattern that has now been replicated many times: Political liberals value care (non-harm) and fairness more than conservatives, whereas conservatives value ingroup, authority, and purity more than liberals. In addition, liberals show a greater preference for care and fairness concerns over the other three kinds of moral concerns, whereas conservatives value all five foundations relatively equally. However, people's scores on all five foundations can vary independently, and variations among many different moral patterns can be modeled as instantiations of different settings on a kind of "moral equalizer" with five sliding controls.[3]

Perhaps because the equalizer metaphor is intuitively appealing, and perhaps because we have frequently presented simple graphs showing how groups differ on the five scores provided by the Moral Foundations Questionnaire, many readers of our work have interpreted moral foundations theory as a kind of multiple regression theory of morality. Like the Big Five theory of personality, all you need to know about a person is his or her static and stable scores on five traits or dimensions. However, from our earliest writings we have emphasized that foundations are just foundations. A morality must be constructed on top of those foundations, and the construction process is always done socially, as part of one's development within specific ecological settings and subcultures.

---

[3]We are indebted to Will Wilkinson for this metaphor.

We have found McAdams's work on narrative to be particularly helpful for understanding this construction process. McAdams (2001) studied *life stories*, which he described as "psychosocial constructions, coauthored by the person himself or herself and the cultural context within which the person's life is embedded and given meaning" (p. 101). Life stories help individuals make sense of their past experiences and guide them as they make choices about their futures. (See McAdams et al., 2008, for evidence that the life stories of liberals and conservatives, coded for foundation-related content, show the same pattern we have found using quantitative methods; see also Chapter 15, this volume, on the life stories of moral heroes.) For our work in political psychology, however, we have found it most useful to move from life stories to *ideological narratives* (Haidt, Graham, & Joseph, 2009).

In *The Political Brain*, Westen (2007) argued that successful political movements must have a story that explains the origins of present problems and shows why the movement offers a solution. He pointed out that coherent stories usually have an initial state ("Once upon a time . . ."), protagonists, a problem or obstacle, villains who stand in the way, a clash, and a denouement. These ideological narratives are clearly like life stories in most ways. For example, they always incorporate a reconstructed past and an imagined future, often telling a story of progress or of decline. But they are different from life stories in one key respect: Each person must be the first author of his or her own life story. More than a little bit of plagiarism would be shameful. But when people join together to pursue political projects—from the demand for civil rights to violent revolution to genocide—they must share a common story, one that they accept as true without having authored it. Ideological narratives, then, by their very nature, are always stories about good and evil. They identify heroes and villains, they explain how the villains got the upper hand, and they lay out or justify the means by which—if we can just come together and fight hard enough—we can vanquish the villains and return the world to its balanced or proper state.

Ideological narratives provide a crucial link between a psychological analysis of moral foundations and the sorts of violent extremists described by Berlin. First, we simply observe that people love stories. All around the world, cultures rely on stories to socialize their children, and narrative thinking has been called one of two basic forms of human cognition (along with logical reasoning; see Bruner, 1986). Second, we note that successful stories—the ones that get transmitted from person to person and decade to decade—are those that fit well with the human mind, particularly by eliciting strong emotions, as found in analyses of successful urban legends (Heath, Bell, & Sternberg, 2001). We think moral foundations theory provides the most comprehensive account of the "hooks" in the moral mind to which a good ideological narrative can attach. Third, we note that intergroup competition, and particularly warfare, causes prevailing ideological narratives to become more extreme, often to the point of being cartoonish (e.g., the frequent charge that one's enemies enjoy killing or even eating children). Such extreme narratives seem to serve the purpose of mobilizing and inspiring one's team and preparing the way for its members to "break eggs," as Berlin lamented. As Baumeister (1997) pointed out,

> One far-reaching difference between idealistic evil and other forms of evil is that idealistic evil is nearly always fostered by groups, as opposed to individuals. . . . To put this more bluntly: It is apparently necessary to have someone else tell you that violent means are justified by high ends. (p. 190)

THE FIVE FOUNDATIONS OF EVIL

Scientific treatments of evil have tended to define it in terms of a single moral foundation: harm/care. For instance, *evil* has been operationalized as "human actions that harm others" (Staub, 2003, p. 5; see also Chapter 21, this volume), "intentional interpersonal harm" (Baumeister, 1997, p. 8; see also Chapter 20, this volume), and "intentionally behaving—or causing others to act—in ways that demean, dehumanize, harm, destroy, or kill innocent people" (Zimbardo, 2004, p. 23). We share the normative intuition of these authors that the prototypes of evil are acts of cruelty and violence and would even agree that these are the most important kinds of evil to understand and prevent. However, as a descriptive account of the psychological underpinnings of positive and negative moral judgments, moral foundations theory suggests that perceptions of evil may be based on concerns other than harm, cruelty, and violence.

If ideological narratives can draw on any combination of the five foundations, then there can be many kinds of heroes and many kinds of villains. Table 1.1 shows how each foundation may be used to support the sacralization and demonization of diverse objects. The *sacred values* column lists the values that are set apart from everyday profane concerns and protected from trade-offs; they are moral concerns imbued with value far beyond practical utilities or self-interest. The *sacred objects* column lists the people, things, and ideas that can become sacralized because they are linked to these sacred values. And just as something is seen as worthy of ultimate protection, there is a vision of what it must be protected from: This is a vision of evil. Note that the visions in the *evil* column aren't simply people or things that go against the foundational concerns, like vices. Evil is something more, something that threatens to hurt, oppress, betray, subvert, contaminate, or otherwise profane something that is held as sacred. Also important to note is that the sacred object prompting the vision of evil is not held by just one person (say, a favorite teddy bear), but by a group who explicitly or implicitly cohere in these twin visions of

TABLE 1.1
Sacredness and Evil in Relation to Moral Foundations

Foundation	Sacred values	Sacred objects	Evil	Examples of idealistic violence
Harm	Nurturance, care, peace	Innocent victims, nonviolent leaders (e.g., Gandhi, M. L. King)	Cruel and violent people	Killing of abortion doctors, Weather Underground bombings
Fairness	Justice, karma, reciprocity	The oppressed, the unavenged	Racists, oppressors, capitalists	Vengeance killings, reciprocal attacks, feuds
Ingroup	Loyalty, self-sacrifice for group	Homeland, nation, flag, ethnic group	Traitors, outgroup members and their culture	Ethnic grudges, genocides, violent punishment for betrayals
Authority	Respect, tradition, honor	Authorities, social hierarchy, traditions, institutions	Anarchists, revolutionaries, subversives	Right-wing death squads, military atrocities, Abu Ghraib
Purity	Chastity, piety, self-control	Body, soul, sanctity of life, holy sites	Atheists, hedonists, materialists	Religious crusades, genocides, killing abortion doctors

sacredness and evil. More than just a very morally bad thing, evil is something special that comes out of a shared narrative and in fact could be said to play the starring role in that narrative. Evil is whatever stands in the way of sacredness.[4] The right column lists *examples of idealistic violence* (what Baumeister, 1997, called *idealistic evil*) and illustrates that the process of sacralizing objects according to sacred values (as well as the attendant process of developing a vision of evil in whatever threatens those objects) can lead to violent actions even if those sacred values are radically opposed to violence, like nurturance, care, or peace.

Our goal in presenting Table 1.1 is not to argue that there are five discrete kinds of evil. Evil emerges as communities construct ideological narratives and converge on a shared understanding of what their problems are, who caused them, and how to fight back. These narratives can build on several foundations—perhaps even on all five. Our goal is rather to show the diversity

---

[4]In Hebrew, the word for devil, *ha-satan*, means "obstacle" or "adversary."

of values and objects that can become sacralized and to show that evil is as diverse as morality. But this is all rather abstract.

QUALITATIVE APPROACH: NARRATIVES CONNECT SACRED PRINCIPLES TO ACTION

In this section, we provide two case studies of extreme ideological narratives, based on very different sets of moral foundations, that motivated people to commit idealistic violence.

Sacred Race: The Turner Diaries

Less than 30 miles from our offices in Virginia, one can find the headquarters of National Vanguard, one of America's largest White supremacist groups. This is a splinter group off the older National Alliance, which was led by William Pierce (author of *The Turner Diaries*, published under the pen name Alexander Macdonald) until his death in 2002. Provided the reader can stomach it, *The Turner Diaries* (Pierce, 1978) offers an in-depth look into the moral worldview of ultra-right-wing White supremacy and anti-Semitism, as its adherents want it to be seen. A narrator from an idealized, post-America Aryan future presents the diaries of Earl Turner, who led a resistance army against the diabolical "System." The System was dominated by Jewish human-rights advocates who outlawed guns and employed Black men to confiscate those guns from White people. White individuals were left defenseless as non-White people raped and pillaged at will. Turner wistfully remembered his "once upon a time" when the White population didn't have to live in fear, when their racial pride wasn't censored as hate speech and their second-amendment rights were upheld. As many have pointed out, *The Turner Diaries* is a compendium of right-wing fears and angers, augmented into a dystopian vision and then finally a utopian denouement as Turner deals the decisive blow to the System by flying a plane with a nuclear warhead into the Pentagon building.

Although one can find evidence of values related to fairness (reciprocity, vengeance) and authority (honor, social order), the book treats as sacred a tight constellation of values related to ingroup and purity above all: Loyalty and self-sacrifice for Turner's underground rebellion are painted as moral ideals, as are the self-control, cleanliness, and purity of the White race (presented in stark contrast to the vile, animalistic, and self-indulgent behavior of other races). The White race (and its "pure" bloodline) is the sacralized object to be protected, and the reader is encouraged to root and hope for its survival into future generations. With this vision of sacredness, of course, comes a vision of evil, and Pierce offered an amplified and even fetishized vision of the all-consuming power and viciousness of the Jewish and Black populations, who threaten the survival of the White race. By giving these exemplars of evil such power in his fictional world, Pierce brought the impulse to protect the sacralized object from evil to a fever pitch, and the reader is asked to cheer for the violence that is necessary (eggs must be broken) to achieve this morally sacred end.

At one point, Turner and his comrades load up a delivery truck with explosives and detonate it under a federal building:

> At 9:15 yesterday morning our bomb went off in the F.B.I.'s national headquarters building. . . . The damage is immense. [W]e gaped with a mixture of horror and elation at the devastation. . . . It is a heavy burden of responsibility for us to bear, since most of the victims of our bomb were only pawns who were no more committed to the sick philosophy of the racially destructive goals of the System than we are. But there is no way we can destroy the System without hurting many thousands of innocent people—no way. It is a cancer too deeply rooted in our flesh. And if we don't destroy the System before it destroys us—if we don't cut this cancer out of our living flesh—our whole race will die. (Pierce, 1978, p. 42)

This scene will sound familiar to American readers because something very similar was carried out by one of the book's biggest fans, Timothy McVeigh, in Oklahoma City on April 19, 1995. McVeigh was deeply committed to the book, selling it at gun shows and sending copies to his friends. When McVeigh carried out his own idealistic violence, he had pages from the book in his car and had mailed others to his sister and to the FBI. This horrific act of violence, which killed 168 people and wounded nearly 500 others, would not have been possible without a shared moral vision of sacred values (White pride, self-sacrifice for one's race, purity), sacred objects (the White race), and a vision of evil (international cabal of non-Whites and Jews), all built upon the foundations of ingroup and purity. It is also important to note that for these White supremacists, the lives of individual White people are valuable but not sacred. *The Turner Diaries* is full of meditations and metaphors (e.g., treating cancer) that justify the killing of individual White people to save and protect what is truly sacred: the White race.

Sacred Victims: The Weather Underground

The ingroup, authority, and purity foundations reinforce each other in many cases of tribal, ethnic, or nationalist fervor, and such causes tend to be supported by more conservative elements within a society. But the propensity for idealistic violence is not limited to the political right; any combination of foundations can be used to support an ideological narrative that motivates violence.

Splitting from the Students for a Democratic Society in the late 1960s, the Weather Underground was a militant left-wing group active throughout the 1970s. Like most student groups at the time, this group was passionately concerned about atrocities happening in Vietnam and about the injustice of the war itself. But their primary area of sacralization was Black victims in White America. Soaking up and producing reams of revolutionary and Communist literatures, the group—many of whom lived together in tightly knit quarters— quickly established an ideological narrative that split the moral world into black and white, and white was bad. Non-White populations, the poor class, and other oppressed peoples around the world were innocent victims deserving of justice, and White dominance (seen in both resistance to civil rights progress in the United States and imperialist actions in other countries) was the ultimate evil, harming and humiliating the sacred victims. Activist rhetoric quickly morphed from the nonviolence espoused by the Student Nonviolent Coordinating Committee to calls for open and armed revolt. After a series of bombings, the group went into hiding from the FBI in 1970 and started delivering communiqués to the press, including the following:

> It is our job to blast away the myths of the total superiority of the man. We did not choose to live in a time of war. We choose only to become guerillas and to urge our people to prepare for war rather than become accomplices in the genocide of our sisters and brothers. We learned from Amerikan [sic] history about policies of exterminating an entire people and their magnificent cultures—the Indians, the blacks, the Vietnamese. . . . Don't be tricked by talk. Arm yourselves and shoot to live! We are building a culture and a society that can resist genocide. (Dohrn, Ayers, & Jones, 2006, p. 157)

The members of the Weather Underground were horrified by the suffering and oppression of victims in their own time, and they wove that suffering into a larger narrative stretching back to the founding of America via genocide of Native Americans and enslavement of Africans. Once victims had been sacralized, the devil was clear: White capitalist America, which must be destroyed by any means available. Even though their morality was based squarely on the harm/care foundation, which generally makes people recoil from violence, the group found a way to justify and motivate violence. They perpetrated dozens of bombings, mostly of police stations and other buildings that could plausibly be said to be part of the "system." At one point they had planned to detonate a bomb at a noncommissioned officers' dance at the Fort Dix U.S. Army base, but the bomb went off in the bomb maker's Greenwich Village townhouse. After that episode, the group tried to avoid killing people and focused on destroying property; nevertheless, several members were involved in a botched 1981 robbery of a Brink's truck that resulted in the killing of two police officers and two security guards (Berger, 2006). The group's leader, Mark Rudd, said of the time, "I cherished my hate as a badge of moral superiority" (Green & Siegel, 2002).

Although the group members' harm and fairness values led them to idealistic violence, those values also contributed to much self-criticism in later years. Some came to denounce the violent tactics, some still support them, but most came to agree with Berlin's warning about the dangers of moral absolutism. "The Vietnam war made us crazy," said Brian Flanagan, years after his involvement with the group. "When you think you have right on your side, you can do some horrific things" (Green & Siegel, 2002). Similarly, Bill Ayers reflected, "One of the great mistakes of 1969 is that we thought we [alone] had it right. The main failures we had were those of smugness and certainty and arrogance" (Berger, 2006, p. 114). Finally, Naomi Jaffe reflected on some of the group's vacillations between extreme positions (whichever seemed more in line with the revolutionary narrative at the time): "It was reflected in the seesawing from dismissing the White working class to glorifying the White working class. Obviously, both those positions are wrong. But they're wrong because what's right is pretty difficult and complicated" (Berger, 2006, p. 282). This vacillation illustrates two features of sacredness: It is all-or-nothing (the object in question is either sacred or profane), and it is constructed by tightly knit moral communities, not by individuals.

QUANTITATIVE APPROACH: THE MORAL FOUNDATIONS SACREDNESS SCALE

If moral sacredness is so important and powerful, can it be brought into the lab? We have found the most useful empirical operationalization of sacredness to be the one in Tetlock's work on taboo trade-offs of sacred values (Tetlock, 2003; Tetlock et al., 2000), which demonstrated that people often refused to exchange sacred values for profane concerns and felt contaminated when they did. Graham et al. (2009) followed Tetlock's method by presenting people with violations of the five moral foundations—for example, "Kick a dog in the head, hard" for harm—and asking how much money they would require to do it (with an option to refuse the taboo trade-off for any amount of money). A major advantage of this approach is that compared to other self-report measures of moral personality (e.g., the Defining Issues Test; Rest, 1979), the very experience of taking the survey triggers some gut-level intuitive reactions (Haidt, 2001), as well as some deliberative reasoning. We have since developed and revised these items into the Moral Foundations Sacredness Scale, which we present here (see Appendix 1.1) in hopes that other researchers in moral psychology may use it to investigate the full range of moral concerns that people can hold sacred.

As Appendix 1.1 shows, the scale gives four items for each foundation, as well as an optional four-item subscale with personally unpleasant outcomes that are not relevant to moral concerns (e.g., having a severe headache for 2 weeks). This nonmoral subscale can be used as a statistical control to remove individual differences in attitudes about money and about trade-offs in general when sacredness is not involved. All items are presented to participants in randomized order, without foundation or item labels.

Many of the items were inspired by previous treatments of sacredness; for example, the item about flag burning reflects the attention Durkheim (1915/1965, pp. 260–262) paid to the national flag as a sacred object, and the item about selling one's soul mirrors Haidt, Bjorklund, and Murphy's (2000) observation that participants (even those who did not believe they had a soul) resisted this offer as a tainting trade-off. In developing and selecting items for the scale, we tried to capture a wide range of content domains for each foundational concern; for instance, instead of maximizing alpha (an index of reliability or unidimensionality), which would have led us to retain only nation-related items for the ingroup scale, we selected a final set of items that concerned loyalty to nation, family, and club or team. For this reason, internal consistencies are relatively low (average $\alpha = .64$ for the four-item subscales) but sufficient, given the lack of redundant items, wide range of topics, and small number of items (for a related discussion, see Graham et al., in press).

The items are responded to on an 8-point scale, beginning with "$0 (I'd do it for free)," then $10, and then increasing by factors of 10 to $1 million, with a top option of "never, for any amount of money." The scale is scored in two ways: One method is simply to average subscale items on the full 8-point scale, and the other is to calculate for each person how many behaviors (out of four) he or she would "never [do] for any amount of money" for each subscale. (This latter method sacrifices a good deal of information, but it is closer to the definition of sacredness as a refusal to make trade-offs.)

The top half of Table 1.2 provides full scale means and standard deviations for a large heterogeneous (and international) sample of more than 27,000 visitors to YourMorals.org (http://yourmorals.org), as well as separate means for gender and political identification groups. The bottom half presents the same data scored by the stricter criterion of number of "never" answers for each subsample. As both halves show, women are more likely than men to sacralize values related to all five foundations in terms of both requiring more money to violate them and being more likely to refuse to violate them for any amount of money ($ts > 17$, $ps < .0001$). Table 1.2 also shows clear political patterns for ingroup, authority, and purity, in that conservatives are the most likely group

TABLE 1.2
Means, Standard Deviations, and Alphas for Sacredness Subscales

Foundation	Total (n = 27,833)		Women (n = 12,082)	Men (n = 15,752)	Liberals (n = 17,795)	Moderates (n = 2,699)	Conservatives (n = 3,073)	Libertarians (n = 2,354)
	Mean	SD	Mean	Mean	Mean	Mean	Mean	Mean
Harm	6.96	1.24	7.36	6.66	7.08	7.05	6.89	6.32
Fairness	6.41	1.32	6.58	6.27	6.43	6.51	6.56	6.06
Ingroup	5.63	1.45	5.90	5.42	5.47	6.00	6.51	5.32
Authority	4.43	1.64	4.71	4.22	4.29	4.87	5.23	4.04
Purity	5.58	(1.47)	5.98	5.28	5.41	6.03	6.40	5.19
Nonmoral	6.01	1.11	6.32	5.78	6.01	6.11	6.18	5.67

Foundation	No. never	SD	No. never	No. never	No. never	No. never	No. never	No. never
Harm	2.51	1.44	2.97	2.17	2.60	2.63	2.47	1.89
Fairness	2.04	1.29	2.20	1.91	2.05	2.10	2.18	1.75
Ingroup	1.30	1.18	1.51	1.13	1.21	1.47	1.86	1.03
Authority	0.93	1.05	1.06	0.84	0.85	1.15	1.38	0.74
Purity	1.53	1.20	1.86	1.28	1.39	1.87	2.22	1.20
Nonmoral	0.96	1.05	1.21	0.77	0.95	1.04	1.08	0.65

Note. Range for all items and subscale means is 1–8 (see Appendix 1.1 for response options). No. never = average number of items (out of four) the subsample indicated they would never do for any amount of money; it is a stricter criterion of sacredness than the overall mean in that it considers only refusals to enter into the taboo trade-off altogether.

to sacralize these values, then moderates, then liberals. However, no such pattern emerges for harm and fairness, which moral foundations theory predicts should be more sacred to liberals than conservatives.

We found something similar with an early version of the scale (Graham et al., 2009, Study 3) and speculated that there might be a general tendency for conservatives to be more likely to refuse monetary trade-offs in general (perhaps seeing such trade-offs as a form of prostitution). The addition of the nonmoral subscale supports this speculation, in that it correlates weakly but reliably with political conservatism ($r = .08$, $p < .001$). When we computed difference scores by subtracting participants' nonmoral scores from their foundation scores (to partial out individual differences in amounts required and propensity to refuse doing things for money in general), political conservatism remained positively correlated with ingroup ($r = .11$, $p < .0001$), authority ($r = .17$, $p < .0001$), and purity ($r = .27$, $p < .0001$) and was weakly negatively correlated with harm ($r = -.12$, $p < .0001$) and fairness ($r = -.05$, $p = .02$). Finally, the right column of the table shows that libertarians are the most profane group of all for every subscale. As this group becomes more vocal in U.S. and international politics, it will be more important to investigate the narrative they are weaving, which seems to sacralize the value of individual liberty linked to the sacred figures of the American founding fathers and the evils of European-style socialism (see Iyer, Koleva, Graham, Haidt, & Ditto, 2010, for further information on libertarian morality).[5]

What can data from this scale tell us about what kinds of sacralization are most likely to lead to violence? As a first pass, we examined whether the Sacredness subscales could predict attitudes toward war as measured by a scale that treated peace and war attitudes as separate constructs (van der Linden, Bizumic, Stubager, & Mellon, 2008). The Attitudes Toward War subscale included items expressing justification for war, such as "Under some conditions, war is necessary to maintain justice." In multiple regression analyses including political identification and gender as covariates, prowar attitudes were negatively predicted by harm ($\beta = -.13$, $p < .001$) and fairness ($\beta = -.11$, $p < .01$) but positively predicted by sacralization of ingroup concerns ($\beta = .15$, $p < .001$). Of course, indicating that wars can sometimes be justified is a far cry from actually perpetrating acts of idealistic violence; we hope that future research can more directly investigate the links between sacralization of specific foundational concerns and idealistic violence in support of those moral ends. More generally, we hope that moral psychologists will begin using the scale as a way to measure individual differences in the tendency to sacralize

---

[5]We have long said that there are more than five psychological foundations. We believe the five we have identified are the five best candidates, but we are now investigating the possibility that liberty/constraint is the sixth.

values and objects. We predict that the differences measured by the scale will interact with many of the manipulations currently used in moral psychology experiments, which frequently pit values against each other.

CONCLUSION: MANY SACRED PATHS TO THE SAME EVIL

Why do absolutist visions of an idealized future so often require, as Isaiah Berlin put it, breaking some eggs? How can moral ends justify violent means? In this chapter, we argued that sacredness is one key to understanding this phenomenon, and we suggested a process whereby strongly held values, in the presence of intergroup conflict or competition, lead to the sacralization of specific people, places, or ideas. This sacralization brings with it an attendant vision of evil as whatever threatens or stands in the way of what is sacred. We have also argued that this process of constructing sacredness and evil is not done by individuals, but by groups, teams, and communities—the visions of sacredness are shared visions, part of ideological narratives in which the evil one or ones play a starring role. We gave two qualitative examples of such narratives based on very different constellations of foundation-related values (one based primarily on ingroup and purity, the other on harm and fairness). Finally, we presented the Moral Foundations Sacredness Scale as a way to measure sacralization of principles related to five different classes of moral concerns.

Future theoretical and empirical investigations will need to address the question of which foundational values most lend themselves to idealistic violence: Can any sacralized values encourage violence in pursuit of their ends, or do some values lead to violence more quickly than others? The example of the Weather Underground shows that harm and fairness concerns can, almost paradoxically, lead to violent actions when sacralized by a moral community with a clear vision of evil. However, their killings were by and large accidental, whereas Timothy McVeigh specifically sought to kill hundreds of innocent civilians to strike a blow at his particular vision of evil, the government. We hope that future work by moral psychologists will reveal how the processes of sacralization leading to violence differ depending on the kind of sacred values and, most importantly, whether interventions intended to stop or reverse this process are differentially effective depending on this as well (for a promising start, see the chapters in Part IV of this volume). Different evils may lead to violent crusades to stop those evils in different ways. It is our hope that moral foundations theory, as applied to sacredness and evil, can help us understand and prevent the perceived necessity of breaking so many eggs.

REFERENCES

Atran, S., & Norenzayan, A. (2004). Religion's evolutionary landscape: Counter-intuition, commitment, compassion, communion. *Behavioral and Brain Sciences*, *27*, 713–730. doi:10.1017/S0140525X04000172

Baron, J., & Spranca, M. (1997). Protected values. *Organizational Behavior and Human Decision Processes*, *70*, 1–16. doi:10.1006/obhd.1997.2690

Baumeister, R. F. (1997). *Evil: Inside human violence and cruelty*. New York, NY: W. H. Freeman.

Berger, D. (2006). *Outlaws of America: The Weather Underground and the politics of solidarity*. Oakland, CA: AK Press.

Berlin, I. (1998, May 14). My intellectual path. *The New York Review of Books*, pp. 53–60.

Boyer, P. (2003). Religious thought and behaviour as by-products of brain function. *Trends in Cognitive Sciences*, *7*, 119–124. doi:10.1016/S1364-6613(03)00031-7

Bruner, J. (1986). *Actual minds, possible worlds*. Cambridge, MA: Harvard University Press.

Darwin, C. (1998). *The descent of man and selection in relation to sex*. Amherst, NY: Prometheus Books. (Original work published 1871)

Dohrn, B., Ayers, B., & Jones, J. (Eds.). (2006). *Sing a battle song: The revolutionary poetry, statements, and communiqués of the Weather Underground, 1970–1974*. New York, NY: Seven Stories Press.

Durkheim, E. (1965). *The elementary forms of religious life* (J. W. Swain, Trans.). New York, NY: Free Press. (Original work published 1915)

Eliade, M. (1959). *The sacred and the profane* (W. R. Trask, Trans.). San Diego, CA: Harcourt.

Glover, J. (1999). *Humanity: A moral history of the twentieth century*. New Haven, CT: Yale University Press.

Graham, J., & Haidt, J. (2010). Beyond beliefs: Religions bind individuals into moral communities. *Personality and Social Psychology Review*, *14*, 140–150. doi:10.1177/1088868309353415

Graham, J., Haidt, J., & Nosek, B. A. (2009). Liberals and conservatives rely on different sets of moral foundations. *Journal of Personality and Social Psychology*, *96*, 1029–1046. doi:10.1037/a0015141

Graham, J., Nosek, B. A., Haidt, J., Iyer, R., Koleva, K., & Ditto, P. (in press). Mapping the moral domain. *Journal of Personality and Social Psychology*.

Green, S. (Producer/Director), & Siegel, B. (Producer/Director). (2002). *The Weather Underground* [Documentary motion picture]. United States: Free History Project.

Haidt, J. (2001). The emotional dog and its rational tail: A social intuitionist approach to moral judgment. *Psychological Review*, *108*, 814–834.

Haidt, J. (2008). Morality. *Perspectives on Psychological Science, 3,* 65–72. doi:10.1111/j.1745-6916.2008.00063.x

Haidt, J., Bjorklund, F., & Murphy, S. (2000). *Moral dumbfounding: When intuition finds no reason.* Unpublished manuscript, University of Virginia, Charlottesville, VA.

Haidt, J., & Graham, J. (2007). When morality opposes justice: Conservatives have moral intuitions that liberals may not recognize. *Social Justice Research, 20,* 98–116. doi:10.1007/s11211-007-0034-z

Haidt, J., Graham, J., & Joseph, C. (2009). Above and below left–right: Ideological narratives and moral foundations. *Psychological Inquiry, 20,* 110–119. doi:10.1080/10478400903028573

Haidt, J., & Joseph, C. (2004). Intuitive ethics: How innately prepared intuitions generate culturally variable virtues. *Daedalus, 133,* 55–66. doi:10.1162/0011526042365555

Haidt, J., & Kesebir, S. (2010). Morality. In S. T. Fiske, D. Gilbert, & G. Lindzey (Eds.), *Handbook of social psychology* (5th ed., pp. 797–832). Hoboken, NJ: Wiley.

Heath, C., Bell, C., & Sternberg, E. (2001). Emotional selection in memes: The case of urban legends. *Journal of Personality and Social Psychology, 81,* 1028–1041. doi:10.1037/0022-3514.81.6.1028

Henrich, N., & Henrich, J. (2007). *Why humans cooperate: A cultural and evolutionary explanation.* Oxford, England: Oxford University Press.

Iyer, R., Koleva, S., Graham, J., Haidt, J., & Ditto, P. H. (2010). *What libertarians believe, and (perhaps) why: Psychological differences among libertarians, liberals, and conservatives.* Manuscript submitted for publication.

Keltner, D., & Haidt, J. (1999). The social functions of emotions at four levels of analysis. *Cognition and Emotion, 13,* 505–521. doi:10.1080/026999399379168

Kirkpatrick, L. (1999). Toward an evolutionary psychology of religion. *Journal of Personality, 67,* 921–952. doi:10.1111/1467-6494.00078

Malinowski, B. (1922). *Argonauts of the Western Pacific.* London, England: Routledge.

McAdams, D. P. (2001). The psychology of life stories. *Review of General Psychology, 5,* 100–122. doi:10.1037/1089-2680.5.2.100

McAdams, D. P., Albaugh, M., Farber, E., Daniels, J., Logan, R. L., & Olson, B. (2008). Family metaphors and moral intuitions: How conservatives and liberals narrate their lives. *Journal of Personality and Social Psychology, 95,* 978–990. doi:10.1037/a0012650

Nisbet, R. A. (1993). *The sociological tradition* (2nd ed.). New Brunswick, NJ: Transaction. (Original work published 1966)

Otto, R. (1958). *The idea of the holy: An inquiry into the non-rational factor in the idea of the divine and its relation to the rational* (J. W. Harvey, trans.). New York, NY: Oxford University Press. (Original work published 1917)

Pierce, W. L. (1978). *The Turner diaries.* Hillsboro, WV: National Vanguard Books.

Rest, J. R. (1979). *Development in judging moral issues*. Minneapolis, MN: University of Minnesota Press.

Richerson, P. J., & Boyd, R. (2005). *Not by genes alone: How culture transformed human evolution*. Chicago, IL: University of Chicago Press.

Ritov, I., & Baron, J. (1999). Protected values and omission bias. *Organizational Behavior and Human Decision Processes, 79*, 79–94. doi:10.1006/obhd. 1999.2839

Shweder, R. A., Much, N. C., Mahapatra, M., & Park, L. (1997). The "big three" of morality (autonomy, community, and divinity), and the "big three" explanations of suffering. In A. Brandt & P. Rozin (Eds.), *Morality and health* (pp. 119–169). New York, NY: Routledge.

Skitka, L. J., & Mullen, E. (2002). The dark side of moral conviction. *Analyses of Social Issues and Public Policy, 2*, 35–41. doi:10.1111/j.1530-2415.2002. 00024.x

Solecki, R. S. (1975). Shanidar IV: A Neanderthal flower burial in northern Iraq. *Science, 190*, 880–881.

Staub, E. (2003). *The psychology of good and evil*. Cambridge, England: Cambridge University Press. doi:10.1017/CBO9780511615795

Tetlock, P. E. (2003). Thinking about the unthinkable: Coping with secular encroachments on sacred values. *Trends in Cognitive Sciences, 7*, 320–324. doi:10.1016/S1364-6613(03)00135-9

Tetlock, P. E., Kristel, O., Elson, B., Green, M., & Lerner, J. (2000). The psychology of the unthinkable: Taboo trade-offs, forbidden base rates, and heretical counterfactuals. *Journal of Personality and Social Psychology, 78*, 853–870. doi:10. 1037/0022-3514.78.5.853

Trivers, R. L. (1971). The evolution of reciprocal altruism. *Quarterly Review of Biology, 46*, 35–57. doi:10.1086/406755

Turiel, E. (1983). *The development of social knowledge: Morality and convention*. Cambridge, England: Cambridge University Press.

Van der Linden, N., Bizumic, B., Stubager, R., & Mellon, S. (2008, July). *Belligerent peaceniks and hippie warmongers: The dimensionality of attitudes towards, and social representations of, war and peace*. Poster presented at the 31st Annual Scientific Meeting of the International Society of Political Psychology, Paris, France.

Westen, D. (2007). *The political brain: The role of emotion in deciding the fate of the nation*. New York, NY: Public Affairs.

Wilson, D. S. (2002). *Darwin's cathedral: Evolution, religion, and the nature of society*. Chicago, IL: University of Chicago Press.

Zimbardo, P. G. (2004). A situationist perspective on the psychology of evil: Understanding how good people are transformed into perpetrators. In A. G. Miller (Ed.), *The social psychology of good and evil* (pp. 21–50). New York, NY: Guilford Press.

APPENDIX 1.1. THE MORAL FOUNDATIONS SACREDNESS SCALE

Instructions: Try to imagine *actually doing* the following things, and indicate how much money someone would have to pay you (anonymously and secretly) to be willing to do each thing. For each action, assume that nothing bad would happen to you afterward. Also assume that you cannot use the money to make up for your action.

Scale: 1 = $0 (I'd do it for free); 2 = $10; 3 = $100; 4 = $1,000; 5 = $10,000; 6 = $100,000; 7 = $1 million; 8 = never, for any amount of money

Harm

DOGKICK: Kick a dog in the head, hard.
ENDANGERED: Shoot and kill an animal that is a member of an endangered species.
OVERWEIGHT: Make cruel remarks to an overweight person about his or her appearance.
PALM: Stick a pin into the palm of a child you don't know.

Fairness

CARDS: Cheat in a game of cards played for money with some people you don't know well.
APARTMENT: Say no to a friend's request to help him move into a new apartment after he helped you move the month before.
BALLOTS: Throw out a box of ballots, during an election, to help your favored candidate win.
RACEPLEDGE: Sign a secret but binding pledge to hire only people of your race in your company.

Ingroup

TALKRADIO: Say something bad about your nation (which you don't believe to be true) while calling in, anonymously, to a talk radio show in a foreign nation.
FAMILYSHUN: Break off all communications with your immediate and extended family for 1 year.
FLAGBURN: Burn your country's flag in private (nobody else sees you).
LEAVECLUB: Leave the social group, club, or team that you most value.

Authority

PARENTCURSE: Curse your parents to their face. (You can apologize and explain 1 year later.)
HANDGESTURE: Make a disrespectful hand gesture to your boss, teacher, or professor.
ROTTENTOMATO: Throw a rotten tomato at a political leader you dislike. (Remember, you will not get caught.)
FATHERSLAP: Slap your father in the face (with his permission) as part of a comedy skit.

Purity

SOULSELL: Sign a piece of paper that says "I hereby sell my soul, after my death, to whoever has this piece of paper."
TAIL: Get plastic surgery that adds a 2-inch tail to the end of your spine (you can remove it in 3 years).
MOLESTERBLOOD: Get a blood transfusion of 1 pint of disease-free, compatible blood from a convicted child molester.
STAGEANIMAL: Attend a performance art piece in which all participants (including you) have to act like animals for 30 minutes, including crawling around naked and urinating on stage.

Nonmoral (optional)

ICEBATH: Sit in a bathtub full of ice water for 10 minutes.
IDIOTSIGN: Wear a sign on your back for 1 month that says, in large letters, "I am an idiot."
HEADACHE: Experience a severe headache for 2 weeks.
LOSEHEARING: Lose your sense of hearing for 1 year.

2

THE PHILOSOPHER IN THE THEATER

FIERY CUSHMAN AND JOSHUA GREENE

The moral principles found in philosophy and embodied in law are often strikingly complex and peculiar, and yet resolutely persistent. For instance, it was long held in Britain that a person could be tried for murder only if the victim died within a year and a day of the crime. And in the United States, if a robber gets into a shootout with a cop and the cop's bullet hits a bystander, the robber can be charged with murdering the bystander. Naively, one might have assumed that murder could be defined simply as "intentionally causing another person to die." In fact, the American Law Institute's Model Penal Code requires pages of fine print.

Our goal in this chapter is to present a model of the origins of moral principles that can explain their complexity, peculiarity, and persistence. According to this model, abstract, general moral principles are constructed from the raw material of intuitive responses to particular cases, as explained in the next section of the chapter. Those intuitive responses depend, in turn, on many psychological capacities that are not specific to morality at all. These include

---

This chapter draws largely from ideas and material in Cushman's (2008b) doctoral thesis, which were revised and extended with assistance by Greene.

attributions of causation ("John harmed Jane") and intent ("on purpose"). Consequently, explicit moral principles reflect the complexity of our psychological processes of causal and intentional attribution. That complexity can seem peculiar because intuitive, automatic attributions of causation and intent are often at odds with more considered, explicit theories of causation and intention. Despite their complexity and peculiarity, these principles persist because they are supported by compelling emotions that are particularly difficult to revise or reject, an issue considered in the final section of this chapter.

INTUITIONS AND PRINCIPLED REASONING

Ordinary people's moral judgments often track philosophers' and lawyers' explicit principles, mirroring their complexity and nuance. For a long while psychologists assumed a simple explanation of this phenomenon: Ordinary people use explicit principles when they make moral judgments (Kohlberg, 1969). (By an *explicit moral principle*, we mean a general moral rule that can be verbalized and is available to conscious reasoning.) However, research in moral psychology forcefully challenges this assumption (Haidt, 2001; see also Chapter 1, this volume). At least in some cases, people make moral judgments that are consistent with prominent philosophical or legal principles, and yet they have no explicit awareness of those principles (Cushman, Young, & Hauser, 2006; Mikhail, 2000). In fact, some of these characteristic patterns of judgment are established by early childhood (Pellizzoni, Siegal, & Surian, 2010; see also Chapter 4, this volume). These findings indicate that moral principles derive their content from moral judgments, rather than the other way around.

To some extent, this should not come as a surprise. Many philosophers commonly test their principles against intuitions about specific cases, and some openly embrace the project of systematizing moral intuition in principles (Fischer & Ravizza, 1992; Kamm, 2006). Also, psychological research shows that ordinary people often attempt to provide post hoc rationalizations of their moral judgments, constructing explicit principles to match their intuitive responses to particular cases (Haidt, 2001; Uhlmann, Pizarro, Tannenbaum, & Ditto, 2009). This suggests that the philosophical practice of constructing intuitively plausible moral principles may be continuous with the commonplace practice of rationalizing emotional moral commitments (Cushman & Young, 2009; Greene, 2007; Mikhail, 2000; Shweder & Haidt, 1993; see also Chapter 3, this volume).

From a certain perspective, this is a decidedly unflattering portrait of moral reasoning. For instance, pioneering experiments by Haidt showed that people are strikingly unable to provide adequate, consistent principles to support the common judgment that sibling incest is wrong (e.g., Haidt & Hersh, 2001). They claim it is wrong because it leads to genetic deficits in children, but they insist that it is still wrong even if the sister is infertile. They claim it is wrong because the family would be embarrassed, but they insist that it is wrong even if kept secret. They claim it is wrong because the siblings will regret it, but they insist it is wrong even if the siblings find it quite enjoyable. Finally, they throw up their hands and say they do not know why incest is wrong, they just know it is. Participants in these experiments appear to be engaged in a desperate and unsuccessful search for any principled basis for their intuitions, a phenomenon that Haidt calls "moral dumbfounding." It appears that their goal is not to develop a rational theory to guide future judgments but instead to paint the veneer of reason over a foregone conclusion.

Yet there is evidence that people's moral justifications are sometimes more considered and constrained than these early studies suggested. Take, for example, the tendency to justify the prohibition against incest by appeal to the possibility of harm (e.g., to the child, the family, or the siblings themselves; Paxton & Greene, 2010). Consistent with these justifications, there is now mounting evidence that people engage in explicit utilitarian moral reasoning favoring actions that minimize harm (Bartels, 2008; Greene, Morelli, Lowenberg, Nystrom, & Cohen, 2008; Greene, Nystrom, Engell, Darley, & Cohen, 2004). People's moral justifications also frequently invoke principles of causal responsibility (it is wrong to cause harm) and intent (it is wrong to harm another intentionally; see Cushman et al., 2006; Kohlberg, 1981; Piaget, 1965/1932), and again their judgments are generally consistent with these principles (e.g., Weiner, 1995).

There are other factors that play an important role in intuitive judgments but that people nevertheless tend to regard as morally irrelevant. For instance, moral intuitions are sensitive to whether a perpetrator acts with direct physical force on a victim (Cushman et al., 2006; Greene et al., 2009): Pushing a person in front of a train is worse than flipping a switch that drops the person in front of a train. But when people recognize the role of force in their intuitive judgments, they often reject this factor as morally irrelevant (Cushman et al., 2006); for instance, one participant wrote, "I guess I was fooled by the line-pulling [i.e., indirect force] seeming more passive than the man-pushing, but that view is hard to justify now" (p. 1087).

These studies suggest that although moral intuitions play an important role in the development of explicit moral theories, people do not endorse intuitively supported moral principles indiscriminately. Rather, people seem to progress toward what philosophers call *reflective equilibrium*, achieved through a tug-of-war between intuitive attitudes and principled commitments. If it is true that the philosopher's method of constructing moral principles is roughly continuous with the ordinary person's, then evidence for reflection is surely welcome news to philosophers. Maybe philosophers are experts in reflection: ordinary in the intuitions they harvest but extraordinary in their capacity to separate the wheat from the chaff.

A recent study tested this proposition by comparing intuitive judgments and moral principles in a large sample of philosophers—about 280 individuals who had earned a master's degree or doctorate in philosophy (Schwitzgebel & Cushman, in press). In an early part of the test, participants judged a pair of specific hypothetical moral dilemmas similar to the well-studied trolley problem (e.g., Fischer & Ravizza, 1992; Foot, 1967; Hauser, Cushman, Young, Jin, & Mikhail, 2007; Kamm, 1998; Petrinovich, O'Neill, & Jorgensen, 1993; Thomson, 1985). In "push"-type cases, the agent had to apply direct physical force to a victim, using him as a tool to save five other people: for example, throwing a man in front of a runaway boxcar to stop it from hitting five people farther down the tracks. In "switch"-type cases, the agent acted at a distance to save five people, with the side effect that one other person would die: for instance, switching a runaway boxcar away from the main track where five people were threatened and onto a side track where one person would die. The critical manipulation was to change the order in which these two cases were presented. Nonphilosophers were more likely to judge switch-type harm to be as bad as push-type harm when viewed in the order push/switch but were more likely to judge switch-type harm to be less bad than push-type harm when the cases were viewed in the order switch/push. It turns out that philosophers were just as susceptible as nonphilosophers to this effect: The order in which they viewed the cases had a statistically significant and surprisingly large effect on their patterns of judgment.

The most important evidence came, however, at the end of the test. We asked philosophers whether they endorsed the doctrine of double effect (DDE), a well-known principle in philosophy that draws a moral distinction between push-type and switch-type cases. The results were striking: Philosophers were about 30% more likely to endorse the DDE—an abstract, explicit moral principle—when they had previously viewed specific moral dilemmas in the order switch/push rather than push/switch. This effect was just as strong among the subset of philosophers who specialized in ethics and had received a PhD.

These results have two important implications. First, they provide evidence that philosophers' endorsements of moral principles can depend substantially on their prior judgments regarding particular cases. Second, they demonstrate that philosophical training does not inoculate against the influence of morally "irrelevant" factors (e.g., the order in which the two cases are presented) on principled reasoning. (At least, we presume that most philosophers would deem order of presentation irrelevant.) Reflective equilibration surely plays a critical role in the construction of explicit moral theories. Nevertheless, it appears that intuitive processes of moral judgment influence philosophical theories in ways that are both powerful and unseen.

COMPLEXITY

In 1997, the U.S. Supreme Court announced a landmark decision upholding New York's ban on physician-assisted suicide (*Vacco v. Quill*, 1997). The case turned on the merits of a simple comparative question: Is killing a person the same as allowing him or her to die? According to law, a physician must respect a patient's wish to withhold lifesaving medication— that is, doctors can be required to allow a patient to die. Defenders of a right to physician-assisted suicide asserted that the distinction between active euthanasia (e.g., administering a lethal dose of morphine) and passive euthanasia (e.g., withholding a lifesaving dose of antibiotics) is nothing more than a semantic sleight of hand. Either way, they argued, the patient's death depends on the doctor's choice. But the Court disagreed. The majority opinion in *Vacco v. Quill* held that there is a significant moral distinction between actively killing and passively allowing a person to die.

The moral distinction between active and passive harm is well represented in the philosophical literature (Fischer & Ravizza, 1992) and has a large influence on ordinary people's moral judgments (Baron & Ritov, 2004; Cushman et al., 2006; Ritov & Baron, 1999; Spranca, Minsk, & Baron, 1991). From a certain perspective, however, it is hard to explain or to justify. Consider again *Vacco v. Quill:* In both cases the doctor's decision is unequivocally responsible for the patient's death. In both cases the doctor is doing what the patient wants. Why does it matter whether the death was caused by performing a physical act or, instead, by failing to act?

We use the distinction between actions and omissions as a case study of complexity in moral principles. We argue that actions typically support more robust, automatic attributions of causation and intention. Because these attributions constitute basic inputs to the process of moral judgment, the action/omission attribution affects moral judgment. In essence, the moral distinction derives from distinctions made by nonmoral cognitive processes such as causal attribution and intentional attribution. More broadly, we suggest that much of the complexity of moral rules ultimately derives from the complexity of nonmoral cognition.

For example, consider John, who rolls a ball toward 12 pins (an action), and Jane, who stands by and allows the ball to roll (an omission). John might be considered more causally responsible for the pins' falling than Jane is and also to have intended the pins to fall more than Jane did. This is an example of the action/omission distinction operating in nonmoral attributions of causation and intention. Possibly, the action/omission distinction carries through to affect moral judgments in the context of harmful behavior because causal responsibility for harm and intent to cause harm are key determinants of moral judgments. Replace the 12 pins with an innocent child, and John might look morally more culpable than Jane because he appears to have directly caused the child harm and intended the harm more than Jane.

Experimental evidence supports this hypothesis. People's judgments of nonmoral actions and omissions (e.g., the bowling case) do reveal systematic discrepancies in causal attribution and intentional attribution (Cushman & Young, in press). Specifically, people assign more causal responsibility to actions than to omissions, and they are more likely to consider actions intentional. Indeed, there is some evidence that actions support more robust causal inferences about an agent's goal (similar to intent) even during infancy (Cushman, Fieman, & Carey, 2011). In the relevant study, 6- to 7-month-old infants watched as a hand repeatedly reached for and grasped a series of objects. In the "consistent action" condition, the hand always reached for one object (e.g., a ball), preferring it to any other object (e.g., a banana, a box, a watch). Infants in the action condition expected the hand to continue reaching for the ball, as revealed by the duration of their gaze to expected versus unexpected events. In the "consistent omission" condition, the hand never reached for the ball, preferring to reach instead for any other object. Infants in the omission condition failed to form any expectation about the hand's future behavior; they were entirely unsurprised to see the hand change course and prefer the ball to future objects. Thus, infants appear to infer goals from consistent actions ("the hand always goes for the ball") but not consistent omissions ("the hand never goes for the ball"), even when the evidence in favor of each inference is equal.

It is well known that moral judgments depend substantially, although not exclusively, on assessments of causal responsibility for harm and intent to harm (Alicke, 1992; Cushman, 2008a; Darley & Shultz, 1990; Piaget, 1965/1932; Royzman & Baron, 2002; Young, Cushman, Hauser, & Saxe, 2007; see also Chapter 5, this volume). Thus, harmful actions may seem morally worse than harmful omissions because the active agent appears to have caused and intended the harm more. To establish this causal connection between nonmoral attributions and moral judgments, Cushman and Young (in press) took advantage of the finding that the judgment of deserved punishment relies significantly more on causal attributions than does the judgment of moral wrongness (Cushman, 2008a). If causal attribution is partially responsible for the moral distinction between actions and omissions, then the action/omission distinction should exert greater influence on punishment judgments than on wrongness judgments. This is precisely what the study revealed.

Further evidence for the role of causal attribution in the action/omission distinction comes from a series of studies by Baron and colleagues (Asch et al., 1994; Baron & Ritov, 2004; Ritov & Baron, 1999; Royzman & Baron, 2002; Spranca et al., 1991). They consistently found that (a) many people explicitly stated that actions are more "causal" than omissions, (b) people who made that assessment were much more likely to judge harmful actions to be morally worse than harmful omissions, and (c) people explained their moral distinction between actions and omissions by appealing to the underlying causal distinction.

This evidence from people's explicit justifications for the action/omission distinction raises a key question: To what extent does the moral distinction between active and passive harm depend on an explicit, principled appeal to causal and intentional concepts rather than on processing features of implicit, automatic attributions of causation and intent? A recent study addressed this question by using functional neuroimaging to infer the cognitive processes underlying the action/omission distinction (Cushman, Murray, Gordon-McKeon, Wharton, & Greene, 2011). Of particular interest was activity in the dorsolateral prefrontal cortex (DLPFC), a region associated with the explicit, controlled application of abstract rules to a problem (Bunge & Wallis, 2007). The DLPFC was found to be significantly more active when subjects judged harmful omissions compared with when they judged harmful actions. Taken alone, this evidence is compatible with either of the hypotheses we considered above. Possibly, activation in the DLPFC reflects the application of an explicit principled rule exonerating omissions: "The doctor is not responsible because he simply allowed the patient to die, but he didn't really cause the death." An alternative possibility is that activation in the DLPFC reflects the need to deploy controlled cognitive processes to condemn omissions: "The doctor is responsible because the patient's death depended on his purposeful decision." According to this latter hypothesis, actions require less controlled, less deliberate DLPFC processing than omissions because automatic psychological mechanisms robustly condemn actions but not omissions.

These two hypotheses make opposite predictions about which participants will show the greatest amount of DLPFC activity when judging omissions. If the activity reflects the application of an explicit moral rule exonerating omissions, then people who show the greatest difference in judgment between actions and omissions should also show the most DLPFC activity. Alternatively, if the activity reflects the necessity of controlled processes to interpret and condemn harmful omissions, then people who show the smallest difference in judgment between actions and omissions should show the most DLPFC activity. This second pattern is what we observed: DLPFC activity during the judgment of omissions was significantly correlated with their condemnation. Thus, although people are able to report an explicit rule that accounts for the action/omission distinction after the fact, this study failed to provide evidence for the deployment of such a rule during the process of judgment itself. Instead, the evidence suggested that additional controlled, cognitive processing is necessary to equate harmful omissions with harmful actions. The automatic processes that support the judgment of harmful actions appear to be insufficient for the condemnation of harmful omissions.

In summary, it appears that the moral distinction between actions and omissions depends in part on nonmoral processes of causal and intentional attribution. People—perhaps even young infants—tend to form more robust causal and intentional attributions from actions than from omissions. Automatic moral judgments rely on attributions of causation and intent as key inputs. Consequently, the nonmoral action/omission distinction leads harmful actions to be judged morally worse than harmful omissions. As we saw earlier, consistent patterns of moral judgment constitute an important basis for the abstraction of general moral principles. In this way, the basic cognitive processes that young infants use to understand actions and events may contribute importantly to the moral doctrines endorsed by the U.S. Supreme Court.

If the general structure of this argument is correct—if explicit moral principles reflect the processing features of relatively automatic, nonmoral processes of causal and intentional attribution—then we can begin to explain the pervasive complexity of explicit moral principles. It derives from the much more general complexity of the cognitive mechanisms we use to interpret actions and events. By analogy, Pinker (2007) argued that many of the complex rules governing the grammaticality of verbs depend on general (i.e., nonlinguistic) processing features of those very same cognitive systems. From this perspective, moral rules and grammatical rules are two windows onto the basic structure of human thought.

PECULIARITY

If the moral distinction between active and passive harm is an explicit formalization of moral intuitions, why can it seem so peculiar? Active harm really does feel worse than passive harm. Yet it still seems strange to say that it is worse for a doctor to fulfill a patient's end-of-life wishes by actively doing something than by deliberately withholding treatment. In this section, we argue that this *two-mindedness* reflects the operations of dissociable cognitive systems that operate with incommensurable conceptions of causation, intention, and (consequently) morality (Cushman & Young, 2009; Cushman et al., 2006; Greene, 2007; Greene, Sommerville, Nystrom, Darley, & Cohen, 2001; Pizarro & Bloom, 2003; Sloman, 1996; White, 1990).

When we construct an explicit theory of morality, we do our best to capture the bases of intuitive judgments. But the concepts available to our explicit thought processes are fundamentally mismatched to the underlying bases of our intuitive, affective responses. Because of this mismatch, intuitive patterns of judgment look peculiar to the explicit reasoning system that constructs moral principles.

To illustrate this phenomenon, we turn from active versus passive euthanasia to another, perhaps less well studied, feature of the law. The Anglo-American legal tradition uses two distinct concepts of causation: factual causation and proximate causation. *Factual causation* has a simple, clear definition that sounds entirely reasonable: A person's behavior caused an event if the event would not have occurred in the absence of the behavior. How do you know if Frank's shot caused Mary's death? It did so if Mary would be alive but for Frank's pulling the trigger. This "but for" criterion gives factual causation its other popular name in law: the sine qua non test.

The problem with factual causation as a legal concept is that it completely fails to capture intuitive judgments about moral responsibility—or, for that matter, causation. To see why, consider the following version of Frank's shot and Mary's death. When Frank pulled the trigger, his bullet hit the bull's eye. Frank, not Bruce, won the shooting competition. Without the $10,000 prize, Bruce cancelled his trip home for Thanksgiving. Too bad, because Bruce's aunt Mary choked on a cranberry, and Bruce's cardiopulmonary resuscitation skills undoubtedly would have saved her. But for Frank pulling the trigger, Mary would still be alive, and yet we not only refuse to hold Frank morally responsible for Mary's death; we don't even want to say that Frank caused Mary's death.

Unlike factual causation, proximate causation is a hopelessly complicated concept that utterly resists definition. As its name implies, one of the critical factors is proximity, which can be understood temporally, spatially, or in terms of intervening events. (Recall that British law long held a person guilty of homicide only if his or her behavior caused death within a year and a day.) But perhaps the most peculiar element of proximate causation—and arguably the most fundamental—is foreseeability. Suppose that Anne's daughter complains of an ear infection and a stomachache. Anne asks her husband, a chemist, what to do. He suggests acetaminophen for the ears and bismuth subsalicylate for the tummy. Now, suppose that these two medications react to produce a very toxic substance, as any chemist would know. But Anne's husband is tired and fails to think very hard about his advice. Anne administers the medicine to their daughter, and her reaction to the toxic compound is fatal. Here is the critical question: Who caused the daughter's death? If your intuitions point toward Anne's husband, then you'll be glad to hear that the law does, too. An agent is typically considered the proximate cause of a harmful outcome only if a reasonable person in that agent's shoes would have foreseen harm as a likely outcome of his behavior. Anne could not reasonably be expected to foresee harm, but her husband could have.

Proximate causation is sometimes maligned by legal scholars who disapprove of a causal concept that cannot be defined and depends on factors, such as foresight, that do not seem to have anything to do with causation at all. Yet the law requires proximate causation because it succeeds brilliantly where factual causation fails: Proximate causation captures our intuitive judgments of causal and moral responsibility. At some level, it does not just capture our intuitions—it is our intuitions. Although attempts have been made to characterize proximate causation, it does not exist as a defined doctrine; rather, it is a collection of legal precedents born in the nuanced peculiarities of individual cases and gerrymandered to suit jurists' needs.

As you might expect, psychological theories of ordinary people's intuitive causal judgments resemble the legal concept of proximate cause. For instance, consider the role of mental state information in assigning causal responsibility. Lombrozo (2007) demonstrated that adults are more likely to assign causal responsibility for an event to an agent who brings it about intentionally rather than accidentally. More recently, Muentener (2009) demonstrated that intentional actions are more likely to support causal inferences in infants. These findings are not an exact fit to the legal doctrine; the psychological studies implicate an agent's intention as a key element of causation, whereas the legal concept of proximate cause depends on what a reasonable person in the defendant's situation would have foreseen. But in each case, mental state representations exert an unexpected influence over intuitive causal judgments.

We have taken this detour through legal concepts of causation because they seem to parallel psychological mechanisms of causal judgment present in ordinary people. As we have seen, proximate causation captures elements of our intuitive causal judgments. Just as important, however, factual causation captures a prominent explicit causal theory (White, 1990). Philosophers and psychologists often refer to the "but for" test that defines factual causation as a *counterfactual* theory of causation. There are other popular explicit theories of causation as well. For instance, *mechanistic* or *production* theories of causation trace causal histories by exclusively tracing the transfer of energy through matter.

Critically, it appears that our explicit theories of causation are incommensurable with the psychological mechanisms that produce intuitive causal judgments. To put the point metaphorically, the words in our explicit causal language simply cannot express the ideas used by our intuitive mechanisms of causal judgments. For instance, neither counterfactual nor production theories of causation have any place for mental state concepts such as foresight or intent, yet mental state factors play a critical role in our intuitive causal judgments. If you try to create an explicit causal theory that captures our intuitive causal judgments using only the conceptual resources available within counterfactual and production theories, the result will be both complicated and insufficient. Alternatively, you could construct an explicit theory that draws on representations of others' mental states, but then you would no longer recognize it as a causal theory. By the lights of our explicit causal theories, foreseeability simply does not belong. This may sound familiar: When legal scholars try to define proximate causation explicitly, what they end up with is complicated, insufficient, and alarmingly uncausal.

The incommensurability of explicit theories and intuitive mechanisms of judgment plays a key role in explaining why complex moral principles are generalized from what may be simple moral rules—and why they can look so peculiar. Let us suppose that intuitive moral judgments of harmful actions are generated by an extremely simple computation: An agent acted wrongly if his or her actions intentionally caused harm. Additionally, let us suppose that the representational inputs into this computation are intuitive attributions of causation and intention. Now, assume that a person attempts to generalize an explicit moral theory over his or her pattern of intuitive judgments. As a first pass, the person constructs the following theory: "An agent acted wrongly if his or her actions intentionally caused harm." But the available explicit theories of causation and intention will produce counterintuitive moral judgments whenever those theories are at variance with their intuitive counterparts. This unfortunate person is now left trying to build an explicit moral theory that captures intuitive moral judgments, but using explicit concepts that are incommensurable with those embodied implicitly by the psychological mechanisms that determine his or her intuitive moral judgments. What the person ends up with is complicated, insufficient, and sometimes alarmingly unmoral. In short, he or she ends up with moral principles that look peculiar, like the distinction between active and passive euthanasia. In the final section, we ask why those peculiar-looking moral principles are so persistent.

PERSISTENCE

If moral principles like the action/omission distinction and proximate causation are so peculiar by lights of our explicit concepts, why do they persist? To bring the question into focus, it helps to contrast moral principles with scientific principles. One of the enduring metaphors of the cognitive revolution is the "person as scientist." The idea is that people have explicit theories (also called *folk theories*) that describe, explain, and predict the world around them. Of course, when we construct explicit theories about the world we are forced to rely on representational input from lower-level, automatic systems. Dennett (1991) argued against the notion of a *Cartesian theater*, a removed vantage point from which a person watches his or her own mental processes. But if we take the notion of the person as scientist seriously, there is such a vantage point: The theater is occupied by a scientist who is using controlled psychological processes to interpret the representational output of automatic psychological systems as they are projected into consciousness.

Consider, for example, an ordinary person's understanding of the laws of physical motion. A large body of evidence suggests that people have an intuitive sense of physical motion that operates with dramatically different properties than Newtonian mechanics (Caramazza, McCloskey, & Green, 1981; McCloskey, 1983). Consequently, when asked to produce an explicit theory of physical motion, people tend to produce an "impetus theory" remarkably similar to pre-Newtonian scientific theories. Just as in the moral cases presented in this chapter, people's explicit theories of physics can reflect processing characteristics of automatic, intuitive psychological mechanisms.

Yet folk theories, like scientific theories, can be revised, rejected, and reconstructed, ultimately moving beyond the structure of any particular automatic mechanism. This kind of conceptual change occurs when people check the predictions of a theory (e.g., an impetus theory) against the actual, represented phenomenon in the world (e.g., the motion of billiard balls). Empirical evidence clearly indicates that Newtonian mechanics explains reality better than impetus theory. So if people are able to revise their explicit theory of physics, moving beyond the input of automatic mechanisms of physical understanding, why doesn't morality work the same way? We propose an answer to this question that depends on a distinction between representational and affective processes.

Explicit theories of scientific domains such as physics, biology, and psychology are representational. That is, *folk theories* are mental structures that map onto structures in the world and are used to describe, explain, and predict those structures. This representational function means that there is a place—the real world—from which new structure can be derived. Consequently, folk theories can take on representational structure exceeding that of the input mechanisms simply by comparing the internal representation (e.g., a folk theory of physics) to external events (actual physical events).

By contrast, affective processes assign value to things and events in the world, providing a basis for choosing between possible courses of actions. Morality is, at its core, an affective system (Haidt, 2001, 2007; see also Chapter 1, this volume). The function of morality is not to provide an accurate working model of events in the world, like a theory of physics. Rather, its functional role is to guide our behavior, telling us which behaviors of our own to inhibit and which to perform, when to punish people and when to reward them, and so forth.

Consequently, an explicit theory of one's affective responses—a theory of what is pleasurable, what is beautiful, or what is moral—will not reflect the structure of the physical world; it will reflect the psychological structure of our evaluations of the world. Consider a moral claim such as "Killing babies for fun is wrong." This moral claim makes no straightforward predictions about the world that can be tested by an experiment. To the extent that it makes a prediction, that prediction concerns the structure of our minds. To say "Killing the baby is wrong" predicts that killing the baby will feel wrong. This is a fundamental difference between theories formed over affective content and theories formed over representational content.

So where does this leave the scientist in the theater? He or she constructs explicit moral principles on the basis of moral intuitions designed to motivate. This process of construction may proceed very similarly to the construction of folk theories, but there is at least one key difference. Our representational folk-scientific theories can be checked against data outside our heads: biological structure, physical structure, and so forth. By contrast, the content of moral principles can be checked only against data inside our heads: the motivational mechanisms we use to make moral judgments. Thus, it is worthwhile to differentiate between two occupants of the theater: (a) the familiar scientist and (b) a philosopher. Like scientists' theories, philosophers' theories are carefully tested and revised. But scientists' questions are answerable by testing and revising theories against data gleaned from the external world. By contrast, philosophers' questions are answerable by testing and revising theories against data gleaned from the mind.

Applying this perspective to the particular case of the action/omission distinction, we are at last in a position to explain its complexity, peculiarity, and persistence. Automatic mechanisms of causal and intentional attribution respond more robustly to actions than to omissions. Consequently, automatic mechanisms of moral judgment yield a greater affective response prohibiting actions as compared with omissions. This introduces some level of complexity to our moral judgments, although our explicit representational theories of causation and intent may reject a bright-line distinction between actions and omissions. Thus, in light of our explicit theories, discrepant moral judgments of actions and omissions look peculiar. The explicit moral distinction is persistent, however, because moral judgment is an affective process. Although the judgment that "active euthanasia feels wrong, but withholding life-saving treatment feels OK" reflects the output of representational processes (e.g., causal and intentional attributions), the judgment itself is not a representation. This makes the explicit moral theory distinguishing actions from omissions difficult to revise or reject.

CONCLUSION

The metaphor of the philosopher in the theater situates philosophy within the ordinary person's mind. On the one hand, it provides a valuable lesson about the psychology of ordinary people. Just as ordinary people act like scientists, constructing, testing, and revising theories about physics and biology, ordinary people also act like philosophers, constructing, testing, and revising theories about right and wrong. On the other hand, this metaphor provides a valuable lesson about the nature of moral philosophy. Just as theories in scientific domains tend to reflect the structure of the world, there is reason to suppose that moral philosophies tend to reflect the structure of the mind. And to the extent that the content of explicit moral theories depends on widely shared patterns of intuitive moral judgments, we can explain three salient properties of law, policy, and philosophy: complexity, peculiarity, and persistence.

We conclude on a more circumspect note, considering a very large body of moral principles that our model does not explain. The rules of evidence in U.S. courts are a useful example. They are certainly very complex and sometimes peculiar, and yet persistent. Among the most peculiar are rules that prevent juries from considering information that is highly reliable and relevant to a case when, for instance, it was improperly collected by police authorities (the exclusionary rule) or when it depends on secondhand rather than direct testimony (the hearsay rule). Although we have not studied other people's intuitive judgments of evidentiary rules, the exclusionary rule and hearsay rule certainly violate our own intuitions. For the sake of argument, suppose that it is strongly counterintuitive to prevent a jury from hearing all the relevant evidence against an accused murderer, as we strongly suspect is the case. How can we explain the rules of evidence?

Our answer is neither surprising nor unique: Complex, peculiar rules of evidence persist because they work. We want to see as much relevant evidence as possible presented in trial; at the same time, we want to see safeguards against unscrupulous police practices or unreliable statements on the witness stand. Our rules of evidence strike a balance between these competing interests. We endure the counterintuitive outcomes of those rules in specific cases because they support a broader system that functions well, meeting our standards for the processes and outcomes of the law. There is a broader issue at stake in this example. We, and many others, have written about the ways that people construct and use moral principles that move beyond the raw material of their intuitive judgments of particular cases (e.g., Cushman & Young, 2009; Greene, 2007; Kohlberg, 1969; Pizarro & Bloom, 2003; Rawls, 1971, to cite only a few). For the purposes of this essay, a simple point suffices: Having situated the philosopher in the theater, we are in a better position to plot his or her escape.

REFERENCES

Alicke, M. (1992). Culpable causation. *Journal of Personality and Social Psychology, 63*, 368–378. doi:10.1037/0022-3514.63.3.368

Asch, D. A., Baron, J., Hershey, J. C., Kunreuther, H., Meszaros, J., Ritov, I., & Spranca, M. (1994). Omission bias and pertussis vaccination. *Medical Decision Making, 14*, 118–123. doi:10.1177/0272989X9401400204

Baron, J., & Ritov, I. (2004). Omission bias, individual differences, and normality. *Organizational Behavior and Human Decision Processes, 94*, 74–85. doi:10.1016/j.obhdp.2004.03.003

Bartels, D. M. (2008). Principled moral sentiment and the flexibility of moral judgment and decision making. *Cognition, 108*, 381–417. doi:10.1016/j.cognition.2008.03.001

Bunge, S. A., & Wallis, J. D. (Eds.). (2007). *Neuroscience of rule-guided behavior*. New York, NY: Oxford University Press. doi:10.1093/acprof:oso/9780195314274.001.0001

Caramazza, A., McCloskey, M., & Green, B. (1981). Naive beliefs in "sophisticated" subjects: Misconceptions about the trajectories of objects. *Cognition, 9*, 117–123. doi:10.1016/0010-0277(81)90007-X

Cushman, F. A. (2008a). Crime and punishment: Distinguishing the roles of causal and intentional analyses in moral judgment. *Cognition, 108*, 353–380. doi:10.1016/j.cognition.2008.03.006

Cushman, F. A. (2008b). *The origins of moral principles*. Unpublished doctoral dissertation, Harvard University, Cambridge, MA.

Cushman, F. A., Fieman, R., & Carey, S. (2011). *Infants' representations of others' goals: A preference for actions over omissions*. Unpublished manuscript.

Cushman, F. A., Murray, D., Gordon-McKeon, S., Wharton, S., & Greene, J. D. (2011). *Judgment before principle: Simultaneous engagement of prefrontal control and default networks in condemning harmful omissions*. Unpublished manuscript.

Cushman, F. A., & Young, L. (2009). The psychology of dilemmas and the philosophy of morality. *Ethical Theory and Moral Practice, 12*, 9–24. doi:10.1007/s10677-008-9145-3

Cushman, F. A., & Young, L. (in press). Patterns of moral judgment derive from nonmoral psychological representations. *Cognitive Science*.

Cushman, F. A., Young, L., & Hauser, M. D. (2006). The role of conscious reasoning and intuitions in moral judgment: Testing three principles of harm. *Psychological Science, 17*, 1082–1089. doi:10.1111/j.1467-9280.2006.01834.x

Darley, J. M., & Shultz, T. R. (1990). Moral rules: Their content and acquisition. *Annual Review of Psychology, 41*, 525–556. doi:10.1146/annurev.ps.41.020190.002521

Dennett, D. C. (1991). *Consciousness explained*. Boston, MA: Little Brown.

Fischer, J. M., & Ravizza, M. (1992). *Ethics: Problems and principles*. New York, NY: Holt, Rinehart & Winston.

Foot, P. (1967). The problem of abortion and the doctrine of double effect. *Oxford Review, 5,* 5–15.

Greene, J. D. (2007). The secret joke of Kant's soul. In W. Sinnott-Armstrong (Ed.), *Moral psychology* (Vol. 3, pp. 35–80). Cambridge, MA: MIT Press.

Greene, J. D., Cushman, F. A., Stewart, L. E., Lowenberg, K., Nystrom, L. E., & Cohen, J. D. (2009). Pushing moral buttons: The interaction between personal force and intention in moral judgment. *Cognition, 111,* 364–371. doi:10.1016/j.cognition.2009.02.001

Greene, J. D., Morelli, S. A., Lowenberg, K., Nystrom, L. E., & Cohen, J. D. (2008). Cognitive load selectively interferes with utilitarian moral judgment. *Cognition, 107,* 1144–1154. doi:10.1016/j.cognition.2007.11.004

Greene, J. D., Nystrom, L. E., Engell, A. D., Darley, J. M., & Cohen, J. D. (2004). The neural bases of cognitive conflict and control in moral judgment. *Neuron, 44,* 389–400. doi:10.1016/j.neuron.2004.09.027

Greene, J. D., Sommerville, R. B., Nystrom, L. E., Darley, J. M., & Cohen, J. D. (2001, September 14). An fMRI investigation of emotional engagement in moral judgment. *Science, 293,* 2105–2108. doi:10.1126/science.1062872

Haidt, J. (2001). The emotional dog and its rational tail: A social intuitionist approach to moral judgment. *Psychological Review, 108,* 814–834. doi:10.1037/0033-295X.108.4.814

Haidt, J., & Hersh, M. A. (2001). Sexual morality: The cultures and emotions of conservatives and liberals. *Journal of Applied Social Psychology, 31,* 191–221. doi:10.1111/j.1559-1816.2001.tb02489.x

Haidt, J. (2007, May 18). The new synthesis in moral psychology. *Science, 316,* 998–1002. doi:10.1126/science.1137651

Hauser, M. D., Cushman, F. A., Young, L., Jin, R., & Mikhail, J. M. (2007). A dissociation between moral judgment and justification. *Mind & Language, 22,* 1–21. doi:10.1111/j.1468-0017.2006.00297.x

Kamm, F. M. (1998). *Morality, mortality: Death and whom to save from it*. New York, NY: Oxford University Press. doi:10.1093/0195119118.001.0001

Kamm, F. M. (2006). *Intricate ethics: Rights, responsibilities, and permissible harm*. New York, NY: Oxford University Press.

Kohlberg, L. (1969). Stage and sequence: The cognitive–developmental approach to socialization. In D. A. Goslin (Ed.), *Handbook of socialization theory and research* (pp. 151–235). New York, NY: Academic Press.

Kohlberg, L. (1981). *Essays on moral development: Vol. 1. The philosophy of moral development*. New York, NY: Harper Row.

Lombrozo, T. (2007, June). *Mechanisms and functions: Empirical evidence for distinct modes of understanding*. Paper presented at the 33rd annual conference of the Society for Philosophy and Psychology, Toronto.

McCloskey, M. (1983). Intuitive physics. *Scientific American, 248,* 122–130. doi:10. 1038/scientificamerican0483-122

Mikhail, J. M. (2000). *Rawls' linguistic analogy: A study of the "generative grammar" model of moral theory described by John Rawls in "A theory of justice"* Unpublished doctoral dissertation, Cornell University, Ithaca, NY.

Muentener, P. (2009). *The origin and development of causal reasoning.* Unpublished doctoral dissertation, Harvard University, Cambridge, MA.

Paxton, J. M., & Greene, J. D. (2010). Moral reasoning: Hints and allegations. *Topics in Cognitive Science, 2,* 511–527. doi:10.1111/j.1756-8765.2010.01096.x

Pellizzoni, S., Siegal, M., & Surian, L. (2010). The contact principle and utilitarian moral judgments in young children. *Developmental Science, 13,* 265–270. doi:10. 1111/j.1467-7687.2009.00851.x

Petrinovich, L., O'Neill, P., & Jorgensen, M. J. (1993). An empirical study of moral intuitions: Towards an evolutionary ethics. *Journal of Personality and Social Psychology, 64,* 467–478. doi:10.1037/0022-3514.64.3.467

Piaget, J. (1965). *The moral judgment of the child.* New York, NY: Free Press. (Original work published 1932)

Pinker, S. (2007). *The stuff of thought.* New York, NY: Viking.

Pizarro, D. A., & Bloom, P. (2003). The intelligence of the moral intuitions: Comment on Haidt (2001). *Psychological Review, 110,* 193–196, discussion 197–198. doi:10.1037/0033-295X.110.1.193

Rawls, J. (1971). *A theory of justice.* Cambridge, MA: Harvard University Press.

Ritov, I. I., & Baron, J. (1999). Protected values and omission bias. *Organizational Behavior and Human Decision Processes, 79,* 79–94. doi:10.1006/obhd.1999.2839

Royzman, E., & Baron, J. (2002). The preference for indirect harm. *Social Justice Research, 15,* 165–184. doi:10.1023/A:1019923923537

Schwitzgebel, E., & Cushman, F. A. (in press). Expertise in moral reasoning? Order effects on moral judgment in professional philosophers and non-philosophers. *Mind & Language.*

Shweder, D., & Haidt, J. (1993). The future of moral psychology: Truth, intuition, and the pluralist way. *Psychological Science, 4,* 360–365. doi:10.1111/j.1467-9280.1993.tb00582.x

Sloman, S. (1996). The empirical case for two systems of reasoning. *Psychological Bulletin, 119,* 3–22. doi:10.1037/0033-2909.119.1.3

Spranca, M., Minsk, E., & Baron, J. (1991). Omission and commission in judgment and choice. *Journal of Experimental Social Psychology, 27,* 76–105. doi:10.1016/0022-1031(91)90011-T

Thomson, J. J. (1985). The trolley problem. *The Yale Law Journal, 94,* 1395–1415. doi:10.2307/796133

Uhlmann, E., Pizarro, D., Tannenbaum, D., & Ditto, P. (2009). The motivated use of moral principles. *Judgment and Decision Making, 4,* 476–491.

Vacco v. Quill, 521 U.S. 793 (1997).

Weiner, B. (1995). *Judgments of responsibility: A foundation for a theory of social conduct.* New York, NY: Guilford Press.

White, P. A. (1990). Ideas about causation in philosophy and psychology. *Psychological Bulletin, 108,* 3–18. doi:10.1037/0033-2909.108.1.3

Young, L., Cushman, F. A., Hauser, M. D., & Saxe, R. (2007). The neural basis of the interaction between theory of mind and moral judgment. *Proceedings of the National Academy of Sciences of the United States of America, 104,* 8235–8240. doi:10.1073/pnas.0701408104

3

DEONTOLOGICAL DISSONANCE AND THE CONSEQUENTIALIST CRUTCH

PETER H. DITTO AND BRITTANY LIU

Partial definition of the adjective form of the word *right:*
2. being in accordance with what is just, good, or proper;
3. conforming to facts or truth: correct
—Merriam-Webster, Inc. (2005)

People have moral beliefs. They believe that some things are morally right and some are morally wrong, just as they believe that other propositions about the state of the world are factually right or factually wrong. In the absence of pressure to justify their positions, people seem to experience prescriptive beliefs such as "Capital punishment is wrong" in much the same way they experience descriptive beliefs like "Cutting taxes stimulates the economy." Interesting differences emerge, however, when people are required to justify their moral beliefs.

In this chapter, we examine the relation between moral beliefs (i.e., what a person believes is morally just, good, or proper) and factual beliefs (i.e., what a person believes is empirically true on the basis of fact, observation, and reason). We make the case that people are both moral intuitionists and moral realists: that our beliefs about right and wrong are more often a product of affective reactions than of deliberative cognitive processing, but that we nonetheless feel a need to justify the "truth" of our moral beliefs with reference to some form of evidence. This becomes tricky for people when faced with classic forms of moral dilemmas, in which the superficial facts of the matter suggest that no course of action is without morally undesirable consequences. It is in these cases, we argue, that factual beliefs come into moral play and are often constructed in ways that minimize the experience of moral conflict. Hence, people rarely take true "moral stands" by asserting that some course of action is morally right, even when facts suggest that other actions are more practically advantageous. Rather, people tend to bring their factual beliefs into line with their moral intuitions, such that the right course of action morally becomes the right course of action practically as well. Our analysis complicates simple distinctions between deontological (rule- or principle-based) and consequentialist (outcome- or consequence-based) morality and identifies a key contributor to the intractability of many moral and political conflicts. It is difficult to resolve differences of opinion when each side has its own facts.

MORAL INTUITIONISM

Over the past several decades, the dominant perspective in moral psychology has evolved from a rationalist view that saw cognitive sophistication and deliberative reasoning as the crucial phenomena in moral judgment (e.g., Kohlberg, 1969) to a recognition that implicit affective processes play a substantial role in establishing beliefs about right and wrong (e.g., see Chapters 1, 2, 9, and 18, this volume). This affective revolution was sparked by two groundbreaking papers published in 2001: Greene, Sommerville, Nystrom, Darley, and Cohen's (2001) empirical demonstration of the involvement of emotional centers of the brain when a person considers classic moral dilemmas and Haidt's (2001) articulation of a social intuitionist model of moral judgment. In sharp contrast to Kohlberg's (1969) rationalist position, this new look in moral psychology posited that right and wrong are judgments more often felt than thought. Haidt in particular argued that moral judgments are less like reasoned inferences than aesthetic preferences; they are evaluations that seem to appear in consciousness unattached to any logical derivation or evidentiary basis (Hume, 1740/1985). Importantly, neither Haidt nor Greene et al. contended that thoughtful deliberation plays no role in moral judgment, but rather that moral reasoning is a special case, usually prompted either by conflict between competing moral intuitions or in the service of explaining one's moral beliefs to others.

MORAL REALISM

People may arrive at moral judgments intuitively, but most do not perceive them as merely idiosyncratic hunches or matters of personal taste. People navigate the world as naive realists, believing that their perceptions reflect the external world as it is, with little appreciation for how top-down construal processes can shape subjective impressions (e.g., Ross & Ward, 1996). Naive realism plays an important role in moral judgment as well.

When presented with matters of aesthetics or social convention, people seldom say that there is a universally "correct" answer to these questions or that someone who gives a different answer from theirs is "wrong." But in matters of scientific fact they assume that there is a correct answer, and they often respond similarly to important moral questions (Goodwin & Darley, 2008). Although people are sensitive to differences between factual and moral judgments, most people most of the time approach the world as moral realists, experiencing the morality of issues such as racial prejudice, stem cell research, and enhanced interrogation techniques as "objective" characteristics of phenomena (Goodwin & Darley, 2008; Skitka, Bauman, & Sargis, 2005; see also Chapter 19, this volume) that apply universally across people and cultures (Nichols & Folds-Bennett, 2003). Even people reading this chapter, for example, despite their sophisticated understanding of the complexities of moral judgment, probably spend the better part of their day believing that embryonic stem cell research really is morally justifiable, that waterboarding really is morally wrong, and that people who disagree with them on these scores are mistaken about the actual moral qualities of those acts. As one would expect, this is particularly true of our most important moral beliefs (Skitka et al., 2005) and, we suspect, is even more true implicitly, outside the glare of psychologists' prodding questions, than when people are explicitly asked by researchers to consider the nature of their beliefs.

In short, people treat morality as more than just a matter of aesthetics or opinion. Although we appreciate that morality is something more subjective than scientifically verifiable fact, our actions nevertheless imply that we endorse some notion of moral "truth," some sense that beliefs about right and wrong can themselves be right or wrong.

MORAL JUSTIFICATION

If our moral reactions are to be treated as something more than mere opinion, however, both philosophers and ordinary people expect them to be justified by some form of evidence. The intuitive nature of moral responses makes us unlikely to generate moral justifications spontaneously (just as we are unlikely to question the validity of visual or auditory perceptions; Gilbert, 1991), but if moral intuitions are challenged by others, or if a situation evokes conflicting moral intuitions, it is not enough just to assert that, for example, capital punishment is wrong and then be done with it. As with matters of fact, we expect other people to agree with our moral positions, and if we are to convince them to do so, we have to provide them with some justification for why they should share our beliefs.

It is in this matter of justification, however, that moral and factual judgments differ. Simply put, descriptive judgments are justified by facts and logic. If we want to argue that cutting taxes stimulates the economy, it is incumbent upon us to provide factual evidence that logically supports the accuracy of this description. But moral judgments have a more complicated relation to descriptive facts, and in particular to cost–benefit logic, than do nonmoral judgments.

First, it has often been argued that the essence of moral thinking is deontological intuitions, that some acts are simply right or wrong in and of themselves, no matter their costs or benefits to self or others (Baron & Spranca, 1997; Kant, 1785/1998). Many people state, for example, that it is morally wrong to use human embryos in medical research, even if that research might produce tremendous benefits in lives saved from serious illness. This notion of the *sacred*, that certain acts are protected from normal cost–benefit valuation (that the "ends do not justify the means"), is often thought to be what separates truly moral judgments from other kinds of thinking (see Chapter 1, this volume).

Most important, because deontological moral judgments are inherently rule based, factual justifications are irrelevant (Tanner, Medin, & Iliev, 2008). What facts could be harnessed to prove that embryonic stem cell research is immoral independent of its consequences? In such cases, people justify their moral intuitions by invoking a principle. Grounding one's specific deontological intuitions as an instantiation of a general moral principle allows moral justification to take a form (e.g., "I believe stem cell research is wrong because it is morally impermissible to deliberately sacrifice innocent human life even for a greater good") very much like fact-based inference (e.g., "I believe cutting taxes improves the economy because data show that tax cuts stimulate business growth and investment"). It is important to note, however, that the principle, like the specific judgment, is a prescriptive value assessment that cannot be supported in any simple way by descriptive facts.

But not all moral justifications are based on pure principle. In many cases for many people, moral beliefs are justified via much the same logical analysis as factual beliefs. The broad set of philosophical positions referred to as *consequentialism* (aka *utilitarianism*) is founded on the notion that the morality of an act is based on some sort of calculation of the benefits it produces (Bentham, 1789/1961). Thus, many people state that capital punishment is morally justified because it deters potential future murderers from committing this crime; that is, that the taking of one life is justified by saving many more. Consequentialism explicitly subsumes moral reasoning within cost–benefit analyses, with the assumption that ends can justify means depending on the moral balance sheet.

In the case of consequentialist moral judgments, factual beliefs are quite relevant to moral justification. If one asserts that capital punishment is permissible because it deters future murders, then one is also asserting (descriptively) that these acts actually do produce these outcomes. Similarly, given that one's moral evaluation is based on the cost–benefit ratio of the act to the outcome, facts about the costs of the action are also relevant. If one believes that waterboarding is not particularly painful and causes no permanent psychological damage, then the low cost means that less benefit in terms of acquired intelligence needs to be assumed for that act to pass muster in a moral cost–benefit calculation.

In summary, there are two primary ways to justify moral beliefs. One is to stand on principle. This kind of deontological stand is theoretically independent of factual belief or rational analysis. The stand is justified by prescriptive beliefs about the inherent (im)morality of the act. The second way to justify moral beliefs is to focus on outcomes. This latter form of judgment, consequentialism, is a kind of rational moral calculus in which descriptive beliefs about the likelihood that an act will bring about particular outcomes play a crucial role. The only prescriptive principle involved in consequentialism is that the morality of acts should be based on their consequences. Once that position is adopted, moral evaluation is just a matter of fact.

MORAL CONFLICT

Moral justification becomes most interesting when principles come into conflict with cost–benefit analyses and factual beliefs. Psychologists and philosophers are fascinated by moral dilemmas, situations in which no moral choice is without undesirable moral consequences. Of particular interest have been dilemmas that pit deontological against consequentialist logic, as in Kohlberg's famous Heinz dilemma, in which a husband must choose whether or not to steal an overpriced drug to save his wife's life (Kohlberg, 1969), or the trolley problem, in which the morality of redirecting a runaway trolley train to kill one individual rather than five must be evaluated (e.g., Foot, 1994; see also Chapter 2, this volume). These dilemmas place people in a difficult moral quandary, requiring them to weigh whether one ostensibly immoral act (committing a robbery or taking a single life) can be justified if it produces what most would consider a greater moral benefit (curing one's wife of a deadly disease or saving the lives of five people in exchange for the life of one).

The conflicting intuitions these puzzles engage make them fun to ponder at cocktail parties or dorm-room bull sessions, but understanding how people deal with moral dilemmas is more than just an academic parlor game or an exercise in frivolous "trolleyology." The value of studying fanciful laboratory puzzles comes from the similarity they share with many real-world moral controversies. Capital punishment, embryonic stem cell research, the use of forceful interrogation techniques, and even whether to promote condom use to teenagers all pose the same essential question of whether (or under what circumstances) undesirable means can be justified to achieve desirable ends. Debates about the proper policies to pursue in these situations have consumed countless hours of debate in halls of government, on 24-hr cable news stations, and in Internet blogs and chat rooms. The intense disagreements these issues engender form the centerpiece of the venomous "culture war" in contemporary American politics (e.g., Hunter, 1991).

And yet an interesting feature of the moral conflict caused by these dilemmas is that the conflict is largely interpersonal rather than intrapersonal. That is, groups and individuals fight endlessly about the morally correct response to the dilemmas posed by the death penalty, enhanced interrogation, and so on. But individuals seldom experience their chosen solution as particularly dilemmatic. Rather, people who believe that capital punishment is inherently immoral also typically contend that it is ineffective at deterring future crime, and it is difficult to find anyone who believes that techniques like waterboarding are morally reprehensible who does not also doubt their effectiveness in producing actionable intelligence. How do people enjoy the best of both worlds, touting their moral imperatives while at the same time believing that the cost–benefit analysis is on their side as well?

MORAL CONFABULATION

Moral dilemmas resemble a classic free-choice cognitive dissonance paradigm in that any choice an individual makes produces, at least temporarily, some level of psychological discomfort (see Chapter 9, this volume). In the classic trolley dilemma, for example, if a person makes the consequentialist choice to sacrifice a single life to save five, that choice necessarily results in both consonant cognitions (that five lives have been saved by one's decision) and dissonant cognitions (that one's decision also resulted in the death of an innocent person). The dissonance resulting from the choice can be made more or less intense depending on other relevant cognitions—for example, whether one has to actively push an innocent person to his death or merely flip a switch to produce the result—but some level of dissonance is virtually inescapable for anyone with normal moral sensibilities (see Chapter 2, this volume).

Moreover, a deontological choice should be particularly dissonance inducing. In this case, the individual chooses to defy rational cost–benefit calculations to take a moral stand, refusing to sacrifice one life even though doing so would save five others. At some level, this kind of principled choice does not make sense (quite literally, it doesn't "add up"). Attributing disproportionate (sometimes infinite) value to certain acts or objects necessarily runs afoul of our sense of moral realism, our need to provide some rational justification for our beliefs. Individuals in these situations can and do appeal to principle as an explanation, but this is a difficult stance that conflicts with firmly entrenched and well-rehearsed economic intuitions. For this reason, true moral stands—when one sees them—are inspiring. We respond positively to persuaders who argue against their own self-interest (Eagly, Wood, & Chaiken, 1978) and to "maverick" politicians who advocate positions that may hurt their standing within their own political party (Ditto & Mastronarde, 2009). But these instances are rare (and thus especially admirable), precisely because they seem to swim upstream against fundamental economic (i.e., consequentialist) sensibilities.

So what are the consequences of this moral dissonance? As we have known since Festinger's (1957) original statement of cognitive dissonance theory, dissonance is an unstable state, and the human mind works to resolve it by adding or adjusting cognitions in a way that moves beliefs toward greater harmony. We would expect morally relevant dissonance processes to operate in a similar fashion, and in fact, dissonance resolution may operate particularly smoothly in moral reasoning. An intuitionist perspective (Haidt, 2001) suggests that individuals recruit reasoning processes to justify their moral intuitions after the fact. The intuitive response to a particular dilemma could be based on moral values rooted in cultural or political socialization (see Chapter 1, this volume) or on details inherent to the specific situation (e.g., revulsion at the thought of having to push a man to his death to stop a trolley), but the key point is that the process of justifying moral intuitions is top down rather than bottom up, and consequently moral reasoning should be relatively easy fodder for confabulation by a motivated moral thinker (Ditto, Pizarro, & Tannenbaum, 2009).

The most obvious manifestation of this dissonance-reducing confabulation process would be manipulation of an act's cost–benefit ratio. Thus, if an individual's intuition favors a consequentialist response in a given situation (that it is permissible to engage in an undesirable act for a greater good), one way to bolster the moral correctness of that response would be to enhance the value and/or likelihood of the benefits of the act (e.g., saving five people, deterring future crime) and downplay the value and/or likelihood of the costs of the act (e.g., sacrificing the life of a railroad worker or a convicted murderer).

We should note two important features of this process. First, the most effective way to reduce the psychological conflict is by constructing factual beliefs that support one's moral intuitions. An individual whose intuition favors the morality of the death penalty, for example, should find it reassuring to believe that capital punishment indeed serves as a deterrent to future murders. This intuition is likely to shape judgment and memory processes in a way that favors this preferred belief in the deterrent efficacy of the death penalty (Ditto & Lopez, 1992; Kunda, 1990). For similar reasons, the costs of capital punishment would seem most effectively downplayed by altering one's descriptive beliefs about the likelihood that innocent individuals are executed by mistake or even the pain involved in executions.[1]

Second, this process has particularly provocative implications for deontological judgment. Theoretically, deontological judgments are independent of facts and cost–benefit considerations, but imagine an individual whose intuitions suggest that the death penalty is inherently immoral, yet who believes that it is an effective deterrent against future murders. Most of us would find this position morally admirable (perhaps even those who disagree with it) but psychologically challenging. And it is for this very reason, we believe, that such purely moral stands occur infrequently in the real world. It is much more likely, we suspect, that an individual who believes in the inherent immorality of capital punishment—and would even maintain that this belief is based on principle rather than consequences—will nonetheless come to believe that capital punishment is ineffective at deterring murder. The same pressure to bolster one's deontological stand is likely to organize beliefs about the undesirable costs of capital punishment, and the same tendency to square moral intuitions with

---

[1]A question that may occur to readers at this point in our argument concerns what role, if any, "objective" reality plays in factual belief. That is, does it matter to our analysis whether capital punishment actually deters crime or the veridical frequency with which innocent people are unjustly executed? For the most part, these questions are well beyond the scope of this chapter and belong more in the realm of metaphysics than psychology. But a few quick points can be made. There is clear evidence from the motivated reasoning literature that people's judgments are generally responsive to the strength of available information and that people do not ignore plausible information to believe whatever they wish to believe just because they wish to believe it (Ditto, Scepansky, Munro, Apanovitch, & Lockhart, 1998; Kunda, 1990). Festinger himself acknowledged such "reality constraints" in his 1957 book introducing cognitive dissonance theory when he noted that "if one sees the grass as green, it is very difficult to think it is not so" (pp. 24–25). Motivated reasoning processes are most pronounced when information is ambiguous or contradictory, but it is crucial to note that this is precisely the epistemic situation typified by virtually every judgment humans make (see Festinger, 1954), and certainly the sorts of sociopolitical judgments that concern us in this chapter. It would take a second chapter of at least this length to review the inconclusive and contradictory scientific data on the deterrent efficacy of capital punishment (e.g., Weisberg, 2005), and at the end we would be little closer to knowing whether capital punishment actually deters future crime. Some experts believe it does; others believe it does not. At that point, who is to judge who is objectively correct? Perhaps more important, only a handful of people who have firm opinions about the death penalty's deterrent effects have more than the most passing acquaintance with the relevant scientific data, so it strains plausibility to believe that the average person's attitudes and beliefs about capital punishment (or any similar issue for that matter) are based in any way on a sensitivity to what is objectively true. Psychologically, it is fair to say that belief is broadly constrained by pseudological reasoning processes, but speculation about whether one set of beliefs is more correct than another is both precarious and a distraction from the more tractable enterprise of specifying the cognitive and affective processes that shape those beliefs.

factual beliefs should characterize any of the host of real-world moral dilemmas in which deontological and consequentialist intuitions collide.

In summary, then, we contend that when individuals have an intuitive moral reaction to a given issue, this intuition guides post hoc attempts to justify that reaction by strategically organizing factual beliefs about the costs and benefits of alternate courses of action. This should hold true even for (or even especially for) deontological intuitions that are typically considered to be independent of cost–benefit considerations. This leads to the interesting prediction that because of the unique dissonance they engender, deontological moral stands often find support in a consequentialist crutch.

PREVIOUS WORK ON MORAL AND FACTUAL BELIEFS

The notion that moral values can shape factual beliefs is not new (Baron & Spranca, 1997; Juth & Lynöe, 2010; Kahan, Braman, Slovic, Gastil, & Cohen, 2007; Skitka & Mullen, 2002). The most extensive empirical work on the subject is that of Kahan and collaborators (2007) examining what they called *cultural cognition*. Rather than examining moral values per se, they focused on how cultural values such as belief in the equal distribution of goods across individuals (individualism vs. egalitarianism) can influence factual beliefs about controversial political topics. In one study, for example, participants' reactions to information about the human papillomavirus (HPV) vaccine polarized along cultural lines, such that individualists believed the HPV vaccine would be less likely to reduce rates of cervical cancer and more likely to encourage vaccinated women to have unprotected sex than did egalitarians. In other words, those least likely to support mandatory HPV vaccinations also thought it was least likely to be effective in producing benefits and most likely to have undesirable costs.

Similarly, in a theoretical analysis that anticipated our own, Baron and Spranca (1997) tested a number of predictions about their notion of *protected values* (i.e., values that "resist trade-offs with other values, particularly economic values"; p. 1). They found that the more individuals characterized a value (e.g., prohibiting euthanasia) as absolute and protected from trade-offs, the more likely they were to deny that anything was lost for the sake of this value. In the authors' words, "People want to have their non-utilitarian cake and eat it too" (Baron & Spranca, 1997, p. 13).

Motivated Consequentialism

Our own empirical work has focused specifically on responses to moral dilemmas that pit deontological against consequentialist intuitions. We examined people's moral choices and the ways in which they shape factual beliefs about both the benefits of an action and its potential costs.

Lifeboats and Trolleys

In our first set of studies, we presented college students with two classic moral dilemmas: the lifeboat dilemma, in which a choice must be made about whether to push an injured man off a lifeboat to prevent it from sinking (and thus killing all of the people aboard); and the footbridge version of the trolley problem, in which the action in question is pushing a large man off a footbridge to stop a runaway trolley. One alteration we made in both scenarios was to remove language asserting certainties between actions and consequences. That is, most previous research on moral judgment simplified moral choices by encouraging participants to assume that, for example, throwing a sick man overboard would definitely save the others in the lifeboat and that he would certainly die even if he were not sacrificed for the lives of the other passengers. We used softer probabilistic language in our scenarios because it was precisely the perception of these likelihoods that we were interested in studying.

In the lifeboat scenario, we asked participants to indicate whether they believed it was morally acceptable to throw the injured man overboard and then to assess (a) the likelihood that throwing him overboard would save the other passengers, (b) the likelihood that the injured man would die if not thrown overboard, and (c) how much pain the injured man would experience if thrown overboard. The pattern of responses we observed was perfectly consistent with our hypotheses based on the theoretical analysis presented earlier in the present chapter. Compared with participants who thought that sacrificing the injured man was morally acceptable, those who believed it was not morally acceptable also believed that sacrificing him had a lower probability of saving the other passengers, gave a higher probability that he was likely to survive if not thrown overboard, and believed that he would experience a more painful death if he was thrown over.

The obvious question about these results concerns their causal direction. We cannot know from this study whether prescriptive moral judgments shaped factual beliefs about costs and benefits or whether participants decided that pushing the injured man overboard was wrong precisely because, for example, the likelihood that this act would save the other passengers was low. Nonetheless, it is worth considering the conceptual implications of this alternative causal scenario. In past moral judgment research (e.g., Bartels, 2008; Tanner et al., 2008), a participant who stated that it was morally unacceptable to sacrifice the injured man would have been characterized as making a deontological judgment (i.e., a judgment based on principle rather than the consequences of the act). But if it was truly the participant's cost–benefit calculations that led to the decision that sacrificing the man would be immoral, that judgment is anything but deontological. Rather, a consequentialist calculus can be posited to underlie both the belief that it is moral to sacrifice the man and the belief that it is not.

The footbridge scenario data push this point a bit farther. In that scenario, we did not specify the number of workmen who would be saved by pushing the large man onto the tracks. Instead, after reading the scenario, participants were asked to indicate how many workmen's lives would need to be saved for them to feel that it was morally acceptable to push him. They were given nine response options ranging from "at least two" to "at least 1,000," with the final option being "I would never push the stranger, no matter how many lives would be saved." As in past studies using the footbridge dilemma, our participants were extremely reluctant to push the man onto the tracks, with 80% indicating that no trade-off in saved lives could justify this action. This allowed us to compare individuals who gave what appears to be a fully deontological response with the smaller set who endorsed some level of consequentialist trade-off. The pattern of descriptive beliefs observed was identical to those found in the lifeboat scenario. Compared with the consequentialist minority, participants who on the surface seemed to be taking a principled stand against sacrificing the large stranger gave a lower likelihood that pushing him onto the tracks would stop the trolley, gave a higher likelihood that the workers might get off the tracks before the trolley struck them, and gave higher estimates of the pain the large stranger would suffer if pushed onto the tracks. Again, these results cannot resist an alternate causal interpretation, but they reveal even more clearly than the lifeboat results that a judgment that past researchers would typically have interpreted as implying a deontological moral stand in our study was actually kept upright by leaning on a consequentialist crutch.

Real-World Dilemmas

Besides the causal direction question (to which we will return shortly), the other clear limitation of this first set of results is their artificiality. We therefore set out to demonstrate a similar conflation of moral and factual beliefs in a set of real-world dilemmas. The four we selected were

1. capital punishment, in which taking the life of a convicted murderer is balanced against the potential deterrence of future crime;
2. forceful interrogation techniques, in which the suffering inflicted on individuals suspected of terrorism is balanced against the potential of collecting information that could prevent future terrorism;

3. embryonic stem cell research, in which the destruction of human embryo cells is balanced against the potential of developing treatments for diseases; and

4. condom promotion in high school sex education classes, in which the (at least implicit) condoning of sexual behavior in teenagers is balanced against the potential benefit of preventing sexually transmitted disease (STD) and unwanted pregnancy.

These four issues have all been the focus of considerable controversy in recent years, and the four are ideologically balanced in that political conservatism is associated with favorable moral beliefs about the first two issues and unfavorable moral beliefs about the last two.

We presented information about these four dilemmas to approximately 1,800 visitors to YourMorals.org (http://yourmorals.org; a data collection website offering participants the chance to complete various psychological, moral, and political scales in exchange for feedback about their responses; see also Chapter 1, this volume). To get a thoughtful assessment of the extent to which participants had deontological intuitions about each issue, participants were first asked to provide a simple moral evaluation (e.g., with a scale judging the death penalty from "morally acceptable in most or all cases" to "morally wrong in most or all cases") and then an agree–disagree scale designed to tap willingness to accept trade-offs with regard to the issue (e.g., "The use of the death penalty as punishment for murder is morally wrong even if it discourages others from committing the same crime"). We believe this procedure made the more nuanced intent of the second scale clearer to participants, and items with this format were used as our measure of deontological intuitions about each of the four issues.

For each issue, we also asked a series of questions that assessed two key factual beliefs: (a) the likelihood that the action in question would produce its assumed beneficial effects and (b) the likelihood that the action in question would produce undesirable consequences (i.e., costs). So, for example, questions about capital punishment focused on perceptions of how likely it was to deter future murders (its main benefit) and whether executions caused suffering and how often they were carried out in error (undesirable costs). In every case but one, three or more questions tapped each construct, and reliable perceived benefit and perceived cost indices were created for each issue.

The results were remarkably consistent, both with each other and with our predictions. For all four issues, regression analyses revealed strong relations between deontological intuitions and perceived benefits and costs. Using forceful interrogations as an example, the more strongly participants endorsed the belief that forceful interrogation was morally wrong even if it was effective in getting terrorist suspects to talk, the less likely they were to believe it actually was effective and the greater estimates they gave of the degree of physical and emotional stress it inflicted on its victims. The results for condom promotion were also fascinating, revealing that participants who most strongly believed that sex education programs encouraging condom use were morally wrong even if they prevented STDs and pregnancy also had the strongest beliefs that such programs were no more effective than abstinence-based programs, that condoms themselves were ineffective in preventing STDs and pregnancy, and that promoting condoms simply made teenagers more likely to have sex.

Manipulating Deontological Intuitions

The results of our first two studies are impressive in their strength and consistency, and their oddly counterintuitive quality is exactly what one would expect if people experienced psychological pressure to reinforce their deontological intuitions with consequentialist logic. But they are still correlational, so we designed a final study to confirm our beliefs about causal direction.

In that study, we picked one issue, capital punishment, and tried to manipulate deontological intuitions to see if this would alter consequentialist beliefs. Participants were college students who began the experimental session with a questionnaire asking them the same types of questions used in our correlational study, including their moral evaluation of capital punishment in its deontological form, their beliefs about its deterrent efficacy, and their beliefs about its undesirable costs (e.g., the likelihood of executing an innocent person). These questions were embedded in similar questions about the other issues to disguise our interest in them. Participants were told they would read an essay about one of the four issues chosen at random. All participants read essays about capital punishment, but some read an essay supportive of its morality and some an essay arguing against its morality. These essays were of a particular kind, however. They were designed to be purely deontological in quality. Neither essay made any arguments for or against the morality of capital punishment based on its effectiveness as a crime deterrent or the likelihood of undesirable costs. The main points in the pro–death penalty essay were (a) justice for a murderer is best and most fairly achieved with capital punishment, (b) premeditated murderers are—by their own choice—subhuman and do not deserve mercy, and (c) favoring capital punishment shows the highest form of regard for human life. The main points in the anti–death penalty essay were (a) capital punishment is wrong because it is barbaric and inhumane, (b) it is wrong to punish violence with further violence, and (c) it is wrong to quantifiably measure death by saying some forms of homicide (e.g., drunk driving) deserve less punishment than other forms (premeditated murder). After reading the essay, participants completed a series of questionnaires in which were embedded the same questions about capital punishment they had completed at the pretest.

Results showed that even though the two measurements were typically taken less than a half hour apart, we were able to change both deontological intuitions about capital punishment and factual beliefs about its costs and benefits. Despite the fact that neither essay mentioned deterrent efficacy—only the principled morality or immorality of capital punishment—participants exposed to the pro–death penalty essay reported significantly stronger beliefs that capital punishment deterred crime than did participants exposed to the anti–death penalty essay. Furthermore, participants who read the anti–death penalty essay became stronger believers that capital punishment causes an executed person significant suffering and that it was frequently carried out mistakenly on innocent individuals than did participants exposed to the pro–death penalty essay.

Moral Naiveté?

Before we discuss the implications of these findings in greater depth, we should address a common question concerning whether the blurring of the lines between deontological and consequentialist thought observed in our studies is merely a product of our study participants' lack of experience in grappling with complex moral issues. Perhaps individuals more practiced and informed, such as professional politicians, are less likely to show such effects.

An intriguing body of research, however, suggests quite the contrary, that more informed and sophisticated individuals are particularly prone to judgmental bias (Federico & Sidanius, 2002; Taber & Lodge, 2006; Vallone, Ross, & Lepper, 1985). Taber and Lodge (2006), for example, found that participants with more political knowledge (e.g., ones who could correctly answer questions about such things as the name of the office held by Antonin Scalia, a U.S. Supreme Court justice) showed more partisan bias when evaluating issues such as affirmative action and gun control policies than did less politically savvy participants. A similar pattern was seen in Vallone et al.'s (1985) famous demonstration of hostile media bias. Examining pro-Arab and pro-Israeli reactions to media coverage of the 1982 Beirut Massacre, they found that greater knowledge of the event and its antecedents was associated with stronger beliefs that one's own side was treated more harshly by the media than the opposition and with memories more biased toward remembering positive references to the other side and negative references to one's own. One way to interpret this pattern is that relative experts in any particular domain have more emotional commitment to their chosen attitudinal position and/or greater cognitive ammunition to defend it.

Our own data on real-world moral dilemmas reveal a similar pattern. One of the limitations of samples collected via YourMorals.org is that visitors to the site tend to be politically informed and highly educated (a substantial percentage have graduate degrees). So it is a sophisticated sample to begin with. More important, however, we collected measures of how informed participants perceived themselves to be about each issue under consideration as well as the degree to which they considered each issue a moral mandate (Mullen & Skitka, 2006). When these measures were included in regression analyses, we found that in almost every case our predicted effects were significantly stronger the more informed participants perceived themselves to be about the issue and frequently stronger the more morally committed the participants were to their particular position on the issue. That is, the more participants felt they knew about the issue and the more they perceived it as a moral mandate, the more their cost–benefit perceptions were consistent with their moral intuitions. These data have obvious limitations, but together with the similar pattern found in previous studies, they suggest a very testable hypothesis that it may be political sophisticates rather than neophytes who are most prone to attitude-justifying biases.

CONCLUSIONS AND CONSEQUENCES

It is an odd coincidence (at least, we think it is a coincidence) that in English we use the same word—*right*—to refer to both moral and factual correctness. In this chapter, however, we have argued that there may actually be some psychological substance to this linguistic homography. Our central point is that because of our desire to reify our moral intuitions—to transform them into moral "beliefs" that can be right or wrong in the same sense that factual beliefs can be right or wrong—we tend to shape our descriptive understanding of the world to fit our prescriptive understanding of it. At this level, the research reported here represents another example of a tendency, long noted by philosophers, for people to have trouble maintaining clear conceptual boundaries between what ought to be and what is (Hume, 1740/1985).

In particular, people seem to experience a fundamental conflict between deontological and consequentialist intuitions. Our sense that certain acts are simply wrong, in and of themselves, often clashes with knowledge suggesting that engaging in those acts is likely to produce moral benefits that seem to outweigh any tangible costs. Why not sell your deceased husband's wedding ring for a hefty profit? Why not sacrifice one life to save five? Our moral selves and our economic selves are not always good bedfellows (e.g., Baron & Spranca, 1997), and thus a rapprochement must be reached in which our moral balance sheet fits better with our moral intuitions.

It is because of this tendency toward deontological dissonance that pure deontological stands, in political discourse at least, are exceedingly rare. Try to imagine an example of a politician or pundit arguing that forceful interrogations are morally wrong while also admitting that they are effective, or that the death penalty is wrong even though it deters crime. Standing on principle is a challenging psychological feat, and it is often seen as both an admired moral virtue and a powerful persuasive tool precisely because it occurs so rarely.

The tendency for moral beliefs to shape factual ones has both theoretical and practical implications. Theoretically, as we noted earlier, it challenges simple distinctions between deontological and consequentialist judgments, especially regarding how these terms are used to describe research findings. A moral intuitionist position suggests that people seldom reason from the bottom up to moral conclusions using deontological or consequentialist logic. Rather, they more typically generate this logic from the top down and thus are likely to latch onto any justification they can find to support their intuitions. Our data confirm this tendency and suggest that characterizing certain moral positions as deontological may be particularly misleading. It is time to stop using reasoning-based terms to describe intuitively based judgments.

Practically, the tendency for people to harness factual beliefs to support entrenched moral commitments can be linked to a number of social and political controversies. For example, abstinence-only sexual education programs have yielded notoriously poor results, typically producing little or no delay in onset of sexual intercourse and often an increased tendency to engage in unsafe sex practices (Santelli et al., 2006). This is precisely the pattern our analysis would predict. It is difficult to maintain the belief that encouraging the use of condoms is morally wrong and also that it is effective in preventing STDs and pregnancy. One way to bolster this belief with consequentialist logic is to come to believe that condoms themselves are ineffective (providing another reason, besides principle, not to promote them). We found exactly this pattern of beliefs in our data, and abstinence-only sexual education programs are well known for disparaging the effectiveness of safe-sex practices (Santelli et al., 2006). In fact, a recent study found that an abstinence-education program that did not denigrate the effectiveness of condoms was effective in delaying students' onset of first intercourse compared with a control health promotion intervention (Jemmott, Jemmott, & Fong, 2010).[2]

---

[2] We cite this example because the current analysis can speculatively explain an odd phenomenon— that abstinence-only sex education programs often produce an increase in unsafe sex—not to imply that political conservatives are more prone to coordinate moral and factual beliefs than are political liberals. As discussed in the first footnote, psychological analyses are for the most part ill-equipped to assess the accuracy of beliefs. Comparing the magnitude of a specific judgmental bias across different groups is potentially more tractable but considerably more difficult than it might initially appear. To date, we have neither the data to support, nor any clear theoretical reason to predict, that the processes discussed in this chapter are more pronounced in individuals of one particular political persuasion than another. We agree that this is a fascinating question for future research to address, but we have tried to take care throughout this chapter to balance our use of examples (e.g., conservative resistance to stem cell research vs. liberal resistance to enhanced interrogation), consistent with our current working presumption that motivated consequentialism is a bipartisan bias.

Finally, and most generally, as avid observers of contemporary American politics, we find it hard not to notice how the vicious partisan battles that dominate political discourse are fueled by huge discrepancies in factual beliefs. Liberals and conservatives have well-documented differences in their moral sensibilities (e.g., Chapters 1 and 7, this volume). Although these present obvious challenges to political compromise, one could imagine an ideal world in which such differences of opinion were settled with reference to data. If conservatives find liberals' support for government intervention in the economy morally distasteful and favor instead across-the-board tax cuts, the solution would seem to require only a simple check of the data to see which strategy was most effective. But what can be done when liberals contend that the recent economic stimulus package created 2 million new jobs and conservatives assert that it has created not a one (Lee, 2010)? Liberals and conservatives similarly have differing moral reactions about forceful interrogation of terrorism suspects but spend almost all of their time disputing their radically different beliefs about its effectiveness (Ackerman, 2010).

It is difficult enough to resolve differences of moral opinion, but when these differences align themselves almost perfectly with differing perceptions of fact, it presents a major obstacle to fruitful negotiation. The tendency for people to shape factual beliefs to reinforce moral and ideological commitments is a compromise killer and conversation stopper. The hypothesis that this may be especially characteristic of people with deep ideological commitments and extensive factual knowledge would explain a lot about the current state of American politics. In the intense partisan bickering that preceded the recent passage of the controversial health care reform bill in the United States, several prominent Democratic politicians, including President Barack Obama, responded to Republican politicians with variants of a line usually attributed to former Senator Daniel Patrick Moynihan: "You are entitled to your own opinion. But you are not entitled to your own facts." One can rest assured that Republicans feel the same way about the Democrats' facts and that each side's moral beliefs seem as real to them as the moral and political conflict they inevitably engender.

REFERENCES

Ackerman, S. (2010, February 22). Marc Thiessen truly has no idea what he's talking about on interrogation. *The Washington Independent*. Retrieved from http://washingtonindependent.com/77302

Baron, J., & Spranca, M. (1997). Protected values. *Organizational Behavior and Human Decision Processes, 70*, 1–16. doi:10.1006/obhd.1997.2690

Bartels, D. M. (2008). Principled moral sentiment and the flexibility of moral judgment and decision making. *Cognition, 108,* 381–417. doi:10.1016/j.cognition.2008.03.001

Bentham, J. (1961). *An introduction to the principles of morals and legislation.* Garden City, NY: Doubleday. (Original work published 1789)

Ditto, P. H., & Lopez, D. F. (1992). Motivated skepticism: Use of differential decision criteria for preferred and nonpreferred conclusions. *Journal of Personality and Social Psychology, 63,* 568–584. doi:10.1037/0022-3514.63.4.568

Ditto, P. H., & Mastronarde, A. J. (2009). The paradox of the political maverick. *Journal of Experimental Social Psychology, 45,* 295–298. doi:10.1016/j.jesp.2008.10.002

Ditto, P. H., Pizarro, D. A., & Tannenbaum, D. (2009). Motivated moral reasoning. In D. M. Bartels, C. W. Bauman, L. J. Skitka, & D. L. Medin (Eds.), *The psychology of learning and motivation* (Vol. 50, pp. 307–338). Burlington, VT: Academic Press. doi:10.1016/S0079-7421(08)00410-6

Ditto, P. H., Scepansky, J. A., Munro, G. D., Apanovitch, A. M., & Lockhart, L. K. (1998). Motivated sensitivity to preference-inconsistent information. *Journal of Personality and Social Psychology, 75,* 53–69. doi:10.1037/0022-3514.75.1.53

Eagly, A. H., Wood, W., & Chaiken, S. (1978). Causal inferences about communicators and their effect on opinion change. *Journal of Personality and Social Psychology, 36,* 424–435. doi:10.1037/0022-3514.36.4.424

Federico, C. M., & Sidanius, J. (2002). Racism, ideology, and affirmative action revisited: The antecedents and consequences of "principled objections" to affirmative action. *Journal of Personality and Social Psychology, 82,* 488–502. doi:10.1037/0022-3514.82.4.488

Festinger, L. (1954). A theory of social comparison processes. *Human Relations, 7,* 117–140. doi:10.1177/001872675400700202

Festinger, L. (1957). *A theory of cognitive dissonance.* Stanford, CA: Stanford University Press.

Foot, P. (1994). The problem of abortion and the doctrine of double effect. In B. Steinbock & A. Norcross (Eds.), *Killing and letting die* (2nd ed., pp. 266–279). New York, NY: Fordham University Press.

Gilbert, D. T. (1991). How mental systems believe. *American Psychologist, 46,* 107–119. doi:10.1037/0003-066X.46.2.107

Goodwin, G. P., & Darley, J. M. (2008). The psychology of meta-ethics: Exploring objectivism. *Cognition, 106,* 1339–1366. doi:10.1016/j.cognition.2007.06.007

Greene, J. D., Sommerville, R. B., Nystrom, L. E., Darley, J. M., & Cohen, J. D. (2001, September 14). An fMRI investigation of emotional engagement in moral judgment. *Science, 293,* 2105–2108. doi:10.1126/science.1062872

Haidt, J. (2001). The emotional dog and its rational tail: A social intuitionist approach to moral judgment. *Psychological Review, 108,* 814–834. doi:10.1037/0033-295X.108.4.814

Hume, D. (1985). *A treatise of human nature*. London, England: Penguin. (Original work published 1740)

Hunter, J. D. (1991). *Culture wars: The struggle to define America*. New York, NY: Basic Books.

Jemmott, J. B., Jemmott, L. S., & Fong, G. T. (2010). Efficacy of a theory-based absti- nence-only intervention over 24 months: A randomized controlled trial with young adolescents. *Archives of Pediatrics & Adolescent Medicine, 164,* 152–159. doi:10.1001/archpediatrics.2009.267

Juth, N., & Lynöe, N. (2010). Do strong value-based attitudes influence estimations of future events? *Journal of Medical Ethics, 36,* 255–256. doi:10.1136/jme. 2009.033506

Kahan, D. M., Braman, D., Slovic, P., Gastil, J., & Cohen, G. L. (2007). *The second national risk and culture study: Making sense of—and making progress in—the Amer- ican culture war of fact* (Research Paper No. 08-26). Cambridge, MA: Harvard Law School Program on Risk Regulation.

Kant, I. (1998). *Groundwork for the metaphysics of morals* (M. J. Gregor, Trans.). New York, NY: Cambridge University Press. (Original work published 1785)

Kohlberg, L. (1969). Stage and sequence: The cognitive–developmental approach to socialization. In D. A. Goslin (Ed.), *Handbook of socialization theory and research* (pp. 347–489). Chicago, IL: Rand McNally.

Kunda, Z. (1990). The case for motivated reasoning. *Psychological Bulletin, 108,* 480–498. doi:10.1037/0033-2909.108.3.480

Lee, D. (2010, February 18). Taking stock a year later, was the stimulus program effec- tive or wasteful? Politicians disagree, of course. *Los Angeles Times,* p. B1.

Merriam-Webster, Inc. (2005). *Merriam-Webster's Collegiate Dictionary* (11th ed.). Springfield, MA: Author.

Mullen, E., & Skitka, L. J. (2006). Exploring the psychological underpinnings of the moral mandate effect: Motivated reasoning, group differentiation, or anger? *Journal of Personality and Social Psychology, 90,* 629–643.

Nichols, S., & Folds-Bennett, T. (2003). Are children moral objectivists? Children's judgments about moral and response-dependent properties. *Cognition, 90,* B23–B32. doi:10.1016/S0010-0277(03)00160-4

Ross, L., & Ward, A. (1996). Naive realism in everyday life: Implications for social conflict and misunderstanding. In T. Brown, E. Reed, & E. Turiel (Eds.), *Values and knowledge* (pp. 103–135). Hillsdale, NJ: Erlbaum.

Santelli, J., Ott, M. A., Lyon, M., Rogers, J., Summers, D., & Schleifer, R. (2006). Abstinence and abstinence-only education: A review of U.S. policies and programs. *Journal of Adolescent Health, 38,* 72–81. doi:10.1016/j.jadohealth. 2005.10.006

Skitka, L. J., Bauman, C. W., & Sargis, E. G. (2005). Moral conviction: Another con- tributor to attitude strength or something more? *Journal of Personality and Social Psychology, 88,* 895–917. doi:10.1037/0022-3514.88.6.895

Skitka, L. J., & Mullen, E. (2002). Understanding judgments of fairness in a real-world political context: A test of the value protection model of justice reasoning. *Personality and Social Psychology Bulletin, 28,* 1419–1429. doi:10.1177/014616702 236873

Taber, C. S., & Lodge, M. (2006). Motivated skepticism in the evaluation of political beliefs. *American Journal of Political Science, 50,* 755–769. doi:10.1111/j.1540-5907.2006.00214.x

Tanner, C., Medin, D. L., & Iliev, R. (2008). Influence of deontological versus consequentialist orientations on act choices and framing effects: When principles are more important than consequences. *European Journal of Social Psychology, 38,* 757–769. doi:10.1002/ejsp.493

Vallone, R. P., Ross, L., & Lepper, M. R. (1985). The hostile media phenomenon: Biased perception and perceptions of media bias in coverage of the Beirut massacre. *Journal of Personality and Social Psychology, 49,* 577–585. doi:10.1037/0022-3514.49.3.577

Weisberg, R. (2005). The death penalty meets social science: Deterrence and jury behavior under new scrutiny. *Annual Review of Law and Social Science, 1,* 151–170. doi:10.1146/annurev.lawsocsci.1.051804.082336

4

MORAL NATIVISM AND MORAL PSYCHOLOGY

PAUL BLOOM

Moral psychology is both old and new. It is old because moral thought has long been a central focus of theology and philosophy. Indeed, many of the theories that psychologists explore today were first proposed by scholars such as Aristotle, Kant, and Hume. It is young because the scientific study of morality—specifically, the study of what goes on in a person's head when making a moral judgment—has been a topic of serious inquiry only for the past couple of decades. Even now, it is just barely mainstream.

This chapter is itself a combination of the old and the new. I am going to consider two broad questions that would have been entirely familiar to philosophers such as Aristotle but are also the focus of considerable contemporary research and theorizing: (a) What is our natural human moral endowment? and (b) To what extent are moral judgments the products of our emotions? I have the most to say about the first question and review a body of empirical work that bears on it; much of this research is still in progress. The answer to the second question is briefer and more tentative and draws in part on this empirical work.

Many leading researchers, including other contributors to this volume, have their own answers to these questions, and at every point in this chapter I will do my best to make contact with their work, being explicit about areas of overlap and disagreement. To anticipate, my conclusions are as follows: Humans possess an innate and universal system for moral evaluation. And emotions play a significant role in moral judgment—but so does deliberative reason.

WHAT IS OUR NATURAL HUMAN MORAL ENDOWMENT?

I will start by putting the question somewhat bluntly: How much of moral understanding is innate? It is important to clarify the terms here; one traditional meaning of *innate* is "present at birth," but this is not how I am using the word—or how anyone else uses it these days. Rather, by *innate* I mean "not learned"—and by *learned,* I mean, roughly, "gotten into the head by means of the extraction of information from the environment."

This is not meant to be an airtight definition (for discussion of some of the subtleties, see Bloom, 2000). But it captures the right intuitive contrast. Nobody thinks that the rules of baseball are innate, and this is because they obviously do not start off inside anyone's head; they become known only through exposure to the relevant information in the world. That is, everyone who knows the rules of baseball does so because he or she has been told about them or read about them or figured them out by watching a baseball game. Indeed, there are cultures without baseball, and children raised in such cultures do not have any baseball knowledge. In contrast, there is considerable evidence that human babies possess certain systems of knowledge that have not been extracted from the environment, such as a foundational understanding of objects and number (e.g., Baillargeon, Spelke, & Wasserman, 1985; McCrink & Wynn, 2008). This knowledge is universal, showing up in all human groups. It is likely to be innate.

This helps frame the question regarding moral beliefs and moral feelings. If they are learned, then one would expect them to emerge as a result of exposure to the right sort of information. They should not be present in children's minds before this information is accessible to them. And they might vary substantially across cultures. Conversely, if they are innate, one might expect cross-cultural universals. Some understanding of morality should emerge without any exposure to relevant information and thus may show up in young children and even babies.

The Question of Moral Universals

Many philosophers and psychologists would defend the view that morality is learned. Perhaps the most thorough defense of this view is the one developed by Jesse Prinz (e.g., Prinz, 2009). I focus here on his argument that there are no substantive moral universals. Prinz started by exploring a specific proposal, which is that we have a universal prohibition against harm, a moral response to the suffering of others (for proposals along these lines, see Turiel, 2006). He then provided several examples that suggested that this claim is mistaken. It is not merely that people harm one another all the time; it is that people are often morally untroubled by harming others. Indeed, in many cases, they believe that harming others is morally praiseworthy.

Prinz (2009) made his case through exotic examples from faraway cultures, such as the brutal customs of the Ilongot of Luzon. But his claim is plausible and is supported by more familiar cases. Most people in industrial societies eat meat that was created through imposing terrible conditions on animals, causing them great pain, but few are morally troubled by it, even if they are fully aware of these conditions. Most people believe it is acceptable to harm or even kill another adult in self-defense, or when defending a loved one, or in times of war, or even to protect one's property or dignity. Some would go further and view such an act as praiseworthy. A police officer who killed a terrorist about to set off a bomb would be seen as a hero. Indeed, for at least some of us, we would find it heroic even if the terrorist's death was not instrumental in stopping the bomb: When such scenes are shown in movies, audiences cheer. Most people think it is fine to cause mild pain or injury during sport. And most believe that it is morally right to harm criminals, such as by taking away their property, putting them in jail cells, or even killing them. Most parents think it is morally obligatory to harm their own children, with the harm being physical, as in spanking, or emotional, as when punishing a child by taking away certain treats. Such examples can easily be multiplied.

Prinz (2009) was right, then, to conclude that there is no general prohibition against causing harm. But there is a reasonable nativist response here. Any plausible hardwired prohibition is going to be more subtle than "Do not harm." This is because any innate moral notion is likely to have evolved through natural selection, and any tenable evolutionary account would predict that harm can be morally neutral or even morally positive under certain circumstances. For instance, no nativist should deny that our moral intuitions are calibrated to the genetic and social distance from whoever is harmed. It is no surprise, then, that we are more outraged by harm to ourselves and to those we love than harm to our neighbors or that we often lack compassion for strangers in faraway lands and for nonhuman animals. Furthermore, no nativist would deny that our moral reaction to harm must be balanced against other moral and nonmoral priorities. This is why it is morally fine to scream at your child—purposefully upsetting her, causing her harm—if she walks into the street without looking for cars. Such examples, then, as well as others raised by Prinz, are consistent with the notion that we have an evolved moral sense; they are not evidence against it.

Prinz (2009) considered this objection and responded with the argument that such nuanced thoughts and actions—the prohibition of "just some harms"—are most parsimoniously explained without nativism through general considerations of rationality and concerns about social stability. He asked, "How would society work if you could punch your neighbor regularly?" If all we have left is the platitude "Harm when and only when the pros outweigh the cons," then we need not appeal to hardwired universals. Prinz went on to make parallel arguments for the moral feelings associated with reciprocity and sharing. There is considerable cross-cultural variation in the extent to which people feel obliged to share, trade, and cooperate with others (Henrich et al., 2005). Even if universals exist, they can be understood as universal cultural constructions, invented and sustained because of the work they do for members of a society.

This is an intriguing view and is surely true to some extent. Moral intuitions do emerge in part as a response to societal conditions. One well-known example is that of so-called cultures of honor. Historically, these are societies in which resources are vulnerable and people cannot rely on external authority to protect these resources and mete out justice. A reputation for toughness matters a lot in such situations, and hence people in such societies, more than most others, are disapproving toward acts of disrespect and forgiving of acts of retribution (see Nisbett & Cohen, 1996, and Cohen & Leung, 2010, for reviews and empirical support). Culture does shape morality, then, sometimes in a rational manner.

In the end, though, it seems unlikely that all moral responses are cultural constructions that work for the good of society. After all, one of the most salient facts about our everyday moral responses is that they often have awful consequences. Consider our intuitions about punishment, which underlie the desire for vengeance. This desire may have been of adaptive value when we lived in small groups, but it is wasteful, at best, in the world in which we now live. People have died, needlessly, in attempts to settle a score, often reacting with violence to an injustice that is, in an objective sense, utterly trivial. Or consider our strongly tribal impulses, which lead us to morally value those who are close to us, particularly those related by blood, far more than anyone else. These impulses make evolutionary sense but often cause savage discord in contemporary nation–states. Many of our moral impulses are maladaptive in the modern world; we would be better off, right now, without them.

In the end, this is an empirical issue; we can explore just how much variation there really is and the extent to which it is best explained as a response to social and economic forces (see, e.g., Henrich et al., 2005). We can also explore whether certain moral notions are present in nonhuman primates (see, e.g., de Waal, 2001; Lakshminarayanan & Santos, 2008). After all, if chimpanzees and monkeys have some of the same moral intuitions as people, it is an excellent bet that these intuitions are not cultural inventions, since these primates do not have culture—at least not the sort that humans have. (The inference works only one way, though: If they lack such intuitions, it does not necessarily support the cultural theory. It might be that they don't have the right innate endowment.)

A different data source comes from my own field of developmental psychology. If moral principles are invented by societies, then they should not be present in babies; they need to be learned. In contrast, if they are innate, they may be present even in prelinguistic babies.

Psychologists have long been interested in moral development, particularly since Lawrence Kohlberg (1984) articulated his classic proposals about stage theories of moral reasoning. Ongoing research programs include studies of the emerging capacity to distinguish between moral and conventional violations, to understand fairness and justice, to understand the role of intentionality in moral responsibility, and to respond with moral disapproval to certain disgusting acts. But there has been little research thus far into moral evaluation by infants or toddlers, and so—unlike domains such as naive physics, naive psychology, and number—the more direct evidence that could support or falsify specific developmental claims of the origin of moral judgments is thin on the ground. It has been only in the past 5 years or so that the relevant experiments have been done, and this is what I discuss below.

The Question of Moral Babies

It has long been known that babies grow anxious when others are in distress. Darwin (1872/1913) told this story of his first son, William:

> When this child was about four months old, I made in his presence many odd noises and strange grimaces, and tried to look savage; but the noises, if not too loud, as well as the grimaces, were all taken as good jokes; and I attributed this at the time to their being preceded or accompanied by smiles. (p. 358)

But then William was fooled by his nurse: "When [he was] a few days over six months old, his nurse pretended to cry, and I saw that his face instantly assumed a melancholy expression, with the corners of his mouth strongly depressed" (p. 358).

Babies cry when they hear other babies cry (Simner, 1971), and once they have enough physical competence, they soothe others in distress. This has been observed both spontaneously and in controlled studies in which an adult (typically, the child's mother) pretends to be in pain (Sagi & Hoffman, 1976; Zahn-Waxler, Radke-Yarrow, Wagner, & Chapman, 1992). This intentional soothing of others is not uniquely human: de Waal (2001) observed that chimpanzees—but not monkeys—"will approach a victim of attack, put an arm around her and gently pat her back, or groom her" (p. 326).

More recent studies have found elaborate altruistic behavior by toddlers, behaviors in which they give up their time and energy to help strangers without being prodded or rewarded. If an adult reaches for something beyond his reach, for instance, the toddler will often just hand it over to him, even if the adult does not ask or even look at her (Warneken & Tomasello, 2006, 2009; see also Wynn, 2009).

How do these sensitivities and inclinations relate to mature morality? The problem here is that there is no consensus about what is distinct about the domain of morality even for adults—no accepted definition or list of criteria. But, presumably, a mature moral psychology entails the capacity to evaluate different acts and different people; this evaluation ties into systems of praise and blame; into emotions such as anger, gratitude, and guilt; and, ultimately, to broader issues of fairness and justice. What we find so far in babies falls far short of this. Perhaps their responses reflect nothing more than a set of reactions and motivations: the pain of others is upsetting to them; they are compelled to help under certain circumstances. It is conceivable that such reactions are no different in kind from purely nonmoral and nonsocial reactions and motivations, such as being frightened at a loud noise or wanting to void a full bladder.

At the same time, though, it is hard to conceive of a moral system that does not have such responses as a starting point: A creature that lacked them might never attain a moral system. The point here is owed to David Hume; pure reason gets you only so far. To have a genuinely moral system, things have to matter: "'Tis not contrary to reason to prefer the destruction of the whole world to the scratching of my finger" (Hume, 1888, p. 416). What we see in these emerging emotions is the development of mattering. The woes of others are painful to children, and when the children are capable of acting, they are motivated to act so as to make others' woes go away.

Do babies also possess the ability to evaluate others' actions? This is the topic of considerable ongoing research (see Wynn, in press, for a review). I can illustrate the logic of many of these studies with the following case: Suppose Individual A is standing halfway up a steep hill and trying to climb to the top. This event continues in one of two ways. In one, Individual B appears on the scene and repeatedly pushes A down the hill until A is at the bottom. In the other, Individual C appears on the scene and repeatedly nudges A up the hill until A reaches the top.

This paradigm is partially based on a classic study by Premack and Premack (1997), who showed babies a series of computer-animated displays in which one intentional agent acted either positively or negatively toward another. The researchers used a looking-time measure to see how the babies grouped the actions together. The babies' pattern of looking times suggested that helping someone push through a gap was grouped along with caressing the person, and preventing someone from going through a gap was grouped along with hitting the person. Premack and Premack suggested that infants appreciated that the former two actions, though perceptually very different from one another, were positive and the second two were negative.

This finding motivated a series of studies in which we explored babies' intuitions about scenes with helping and scenes with hindering (Hamlin, Wynn, & Bloom, 2007; Kuhlmeier, Wynn, & Bloom, 2003). Our initial studies asked about babies' expectations of how Individual A would behave with regard to the hinderer (B) versus the helper (C). As an adult, if you were to witness such scenes, you would likely expect A to later tend to avoid B and to approach C. Using a looking-time method, the researchers found that 12-month-olds and even 9-month-olds had these same intuitions.

What about babies' own preferences for these two characters? In Hamlin et al. (2007), we looked into this matter by showing babies a three-dimensional display in which real objects acted out the interactions, again with B hindering A and C helping A. Then we offered the babies themselves the choice between reaching for B or C. We found that both 6- and 10-month-old infants overwhelmingly preferred the helpful individual to the hindering individual.

Now, this preference result is ambiguous. It could mean that babies are attracted to the helpful individual, repelled by the hinderer, or both. We explored this in a further series of studies that introduced a neutral character, one that neither helps nor hinders. We found that during choice, infants prefer a helpful character to a neutral one and prefer a neutral character to a hindering one. This shows that both inclinations are at work—infants are both drawn to the nice guy and repelled by the mean guy.

Our preferred interpretation of these results is that they reflect a social competence in which babies' expectations about others and their own preferences are motivated by the perceived goodness and badness of the characters. But there is always the worry that perhaps some other nonsocial feature particular to the stimuli was triggering these responses. Of course, our experiments were designed in the hopes of avoiding such confounds by counterbalancing the colors and shapes of the characters, matching the intensities of the helping and hindering movements, and so on. In addition, we included "nonsocial" controls in which the characters exhibited similar movement patterns but were not depicted as animate beings. As predicted, these did not elicit the same preferences (see Hamlin et al., 2007, for details). But, still, it is useful to see whether these findings replicate more generally across different sorts of stimuli.

This concern motivated a series of studies with 5-month-olds by Hamlin and Wynn (in press). The studies involved actions that were, by adult lights, positive or negative, but in very different contexts than the hill. In the first study, an individual struggled to open a box, getting it partially open but then watching the lid fall back down. Then, on alternating trials, one puppet would grab the lid and open it all the way, and another puppet would jump on the box and slam it shut. Would babies prefer the puppet that (by adult intuitions) was the prosocial one and avoid the one that (by adult intuitions) was antisocial? In a second study, an individual played with a ball. On alternating trials, the individual would either roll the ball to a puppet that would roll it back or roll the ball to a puppet that would run away with it. Again, the question was whether babies would prefer to interact with the character that was (by adult intuitions) helpful as opposed the one that was nasty.

As predicted, in both scenarios, 5-month-olds preferred the prosocial character over the antisocial one. In other research, using a preferential looking paradigm, we replicated this finding with infants as young as 3 months of age (Hamlin, Wynn, & Bloom, 2010).

Further studies have explored responses more elaborate than simple preference. Part and parcel of adult morality is the notion that good acts should meet with a positive response and bad acts with a negative response. To see whether babies have the same intuition, we exposed 21-month-olds to the good guy/bad guy situations described previously and gave them an opportunity to hand over a treat to either of the characters. They overwhelmingly chose to give it to the positive character. In contrast, when asked to take a treat from one of the characters, they tended to take it from the bad guy (Hamlin, Wynn, Bloom, & Mahajan, 2011).

We then extended this paradigm by exploring reward and punishment once removed (Hamlin et al., 2011). In one condition, we showed babies a set of scenarios in which a puppet was trying to open a box; on some occasions a helpful puppet joined in and helped get the box open, and on other occasions a hindering puppet jumped on the box lid, slamming it shut. This is one of the good guy/bad guy situations tested by Hamlin and Wynn (in press), who found that babies preferred the helpful puppet. But here we took an additional step. We showed babies a second set of scenarios with these same characters as the targets of other actions. That is, we showed babies either the original helper or the original hinderer in a different situation in which the character was treated positively by one new character and negatively by another new character. The babies were then asked to choose between the two new characters.

Did they prefer the character who rewarded the good guy over the one who punished the good guy? They did—even 8-month-olds preferred the rewarder. In itself this is not very surprising, given the other studies showing a preference for those who act prosocially. That is, they would likely have shown the same preference even if they forgot, or had never encoded, the fact that the character who was rewarded and punished had behaved well in the past. What is far more interesting is the condition in which they watched the bad guy being rewarded or punished. Here they chose to interact with the punisher. Infants like those who harm bad guys. They like punishers.

To sum up, the results so far suggest that even young babies make sense of a range of interactions—helping someone up a hill versus hindering the character's progress, helping someone open a box versus slamming it shut, passing back a ball versus absconding with it—the same way that adults do, in terms of prosocial and antisocial behavior. Babies expect whoever was the target of such behavior to later associate with the prosocial character over the antisocial one, and they themselves prefer to reach for (or, for the younger babies, to look at) the good guy over the bad guy. They prefer to reward the good and punish the bad and prefer others who reward the good and punish the bad.

But Is It Moral?

This is evidence for early social evaluation. But a critic might point out that none of this has to be moral in any interesting sense. It could just be a social preference. To see the difference, consider an adult example: Suppose you observe that Jane always hands out candies to those she meets, whereas Joe tries to hit people with an axe. You might reasonably infer that people would prefer to socialize with Jane over Joe, and you yourself would prefer Jane over Joe. If forced to choose, you would prefer to reward Jane and punish Joe and would prefer characters who do the same. After all, you would like to encourage Jane's actions and discourage Joe's actions. But all of this might just draw on a rudimentary understanding of others and a healthy allotment of basic self-interest. Your expectation and preference would not necessarily demonstrate that you thought that Jane was somehow good (moral) and Joe was somehow bad (immoral) or that you attributed moral value to their actions of candy giving and axe waving. Indeed, even a pure psychopath—a hypothesized individual with no moral sense at all, but with normal intelligence and social understanding—might have the same responses. So how can we draw conclusions about the moral lives of babies?

For adults, distinctive aspects of moral intuitions can be expressed in language. For instance, when describing Joe and Jane and what they are up to, adults would likely use terms like *right* and *wrong* and express notions such as *should* and *shouldn't*. Adults can explicitly separate morality from preference, acknowledging that there are cases in which one prefers X to Y (people or actions) but thinks that Y is more moral than X. You might say, "I like when X does such-and-so, but I don't approve of it" or "It really annoys me when Y does such-and-so, but I have to admit that she is doing the right thing" or that "Nobody should do such a thing." You might express second-order desires: "I disapprove of X, and I want to disapprove of X." But of course, the expression of this sort of sophisticated understanding is far beyond the capacity of babies or even young children.

The question remains, then, whether babies already possess the core of what we would describe in adults as a moral sense. It would be premature to answer this with confidence, but there are three considerations that bear on the question, and, taken together, they favor an affirmative answer.

First, babies respond to (what for adults are) morally relevant properties of the actions. Babies were not reacting to the characters' prettiness, their rapidity of movement, or anything like that. They were responding to how one individual treated another, either helping or hindering the individual in attaining a goal. They were resonating to the difference that adults would describe as "nice guys" versus "mean guys," and, indeed, when we ask 18-month-olds "Who is the nice guy?" and "Who is the mean guy?" they respond in adultlike ways. Keep in mind also that in all of these studies, the babies are never themselves helped or harmed by these characters; their intuitions and predictions are based on observations of third-person interactions among characters that are not even human: animated figures, blocks of wood with eyes on them, or small puppets. Their responses and expectations, then, are not based on either self-interest or personal experience.

Second, the competences that we chose to explore were not pulled from the air. They are just what you would expect from theories of the evolution of social and moral behavior. It is plainly useful to distinguish supportive and friendly individuals from harmful and malicious ones and to respond accordingly. Indeed, some ability to evaluate others is essential for navigating the social world—perhaps just as essential as the predictive and interpretative capacities that are the topic of so much developmental research. Furthermore, it has long been noted that cooperative behavior such as group hunting and food sharing can be beneficial to the individual members of a group, but it can successfully emerge in populations of unrelated individuals only if they have the capacity to distinguish free riders (or "cheaters") from those willing to do their fair share (e.g., Axelrod, 1984; Cosmides, 1989; Trivers, 1971, 1985). It makes sense, then, for us to evolve a particular sensitivity to "bad guys" along with a wish to punish them and to approve of others who punish them. For many scholars, this is the explanation of the foundation of morality.

Note, however, that even if this evolutionary analysis is correct, it does not mean that these notions are therefore necessarily innate. It is one of the axioms of evolutionary developmental biology that adaptations need not be hardwired; evolution can work so that an adaptive capacity emerges in the course of normal development. All natural selection cares about (to put it metaphorically) is that we end up with such capacities; it makes no claim about how they get there. It is possible, then, that the foundations of moral evaluation are evolutionary adaptations, but that, contrary to our hypothesis, these foundations are learned. Innateness is a hypothesis, not a logical truth.

Third, there is some tentative evidence that the babies responded to our characters with the same emotions that are, for adults, infused with morality—emotions such as disapproval, concern, and even anger. I discuss this in more detail in the next section.

Finally, our findings mesh well with previous proposals about the developmental origins of morality. I will end this section by considering two of them.

One theory is that there exists an innate moral grammar, an analogy with Noam Chomsky's proposals concerning an innate language faculty. This analogy was initially proposed by both the political philosopher John Rawls and by Chomsky himself. It was developed extensively in the dissertation of Mikhail (see Mikhail, 2007, for discussion) and then was extended by Hauser, both with Mikhail and independently (e.g., Hauser, 2006).

According to this intriguing idea, there are certain suggestive parallels between language and morality. For one, Chomsky has long observed that our linguistic knowledge (competence) can be distinguished from how we use this knowledge in everyday life (performance). For another, linguistic knowledge is unconscious or tacit—every English speaker knows that something is wrong with the sentence "John seems sleeping," but few of us can explain why it is wrong. Similarly, moral intuitions are imperfectly linked to action; you can know the right thing to do (competence) but choose not to do it (performance). And the reasons for our moral judgments are typically not accessible to us; indeed, much of the program in moral philosophy and moral psychology is to explain precisely why we find some acts and people morally wrong. These similarities suggest that the same methodological approaches and theoretical ideas that work well for the study of language can be productively applied to the domain of moral thought (Hauser, 2006).

There are also reasons to doubt the aptness of this analogy (see Bloom & Jarudi, 2006). Language is a generative system, where units such as words and phrases are combined through recursive rules to generate a potential infinity of sentences. Morality does not seem to work that way. Universals of moral knowledge, should they exist, might therefore be better characterized as a small list of evolved rules, very different in character from linguistic knowledge.

Our developmental results favor the generative grammar analogy in at least one regard, however. This is in its claim that, similar to core aspects of language, moral intuitions are not entirely learned. Our own experiments thus far have explored only the early understanding of fairly crude distinctions, such as the contrast between aiding one's goal versus hindering one's goal. It would be interesting for further research to explore whether the subtler distinctions explored by Hauser and colleagues—such as the contrast between a harmful event being a side effect rather than being a means to an end—also show early emergence. If they do, the question would then arise as to whether these subtleties are specific to morality, along the lines of language-specific constraints proposed by Chomsky and his colleagues, or whether they emerge from more general properties of action comprehension (see Cushman, Young, & Hauser, 2010; and Chapter 2, this volume).

Another proposal about the innate capacity for morality emerges from the work of Haidt and his colleagues (e.g., Haidt, 2001; Haidt & Joseph, 2004; Haidt & Kesebir, 2010; see also Chapter 1, this volume). This is motivated by observations of cross-cultural and individual differences in moral notions (see also Shweder, Much, Mahapatra, & Park, 1997). Haidt's theory posits five innate domains of morality: harm/care, fairness/reciprocity, ingroup/loyalty, authority/respect, and purity/sanctity.

How does that theory mesh with the developmental data presented above? So far, quite well. The research I have summarized in this chapter can be seen as showing early competence in the domain of harm/care. Other recent studies suggest a rudimentary grasp of fairness/reciprocity: Babies and toddlers prefer characters who equally distribute resources to other people (Geraci & Surian, 2010). There is suggestive evidence for some sort of ingroup/loyalty bias: Put crudely, babies prefer their own kind, with "kind" being based on physical similarity, sameness of language, or similarity of preference (e.g., Kinzler, Shutts, DeJesus, & Spelke, 2009).

The studies summarized above bear on the first three domains. There are little data, so far, that bear on the other two domains discussed by Haidt: authority/respect and purity/sanctity. These domains emerge late in development, but it is nevertheless possible that they also have some unlearned, universal basis (for discussion of the moral roots of disgust, see Bloom, 2004; Danovitch & Bloom, 2009).

TO WHAT EXTENT ARE MORAL JUDGMENTS THE PRODUCTS OF EMOTIONS?

There is a popular view about morality, developed by, among others, the philosopher Jesse Prinz, the neuroscientist Antonio Damasio, and the social psychologist Jonathan Haidt, that lies close to the position laid out by the 18th-century Scottish philosopher David Hume, who argued that reason, and particularly moral reason, is nothing more than "the slave of the passions" (Hume, 1888, p. 415).

A mild version of this view is uncontroversial. Few would doubt that our moral judgments can be influenced by our emotions. There are numerous findings from social psychology and social neuroscience suggesting that our judgments of good and evil are influenced by emotions such as empathy and disgust (see Haidt & Kesebir, 2010, for a review). And there is a consensus that Hume's deeper point is right as well, that there are moral intuitions that cannot themselves be justified by reason—"self-evident" truths, as Thomas Jefferson put it. Indeed, as Pizarro and Bloom (2003) noted, this is the case for all domains of reasoning, including deductive inference and inductive generalization.

But the Humean theory that many contemporary scholars hold is stronger than this. It largely rejects rational deliberation as playing an important role in moral judgment. Haidt (2001) made this point with vigor, arguing that the reasoned arguments we often use concerning why we hold certain moral positions are mostly post hoc justifications for the gut reactions that really matter: "Moral reasoning does not cause moral judgment; rather, moral reasoning is usually a post hoc construction, generated after a judgment has been reached" (p. 814). To use Haidt's analogy, we like to think of ourselves as judges, reasoning through cases according to deeply held principles, but in reality we are more like lawyers, making arguments for positions that have already been established (see Chapter 3, this volume). With the exception of professional philosophers, conscious deliberation plays little role in determining our moral judgments.

What does the developmental evidence reviewed in the first section have to say about this? To a large extent, it supports it. Recall that I discussed two foundations of early moral understanding. The first foundation was a set of emotional reactions, such as empathy. Plainly, this fits the Humean picture. The second was a rich capacity for moral evaluation, with which babies appear to judge different characters as moral or immoral and reason and act accordingly. Interestingly, these evaluations give the impression of being emotional. As Hamlin (2010) summarized it, "Anecdotally, babies appear to be more likely to smile, clap, etc. during prosocial events, and to frown, shake their heads, and look sad or otherwise upset during antisocial events" (p. 138). In addition, at least some babies are aggressive toward the antisocial character. In one of our punishment studies, a toddler took a treat from the antisocial puppet and then leaned forward and smacked him in the head.

Now, as Huebner, Dwyer, and Hauser (2009) emphasized, the fact that an emotion corresponds to a moral judgment does not entail that emotions cause the judgment. It is possible, as a Humean would argue, that the baby gets angry at the behavior of the antisocial character, and this drives the judgment that the behavior is wrong. But it is also possible that the baby judges the behavior to be wrong, and this in turn motivates the anger. The emotion might be relevant only to the motivation of moral action, or possibly it plays no role at all.

Keep in mind also that even if the emotional response is the cause of the moral judgment, the emotion itself is based on a fairly sophisticated analysis of the scene. How can the baby get angry if he or she does not believe that the character did something wrong? If the baby sympathizes with a victim, cheers on a rescuer, and avoids someone who rewards a bad guy, this entails that the baby is able to figure out who the victim, rescuer, and bad guy are, and this requires a rich understanding of human action. Emotions must be smart. This is true of gut feelings as a whole—how you think about something affects how you respond emotionally to it. Finding a telephone number in one's spouse's pocket can engender intense jealousy in one individual but mere curiosity in another, depending on how the situation is construed. You do not normally respond with fear when you hear someone start to whistle—but you might do so if it was 3 a.m. and you had thought you were alone in the house (Pizarro & Bloom, 2003).

Still, caveats aside, the baby data are at least consistent with the intuitionist analysis. Babies are making moral (or quasi-moral) evaluations, and there is some evidence that these are associated with emotional responses. Surely their evaluations are not the product of deliberative reason. Babies are Humeans. If there were no subsequent development, then the strong Humean view would be correct for humans in general. The only difference is that babies' intuitions are the product of evolution plus some personal experience, whereas adults have the additional influence of culture. This affects the scope of moral response: Babies respond to hindering and hitting; adults respond as well to treason, necrophilia, and insider trading.

Unlike babies, though, children and adults have the capacity for rational deliberation. This underlies one of the most significant aspects of human nature, the existence of moral progress—or, to put it less contentiously, of directional moral change (Bloom, 2004, 2010).

The sort of change I am talking about has been explored by many scholars (Pinker, 2002; Singer, 1981; Wright, 2000). Consider Singer's (1981) discussion of the expansion of the moral circle. There is no doubt that the average person's sympathies have grown substantially over our history. There was a time when human sympathies never extended beyond the immediate group. Now some of us donate money and even blood to people with whom we have no contact and little in common. Contemporary readers of this chapter have profoundly different beliefs about the rights of women, racial minorities, homosexuals, and nonhuman animals than readers in the late 1800s. In 1960, for instance, most Americans thought interracial marriage was wrong; now very few do. A hundred years before this, many Americans thought slavery was morally justified; now very few do.

I am happy to describe this as "progress" but am aware that this assumes a moral realism that many readers would reject, and the relevant phenomenon can be characterized in more neutral terms. It is that the change is directional. It is not that the circle has remained constant or that it randomly grows and shrinks. It started off small and, over a long history, has grown. This is a critical way in which the history of morality is sharply different from domains such as fashion in clothing and taste in food, regarding which there is no directionality. Indeed, in its cumulative nature, morality looks a lot more like science.

What drives this directional moral change? There are many possible factors, some of them fully consistent with a Humean theory of human morality. One main driver, for instance, is contact: When we associate with other people and share common goals with them, we extend them our affection (see Stephan, 1987). In recent times, increased political and economic interdependence has ensured that we associate with many more people than our grandparents and even our parents ever did, and this trend has accelerated through the virtual contact enabled by television and the Internet. Wright (2000), in particular, outlined the argument that the cold-blooded forces of increased populations and interactions with others have led to greater niceness. As he once put it, "Among the many reasons I don't think we should bomb the Japanese is that they built my minivan" (quoted in Pinker, 2002, p. 329). Because the extent of interdependence tends to grow over human history, moral change takes on a certain positive direction, all without any sort of rationality or reason.

But this explanation is incomplete. It does not explain the shifts in opinions on issues such as slavery and animal rights. Contact and interdependency are not enough: Owning slaves did not turn people into abolitionists, and running a factory farm does not increase sympathy for cows, pigs, and chickens. And these nonrational processes do not explain certain genuinely new moral notions, such as the immorality of torture as a form of punishment or the morality of democracy as a form of governance.

I propose that some people generate—through the interplay of reason and emotion and imagination—novel moral insights. This process is similar to what goes on when we generate other sorts of ideas, including philosophical and scientific ones. As a core example of this, Singer (1981) argued that the great insight about morality is the notion that it should be built from an objective position. Put crudely, the idea here is that nobody is special, which is an insight enshrined in the Golden Rule, the "impartial spectator" of Adam Smith, and the "original position" of John Rawls. We have the capacity to generate such ideas, and they really do matter, shaping the societies in which we live.

This is a claim about where ideas originally come from, not how they are usually acquired. And so I agree with the Humean position that people are often swayed more by emotional appeals than by rational arguments. Indeed, it is likely that certain moral views, such as the wrongness of slavery, become commonplace through processes that are, for the most part, nondeliberative. Most of us were never persuaded that slavery is wrong; we acquired this belief in much the same way that we learned what language to speak or what clothes to wear. But still, as psychologists, we also need to explain how it was that someone once came to the moral insight that slavery is wrong and, just as impressive, was able to convey this moral insight in such a way that it persuaded others. Explaining this process requires going beyond Hume.

CONCLUSION

In sum, the existence of moral progress shows that humans have the capacity for moral generativity—that is, for coming to novel moral views. Psychologists often miss this, in large part because we rarely look for it. In moral psychology, as in other domains of psychology, there is a nearly exclusive focus on how people respond to various situations, and so there are countless studies in which various populations (mostly undergraduates, but also children, psychopaths, and the like) are exposed to artificial moral dilemmas. (This is surely true of my own research.) But it is unusual for us to study how people naturally arrive at their moral judgments, including ones that clash with those of the communities around them. We should do more of this, because at present the nature of this critically important process is almost entirely mysterious.

REFERENCES

Axelrod, R. (1984). *The evolution of cooperation*. New York, NY: Basic Books.

Baillargeon, R., Spelke, E. S., & Wasserman, S. (1985). Object permanence in five-month-old infants. *Cognition, 20*, 191–208. doi:10.1016/0010-0277(85)90008-3

Bloom, P. (2000). *How children learn the meanings of words*. Cambridge, MA: MIT Press.

Bloom, P. (2004). *Descartes' baby: How the science of child development explains what makes us human*. New York, NY: Basic Books.

Bloom, P. (2010, March 25). How do morals change? *Nature, 464*, 490. doi:10.1038/464490a

Bloom, P., & Jarudi, I. (2006, October 26). The Chomsky of morality? *Nature, 443*, 909–910. doi:10.1038/443909a

Cohen, D., & Leung, A. K.-Y. (2010). Violence and character: A CUPS (Culture × Person × Situation) perspective. In P. R. Shaver & M. Mikulincer (Eds.), *Human aggression and violence: Causes, manifestations, and consequences* (pp. 187–200). Washington, DC: American Psychological Association.

Cosmides, L. (1989). The logic of social exchange: Has natural selection shaped how humans reason? Studies with the Wason selection task. *Cognition, 31*, 187–276. doi:10.1016/0010-0277(89)90023-1

Cushman, F. A., Young, L., & Hauser, M. (2010). *Patterns of moral judgment derive from non-moral psychological representations: A study of the action/omission distinction*. Manuscript submitted for publication.

Danovitch, J., & Bloom, P. (2009). Children's extension of disgust to physical and moral events. *Emotion*, *9*, 107–112. doi:10.1037/a0014113

Darwin, C. (1913). *The expression of the emotions in man and animals.* New York, NY: D. Appleton. (Original work published 1872)

de Waal, F. (2001). *The ape and the sushi master: Cultural reflections of a primatologist.* New York, NY: Basic Books.

Geraci, A., & Surian, L. (2010). *The developmental roots of fairness: Infants' reactions to equal and unequal distributions of resources.* Manuscript submitted for publication.

Haidt, J. (2001). The emotional dog and its rational tail: A social intuitionist approach to moral judgment. *Psychological Review*, *108*, 814–834. doi:10.1037/0033-295X.108.4.814

Haidt, J., & Joseph, C. (2004). Intuitive ethics: How innately prepared intuitions generate culturally variable virtues. *Daedalus*, *133*, 55–66. doi:10.1162/00115 26042365555

Haidt, J., & Kesebir, S. (2010). Morality. In S. Fiske & D. Gilbert (Eds.), *Handbook of social psychology* (5th ed., pp. 797–832). New York, NY: Oxford University Press.

Hamlin, J. K. (2010). *Social evaluation in infancy.* Unpublished doctoral dissertation, Yale University.

Hamlin, J. K., & Wynn, K. (in press). Young infants prefer prosocial to antisocial others. *Child Development.*

Hamlin, J. K., Wynn, K., & Bloom, P. (2007, November 22). Social evaluation by preverbal infants. *Nature*, *450*, 557–559. doi:10.1038/nature06288

Hamlin, J. K., Wynn, K., & Bloom, P. (2010). Three-month-old infants show a negativity bias in social evaluation. *Developmental Science*, *13*, 923–929.

Hamlin, J. K., Wynn, K., Bloom, P., & Mahajan, N. (2011). *Third-party reward and punishment in infants and toddlers.* Manuscript submitted for publication.

Hauser, M. (2006). *Moral minds.* New York, NY: Ecco.

Henrich, J., Boyd, R., Bowles, S., Gintis, H., Fehr, E., Camerer, C., . . . Tracer, D. (2005). "Economic man" in cross-cultural perspective: Ethnography and experiments from 15 small-scale societies. *Behavioral and Brain Sciences*, *28*, 795–855. doi:10.1017/S0140525X05000142

Huebner, B., Dwyer, S., & Hauser, M. (2009). The role of emotion in human psychology. *Trends in Cognitive Sciences*, *13*, 1–6. doi:10.1016/j.tics.2008.09.006

Hume, D. (1888). *A treatise of human nature.* Oxford, England: Clarendon Press. (Original work published 1740)

Kinzler, K. D., Shutts, K., De Jesus, J., & Spelke, E. S. (2009). Accent trumps race in guiding children's social preferences. *Social Cognition*, *27*, 623–634. doi:10.1521/soco.2009.27.4.623

Kohlberg, L. (1984). *The psychology of moral development: The nature and validity of moral stages.* New York, NY: Harper & Row.

Kuhlmeier, V., Wynn, K., & Bloom, P. (2003). Attribution of dispositional states by 12-month-old infants. *Psychological Science*, *14*, 402–408. doi:10.1111/1467-9280.01454

Lakshminarayanan, V., & Santos, L. R. (2008). Capuchin monkeys are sensitive to others' welfare. *Current Biology*, *18*, R999–R1000. doi:10.1016/j.cub.2008.08.057

McCrink, K., & Wynn, K. (2008). Mathematical reasoning. In M. Haith & J. Benson (Eds.), *The encylopedia of infant and early childhood development* (Vol. 2, pp. 280–289). New York, NY: Elsevier Press.

Mikhail, J. (2007). Universal moral grammar: Theory, evidence, and the future. *Trends in Cognitive Sciences*, *11*, 143–152. doi:10.1016/j.tics.2006.12.007

Nisbett, R. E., & Cohen, D. (1996). *Culture of honor: The psychology of violence in the South*. Denver, CO: Westview Press.

Pinker, S. (2002). *The blank slate*. New York, NY: Norton.

Pizarro, D. A., & Bloom, P. (2003). The intelligence of the moral intuitions: Comment on Haidt (2001). *Psychological Review*, *110*, 193–196. doi:10.1037/0033-295X.110.1.193

Premack, D., & Premack, A. J. (1997). Infants attribute value ± to the goal-directed actions of self-propelled objects. *Journal of Cognitive Neuroscience*, *9*, 848–856. doi:10.1162/jocn.1997.9.6.848

Prinz, J. (2009). Against moral nativism. In D. Murphy & M. A. Bishop (Eds.), *Stich and his critics* (pp. 167–189). New York, NY: Wiley-Blackwell.

Sagi, A., & Hoffman, M. (1976). Empathic distress in the newborn. *Developmental Psychology*, *12*, 175–176. doi:10.1037/0012-1649.12.2.175

Shweder, R., Much, N., Mahapatra, N., & Park, L. (1997). The "big three" of morality (autonomy, community, and divinity), and the "big three" explanations of suffering, as well. In A. Brandt & P. Rozin (Eds.), *Morality and health* (pp. 119–169). New York, NY: Routledge.

Simner, M. L. (1971). Newborn's response to the cry of another infant. *Developmental Psychology*, *5*, 136–150. doi:10.1037/h0031066

Singer, P. (1981). *The expanding circle: Ethics and sociobiology*. New York, NY: Farrar, Straus, & Giroux.

Stephan, W. G. (1987). The contact hypothesis in intergroup relations. In C. Hendrick (Ed.), *Group processes and intergroup relations* (pp. 229–257). Orlando, FL: Academic Press.

Trivers, R. L. (1971). The evolution of reciprocal altruism. *Quarterly Review of Biology*, *46*, 35–57. doi:10.1086/406755

Trivers, R. L. (1985). *Social evolution*. Reading, MA: Benjamin/Cummings.

Turiel, E. (2006). The development of morality. In W. Damon & R. M. Lerner (Series Ed.) & N. Eisenberg (Vol. Ed.), *Handbook of child psychology: Vol. 3. Social, emotional, and personality development* (6th ed., pp. 789–857). New York, NY: Wiley.

Warneken, F., & Tomasello, M. (2006, March 3). Altrustic helping in human infants and young chimpanzees. *Science, 311*, 1301–1303. doi:10.1126/science.1121448

Warneken, F., & Tomasello, M. (2009). The roots of human altruism. *British Journal of Psychology, 100*, 455–471. doi:10.1348/000712608X379061

Wright, R. (2000). *Nonzero: The logic of human destiny.* New York, NY: Vintage Press.

Wynn, K. (2009). Constraints on natural altruism. *British Journal of Psychology, 100*, 481–485. doi:10.1348/000712609X441312

Wynn, K. (in press). Developmental origins of social and moral evaluation. In A. Leslie & T. German (Eds.), *The handbook of theory of mind.* Hillsdale, NJ: Erlbaum.

Zahn-Waxler, C., Radke-Yarrow, M., Wagner, E., & Chapman, M. (1992). Development of concern for others. *Developmental Psychology, 28*, 126–136. doi:10.1037/0012-1649.28.1.126

5

BRINGING CHARACTER BACK: HOW THE MOTIVATION TO EVALUATE CHARACTER INFLUENCES JUDGMENTS OF MORAL BLAME

DAVID A. PIZARRO AND DAVID TANNENBAUM

Human beings are deeply moral creatures. Perhaps nowhere is this more evident than in the stories we tell. Literature, cinema, and television are replete with tales that (either literally or metaphorically) describe the battle between good and evil and tell the stories of the heroes and villains fighting for each side. But although we may root for the heroes, it is the villains who often capture most of our attention. Like audiences in the silent movie era, who would boo and hiss loudly when the villain appeared on screen, we are motivated to condemn the villains for their immoral actions; in fact, we seem to take great pleasure in doing so. For those of us of a certain age, there was one villain who allowed us this pleasure more than any other: Darth Vader, the antagonist of the original *Star Wars* films. From the moment he stepped onto the screen, there could be no doubt in the audience's mind that he was the bad guy. Vader exuded all of the cues used by moviemakers to communicate "evil": He was clad entirely in black; spoke with a deep, ominous voice; and was as much a machine as a human being. To be sure, if we ever encountered him in real life, we would have been very motivated to keep a safe distance.

The motivation to identify and condemn villains is not limited to our role as audience members, however. Few tasks are as important to our social well-being as figuring out who the "good guys" and the "bad guys" are in our everyday lives. Many social decisions require us to make an evaluation regarding a person's underlying traits—such as trustworthiness, honesty, compassion, or hostility—that together constitute an individual's moral character. For instance, how do I know whether or not to trust the person trying to sell me a car? Should I accept a date with someone I've just met, or is he or she a creep? Should I believe the teenager at my door who says his car broke down and he just needs to use my phone? Getting these evaluations right is important; misreading a person's character not only might lead to poor financial or romantic decisions, it might also get one killed. And these judgments are not just one-shot deals. Keeping track of the good people and the bad people over time is just as important, lest we get cheated again by the same person or unwittingly offer help to someone who might never help in return.

Unfortunately, unlike Darth Vader, the bad characters we encounter in everyday life do not always dress in black or speak in ominous voices, so figuring out whether someone possesses negative character traits is more complicated than spotting cinematic villains (who are more akin to caricatures of "pure evil"; see Chapter 20, this volume). Yet despite the lack of such overt cues, we seem motivated and well-equipped to evaluate other people's underlying character traits. In fact, there is a great deal of evidence that these evaluations are psychologically primary. We evaluate agents on the dimension of goodness or badness automatically and with little effort starting remarkably early in life, and this seems to be true of individuals across cultures (Fiske, Cuddy, & Glick, 2007; Hamlin, Wynn, & Bloom, 2007; Willis & Todorov, 2006; see also Chapter 4, this volume). Before we shake a person's hand for the first time, we have most likely already made a judgment about his or her trustworthiness (Todorov, Said, Engell, & Oosterhof, 2008) and have noticed whether he or she appears hostile or threatening (Bar, Neta, & Linz, 2006).

Moreover, we continue evaluating others' character long after our first encounter through a variety of methods, such as observing their emotional signals (Ames & Johar, 2009; Frank, 1988) or gossiping with friends about the others' moral failings (Foster, 2004). This desire to track others' character is also evident in our concern for people's reputations. Reputations affect our ability to succeed in games based on trust and cooperation (e.g., Rand, Dreber, Ellingsen, Fudenberg, & Nowak, 2009). The motivation to keep track of the other's character is evident even in memory: We have better memory for the faces of people who cheated us unexpectedly (or helped us unexpectedly; Chang & Sanfey, 2009).

This ability and motivation to evaluate others on the basis of moral character was likely of such fundamental importance during primate and human evolution that it is most likely a product of natural selection. For instance, to the extent that moral character was predictive of whether a person would cooperate in or defect from joint endeavors, character assessment was invaluable when making social decisions that directly affected survival and reproduction (Gintis, Henrich, Bowles, Boyd, & Fehr, 2008). More generally, individuals who were able to detect the presence of underlying moral traits in others would have been better able to avoid cheaters, psychopaths, and murderers and would have benefited from forming reliable social relationships with trustworthy individuals who could provide help when needed. Miller (2007) argued that sexual selection pressures may have favored the ability to evaluate the character traits of potential mates. To the extent that these traits were correlated with future choices, such as parental investment, the survival and reproduction chances of one's offspring might depend on valid character assessments during mate selection.

In short, the motivation to evaluate others' character appears to be a fundamental feature of human social cognition, and for good reasons. Accordingly, one would expect that theories of moral judgment—particularly those that focus on how we evaluate others' moral actions—might place great emphasis on how such character evaluations influence moral judgment. Yet this is not the case. In this chapter, we argue that theories of moral judgment (specifically, theories of moral blame) are fundamentally incomplete because they disregard the primacy of character evaluations. We then outline an alternative character-based theory of moral blame that may explain recent findings in the literature on moral responsibility that were incorrectly viewed, in terms of previous theories, as judgment errors but appear natural in light of motivation to evaluate others' moral character. By integrating character into the psychology of moral judgment, we hope to arrive at a more accurate account of *how* we make judgments of moral blame by taking into account *why* we make these judgments in the first place.

THE PSYCHOLOGY OF MORAL BLAME

A quick read of a daily newspaper, or a few minutes eavesdropping at the office water cooler, is probably sufficient to convince anyone that moral judgments come quickly and easily to most human beings. Yet figuring out how we make these judgments has proved difficult. One long-standing puzzle in the study of morality has been the wide variety of beliefs among individuals and across cultures concerning which acts are immoral. Why, for instance, do some people believe that aborting a fetus, torturing a prisoner for information, and pirating music are moral don'ts, whereas others not only disagree with these beliefs but go to great lengths to defend their opposites? Answering this question—how and why we come to believe that certain acts are morally taboo, permissible, or obligatory—has been a central concern of many moral psychologists (Greene, 2007; Haidt, 2001; see also Chapters 1 and 2, this volume). But even when an act is uncontroversially perceived to be morally wrong, we often have to make an additional moral judgment to determine whether the person who has committed the act should be held morally responsible. These two judgments—moral acceptability and responsibility—are the basis for judgments of blame (*blame* being an ascription of responsibility for a morally bad action). A number of highly influential theoretical accounts have been proposed to describe and explain how such judgments are made (Shaver, 1985; Weiner, 1995). It is to these accounts of blame that we now turn.

Moral Blame: The Standard Account

Most moral infractions we encounter in everyday life are minor: Someone cuts in front of you in line at the grocery store, unfairly insults a sensitive coworker, or spreads questionable rumors about a friend. But we are also confronted not infrequently with more serious infractions, even if only when watching the nightly news or reading the newspaper (e.g., a mother drowns her child, a man is convicted of embezzling company funds). Although we generally believe that cutting in line is wrong and killing a child is very wrong, we do not always hold people responsible for such acts. Maybe the person who cut in front of you failed to see you; maybe the mother who drowned her child had a mental illness. It is important to get these judgments right, because judgments of right and wrong carry social sanctions such as exclusion, imprisonment, and in some cases even death.

The normative answer to this question of how blame should be assigned—that is, how we ought to make these judgments—has been discussed by philosophers and legal scholars for centuries (Hart, 1968). For psychologists, these normative theories have served as a starting point for developing more complete theories of responsibility and blame. For instance, the earliest and most influential theories of moral psychology, the developmental theories of Piaget and Kohlberg, were heavily influenced by Kant's (1796/2002) deontological ethics, according to which the moral status of an act is evaluated in relation to rules, duties, or obligations viewed as a set of constraints on action (Kagan, 1997; see also Chapter 3, this volume). In a deontological approach, actions are viewed as morally impermissible if they violate these constraints (e.g., the prohibition against knowingly taking an innocent life). This view implies that to be held responsible for an act, an individual must have had the ability to do otherwise. In the absence of the freedom to act differently, holding an individual blameworthy would be unjustified. In Kant's view, *ought* implies *can*. If an individual had no control over an action, or did not intend or foresee the infraction, he or she could not have acted otherwise and is therefore not blameworthy (Bayles, 1982).

The deontological approach has been contrasted with the equally influential consequentialist approach to ethics (e.g., Smart & Williams, 1973; see also Chapter 3, this volume), which makes no distinctions regarding rules, duties, and obligations but proposes one criterion for evaluating the moral "rightness" or "wrongness" of an act—whether or not it brings about a favorable outcome. Moral acts, then, are defined as ones that maximize "good" consequences and avoid negative consequences. One upshot of this view is that moral blame is relevant only insofar as it might socially sanction and deter future negative acts. For the consequentialist, it is permissible for sanctions to be imposed whether or not the offender could have done otherwise. Features important from a deontological perspective, then, such as the specifics of an individual's mental state, are in and of themselves meaningless for determining sanctions.

Of importance to the argument we are advancing here, both of these normative approaches place little (if any) emphasis on evaluations of a person—they are fundamentally act based rather than person based. They propose that moral evaluations should focus on local features of an act and agent (e.g., whether the action violates a rule, whether the agent's mental state at the time of the action allowed for alternative actions, or whether the act caused harm). In contrast, a person-based approach would take the person as the unit of analysis when judging blame—their underlying traits, dispositions, and character (Bayles, 1982). Such an approach seems to fit our normal (and biologically ancient) reasons for blaming because it takes into account the goal of removing "bad people" from important positions in our social lives. And there is a theory in normative ethics that takes this view: virtue ethics (e.g., Anscombe, 1958). This approach emphasizes the character of the agent, rather than whether an act complies with rules or has good consequences. In fact, the claim that morality is fundamentally about possessing the right kind of character can be traced (at least in Western thought) to the views of Plato and Aristotle, who argued that to be a moral person means to have a moral character or to possess desired virtues. Although this view fell out of favor among philosophers as the deontological and consequentialist approaches gained ground, the virtue-based approach has enjoyed a resurgence in philosophy, and in legal theory as well (this resurgence has been referred to as the *aretaic turn*; Solum, 2004). So far, however, this virtue-based approach to ethics has gained little ground in moral psychology (but see Monin, Pizarro, & Beer, 2007).

By building on deontological and consequentialist normative approaches, psychological theories of blame have inherited their act-based approach to moral assessment inasmuch as they outline a set of local criteria for determining responsibility for a moral infraction (and hence blame; Shaver, 1985; Weiner, 1995). In addition, consistent with the attribution theories from which they emerged (e.g., the theories of Heider, 1958, and Kelley, 1967), psychological theories of blame have assumed that when given the necessary information, lay judges are capable of determining whether these criteria were met in any given act. That is, when presented with an instance in which a moral infraction was committed, the lay judge is presumed to work his or her way through the criteria in a stagelike fashion, asking a series of questions about features of the act, such as whether the actor intended the outcome, had control over the outcome, or could foresee the results of the action. If these conditions are met, there is nothing to prevent a confident judgment that the person should be held responsible and blamed (or praised, in the case of positive actions) accordingly. However, if some of these criteria are not met (e.g., the agent did not intend the outcome), these theories predict that the lay judge will either attenuate blame or ascribe no blame at all. It should be noted that these theories assume an invariant application of these decision rules across similar judgments; the same criteria should be applied regardless of time, place, or individual (Knobe & Doris, 2010; see also Chapter 3, this volume). For instance, when determining whether an individual should be blamed for stealing a car, his capacity to distinguish right from wrong and his ability to form intentions matter, but whether he is the judge's best friend or worst enemy should not matter. Likewise, if a person accidentally trips and knocks another in the face with her arm, whether or not she has a criminal record bears little on the assessment of blame because she had little control over the outcome.

The criteria outlined by these theories of blame seem intuitively reasonable, and the theories have fared quite well in predicting judgments of responsibility across a wide range of cases. When one or more of the designated criteria for blame are absent in a given case, research participants tend to reduce the amount of blame they assign to the agent. For instance, relatives of individuals with schizophrenia reduce the blame they assign for harmful actions undertaken as a result of the individual's (uncontrollable) hallucinations and delusions (Provencher & Fincham, 2000). And research participants are more likely to assign blame to AIDS patients if they contracted the disease through controllable means (licentious sexual practices) than if they contracted it uncontrollably (receiving a tainted blood transfusion; Weiner, 1995). In addition, unintentional acts, such as accidental harms, are seen as less blameworthy than intentional acts and acts that are unforeseeable as less blameworthy than foreseeable acts (Weiner, 1995).

When it comes to the issue of causality, people are more sensitive than even these classic theories might have predicted. For instance, individuals seem to care not only whether an agent caused an outcome but also whether the agent caused it in the specific manner in which he or she intended. If an act was intended and caused, but caused in a manner other than the one intended (acts are "causally deviant"), research participants view the acts as less blameworthy. For example, Pizarro, Uhlmann, and Bloom (2003) presented participants with the story of a woman who desired to murder her husband by poisoning his favorite dish at a restaurant, but she succeeded in causing his death only because the poison made the dish taste bad, which led to him to order a new dish to which he was (unbeknownst to all) deathly allergic. In cases like these, participants did not assign the same degree of blame as if the outcome had been caused directly in the manner the agent had intended. It seems, in short, that people often pay very close attention to the features of an action in just the manner described by deontological and consequentialist theories of blame.

A Character-Based Alternative to Understanding Blame

Despite the empirical support these theories have received, a number of recent findings have called their accuracy into question. For instance, judgments of moral blame are often disproportionate to the actual harm an agent caused; relatively harmless acts can receive harsh moral judgments. In addition, the mental-state criteria used to determine blame do not always fit the stagelike pattern predicted by the traditional approaches. In fact, research participants' judgments are often influenced by information that the traditional theories consider extraneous and irrelevant, such as the outcome of the act or the characteristics of the person performing the act (e.g., Alicke, 2000; Knobe, 2006).

One way to interpret these findings is to take them as evidence that, as in other judgmental domains, people are prone to error and bias in their judgments of moral blame. For example, rather than carefully taking the proper criteria into account before making a judgment of blame, people are affected by the emotions aroused by certain acts (e.g., Alicke, 2000). We believe, however, that such findings represent more than just a growing catalog of "errors" in moral judgment—simple deviations from otherwise accurate theories of blame. We believe that there are systematic patterns in the "errors" suggesting that the theoretical approaches themselves are error prone rather than the people making the judgments. This is why we are proposing a person-based character approach as an alternative to the act-based theories. This approach can explain putative judgmental errors as the systematic (and often rational) output of a system that is primarily concerned with evaluating others' character traits. A simple way of highlighting the difference is to wonder whether the person making a judgment of blame is asking himself or herself, "Was this particular action wrong?" or "Is the person who committed this act a bad person?"

We want to argue that the motivation to evaluate an agent's character manifests itself in at least two related ways when one is presented with a moral infraction. First, to the extent that a given act seems diagnostic of negative character traits, the agent of the act is more likely to be seen as deserving of blame. This may lead to harsh judgments for actions that seem fairly harmless in themselves but are indicative of a "bad" character. Second, if there is information about an individual's character that is extrinsic to the features of a particular act, it will be applied in judgments of blame (including judgments of such issues as control, causality, and intentionality). For instance, if there is evidence that an individual is a bad person, the inference that he or she intended a negative outcome seems reasonable (because bad people, by definition, are likely to desire and intend bad things).

ASYMMETRIES IN JUDGMENTS OF CONTROL, INTENTIONALITY, AND BLAME

Extant theories of blame make a straightforward prediction that criteria such as control, intention, and causality feed directly into judgments of blame. If, for example, an individual has absolutely no control over an action (and simply could not have done otherwise), he or she should not be held responsible. If caffeine jitters cause you to accidentally donate money to charity by clicking on the wrong computer key, or you accidentally scratch your friend's car with your key because someone bumped into you, you are not a candidate for praise or blame.

A number of studies have indicated that the relation between these criteria and judgments of blame is not so simple (Alicke, 1992; Knobe, 2006; Pizarro, Uhlmann, & Salovey, 2003). Despite evidence that humans are capable of making fairly careful distinctions regarding the presence of intentions, causality, and control, these distinctions may be overshadowed by a negative evaluation of character. This evaluation may cause "inflated" judgments of intentionality, causality, and control in cases where an agent seems particularly nefarious. Given the argument that these good–bad character judgments are psychologically primary (perhaps for evolutionary reasons), this should come as little surprise, but this asymmetric ascription of increased intentionality, causality, and control is puzzling given a standard act-based account of moral judgments.

Alicke and colleagues (e.g., Alicke, 1992, 2000) showed that participants made differential judgments about how much control a person had over an outcome if they had reason to think of him or her as a bad person. In one study, participants were told that a man was speeding home in a rainstorm and got into an accident that injured others. When asked whether the accident was due to factors under the driver's control (e.g., he was driving irresponsibly), participants were more likely to agree if they were previously told that he was speeding home to hide cocaine from his parents than if they were told he was speeding home to hide an anniversary gift, despite being given identical information regarding the factors that led to the accident. According to Alicke, our desire to blame the nefarious "cocaine driver" is what leads us to distort the criteria of controllability to validate this blame. Again, in the standard act-based view of responsibility, this appears to be a bias in judgment.

But in the character-based account, this makes sense. If we have just been provided with information that an individual is the sort of person to be hiding cocaine in his parents' house, it seems reasonable to assume that he might be the sort of person who drives recklessly. That is, given minimal, incomplete, or ambiguous information about controllability or intentionality, we are likely to take character information into account when asked to arrive at an estimate of these features. In fact, because we rarely have a window into factors such as the mental state of the individual at the time of the infraction (there often is not an easily identifiable, objective answer to the question of how much control an individual actually possessed), it seems as if applying information about an individual's previous acts, his or her known behavioral tendencies, or his or her character traits is a valid (albeit not perfect) way to make an assessment, much as we would apply base rate information when making other kinds of judgments under uncertainty.

This filling in the gaps using information about an individual's character may also be at work in intentionality judgments. Knobe and his colleagues (e.g., Leslie, Knobe, & Cohen, 2006; see Knobe, 2006, for a review) have shown that people are more likely to say that an act was performed intentionally if they perceive it to be morally wrong. In many of Knobe and colleagues' examples, individuals were provided with a scenario in which a foreseeable side effect results in a negative outcome. They were then asked if the side effect was brought about intentionally. For instance, in one scenario participants were told that the CEO of a company decided to implement a new policy but that the policy would have the side effect of either harming or helping the environment. Across both versions of the scenario (harm the environment or help the environment), participants were told that the CEO explicitly cared only about increasing profits, not about the incidental side effect of harming or helping the environment ("I don't care at all about harming the environment. I just want to make as much profit as I can"). Nonetheless, participants judged the side effect of harming the environment as intentional, but not the side effect of helping. This pattern of findings (with simpler scenarios) is evident in studies involving children as young as 6 or 7 years old (Leslie et al., 2006).

From an act-based approach, this so-called side-effect effect is puzzling, because judgments of intentionality are thought to be descriptive judgments about an agent's state of mind, and they should therefore be independent of the moral implications associated with the act. For these reasons, several researchers (including one of the authors; Pizarro & Helzer, 2010) have concluded that the side-effect effect is the result of a bias or "performance error" in the way our intentionality judgments are made. However, other researchers (including Knobe, 2006) have suggested that intentionality judgments may be more than just assessments of mental state and instead may be fundamentally imbued with normative considerations of praise and blame.

In a similar vein, Wellman and Miller (2008) argued that deontological considerations (judgments of permissibility or obligation) are fundamental to reasoning about intentionality (or belief–desire reasoning, which is usually thought to be a core component of intentionality; see Malle & Knobe, 1997). That is, obligations regarding harming and helping—obligations held to be especially important for morality—are asymmetric, such that we perceive a greater duty not to cause harm than we do to help (Grueneich, 1982). It makes sense, then, that we perceive acts in which an agent foresees a potential harm as different from those in which the agent foresees a potential benefit. The CEO in the "harm" side effect example above is performing a behavior that runs counter to the strong obligation to avoid knowingly causing harm. Because he continues to carry out his chosen action despite this obligation, it is reasonable to infer that his behavior was performed intentionally (overriding a strong obligation seems to require greater intentionality than overriding a weak one). However, because the CEO in the "help" condition does not have a strong obligation to help, it is reasonable to infer that his behavior is less intentional.

What this means from a character-based approach is that people judge cases in which a side effect causes harm as being particularly diagnostic of their character traits. This is consistent with what attribution theorists have noted: Some behaviors are more diagnostic of an individual's character than others. Reeder and Brewer (1979), for instance, argued that some dimensions of behavior are asymmetrically informative about the character of the actor. This asymmetric diagnosticity is especially true for moral behaviors. For example, dishonest people often tell the truth, but genuinely honest people rarely lie (Reeder & Brewer, 1979). Likewise, violating a strong moral obligation (e.g., not to cause harm) is perceived as more reflective of personal dispositions than violating a weaker moral obligation (e.g., failing to help; Trafimow & Trafimow, 1999). This is consistent with research demonstrating the side-effect effect: Obligations to prevent foreseeable harms are treated differently than obligations to help. Bringing about harm that one foresees is therefore perceived as intentional, and such acts are seen as more informative about a person's character.

More generally, from a character-based perspective it makes sense to hold someone fully accountable—that is, to treat his or her actions as though they were intentional—for a decision made when the person could foresee that it would cause harm. Such an act sends a clear signal as to what the agent does and does not value. And if, as we have been arguing, judgments of blame are in the service of character evaluations, there is a world of difference between someone knowingly allowing or causing harm to occur and someone taking potential harm seriously and ensuring that it does not occur.

An actor's intentions provide us with information about both the nature of the act itself and the agent who performed it. Accordingly, intentions may play an independent causal role in our perception of the outcomes (see Chapter 6, this volume). This was demonstrated recently by Gray and Wegner (2008), who found that when participants received shocks that they thought were intentional, they found them more painful than unintended shocks of equal magnitude. Moreover, whereas continued administration of unintentional shocks led to a reported decrease in the severity of pain (consistent with psychophysical laws of habituation), participants who perceived the shocks as intentional continued to report the same severity throughout the testing procedure, suggesting that the pain of intentional harm is more difficult to accommodate.

In sum, intentions matter to moral judgment above and beyond the specifics of a given action; they are important because we see ourselves and others as rational and purposeful agents, and intentions are the clearest ways of understanding what causes a person to do what he or she does; they reflect the person's attitudes, traits, and general moral character (Morse, 2003).

Beyond intentional behaviors, other kinds of behavior are also considered to be diagnostic of bad moral character—for example, acts that seem to indicate emotional callousness or a failure to consider the welfare of others when making a decision. Even when an act produces a net benefit for others, in some cases we find it difficult *not* to blame the agent. This again poses a real puzzle for standard accounts of blame because it means that even though a person may perform a morally permissible (or even obligatory) act, and one that fails to harm others or even ends up helping others, the person may be considered blameworthy.

One way to understand this from a character-based perspective is that we do not just want individuals to perform the right act; we want them to do it in the right way and for the right reasons. Consider the example of research on the footbridge dilemma, Thomson's (1976) scenario in which a person is faced with the decision of throwing a large man off a footbridge to his death in order to save the lives of five other people. Although most people view this act as morally forbidden (Mikhail, 2007), upon reflection many people agree that it might actually be the most ethical choice (Greene, Morelli, Lowenberg, Nystrom, & Cohen, 2008; Greene, Nystrom, Engell, Darley, & Cohen, 2004). But there are different ways in which the decision process can be described. In some cases, the person making the decision is described as painfully deliberating until the very last moment (with a train rapidly approaching), when he finally decides it is the right thing to do. In other cases, the person making the decision immediately shoves the large man to his death—while laughing. Although both men performed the same kind of act, with the same consequences—killing one to save five—it is difficult not to think that the "laughing utilitarian" deserves a negative moral evaluation. Indeed, recent research indicates that people often evaluate a person based not on the specific consequences of the act, but rather—independent of consequences—on what the act reveals about the person's character.

One piece of information often thought to be diagnostic of an agent's mental state is his or her emotional state at the time of the action. Was the person in a calm, rational state of mind, or was the person acting impulsively? Emotionally impulsive acts are generally seen as less controllable (which is one reason premeditated murders are punished more harshly than "crimes of passion"). Yet actions that are viewed as equally impulsive—where controllability is held constant—can lead to differential judgments of responsibility depending on the valence of the act. For instance, Pizarro, Uhlmann, and Salovey (2003) found that, consistent with an act-based approach to moral decision making, participants tended to reduce blame if a negative act was committed impulsively rather than deliberately. A person who impulsively hit someone in a fit of anger was seen as less responsible than someone who deliberately decided to hit someone. However, contrary to the invariance predicted by the act-based approach, positive acts that were committed impulsively received no such reductions in responsibility compared with positive acts committed deliberately. For example, impulsively donating money to charity because of a strong sympathetic reaction did not result in lower responsibility judgments or praise than donating the same amount after having deliberated about it. The authors argued that participants were making inferences about the actor's *metadesires* (the extent to which the donor had a second-order desire to entertain positive or negative impulses) and that the observed asymmetry arose because, unlike positive impulses, negative impulses were assumed to be unwanted by the participant. Consistent with this interpretation, follow-up studies revealed that when positive impulses were described as unwanted, the asymmetry disappeared. These metadesires—the evaluations an individual makes regarding his or her first-order impulses—are indicators of what the person truly values or of the "deep" self (Wolf, 1987).

Woolfolk, Doris, and Darley (2006) found that actors can sometimes be judged as morally responsible even if their actions were completely constrained by external circumstances. According to act-based models, acts committed because of situational constraints (indicating less controllability over the act) should cause research participants to reduce perceived responsibility for the action. But when Woolfolk and colleagues presented a scenario in which a man was under a clear situational constraint that forced him to murder an airplane passenger (he was forced by hijackers to kill the person or else he and 10 others would be killed), they held him responsible for the murder if it was something he had wanted to do anyway (i.e., if he "identified" with the act). In contrast, if participants believed that, while under identical situational constraints, the agent did not identify with the action—that in some sense the behavior felt "alien" to him—they reduced their attributions of responsibility. On the standard account of moral reasoning this is an anomaly, but on the character-based account it is quite reasonable. Embracing or identifying with murderous behavior is perceived as particularly indicative of an individual's negative character.

But not all impulsive acts provide the same information about an individual's character. Critcher, Inbar, and Pizarro (2011) found that only certain kinds of negative impulses led to a reduction in blame compared with identical deliberate acts. Some negative impulses actually led to increased blame. Consistent with the findings of Pizarro, Uhlmann, and Salovey (2003), a negative behavior committed while an actor was enraged resulted in lower blame than a similar but deliberate act. However, negative acts committed in a "rash" manner—equally impulsive, but without the presence of strong negative emotions—led to amplified blame when compared with a deliberate action. Critcher et al. found that this effect resulted from differing assumptions regarding the metadesires of individuals who act impulsively due to "rashness" compared with those who act impulsively out of "rage." Consistent with the character-based approach to moral reasoning, this effect was shown to occur because acts of rashness are perceived as more diagnostic of the underlying intentions and character attributes of the individual than acts of "rage" and are perceived as less situationally determined than acts of rage.

In another set of studies that resemble the laughing utilitarian example discussed earlier (Critcher, Helzer, Tannenbaum, & Pizarro, 2011), we demonstrated another way in which acts that result in the same—or in some cases better—consequences can be seen as blameworthy. We showed that the manner in which the decision is carried out—not just the decision itself—affects judgments of praise and blame. To the extent that the materials presented to participants provided information about the agent—what he or she valued and knew about what other people value—research participants incorporated these cues into their moral judgments. In one study, we presented participants with a common moral dilemma in which a group of Jewish people must remain quietly hidden lest nearby Nazi soldiers hear them and kill them. In this dilemma, a crying baby must be silenced or the group will be discovered and killed. The group realizes that the only way to save everyone's life is to kill the crying baby (by suffocating him). One group of subjects receives the information that the Nazi soldiers are next door, and a decision about the baby must be made quickly, whereas the other group is told that the Nazis are a few houses away and the potential victims have time to deliberate. When told that the person in charge of making the decision chose to sacrifice the baby, participants judged him significantly more harshly if he made this decision immediately than if he made it after having had a chance to deliberate. In fact, choosing to sacrifice the baby immediately garnered the most negative moral evaluations, and the other three conditions were evaluated less negatively and to the same extent. When making a difficult decision about morality in a situation like this, it appears that people want the decision to be made with difficulty, because this indicates that the decision maker has sentiments we value.

Finally, consider another set of studies by Tannenbaum, Uhlmann, and Diermeier (2010) showing that evaluations of character can result in greater blame for acts that cause less harm. In one of their experiments, participants were given one of two descriptions of a company manager who causes harm to his employees (by cutting the number of their vacation days in half). One condition described a "misanthropic" manager who cuts vacation days for all of his employees. In another condition he was described as cutting vacation days only for his African American employees ("bigot" manager). (In both cases, the description stated that about 20% of the company's employees were African American, and in the bigot version only the manager knew that some employees received fewer vacation days). Not surprisingly, although the bigoted manager caused material harm to far fewer individuals, he was judged as more blameworthy than the misanthropic manager. Moreover, participants were more likely to believe that the behavior of the bigot was diagnostic of his character than the behavior of the misanthrope. Of importance for the character-based theoretical perspective, judgments of the diagnosticity of the bigot's behavior were significantly correlated with judgments of blameworthiness. Once again, judgments of character seemed to affect moral blame in a manner inconsistent with act-based approaches to moral reasoning but quite consistent with a character-based approach.

CONCLUSION

A growing body of evidence suggests that the ways in which people make attributions of control, intentionality, responsibility, and blame are more complex and potentially important than one would assume on the basis of an act-based model of moral judgment. Although traditional act-based approaches recognize that these criteria are sometimes important for determining blame, they fail to explain why. We have argued that their importance is based on their being informative in that they indicate who the actor is and what he or she values and considers when performing morally relevant actions. In short, they reveal an agent's moral character, and data from several studies indicate that character is an important consideration when people assess others on moral grounds. Moreover, given the ability of the character-based approach to moral judgments to explain findings that seem puzzling from an act-based perspective, there is reason to take this approach seriously.

REFERENCES

Alicke, M. D. (1992). Culpable causation. *Journal of Personality and Social Psychology, 63*, 368–378. doi:10.1037/0022-3514.63.3.368

Alicke, M. D. (2000). Culpable control and the psychology of blame. *Psychological Bulletin, 126*, 556–574. doi:10.1037/0033-2909.126.4.556

Ames, D. R., & Johar, G. V. (2009). I'll know what you're like when I see how you feel. *Psychological Science, 20*, 586–593. doi:10.1111/j.1467-9280.2009.02330.x

Anscombe, G. E. M. (1958). Modern moral philosophy. *Philosophy, 33*, 1–19. doi:10.1017/S0031819100037943

Bar, M., Neta, M., & Linz, H. (2006). Very first impressions. *Emotion, 6*, 269–278. doi:10.1037/1528-3542.6.2.269

Bayles, M. (1982). Character, purpose and criminal responsibility. *Law and Philosophy, 1*, 5–20. doi:10.1007/BF00143144

Chang, L. J., & Sanfey, A. G. (2009). Unforgettable ultimatums? Expectation violations promote enhanced social memory following economic exchange. *Frontiers in Behavioral Neuroscience, 3*, 1–12. doi:10.3389/neuro.08.036.2009

Critcher, C., Helzer, E., Tannenbaum, D., & Pizarro, D. A. (2011). *Moral judgments stem not from the goodness of acts, but from the goodness of the principles motivating them.* Manuscript in preparation.

Critcher, C., Inbar, Y., & Pizarro, D. A. (2011). *When impulsivity illuminates moral character: The case of rashness.* Manuscript submitted for publication.

Fiske, S. T., Cuddy, A. J. C., & Glick, P. (2007). First judge warmth, then competence: Fundamental social dimensions. *Trends in Cognitive Sciences, 11*, 77–83. doi:10.1016/j.tics.2006.11.005

Foster, E. K. (2004). Research on gossip: Taxonomy, methods, and future directions. *Review of General Psychology, 8*, 78–99. doi:10.1037/1089-2680.8.2.78

Frank, R. H. (1988). *Passions within reason: The strategic role of the emotions.* New York, NY: Norton.

Gintis, H., Henrich, J., Bowles, S., Boyd, R., & Fehr, E. (2008). Strong reciprocity and the roots of human morality. *Social Justice Research, 21*, 241–253. doi:10.1007/s11211-008-0067-y

Gray, K., & Wegner, D. M. (2008). The sting of intentional pain. *Psychological Science, 19*, 1260–1262. doi:10.1111/j.1467-9280.2008.02208.x

Greene, J. D. (2007). Why are VMPFC patients more utilitarian? A dual-process theory of moral judgment explains. *Trends in Cognitive Sciences, 11*, 322–323.

Greene, J. D., Morelli, S. A., Lowenberg, K., Nystrom, L. E., & Cohen, J. D. (2008). Cognitive load selectively interferes with utilitarian moral judgment. *Cognition, 107,* 1144–1154. doi:10.1016/j.cognition.2007.11.004

Greene, J. D., Nystrom, L. E., Engell, A. D., Darley, J. M., & Cohen, J. D. (2004). The neural bases of cognitive conflict and control in moral judgment. *Neuron, 44,* 389–400. doi:10.1016/j.neuron.2004.09.027

Grueneich, R. (1982). The development of children's integration rules for making moral judgments. *Child Development, 53,* 887–894. doi:10.2307/1129125

Haidt, J. (2001). The emotional dog and its rational tail: A social intuitionist approach to moral judgment. *Psychological Review, 108,* 814–834. doi:10.1037/0033-295X.108.4.814

Hamlin, J. K., Wynn, K., & Bloom, P. (2007, November 22). Social evaluation by preverbal infants. *Nature, 450,* 557–559. doi:10.1038/nature06288

Hart, H. L. A. (1968). *Punishment and social responsibility.* Oxford, England: Clarendon Press.

Heider, F. (1958). *The psychology of interpersonal relations.* New York, NY: Wiley. doi:10.1037/10628-000

Kagan, S. (1997). *Normative ethics.* Boulder, CO: Westview Press.

Kant, I. (2002). *Groundwork for the metaphysics of morals* (A. Zweig, Trans.). New York, NY: Oxford University Press. (Original work published 1796)

Kelley, H. H. (1967). Attribution theory in social psychology. In D. Levine (Ed.), *Nebraska symposium on motivation* (pp. 129–238). Lincoln: University of Nebraska Press.

Knobe, J. (2006). The concept of intentional action: A case study in the uses of folk psychology. *Philosophical Studies, 130,* 203–231. doi:10.1007/s11098-004-4510-0

Knobe, J., & Doris, J. (2010). Strawsonian variations: Folk morality and the search for a unified theory. In J. Doris (Ed.), *The handbook of moral psychology* (pp. 321–353). Oxford, England: Oxford University Press.

Leslie, A. M., Knobe, J., & Cohen, A. (2006). Acting intentionally and the side-effect effect: Theory of mind and moral judgment. *Psychological Science, 17,* 421–427. doi:10.1111/j.1467-9280.2006.01722.x

Malle, B. F., & Knobe, J. (1997). The folk concept of intentionality. *Journal of Experimental Social Psychology, 33,* 101–121. doi:10.1006/jesp.1996.1314

Mikhail, J. (2007). Universal moral grammar: Theory, evidence, and the future. *Trends in Cognitive Sciences, 11,* 143–152. doi:10.1016/j.tics.2006.12.007

Miller, G. F. (2007). Sexual selection for moral virtues. *Quarterly Review of Biology, 82,* 97–125. doi:10.1086/517857

Monin, B., Pizarro, D., & Beer, J. (2007). Deciding vs. reacting: Conceptions of moral judgment and the reason–affect debate. *Review of General Psychology, 11,* 99–111. doi:10.1037/1089-2680.11.2.99

Morse, S. J. (2003). Diminished rationality, diminished responsibility. *Ohio State Journal of Criminal Law, 1*, 289–308.

Pizarro, D. A., & Helzer, E. (2010). Freedom of the will and stubborn moralism. In R. F. Baumeister, A. R. Mele, & K. D. Vohs (Eds.), *Free will and consciousness: How might they work?* (pp. 101–120). New York, NY: Oxford University Press.

Pizarro, D. A., Uhlmann, E., & Bloom, P. (2003). Causal deviance and the attribution of moral responsibility. *Journal of Experimental Social Psychology, 39*, 653–660. doi:10.1016/S0022-1031(03)00041-6

Pizarro, D. A., Uhlmann, E., & Salovey, P. (2003). Asymmetry in judgments of moral blame and praise: The role of perceived metadesires. *Psychological Science, 14*, 267–272. doi:10.1111/1467-9280.03433

Provencher, H. L., & Fincham, F. D. (2000). Attributions of causality, responsibility, and blame for positive and negative symptom behaviors in caregivers of persons with schizophrenia. *Psychological Medicine, 30*, 899–910. doi:10.1017/S003329 1799002342

Rand, D. G., Dreber, A., Ellingsen, T., Fudenberg, D., & Nowak, M. A. (2009, September 4). Positive interactions promote public cooperation. *Science, 325*, 1272–1275. doi:10.1126/science.1177418

Reeder, G. D., & Brewer, M. (1979). A schematic model of dispositional attribution in person perception. *Psychological Review, 86*, 61–79. doi:10.1037/0033-295X. 86.1.61

Shaver, K. G. (1985). *The attribution of blame: Causality, responsibility, and blameworthiness.* New York, NY: Springer-Verlag.

Smart, J. J. C., & Williams, B. (1973). *Utilitarianism: For and against.* Cambridge, England: Cambridge University Press.

Solum, L. B. (2004). *The aretaic turn in constitutional theory* (Working Paper 3, Legal Working Paper Series, Public Law and Legal Theory Research Paper Series). University of San Diego, San Diego, CA.

Tannenbaum, D. T., Uhlmann, E. L., & Diermeier, D. (2010). *Moral signals, public outrage, and immaterial harms.* Manuscript submitted for publication.

Thomson, J. (1976). Killing, letting die, and the trolley problem. *The Monist, 59*, 204–217.

Todorov, A., Said, C. P., Engell, A. D., & Oosterhof, N. N. (2008). Understanding evaluation of faces on social dimensions. *Trends in Cognitive Sciences, 12*, 455–460. doi:10.1016/j.tics.2008.10.001

Trafimow, D., & Trafimow, S. (1999). Mapping imperfect and perfect duties on to hierarchically and partially restrictive trait dimensions. *Personality and Social Psychology Bulletin, 25*, 686–695. doi:10.1177/0146167299025006004

Weiner, B. (1995). *Judgments of responsibility: A foundation for a theory of social conduct.* New York, NY: Guilford Press.

Wellman, H. M., & Miller, J. G. (2008). Including deontic reasoning as fundamental to theory of mind. *Human Development, 51*, 105–135. doi:10.1159/000115958

Willis, J., & Todorov, A. (2006). First impressions: Making up your mind after 100 ms exposure to a face. *Psychological Science, 17*, 592–598. doi:10.1111/j.1467-9280.2006.01750.x

Wolf, S. (1987). Sanity and the metaphysics of responsibility. In F. Schoeman (Ed.), *Responsibility, character, and the emotions: New essays in moral psychology* (pp. 363–373). Cambridge, England: Cambridge University Press.

Woolfolk, R. L., Doris, J. M., & Darley, J. M. (2006). Identification, situational constraint, and social cognition: Studies in the attribution of moral responsibility. *Cognition, 100*, 283–301. doi:10.1016/j.cognition.2005.05.002

6

MORALITY TAKES TWO: DYADIC MORALITY AND MIND PERCEPTION

KURT GRAY AND DANIEL M. WEGNER

One Friday night, you are out on a date at a restaurant, when your friends walk in. You wave hello, but when they come over, they look confused. One mentions that she thought you were on a date. You reply that you are. She points out that you're sitting alone and asks if you've been stood up. You say no, that you're just on a date by yourself, and that you never even intended there to be another person. Another friend asks if you just mean that you're treating yourself, and you get a little testy when you have to repeat yourself—"No, I'm on a date. A real, honest-to-goodness date—just by myself."

If your fictional self sounds a little ridiculous in this story, that's because our concept of *date* requires two people. Two people to gaze affectionately at each other, or two people to have awkward conversation, but nevertheless the core of a date is two. Although dating may be a trivial example, we suggest that the core of morality is also two—a *dyad*. However, unlike a date, where both people have equivalent roles, the two people in a moral dyad have different roles. One person in the dyad—the *moral agent*—does the moral action, and the other person—the *moral patient*—receives it. For example, in a theft, one person is the thief and the other the victim; in a donation, one person is the donor and the other the beneficiary. We propose that all moral acts are (at least

109

implicitly) dyadic, involving two different people, one as a moral agent and one as a moral patient.

The idea that people cleave the moral world into agents and patients is as old as Aristotle (Freeland, 1985), but out of this simple claim—that morality takes two—grows a theory of morality with a host of implications for psychology and the real world. *Dyadic morality* can help explain, for instance, why victims escape blame, why people believe in God, why people harm saints, why some advocate torture, and why those who do good become more physically powerful. In this chapter, we explore the idea of dyadic morality, its extensions and implications. In particular, we examine the following four tenets of dyadic morality:

1. Morality involves a moral agent helping or harming a moral patient.
2. Morality and mind perception are linked: Agency is tied to moral agents; experience is tied to moral patients.
3. Morality requires a complete dyad: An isolated moral agent creates a moral patient; an isolated moral patient creates a moral agent.
4. Morality requires two different people as agent and patient, which means that people are perceived as either agents or patients, both in moral acts and more generally, a phenomenon called *moral typecasting*.

We first explore the link between mind and morality, then examine dyadic help and harm, then explain how moral dyads complete themselves, and finally consider moral typecasting. Why start first with mind perception? Perceptions of mind are tightly bound to moral judgments, and as we show, the structure of mind perception is split into two complementary parts that correspond to the two parts of morality. Perceptions of mind underlie the most fundamental of moral decisions: who deserves moral rights and who deserves moral responsibility.

MORALITY AND MIND PERCEPTION

Morality and mind perception are linked: Agency is tied to moral agents; experience is tied to moral patients. In 2007, the Spanish government voted to extend basic human rights to chimpanzees and other great apes. These inviolable rights made it illegal to abuse or kill these creatures, protecting them from harmful medical experiments and subhuman living conditions in zoos. In contrast, every year, the Canadian, Norwegian, and Russian governments hand out thousands of licenses to hunt harp seal pups, whose silky white fur and big brown eyes make them the darlings of furriers and animal rights activists, respectively.

In 2005, 12-year-old Bryan Sturm became angry with his grandmother and aunt for verbally putting him down and enacted vengeance with a double-barreled shotgun, shooting his aunt in the head and—after reloading—his grandmother in the chest. An Ohio jury convicted him of two counts of murder, but because of his age, he was sentenced to only a few years in prison. Years earlier, in Oregon, 15-year-old Kip Kinkel murdered his parents and two classmates and wounded 25 others. In contrast to Bryan's light sentence, Kip was handed 111 years in prison.

Why are apes protected from harm while seal pups are hunted by the millions? What makes a 15-year-old responsible for his crimes but not a 12-year-old? What distinguishes those with moral rights and moral responsibilities from those lacking these attributes? The answer is mind: An entity's or person's mental capacities place the entity or person either inside or outside the moral circle. But what mental capacities specifically? The ability to critique Shakespeare and appreciate Wilde? The ability to speak or to cry "Ouch!" when poked? And what exactly is the moral circle to which having a mind gains one entrance? There seem to be two important moral circles involved: the first qualifies an entity for inviolable moral rights, and the second qualifies an entity for moral responsibility (see Chapter 11, this volume). Membership in these circles is exactly what is at stake when we discuss the fates of chimps versus seals and the responsibility of murdering adolescents. Research suggests that minds are perceived along two unique dimensions, each corresponding to one moral circle.

The Mind Survey

To investigate the link between perceived mind and moral rights and responsibilities, we conducted an international study in which more than 2,000 respondents evaluated both the mental abilities and the moral standing of a number of different entities, including a dog, a normal adult, a child, a person in a persistent vegetative state, a fetus, a robot, a dead person, a chimpanzee, and God (H. M. Gray, Gray, & Wegner, 2007). Each respondent evaluated entities on either a specific mental capacity (e.g., the capacity to feel pain, the capacity to communicate) or on one of two moral questions. The first moral question tapped moral rights and asked which entities would be most difficult for the participant to harm—in other words, which entities deserved more protection from harm. The second tapped moral responsibility and asked which entities should be most punished for causing someone's death.

When the survey responses were analyzed, the results were striking (Figure 6.1). First, people perceived the minds of these entities along two broad

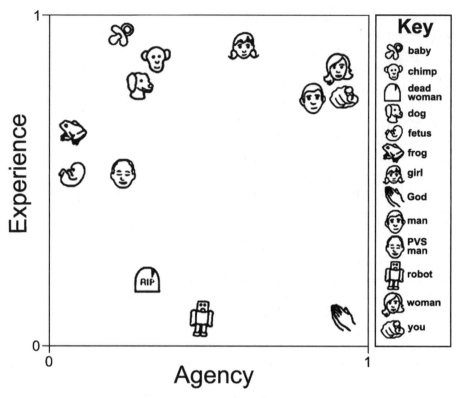

Figure 6.1. Dimensions of mind perception. Reprinted from "Dimensions of Mind Perception," by H. M. Gray, K. Gray, and D. M. Wegner, 2007, *Science, 315,* p. 619. Copyright 2007 by the American Association for the Advancement of Science. Reprinted with permission.

dimensions, which we labeled *experience* and *agency.* Experience is the general capacity for sensation and feeling and includes the capacities for hunger, fear, pain, and pleasure. Agency, in contrast, is the capacity to do and intend and includes the capacities for self-control, judgment, communication, and memory. These dimensions are generally independent, which means that an entity can have agency without experience or experience without agency. More broadly, this demonstrates that mind-having is not simply a matter of degree (less vs. more) but of type (agency, experience, or both). These two dimensions of mind map onto other dimensions by which we perceive others, including warmth (experience) and competence (agency; Fiske, Cuddy, & Glick, 2007) as well as human nature (experience) and human uniqueness (agency; Haslam, Loughnan, Kashima, & Bain, 2008; see also Chapter 11, this volume).

Of special importance, the survey indicated that the two types of moral standing were each uniquely predicted by one of the two dimensions of mind.

Experience (the capacity to feel) determined whether an entity deserved moral rights and protection from harm, whereas agency (the capacity to do and intend) endowed an entity with moral responsibility and warranted punishment for killing another. In the words of Aristotle, those with agency are moral agents—entities capable of doing good or evil, right or wrong—and those with experience are moral patients—capable of having good or evil, right or wrong, done to them. Only entities with self-control and judgment are truly capable of doing evil and able to be held accountable for their actions. Compare the wrongness of an adult killing a puppy with a toddler doing the same—the actions of the adult can be labeled evil, but it is much harder to call the toddler evil because he or she lacks the mental capacities that confer moral agency. Similarly, only someone with the capacity to feel pain and pleasure can truly be wronged. Both a tin can and a mailman might be punctured by a gunshot, but because only the mailman feels pain, only he is a moral patient who can be a victim of evil.

Types of Mind

When the characters from the mind survey were plotted according to how much experience or agency each was seen to possess, clusters were revealed (Figure 6.1). Possessing both agency and experience, and so qualifying as both moral agents and moral patients, were adult humans, who can be both the perpetrators and victims of evil. Animals and children were seen to be solely moral patients, with experience but reduced agency, explaining both why it is wrong to harm them and why they are not held morally accountable for their actions. Opposite to this corner of the graph was God, who can undertake moral deeds (and possibly immoral deeds, depending on what you believe about God's justness) but cannot be harmed by the actions of others—an omnipotent but unfeeling deity. In a replication, Google was also found to live in this corner, suggesting that corporations can act and do evil but cannot themselves be harmed (though, of course, individual employees can; see also Knobe & Prinz, 2008). The dead person, who lacked both experience and agency, was neither a moral agent nor a moral patient.

Perceptions of mind concerning other targets—and therefore the moral judgments concerning them—were less clear-cut. For example, fetuses and people in persistent vegetative states were seen to have intermediate amounts of experience, therefore leaving open the question of whether they are moral patients and deserve protection. Nowhere is this ambiguity more salient than in debates about abortion and the right of patients to remain indefinitely on life support, with those attributing mind to these entities arguing for human rights and those not attributing mind to them arguing against such rights.

That the two dimensions of mind link to two moral roles suggests that if there were more dimensions of mind, there might also be more moral roles, but we propose that, in both morality and mind, two is the magic number. The dyadic roles of moral doer and recipient, agent and patient, are not simply aspects of the moral world; they define its very structure.

THE DYADIC STRUCTURE OF MORALITY

Morality involves a moral agent helping or harming a moral patient. Imagine a typical moral event, such as assault, murder, and theft (on the side of evil) or charity and rescue (on the side of good). Each of these acts requires at least two people—a person to assault, murder, steal, give, or rescue, and a person to be assaulted, murdered, stolen from, given to, or rescued. Indeed, without two people, these actions lose their moral status. Without a moral agent (e.g., a thief), stealing becomes losing something; without a moral patient (e.g., a victim), stealing becomes finding something. Even the language of morality reflects this dyadic structure—you cannot simply kill or assault; you must kill or assault *someone*.

Some evidence for the necessity of both agent and patient for (im)morality comes from the work of Nichols and Knobe (2007), who presented people with a variety of potentially moral scenarios and found that only those with both a clear perpetrator and a clear victim were judged as wrong. For example, rape but not tax evasion was seen as wrong because rape has a clear victim, whereas the harm of tax evasion is less obvious. If moral acts need both an agent and a patient, the link between mind and morality implies that wrongdoing should involve both an evil intention on the part of a perpetrator (agency) and suffering on the part of a victim ("patiency"). In fact, these two criteria are explicitly stated by the law as necessary for wrongdoing under the terms *mens rea* and *actus reus*, respectively (Hart & Honoré, 1985).

Mens rea is translated as "guilty mind" and means that the person who perpetrated the act must have recognized the wrongness of the misdeed and must have been able to act otherwise. In other words, the person had to be able to appreciate the distinction between right and wrong and be able to exert self-control—both capacities of agency. *Actus reus* is Latin for "guilty act" and means that someone must have done something wrong—usually by harming another person. Psychological research on moral decision making has further confirmed the importance of these two components by finding that intentions (agency) and outcomes (patiency) serve as the basis for judgments of wrongness (Cushman, 2008; see also Chapter 2, this volume).

Defining morality as involving a dyad in which one member (the agent) harms or helps the other member (the patient) may seem overly restrictive, especially in light of research that finds that moral judgment extends beyond harm and justice to other domains, such as purity and respect for authority (Haidt & Graham, 2007; see also Chapter 1, this volume). We, along with others (e.g., DeScioli & Kurzban, 2009), suggest that these additional domains build on a harm-centered dyadic core of morality. Evidence for this suggestion comes from developmental science, which has shown that young infants are attuned to helping and harming behaviors (Hamlin, Wynn, & Bloom, 2007; see also Chapter 4, this volume). Infants and young children are also distressed by others' expressions of pain (Eisenberg, 2000; Martin & Clark, 1982; Zahn-Waxler, Robinson, & Emde, 1992), but presumably not by other moral violations. Anyone who has seen what young children put in their mouths may suspect that purity concerns and moral disgust are not innate.

Older children also provide support for the centrality of harm in moral judgments. For example, Turiel (2002) and Nucci (1981) found that although children see transgressions involving harm as morally wrong, other violations (e.g., defying authority, eating in a disgusting manner) are more often seen as violations of societal rules, customs, or norms rather than morality. Interestingly, the relative wrongness of these nonmoral transgressions seems to depend on the presence of another person affected by them (i.e., a victim or moral patient). Of course, the harm-based evolution of morality does not bar people from developing additional domains of morality, and in fact, the moral innateness of harm provides a way for other moral domains to be established. For example, violations of purity can be likened to something that induces physical or mental harm to the self or society. This is probably why when people talk about moral violations of other domains, they often fall back on the perceived harm it causes (Haidt, 2001; see also Chapter 1, this volume).

COMPLETING THE MORAL DYAD

Morality requires a complete dyad: An isolated moral agent creates a moral patient; an isolated moral patient creates a moral agent. Although we have proposed that the core of morality is a dyad in which one person helps or harms another, it is possible to think of acts that seem wrong but involve only one person. Haidt and colleagues' example of someone having sex with a dead chicken and then eating it (Haidt, Koller, & Dias, 1993) initially seems wrong, harmless, and something one can do alone. Although these actions initially seem to involve no moral patient, we suggest that people typically do infer the presence of a victimized moral patient. In the case of dead-chicken sex buffets, the victim could be the memory of the chicken; the children whose morals might be twisted by learning about this episode; or you, gentle reader, who becomes psychologically scarred from thinking about how exactly you would have to position a chicken carcass for intercourse. Of course, examples can be constructed that explicitly deny the presence of a victim, but the point is that dyadic morality gives us an automatic victim detector—a reflex, like our leg jerking after being tapped on the knee. If something seems wrong, there must be someone harmed by it.

Informal evidence exists for this automatic moral patient detector. For example, those who think that homosexuality is wrong frequently cite the harm done to others, such as children (Bryant, 1977), and those who see the wrongness in flag burning point to the harm it indirectly causes our veterans (Welch, 2000, p. 173). In terms of psychological evidence, DeScioli (2008) found that people cannot help but see victims in response to perceived wrongdoing, even for victimless offenses—a phenomenon he called the *indelible victim effect*. In his studies, participants were presented with a variety of transgressions (e.g., eating dog meat, flag burning, grave desecration, homosexuality, suicide) and were asked to rate both the wrongness of each transgression and the extent to which each involved a victim. He found that when people rated an offense as wrong, they perceived a victim 89% of the time, but when they did not perceive the offense as wrong, they perceived a victim only 15% of the time (DeScioli, 2008, p. 48), which suggests a strong link between moral wrongness and there being a moral patient. These studies suggest that even nondyadic moral situations are automatically squeezed into a dyadic template. Just as people twist objective facts to support their moral judgments (Chapter 3, this volume), so, too, will they create a moral dyad to account for actions that seem wrong.

Suffering Needs a God

Dyadic morality suggests that when we see an isolated moral agent, someone being immoral alone, we fill in the moral dyad by seeing a suffering victim. But if perpetrators need victims, it should also be the case that victims need perpetrators. In other words, people should complete the moral dyad for isolated moral patients by seeking moral agents to blame for unfair suffering. Anecdotally, it certainly appears that people are only too ready to blame (and sue) someone for their misfortune. Someone trips on the sidewalk and sues the homeowner, someone chokes on a hamburger and sues the cook, someone spills hot coffee on himself and sues the company for not having sufficient warning labels. What happens, though, when harm befalls someone and there is no person or corporation to blame? If morality is dyadic, moral patients should need to find a moral agent, even if none is readily apparent. Luckily, there appears to be one entity powerful enough to accept blame for an entire universe of suffering—God.

There are lots of reasons to believe in God. He gives meaning to a potentially meaningless life (Paloutzian, 1981), He provides control in a chaotic world (Kay, Gaucher, McGregor, & Nash, 2010), and He even acts as a surrogate parent by filling attachment needs (Kirkpatrick & Shaver, 1992; see also Chapter 14, this volume). On top of these functions, we suggest that God is also the ultimate moral agent, the entity to which people attribute otherwise unattributable helps and harms. In this view, the main reason people see God acting in the world is not to explain the marvel of sunsets or the wonder of life, but rather to explain otherwise inexplicable salvation and suffering (K. Gray & Wegner, 2010a).

Evidence suggests that people do see the hand of God in beneficial events. God is held responsible, for example, when a person is suddenly cured of disease or survives a potentially lethal "accident" (Pargament & Hahn, 1986; Pepitone & Saffiotti, 1997; Spilka & Schmidt, 1983), but there is reason to suspect that people are more likely to perceive God in cases of suffering than in cases of salvation, because negative events are consistently more powerful and in need of explanation than positive events (Baumeister, Bratslavsky, Finkenauer, & Vohs, 2001; Taylor, 1991). Imagine the difference between getting a job and losing a job: Getting a job feels good, but not as good as losing a job feels bad. So although people may thank God for benefits received, they may be even more likely to view Him as the cause of a catastrophe. In the frame provided by Janoff-Bulman (Chapter 7, this volume), people should be less inclined to see God for things that should happen and more inclined to see Him for things that simply should not happen.

There is certainly anecdotal evidence to support this claim; just look at newspapers and blogs after natural disasters, and you will see the Almighty frequently invoked. People saw God's divine wrath behind the Haitian earthquake of 2010, with one televangelist suggesting that God was punishing the nation for a "pact with the devil" that Haitians made in the 17th century concerning slavery (Foser, 2010). In 2005, Ray Nagin, the mayor of New Orleans, saw evidence of God's hand in the devastation of Hurricane Katrina (Martel, 2006); in 2004, many saw evidence of God's displeasure in the Indonesian tsunami (de Borchgrave, 2005).

In a more controlled study, we examined the link between suffering and belief in God in the United States (K. Gray & Wegner, 2010a). The Pew Foundation collects statistics on the average level of religious belief in each state, and the United Health Foundation computes a "health index" for each state that incorporates levels of infant mortality, cancer deaths, environmental pathogens, and even violent crime victimization. Taking the reverse of this health index yields a "suffering index," and the correlation between this measure and the proportion of people in each state who believe strongly in God is $r(48) = .69$, $p < .001$. This link remains significant even after controlling for median income and education (percentage of people with bachelor's degrees), $\beta = .37$, $p < .01$ (K. Gray & Wegner, 2010a).

These results suggest that when people suffer, they tend to hold God responsible for their plight. Of course, people should blame God for their suffering only when they cannot complete the moral dyad with another person, and one study suggests that this is the case (K. Gray & Wegner, 2010a). In this study, participants read one of four stories about a family on a picnic in the bottom of a ravine when water suddenly floods the valley. In half of the stories, the family escapes with no ill effects; in the other half, the entire family (including the dog) drowns in the flood. The stories are further divided such that sometimes the flood is caused by a dam worker upstream and sometimes there is no clear explanation for the flood. When people were asked to say how much the events in the story were "part of God's higher plan," they saw a significant role for the Almighty only when the family died and there was no other person to blame. This suggests that God serves as a surrogate moral agent to whom the cause of suffering is ascribed when no other person can be found.

Although people may believe in God for many reasons, suffering may prompt belief in God because of the dyadic nature of morality. Suffering may also evoke religious belief for additional reasons: People go to God for relief, and even when God is seen as causing suffering, he is often also ascribed a reasonable rationale for doing so. Nevertheless, it seems that an isolated moral patient needs a moral agent.

Intention and Suffering

The dyadic nature of morality suggests that suffering needs to be ascribed to an intentional harm, but the link between suffering and intention also seems to function in reverse, whereby intention leads to suffering. This may seem odd, for unless someone possesses evil telekinetic powers, how can intention by itself harm another person? Barring the existence of mental death rays, it is still possible that the perceived intention of a moral agent can influence the experience of a moral patient. Imagine yourself receiving a slap from either a jilted lover or a friend trying to kill a mosquito—the insect-targeted slap would seem to hurt less because it lacks the emotional affront of the harmful one. Of course, the unintentional slap would also likely be softer, but even an identical harm (e.g., a 50-V electric shock) might hurt differently depending on the perceived intention behind it.

Perceived intention can change pain because pain represents not only the physical parameters of a harm but also its emotional meaning. Intentional harms inflict not only the pain of the stimuli but also the emotional sting of malice. Studies suggest that this is the case (K. Gray & Wegner, 2008). In one experiment, participants who received intentional electric shocks felt more pain than those who received accidental shocks. Moreover, follow-up studies suggested that intentional shocks not only hurt more but also engender a greater skin conductance response, suggesting that this effect extends beyond subjective experience to physiology.

These studies indicate, then, that not only does suffering lead to the perception of intentional agency but also that perceptions of intentional agency lead to increased suffering. This further supports the idea of dyadic morality—the notion that people possess a moral template that links agency and patiency, intention and outcomes, and evil and suffering.

MORAL TYPECASTING

Morality requires two different people as agent and patient, which means that people are perceived as either agents or patients, both in moral acts and more generally. So far, we have discussed three parts of dyadic morality: the link between the two dimensions of mind perception and the two moral roles; dyadic help and harm; and the power of the moral dyad to complete itself, whether by finding patients to receive moral wrongs or by finding agents to account for suffering. In the remainder of the chapter, we focus on the final part of dyadic morality: moral typecasting.

Picture a typical immoral act, such as a theft, in which one person (the thief) takes money from another person (the victim). Now imagine that the thief and the victim were the same person. The theft now turns into a person taking money from himself or herself—perhaps out of a wallet or bank account—but in either case, the act loses its moral punch. This thought experiment suggests that moral acts require a dyad consisting of two different people and that for any single act, a person can be either the moral agent or the moral patient, but not both. Although this either/or restriction may seem obvious for a single moral act, research suggests that people perceive others more generally as either moral agents or moral patients, but not both (K. Gray & Wegner, 2009). This is called *moral typecasting,* for just as actors are typecast into certain roles, making it difficult to see them in other roles (just try to imagine a cute child actor as a villain), so too are people typecast into the mutually exclusive moral roles of agent and patient. These roles of agent and patient are not simply momentary viewpoints but more enduring perceptions of character (see Chapter 5, this volume).

Most fundamentally, moral typecasting means that the more someone is seen as a moral agent (a hero or villain), the less he or she can be seen as a moral patient (beneficiary or victim). Given the link between morality and mind, this means that the more someone is seen as capable of acting intentionally and earning blame or praise (moral agency), the less he or she should be seen as capable of feeling pain and pleasure (moral patiency). Indeed, when participants are asked to rate a variety of targets on their capacity for blame or praise and pain, an inverse relation is found: Those who earn blame (e.g., Hitler) and praise (e.g., Mother Teresa) are seen to be insensitive to pain, and those who are sensitive to pain (e.g., victims of crimes, orphans) are viewed as incapable of earning blame or praise (K. Gray & Wegner, 2009).

Blame, Pain, and Typecasting

The inverse relation between moral agency and patiency can have some surprising effects. For example, perceiving moral agents to be less sensitive to pain may license people to harm them. Although this would be unsurprising in the case of evil agents—who wouldn't want to heap pain on Hitler?—it would be more interesting if people allot more pain to Mother Teresa simply because she seems relatively insensitive. Of course, people would be unlikely to spontaneously harm the saintly, but the idea is that if people *had* to harm someone, they would sooner do it to Mother Teresa than to an ordinary person.

To test this idea, we asked participants to imagine that they had three pain-producing pills to divide between pairs of people (an odd number was chosen so that someone would have to receive more pills). These potential pain recipients were drawn from a population of moral patients (e.g., an orphan), neutral people (e.g., a bank teller), good agents (e.g., Mother Teresa), and bad agents (e.g., Hitler). When we looked at people's pill allocations, we found that, unsurprisingly, bad agents were assigned the most pain and patients the least. As predicted, however, Mother Teresa and her crew of altruists received more pain than ordinary people, suggesting that despite all of the good that heroes do, people are willing to assign them pain when someone has to be harmed (K. Gray & Wegner, 2009).

These findings suggest that people harm good doers not despite their good deeds, but because of them. By doing good, they appear less sensitive to pain and therefore are more likely to receive it from others. These results stand against the idea of karma and belief in a just world (Lerner, 1980), as instead of being rewarded with pleasure, good doers are paid back with pain. Additionally, since both good and bad agents received more pain, it suggests that a hero's role as a moral agent may be more salient than his or her goodness. And although this assignment of suffering seems unfair, the concept of typecasting suggests that there are even more ways in which virtue fails to pay.

Typecasting and Blame

People say that doing good is its own reward, but many of us intuitively believe that doing good is good for other reasons as well. Indeed, those who do good are admired and revered, and they often receive rewards in the form of accolades and medals (see Chapter 15, this volume). What happens, however, when doers of good succumb to temptation and act immorally?

It would make sense for the misdeeds of heroes to be measured against their contributions to society, such that the more good people do, the less blame and punishment they receive for their mistakes. Typecasting suggests, however, that previous heroes should earn just as much blame as everyone else, if not more, because heroes are moral agents who not only earn praise but are also capable of earning blame. Moral typecasting suggests that in the conceptual space of morality, villains are close enough to heroes that it should take little to turn adoration into revulsion. Evidence for the futility of virtue in escaping blame comes from studies showing that heroes are punished at least as much as ordinary people for misdeeds, even when the misdeeds can be interpreted more charitably (K. Gray & Wegner, 2011). For example, if someone with a long history of charitable donations and an ordinary person both take $10 that does not belong to them, people show no leniency toward the hero. Although some may see the misdeeds of heroes as acts of hypocrisy (see Chapter 9, this volume), the ultimate use of the money is unspecified, leaving space for a more charitable interpretation of the theft; it could be that our hero is using the money to feed the homeless, but people withhold the benefit of the doubt and heap on blame. In another study, people even remembered the misdeeds of heroes faster, suggesting that we just can't wait to blame them (K. Gray & Wegner, 2011).

The fine line between hero and villain stands in contrast to the psychological distance between moral agents and patients. Because perceptions of moral agency and patiency oppose each other, moral patients (e.g., victims) should best escape blame. The same studies documenting the futility of heroism also highlight the power of victimhood; in contrast to heroes, who often received more blame than neutral targets, victims consistently received less blame (K. Gray & Wegner, 2011). Whether in the case of theft, negligence, or simple callousness, when people's victimhood was made salient, they were assigned less blame. These results suggest that when a person wishes to shirk blame, he or she should bemoan the difficulty of life and the harms received at the hands of others. Importantly, the ability of victims to escape blame does not stem simply from sympathy but from altered mind perception. Because victims are moral patients, we think of them as incapable of planning and self-control—past suffering makes people seem incapable of evil.

Typecasting and Torture

The recommendation that one should play the victim to escape blame seems to run counter to the research showing that people blame victims in order to believe that the world is just (Lerner, 1980; Lerner & Simmons, 1966). For example, victims of rape are frequently blamed for their misfortune because people do not want to believe that terrible things can happen to innocents (Furnham, 2003). But if just world theory says that victims earn more blame, and moral typecasting says that victims receive less blame, which is right? It turns out that both are right, depending on the circumstances. Blaming the victim depends on being emotionally involved with the victim's plight, so it is only when people feel uneasy that they view victims as guilty (Cialdini, Kenrick, & Hoerig, 1976). This suggests that putting some psychological distance between people and the suffering other will reduce dissonance and lead them to see that victim as less rather than more guilty.

People ascribing blame to victims is more than just an academic issue; it underlies the current debate about torture. Torture is supposed to reveal its victims' guilt, but it may instead just lead to the inference of guilt (Greenberg & Dratel, 2005). When people see another person in pain, their discomfort at the victim's suffering may cause them to perceive the victim as blameworthy and hence deserving of pain. In contrast, those who are relatively distant from torture may follow the rules of typecasting and see the victims' suffering as evidence of innocence because pain and blame are inconsistent with each other. The different predictions of just world/dissonance and typecasting may explain the debate on torture, with those who feel closely associated with the torture—or at least somewhat complicit—justifying it and those at greater distance condemning it.

We conducted a study to examine torture in the lab and manipulated physical distance. Participants learned of a young woman suspected of stealing and then listened as she was ostensibly tortured by having her hand submerged in ice water. Half of the participants met this suspect face to face and sat next door during the torture, whereas the other half did not meet her and listened only to a recording of previous torture. Thus, although both were exposed to torture, only the first group of participants were nearby and felt complicit in the victim's suffering. After the presumably painful torture, participants rated the likely guilt of the victim. As predicted, those nearby the torture acted in line with just world/dissonance predictions and ascribed more blame following the painful torture, whereas those at a greater distance did the opposite, in line with typecasting predictions (K. Gray & Wegner, 2010b).

Thus, those far from suffering appear to sympathize with victims, whereas those involved react harshly. We found this difference by manipulating physical distance, but psychological distance should work similarly: Feeling complicit with torture because of voting behavior or political affiliation should also increase blame for torture victims. In more general terms of escaping blame, these results suggest that victimhood helps except when those doing the blaming are close to or feel responsible for a victim's suffering. In addition to exploring the moderators of typecasting, this study demonstrates the flexibility of important moral judgments. Most of us would like to think we take strong stands on moral issues, but these data and the work of others in this volume suggest that both moral judgments and behavior hinge on situational factors (see Chapters 2, 8, 10, and 19, this volume).

Becoming Agentic

The research on typecasting reviewed so far examines when other people perform or receive moral deeds. What happens when we ourselves do good or evil? Does moral typecasting apply to oneself? Research suggests not only that typecasting applies to oneself but also that it can change people's capacity for physical agency.

It has long been known that self-perceptions can act as self-fulfilling prophecies, such as when people who are led to see themselves as extroverted actually become more extroverted (Bem, 1967; Fazio, Effrein, & Falender, 1981). It may be that self-perceptions of moral agency are also self-fulfilling, such that when people are led to see themselves as moral agents, they actually become more agentic. If this is the case, it would suggest that agency—self-control, tenacity, and willpower—is a consequence and not a precursor of good deeds. Perhaps someone like Gandhi was not born with the capacity for heroism but acquired it by attempting to do good. This may be one reason why moral agents differ from normal people (Chapter 15, this volume)—their moral deeds have transformative power.

The power of moral deeds to increase agency was tested by allowing people to do good before measuring their physical self-control. Study participants were given a dollar and told they could either keep it or donate it to charity. They were then asked to hold up a 5-lb weight for as long as possible. Those who did good by donating the dollar to charity were able to hold up the weight significantly longer (K. Gray, 2010), suggesting that doing good may not just feel good (Dunn, Aknin, & Norton, 2008); it may also increase agency. Of course, because moral agents can be either good or evil, doing (or thinking of oneself doing) evil should also increase agency. This appears to be the case, as people who wrote fictional stories about themselves doing good or evil could hold a weight longer than those who wrote about a more neutral deed (K. Gray, 2010). In fact, people who wrote evil stories held the weight somewhat longer, suggesting that evil deeds—like violence—not only may get people what they want (Chapter 20, this volume) but may also confer an agency boost. Of course, there are other reasons to recommend good deeds over evil ones, but whether a person does good or evil, moral typecasting seems to work through moral deeds, transforming the weak into the mighty. This suggests that perhaps the best route to increased self-control and physical endurance or recovery from trauma (Chapter 17, this volume) and psychopathology (Chapter 16, this volume) is to do moral deeds.

CONCLUSION

Morality is complex. The ways in which people make moral judgments, the reasons people behave badly, and society's options for making people do good are all difficult issues. Nevertheless, we have shown that many questions about morality can be answered by focusing on its dyadic nature, which affects how people ascribe moral rights and responsibilities, why people harm saints and free victims, why many believe in God, and how moral deeds can change people's agency.

In particular, the dyadic approach to morality suggests that (a) morality involves an agent helping or harming a patient, (b) conceptions of mind and morality are related, (c) moral dyads need to be completed, and (d) any one person is viewed as either a moral agent or a moral patient. Of course, morality can take a variety of forms, many of which are discussed elsewhere in this volume, but the dyadic perspective on morality suggests that despite appearances, all moral situations share a fundamental structure. Inside every instance of right or wrong beat two hearts.

REFERENCES

Baumeister, R. F., Bratslavsky, E., Finkenauer, C., & Vohs, K. D. (2001). Bad is stronger than good. *Review of General Psychology, 5*, 323–370. doi:10.1037/1089-2680.5.4.323

Bem, D. J. (1967). Self-perception: An alternative interpretation of cognitive dissonance phenomena. *Psychological Review, 74*, 183–200. doi:10.1037/h0024835

Bryant, A. (1977). *The Anita Bryant story: The survival of our nation's families and the threat of militant homosexuality.* Grand Rapids, MI: Revell.

Cialdini, R. B., Kenrick, D. T., & Hoerig, J. H. (1976). Victim derogation in the Lerner paradigm: Just world or just justification? *Journal of Personality and Social Psychology, 33*, 719–724. doi:10.1037/0022-3514.33.6.719

Cushman, F. (2008). Crime and punishment: Distinguishing the roles of causal and intentional analyses in moral judgment. *Cognition, 108*, 353–380. doi:10.1016/j.cognition.2008.03.006

de Borchgrave, A. (2005, January 9). Allah off the Richter scale. *Washington Times.* Retrieved from http://www.washingtontimes.com/news/2005/jan/09/20050109-102911-9121r/

DeScioli, P. (2008). *Investigations into the problems of moral cognition*. Philadelphia, PA: University of Pennsylvania.

DeScioli, P., & Kurzban, R. (2009). Mysteries of morality. *Cognition, 112*, 281–299. doi:10.1016/j.cognition.2009.05.008

Dunn, E. W., Aknin, L. B., & Norton, M. I. (2008, March 21). Spending money on others promotes happiness. *Science, 319*, 1687–1688. doi:10.1126/science.1150952

Eisenberg, N. (2000). Emotion, regulation, and moral development. *Annual Review of Psychology, 51*, 665–697. doi:10.1146/annurev.psych.51.1.665

Fazio, R. H., Effrein, E. A., & Falender, V. (1981). Self-perceptions following social interactions. *Journal of Personality and Social Psychology, 41*, 232–242. doi:10.1037/0022-3514.41.2.232

Fiske, S. T., Cuddy, A. J. C., & Glick, P. (2007). Universal dimensions of social cognition: Warmth and competence. *Trends in Cognitive Sciences, 11*, 77–83. doi:10.1016/j.tics.2006.11.005

Foser, J. (2010, January 14). The right-wing media react to Haiti. *Media Matters for America*. Retrieved from http://mediamatters.org/columns/201001140050

Freeland, C. A. (1985). Aristotelian actions. *Nous, 19*, 397–414. doi:10.2307/2214949

Furnham, A. (2003). Belief in a just world: Research progress over the past decade. *Personality and Individual Differences, 34*, 795–817. doi:10.1016/S0191-8869(02)00072-7

Gray, H. M., Gray, K., & Wegner, D. M. (2007, February 2). Dimensions of mind perception. *Science, 315*, 619. doi:10.1126/science.1134475

Gray, K. (2010). Moral transformation: Good and evil turn the weak into the mighty. *Social Psychological and Personality Science, 1*, 253–258. doi:10.1177/1948550610367686

Gray, K., & Wegner, D. M. (2008). The sting of intentional pain. *Psychological Science, 19*, 1260–1262. doi:10.1111/j.1467-9280.2008.02208.x

Gray, K., & Wegner, D. M. (2009). Moral typecasting: Divergent perceptions of moral agents and moral patients. *Journal of Personality and Social Psychology, 96*, 505–520. doi:10.1037/a0013748

Gray, K., & Wegner, D. M. (2010a). Blaming God for our pain: Human suffering and the divine mind. *Personality and Social Psychology Review, 14*, 7–16. doi:10.1177/1088868309350299

Gray, K., & Wegner, D. M. (2010b). Torture and judgments of guilt. *Journal of Experimental Social Psychology, 46*, 233–235. doi:10.1016/j.jesp.2009.10.003

Gray, K., & Wegner, D. M. (2011). To escape blame, don't be a hero—be a victim. *Journal of Experimental Social Psychology, 47*, 516–519.

Greenberg, K. J., & Dratel, J. L. (Eds.). (2005). *The torture papers: The road to Abu Ghraib*. Cambridge, England: Cambridge University Press.

Haidt, J. (2001). The emotional dog and its rational tail: A social intuitionist approach to moral judgment. *Psychological Review, 108,* 814–834. doi:10.1037/0033-295X.108.4.814

Haidt, J., & Graham, J. (2007). When morality opposes justice: Conservatives have moral intuitions that liberals may not recognize. *Social Justice Research, 20,* 98–116. doi:10.1007/s11211-007-0034-z

Haidt, J., Koller, S. H., & Dias, M. G. (1993). Affect, culture, and morality, or is it wrong to eat your dog? *Journal of Personality and Social Psychology, 65,* 613–628. doi:10.1037/0022-3514.65.4.613

Hamlin, J. K., Wynn, K., & Bloom, P. (2007, November 22). Social evaluation by preverbal infants [Letter]. *Nature, 450,* 557–559. doi:10.1038/nature06288

Hart, H. L. A., & Honoré, T. (1985). *Causation in the law.* New York, NY: Oxford University Press.

Haslam, N., Loughnan, S., Kashima, Y., & Bain, P. (2008). Attributing and denying humanness to others. *European Review of Social Psychology, 19,* 55–85. doi:10.1080/10463280801981645

Kay, A. C., Gaucher, D., McGregor, I., & Nash, K. (2010). Religious belief as compensatory control. *Personality and Social Psychology Review, 14,* 37–48. doi:10.1177/1088868309353750

Kirkpatrick, L. A., & Shaver, P. R. (1992). An attachment-theoretical approach to romantic love and religious belief. *Personality and Social Psychology Bulletin, 18,* 266–275. doi:10.1177/0146167292183002

Knobe, J., & Prinz, J. (2008). Intuitions about consciousness: Experimental studies. *Phenomenology and the Cognitive Sciences, 7,* 67–83. doi:10.1007/s11097-007-9066-y

Lerner, M. J. (1980). *The belief in a just world: A fundamental delusion.* New York, NY: Springer.

Lerner, M. J., & Simmons, C. H. (1966). Observer's reaction to the "innocent victim": Compassion or rejection? *Journal of Personality and Social Psychology, 4,* 203–210. doi:10.1037/h0023562

Martel, B. (2006, January 17). Storms payback from God, Nagin says. *Washington Post,* p. A04.

Martin, G. B., & Clark, R. D. (1982). Distress crying in neonates: Species and peer specificity. *Developmental Psychology, 18,* 3–9. doi:10.1037/0012-1649.18.1.3

Nichols, S., & Knobe, J. (2007). Moral responsibility and determinism: The cognitive science of folk intuitions. *Nous, 41,* 663–685. doi:10.1111/j.1468-0068.2007.00666.x

Nucci, L. (1981). Conceptions of personal issues: A domain distinct from moral or societal concepts. *Child Development, 52,* 114–121. doi:10.2307/1129220

Paloutzian, R. F. (1981). Purpose in life and value changes following conversion. *Journal of Personality and Social Psychology, 41,* 1153–1160. doi:10.1037/0022-3514.41.6.1153

Pargament, K. I., & Hahn, J. (1986). God and the just world: Causal and coping attributions to God in health situations. *Journal for the Scientific Study of Religion, 25,* 193–207. doi:10.2307/1385476

Pepitone, A., & Saffiotti, L. (1997). The selectivity of nonmaterial beliefs in interpreting life events. *European Journal of Social Psychology, 27,* 23–35. doi:10.1002/(SICI)1099-0992(199701)27:1<23::AID-EJSP805>3.0.CO;2-B

Spilka, B., & Schmidt, G. (1983). General attribution theory for the psychology of religion: The influence of event-character on attributions to God. *Journal for the Scientific Study of Religion, 22,* 326–339. doi:10.2307/1385771

Taylor, S. E. (1991). Asymmetrical effects of positive and negative events: The mobilization–minimization hypothesis. *Psychological Bulletin, 110,* 67–85. doi:10.1037/0033-2909.110.1.67

Turiel, E. (2002). *Culture of morality: Social development, context, and conflict.* West Nyack, NY: Cambridge University Press. doi:10.1017/CBO9780511613500

Welch, M. (2000). *Flag burning: Moral panic and the criminalization of protest.* New York, NY: Aldine de Gruyter.

Zahn-Waxler, C., Robinson, J. L., & Emde, R. N. (1992). The development of empathy in twins. *Developmental Psychology, 28,* 1038–1047. doi:10.1037/0012-1649.28.6.1038

II

MOTIVATIONAL AND COGNITIVE PROCESSES

7

CONSCIENCE: THE DOS AND DON'TS OF MORAL REGULATION

RONNIE JANOFF-BULMAN

Recent years have witnessed a proliferation of books invoking the word *conscience*, including *The Conscience of a Liberal* (Krugman, 2007), *Conservatives Without Conscience* (Dean, 2006), *Liberty of Conscience* (Nussbaum, 2008), *The Conscience of a Libertarian* (Root, 2009), *Conscience and Corporate Culture* (Goodpaster, 2006), *The Secular Conscience* (Dacey, 2008), and a reissue of *Conscience of a Conservative* (Goldwater, 2009). Apparently attractive in marketing books, the word *conscience* appeals to our interest in human behavior and in moral conduct in particular. As morality has increasingly been implicated as a basis for rifts in politics and business, *conscience* has become a catchall term implying moral legitimacy.

Yet conscience remains an underdeveloped construct in psychology. It has a long history in human discourse but a brief résumé in psychological investigations. Derived from the Latin word *conscientia*, conscience was originally identical to *consciousness* in English, German, and the Romance languages, suggesting the self-awareness common to both terms. Before it was the *lumen natural* of Kant's practical reason, conscience was the voice of God (Arendt, 2003); as Milton wrote in *Paradise Lost*, "And I will place within them as a guide / My umpire Conscience" (III: 194–195). Metaphors for conscience abound. For Victor Hugo, it was the "gazing eye," whereas for Herman Melville conscience was akin to the "heaving tides of the sea" (Feldman, 2006). Freud (1961) focused on its punitive nature as the "garrison in a conquered city" (p. 84). In contrast, Becker (1973) recognized our yearning to be good and noted that this "inner sensitivity" is conscience, which should be treated with the "highest reverence" (p. 150).

Early perspectives supported the view that there is no misinformed conscience. As the voice of God, conscience was unerring, and Kant believed that our natural rationality leads us to know right from wrong—that the "law of morality" is a "categorical imperative" (Kant, 1785/1964). The shift to "moral sentiments" in the work of David Hume, Adam Smith, and Charles Darwin not only placed feelings and emotions at the center of morality ("morality . . . is more properly felt than judged of"; Hume, 1739/1978, p. 470) but also stressed the social bases of conscience. Thus, Smith attributed our awareness of right and wrong to "sympathetic understanding" and Darwin to our "instinctive sympathy" (see Hyde, 2001).

In social psychology, too, conscience has long been understood as socially derived, for it is the internalized representation of normative standards (e.g., Baldwin, 1906; Newcomb, 1950). The liberalist tradition (e.g., Kohlberg, 1981; Turiel, 1983), with its focus on rationality, conceives of morality as based in our understanding of justice, rights, fairness, and people's welfare. More recently, moral psychology has embraced more intuitive processes and has expanded the domain of morality to include sexual behavior, cleanliness, work ethic, and other instances of personal conduct (e.g., Haidt, 2007; Shweder, Much, Mahapatra, & Park, 1997; see also Chapter 1, this volume).

Psychologically, conscience is a regulator of conduct in these moral domains. It functions as guide, witness, and judge. Although people regulate their actions in many ways, conscience is the only name given to a particular sort of self-regulation, suggesting its centrality—and the centrality of morality—in human experience. This chapter explores the nature of moral regulation, popularly understood as conscience. On the basis of past work on self-regulation more generally, two types of moral regulation are distinguished. The features of each moral regulatory system are presented, and the utility of distinguishing between them is then explored through applications to two markedly different domains: moral emotions and politics. More specifically, this dual regulatory approach to morality is used to inform differences between shame and guilt, which are implicated in the self-regulation of morality, and between political liberalism and conservatism, which involve the social regulation of morality.

SELF-REGULATION: APPROACH VERSUS AVOIDANCE

On the basis of studies of animal conditioning, human learning, neuroscience, and psychopathology, contemporary psychologists distinguish between two systems of self-regulation: a behavioral inhibition system based in avoidance motivation and a behavioral activation system based in approach motivation (for reviews, see Carver & Scheier, 1998; Gable, Reis, & Elliot, 2003). Overall, there are two primary characteristics—end states and action tendencies—that differentiate approach and avoidance motivational systems. The approach system has a *positive* end state and an *activation* action tendency, whereas the avoidance system has a *negative* end state and an *inhibition* action tendency. As Carver and Scheier (1998) noted, the approach system involves movement toward a goal or desired referent, whereas the avoidance system involves withdrawal from an "antigoal" or undesired referent. They build on Gray's (1990) distinction between the behavioral activation system (BAS) and the behavioral inhibition system (BIS). The BAS is an appetitive motivational system sensitive to reward, whereas the BIS is an aversive motivational system sensitive to punishment. Recent neuroscience research has found that the BIS and BAS are associated with distinct neural substrates (e.g., Davidson, 1998; Sutton & Davidson, 1997), and numerous studies support the conclusion that greater relative left frontal activity is involved in approach motivation, whereas greater relative right frontal activity is involved in avoidance motivation (see Coan & Allen, 2004; Davidson, 1992; Harmon-Jones, 2003).

The distinction between an approach-based BAS and an avoidance-based BIS is a fundamental feature of self-regulatory processes broadly considered. It seems likely, then, that it will also characterize self-regulatory processes in the moral domain more specifically.

TWO MODES OF MORAL REGULATION

On the basis of fundamental differences in self-regulation, Janoff-Bulman, Sheikh, and Hepp (2009) recently proposed two systems of moral regulation: a *proscriptive* system, sensitive to negative outcomes (i.e., antigoals, threats, punishments, and other undesirable end states) and based in behavioral inhibition; and a *prescriptive* system, sensitive to positive outcomes (i.e., goals, rewards, incentives, and other desirable end states) and based in behavioral activation. Proscriptive regulation focuses on what we should not do, whereas prescriptive regulation focuses on what we should do. Proscriptive morality involves avoidance motives and inhibiting a motivation to do something bad;

prescriptive morality involves approach motives and activating a motivation to do something good.

Proscriptive and prescriptive morality therefore involve different motivational tasks, for the former requires overcoming or curbing "tempting" negative desires, whereas the latter requires catalyzing or establishing a positive desire by overcoming inertia. Proscriptive immorality involves a failure to inhibit a negative moral outcome, whereas prescriptive immorality involves a failure to activate a positive moral outcome. It follows that the two systems of moral regulation are generally concerned with different behavioral domains. Proscriptive morality is focused on dangers to the self and others and involves the restraint of harm, including physical harm and behaviors believed to violate valued group norms. This is also the realm of many of the popularized deadly sins, which involve excesses or indulgences that presumably call for self-control. Prescriptive morality focuses on providing positive outcomes and includes behaviors that help others by relieving their suffering or advancing their well-being; examples are acts of benevolence, charity, and generosity. Also included are activation-based traits and behaviors associated with the Protestant ethic—industriousness, self-reliance, and hard work (see Janoff-Bulman, Sheikh, & Baldacci, 2008).

Largely the legacy of thinkers as diverse as Kant (1785/1964) and Freud (1923/1960), morality has typically been viewed monolithically, as a conflict between duty and desire; immorality is regarded as having its source in desire, which must be restrained and overcome. This is the domain of proscriptive morality, which involves the inhibition of harmful behaviors. Yet not harming another is not equivalent to helping another, just as not lying is not the same as telling the truth (as recognized in U.S. courts of law, which permit silence rather than self-incrimination via the truth). Although there is considerable work on prosocial behavior in social and developmental psychology (see, e.g., Batson, Ahmad, & Powell, 2008; Eisenberg & Fabes, 1998), it exists as a separate literature and has not been integrated into research and theory on morality. Interestingly, the importance of recognizing a distinction between moral rules that "prohibit harming others" and those that "enjoin one to help others" was recently acknowledged in moral philosophy by Gert (2001), who claimed that this difference "has not been sufficiently appreciated" (p. 1169).

Although there is a dearth of research examining this distinction, one important exception is a study by Kochanska, Coy, and Murray (2001), who investigated "dos" and "don'ts" in their longitudinal research on the early development of morality in children. They found that dos were more challenging than don'ts for children at all ages studied (14, 22, 33, and 45 months), and fearfulness was associated with don'ts but not dos. They concluded that their data provide "impressive evidence of substantial differences" (Kochanska et al., 2001, p. 1106) between dos and don'ts in early self-regulation.

A more recent study by Wiltermuth, Monin, and Chow (2010) also supported a dual regulatory perspective on morality, for these researchers found that praising others for moral behaviors and condemning them for immoral behaviors are orthogonal tendencies influenced by different conceptions of morality.

In our own research, we have found evidence of the distinct approach versus avoidance bases of prescriptive and proscriptive morality in studies involving approach–avoidance priming, linguistic representations, and individual-difference measures of approach–avoidance sensitivity (see the seven studies reported in Janoff-Bulman et al., 2009). Thus, a threat-based avoidance prime resulted in increased moral proscriptions but not increased moral prescriptions. Further, following work by Semin and Fiedler (1988), which demonstrated that concrete versus abstract language reflects avoidance versus approach orientations, respectively, we found that proscriptive morality was represented in more concrete verb terms, whereas prescriptive morality was represented in more abstract adjective terms. Such linguistic associations may help us better understand differences underlying the moral philosophies of Kant (1785/1964), who focused on duties, which are primarily proscriptive, and Aristotle (350 BCE/1989), who emphasized virtues, which appear to be primarily prescriptive. Moving beyond language, we found that BIS scores (Carver & White, 1994) were positively associated with proscriptive morality, whereas BAS scores were positively associated with prescriptive morality.

MORAL ASYMMETRY

Work on the negativity bias in psychology suggests a moral asymmetry—that is, that proscriptive regulation is likely to be harsher and more demanding than prescriptive regulation. Past work on the negativity bias demonstrates that the motivation to avoid a negative entity is stronger than the motivation to approach a positive entity, and the failure to avoid incurs greater psychological distress than the failure to approach (for reviews, see Baumeister, Brataslavsky, Finkenauer, & Vohs, 2001; Rozin & Royzman, 2001). Further, Knobe (2003; Leslie, Knobe, & Cohen, 2006) found that negative side effects have a greater impact and are seen as more intentional than positive side effects in moral dilemmas.

Consistent with this work, Janoff-Bulman et al. (2009) found that the greater potency of negative consequences is reflected in a stronger motivation to avoid "errors" in the proscriptive than in the prescriptive system. Proscriptive morality was regarded as more mandatory, whereas prescriptive morality was perceived as more discretionary, and this was the case even when the behaviors involved were "imperfect" duties (see Kant, 1785/1964). Further, greater blame was attributed for proscriptive immorality than for prescriptive immorality, but greater moral credit was attributed for prescriptive morality than for proscriptive morality. The concrete–abstract linguistic differences noted above also support the moral asymmetry of the two regulatory modes. The stricter, more mandatory nature of proscriptive morality depends on greater specificity; we need to know precisely what behaviors to avoid in order to escape the harsher consequences of proscriptive errors. The more discretionary nature of prescriptive regulation allows for more abstract representations of positive behaviors.

Overall, proscriptive morality is condemnatory and strict, whereas prescriptive morality is commendatory and less strict. Given the asymmetry of the two moral regulatory systems, it is perhaps not surprising that at the societal level, proscriptive morality is primarily regulated via legal systems. The mandatory, concrete, restraint-based nature of proscriptive morality readily lends itself to a system of laws that is focused on what we should not do, and it can apply to everyone in a society. For any individual, conscience is likely to operate on the basis of both forms of regulation, for we are generally sensitive to "shoulds" and "should nots." Nevertheless, one or the other system may be dominant at a given time or for a given person, with implications for domains as diverse as moral emotions and political orientation, as is discussed below.

MORAL EMOTIONS: SHAME VERSUS GUILT

When we consider moral regulation, we naturally think about shame and guilt, for these are the emotional consequences of failing to follow the dictates of our conscience. Whether actually felt or anticipated, both function as moral motivators and involve self-evaluation and negative valence. Yet shame and guilt are nevertheless distinct constructs and experiences. In attempts to differentiate between the two, psychologists have emphasized descriptive differences, and to date the dominant basis for distinguishing between them has been a focus on the self versus behavior. As originally proposed by Lewis (1971), shame follows a transgression attributed to the wrongdoer's global self, whereas guilt follows a transgression attributed to a specific behavior. Tangney (1991; Tangney & Dearing, 2002; Tangney, Stuewig, & Mashek, 2007) further developed and advanced these ideas; when we feel guilt, we are focused on what we did (i.e., the "bad" act), whereas when we feel shame, we are focused on who we are (i.e., the "bad" self).

Interestingly, past research has also found that shame and guilt are associated with distinct motivations to hide and amend. Guilt motivates attempts to repair damaging consequences, including apologies, confessions, and prosocial actions; in contrast, shame motivates hiding, withdrawal, and escape (for reviews, see Tangney & Dearing, 2002; Tangney et al., 2007). Despite recognition of these avoidance versus approach action tendencies, to date differences between shame and guilt have not been informed by self-regulation theory. The most common explanation for these divergent action orientations has been the posited self versus behavior appraisals associated with shame versus guilt. Thus, Tangney and Dearing (2002) wrote that these self-behavior differences have "far-reaching implications . . . for subsequent motivation" (p. 24), for when specific behavior is the problem, its malleability and controllability enable us to make changes and remedy the consequences of the bad action. However, with global attributions to the self, no action can repair the inadequacies of the "bad" self, and we are motivated to hide or withdraw (see also Tangney, 1991, 1993).

We have proposed an alternative framework for understanding differences between shame and guilt, one that links these emotions more directly to self-regulation in the moral domain (see Sheikh & Janoff-Bulman, 2010a, 2010b). Specifically, we maintain that guilt is experienced when we interpret our transgressions via the prescriptive system—by attending to positive end states and moral shoulds (the right, good, or moral). Shame, in contrast, is experienced when we interpret our transgressions via the proscriptive system—by attending to negative end states and moral should nots (the wrong, bad, or immoral). Our transgressive act or omission is recognized in both instances, yet we feel guilt when we realize that we did not act morally, for we failed to engage in a positive, moral act; that is, we did not act like an honest person or caring partner. And we feel shame when we realize that we acted immorally, for we engaged in a negative immoral act; that is, we acted like a liar or a cheat. Guilt highlights positive, rewarding moral referents (shoulds) and impels us forward toward the possibility of repair, redemption, and future moral outcomes; we want to right the wrong. Shame highlights negative, punishing moral referents (should nots) and leaves us confronting our immorality; we want to escape and withdraw. Consistent with the end states and action tendencies associated with prescriptive and proscriptive morality, respectively, guilt involves a focus on positive outcomes and is based in activation, whereas shame involves a focus on negative end states and is based in inhibition.

In three empirical studies (Sheikh & Janoff-Bulman, 2010a), we found support for the proscriptive–shame link and the prescriptive–guilt link. In Study 1, individual differences in approach versus avoidance orientation differentially predicted proneness to guilt versus shame respectively, over and above the predictive value of self-esteem. More specifically, we found that BAS scores were associated with proneness to guilt but not shame, and BIS scores were associated with proneness to shame but not guilt. Study 2 found that situationally priming proscriptive morality increased state shame but not guilt, whereas priming prescriptive morality increased state guilt but not shame.

In a third study (Sheikh & Janoff-Bulman, 2010a), we found that the types of transgressions most apt to engage proscriptive regulation engendered more shame than guilt, and transgressions most apt to engage prescriptive regulation engendered more guilt than shame. Hypothetically, any transgression can be interpreted via the proscriptive or prescriptive system, or both; this no doubt accounts in part for the positive correlations often found between shame and guilt in past research. Nevertheless, as discussed earlier, some behaviors are more likely to be associated with one system or the other (Janoff-Bulman et al., 2008). Thus, helping and caring behaviors involving the well-being of others and behaviors reflecting industriousness and self-reliance are most likely to engage the prescriptive system; transgressions here should result in guilt rather than shame. Proscriptive regulation involves overcoming temptations and restraining from bad behavior, and thus more shame than guilt should result from self-perceived indulgences and excesses often associated with eating, drinking, gambling, and the body more generally. These transgression-based differences in guilt and shame were supported in our third study, both in participants' responses to experimenter-created scenarios and in their own self-reported narratives as well.

Together, the three studies provide support for self-regulatory differences in shame and guilt. An individual's dispositional orientation in terms of approach–avoidance motivation appears to affect proneness to shame versus guilt, but situational variables (as demonstrated via experimental priming) and the nature of the transgression itself also have an impact on the specific self-evaluative moral emotion experienced. This self-regulatory framework does not negate previous perspectives on shame and guilt (e.g., Lewis, 1971; Tangney, 1991; Tangney & Dearing, 2002; Tangney et al., 2007), but rather provides a theoretical framework within which to understand them. The more severe, condemnatory proscriptive system of morality naturally leads to harsher, more negative self-evaluations likely to generalize to the global self. It also follows that shame is the more painful of the two emotions (e.g., Lewis, 1971; Lindsay-Hartz, 1984; Tangney, Wagner, Fletcher, & Gramzow, 1992; Tangney & Dearing, 2002). Guilt's emphasis on rewarding outcomes and positive referents is likely to limit the negative evaluation following a transgression and activate alternative, reparative behaviors; a more specific focus on behavior rather than the self would be the likely attribution, for it is a focus on specific behavior that best provides an opportunity to advance subsequent morality.

Interestingly, much past work on self-regulation has assumed that approach motivation is necessarily associated with positive-valence emotions and avoidance motivation with negative-valence emotions. As Carver and Harmon-Jones (2009) noted, motivation and valence have been confounded in the past, particularly in research on cortical asymmetry. Yet their own work on anger has clearly demonstrated the independence of the two. More specifically, based largely on studies of neural substrates, they found that anger is associated with approach-based motivation despite its negative valence and involves left rather than right frontal activation. Our own work suggests that from a regulatory perspective, guilt is very similar to anger in that it, too, is based in approach and activation and yet is an emotion with negative valence.

A FEW WORDS ABOUT PARENTING

A self-regulatory perspective on shame and guilt receives additional support from work on parenting. Parents are undoubtedly prime influences in the development of conscience and are instrumental in producing early orientations toward morality and immorality. It follows that parents who focus primarily on prohibitions, relying on threats and punishment (emphasizing Baumrind's [1971] restrictive parenting dimension), are likely to produce proscriptively oriented children who are also high in shame. Parents who focus on positive behaviors, relying on emotional incentives and rewards (emphasizing Baumrind's [1971] nurturant dimension), are likely to produce prescriptively oriented children who are more apt to experience guilt than shame. From our perspective, with high restrictiveness the parent focuses the child on immorality and bad conduct, and the goal is obedience and inhibition. Nurturing interactions, in contrast, focus on morality and communicate that the child is inclined to be moral and engage in positive, prosocial acts (see also Chapters 13 and 14, this volume, on the effects of parenting on morality).

Past research has found that recurrent positive, rewarding interactions with parents who rely on warmth and affection rather than punishment are associated with the development of guilt in children (e.g., Hoffman, 1982; Zahn-Waxler & Kochanska, 1990). In contrast, the children of punitive parents who use putdowns and emotional abuse are prone to high levels of shame (Hoglund & Nicholas, 1995; Lutwak & Ferrari, 1997; for a summary, see Tangney & Dearing, 2002), and parents' own shame proneness predicts their use of psychological restrictiveness (Mills et al., 2007). Although parenting surely is not wholly determinative of regulatory orientation, it is nevertheless of fundamental importance in the development of conscience and the moral emotions.

POLITICS: LIBERALISM AND CONSERVATISM

Proscriptive morality, the more condemnatory system, results in the harsher of the two emotional experiences, shame. The more commendatory prescriptive morality results in guilt and the motivation to repair ruptures in the moral fabric. As moral emotions, shame and guilt are bound to these systems and become engines of moral regulation themselves. Yet in making a claim for the utility of a dual regulatory system of morality, it would seem advantageous to move farther afield and use the prescriptive–proscriptive distinction to unpack differences in an entirely different domain. We therefore turn to politics, and in particular to the distinction between political liberalism and conservatism.

In focusing on politics, we move from self-regulation to social regulation, from a consideration of morality in terms of one's own shoulds and should nots to a consideration of morality in terms of broader societal shoulds and should nots. It is therefore not surprising that books representing the left and right invoke conscience, as evident in the list of titles presented at the beginning of this chapter. In recent work we have argued that liberalism and conservatism reflect distinct self-regulatory systems, with liberalism based in approach regulation and conservatism in avoidance regulation (Janoff-Bulman, 2009; Janoff-Bulman et al., 2008; Rock & Janoff-Bulman, 2010). Yet politics fundamentally involves regulation at the societal level, and in particular moral regulation, and thus it seems likely that liberalism and conservatism reflect regulatory differences in the moral domain in particular.

It follows that conservatism, based in avoidance regulation, primarily reflects a proscriptive moral orientation focused on should nots, whereas liberalism, based in approach regulation, primarily reflects a prescriptive moral orientation focused on shoulds. Most generally, liberals are motivated to provide for the welfare of societal members, whereas conservatives are motivated to protect societal members. Despite each side's certainty regarding the other side's immorality, both of these are moral motivations intended to benefit the group and contribute to its survival. Nevertheless, their prescriptive–proscriptive differences have major implications for social goals and policy preferences.

Reflecting their distinct regulatory orientations, liberals focus on positive outcomes, specifically societal gains, and conservatives focus on negative outcomes, particularly societal losses (Janoff-Bulman, 2009). Conservatives are particularly sensitive to threat, whereas liberals are more willing to embrace novelty and change (e.g., Altemeyer, 1998; Braithwaite, 1997; Duckitt, 2001; Jost, Glaser, Kruglanski, & Sulloway, 2003; Jost, Nosek, & Gosling, 2008). In provocative recent research, conservatives showed higher physiological reactivity to threat (i.e., sudden noises and threatening visual images) than liberals (Oxley et al., 2008). Moreover, a 20-year longitudinal study of personality found that conservatives at the age of 23 were likely to have been fearful and overcontrolled preschoolers 2 decades earlier, and liberals at 23 were more often described as energetic and resilient as preschoolers (Block & Block, 2006). These findings support the posited differences in approach/activation and avoidance/inhibition we believe underlie liberalism and conservatism.

The conservative focus on threats and losses produces a protective orientation reflected in an emphasis on stability and security. The liberal focus on positive outcomes produces a forward-looking orientation that strives to provide for group members via social initiatives and interventions. These differences are reflected in the primary moral agendas advocated by the two political orientations: Liberals strive for social justice; conservatives strive for social order. Liberals are particularly attuned to fairness and social equity, whereas conservatives particularly value norm adherence and stability (e.g., Bobbio, 1996; Janoff-Bulman, 2009; Jost et al., 2008; Kerlinger, 1984; Skitka, Mullen, Griffin, Hutchinson, & Chamberlin, 2002; see also Chapter 12, this volume, on the relationship between morality and cultural values).

In past research, we have consistently found that contemporary social issues factor into two clusters (e.g., Janoff-Bulman et al., 2008; see also Lewis-Beck, Jacoby, Norpoth, & Weisberg, 2008). One set of issues, which we have labeled *equity issues*, includes items such as affirmative action and government welfare for the poor population. The other, labeled *lifestyle issues*, includes items such as abortion and gay marriage. Positions on both factors are strongly associated with political orientation. However, the lifestyle issues are strongly correlated with beliefs about social order, but not social justice, whereas the equity issues are strongly associated with beliefs about social justice, but not social order (Janoff-Bulman et al., 2008). That is, positions on abortion and gay marriage depend on how much a person strives for social order; social justice beliefs do not predict these lifestyle attitudes. In contrast, social justice beliefs predict attitudes toward equity issues, which are not associated with social order beliefs.

Further, we found that the two domains are differentially associated with proscriptive and prescriptive morality, as measured by an instrument that has nothing to do with political orientation (i.e., the Moralisms Scale; Janoff-Bulman et al., 2009). Proscriptive morality scores were significantly associated with positions regarding lifestyle but not equity issues, and proscriptive scores were positively associated with more conservative positions. Prescriptive morality scores were significantly associated with equity but not lifestyle issues, and prescriptive scores were positively associated with more liberal positions.

The prescriptive link to social justice goals and the proscriptive link to social order goals are evident in the domains of social regulation advocated by liberals and conservatives. Liberals seek to regulate social and economic goods in hopes of approaching a more equal distribution of resources in society, whereas conservatives seek to regulate the domain of lifestyles and personal behaviors in hopes of minimizing deviance from acceptable social norms. At first glance we might also believe that liberals want to regulate lifestyles—just differently from conservatives—and conservatives want to regulate social and economic goods—just differently from liberals. However, these are domains of autonomy (based on individual freedom and choice), not regulation, for the respective groups; thus, liberals don't want to regulate abortion and gay marriage, and conservatives don't want to regulate the distribution of social and economic goods. (Clearly, some people are not pure liberals or conservatives but have a foot in both camps; thus, libertarians prefer no regulation in either domain, whereas communitarians prefer regulation in both domains; Janoff-Bulman et al., 2008).

It is in the mode of preferred regulation—the *how*—associated with their respective domains of regulation that proscriptive and prescriptive orientations become particularly evident. Regarding moral social regulation, the activation and inhibition action tendencies associated with prescriptive and proscriptive morality translate into positive obligations and prohibitions. For liberals, social regulation involves a primary focus on positive obligations; they strive to intervene and establish programs (e.g., affirmative action, welfare programs, publicly funded day care) aimed at advancing social welfare and producing greater social justice. For conservatives, social regulation involves a primary focus on prohibitions; conservatives seek to prohibit stem cell research, abortion, and gay marriage. Proscriptive regulation focuses on the should nots that restrain people from behaviors that violate group norms; prescriptive regulation focuses on the shoulds that activate positive obligations toward others and foster group interdependence.

When protection, social order, and adherence to group norms are paramount, as they are for conservatives, there is a concomitant focus on ingroup–outgroup boundaries and group loyalty (see Chapter 1, this volume). Who is in the group, and who is not? Who can be trusted? In this context, lifestyle behaviors become signals of commitment and allegiance to the community—social identity markers indicating warranted inclusion in the group. For conservatives, the basis for group membership is common social identity, which is restrictive; for liberals, it is a sense of shared responsibilities and is relatively inclusive. These differences are evident in responses to illegal immigrants, for example. Restrictive and attuned to transgressions with their proscriptive orientation, conservatives respond with harsh, punishing responses. Liberals, with their prescriptive moral orientation and consequent emphasis on positive obligations, are more forgiving and accepting of illegal immigrants. In recent research we found evidence of conservatives' category restrictiveness even on a purely cognitive, nonpolitical task involving judgments of category membership following proscriptive, prescriptive, or neutral primes (Rock & Janoff-Bulman, 2010); for example, participants indicated whether items such as car, bus, tractor, go-cart, yacht, and elevator were members (yes or no) of the category "vehicle." Conservatives, but not liberals, were sensitive to proscriptive morality, for when proscriptively primed, conservatism was associated with greater category restrictiveness; in contrast, liberalism was associated with (high) category inclusiveness across conditions.

Overall, prescriptive and proscriptive morality appear to underlie the social regulatory orientations of liberals and conservatives, respectively. Liberals aim to advance the good via providing for group members; they are inclusive and focus on group interdependence. Conservatives aim to prevent the bad via protecting group members; they are restrictive and focus on common social identity. Oriented toward positive morality and shoulds, liberals rely on positive obligations as their primary mode of social regulation. Conservatives emphasize immorality and should nots and rely on prohibitions as their primary mode of social regulation.

FINAL THOUGHTS AND CURRENT WORK ON REGULATORY BALANCE

The distinction between proscriptive and prescriptive morality provides one means of exploring conscience and moral regulation. This dual perspective offers new ways of understanding old divisions such as shame versus guilt and political liberalism versus conservatism. Both forms of regulation are typically used in the self-regulation of morality (although one system may certainly be dominant); the two orientations are complementary rather than antagonistic. In the social regulation of morality, and politics in particular, this complementarity is far less evident, as deep antagonisms and dueling "facts" increasingly define the relationship between liberals and conservatives (e.g., Chapter 3, this volume). Nevertheless, it is conceivable that from a societal perspective, as unpalatable as it might seem to those on both sides, each political orientation may function as a counterweight to the other's proscriptive or prescriptive orientation.

In our current work we are particularly interested in this matter of regulatory balance. In two separate research programs, we have begun to focus on problems associated with imbalances in moral self-regulation. Thus, we are investigating the overregulation of proscriptive morality (and the underregulation of prescriptive morality) to better understand the increased incidence of children's behavioral transgressions associated with very restrictive, punitive parents. High levels of shame in these children suggest that traditional attribution-based explanations (i.e., strong external justification precludes internalization of norms) are inadequate. Hence we are testing an ego depletion model based on monitoring and suppression effects, which we believe may result from the increased shame and greater salience and potency of negative temptations associated with proscriptive regulation.

We have also begun to explore power and moral corruption in terms of the overregulation of prescriptive morality and underregulation of proscriptive morality (given that power involves approach motivation; e.g., Keltner, Gruenfeld, & Anderson, 2003). High power may have the dual effect of licensing moral credentials (Monin & Miller, 2001; see also Chapter 9, this volume) while minimizing the importance of proscriptive morality, thereby increasing the likelihood of proscriptive transgressions. At the risk of resembling the child with a hammer who believes everything looks like a nail and requires pounding, in this and other work we hope to use the proscriptive–prescriptive distinction in the moral domain to expand our understanding of diverse psychological and social phenomena.

REFERENCES

Altemeyer, R. A. (1998). The other "authoritarian personality." *Advances in Experimental Social Psychology, 30*, 47–92. doi:10.1016/S0065-2601(08)60382-2

Arendt, H. (2003). *Responsibility and judgment.* New York, NY: Schocken Books.

Aristotle. (1989). *Nichomachean ethics.* Oxford, England: Blackwell. (Original work published 350 BCE)

Baldwin, J. M. (1906). *Social and ethical interpretations in mental development* (4th ed.). London: Macmillan.

Batson, C. D., Ahmad, N., & Powell, A. A. (2008). Prosocial motivation. In J. Y. Shah & W. L. Gardner (Eds.), *Handbook of motivation science* (pp. 135–149). New York, NY: Guilford Press.

Baumeister, R. F., Brataslavsky, E., Finkenauer, C., & Vohs, K. D. (2001). Bad is stronger than good. *Review of General Psychology, 5*, 323–370. doi:10.1037/1089-2680.5.4.323

Baumrind, D. (1971). Current patterns of parental authority. *Developmental Psychology Monographs, 4* (No. 1, Pt. 2).

Becker, E. (1973). *The denial of death.* New York, NY: Free Press.

Block, J., & Block, J. H. (2006). Nursery school personality and political orientation two decades later. *Journal of Research in Personality, 40*, 734–749. doi:10.1016/j.jrp.2005.09.005

Bobbio, N. (1996). *Left and right.* Cambridge, England: Polity Press.

Braithwaite, V. (1997). Harmony and security value orientations in political evaluation. *Personality and Social Psychology Bulletin, 23*, 401–414. doi:10.1177/0146167297234006

Carver, C. S., & Harmon-Jones, E. (2009). Anger is an approach-related affect: Evidence and implications. *Psychological Bulletin, 135*, 183–204. doi:10.1037/a0013965

Carver, C. S., & Scheier, M. F. (1998). *On the self-regulation of behavior*. New York, NY: Cambridge University Press.

Carver, C. S., & White, T. L. (1994). Behavioral inhibition, behavioral activation, and the affective responses to impending reward and punishment: The BIS/BAS Scales. *Journal of Personality and Social Psychology, 67*, 319–333. doi:10.1037/0022-3514.67.2.319

Coan, J. A., & Allen, J. J. B. (2004). Frontal EEG asymmetry as a moderator and mediator of emotion. *Biological Psychology, 67*, 7–50. doi:10.1016/j.biopsycho.2004.03.002

Dacey, A. (2008). *The secular conscience*. New York, NY: Prometheus Books.

Davidson, R. J. (1992). Emotion and affective style: Hemispheric substrates. *Psychological Science, 3*, 39–43. doi:10.1111/j.1467-9280.1992.tb00254.x

Davidson, R. J. (1998). Anterior electrophysiological asymmetries, emotion, and depression: Conceptual and methodological conundrums. *Psychophysiology, 35*, 607–614. doi:10.1017/S0048577298000134

Dean, J. W. (2006). *Conservatives without conscience*. New York, NY: Viking.

Duckitt, J. (2001). A dual-process cognitive–motivational theory of ideology and prejudice. *Advances in Experimental Social Psychology, 33*, 41–113. doi:10.1016/S0065-2601(01)80004-6

Eisenberg, N., & Fabes, R. A. (1998). Prosocial development. In W. Damon & N. Eisenberg (Eds.), *Handbook of child psychology: Vol. 3. Social, emotional, and personality development* (pp. 701–778). Hoboken, NJ: Wiley.

Feldman, K. (2006). *Binding words: Conscience and rhetoric in Hobbes, Hegel, and Heidegger*. Evanston, IL: Northwestern University Press.

Freud, S. (1960). *The ego and the id*. New York, NY: Norton. (Original work published 1923)

Freud, S. (1961). *Civilization and its discontents*. New York, NY: Norton.

Gable, S. L., Reis, H. T., & Elliot, A. J. (2003). Evidence for bivariate systems: An empirical test of appetition and aversion across domains. *Journal of Research in Personality, 37*, 349–372. doi:10.1016/S0092-6566(02)00580-9

Gert, B. (2001). Moral rules. In L. C. Becker & C. B. Becker (Eds.), *Encyclopedia of ethics* (2nd ed., pp. 1168–1170). New York, NY: Routledge.

Goldwater, B. M. (2009). *Conscience of a conservative*. New York, NY: CreateSpace.

Goodpaster, K. E. (2006). *Conscience and corporate culture*. New York, NY: Wiley-Blackwell.

Gray, J. A. (1990). Brain systems that mediate both emotion and cognition. *Cognition and Emotion, 4*, 269–288. doi:10.1080/02699939008410799

Haidt, J. (2007). The new synthesis in moral psychology. *Science, 316*, 998–1002. doi:10.1126/science.1137651

Harmon-Jones, E. (2003). Anger and the behavioral approach system. *Personality and Individual Differences, 35*, 995–1005. doi:10.1016/S0191-8869(02)00313-6

Hoffman, M. L. (1982). Development of prosocial motivation: Empathy and guilt. In N. Eisenberg-Berg (Ed.), *Development of prosocial behavior* (pp. 281–313). New York, NY: Academic Press.

Hoglund, C. L., & Nicholas, K. B. (1995). Shame, guilt, and anger in college students exposed to abusive family environments. *Journal of Family Violence, 10,* 141–157. doi:10.1007/BF02110597

Hume, D. (1978). *A treatise of human nature.* Oxford, England: Clarendon. (Original work published 1739)

Hyde, M. J. (2001). *The call of conscience.* Columbia, SC: University of South Carolina Press.

Janoff-Bulman, R. (2009). To provide or protect: Motivational bases of political liberalism and conservatism. *Psychological Inquiry, 20,* 120–128. doi:10.1080/10478400903028581

Janoff-Bulman, R., Sheikh, S., & Baldacci, K. (2008). Mapping moral motives: Approach, avoidance, and political orientation. *Journal of Experimental Social Psychology, 44,* 1091–1099. doi:10.1016/j.jesp.2007.11.003

Janoff-Bulman, R., Sheikh, S., & Hepp, S. (2009). Proscriptive versus prescriptive morality: Two faces of moral regulation. *Journal of Personality and Social Psychology, 96,* 521–537. doi:10.1037/a0013779

Jost, J. T., Glaser, J., Kruglanski, A. W., & Sulloway, F. J. (2003). Political conservatism as motivated social cognition. *Psychological Bulletin, 129,* 339–375. doi:10.1037/0033-2909.129.3.339

Jost, T. J., Nosek, B. A., & Gosling, S. D. (2008). Ideology: Its resurgence in social, personality, and political psychology. *Perspectives on Psychological Science, 3,* 126–136. doi:10.1111/j.1745-6916.2008.00070.x

Kant, I. (1964). *Groundwork for the metaphysics of morals* (H. J. Paton, Trans.). New York, NY: Harper & Row. (Original work published 1785)

Keltner, D., Gruenfeld, D. H., & Anderson, C. (2003). Power, approach, and inhibition. *Psychological Review, 110,* 265–284. doi:10.1037/0033-295X.110.2.265

Kerlinger, F. N. (1984). *Liberalism and conservatism: The nature and structure of social attitudes.* Hillsdale, NJ: Erlbaum.

Knobe, J. (2003). Intentional action in folk psychology: An experimental investigation. *Philosophical Psychology, 16,* 309–324. doi:10.1080/09515080307771

Kochanska, G., Coy, K. C., & Murray, K. T. (2001). The development of self-regulation in the first four years of life. *Child Development, 72,* 1091–1111. doi:10.1111/1467-8624.00336

Kohlberg, L. (1981). *Essays on moral development: Vol. 1. The philosophy of moral development.* San Francisco, CA: Harper & Row.

Krugman, P. (2007). *The conscience of a liberal.* New York, NY: Norton.

Leslie, A. M., Knobe, J., & Cohen, A. (2006). Acting intentionally and the side-effect effect: Theory of mind and moral judgment. *Psychological Science, 17,* 421–427. doi:10.1111/j.1467-9280.2006.01722.x

Lewis, H. B. (1971). Shame and guilt in neurosis. *Psychoanalytic Review, 58,* 419–438.

Lewis-Beck, M. S., Jacoby, W. G., Norpoth, H., & Weisberg, H. F. (2008). *The American voter revisited.* Ann Arbor, MI: University of Michigan Press.

Lindsay-Hartz, J. (1984). Contrasting experiences of shame and guilt. *American Behavioral Scientist, 27,* 689–704. doi:10.1177/000276484027006003

Lutwak, N., & Ferrari, J. R. (1997). Understanding shame in adults: Retrospective perceptions of parental-bonding during childhood. *Journal of Nervous and Mental Disease, 185,* 595–598. doi:10.1097/00005053-199710000-00001

Mills, R., Freeman, W., Clara, I., Elgar, F., Walling, B., & Mak, L. (2007). Parents' proneness to shame and the use of psychological control. *Journal of Child and Family Studies, 16,* 359–374.

Monin, B., & Miller, D. T. (2001). Moral credentials and the expression of prejudice. *Journal of Personality and Social Psychology, 81,* 33–43. doi:10.1037/0022-3514.81.1.33

Newcomb, T. M. (1950). *Social psychology.* New York, NY: Dryden. doi:10.1037/11275-000

Nussbaum, M. C. (2008). *Liberty of conscience.* New York, NY: Basic Books.

Oxley, D. R., Smith, K. B., Alford, J. R., Hibbing, M. V., Miller, J. L., Scalora, M., . . . Hibbing, J. R. (2008, September 19). Political attitudes vary with physiological traits. *Science, 321,* 1667–1670. doi:10.1126/science.1157627

Rock, M. S., & Janoff-Bulman, R. (2010). Where do we draw our lines? Politics, rigidity, and the role of self-regulation. *Social Psychological and Personality Science, 1,* 26–33. doi:10.1177/1948550609347386

Root, W. A. (2009). *The conscience of a libertarian.* New York, NY: Wiley.

Rozin, P., & Royzman, E. B. (2001). Negativity bias, negativity dominance, and contagion. *Personality and Social Psychology Review, 5,* 296–320. doi:10.1207/S15327957PSPR0504_2

Semin, G. R., & Fiedler, K. (1988). The cognitive functions of linguistic categories in describing persons: Social cognition and language. *Journal of Personality and Social Psychology, 54,* 558–568. doi:10.1037/0022-3514.54.4.558

Sheikh, S., & Janoff-Bulman, R. (2010a). A self-regulatory perspective on shame and guilt. *Personality and Social Psychology Bulletin, 36,* 213–224. doi:10.1177/0146167209356788

Sheikh, S., & Janoff-Bulman, R. (2010b). Tracing the self-regulatory bases of moral emotions. *Emotion Review, 2,* 386–396.

Shweder, R. A., Much, N. C., Mahapatra, M., & Park, L. (1997). The "big three" of morality (autonomy, community, divinity) and the "big three" explanations of suffering. In A. Brandt & P. Rozin (Eds.), *Morality and health* (pp. 119–169). New York, NY: Routledge.

Skitka, L. J., Mullen, E., Griffin, T., Hutchinson, S., & Chamberlin, B. (2002). Dispositions, scripts or motivated correction? Understanding ideological differences in explanations for social problems. *Journal of Personality and Social Psychology, 83,* 470–487. doi:10.1037/0022-3514.83.2.470

Sutton, S. K., & Davidson, R. J. (1997). Prefrontal brain asymmetry: Biological substrate of the behavioral approach and inhibition systems. *Psychological Science, 8,* 204–210. doi:10.1111/j.1467-9280.1997.tb00413.x

Tangney, J. P. (1991). Moral affect: The good, the bad, and the ugly. *Journal of Personality and Social Psychology, 61,* 598–607. doi:10.1037/0022-3514.61.4.598

Tangney, J. P. (1993). Shame and guilt. In C. G. Costello (Ed.), *Symptoms of depression* (pp. 161–180). Oxford, England: Wiley.

Tangney, J. P., & Dearing, R. L. (2002). *Shame and guilt.* New York, NY: Guilford Press.

Tangney, J. P., Stuewig, J., & Mashek, D. J. (2007). Moral emotions and moral behavior. *Annual Review of Psychology, 58,* 345–372. doi:10.1146/annurev.psych.56.091103.070145

Tangney, J. P., Wagner, P., Fletcher, C., & Gramzow, R. (1992). Shamed into anger? The relation of shame and guilt to anger and self-reported aggression. *Journal of Personality and Social Psychology, 62,* 669–675.

Turiel, E. (1983). *The development of social knowledge: Morality and convention.* Cambridge, England: Cambridge University Press.

Wiltermuth, S., Monin, B., & Chow, R. (2010). The orthogonality of praise and condemnation in moral judgment. *Social Psychological and Personality Science, 2,* 302–310.

Zahn-Waxler, C., & Kochanska, G. (1990). The origins of guilt. In R. A. Thompson (Ed.), *Nebraska symposium on motivation: Socioemotional development* (pp. 183–258). Lincoln, NE: University of Nebraska Press.

8

HONEST RATIONALES FOR DISHONEST BEHAVIOR

SHAHAR AYAL AND FRANCESCA GINO

Cheating, fraud, racketeering, and other forms of dishonesty are among the greatest personal and societal challenges of our time. While the media commonly highlight extreme examples and focus on the most sensational scams (e.g., those by Enron and Bernard Madoff), less exposure is given to the prevalence of "ordinary" unethical behavior—dishonest acts committed by people who value morality but act immorally when they have an opportunity to cheat. Examples include cheating on one's taxes and engaging in "wardrobing" (the practice of purchasing an item of clothing, wearing it, and then returning it to the store for a refund). When considered cumulatively, this seemingly innocuous and ordinary unethical behavior causes considerable societal damage (Ariely, 2008; DePaulo, Kashy, Kirkendol, Wyer, & Epstein, 1996; Feldman, 2009). Wardrobing alone costs retailers over $10 billion per year, according to a recent estimate by the National Retail Federation.

A growing body of empirical research shows how frequently such ordinary dishonesty occurs. For example, in two diary studies, participants recorded their social interactions and lies for a week, including self-serving lies and altruistic ones. On average, people reported telling one to two lies per day (DePaulo & Kashy, 1998). Although not all lies are harmful, people do engage in a great deal of dishonest behavior that negatively affects others, and they do so in many different contexts, such as personal relationships (Canner, 2008), the workplace (Murphy, 1993), and sports. As an example, consider the "Spygate" incident that occurred during the 2007 National Football League (NFL) season. The New England Patriots were disciplined by the NFL for secretly videotaping New York Jets defensive coaches' signals during a game, a violation of league rules.

Real-world stories and empirical evidence are consistent with recent laboratory experiments showing that many people cheat slightly when they think they can get away with it (Gino, Ayal, & Ariely, 2009; Mazar, Amir, & Ariely, 2008). In these experiments, people misreported their performance to earn more money, but only to a certain degree (about 10%–20%) above their actual performance and far below the maximum payoff possible. That is, most of the cheating was not committed by "a few bad apples" that were totally rotten. Rather, many apples in the barrel turned just a little bit bad. The evidence from such studies paints a troubling picture of human nature: People are often tempted by the potential benefits of cheating and commonly succumb to temptation by behaving dishonestly, but only "a little bit."

The evidence is striking in light of social psychological research that, for decades, has robustly demonstrated that people strive to maintain a positive self-image both privately and publicly (Allport, 1955; Rosenberg, 1979). Social identity theorists, such as Schlenker (1982) and Tajfel (1982a), have argued that people want to feel good about themselves and strive to maintain a positive self-image, which presumably includes viewing themselves as moral. But sometimes this requires a little immorality combined with self-deception. For example, people embrace successes as their own and reject failures as circumstantial (Miller & Ross, 1975), maintain an illusion of control over unpredictable events (Langer, 1975), and, on average, rank themselves as better than average on positive traits (Alicke, Klotz, Breitenbecher, Yurak, & Vredenburg, 1995; Klar, 2002). In the same vein, people typically value honesty, believe strongly in their own morality, and strive to maintain a moral self-image (Greenwald, 1980; Sanitioso, Kunda, & Fong, 1990). For instance, approximately 84% of individuals in one sample self-reported that they are moral and honest (Aquino & Reed, 2002).

The gap between people's actual dishonest behavior and their desire to maintain a positive moral self-image has not been carefully investigated. We call this gap *ethical dissonance* (Barkan, Ayal, Gino, & Ariely, 2010). Ethical dissonance is similar to the familiar concept of cognitive dissonance (Festinger, 1957)—the feeling of uncomfortable tension that comes from holding two conflicting thoughts at the same time. Ethical dissonance is the tension that arises from the inconsistency between one's actual cheating behavior and one's ethical values or attitudes. We argue that the discomfort produced by ethical dissonance, similar to the consequences of cognitive dissonance, calls for some kind of adjustment. Prior research has examined situations in which observing the behavior of others leads people to think differently about their own moral character (see Chapter 9, this volume). For instance, recent studies on moral compensation show that people may boost their moral self-regard and be critical of others' morality to compensate for a threat to their self-concept in a nonmoral domain (Jordan & Monin, 2008). Departing from this body of work, we focus in this chapter on situations in which ethical dissonance results from reflecting on one's own past deeds.

Importantly, ethical dissonance is a specific form of cognitive dissonance that calls for a unique kind of solution. A key aspect of many cognitive dissonance experiments is that behavior that contradicts a belief or attitude is public and cannot be denied or changed (e.g., eating meat during a meal with others who know you have a strong belief in animal rights). As a result, people reconcile the tension they experience by adjusting their attitudes to be consistent with a behavior that has already been performed. By contrast, in the case of ethical dissonance, the unethical behavior, such as a minor instance of cheating, is hidden from other people. Thus, the adjustments and corrections people make to cope with ethical dissonance do not necessarily require them to relax their contradictory internal code.

In this chapter, we identify the main adjustment strategies people use to reduce ethical dissonance. We seek to understand how people can seemingly benefit from dishonest behavior while simultaneously preserving a moral self-image. Specifically, we discuss three psychological mechanisms that enable people to rationalize and condone their unethical behavior: moral cleansing, local social utility, and social comparisons of one's own behavior with that of others. Before presenting evidence in support of these three mechanisms, we discuss the role of ambiguity in people's reinterpretation of their bad deeds.

REINTERPRETATION OF AMBIGUOUS UNETHICALITY

One way to resolve the tension between unethical behavior and moral self-image is to creatively interpret an incriminating behavior as an honest one. In many situations, people behave dishonestly enough to profit from their unethicality but restrict the magnitude of their dishonesty. This restriction allows them to maintain a positive self-concept (Mazar et al., 2008) by noting their actions (e.g., "I am overclaiming") but not necessarily categorizing them as unethical or immoral (e.g., "I am dishonest").

In their self-concept maintenance theory, Mazar et al. (2008) identified two contextual variables that can affect a person's freedom to engage in creative reinterpretation of unethical behavior. The first is the behavior's degree of malleability (i.e., the level of flexibility people have in rationalizing this behavior). Previous research has shown that when moral categorization of a particular behavior is malleable rather than clear-cut (e.g., taking office supplies from work), people can, and in fact often do, conceptualize their actions in acceptable terms and thus avoid having to challenge or change their moral self-image (Baumeister, 1998; Schweitzer & Hsee, 2002). In one study demonstrating this tendency (Ariely, 2008), the experimenter left a six-pack of a popular soft drink in each of several communal refrigerators on a university campus. In some of the refrigerators, the experimenter also left a plate containing six $1 bills. The cans of soft drink quickly disappeared (within 72 hr), but the plates of $1 bills remained untouched. In a similar vein, participants in laboratory experiments tended to inflate their performance on a problem-solving task more when they were instructed to take tokens from a jar (later replaced by money) as a reward for good performance than when they were instructed to take dollar bills from a jar (Mazar et al., 2008). That is, being able to take tokens (or cans of soda) rather than cash offered more categorization malleability such that people could interpret their dishonesty in a more self-serving manner, reducing the negative self-signal they otherwise would have received from directly stealing money. Consequently, distancing participants one step from cash by using tokens increased the threshold for the acceptable magnitude of dishonesty.

A second contextual variable that may affect a person's ability to reinterpret unethical behavior is the saliency of ethicality at the moment a particular behavior is considered. The concept of *bounded ethicality* (Banaji, Bazerman, & Chugh, 2003) applies to situations in which people make unconscious decision errors that serve their self-interest but are inconsistent with their consciously espoused beliefs and preferences (e.g., engaging in ingroup favoritism)—decisions they would condemn upon further reflection or greater awareness. For example, accounting firms have their own ethical code but also numerous reasons to view their clients' books in a positive light, including the auditing and consulting fees they receive from their client firms. Bazerman, Loewenstein, and Moore (2002) tested this conflict of interest by giving participants a complex body of information about the potential sale of a fictitious company. Participants were strongly biased toward the interests of their own clients. Moreover, they assimilated information about the target company in a biased way and were unable to adjust their biased evaluations even for monetary rewards.

If a lack of awareness helps people reinterpret their dishonest behavior as honest, drawing their attention to moral standards should reduce dishonesty. Indeed, Mazar et al. (2008) found that after being asked to recall the Ten Commandments, participants who were given the opportunity to gain financially by cheating did not cheat at all, whereas those who had the same opportunity to cheat but were not given the moral reminder cheated significantly. Gino et al. (2009) also found that a subtle reminder of the possibility of cheating in a specific setting was sufficient to reduce levels of dishonesty.

Taken together, these findings suggest that cheating only a little (rather than to the maximum extent possible), engaging in highly malleable behavior, and lacking full awareness introduce ambiguity that blurs the criteria for judging what is right and what is wrong. Such ambiguity allows people to reinterpret their unethical behavior and whitewash it. However, when such ambiguity is absent, people's dishonest behavior becomes undeniably wrong. In the following sections, we focus on these kinds of unambiguous situations.

HONEST RATIONAL MECHANISMS

The following sections discuss three psychological mechanisms that people use to rationalize their unethical behavior and reduce ethical dissonance: moral cleansing, local social utility, and social comparisons of one's own behavior with that of others.

Moral Cleansing

The first of these mechanisms is *moral cleansing*. According to Tetlock, Kristel, Elson, Green, and Lerner (2000), moral cleansing is an attempt to rid oneself of negative feelings after committing an unethical act by mental appeasement. This conscious process enables individuals to distance themselves from transgressions and turn a new page in their moral ledger. Moral cleansing can take place in at least three ways: physical washing and pain, moral licensing, and confession.

Physical Washing and Pain

Physical cleansing, such as bathing or washing hands, is a common religious ritual. For example, Christians practice baptism, a water purification ritual, in the belief that through the symbolic cleansing of their bodies they can also achieve a cleansing of conscience and soul (Zhong & Liljenquist, 2006). In the Jewish tradition, several biblical regulations specify that full immersion in a *mikve* (ritual pool) is required to regain ritual purity following ritually impure events. Physical cleansing is also central to Islam; *ablution* is the Muslim act of washing parts of the body in clean water to prepare for worship. Thus, major religions include bodily purity rituals in the belief that physical cleansing ceremonies can purify the soul (see also Chapter 1, this volume).

Zhong and Liljenquist (2006) provided evidence for this association between physical cleansing and moral purification. In one experiment, participants were asked to hand copy a short story written in the first person. The story described either an ethically selfless deed (control group) or an unethical act (experimental group). Participants were then offered a free gift and given a choice between an antiseptic wipe and a pencil. Those who copied the story describing an unethical deed were more likely to choose an antiseptic wipe than were those who copied an ethical deed. Furthermore, Zhong and Liljenquist found that within the experimental group in which participants recalled unethical behavior, those who washed their hands with an antiseptic wipe reported experiencing fewer moral emotions (e.g., guilt) than those who did not wash their hands. This result suggests that the sanitation wipes had psychologically washed away the participants' moral stains and restored a suitably moral self. Extending these results, Schnall, Benton, and Harvey (2008) demonstrated that when the notion of physical purity is made salient to individuals, moral judgments of others become less severe.

Related research has suggested that pain has positive qualities, as it provides a means of spiritual and moral cleansing (Klaassen, 2008). The Jewish people, for instance, use Yom Kippur to attempt to atone for immoral behavior during the previous year and seek forgiveness for wrongs committed against God and human beings. They do so by fasting and intensive praying for a period of 25 hr in the hope that God will inscribe their names in the "Good Book." And Wallington (1973) showed that people who violated moral rules tended to cause themselves to suffer in other domains (by giving themselves electric shocks) as a way of redeeming themselves from their previous unethical acts, even though no restitution resulted from their suffering.

Moral Licensing

John Gotti, New York City's most infamous mob boss throughout the 1980s, created a charity in his name. As many have argued (e.g., Capeci & Mustain, 1996; Raab, 2006), the charity included genuine intentions and was not used merely as a front to make him seem more legitimate. What drives criminals to engage in humanitarian acts? One explanation is what Levav and McGraw (2009) called *emotional accounting*. When people receive money under ethically questionable circumstances, they may feel bad, and they can sometimes reduce the negative feelings by engaging in ethical behavior. In a series of studies, Levav and McGraw found that people avoided spending money they received under unethical circumstances ("negatively tagged" money) on hedonistic expenditures (e.g., beach parties) and instead made virtuous expenditures (e.g., paying for someone's education). They hoped that their virtuous conduct would reduce or "launder" their negative feelings about the windfall.

Likewise, early studies of compliance following a transgression suggested that participants were likely to engage in altruistic reparation. In a study by Darlington and Macker (1966), for example, some participants were led to believe they had harmed another person, whereas participants in the control group were not. All participants were then given an opportunity to engage in altruistic behavior toward a third party in the form of agreeing to donate blood to a local hospital. The experimental group proved to be more altruistic than the control group. Participants seemed to reduce or balance their ethical dissonance by engaging in behavior on the other side of the moral scale.

Additional evidence for the tendency to balance the scales comes from studies of the reverse phenomenon, in which altruistic behavior releases people from their moral shackles and allows them to cross over into the realm of unethical behavior. According to Sachdeva, Iliev, and Medin (2009), people who feel sufficiently moral may lack an incentive to engage in moral action because of its costliness. They referred to this effect as *moral licensing*, which is a component of a larger system of moral self-regulation (Zhong, Liljenquist, & Cain, 2009). People may feel licensed to refrain from good behavior when they have amassed a surplus of moral currency. This effect has been studied and supported in different domains, such as stereotyping behavior (Monin & Miller, 2001) and consumer decision making (Khan & Dhar, 2006). Extending these findings to charitable giving and corporate ethical decisions, Sachdeva et al. (2009) found that a sense of moral superiority limited additional future moral behavior. Finally, the hand cleansing study mentioned above (Zhong & Liljenquist, 2006) also showed that participants who washed their hands after recalling unethical behavior were less motivated to volunteer to help a "desperate" student than were those who did not wash their hands.

Promise of Confession

The acts of apologizing, asking for forgiveness, and turning over a new leaf intersect at the points where religion and psychology meet guilt and shame. As we have noted, Jewish people view Yom Kippur as a time to seek forgiveness for wrongs committed against other human beings and God. In the Catholic Church, confession to a priest is perceived as a curative act of faith and absolution (Todd, 1985). A priest we interviewed as part of a research project described the function of the Sacrament of Penance, or confession, as follows:

> People come to confession for the purpose of regaining the order in their lives, getting relieved as much as forgiven and redeemed. When you are worried about something, you need relief. . . . The difference between

talking to a priest and talking to your Mom or Dad is that you're actually talking to God through the priest.

There are advantages to viewing confession as a rationalization mechanism. First, by providing relief to the confessor (Kettunen, 2002), confession offers an effective way to resolve the dissonance between one's perception of oneself as a moral person and any dishonest behaviors one has committed. Confession can also help reduce the likelihood of future dishonest behavior. This optimistic prediction is supported by research, which has found that drawing people's attention to moral standards can reduce dishonest behavior (Mazar et al., 2008). Thus, when unethical behavior is made salient via expectation or actual confession, people may subsequently (at least for a while) bear in mind the importance of ethical behavior and moral standards and may try to be consistent with their moral values.

To test the effect of confession, Ayal, Gino, Mazar, and Ariely (2010) simulated a confession in a laboratory setting and measured its influence on people's dishonest behavior. The study used a computerized perceptual task in which participants were placed in situations that induced a conflict between behaving honestly (i.e., click on the accurate response) and maximizing self-interest (i.e., click on the most profitable but inaccurate response). The number of profitable but inaccurate responses was our measure of dishonesty. That is, participants could behave dishonestly by interpreting evidence in a self-serving manner (by choosing an answer that was inaccurate but that led to higher payment). The perceptual task was divided into two phases, and the manipulation was introduced between the two phases. Half of the participants were assigned to the confession condition. They wrote about one bad thing they had done and then were asked to close their eyes and ask "God" or any other entity for forgiveness for that event. The other half, assigned to the control condition, wrote about their typical evening activities. In Phase 1, the two groups exhibited very similar levels of dishonesty. However, in Phase 2, after the manipulation occurred, participants in the confession condition reduced their level of dishonest behavior, whereas participants in the control condition continued to cheat. Moreover, in a follow-up experiment, when participants in the confession condition were informed at the beginning of the study about the confession manipulation, the reduction of the dishonest behavior started at the beginning of the experiment and continued after the confession manipulation. These findings suggest that expectation of confession and forgiveness as well as the actual act of confessing and receiving forgiveness have beneficial effects on honest behavior, at least for a while.

Yet confession may have negative effects on morality in the long run. If people are concerned about their moral self, a confession experienced as achieving forgiveness may act as a moral offset that allows them to transgress again without disturbing their overall moral self-concept. Consistent with this idea, Ayal et al. (2010) found that the positive effect of confession was eliminated and even reversed with temporal distance. In the same vein, Harris, Benson, and Hall (1975) examined people's willingness to donate money before and after engaging in confession at a church. They found that people were significantly more likely to donate money to charity before rather than after making a confession. These findings support the notion of moral licensing. That is, after confession, people feel they have already restored their shattered moral self and thus have no need for the reparation that might otherwise be made by engaging in prosocial activities.

Local Social Utility

Not only is altruistic behavior observed after an unethical act has occurred (e.g., donating blood after engaging in wrongdoing), but at times altruistic motivation can also serve as a justification for later unethical behavior. In many cases, when people cheat, they benefit not only themselves but other people as well. By focusing on the benefits that cheating may provide to others rather than emphasizing their own self-interest, people may be able to view their actions in positive terms, avoiding a tarnished moral self-image (Baumeister, 1998; Schweitzer & Hsee, 2002). The archetypical example of such reframing is Robin Hood, the folkloric hero who robbed from the rich to give to the poor. Gino and Pierce (2010) found support for this type of reframing in their study of the ways in which an employee's perception of a customer's relatively low socioeconomic status may influence illegal helping behavior in the context of vehicle emissions testing. They found that a large number of car inspectors illegally passed customers who drove standard ("poor looking") cars that should have failed the emissions test, but drivers of luxury vehicles were helped less often. The inspectors evidently empathized with customers who shared their modest economic status.

This phenomenon may be particularly relevant when people work in group settings in which others can benefit from their dishonesty. There are two ways in which focusing on others' gains from one's own cheating or dishonesty may help reduce ethical dissonance and enable one to benefit from unethical behavior without having to debit their moral account. The first is related to social psychological research on *diffusion of responsibility* (Latané, 1981). This concept refers to the possibility that the presence of others in group settings enables people to deindividuate and distribute responsibility among group members, thereby reducing their own responsibility and guilt (Diener, 1977; Zimbardo, 1969). For instance, Diener, Fraser, Beaman, and Kelem (1976) found that Halloween trick-or-treaters who were given the opportunity to steal candy and money did so more often when they were part of a group than when they were trick-or-treating alone. The concepts of diffusion of responsibility and deindividuation have been used to explain antinormative social behavior in various domains, including social atrocities (Staub, 1996), computer-mediated communication (Kiesler, Siegel, & McGuire, 1984), and group decision support systems (Jessup, Connolly, & Tansik, 1990).

The second way in which the potential benefits to others of one's own cheating can help reduce ethical dissonance derives from the advantages people accrue from altruistic behavior (Loewenstein, Thompson, & Bazerman, 1989). Several studies have demonstrated that people care not only about their own benefits but also about their utility to others (i.e., social utility; Loewenstein et al., 1989). For instance, Gino and Pierce (2009) showed that individuals were willing to forgo some of their pay to help a peer who was relatively disadvantaged.

In many cases, social utility is in line with self-interest, and both are located in the gray region of the ethical-to-unethical continuum. Gino, Ayal, and Ariely (2010) conducted a series of laboratory experiments to simulate these kinds of situations. Participants were asked to solve simple mathematical problems for pay as individuals, as part of a dyad, or as part of a three-person group. Performance overreporting was used as a measure of dishonesty. In the dyad condition, the individual performance of each member was totaled, and each individual's payment equaled half of the dyad's total payoff. In the group condition, the individual performance of each member in the three-person group was totaled, and payment for each individual was equal to a third of the group's total payoff. In addition, the level of communication among the group members was manipulated.

Participants cheated more when their partners could benefit from their cheating, and they cheated even more when the group was larger and when there was more communication among group members. Moreover, this increase was due to the growth in the number of cheaters, whereas the average magnitude of cheating remained unchanged. These findings suggest that people may care about other group members' benefits, but they are also tempted to use social utility to rationalize their behavior. That is, individuals have the opportunity to cheat and then freely categorize their own bad actions (dishonest behavior) in positive terms (creating financial benefits for others). Consequently, more people fall prey to this temptation when operating in groups because it is easier to justify, or rationalize, their unethical behavior as acceptable.

Social Comparisons

The presence of others is relevant to ethical decision making not only when individuals share in the social utility of their behavior but also when others help to establish a standard for "ethical" behavior. By observing other people's unethical behavior, individuals can assess the costs and benefits of particular transgressions (Becker, 1968). They may determine how frequent this behavior is in a particular environment and, most important, where to draw the line between ethical and unethical behavior (Cialdini & Trost, 1998; Gino et al., 2009). In short, people learn the social norms related to dishonesty by interacting with others (Campbell, 1964) and observing their behavior.

Cialdini, Reno, and Kallgren (1990) defined two kinds of social norms: *descriptive norms*, which specify how most people behave in a given situation, and *injunctive norms*, which specify the particular behaviors approved or disapproved of by most people. According to social norm theory (Cialdini et al., 1990; Reno, Cialdini, & Kallgren, 1993), the social context determines which of these two types of norms people attend to at a particular time and how they impinge on an individual's immediate behavior.

This kind of social learning by observing other people's behavior suggests that when people behave unethically, different social contexts can raise or lower the ethical dissonance they experience. When the social context highlights descriptive norms (e.g., littering in a dirty environment), it helps people justify their behavior and reduce dissonance. In contrast, when the social context highlights injunctive norms (e.g., littering in a clean environment), it might exacerbate the dissonance. Other examples can be found in Bandura's classic studies (Bandura, 1965; Bandura, Ross, & Ross, 1961) in which children exposed to an aggressive model produced considerably more aggressive behavior toward a doll than did children who were not exposed to the aggressive model. Moreover, this effect was stronger when an adult did not comment on the aggressive model's actions or when an adult was not present in the room (Hicks, 1968; Siegel & Kohn, 1959). Children in these studies may have interpreted the lack of evaluative comments about the model's aggressive behavior and the absence of an adult in the room as signs of permission, which they then saw as justifying their own aggressive behavior.

This social norm theory hints at another important factor that could influence the way people interpret the unethical behavior of others—the degree to which they identify with the others (Tajfel, 1982b). When identification is strong, the behavior of others should have a larger influence on observers than when identification is weak. In other words, when individuals observe the unethical misdeeds of ingroup members, they should feel more comfortable in loosening their own ethical code. Field evidence for this theory was obtained in a large-scale survey of Australian citizens (Wenzel, 2004), which found that the presence of social norms elicited consistent behavior (i.e., tax compliance), but only when respondents identified with the group to which the norms were attributed.

Gino et al. (2009) investigated whether the effect of others' unethical behavior is contagious. They asked college students to solve simple math problems in the presence of others. In some of the conditions, participants were given the opportunity to cheat by misreporting their performance and earning undeserved money. More important, in some conditions, participants were exposed to a confederate who cheated ostentatiously by finishing a task impossibly quickly and leaving the room with the maximum reward. In line with social norm theory, the level of unethical behavior among group members increased when the confederate was an ingroup member (indicated by wearing a regular T-shirt) but decreased when the confederate was an outgroup member (wearing a T-shirt from a rival university).

Altogether, these findings support the intersection between social norm theory (Cialdini et al., 1990; Reno et al., 1993) and social identity theory (Tajfel, 1982a). Group members use comparisons with their own group to maintain or enhance positive social identity and self-esteem, and as a consequence they are motivated to perceive an ingroup member's transgression as a descriptive norm, making it less objectionable than if an outgroup member performed the same act. Moreover, instead of using an outgroup confederate's behavior as a model, people tend to highlight the injunctive norm and distance themselves from this "bad apple." This helps them to maintain a distinctive and positive social identity for their ingroup (Brewer, 1993; Tajfel, 1982b). Basically, people use the same behavior to maintain their self-esteem in both cases (ingroup or outgroup confederate), but in two very different ways.

This flexibility in reframing both others' and one's own behavior is also demonstrated by *moral hypocrisy*—an individual's ability to hold onto a belief while acting contrary to it (Batson, Kobrynowicz, Dinnerstein, Kampf, & Wilson, 1997; see also Chapter 9, this volume). More specifically, moral hypocrisy occurs when individuals' evaluations of their own moral transgressions differ substantially from their evaluations of the same transgressions enacted by others. In a study by Valdesolo and DeSteno (2007), participants in one condition were required to distribute a resource (e.g., time, energy) to themselves and another person by choosing to perform one of two tasks, an easy one or a complicated one. They could make the distribution either fairly (i.e., through a random allocation procedure) or unfairly (i.e., selecting the better option for themselves). They were then asked to evaluate the morality, or fairness, of their actions. In another condition, participants viewed a confederate acting in an unfair manner and subsequently evaluated the morality of this act. In line with moral hypocrisy theory, individuals who chose the easier task for themselves perceived their own transgression to be less objectionable than the same transgression enacted by another person. Although this research tested for moral hypocrisy by using a between-subjects design, other research has demonstrated similar effects using within-subjects designs (e.g.,

Lammers, Stapel, & Galinsky, 2010). Testing this idea beyond the bounds of the self, Valdesolo and DeSteno (2007) found that the boundaries of hypocrisy fluctuate as a function of the self's affiliation with the target. Here again, hypocrisy targeted outgroup members more than ingroup members.

Finally, people's moral self-esteem can benefit directly from applying a strict ethical code to others' behavior. A recent study by Barkan et al. (2010) suggests that when people experience ethical dissonance created by their own past misdeeds, they develop a special sensitivity to others' unethical behavior; as a result, they judge it using stricter and harsher criteria than they apply to themselves. In a series of studies, participants were asked to write about a past wrongdoing that they regretted having committed. This manipulation created ethical dissonance. Alternatively, participants in a control group were asked to recall and write about a good deed they were proud of. People in the ethical dissonance group exhibited greater harshness and lower tolerance toward others' cheating than did the members of the control group. By being morally harsh on others who fell prey to temptations, individuals were able to distance themselves from this weakness and protect their self-image.

CONCLUSION

The research discussed in this chapter calls attention to a variety of situations in which people experience tension between behaving honestly and maximizing their own self-interest. The findings suggest that people reduce this tension in a variety of creative ways. They behave unethically enough to benefit but ethically enough to maintain a positive self-image and a defensible balance of ethical and unethical behavior. We identified three mechanisms that people use to achieve this balance. First, they take advantage of the ambiguity surrounding dishonest behavior and make do with a loose interpretation of the relevant ethical code. Second, when their actions are undeniably unethical, people use the social context to justify or excuse their unethical behavior or to balance it with prosocial behavior. Finally, people distance themselves from their misdeeds by confessing and turning over a new leaf.

Although we distinguish between different kinds of mechanisms, the relations between them are interesting. First, some behaviors could be placed in more than one category. For example, altruistic donations of time or money might be viewed as part of moral cleansing. Alternatively, if people such as Robin Hood think about their past contributions to their ingroup before committing an unethical act, the contributions might fit in the local social utility category. Second, people can use more than one mechanism at a time. For example, when a man takes tax deductions that are not actually related to his work, he can justify this decision by using descriptive norms ("Everybody does it"). At the same time, he could also reinterpret the unethical nature of the behavior ("I talked with my aunt about work during this dinner"). Finally, the Harris et al. (1975) study shows that one mechanism can affect the use of another: People's willingness to donate money was higher before going to confession in a Catholic church than after such a confession. That is, after confessing, people felt they had restored their moral self and had no need burnish it further.

In closing, we consider a question Plato posed around 360 BCE: Is there anyone alive who could resist taking advantage of the power of invisibility, given that being monitored by other people may be the only thing that prevents us from committing immoral acts? The literature we reviewed here suggests that others' presence does not always help increase ethicality, because the others' needs and behavior may be used to justify our dishonesty. However, the fact that the psychological mechanisms discussed in this chapter function mainly to enhance our self-esteem and reduce internal dissonance suggests that we might experience dissonance even if we could become invisible at will.

REFERENCES

Alicke, M. D., Klotz, M. L., Breitenbecher, D. L., Yurak, T. J., & Vredenburg, D. S. (1995). Personal contact, individuation, and the better-than-average effect. *Journal of Personality and Social Psychology, 68*, 804–825. doi:10.1037/0022-3514. 68.5.804

Allport, G. W. (1955). *Becoming: Basic considerations for a psychology of personality.* New Haven, CT: Yale University Press.

Aquino, K., & Reed, I. A. (2002). The self-importance of moral identity. *Journal of Personality and Social Psychology, 83*, 1423–1440. doi:10.1037/0022-3514. 83.6.1423

Ariely, D. (2008). *Predictably irrational.* New York, NY: HarperCollins.

Ayal, S., Gino, F., Mazar, N., & Ariely, D. (2010). *Finding balance on the moral scale: Dishonest behavior and the promise of confession.* Manuscript in preparation.

Banaji, M. R., Bazerman, M. H., & Chugh, D. (2003). How (un)ethical are you? *Harvard Business Review, 81*, 56–64.

Bandura, A. (1965). Influence of models' reinforcement contingencies on the acquisition of imitative responses. *Journal of Personality and Social Psychology, 1*, 589–595. doi:10.1037/h0022070

Bandura, A., Ross, D., & Ross, S. A. (1961). Transmission of aggression through imitation of aggressive models. *Journal of Abnormal and Social Psychology, 63*, 575–582. doi:10.1037/h0045925

Barkan, R., Ayal, S., Gino, F., & Ariely, D. (2010). *The pot calling the kettle black: Seeing evil after experiencing ethical dissonance* (Working Paper No. 10-03-01). Durham, NC: Center for Behavioral Economics, Duke University.

Batson, C. D., Kobrynowicz, D., Dinnerstein, J. L., Kampf, H. C., & Wilson, A. D. (1997). In a very different voice: Unmasking moral hypocrisy. *Journal of Personality and Social Psychology, 72*, 1335–1348. doi:10.1037/0022-3514.72.6.1335

Baumeister, R. F. (1998). The self. In D. T. Gilbert, S. T. Fiske, & G. Lindzey (Eds.), *Handbook of social psychology* (Vol. 1, pp. 680–740). New York, NY: McGraw-Hill.

Bazerman, M. H., Loewenstein, G., & Moore, D. A. (2002). Why good accountants do bad audits. *Harvard Business Review, 80*, 96–102.

Becker, G. S. (1968). Crime and punishment: An economic approach. *The Journal of Political Economy, 76*, 169–217. doi:10.1086/259394

Brewer, M. B. (1993). Social identity, distinctiveness, and in-group homogeneity. *Social Cognition, 11*, 150–164. doi:10.1521/soco.1993.11.1.150

Campbell, E. Q. (1964). The internalization of moral norms. *Sociometry, 27*, 391–412. doi:10.2307/2785655

Canner, E. (2008). Sex, lies, and pharmaceuticals: The making of an investigative documentary about "female sexual dysfunction." *Feminism & Psychology, 18*, 488–494. doi:10.1177/0959353508095531

Capeci, J., & Mustain, G. (1996). *Gotti: Rise and fall.* New York, NY: Onyx.

Cialdini, R. B., Reno, R. R., & Kallgren, C. A. (1990). A focus theory of normative conduct: Recycling the concept of norms to reduce littering in public places. *Journal of Personality and Social Psychology, 58*, 1015–1026. doi:10.1037/0022-3514.58.6.1015

Cialdini, R. B., & Trost, M. R. (1998). Social influence: Social norm, conformity, and compliance. In D. T. Gilbert, S. T. Fiske, & G. Lindzey (Eds.), *Handbook of social psychology* (Vol. 2, pp. 151–192). New York, NY: McGraw-Hill.

Darlington, R. B., & Macker, C. (1966). Displacement of guilt-produced altruistic behavior. *Journal of Personality and Social Psychology, 4*, 442–443. doi:10.1037/h0023743

DePaulo, B. M., & Kashy, D. A. (1998). Everyday lies in close and casual relationships. *Journal of Personality and Social Psychology, 74*, 63–79. doi:10.1037/0022-3514.74.1.63

DePaulo, B. M., Kashy, D. A., Kirkendol, S. E., Wyer, M. M., & Epstein, J. A. (1996). Lying in everyday life. *Journal of Personality and Social Psychology, 70*, 979–995. doi:10.1037/0022-3514.70.5.979

Diener, E. (1977). Deindividuation: Causes and consequences. *Social Behavior and Personality, 5*, 143–155. doi:10.2224/sbp.1977.5.1.143

Diener, E., Fraser, S., Beaman, A., & Kelem, R. (1976). Effects of deindividuation variables on stealing among Halloween trick-or-treaters. *Journal of Personality and Social Psychology, 33*, 178–183. doi:10.1037/0022-3514.33.2.178

Feldman, R. (2009). *The liar in your life*. London, England: Virgin Books.

Festinger, L. (1957). *A theory of cognitive dissonance*. Palo Alto, CA: Stanford University Press.

Gino, F., Ayal, S., & Ariely, D. (2009). Contagion and differentiation in unethical behavior: The effect of one bad apple on the barrel. *Psychological Science, 20*, 393–398. doi:10.1111/j.1467-9280.2009.02306.x

Gino, F., Ayal, S., & Ariely, D. (2010). *Altruistic cheating: Behaving dishonestly for the sake of others*. Manuscript in preparation.

Gino, F., & Pierce, L. (2009). Dishonesty in the name of equity. *Psychological Science, 20*, 1153–1160. doi:10.1111/j.1467-9280.2009.02421.x

Gino, F., & Pierce, L. (2010). Robin Hood under the hood: Wealth-based discrimination in illicit customer help. *Organization Science, 21*, 1176–1194.

Greenwald, A. G. (1980). The totalitarian ego: Fabrication and revision of personal history. *American Psychologist, 35*, 603–618. doi:10.1037/0003-066X.35.7.603

Harris, M. B., Benson, S. M., & Hall, C. L. (1975). The effects of confession on altruism. *Journal of Social Psychology, 96*, 187–192. doi:10.1080/00224545.1975.9923284

Hicks, D. J. (1968). Effects of co-observer's sanctions and adult presence on imitative aggression. *Child Development, 39*, 303–309. doi:10.2307/1127381

Jessup, L. M., Connolly, T., & Tansik, D. (1990). Toward a theory of automated group work: The deindividuating effects of anonymity. *Small Group Research, 21*, 333–348. doi:10.1177/1046496490213003

Jordan, A. H., & Monin, B. (2008). From sucker to saint: Moralization in response to self-threat. *Psychological Science, 19*, 809–815. doi:10.1111/j.1467-9280.2008.02161.x

Kettunen, P. (2002). The function of confession: A study based on experiences. *Pastoral Psychology, 51*, 13–25. doi:10.1023/A:1019722307142

Khan, U., & Dhar, R. (2006). Licensing effect in consumer choice. *Journal of Marketing Research, 43*, 259–266. doi:10.1509/jmkr.43.2.259

Kiesler, S., Siegel, J., & McGuire, T. W. (1984). Social psychological aspects of computer-mediated communication. *American Psychologist, 39*, 1123–1134. doi:10.1037/0003-066X.39.10.1123

Klaassen, J. A. (2008). Punishment and the purification of moral taint. *Journal of Social Philosophy, 27*(2), 51–64. doi:10.1111/j.1467-9833.1996.tb00237.x

Klar, Y. (2002). Way beyond compare: Nonselective superiority and inferiority biases in judging randomly assigned group members relative to their peers. *Journal of Experimental Social Psychology, 38*, 331–351. doi:10.1016/S0022-1031(02)00003-3

Lammers, J., Stapel, D. A., & Galinsky, A. D. (2010). Power increases hypocrisy: Moralizing in reasoning, immorality in behavior. *Psychological Science, 21*, 737–744. doi:10.1177/0956797610368810

Langer, E. J. (1975). The illusion of control. *Journal of Personality and Social Psychology, 32*, 311–328. doi:10.1037/0022-3514.32.2.311

Latané, B. (1981). The psychology of social impact. *American Psychologist, 36*, 343–356. doi:10.1037/0003-066X.36.4.343

Levav, J., & McGraw, P. (2009). Accounting: How feelings about money influence consumer choice. *Journal of Marketing Research, 46*, 66–80. doi:10.1509/jmkr.46.1.66

Loewenstein, G. F., Thompson, L., & Bazerman, M. H. (1989). Social utility and decision making in interpersonal contexts. *Journal of Personality and Social Psychology, 57*, 426–441. doi:10.1037/0022-3514.57.3.426

Mazar, N., Amir, O., & Ariely, D. (2008). The dishonesty of honest people: A theory of self-concept maintenance. *Journal of Marketing Research, 45*, 633–644. doi:10.1509/jmkr.45.6.633

Miller, D. T., & Ross, M. (1975). Self-serving biases in attribution of causality: Fact or fiction? *Psychological Bulletin, 82*, 213–225. doi:10.1037/h0076486

Monin, B., & Miller, D. T. (2001). Moral credentials and the expression of prejudice. *Journal of Personality and Social Psychology, 81*, 33–43. doi:10.1037/0022-3514.81.1.33

Murphy, K. R. (1993). *Honesty in the workplace.* Pacific Grove, CA: Brooks/Cole.

Raab, S. (2006). *Five families: The rise, decline, and resurgence of America's most powerful mafia empires.* London, England: Robson Books.

Reno, R. R., Cialdini, R. B., & Kallgren, C. A. (1993). The transsituational influence of social norms. *Journal of Personality and Social Psychology, 64*, 104–112. doi:10.1037/0022-3514.64.1.104

Rosenberg, M. (1979). *Conceiving the self.* New York, NY: Basic Books.

Sachdeva, S., Iliev, R., & Medin, D. L. (2009). Sinning saints and saintly sinners: The paradox of moral self-regulation. *Psychological Science, 20*, 523–528. doi:10.1111/j.1467-9280.2009.02326.x

Sanitioso, R., Kunda, Z., & Fong, J. T. (1990). Motivated recruitment of autobiographical memories. *Journal of Personality and Social Psychology, 59*, 229–241. doi:10.1037/0022-3514.59.2.229

Schlenker, B. R. (1982). Translating actions into attitudes: An identity-analytic approach to the explanation of social conduct. In L. Berkowitz (Ed.), *Advances in experimental social psychology* (Vol. 15, pp. 194–248). New York, NY: Academic Press.

Schnall, S., Benton, J., & Harvey, S. (2008). With a clean conscience: Cleanliness reduces the severity of moral judgments. *Psychological Science, 19*, 1219–1222. doi:10.1111/j.1467-9280.2008.02227.x

Schweitzer, M. E., & Hsee, C. K. (2002). Stretching the truth: Elastic justification and motivated communication of uncertain information. *Journal of Risk and Uncertainty, 25*, 185–201. doi:10.1023/A:1020647814263

Siegel, A. E., & Kohn, L. G. (1959). Permissiveness, permission, and aggression: The effect of adult presence or absence on aggression in children's play. *Child Development, 30,* 131–141. doi:10.2307/1126136

Staub, E. (1996). Altruism and aggression: Origins and cures. In R. Feldman (Ed.), *The psychology of adversity* (pp. 115–147). Amherst, MA: University of Massachusetts Press.

Tajfel, H. (1982a). *Social identity and intergroup relations.* Cambridge, England: Cambridge University Press.

Tajfel, H. (1982b). Social psychology of intergroup relations. *Annual Review of Psychology, 33,* 1–39. doi:10.1146/annurev.ps.33.020182.000245

Tetlock, P. E., Kristel, O. V., Elson, S. B., Green, M. C., & Lerner, J. S. (2000). The psychology of the unthinkable: Taboo trade-offs, forbidden base rates, and heretical counterfactuals. *Journal of Personality and Social Psychology, 78,* 853–870. doi:10.1037/0022-3514.78.5.853

Todd, E. (1985). The value of confession and forgiveness according to Jung. *Journal of Religion and Health, 24,* 39–48. doi:10.1007/BF01533258

Valdesolo, P., & DeSteno, D. (2007). Moral hypocrisy: Social groups and the flexibility of virtue. *Psychological Science, 18,* 689–690. doi:10.1111/j.1467-9280.2007.01961.x

Wallington, S. A. (1973). Consequences of transgression: Self-punishment and depression. *Journal of Personality and Social Psychology, 28,* 1–7. doi:10.1037/h0035576

Wenzel, M. (2004). An analysis of norm processes in tax compliance. *Journal of Economic Psychology, 25,* 213–228. doi:10.1016/S0167-4870(02)00168-X

Zhong, C. B., & Liljenquist, K. (2006). Washing away your sins: Threatened morality and physical cleansing. *Science, 313,* 1451–1452. doi:10.1126/science.1130726

Zhong, C. B., Liljenquist, K., & Cain, D. M. (2009). Moral self-regulation: Licensing and compensation. In D. De Cremer (Ed.), *Psychological perspectives on ethical behavior and decision making* (pp. 75–89). New York, NY: Information Age Publishing.

Zimbardo, P. G. (1969). The human choice: Individuation, reason, and order vs. deindividuation, impulse, and chaos. In W. J. Arnold & D. Levine (Eds.), *Nebraska symposium on motivation* (pp. 237–307). Lincoln, NE: University of Nebraska Press.

9

MORAL HYPOCRISY, MORAL INCONSISTENCY, AND THE STRUGGLE FOR MORAL INTEGRITY

BENOÎT MONIN AND ANNA MERRITT

If future archaeologists unearthed an untitled social psychology text-book, its cover eaten by discerning worms, they would have to figure out what social psychologists studied from the papers they most prominently featured and the topics that recurrently received the field's attention. One reasonable hypothesis might be that ours was the science of moral hypocrisy. Social psychologists are suspicious of actors' self-reported motives, in part because people are surprisingly unaware of their actual motives (Nisbett & Wilson, 1977), but also because two central features of the social psychological model of human behavior, that people care deeply about making a good impression on others (e.g., Schlenker, 1980) and also wish to hold positive views of themselves (e.g., Greenwald, 1980), contribute to their claiming purer moral intentions than they actually have. More than any other social scientists, social psychologists make a living by showing that proclaimed moral intentions cannot be taken at face value.

DISTINGUISHING MORAL HYPOCRISY
AND MORAL INCONSISTENCY

Hypocrisy is often defined in social psychology as not practicing what you preach (e.g., Stone & Fernandez, 2008), saying one thing and doing another (e.g., Barden, Rucker, & Petty, 2005), or publicly upholding moral norms, especially for others to follow, but personally violating them in private (e.g., Lammers, Stapel, & Galinsky, 2010). Although this has been a useful working definition, and one that has yielded many valuable insights and research findings, we propose to expand the definition of moral hypocrisy beyond behavioral inconsistency.

How can hypocrisy not require inconsistency? The etymology of the term is traced back to the Greek, where it referred to playing a part on a stage. The *Oxford English Dictionary* defines hypocrisy as "the assuming of a false appearance of virtue or goodness, with dissimulation of real character or inclinations, esp. in respect of religious life or beliefs; hence in general sense, dissimulation, pretence, sham" (Hypocrisy, n.d.). This means, first, that the term *moral hypocrisy* is somewhat redundant: Hypocrisy, by definition, refers to virtue or goodness, and it is used in other domains only by extension. In fact, even when used to refer to deception in a nonmoral domain, hypocrisy is still ethically problematic because it involves dishonesty. Second, hypocrisy does not necessarily refer to failing to practice what one preaches. Although that particular behavioral inconsistency is a classic cue for hypocrisy, this is so only because it signals that a speaker may not have believed what he or she was preaching at the time. The central issue is preaching in bad faith, not the failure to practice per se.

Table 9.1 illustrates the disjunction between moral hypocrisy and moral consistency and provides a rough outline for the rest of this chapter. We review studies looking at actors (e.g., Do people practice what they preach? What are the psychological consequences of moral hypocrisy?) and ones in which the focus was reactions to other people's behavior (e.g., When do people perceive inconsistency as hypocrisy?). We propose to review various explorations of (moral) hypocrisy in the social psychological literature and to

TABLE 9.1
Mapping Moral Hypocrisy and Behavioral Inconsistency

	No behavioral inconsistency	Behavioral inconsistency
No hypocrisy	Moral integrity, credentials	Weakness of will, overweighing intentions, balancing, confession
Hypocrisy	Bad faith—ulterior motives, double standards, strategic (de)moralization	Not practicing what one preaches

organize them according to this 2 × 2 framework. We begin with the most familiar case of hypocrisy as inconsistency, or not practicing what one preaches. We then extend our definition of moral hypocrisy by considering cases of hypocrisy without behavioral inconsistency. Next we look at cases of inconsistency without hypocrisy, and we finish with *moral integrity*, which we define as a lack of hypocrisy in the context of consistency. By exploring and expanding the definition of moral hypocrisy, this chapter proposes a novel framework to review the disparate literature on the topic, to identify convergences and divergences between existing findings, and to serve as a starting point for future work in this area.

NOT PRACTICING WHAT ONE PREACHES: MORAL HYPOCRISY AS BEHAVIORAL INCONSISTENCY

The first version of hypocrisy is exemplified in the New Testament, when Jesus says of the "scribes and Pharisees," whom he calls "hypocrites," "Therefore all that they tell you, do and observe, but do not do according to their deeds; for they say things and do not do them" (Matthew 23:3). Not practicing what one preaches has served as the working definition of moral hypocrisy in many social psychological investigations, to which we now turn.

Moral Posturing Without Paying the Price

We argued that demonstrations of moral hypocrisy are plentiful in the social psychological literature, replete as it is with demonstrations of attitude–behavior inconsistencies, rationalizations of problematic behavior, and psychological cover-ups of illicit intentions (see also Chapter 8, this volume). One of the consistent contributors to this long tradition, Daniel Batson, defined *moral hypocrisy* as "morality [being] extolled—even enacted—not with an eye to producing a good and right outcome but in order to appear moral yet still benefit oneself" (Batson, Kobrynowicz, Dinnerstein, Kampf, & Wilson, 1997, p. 1335; see also Batson, Thompson, Seuferling, Whitney, & Strongman, 1999; and Batson, Thompson, & Chen, 2002). Batson and his colleagues asked participants to assign experimental tasks to themselves and an unknown participant, knowing that one task was more fun and rewarding than the other. Participants were given an opportunity to flip a coin while alone to make the decision, but it was made clear that this was not required. In a typical study (Batson et al., 1997, Study 2), half of the participants decided to flip the coin and declared it the fairest way to allocate roles, but the biased proportion of flippers who claimed to obtain the better result for themselves by chance (90%) was the same as the proportion of nonflippers who just grabbed the better task for themselves. Although the deception involved in this second maneuver is striking, the choice to flip a coin when it was not required (knowing it was going to lead to deception, if necessary) is just as surprising and speaks to the desire to appear fair and just, even when one may not be planning to pay the consequences. Hypocritical participants preached fairness but fudged their coin-toss results to make sure that they, and not another unsuspecting participant, got the better of the two tasks.

Ascribing Hypocrisy to Others Who Do Not Practice What They Preach

Another productive line of research has documented factors contributing to judgments of hypocrisy by observers. For example, an individual who makes grand claims about the importance of morality and is then found cheating is seen as hypocritical (Gilbert & Jones, 1986), as is someone who publicly commits to diet and exercise and is subsequently found to be a junk-food-eating slouch (Barden et al., 2005). Hypocrisy also wipes out the positive effects of prior good deeds, which would otherwise make even blatant violations in the same domain seem more acceptable in the eyes of observers—as they do when hypocrisy is controlled for, proving that hypocrisy undoes the licensing effect of prior good deeds (Effron & Monin, 2010).

The Consequences of Not Practicing What One Preaches

What are the consequences of hypocrisy for the self? Early cognitive dissonance researchers (Festinger & Carlsmith, 1959; Mills, 1958) showed that lying and cheating are uncomfortable and that people attempt to alleviate this discomfort. One of the early members of the initial dissonance research group, Elliot Aronson, later looked directly at hypocrisy, defined as not practicing what one preaches (Aronson, Fried, & Stone, 1991; for a review, see Stone & Fernandez, 2008). Whereas early dissonance research had focused on the darker side of rationalization, Aronson and his student Jeff Stone aimed to harness dissonance for positive change by inducing a feeling of hypocrisy. For example, individuals who both publicly advocated safe sex and were later reminded of past failures to use condoms were more than twice as likely to buy condoms for future use (Stone, Aronson, Crain, Winslow, & Fried, 1994), as were various control groups, establishing the need for both advocacy and failure reminders. The need to resolve this hypocrisy directly was demonstrated by showing that when given the choice, individuals preferred to engage in behavior that matched what they preached. Participants reminded of their lack of volunteerism after advocating for it chose to donate to the Student Volunteer Council more than they chose to buy condoms, even though using condoms was more important to their global self-worth than donating (Stone, Wiegand, Cooper, & Aronson, 1997).

BAD FAITH AND ULTERIOR MOTIVES: MORAL HYPOCRISY WITHOUT BEHAVIORAL INCONSISTENCY

Although this first definition of moral hypocrisy as behavioral inconsistency has inspired some important research, there are also cases, which we address next, in which hypocrisy occurs in the absence of behavioral inconsistency. The reason why behavioral inconsistency is a convenient proxy for hypocrisy is that it suggests disingenuousness at the time of the "preaching." As the dictionary definition of hypocrisy (the "false appearance of virtue") reminds us, however, it is disingenuousness that is the main issue, not the "practice" itself. We therefore propose to broaden the study of moral hypocrisy to include any claim of morality made to satisfy ulterior (nonmoral), self-serving motives. Batson et al.'s (1997) coin flippers were exposed by the departure of their outcomes from mathematical odds, which is how we know that they did not practice what they preached, but their hypocrisy lay in claiming the moral high road with little resolve to follow through. Moral hypocrisy was thus exposed within subjects—the paradigmatic case of not practicing what one preaches, or behavioral inconsistency. In the cases reviewed in this section, the hypocrisy is often exposed between subjects in that moral judgments and intentions are influenced by situational manipulations demonstrating the opportunistic, self-serving use of morality, or moral hypocrisy in the absence of behavioral inconsistency.

Moral Hypocrisy as Applying a Double Standard

One way to pursue this approach is to show that individuals hold themselves and others to different moral standards. In a paradigm inspired by Batson et al.'s task allocation studies, Valdesolo and DeSteno (2007) found that participants rated other participants who assigned themselves the better task as significantly less fair than they rated themselves when they did the same thing. A similar double standard applied when judging an outgroup member rather than an ingroup member. Moreover, this difference disappeared under a cognitive load, suggesting that the double standard involves effortful rationalization when the self is involved (Valdesolo & DeSteno, 2008), and it was enhanced when individuals imagined themselves in high-power roles (Lammers et al., 2010). Note that, within participants, these results would have been cases of not practicing what one preaches, but because self–other comparisons were always between participants (some participants judged their own behavior, whereas others judged the same choice made by others), the moral hypocrisy exposed across experimental conditions did not involve behavioral inconsistency. Instead, what strikes readers as hypocritical is the fact that individuals did not seem to be making objective decisions or applying ethical standards in good faith. They allowed self-interest to affect their judgments of fairness, even expending cognitive effort to do so.

Strategic Moralization: Moral Hypocrisy as Jealousy With a Halo

Another form of moral bad faith and standard shifting involves moral indignation that does not come from a sincere concern for ethical principles but instead serves to make a person feel better about another form of inadequacy. If I follow silly rules, abide by nonsensical norms, or agree to do undeserved favors, I might feel a sting to my sense of being a rational, independent person when I see someone else acting in more self-interested ways. Whereas I might have admired this rebellion in the abstract, the threat to my self-worth may cause me to moralize my conformity and condemn the rule breaker for the expedient results he or she obtained and that I wish I had. In the words of H. G. Wells (1914), this kind of moral indignation boils down to "jealousy with a halo" (p. 299). Assuming a false appearance of virtue serves a very real self-protective function of compensating for felt inferiority on another dimension. Here hypocrisy does not result from an inherent lack of virtue; it reflects instead that the claim to virtue comes from an unsavory place.

A. H. Jordan and Monin (2008) found that when individuals agreed to perform a tedious task as a favor to an experimenter and then discovered that another participant had refused to do the same thing, they rated themselves as more moral and rated the other as less moral than when they simply witnessed the refusal without doing the task themselves or did the task without observing the refusal. Furthermore, this "sucker-to-saint" compensation effect disappeared when participants were first self-affirmed (Sherman & Cohen, 2006; Steele, 1988) by reflecting on one of their important traits or values, suggesting that the function of moralization was indeed to shore up a threatened ego. This strategic moralization is a case of moral hypocrisy without inconsistency; the moral calculus seems to be based on self-serving considerations, but it is not a case of not practicing what one preaches.

Strategic Demoralization: Moral Hypocrisy as the Denial of Virtue

Another case of hypocrisy without inconsistency involves the bad-faith denial of virtue. The same exemplary behavior that is recognized as morally superior by uninvolved observers is received with considerably less respect from individuals whose self-image is threatened by comparison. Participants in a study by Monin, Sawyer, and Marquez (2008, Study 2) discovered that the peer whose responses they were to evaluate had refused to complete a task because he considered it offensively racist (the obvious culprit in a whodunit story was the sole Black suspect). As expected, observers rated this rebel as more moral than an obedient control. Moral hypocrisy came into play when participants had themselves completed the task beforehand: Having overwhelmingly accused the Black suspect, they now denied the morality of the rebel's stance and in fact liked and respected him less than an obedient control. Note that the fact that observers who did not themselves make the choice liked the rebel more than an obedient control suggests that it is not simply the rebel's apparent disregard for the facts of the case that made the rebel unlikable. As with moralization, the self-protective nature of demoralization was demonstrated by the fact that self-affirmed individuals readily acknowledged the greater morality (and agency) of rebels and also liked them more (Monin et al., 2008, Study 4). In both cases, judgments of morality (high or low) seemed less based on real moral convictions and more based on the situational expediency of self-defense (see the related discussion of "inauthentic" moral choices in Chapter 14, this volume).

Suspicion and the Ascription of Bad Faith and Ulterior Motives to Others

We have seen how individuals who do not practice what they preach are taxed with hypocrisy. We now turn to hypocrisy without inconsistency. Suspicion about virtuous motives is easily elicited (Fein, Hilton, & Miller, 1990), and moral behavior is spontaneously chalked up to situational demands instead of moral dispositions (Ybarra, 2002), so any moral behavior exposes one to the charge of moral hypocrisy, especially if it makes others feel less morally adequate (Monin, 2007). Wiltermuth, Monin, and Chow (2010) found that the willingness to give moral credit to individuals who engaged in proactive moral behavior (e.g., volunteering) was unrelated to the general tendency to condemn immoral behavior (for a related discussion, see Chapter 7, this volume). Many cynical respondents were quite condemning of moral violations but saw little evidence of morality in even the most exemplary civic-minded behavior, suggesting that moral displays can be taken with a grain of salt even by people who otherwise care deeply about morality.

Furthermore, the importance given to holding "appropriate" mental states congruent with one's public behavior depends on cultural frameworks such as religion. Cohen and Rozin (2001) found that American Protestants were significantly more likely than Jews, for example, to attribute hypocrisy to an actor who treats his parents well despite not liking them, which the authors ascribed to a Protestant belief that people can control their thoughts and should be held morally accountable for them (cf. Jimmy Carter's famous "I have committed adultery in my heart").

Thus, hypocrisy can be ascribed to actors even if they do not meet the classic criterion of not practicing what they preach. Individuals grant morality to others only reluctantly and readily attribute moral hypocrisy, bad faith, and ulterior motives when they encounter putative moral behavior.

THE COMPLEXITIES OF MORAL LIFE: INCONSISTENCY WITHOUT HYPOCRISY

We have discussed hypocrisy without inconsistency to contrast it with the more classic case of not practicing what one preaches. But when people do act inconsistently, does hypocrisy necessarily follow? We suggest that there are many situations in which people act in opposition to their moral values without feeling hypocritical; for example, when preaching has intrinsic value whether or not the preacher adheres to his or her own guidelines, when people behave badly but had the best of intentions, when good deeds license bad ones by balancing them out, and when inconsistency occurs across differing construal levels.

Is It Always Wrong to Preach Without Practicing?

The self-evident wrongness of not practicing what one preaches deserves a second look. If someone endorses a given course of action but is unable to follow through with it, does that necessarily invalidate the appropriateness of that course of action and make the preaching worthless? Note that in Jesus's admonition to do as the Pharisees say but not as they do, he still advises his audience to follow the Pharisees' edicts: As experts in the law, they should be turned to for guidance. Would it be better if, knowing they could not follow through in their deeds, they avoided the charge of hypocrisy by staying quiet and offering no prescriptions?

The utilitarian philosopher Peter Singer presents an interesting case. Following utilitarianism to its ultimate conclusions, and taking into account marginal utility, he argued (e.g., Singer, 1972) that it would be more ethical for citizens of the developed world to spend the vast sums of money they spend keeping their parents alive in old age on children in developing countries, where that wealth would have a much greater beneficial effect. When Singer came to the United States to take a position at Princeton University, much was made of the fact (e.g., Berkowitz, 2000; Specter, 1999) that he was spending considerable funds tending to his sick mother, in apparent violation of his own edicts. Likewise, Al Gore was famously criticized for owning several energy-guzzling houses despite having preached the "inconvenient truth" of global warming. As with the Pharisees, do these apparent failures to follow through make Peter Singer and Al Gore wrong for arguing as they did? Assuming they knew that their own behavior would not change, was it better for the world if they kept their theories to themselves, avoiding the charge of hypocrisy, or if they preached long and loud, hoping to affect other people's behavior?

We argue that there is great value in Singer's working through the complex ethical arguments that would produce a clear utilitarian prescription suitable to contemporary readers, even if he did not always follow his own prescriptions. Otherwise, it would be like faulting an ice skating judge for not being able to perform a triple Salchow or dismissing a physician's recommendation to stop smoking because his or her breath smells of tobacco. When one can make inherently valuable recommendations, it might be one's moral duty to preach—even if one is not always practicing. We view this as a case of inconsistency without hypocrisy.

Weakness of the Will and Unrealistic Intentions

A common explanation for inconsistency between one's stated intention and one's subsequent behavior is a simple inability to follow through for lack of ability, resources, or willpower. This differs from hypocrisy in that the intentions may have been stated in good faith while overestimating one's ability to implement them. Rest (1984), in his four-step model of moral behavior, incorporated follow-through or implementation as Step 4, after (1) interpreting the situation, (2) identifying the morally ideal course of action, and (3) intending to try to live up to one's moral ideal. Here the vast literature on self-regulation provides an abundance of models (e.g., Baumeister, Bratslavsky, Muraven, & Tice, 1998; Fishbach, Zhang, & Koo, 2009) explaining why individuals do not always follow through on their laudable intentions. The important point for our purposes is not that people suffer from weakness of the will, but rather that this type of behavior–intention inconsistency may not be as problematic for people as preaching one thing and practicing another. Falling short of good intentions does not strike us as hypocritical because the intentions were not expressed in bad faith; instead, the inconsistency results from weakness of the will, what philosophers call *incontinence* or *akrasia* (see also Monin, Pizarro, & Beer, 2007).

Moral talk is cheap compared to moral action, which explains why stated intentions may not always be implemented. This disjunction may be due in part to a common planning fallacy—people generally overestimate the time and resources available in the future and underestimate other practical demands (Liberman & Trope, 1998). For example, Epley and Dunning (2000) showed that students overestimated their likelihood of donating to a fraternity fundraiser and the amount they would donate. One ambiguity with asking respondents to indicate their likelihood of performing desirable behaviors is that it confounds two separate questions: asking them how much they care about the cause (and what they would want to do in an ideal world) and asking them to generate realistic predictions about their own behavior. When Tanner and Carlson (2009) specifically separated these two questions by asking a group of participants both what they would do in an ideal world and what they were realistically going to do, they found that ideal answers were very much in line with what participants reported when simply asked to state their intentions. However, after the ideal world question, participants' predictions about their future behavior were much less rosy and more in line with what they predicted for others in the original version. Liberman and Trope (1998) suggested that one reason for the mismatch between present intentions and future behavior involves level of construal: Whereas donating in the future relates mostly to the kind of person one wants to be and is therefore free of reality constraints, being asked to donate now forces one to question whether one has the time, ready cash, or other demands on one's attention and is therefore likely to yield a very different result (see Chapter 10, this volume). These factors can lead people not to follow through on their intentions despite having formulated them in perfectly good faith.

Giving More Weight to One's Moral Intentions

The very fact of holding laudable intentions may allow some people to feel they have already done their share, paradoxically relaxing the need to implement these intentions. In some surveys, individuals readily reported gaps between their moral concerns and their moral behavior. White and Plous (1995) found both that a large majority of respondents reported caring about issues such as homelessness or animal protection more than average and that the majority also reported doing less than average on these same issues. Respondents seemed unbothered by this apparent failure to practice what they preached; in fact, they generally said that whereas the public was not worried enough about these issues, they personally showed the right level of concern.

How do people manage to acknowledge such inconsistencies without feeling hypocritical? One explanation seems to be that they place greater weight on their intentions than on their actions when evaluating their own morality, but not when evaluating the morality of other people. In one study, participants estimated how long they would hold their hand in painfully cold water when experimenters pledged to donate 50 cents to a charity of each participant's choice for every minute of suffering (Kruger & Gilovich, 2004).

When participants actually had to submerge their hands in the icy water, many fell short of their altruistic intentions. However, participants' estimates of their own altruism were driven by their intentions, not by the time they actually held their hand in the water. Observers, by contrast, assessed the participants' altruism based on submersion time alone and did not place much weight on intentions. This egocentric bias is compounded by a difference in availability; we know a great deal about our own intentions and how genuine they are, but we often know little about others' intentions and nothing about their good faith.

Redemption and the Possibility of Positive Change

Another case in which behavioral inconsistency is not necessarily hypocritical is when there is a possibility of personal change or redemption between one's practicing and one's preaching. Indeed, the order in which someone practices and preaches determines whether observers judge the person as hypocritical. As we have seen, if a target first makes a statement about a personal standard (e.g., promoting a get-fit campaign) and then engages in behavior that goes against that standard (e.g., sitting on the couch and eating junk food for the next week), the person will be judged a hypocrite—but much less so if he or she commits to the standard only after violating it, because observers interpret this inconsistency as "turning a new leaf" (Barden et al., 2005). The fact that this behavioral inconsistency (not practicing and then preaching) is not encoded as moral hypocrisy reveals once more that the real issue when one fails to practice what one preaches is not the behavioral inconsistency but instead the good faith of the preaching. Given that the redemption template assumes good faith despite previous failings, inconsistency is unimportant in determining hypocrisy.

This analysis of the temporal sequence of preaching and practicing casts a new light on Stone et al.'s (1994, 1997) induced hypocrisy studies mentioned earlier. In these studies, participants were made aware that they had acted inconsistently—for example, by first promoting condom use to prevent AIDS but then recalling that they had had unprotected sex in the past. Because these failures preceded the preaching, they might have raised doubts about the participants' good faith when promoting safe sex, but without quite invalidating it yet. In fact, by subsequently choosing to buy condoms, participants replaced a potential narrative of hypocrisy with a narrative of redemption. They saw the error of their ways and were now acting in line with what they preached.

Moral Licensing, Moral Credits, and Moral Balance

Inconsistency may also avoid being viewed as hypocrisy if good and bad deeds are perceived as balancing each other. For example, someone who cares about being healthy could reasonably exercise vigorously in the morning (a "good" deed) and eat a big piece of chocolate cake in the afternoon (a "bad" deed) without feeling hypocritical. The actions are inconsistent, but because they balance each other out, they do not interfere too much with the higher level goal of being healthy. In the moral domain, Nisan (1991) argued that people are just concerned with maintaining some "good enough" level of morality and will balance good and bad deeds to remain at that baseline. In a sense, this moral balance model works like a bank account—one earns moral credits (not to be confused with *credentials*, discussed later) by acting morally and can make withdrawals through immoral actions as long as the balance does not drop below baseline. People who remember their past moral behavior feel less compelled to give for a good cause, as if they had already done enough good deeds for the day (Sachdeva, Iliev, & Medin, 2009; see also J. Jordan, Mullen, & Murnighan, in press). In the eyes of observers, moral credits need to be accrued in a different moral domain, or they will be seen as hypocritical and therefore ineffective at licensing a blatant transgression (Effron & Monin, 2010). For example, a person renowned for promoting ethnic diversity in the workplace was judged more leniently when accused of blatant sexual harassment but was not helped in a case of blatant racial discrimination.

Behavioral Inconsistency and Construal Levels

Behavioral inconsistency can also result from differing levels of construal. Behaviors can be construed at various levels of abstraction, with greater distance (spatial or temporal) leading to higher level construal (Liberman & Trope, 1998; see also Chapter 10, this volume). Psychological distance increases when an event or behavior is farther away in time, does not directly affect the self, or is conceptualized in terms of its abstract, higher order qualities (Ledgerwood, Trope, & Liberman, 2010), and people are more likely to reflect their underlying ideology when the event or behavior is psychologically distant rather than near (Ledgerwood, Trope, & Chaiken, 2010).

As a result, individuals are more value driven about the future than about the present (Liberman & Trope, 1998). In one study, people evaluated offensive but harmless transgressions (e.g., eating the family dog after it got run over by a car) as less wrong when they were supposedly going to occur tomorrow (low construal level) than when they were going to occur next year (high, or abstract, construal level; Eyal, Liberman, & Trope, 2008; see also Chapter 10, this volume). To the extent that preaching (future) and practicing (present) tap into different levels of construal, inconsistency is thus to be expected even in the absence of bad faith.

Construal level also moderates inconsistency concerns when two behaviors that appear inconsistent on the surface can be framed as serving the same higher level moral goal, as in the case of confessing one's bad deeds. Writing down one's failures after claiming good intentions supposedly elicits feelings of hypocrisy (Stone et al., 1994), so people should want to avoid listing many failures to avoid feeling more hypocritical; yet participants who advocated safe sex listed more instances of failure to use condoms than those who did not take a public stand (Aronson et al., 1991). How can we resolve this apparent inconsistency? The key may be that stating one's values elevates the level of construal, highlighting that although the behaviors being confessed are at odds with the value being espoused, the act of confessing is actually in line with the value.

Consistent with this prediction, Merritt and Monin (2010) found that people listed more environmentally unfriendly behaviors (by either themselves or a peer) after writing about why they cared about the environment than after writing about their "green" habits or about a control topic. Presumably, people who wrote about their abstract concern for the environment construed confession at a higher level and were motivated to list environmentally harmful behaviors to show their commitment and to demonstrate their vigilance and low tolerance for harmful behavior. By contrast, people who wrote about their environmentally friendly behaviors may have felt that subsequently listing environmentally harmful behaviors would make them appear hypocritical, as good and bad environmental behaviors were at the same low level of construal and thus readily comparable. And indeed, in contrast to the effect of writing why they cared, listing green habits reduced the number of harmful behaviors listed only for the self but not for a peer.

THE STRUGGLE FOR MORAL INTEGRITY

We stressed the difference between moral inconsistency and moral hypocrisy, highlighting the novel cases of hypocrisy without inconsistency and inconsistency without hypocrisy. The remaining cell in Table 9.1 represents the ideal of moral integrity, in which moral intentions are pure and based solely on noble and just considerations and in which moral behavior is consistent, in line with one's public pronouncements and best intentions.

Confidence in one's moral integrity can license one to engage in otherwise problematic behavior without appearing or feeling inconsistent because one has demonstrated one's moral credentials (Effron, Cameron, & Monin, 2009; Merrit, Effron, & Monin, 2010; Monin & Miller, 2001) or because one feels one's group is especially moral (see Chapter 18, this volume). In a study by Effron and Monin (2010), observers judged a target who had an established record of fostering diversity at his firm. When he later failed to promote African American employees and a leaked e-mail revealed that he thought their race made them unsuitable for management (a blatant transgression), raters viewed him as a hypocrite and gave him no credit for his prior good deeds. However, when the transgression was ambiguous—he claimed the African American employees had not performed as well as others and denied discrimination—then his past good deeds caused judges to rate him more positively than a control who did not have credentials, and this was mediated by a change in their perception of the potential transgression. They did not say it was acceptable for him to discriminate (as a moral balance model would), but they construed the behavior differently, as not being a case of discrimination in the first place. Thus, in a top-down fashion, the perception of integrity takes inconsistency off the table. Individuals seem to use a similar logic when deciding if their own past behavior licenses them to make seemingly inconsistent choices (Monin & Miller, 2001).

Another factor that contributes to less opportunistic or self-serving uses of morality, and therefore fosters moral integrity, is whether individuals feel secure that they are good, effective people, as they do when they are self-affirmed by reflecting on values or traits that are important to them (Steele, 1988). Sherman and Cohen (2006) emphasized that self-affirmation manipulations might be shoring up personal integrity, allowing individuals to be less defensive in the face of ego threats. We described previously how, in two experimental paradigms that elicited moral hypocrisy—strategic moralization, or the sucker-to-saint effect (A. H. Jordan & Monin, 2008), and strategic demoralization, or the denial of virtue (Monin et al., 2008)—the simple addition of a self-affirming essay was enough to wipe out moral hypocrisy. Thus, to the extent that moral hypocrisy often serves self-protective functions, buttressing the integrity of the self is one avenue to greater moral integrity.

CONCLUSION

In this chapter, we have attempted to deconstruct the notion of not practicing what one preaches, which is a common working definition of moral hypocrisy, as a way of questioning the link between hypocrisy and inconsistency and as a framework for reviewing recent research bearing on this issue. This strategy gave us license to analyze the two novel categories of hypocrisy without inconsistency and inconsistency without hypocrisy. The first, hypocrisy without inconsistency, broadens the scope of moral hypocrisy research to encompass the bad-faith invocation of moral claims by actors whose real motivation is self-serving or the toning down of moral concerns when they threaten the self. The second category, inconsistency without hypocrisy, drew our attention to the complexity of moral life and the fact that individuals constantly face moral inconsistency without necessarily feeling like hypocrites or being perceived as such by other people.

In general, moral hypocrisy involves claiming to be moral for nonmoral reasons. Although we began by arguing that moral hypocrisy was central to social psychology, at the same time social psychology finds itself in an awkward position to comment on moral hypocrisy. Even if a person displayed perfectly good-faith moral integrity, psychologists, depending on their leaning, would want to dissect the motivating, status-earning, self-actualizing, evolutionarily adaptive, and so forth, functions of such a mental state. In other words, for a deterministic, descriptive scientist, there will always be a nonmoral intention prior to a moral intention, even if it is one that people are unaware of. In their everyday lives, social psychologists need to reconcile their knowledge that moral judgments are shaped by situational factors and self-serving biases with the hope that good intentions can be trusted and accept that individuals are often in good faith even when they erroneously believe that their intentions are moral.

REFERENCES

Aronson, E., Fried, C., & Stone, J. (1991). Overcoming denial and increasing the intention to use condoms through the induction of hypocrisy. *American Journal of Public Health, 81*, 1636–1638. doi:10.2105/AJPH.81.12.1636

Barden, J., Rucker, D. D., & Petty, R. E. (2005). "Saying one thing and doing another": Examining the impact of event order on hypocrisy judgments of others. *Personality and Social Psychology Bulletin, 31*, 1463–1474. doi:10.1177/0146167205276430

Batson, C. D., Kobrynowicz, D., Dinnerstein, J. L., Kampf, H. C., & Wilson, A. D. (1997). In a very different voice: Unmasking moral hypocrisy. *Journal of Personality and Social Psychology, 72*, 1335–1348. doi:10.1037/0022-3514.72.6.1335

Batson, C. D., Thompson, E. R., & Chen, H. (2002). Moral hypocrisy: Addressing some alternatives. *Journal of Personality and Social Psychology, 83*, 330–339. doi:10.1037/0022-3514.83.2.330

Batson, C. D., Thompson, E. R., Seuferling, G., Whitney, H., & Strongman, J. A. (1999). Moral hypocrisy: Appearing moral to oneself without being so. *Journal of Personality and Social Psychology, 77*, 525–537. doi:10.1037/0022-3514.77.3.525

Baumeister, R. F., Bratslavsky, E., Muraven, M., & Tice, D. M. (1998). Ego depletion: Is the active self a limited resource? *Journal of Personality and Social Psychology, 74*, 1252–1265. doi:10.1037/0022-3514.74.5.1252

Berkowitz, P. (2000, January 10). Other people's mothers: The utilitarian horrors of Peter Singer. *New Republic*, 27–37.

Cohen, A. B., & Rozin, P. (2001). Religion and the morality of mentality. *Journal of Personality and Social Psychology, 81,* 697–710. doi:10.1037/0022-3514.81.4.697

Effron, D. A., Cameron, J. S., & Monin, B. (2009). Endorsing Obama licenses favoring Whites. *Journal of Experimental Social Psychology, 45,* 590–593. doi:10.1016/j.jesp.2009.02.001

Effron, D. A., & Monin, B. (2010). Letting people off the hook: When do good deeds excuse transgressions? *Personality and Social Psychology Bulletin, 36,* 1618–1634. doi:10.1177/0146167210385922

Epley, N., & Dunning, D. (2000). Feeling "holier than thou": Are self-serving assessments produced by errors in self or social prediction? *Journal of Personality and Social Psychology, 79,* 861–875. doi:10.1037/0022-3514.79.6.861

Eyal, T., Liberman, N., & Trope, Y. (2008). Judging near and distant virtue and vice. *Journal of Experimental Social Psychology, 44,* 1204–1209. doi:10.1016/j.jesp.2008.03.012

Fein, S., Hilton, J. L., & Miller, D. T. (1990). Suspicion of ulterior motivation and the correspondence bias. *Journal of Personality and Social Psychology, 58,* 753–764. doi:10.1037/0022-3514.58.5.753

Festinger, L., & Carlsmith, J. M. (1959). Cognitive consequences of forced compliance. *Journal of Abnormal and Social Psychology, 58,* 203–210. doi:10.1037/h0041593

Fishbach, A., Zhang, Y., & Koo, M. (2009). The dynamics of self-regulation. *European Review of Social Psychology, 20,* 315–344. doi:10.1080/10463280903275375

Gilbert, D. T., & Jones, E. E. (1986). Exemplification: The self-presentation of moral character. *Journal of Personality, 54,* 593–615. doi:10.1111/j.1467-6494.1986.tb00414.x

Greenwald, A. G. (1980). The totalitarian ego: Fabrication and revision of personal history. *American Psychologist, 35,* 603–618. doi:10.1037/0003-066X.35.7.603

Hypocrisy. (n.d.). In *Oxford English Dictionary.* Retrieved from http://www.oed.com/

Jordan, A. H., & Monin, B. (2008). From sucker to saint: Moralization in response to self-threat. *Psychological Science, 19,* 809–815. doi:10.1111/j.1467-9280.2008.02161.x

Jordan, J., Mullen, E., & Murnighan, J. K. (in press). Striving for the moral self: The effects of recalling past moral actions on future moral behavior. *Personality and Social Psychology Bulletin.*

Kruger, J., & Gilovich, T. (2004). Actions, intentions, and self-assessment: The road to self-enhancement is paved with good intentions. *Personality and Social Psychology Bulletin, 30,* 328–339. doi:10.1177/0146167203259932

Lammers, J., Stapel, D. A., & Galinsky, A. D. (2010). Power increases hypocrisy: Moralizing in reasoning, immorality in behavior. *Psychological Science, 21,* 737–744. doi:10.1177/0956797610368810

Ledgerwood, A., Trope, Y., & Chaiken, S. (2010). Flexibility now, consistency later: Psychological distance and construal shape evaluative responding. *Journal of Personality and Social Psychology, 99,* 32–51.

Ledgerwood, A., Trope, Y., & Liberman, N. (2010). Flexibility and consistency in evaluative responding: The function of construal level. *Advances in Experimental Social Psychology, 43,* 257–295.

Liberman, N., & Trope, Y. (1998). The role of feasibility and desirability considerations in near and distant future decisions: A test of temporal construal theory. *Journal of Personality and Social Psychology, 75,* 5–18. doi:10.1037/0022-3514.75.1.5

Merritt, A. C., Effron, D. A., & Monin, B. (2010). Moral self-licensing: When being good frees us to be bad. *Social and Personality Psychology Compass, 4,* 344–357.

Merritt, A., & Monin, B. (2010, January). *Coming clean about (not) being green: Value assertions increase admissions of environmentally unfriendly behavior.* Poster session presented at the annual meeting of the Society for Personality and Social Psychology, Las Vegas, NV.

Mills, J. (1958). Changes in moral attitudes following temptation. *Journal of Personality, 26,* 517–531. doi:10.1111/j.1467-6494.1958.tb02349.x

Monin, B. (2007). Holier than me? Threatening social comparison in the moral domain. *Revue Internationale de Psychologie Sociale, 20,* 53–68.

Monin, B., & Miller, D. T. (2001). Moral credentials and the expression of prejudice. *Journal of Personality and Social Psychology, 81,* 33–43. doi:10.1037/0022-3514.81.1.33

Monin, B., Pizarro, D., & Beer, J. (2007). Emotion and reason in moral judgment: Different prototypes lead to different theories. In K. D. Vohs, R. F. Baumeister, & G. Loewenstein (Eds.), *Do emotions help or hurt decision making? A hedgefoxian perspective* (pp. 219–244). New York, NY: Russell Sage.

Monin, B., Sawyer, P., & Marquez, M. (2008). The rejection of moral rebels: Resenting those who do the right thing. *Journal of Personality and Social Psychology, 95,* 76–93. doi:10.1037/0022-3514.95.1.76

Nisan, M. (1991). The moral balance model: Theory and research extending our understanding of moral choice and deviation. In W. M. Kurtines & J. L. Gewirtz (Eds.), *Handbook of moral behavior and development* (pp. 213–249). Hillsdale, NJ: Erlbaum.

Nisbett, R. E., & Wilson, T. D. (1977). Telling more than we can know: Verbal reports on mental processes. *Psychological Review, 84,* 231–259. doi:10.1037/0033-295X.84.3.231

Rest, J. (1984). The major components of morality. In W. Kurtines & J. Gerwitz (Eds.), *Morality, moral development, and moral behavior* (pp. 24–38). New York, NY: Wiley.

Sachdeva, S., Iliev, R., & Medin, D. L. (2009). Sinning saints and saintly sinners: The paradox of moral self-regulation. *Psychological Science, 20,* 523–528. doi:10.1111/j.1467-9280.2009.02326.x

Schlenker, B. R. (1980). *Impression management: The self-concept, social identity, and interpersonal relations.* Monterey, CA: Brooks/Cole.

Sherman, D. K., & Cohen, G. L. (2006). The psychology of self-defense: Self-affirmation theory. In M. P. Zanna (Ed.), *Advances in experimental social psychology* (Vol. 38, pp. 183–242). San Diego, CA: Academic Press.

Singer, P. (1972). Famine, affluence, and morality. *Philosophy & Public Affairs, 1,* 229–243.

Specter, M. (1999, September 6). The dangerous philosopher. *New Yorker,* pp. 46–55.

Steele, C. M. (1988). The psychology of self-affirmation: Sustaining the integrity of the self. In L. Berkowitz (Ed.), *Advances in experimental social psychology* (Vol. 21, pp. 261–302). San Diego, CA: Academic Press.

Stone, J., Aronson, E., Crain, A. L., Winslow, M. P., & Fried, C. B. (1994). Inducing hypocrisy as a means of encouraging young adults to use condoms. *Personality and Social Psychology Bulletin, 20,* 116–128. doi:10.1177/0146167294201012

Stone, J., & Fernandez, N. C. (2008). To practice what we preach: The use of hypocrisy and cognitive dissonance to motivate behavior change. *Social and Personality Psychology Compass, 2,* 1024–1051. doi:10.1111/j.1751-9004.2008.00088.x

Stone, J., Wiegand, A. W., Cooper, J., & Aronson, E. (1997). When exemplification fails: Hypocrisy and the motive for self-integrity. *Journal of Personality and Social Psychology, 72,* 54–65. doi:10.1037/0022-3514.72.1.54

Tanner, R. J., & Carlson, K. A. (2009). Unrealistically optimistic consumers: A selective hypothesis testing account for optimism in predictions of future behavior. *Journal of Consumer Research, 35,* 810–822. doi:10.1086/593690

Valdesolo, P., & DeSteno, D. A. (2007). Moral hypocrisy: Social groups and the flexibility of virtue. *Psychological Science, 18,* 689–690. doi:10.1111/j.1467-9280.2007.01961.x

Valdesolo, P., & DeSteno, D. A. (2008). The duality of virtue: Deconstructing the moral hypocrite. *Journal of Experimental Social Psychology, 44,* 1334–1338. doi:10.1016/j.jesp.2008.03.010

Wells, H. G. (1914). *The wife of Sir Isaac Harman.* New York, NY: Macmillan.

White, J., & Plous, S. (1995). Self-enhancement and social responsibility: On caring more, but doing less, than others. *Journal of Applied Social Psychology, 25,* 1297–1318. doi:10.1111/j.1559-1816.1995.tb02619.x

Wiltermuth, S., Monin, B., & Chow, R. (2010). The orthogonality of praise and condemnation in moral judgment. *Social Psychological and Personality Science, 1,* 302–310. doi:10.1177/1948550610363162

Ybarra, O. (2002). Naïve causal understanding of valenced behaviors and its implication for social information processing. *Psychological Bulletin, 128,* 421–441. doi:10.1037/0033-2909.128.3.421

10

MORALITY AND PSYCHOLOGICAL DISTANCE: A CONSTRUAL LEVEL THEORY PERSPECTIVE

TAL EYAL AND NIRA LIBERMAN

People often think in terms of moral principles, values, and ideologies. For example, a woman might characterize herself as someone who values loyalty, social power, or a sustainable environment. Another person might think of donating money to the poor as a way of promoting social justice or fighting inequality. Moral principles and values often guide people's actions, judgments, and predictions. Once a moral rule is invoked, an action is likely to be judged positively when it follows the rule and negatively when it violates the rule. Clearly, however, moral principles and values are not always invoked and often fail to guide people's choices and judgments. Individuals often fail to see the relevance of a value to a particular situation and hence act in ways that reflect situational constraints, local pressures, self-interest, or other considerations that have nothing to do with moral values.

In this chapter, we explore the possibility that values and moral principles are more prominent in judgments and predictions regarding psychologically more distant events. This perspective is based on construal level theory (CLT; Liberman & Trope, 2008; Trope & Liberman, 2010), according to which the construal of psychologically more distant situations highlights their abstract, higher level features. Because values and moral rules tend to be abstract and general, people are more likely to use them in construing, judging, and planning with respect to psychologically more distant situations.

In this chapter, we present the basic assumptions of CLT and explain how they apply to values and moral principles. We then discuss research examining how psychological distance affects (a) judgments of moral and immoral acts, (b) value-based plans, and (c) value-based persuasion. We also examine novel predictions of CLT with respect to the place of values and principles in people's lives.

CONSTRUAL LEVEL THEORY

CLT (Liberman, Trope, Macrea, & Sherman, 2007; Liberman & Trope, 2008; Trope & Liberman, 2010) rests on the notion, shared by many social psychological and cognitive theories, that any object can be mentally represented in different ways (e.g., Ross & Nisbett, 1991). CLT further distinguishes between high-level and low-level construals. Lower level construals are concrete, contextualized representations that include subordinate and incidental features of events. Higher level construals are abstract, schematic, and decontextualized representations that extract the gist from the available information. They emphasize superordinate, essential features of events and omit incidental features that may vary without significantly changing the events' meaning. Consider, for example, the behavior "taking notes in class." A low-level construal of that action might include details of the pen used for writing, the type of paper written on, and the speed of writing. A high-level construal of the same action, however, would omit these details and represent it as "summarizing the lecture" and even "being conscientious."

A central contention of CLT is that psychologically more distant objects are construed on a higher, more abstract level. An object is psychologically distant to the extent that it is remote from direct sensual experience in time (future or past) or in space, refers to the experiences of other people (e.g., relatives, acquaintances, strangers), and is unlikely to occur. According to CLT, objects that are more distant on any dimension will be represented more abstractly because higher-level construals capture the features of objects that remain relatively invariant with increasing distance and thus maintain consistency and enable prediction across distance. Well in advance, the person in our classroom example might have intended to take notes, but he might not have known which pen he would use. Similarly, high-level features tend to change less than low-level features across social distance: Many people take notes, but some use laptop computers or pencils rather than pens.

The effect of psychological distance on construal level has been demonstrated in many studies with all four dimensions of psychological distance (for recent reviews, see Liberman et al., 2007; Trope & Liberman, 2010). For example, Liberman and Trope (1998, Study 1) used an adapted version of Vallacher and Wegner's (1989) Levels of Personal Agency questionnaire. The questionnaire lists 19 activities (e.g., "locking a door") each followed by two restatements, one corresponding to the *why* (high-level) aspects of the activity (e.g., "securing the house") and the other corresponding to the *how* (low-level) aspects of the activity (e.g., "putting a key in the lock"). As predicted, participants chose more high-level, *why* restatements when the activities were described as occurring in the distant future than when the same activities were described as occurring in the near future. Similar results emerged when spatial distance (Fujita, Henderson, Eng, Trope, & Liberman, 2006), probability (Wakslak, Trope, Liberman, & Alony, 2006), and social distance (Liviatan, Trope, & Liberman, 2008; Stephan, Liberman, & Trope, 2010) were manipulated. Other aspects of construal level include using broader, more abstract categories (Rosch & Lloyd, 1978) and using larger chunks to segment ongoing events (Newtson, 1976). Studies conducted within the CLT framework have shown that psychological distance affects these aspects of construal level (Liberman, Sagristano, & Trope, 2002; Wakslak et al., 2006).

CLT further proposes that evaluations and judgments reflect construal such that psychological distancing increases the impact of abstract, super-ordinate aspects of the situation and reduces the impact of secondary, contextual aspects. As a result, psychological distance moves the evaluation of an event closer to the value reflected in its high-level construal than to the value reflected in its low-level construal. Liberman and Trope (1998) reasoned that desirability judgments involve the value of the action's end state and therefore reflect a high-level construal of a situation, whereas feasibility concerns involve the means used to reach the end state and therefore reflect a low-level construal. As predicted, they found that desirability issues received greater weight over feasibility issues as psychological distance increased. For example, as temporal distance from an activity (e.g., attending a lecture) increased, the attractiveness of the activity depended more on its desirability (e.g., how interesting the lecture was) and less on its feasibility (e.g., how convenient the timing of the lecture was). Similar results emerged with probability (Todorov, Goren, & Trope, 2007), social distance (Liviatan et al., 2008), and spatial distance (Henderson, Fujita, Trope, & Liberman, 2006) as the psychological distance dimensions. These findings suggest that psychological distance increases the attractiveness of desirable but difficult-to-obtain alternatives but decreases the attractiveness of less desirable but easy-to-obtain alternatives.

Other research has demonstrated effects of psychological distance on predictions and plans. For example, Nussbaum, Trope, and Liberman (2003, Study 2) conceptualized personal dispositions as high-level construals and situational constraints as low-level construals and found that people expect others to express their personal dispositions and act consistently across different situations in the distant future more than in the near future. In the study, participants imagined an acquaintance's behavior in four different situations (e.g., a birthday party) in either the near future or the distant future and rated the extent to which the acquaintance would display 15 traits (e.g., behave in a friendly vs. an unfriendly manner) representative of the Big Five personality dimensions. Cross-situational consistency was assessed by computing, for each of the 15 traits, the variance in each predicted behavior across the four situations and the correlations among the predicted behaviors in the four situations. As predicted, participants expected others to behave more consistently across distant-future situations than across near-future situations. This finding was replicated with ratings of participants' own behavior in different situations: Participants anticipated exhibiting more consistent traits in the distant future than in the near future (Wakslak, Nussbaum, Liberman, & Trope, 2008, Study 5).

With this background established, we can consider how CLT may apply to moral judgments and value-based plans and decisions. We first examine various definitions of values and suggest that values, by their very definition, typically involve high-level construals. Based on that notion, we examine research on how psychological distance affects the tendency to construe situations in terms of values and to make judgments and decisions based on values. Finally, we consider how thinking in terms of values may affect one's psychological horizons (i.e., one's perception of psychological distance) and whether values may, in some cases, involve low-level construals.

MORAL PRINCIPLES AND VALUES AS HIGH-LEVEL CONSTRUCTS

Personal values (e.g., social equality, respect for tradition, security) are commonly viewed as abstract, superordinate cognitive constructs that provide continuity and meaning under changing environmental circumstances and serve as transsituational goals that guide action (Feather, 1995; Maio, Hahn, Frost, & Cheung, 2009; Rohan, 2000; Rokeach, 1973; Schwartz, 1992; Tetlock, 1986; Verplanken & Holland, 2002; see also Chapter 12, this volume). For example, valuing security implies diverse actions such as striving for safety and protection at home, being careful while driving, and caring about national security. Values concern what is important to people in their lives, and as such they are central parts of each person's self-definition and identity (Kristiansen & Hotte, 1996; Rokeach, 1973).

Moreover, according to a rule-based (deontological) perspective on moral reasoning, global moral principles underlie moral decisions (Lammers & Stapel, 2009; Tanner, Medin, & Iliev, 2008). An act is judged to be right or wrong on the basis of the degree to which it complies with existing moral principles, laws, norms, and rules (e.g., the incest taboo, laws against stealing), irrespective of specific and changing circumstances (see Chapter 3, this volume, for a discussion of deontological vs. consequentialist perspectives on morality).

We propose that because of their superordinate and broadly applicable nature, values are high-level constructs. Based on CLT, we predict that values and moral principles will be more likely to be activated when a person considers more psychologically distant situations. This prediction was examined by Eyal, Liberman, and Trope (2008, Study 1). Participants imagined situations involving moral transgressions taking place either in the near future or in the distant future. One situation involved a woman who cut an old national flag into pieces to be used as rags to clean her house; a second situation involved a family whose pet dog was hit by a car, after which they decided to cook it and eat it; and a third situation involved two siblings who engaged in sexual intercourse with no chance of reproduction (see Haidt, 2001; Haidt, Koller, & Dias, 1993). For each scenario (e.g., national flag), participants chose between two restatements of each action. One restatement referred to an abstract moral principle (high-level construal; e.g., desecrating a national symbol), and the other restatement referred to the means of carrying out the action (low-level construal; e.g., cutting a flag to form rags). We found that distant-future transgressions were identified in moral terms more often than near-future transgressions.

These findings suggest that people are more likely to think of a temporally distant action, rather than one in the near term, as having moral implications. CLT predicts similar results for other forms of psychological distance: Situations should be more readily construed in terms of moral principles when they have occurred further back in the past, apply to more socially or spatially distant individuals or groups, and are less likely to occur. When the same actions are proximal, they are more likely to be construed in terms that are devoid of moral implications. For example, accepting minority students with low grades into one's university would be seen as "endorsing affirmative action" when it is unlikely to be implemented but would be seen in more concrete terms (e.g., as "making acceptance rules more complicated") when it becomes more likely. In the next section we discuss the implications of this tendency for judging the moral rightness or wrongness of near and distant acts.

JUDGMENTS OF MORAL AND IMMORAL ACTS

Most people would agree that it is wrong to make love with a sibling, eat the family's pet, or clean the house with one's national flag. Recent research on moral judgment has shown that even when information about the context indicates that such actions are harmless (e.g., the siblings used contraceptives, the family's pet was dead, the flag was old and worn out and was used as a rag in private), people still feel that the actions are wrong (Haidt, 2001). It appears that people hold general moral rules and intuitions that, when violated, evoke a harsh moral judgment (Haidt, 2001; Horberg, Oveis, Keltner, & Cohen, 2009; Sunstein, 2005; Valdesolo & DeSteno, 2008; see also Chapter 1, this volume).

Indeed, research on morality suggests that people often base their judgments on simple, intuitive moral rules (e.g., lying is wrong) and tend to ignore moderating contextual information (Haidt, 2001; Sunstein, 2005). These moral heuristics represent generalizations from a range of problems for which they are well suited (Baron, 1994). These generalizations, however, are often taken out of context and applied to situations to which they are not appropriate (e.g., when lying might save a human life). According to Haidt (2001), the application of moral rules is immediate and spontaneous, and only if a person subsequently engages in reflective reasoning is he or she likely to take mitigating contextual factors into account (see Chapter 2, this volume, for related comments).

In a similar vein, research on personal values has demonstrated that certain values, such as honor, love, justice, and life, which are called *sacred values* by Tetlock, Kristel, Elson, Green, and Lerner (2000) and *protected values* by Baron and Leshner (2000), are considered inviolate. Similarly, *sacredness* has been defined as a tendency to invest people, places, times, and ideas with importance far beyond the utility they possess (see Chapter 1, this volume). Individuals tend to protect these values and ideas from trade-offs, no matter how small the sacrifice or how large the benefit might be. This is because thinking in terms of such values involves an overgeneralization of the no-trade-off principle (e.g., never trade life for money), which does not allow a person to think about specific situations that violate the rule (e.g., risking one's life crossing a busy street to pick up paper currency lying on the street). However, as Baron and Leshner (2000) argued, when people think about concrete situations, they may become less rigid in implementing protected values. Thus, people may compromise protected values when the probability or amount of harm is small relative to the probability or magnitude of benefit.

We propose, based on CLT, that psychological distance is an important moderator of the choice between values and mitigating circumstances. We predict that more distant misdeeds will seem more immoral and that more distant good deeds will seem more moral.

A series of studies tested this prediction (Eyal et al., 2008). For example, in one of the studies, participants read vignettes adapted from Haidt et al. (1993) describing moral transgressions (e.g., two siblings engaging in sexual intercourse) against widely accepted moral rules (high-level values, e.g., the incest taboo). The vignettes also included situational details that rendered the transgressions harmless (low-level information; e.g., the siblings used contraceptives and kept it a secret). Participants were instructed to imagine that the transgressions would occur tomorrow (the near-future condition) or next year (the distant-future condition) and judged the extent of their wrongness. We found that moral transgressions were judged more severely when imagined in the distant future than in the near future. The same pattern occurred with social distance (Eyal et al., 2008, Study 3), which was manipulated by asking participants to focus either on the feelings and thoughts they experienced while reading about the events (low social distance) or to think about another person they knew, such as a colleague, a friend, or a neighbor, and focus on the feelings and thoughts this person would experience while reading about the events (high social distance). Notice that the social distance manipulation did not involve judging one's own rather than another person's actions, only one's imagined perspective. As predicted, moral transgressions were judged more harshly when imagined from a third-person perspective (high social distance) than from one's own perspective (low social distance). Notably, this social distance manipulation does not support interpreting the results in terms of moral hypocrisy, according to which people judge their own moral transgressions less harshly than another person's transgressions because they wish to appear better than others (see also Chapters 8 and 9, this volume).

Another study (Eyal et al., 2008, Study 4) examined the effects of temporal distance on judgments of moral acts. Participants read vignettes that described virtuous acts related to widely accepted moral principles (high-level information; e.g., adopting a disabled child) as well as low-level, situational details that rendered the acts less noble (e.g., the government offering large adoption payments). It was found that these behaviors were judged to be more virtuous when described as happening in the distant future rather than the near future.

Temporal distance from moral transgressions was also found to affect people's emotional responses. Agerström and Björklund (2009, Studies 1 and 2) asked Swedish participants to imagine situations that involved a threat to human welfare taking place in the near future (today) or in the distant future (in 30 years). For example, one scenario, set in Darfur, Sudan, described a woman who was raped and beaten by the Janjaweed militia. Each scenario was followed by a description of a prosocial action that, if taken, could improve the situation (e.g., donate money). Participants rated how wrong it would be for another Swedish citizen not to take the proposed prosocial action given that they had the means to do so. They also rated how angry they would feel if the target person failed to take the prosocial action. It was found that distant-future moral failures were judged more harshly and invoked more anger than near-future moral failures.

Taken together, these findings suggest that general and uncontextualized moral rules are more likely to guide people's judgments of distant rather than proximal behaviors. Our research has focused on psychological distance effects on judgments of situations in which high-level moral principles are violated in which low-level mitigating information renders the situations less harmful. It might be interesting to examine psychological distance effects on judging situations in which higher-level deontological intuitions conflict with lower-level consequentialist intuitions (cf. Chapter 3, this volume). For example, in the classic Heinz dilemma (Kohlberg, 1969), in which a husband must choose whether to steal an overpriced drug to save his wife's life, we would predict that when considering this dilemma from a psychologically distant perspective, people are more likely to be influenced by a deontological view ("robbery is wrong"), whereas from a psychologically near perspective, people are more likely to be influenced by a consequentialist view (curing one's wife of a deadly disease).

It would also be interesting to apply our logic to sacredness (cf. Chapter 1, this volume). We predict that, when completing the Moral Foundation Sacredness Scale, people are more likely to be willing to compromise their sacred values for money (e.g., kick a dog in the head) when trade-offs are considered from a proximal vantage point (e.g., when offered a check for a million dollars if they will kick the dog in the head). But when trade-offs are considered from greater psychological distance (e.g., when the actions are hypothetical, distal in time or space, or performed by other people), they are more likely to say they would never do it, for any amount of money.

Finally, it would be interesting to examine whether psychological distance affects people's responses to classic moral dilemmas. Consider, for example, the trolley problem (Foot, 1967; see also Chapter 2, this volume). In this dilemma, a decision maker can save the lives of five people who are stuck on a trolley track by killing another (innocent) person and can do this either by switching a runaway boxcar away onto a different track or by directly pushing the person to be sacrificed off a bridge. It has been repeatedly found that most people say they would pull the switch but not push the man off the bridge. We would like to propose that a high-level construal of the situation favors saving five lives by sacrificing one but that killing one person directly by pushing him to his death involves concrete, low-level construal. We predict, therefore, that when adopting a psychologically more distant perspective (e.g., by imagining the situation at a remote location or in the distant future), people would be more likely to indicate that they would push the single person off the bridge in order to save five people and would under those conditions be more likely to think that doing so is not very different from pulling a switch with the same result.

Values-Based Behavioral Plans

People often try to live up to their values. For instance, a person who values preserving the natural environment may be quite receptive to the idea of cleaning up a highway or donating money to restore the Everglades wilderness in Florida. Indeed, much values research suggests that people are likely to use their values as behavioral guides (e.g., Feather, 1995; Rokeach, 1973; Schwartz, 1992; Verplanken & Holland, 2002). Yet the associations reported in the literature between values and behaviors, and between values and behavioral intentions, have varied greatly in magnitude. Whereas some research finds high correlations between values and both intentions and behaviors (e.g., Bardi & Schwartz, 2003), other research has found values to be poor predictors of both outcomes (e.g., Kristiansen & Hotte, 1996). These findings parallel the large body of research showing that people's attitudes and personality traits, like values, often fail to predict behavior.

Values researchers have identified several factors that affect the correspondence between values and behavior, such as the valence of actions and their possible outcomes (Feather, 1995), level of moral reasoning (Kristiansen & Hotte, 1996), centrality to the self (Verplanken & Holland, 2002), and level at which the predicted action is construed (Maio et al., 2009; Vallacher & Wegner, 1989). Based on CLT, we propose that because of their high-level nature, values are more likely to be activated when considering more psychologically distant situations. For example, getting a medical checkup in the relatively distant future is more likely to be represented as an opportunity to improve one's health, whereas arranging for a medical checkup in the immediate future is more likely to be represented in terms of the discomfort it involves or the time it takes. Thus, the value that individuals place on their health is more likely to guide their decision to sign up for a medical checkup in the distant rather than in the near future. The same should hold for any value, not only those that are socially desirable or that involve an immediate sacrifice. For example, individuals' hedonic values are more likely to be expressed in the leisure activities they plan for a distant weekend than for a near-term weekend. In general, we expect values to predict intentions better for distant than for immediate behaviors.

This prediction is consistent with Ajzen and Fishbein's (1977) compatibility principle, which states that attitudes predict behavior to the extent that the two are at comparable levels of specificity. Ajzen and Fishbein proposed that behaviors could be made to correspond more closely to general attitudes by presenting behaviors more abstractly. Consistent with this notion, their research has shown that general attitudes predict behavioral measures that match the attitudes in level of abstraction. For example, an attitude toward religion predicts an aggregate measure of attending church better than it predicts attending service on a particular day. Eliminating low-level incidental features and retaining central, essential features of the behavior, both of which are achieved by aggregating across multiple instances of the behavior, make it possible to predict behavior from general attitudes.

An important difference between Ajzen and Fishbein's (1977) compatibility principle and CLT should be noted, however. The compatibility principle assumes that the objective properties of the behavior determine its level of specificity; general or aggregated behaviors are objectively different from specific behaviors. In contrast, CLT proposes that the same behavior may be construed abstractly or concretely, which in turn determines whether the intention to engage in that behavior will be predicted by one's general attitudes and values or not.

Eyal, Sagristano, Trope, Liberman, and Chaiken (2009) recently obtained evidence for CLT's view of the value–behavior relation. One study used Schwartz's (1992) value questionnaire to assess the importance participants assigned to each of the 10 values identified by Schwartz (power, achievement, hedonism, stimulation, self-direction, universalism, benevolence, tradition, conformity, security) and then asked participants to imagine 30 behaviors, with three behaviors corresponding to each of the 10 values (e.g., "rest as much as I can" corresponded with hedonism, "use environmentally friendly products" corresponded with universalism, "examine the ideas behind rules and regulations before obeying them" corresponded with self-direction; see Bardi & Schwartz, 2003). Participants indicated the likelihood of performing each behavior either in the near future or in the distant future. Eyal, Sagristano, et al. (2009) correlated the rated importance of each value and the mean likelihood of performing the behaviors corresponding to that value. As expected, these correlations were higher when the behaviors were planned for the distant future rather than the near future, suggesting that people's values are better reflected in their intentions for the distant future.

Another study by Eyal, Sagristano, et al. (2009, Study 3) examined the determinants of people's behavioral intentions for psychologically near situations. It was predicted that behavioral intentions for the near future would be influenced by low-level aspects of the event, such as feasibility aspects, rather than by a person's values. Participants first completed a paid experiment in which they reported the importance they assigned to different values as guiding principles in their lives (Schwartz, 1992). They were then asked to volunteer for another experiment, which offered neither payment nor course credit and was to take place in either the near or the distant future. Participants read that the experiment was to take place early in the morning, an inconvenient time for most students (low-feasibility condition), or in the afternoon, a convenient time for most students (high-feasibility condition). It was found that whereas benevolence values better predicted the number of hours participants volunteered for a distant-future experiment than for a near-future experiment, feasibility concerns better predicted volunteering for a near-future experiment than for a distant-future experiment.

Recent research by Ledgerwood, Trope, and Chaiken (2010) examined how high-level ideological considerations versus low-level incidental social influence predicted near- versus distant-future voting intentions. The researchers used an anticipated interaction paradigm in which participants expected to discuss a proposed social policy with another person (Chen, Shechter, & Chaiken, 1996). For example, in one study, participants read about a policy that would increase the deportation of illegal immigrants starting the next week (near future) or a year into the future (distant future) and learned that their discussion partner was either in favor of or against deporting illegal immigrants. They then reported how likely they would be to vote in favor of the policy. It was found that participants' voting intentions were guided by their ideological values to a greater extent when the policy was to be implemented in the distant rather than the near future. However, voting intentions reflected the discussion partner's attitude (low-level consideration) to a greater extent when the policy would be implemented in the near future.

These findings suggest that adopting a distal versus a proximal perspective changes the way people make behavioral plans. Values, a core feature of people's self-concepts, guide plans for psychologically distant situations. However, as people get psychologically closer to a situation, their values and principles are only weak determinants of their intentions. Instead, people's immediate plans are increasingly influenced by incidental aspects of the situation. A person who values adventures and risk taking may plan activities that express this value (e.g., bungee jumping) for the future but rarely actually engage in those activities because of incidental constraints. This implies that people with different and even opposing values may differ more in the behaviors they plan to enact and the ways in which they construe the distal situation than in what they actually do once a concrete occasion presents itself.

It would be interesting to determine whether the effects of temporal distance on using values as guides for behavioral intentions generalize to other distance dimensions. For example, we would predict that a person's cherished values and principles would be more readily applied when giving advice to others than when making personal decisions. Individuals may reason that other people act in accord with their stated values, because the incidental hindrances to acting on such values are not salient when one imagines what someone else might do. But when it comes, say, to choosing the lowest priced product rather than a more expensive but environmentally friendly option, a person's values may not be the most salient consideration. Personal values may also guide decisions about unlikely situations more than decisions about likely situations. For example, people who score high on measures of prosocial values may feel willing to donate to charity some of the money they might win in a lottery, given that the chances of winning are small.

Persuasiveness of Values-Based Messages

Building on the notion that values and principles are high-level constructs, Fujita, Eyal, Chaiken, Trope, and Liberman (2008) reasoned that a message referring to values would be more persuasive if it concerned more distant future issues. To test this idea, participants imagined finding a sale on the Internet for DVD players either that week (near-future condition) or in 3 months (distant-future condition). They then viewed a number of arguments favoring the purchase of a particular DVD player. Six of the arguments were the same in both conditions (e.g., high-quality digital sound system, 2-year warranty, special student discounts). But participants in the high-level appeal condition were presented with a seventh argument that stressed an additional feature related to a positive value (the DVD player is made of environmentally friendly materials), whereas participants in the control condition were presented with a seventh argument that stressed a more value-neutral feature (the manual is easy to use). As expected, in the distant-future condition, but not in the near-future condition, evaluations were more positive when the message included a value-related argument than when it included a value-neutral argument. Thus, persuasive arguments appealing to idealistic values appear to be more persuasive for temporally distant than for temporally near attitude objects.

The effect of psychological distance on persuasion related to moral issues was demonstrated in another study by Fujita et al. (2008, Study 3) in which it was found that participants, given a near-term perspective, were more willing to donate money to save a specific beached whale than to save whales more generally. But when given a long-term perspective, people were more willing to donate money to save whales in general. In other words, in the short term, messages that stress a low-level subordinate exemplar are more persuasive than ones that stress an abstract category, but when considering the long term, messages that emphasize a high-level superordinate category produce greater attitude change.

These results suggest that consumer evaluations (planning to make or not make a particular purchase in the distant future) may be based on values and ideals, but ideals and values may not matter so much when purchase decisions are made on the spot. When applied to other psychological distances, the same notion gives rise to a number of interesting predictions. For example, messages that invoke values should be more influential for products from foreign countries than for local products, for other people more than for oneself, and for members of outgroups more than for members of one's own group.

Effect of Values on Perception of Distance

According to CLT, the relation between psychological distance and level of construal is bidirectional: Not only does distance affect level of construal, but level of construal affects distance. This is because construing an object at a higher level connects it to other objects that span wider ranges of time, space, social perspective, and hypothetical situations, which bring to mind more distal times, places, people, and alternatives. In that sense, high-level construals widen a person's psychological horizon. For example, "being conscientious" would bring to mind experiences that span greater ranges of time and space, pertain to more diverse individuals, and apply even to hypothetical events more readily than would "taking notes in class" Research conducted in the framework of CLT supports this prediction. For example, Liberman et al. (2007) found that thinking about an activity in high-level *why* terms rather than low-level *how* terms led participants to think of the activity as taking place further into the future (see also Macrea, Liberman, Trope, & Sherman, 2008).

An interesting question is whether thinking in terms of values and ideals might expand one's psychological horizons. For example, does thinking of a decision situation in terms of values rather than in terms of concrete situational constraints cause people to consider more far-reaching consequences of the decision? Does thinking in terms of values cause a person to feel more powerful? Do people perceive others who are thinking in terms of values as more socially powerful? These predictions await empirical tests.

Do All Values Involve High-Level Construals?

Although values, in general, tend to involve a higher level of construal than situational circumstances, they may differ in level of construal, with some values being higher level than others. Of particular interest is the CLT notion that central features are higher in level than secondary features, because representing an object more abstractly involves retaining central features and omitting secondary features (see Liberman et al., 2007). Possibly, then, central values could be conceptualized as higher-level constructs than less-central values.

In many situations, different values apply to the same choice (Feather, 1995; Tetlock, 1986). For example, deciding whether to help a fellow student or work on one's own assignment may pit altruism and achievement values against each other. Past research has shown that individuals resolve value conflicts in favor of the value that is deemed more central. For example, Tetlock (1986) found that the participants valued personal prosperity over social equality the more they opposed higher taxes to assist the poor.

If, as proposed by CLT, central values constitute a higher-level construal than more peripheral or secondary values, then central values should guide choices when considering psychologically distant situations. As one gets closer to a situation, choices should become increasingly likely to be based on secondary values. Initial support for this idea comes from research by Eyal, Liberman, Sagristano, and Trope (2009). They found that when a situation is related to different values, the individual's central values are more likely than his or her secondary values to guide a choice made from a psychologically distant perspective. For example, individuals who valued altruism more than achievement were more likely to help a fellow student rather than promote themselves in the distant future than in the near future, whereas individuals who valued achievement more than altruism were more likely to help a fellow student rather than promote themselves in the near future than in the distant future. These findings show that secondary values, which are nonetheless part of one's self-identity, may mask the influence of central values in the short run.

Centrality of values may be defined not only within an individual but also within a situation. For example, when providing medical treatment to someone from a rival group during a war, competition is central and mercy is secondary, whereas in a hospital, the reverse is true. An interesting prediction is that the secondary value will guide behavioral intentions in the near future more than in the distant future. Thus, in a war, benevolence will come into play in near-future plans more than in distant-future plans, leading people to be more merciful than would otherwise be expected. In his poem "After the Battle," Victor Hugo (1859) told about his father ("that hero with the sweetest smile"), an officer in the war against Spain, who encountered a Spanish soldier asking for something to drink. Although on the battlefield, and although the Spaniard tries to kill Hugo's father, the father orders, "All the same, give him something to drink."

CONCLUSION

CLT proposes that psychological distance changes people's moral judgments and value-laden plans by changing the way they mentally represent situations in terms of moral rules and values. The research reviewed here shows that moral principles and values guide judgments and plans for psychologically distant situations more than for psychologically near situations. These results reveal an intriguing phenomenon: Highly cherished concerns and values important for one's self-concept may influence judgments and plans regarding distant situations (e.g., distant future, distant others, distant places, unlikely events) but then fail to be enacted when the time and place of implementation approach. A true believer in altruism, for example, might plan to perform altruistic behaviors in the distant future or think that other people should perform altruistic behaviors, but unless he or she has pre-committed, the person himself or herself may fail to act on these beliefs when the opportunity actually presents itself. This odd slippage between values and behavior may be as much a matter of construal level as it is of moral hypocrisy.

REFERENCES

Agerström, J., & Björklund, F. (2009). Temporal distance and moral concerns: Future morally questionable behavior is perceived as more wrong and evokes stronger prosocial intentions. *Basic and Applied Social Psychology, 31,* 49–59. doi:10.1080/01973530802659885

Ajzen, I., & Fishbein, M. (1977). Attitude–behavior relations: A theoretical analysis and review of empirical research. *Psychological Bulletin, 84,* 888–918. doi:10.1037/0033-2909.84.5.888

Bardi, A., & Schwartz, S. H. (2003). Values and behaviors: Strength and structure of relations. *Personality and Social Psychology Bulletin, 29,* 1207–1220. doi:10.1177/0146167203254602

Baron, J. (1994). Nonconsequentialist decisions. *Behavioral and Brain Sciences, 17,* 1–10. doi:10.1017/S0140525X0003301X

Baron, J., & Leshner, S. (2000). How serious are expressions of protected values? *Journal of Experimental Psychology: Applied, 6,* 183–194. doi:10.1037/1076-898X.6.3.183

Chen, S., Shechter, D., & Chaiken, S. (1996). Getting at the truth or getting along: Accuracy- versus impression-motivated heuristic and systematic processing. *Journal of Personality and Social Psychology, 71,* 262–275. doi:10.1037/0022-3514.71.2.262

Eyal, T., Liberman, N., Sagristano, M. D., & Trope, Y. (2009). *Resolving value conflicts in making choices for the future.* Unpublished manuscript.

Eyal, T., Liberman, N., & Trope, Y. (2008). Judging near and distant virtue and vice. *Journal of Experimental Social Psychology, 44,* 1204–1209. doi:10.1016/j.jesp.2008.03.012

Eyal, T., Sagristano, M. D., Trope, Y., Liberman, N., & Chaiken, S. (2009). When values matter: Expressing values in behavioral intentions for the near vs. distant future. *Journal of Experimental Social Psychology, 45,* 35–43. doi:10.1016/j.jesp. 2008.07.023

Feather, N. T. (1995). Values, valences, and choice: The influence of values on the perceived attractiveness and choice of alternatives. *Journal of Personality and Social Psychology, 68,* 1135–1151. doi:10.1037/0022-3514.68.6.1135

Foot, P. (1967). The problem of abortion and the doctrine of the double effect. *Oxford Review, 5,* 5–15.

Fujita, K., Eyal, T., Chaiken, S., Trope, Y., & Liberman, N. (2008). Influencing attitudes toward near and distant objects. *Journal of Experimental Social Psychology, 44,* 562–572. doi:10.1016/j.jesp.2007.10.005

Fujita, K., Henderson, M. D., Eng, J., Trope, Y., & Liberman, N. (2006). Spatial distance and mental construal of social events. *Psychological Science, 17,* 278–282. doi:10.1111/j.1467-9280.2006.01698.x

Haidt, J. (2001). The emotional dog and its rational tail: A social intuitionist approach to moral judgment. *Psychological Review, 108,* 814–834. doi:10.1037/ 0033-295X.108.4.814

Haidt, J., Koller, S., & Dias, M. (1993). Affect, culture, and morality, or is it wrong to eat your dog? *Journal of Personality and Social Psychology, 65,* 613–628. doi:10.1037/0022-3514.65.4.613

Henderson, M. D., Fujita, K., Trope, Y., & Liberman, N. (2006). Transcending the "here": The effect of spatial distance on social judgment. *Journal of Personality and Social Psychology, 91,* 845–856. doi:10.1037/0022-3514.91.5.845

Horberg, E. J., Oveis, C., Keltner, D., & Cohen, A. B. (2009). Disgust and the moralization of purity. *Journal of Personality and Social Psychology, 97,* 963–976. doi:10.1037/a0017423

Hugo, V. M. (1859). *La Légende des siècles.* Paris, France: Hetzel.

Kohlberg, L. (1969). *Stages in the development of moral thought and action.* New York, NY: Holt, Rinehart & Winston.

Kristiansen, C. M., & Hotte, A. (1996). Morality and the self: Implications for the when and how of value–attitude–behavior relations. In C. Seligman, J. M. Olson, & M. P. Zanna (Eds.), *The psychology of values: The Ontario symposium* (pp. 77–105). Hillsdale, NJ: Erlbaum.

Lammers, J., & Stapel, D. A. (2009). How power influences moral thinking. *Journal of Personality and Social Psychology, 97,* 279–289. doi:10.1037/a0015437

Ledgerwood, A., Trope, Y., & Chaiken, S. (2010). Flexibility now, consistency later: Psychological distance and construal shape evaluative responding. *Journal of Personality and Social Psychology, 99,* 32–51. doi:10.1037/a0019843

Liberman, N., Trope, Y., Macrea, S., & Sherman, S. J. (2007). The effect of level of construal on the temporal distance of activity enactment. *Journal of Experimental Social Psychology, 43,* 143–149. doi:10.1016/j.jesp.2005.12.009

Liberman, N., Sagristano, M., & Trope, Y. (2002). The effect of temporal distance on level of mental construal. *Journal of Experimental Social Psychology, 38*, 523–534. doi:10.1016/S0022-1031(02)00535-8

Liberman, N., & Trope, Y. (1998). The role of feasibility and desirability considerations in near and distant future decisions: A test of temporal construal theory. *Journal of Personality and Social Psychology, 75*, 5–18. doi:10.1037/0022-3514.75.1.5

Liberman, N., & Trope, Y. (2008, November 21). The psychology of transcending the here and now. *Science, 322*, 1201–1205. doi:10.1126/science.1161958

Liviatan, I., Trope, Y., & Liberman, N. (2008). Interpersonal similarity as a social distance dimension: Implications for perception of others' actions. *Journal of Experimental Social Psychology, 44*, 1256–1269. doi:10.1016/j.jesp.2008.04.007

Macrea, S. M., Liberman, N., Trope, Y., & Sherman, S. J. (2008). Construal level and procrastination. *Psychological Science, 19*, 1308–1314. doi:10.1111/j.1467-9280.2008.02240.x

Maio, G. R., Hahn, U., Frost, J. M., & Cheung, W. Y. (2009). Applying the value of equality unequally: Effects of value instantiations that vary in typicality. *Journal of Personality and Social Psychology, 97*, 598–614. doi:10.1037/a0016683

Newtson, D. (1976). Foundations of attribution: The perception of ongoing behavior. In J. H. Harvey, W. J. Ickes, & R. F. Kidd (Eds.), *New directions in attribution research* (pp. 223–248). Hillsdale, NJ: Erlbaum.

Nussbaum, S., Trope, Y., & Liberman, N. (2003). Creeping dispositionism: The temporal dynamics of behavior prediction. *Journal of Personality and Social Psychology, 84*, 485–497. doi:10.1037/0022-3514.84.3.485

Rohan, M. J. (2000). A rose by any name? The values construct. *Personality and Social Psychology Review, 4*, 255–277. doi:10.1207/S15327957PSPR0403_4

Rokeach, M. (1973). *The nature of human values.* New York, NY: Free Press.

Rosch, E., & Lloyd, B. B. (1978). *Cognition and categorization.* Oxford, England: Erlbaum.

Ross, L., & Nisbett, R. E. (1991). *The person and the situation: Perspectives of social psychology.* New York, NY: McGraw-Hill.

Schwartz, S. H. (1992). Universals in the content and structure of values: Theoretical advances and empirical tests in 20 countries. In M. P. Zanna (Ed.), *Advances in experimental social psychology* (Vol. 25, pp. 1–65). San Diego, CA: Academic Press.

Stephan, E., Liberman, N., & Trope, Y. (2010). Politeness and psychological distance: A construal level perspective. *Journal of Personality and Social Psychology, 98*, 268–280. doi:10.1037/a0016960

Sunstein, C. R. (2005). Moral heuristics. *Behavioral and Brain Sciences, 28*, 531–542.

Tanner, C., Medin, D., & Iliev, R. (2008). Influence of deontological versus consequentialist orientations on act choices and framing effects: When principles are more important than consequences. *European Journal of Social Psychology*, *38*, 757–769. doi:10.1002/ejsp.493

Tetlock, P. E. (1986). A value pluralism model of ideological reasoning. *Journal of Personality and Social Psychology*, *50*, 819–827. doi:10.1037/0022-3514.50.4.819

Tetlock, P. E., Kristel, O. V., Elson, S. B., Green, M. C., & Lerner, J. S. (2000). The psychology of the unthinkable: Taboo trade-offs, forbidden base rates, and heretical counterfactuals. *Journal of Personality and Social Psychology*, *78*, 853–870. doi:10.1037/0022-3514.78.5.853

Todorov, A., Goren, A., & Trope, Y. (2007). Probability as a psychological distance: Construal and preferences. *Journal of Experimental Social Psychology*, *43*, 473–482. doi:10.1016/j.jesp.2006.04.002

Trope, Y., & Liberman, N. (2010). Construal level theory of psychological distance. *Psychological Review*, *117*, 440–463.

Valdesolo, P., & DeSteno, D. (2008). The duality of virtue: Deconstructing the moral hypocrite. *Journal of Experimental Social Psychology*, *44*, 1334–1338. doi:10.1016/j.jesp.2008.03.010

Vallacher, R. R., & Wegner, D. M. (1989). Levels of personal agency: Individual variation in action identification. *Journal of Personality and Social Psychology*, *57*, 660–671. doi:10.1037/0022-3514.57.4.660

Verplanken, B., & Holland, R. W. (2002). Motivated decision making effects on activation and self-centrality of values on choices and behavior. *Journal of Personality and Social Psychology*, *82*, 434–447. doi:10.1037/0022-3514.82.3.434

Wakslak, C. J., Nussbaum, S., Liberman, N., & Trope, Y. (2008). Representations of the self in the near and distant future. *Journal of Personality and Social Psychology*, *95*, 757–773. doi:10.1037/a0012939

Wakslak, C. J., Trope, Y., Liberman, N., & Alony, R. (2006). Seeing the forest when entry is unlikely: Probability and the mental representation of events. *Journal of Experimental Psychology: General*, *135*, 641–653. doi:10.1037/0096-3445.135.4.641

11

HUMANNESS, DEHUMANIZATION, AND MORAL PSYCHOLOGY

NICK HASLAM, BROCK BASTIAN, SIMON LAHAM,
AND STEPHEN LOUGHNAN

In principle, we all have moral worth and deserve moral treatment simply by virtue of being human. Philosophers ground moral status in our shared humanity or personhood, declarations of human rights are explicitly universal in their coverage, and laypeople believe that moral rules hold universally. In addition to her sword, scales, and flowing gowns, Lady Justice wears a blindfold to assure us that moral and legal rules apply impartially to everyone.

In practice, of course, some people are considered to be more human than others and more deserving of moral treatment. Humanness is not universally and categorically ascribed to everyone, but is bestowed unevenly across individuals and groups. Metaphorical blindfolds of a different kind allow some people to fail to see the humanity of others, enabling the blindfolded to commit acts of cruelty, to ignore or deny the harm done by third parties, or to minimize the harm they themselves have caused.

Moral action and moral judgment seem to depend on an appreciation of the humanness of others. If others are understood as fully human, then we feel bound to consider and care about their interests, prevent or alleviate their suffering, and experience moral emotions when we have wronged them (see Chapter 21, this volume). When their humanness is denied, either subtly or in extreme cases totally and overtly, their interests and suffering become less visible, and our moral compunction evaporates. Arguably, people must also understand themselves to be fully human in order to act morally, and failing to do so can enable them to behave badly. Moral standing and moral action are therefore entwined with humanness. But what is humanness, and how can we capture this elusive concept in a way that clarifies the psychology of morality?

In this chapter, we review several lines of work that bear on moral psychology. This work has been at least partly inspired by a new model of dehumanization that our group has developed, which derives from a framework for understanding humanness in social perception and judgment. We argue that humanness has two distinct meanings with distinct implications for moral judgment. Understanding that humanness can be denied—that people can be dehumanized—in these two distinct ways may help to illuminate some of the processes that lead to immoral conduct.

The chapter contains four sections. In the first, we lay out our model of humanness and dehumanization. In the second, we review several studies that show how the two dimensions of humanness align with concepts of moral patiency, agency, and responsibility. In the process we show that subtly denying humanness to people has implications for whether they are blamed, praised, or considered worthy of moral concern and rehabilitation. In the third section, we describe our recent work on the moral circle and explain how considerations of humanness are implicated in how and where the boundaries of this circle of moral concern are drawn. Finally, in the fourth section, we discuss how objectification, arguably a form of dehumanizing perception, allows a person to deny others' mental states and, as a result, accord them less moral concern.

A MODEL OF HUMANNESS AND DEHUMANIZATION

The psychology of dehumanization has regained prominence in social psychology after a relatively long hiatus following classic works by Bandura, Underwood, and Fromson (1975); Kelman (1976); Opotow (1990); and Staub (1992). This work was notable for its linkage of dehumanization to violence, aggression, moral exclusion, and organized evil. However, it tended to lack an explicit understanding of what is denied to people when they are dehumanized; to present dehumanization as a single, monolithic phenomenon; and to portray dehumanization as something relevant to extreme situations such as war and genocide rather than to more everyday forms of immorality. The emergence of a new look at dehumanization helped to overcome these limitations and can largely be credited to the work of Jacques-Philippe Leyens and colleagues (e.g., Leyens et al., 2001), who documented the *infrahuman-*

ization effect, in which people tend to ascribe more human qualities to their ingroup than to outgroups. Leyens and colleagues defined *humanness* as characteristics that are unique to our species, exemplified by secondary emotions, and found that people tend to reserve these uniquely human emotions to their own national group and deny them to outgroups. By implication, the ingroup is seen as more human than the outgroup, and the outgroup is seen as more animal-like than the ingroup.

The infrahumanization effect is important for a variety of reasons. First, it recognizes that dehumanization-like phenomena can take relatively mild forms; that is, they fall along a severity continuum that extends upward to the harshest, most degrading denials of humanity. Second, Leyens and colleagues demonstrated that humanness is a fundamental dimension of social perception. Third, the infrahumanization researchers produced a working definition of humanness, in the absence of which the concept of dehumanization is vague and ethereal. Fourth, by recognizing the banal and subtle nature of some dehumanizationlike phenomena, they rendered these phenomena tractable to experimental social psychologists.

Our group's work on dehumanization was stimulated by Leyens's research program but departed from it in an important respect. Whereas researchers in the infrahumanization tradition identify humanness as that which distinguishes humans from (other) animals, we discovered that people distinguish this sense of human uniqueness from an equally accessible sense of humanness as "human nature." Uniquely human attributes tend to revolve around civility, refinement, and higher cognition, whereas human nature tends to involve emotionality, interpersonal warmth, and openness. Moreover, uniquely human attributes are understood to reflect gradual social learning, whereas human nature is seen as innate, essencelike (i.e., deep seated and fundamental), cross-culturally universal, and typical of the human population. *Human uniqueness* thus corresponds to encultured humanity and *human nature* to common or shared humanity (Haslam, Bain, Douge, Lee, & Bastian, 2005). Some evidence indicates that these dimensions of humanness are cross-culturally valid but with some interesting discrepancies (Bain, Vaes, Haslam, Kashima, & Guan, 2010; Haslam, Kashima, Loughnan, Shi, & Suitner, 2008).

If humanness has two distinct senses, then there should be two distinct ways in which it can be denied. This simple insight was the basis for our group's new theoretical framework for understanding dehumanization processes (Haslam, 2006). Individuals or groups that are denied human uniqueness are perceived as lacking civility, refinement, and rationality, and hence are seen as coarse, unintelligent, immoral: in a word, bestial. Because nonhuman animals represent the contrast against which this sense of humanness is defined, people who are denied uniquely human attributes are likened to animals. People who are denied human nature, in contrast, are perceived as lacking emotion, warmth, and openness and thus are seen as mechanical, cold, rigid, and lacking in vitality and animation. The contrastive nonhuman entity is less self-evident than in the case of human uniqueness, but we propose that when people are denied human nature they are implicitly or explicitly likened to objects, automatons, robots, or machines.

We have found evidence of these animalistic and mechanistic forms of dehumanization in the perceptions of a variety of social groups (e.g., Bain, Park, Kwok, & Haslam, 2009; Saminaden, Loughnan, & Haslam, 2010). A variant of the mechanistic form occurs in the self-humanizing effect (Haslam et al., 2005; Haslam & Bain, 2007; Loughnan, Leidner, et al., 2010), in which others are seen as lacking in human nature compared with oneself, independent of the general tendency for people to self-enhance (i.e., view themselves as more worthy than others). The relevance of the dimensions for perceptions of individuals as distinct from groups is also demonstrated by recent findings that people feel they are personally lacking in human nature when they are socially excluded, believe that the person who excluded them sees them as lacking in human nature, and perceive that person as lacking in human nature as well (Bastian & Haslam, 2010).

In sum, our model offers a two-dimensional framework for organizing the diverse forms of dehumanization in terms of a model of humanness. Its fundamental claim is that the dimensions of humanness are implicated in everyday social perception, and the model is intended to encompass phenomena that are mild, everyday, and subtle, as well as those at the other end of the severity continuum that involve clear repudiations of people's humanity.

MAPPING HUMANNESS ONTO MORAL CONCEPTS

Armed with our model of humanness, we may ask how perceptions of humanness relate to perceptions of moral status. For our model to be useful in moral psychology, and for it to clarify how moral standing is ascribed or denied to individuals and groups, we need to know how aspects of moral status align with the dimensions of humanness. A review of relevant literatures suggests at least three different ways that people may be viewed as having moral status. People may be perceived (a) as having the capacity to be responsible for immoral behavior (e.g., requiring inhibition and self-control) and therefore as deserving blame for bad deeds (Alicke, 2000; Knobe, 2003; Shaver, 1985; see also Chapter 6, this volume), (b) as having the desire to engage in moral behavior (e.g., to act prosocially; Bandura, 1999) and therefore as deserving praise for good deeds (Pizarro, Uhlmann, & Salovey, 2003; see also Chapter 5, this volume), or (c) as having the capacity to be recipients of morally relevant actions (e.g., the capacity to experience pain) and therefore as having the right to be protected from harm (H. M. Gray, Gray, & Wegner, 2007; K. Gray & Wegner, 2009). We use the terms *inhibitive agency, proactive agency,* and *moral patiency,* respectively, to refer to these different aspects of moral status (see also Chapter 6, this volume).

These aspects would be expected to align with our dimensions of humanness. A basis for expecting links between inhibitive agency and human uniqueness, and between moral patiency and human nature, is suggested by the work of H. M. Gray et al. (2007). From ratings of the degree to which an assortment of entities—including diverse humans (including fetuses, children, adults, and dead persons), animals, robots, and God—had a variety of mental capacities, H. M. Gray et al. derived a two-dimensional mind perception space (see Figure 6.1, this volume). One dimension, which they called "agency," primarily differentiated adult humans from animals and was constituted by capacities such as foresight, thinking, and self-control. Although it was presented as a dimension of mind rather than humanness, the agency dimension clearly signifies the human–animal distinction and corresponds to our understanding of human uniqueness, so we expect the inhibitive form of moral agency to be associated with it. People who are ascribed more uniquely human attributes should therefore be ascribed greater inhibitive agency, and hence they should be judged as more deserving of blame for morally wrong actions. This prediction was supported by H. M. Gray et al.'s finding that the agency dimension was positively correlated with judgments of the deservingness of punishment for wrongdoing.

H. M. Gray et al.'s (2007) second dimension was labeled *experience* and comprised mental capacities such as emotion, desire, appetite, and suffering. The dimensions primarily differentiated living humans and animals from inanimate, mechanical, and disembodied entities such as dead people, robots, and God. In its composition and its opposition between humans and mechanistic entities, experience corresponds closely to our dimension of human nature. Gray et al. found that experience correlated strongly with perceptions of entities' moral patiency, assessed by judgments of how unpleasant it would be to harm them, so we would predict that this aspect of moral status should be associated with human nature. People who are ascribed more human nature should therefore be seen as having greater rights to be protected from harm.

The third proposed aspect of moral status, proactive moral agency, arguably does not have such clear links to our dimensions of humanness. Its agentic component might suggest a link to H. M. Gray et al.'s (2007) agency dimension, and hence to human uniqueness, but we propose that the capacity to do good is seen as associated with human nature instead. Human nature tends to be seen as involving interpersonal warmth and would therefore be expected to be linked to prosocial intentions. We therefore predicted that proactive moral agency would be associated with human nature and, hence, that people to whom human nature was ascribed would be seen as more deserving of praise for morally good actions.

Bastian, Laham, Wilson, Haslam, and Koval (in press) conducted three studies to test these predictions. In the first study, we constructed descriptions of two fictitious groups of people. One group was described using traits that were high in human nature but low in human uniqueness, and the other group was described with the opposite pattern of traits. Equal numbers of desirable and undesirable traits were used to describe each group. Each participant rated one group on scales assessing inhibitive agency, proactive agency, and moral patiency. Inhibitive agency was measured using the scale from K. Gray and Wegner (2009; e.g., how much members of the group had the capacity for "responsible action," "acting intentionally," "self-control"), proactive agency with scales based on Bandura (1999; e.g., how much members of the group "have the desire to do good things in the world," "want to treat others well," and "want to help other people," as well as the Prosocialness Scale for Adults; Caprara, Steca, Zelli, & Capanna, 2005), and moral patiency with scales based on K. Gray and Wegner's (2009) experience scale and a modified version of the Wong–Baker Pain Scale (Wong & Baker, 1988) to assess the extent to which members of each group would experience pain if they were to experience an injury.

Consistent with our predictions, we found that the high human nature group was rated higher on both measures of proactive agency and both measures of moral patiency and that the high human uniqueness group was rated higher on the inhibitive agency scale. Thus, independent of the perceived desirability of the two groups, two dimensions of their perceived humanness were associated in distinctive ways with aspects of their moral status.

Our second study extended the first study to examine moral judgments of blame, praise, and willingness to protect others. Pizarro et al. (2003) demonstrated that judgments of blame are associated with the perceived intentionality of people's actions, linked to inhibitive agency, whereas judgments of praise are made when people are attributed the desire to act morally toward others, or proactive agency. H. M. Gray et al. (2007) suggested that when people are ascribed moral patiency, our willingness to protect them from immoral actions increases. Investigating stereotypes of real-world social groups rather than fictitious ones, we therefore predicted that groups ascribed more human nature traits would receive more praise and protection, and groups ascribed more human uniqueness traits would receive more moral blame. Related to this, we further predicted that high human nature groups would be seen as meriting rehabilitation after wrongdoing, whereas high human uniqueness groups, because of their greater perceived intentional control or inhibitive agency, would be seen as meriting punishment.

Participants rated 24 diverse social groups on the two dimensions of humanness and imagined that a member of each group had performed a particular moral or immoral act (from Chadwick, Bromgard, Bromgard, & Trafimow, 2006) or had been mistreated in certain ways. Participants judged whether people would judge the person "morally responsible" for performing the immoral behaviors, whether people would give "personal credit" for performing the moral behaviors, and whether people would feel like "intervening" or taking a "moral stand" on behalf of the person when he or she was treated immorally. Finally, participants rated how much people would endorse punishment or rehabilitation (e.g., through education programs) for the group member as a way of dealing with the group member's wrongful behavior. As we predicted, attributions of moral blame were associated only with the human uniqueness of the group, and moral praise and protection were associated only with a group's perceived human nature. Punishment was endorsed more for high human uniqueness groups and rehabilitation more for high human nature groups. As in the first study, indices of inhibitive agency aligned with one sense of humanness, and indices of proactive agency and moral patiency aligned with the other.

Our third study replicated the second one but used experimental manipulation of the humanness dimensions rather than naturally occurring variations in perceived humanness among real-world groups. Four trait-based character descriptions were constructed that factorially varied high and low human uniqueness and human nature. As in the previous study, human uniqueness was associated with judgments of blame for immoral actions, and human nature was associated with judgments of praise for moral actions as well as protection (i.e., intention to intervene and to feel indignation if the person were being mistreated). These findings were not reducible to the general evaluation or liking of the characters.

Results of these three studies indicate that basic aspects of moral status are associated in distinctive ways with the dimensions of humanness. The extent to which individuals or groups are ascribed or denied humanness is therefore likely to affect everyday moral judgments involving them. It may help to clarify why some people are less socially valued than others—a fundamental factor in moral judgment (Cikara, Farnsworth, Harris, & Fiske, 2010). Groups that are seen as embodying human nature, such as children, are apt to receive more protection and praise, and less blame and punishment, than groups that are seen as embodying human uniqueness, such as businesspeople or the rich. Perhaps more important, individuals or groups that are subtly or not so subtly dehumanized are likely to elicit different patterns of moral disengagement depending on the form the dehumanization takes. People who are denied human nature would receive diminished protection, would not receive praise for their good actions, and would not be seen as meriting rehabilitation in response to their misdeeds. People who are denied human uniqueness, in contrast, may tend not to be morally blamed for their wrongdoings on account of the perceived limitations in their capacity for intentional action and inhibition. This may superficially appear to be a desirable state of affairs, but it is likely to be accompanied by a view that such people are childlike and lack the capacity for autonomy. Paternalistic control and benign neglect are two possible responses.

HUMANNESS AND THE MORAL CIRCLE

One role that a theory of humanness might play, in addition to making conceptual links to dimensions of moral judgment such as blame and praise, is to clarify the boundaries of moral concern. People feel morally obligated to show concern for a variety of creatures: their children, other adults, perhaps fetuses, and some nonhuman animals. These entities are said to reside within the *moral circle*, or moral community (Deutsch, 1985; Singer, 1981; see also Chapter 21, this volume). Importantly, inclusion in the moral circle entails, at least in theory, respectful, moral treatment. Circle membership is, therefore, not without consequence. Entities said to reside at the margins of life, such as fetuses and people in permanent vegetative states, may be granted moral status by some but not by others, and the consequences of such disagreements can have serious implications for social policy and legislation (e.g., abortion, euthanasia). In addition, the question of which animals to include in the circle has real implications for the humane treatment of animals in farming and other industries (Lund, Mejdell, Röcklinsberg, Anthony, & Håstein, 2007).

For philosophers, moral circle membership depends on the possession of an attribute, or set of attributes, that resembles components of human uniqueness and human nature. For example, inclusion has been argued based on human nature factors such as sentience or suffering (e.g., Singer, 1981), as well as human uniqueness factors such as language (Frey, 1980) and rationality (Kant, 1888/1980).

Philosophers' accounts of the moral circle are typically prescriptive (e.g., Singer, 1981): We are urged, for example, to include all entities that experience pain or possess rationality. Very little is known about the descriptive content of the layperson's moral circle or about the psychological processes involved in its use in thinking and behavior. Recent work from our lab has begun to consider the properties of the moral circle as a psychological construct and its relationship with human uniqueness and human nature.

One important property of the moral circle as a psychological construct is that its boundary is moveable. The moral circle has generally expanded over history, the boundary shifting outward (Singer, 1981), although it contracts or dilates as a result of large-scale social factors such as economic hardship, war, political turmoil, and violence (Staub, 1992; see also Chapter 21, this volume). Like other psychological categories, the moral circle is also subject to more subtle influences. Work from our lab shows that variations in task framing influence the size of the moral circle. Laham (2009b), for example, gave people a list of entities that were potential members of the moral circle (e.g., young girl, fetus, brain-dead person, adult man, and baby). He then asked them to delimit morally worthy entities either by circling those on the list they deemed worthy of moral consideration (inclusion mind-set) or by crossing out those they did not deem worthy (exclusion mind-set). Across three studies, people in an exclusion mind-set retained more entities (i.e., had larger moral circles) than those in an inclusion mind-set.

A similar effect emerges as a consequence of another subtle cognitive manipulation: subjective ease of retrieval. Laham (2009a) showed, in two studies, that people's moral circles expand if they have a subjectively easy time generating circle exemplars. Participants were asked to think of three or 15 animals that they deemed worthy of moral consideration and to then indicate the size of their moral circles by estimating the proportion of the world's animals deemed worthy of moral treatment. Because subjective ease of retrieval is linked with exemplar prevalence via a naive theory (easy generation experience, more exemplars; Schwarz, 2004), those who had the subjectively easy time of generating three exemplars subsequently had larger moral circles.

Not only are people's nominal moral circles influenced by subtle cognitive manipulations; so, too, are subsequent moral judgments and behaviors. In Laham's (2009b) study, people who adopted an exclusion mind-set were subsequently more likely to treat a range of outgroups with more moral consideration than people in the inclusion mind-set condition. In these studies, task framing increased the size of the moral circle for people in an exclusion mind-set, which in turn made them extend moral concern to a wider range of targets. Laham (2009a) further showed that moral circle size also affects behavior. Participants who had the subjectively easy experience of generating three circle exemplars were 4 times more likely to accept an information sheet about how to donate money to help endangered species than were participants who generated 15 exemplars. This effect was accounted for by moral circle size.

The malleability of the moral circle boundary demonstrated by these studies undermines to some extent the intuition that people determine circle membership via some rational, rule-based process of the kind "if entity X possesses morally relevant property Y, then include it in the moral circle." Rather, people seem subject to influence from various morally irrelevant properties of the decision process. But if people are not necessarily using morally relevant properties such as human uniqueness or human nature to decide on circle membership, what is the relation between these dimensions of humanness and the moral circle? Under some circumstances, it is likely that people do indeed try to assign circle status based on the possession of human uniqueness and human nature attributes. However, we argue that sometimes the process may be reversed: People may come to attribute human uniqueness and human nature to entities based on their (previously decided) circle membership.

To test this possibility, Laham and Haslam (2009) gave people an inclusion–exclusion discrepancy (IED) task similar to that used by Laham (2009b). After including or excluding creatures from the moral circle, participants subsequently rated some of these creatures on mental states and traits representing human uniqueness and human nature. Results showed that the likelihood of inclusion of a creature in the moral circle was a function of mind-set, with creatures more likely to be included under an exclusion mind-set. In addition, people were more likely to attribute rationality (representing human uniqueness) and experience (representing human nature) to creatures included in the circle. As a result, people in an exclusion mind-set came to see more creatures as possessing rationality and experience than did those in an inclusion mind-set. In short, the perceived humanness of a creature may be a criterion on which moral concern is based, but creatures that are granted moral concern also tend to be humanized. By implication, people may be dehumanized as a consequence of moral disengagement, and not only as a cause of it. This possibility accords with research findings that people tend to deny humanness to groups when they learn that their own group has acted inhumanely toward them (Castano & Giner-Sorolla, 2006).

DENIALS OF MORAL STATUS:
OBJECTIFICATION AND MEAT EATING

The previous sections of this chapter explored the relation between humanness and dimensions of moral judgment in general, abstract terms. We now turn to two recent lines of research in which we demonstrated that denials of humanity are associated with diminished moral concern. We focus on two groups that are typically denied full moral consideration: objectified people and nonhuman animals.

Objectification occurs when an individual is viewed or treated as a body and stripped of his or her mind, personality, and personhood (Fredrickson & Roberts, 1997; Nussbaum, 1995). Although this definition contains two elements—to be a body and not to be a person—psychological research has typically examined only body focus. By adopting a humanness perspective, recent questionnaire and neurological research has shown that objectification is associated with denials of both humanness and moral standing.

Adopting a questionnaire-based approach, Loughnan, Haslam, Murnane, et al. (2010) presented people with a series of objectified and nonobjectified images (i.e., men and women either fully clothed or dressed revealingly in swimming costumes). Participants were asked to rate each image on a range of mental states associated with human nature (e.g., emotionality) and human uniqueness (e.g., rationality). Objectified images were rated lower on both dimensions of humanness, indicating a subtle dehumanization. This finding replicates work by Heflick and Goldenberg (2009), who asked participants to focus on either the appearance or personhood of Angelina Jolie or Sarah Palin. Following this prime, they asked participants to rate the women on a series of personality traits and then indicate how much each trait was part of our shared "human nature." They found that participants who focused on appearance rated the women lower on human nature than did participants who focused on the women's personhood.

Questionnaire studies have indicated that people dehumanize the objectified. However, they have not determined whether people attribute and then withdraw humanity from the objectified or fail to attribute it in the first place. Social neuroscience research has provided evidence for the latter, suggesting that objectified targets simply fail to elicit social processing in perceivers. Cikara, Eberhardt, and Fiske (2011) placed men in a magnetic resonance imaging scanner and measured their brain activity when viewing images of objectified and nonobjectified women. They found that objectified images did not activate the brain regions involved in processing social targets (i.e., the medial prefrontal cortex, posterior cingulate, and temporal poles). Put simply, men did not see objectified women as social agents.

If the objectified are not seen as fully human, might they be denied the moral status normally afforded to humans? To test this notion, we measured attribution of moral concern in two studies (Loughnan, Haslam, Murnane, et al., 2010). In Study 1, participants were presented with objectified and nonobjectified women and were asked to rate the women's capacity for experience in H. M. Gray et al.'s (2007) sense, which is closely aligned with perceived moral patiency. The objectified women were judged to possess less experience and therefore to lack moral patiency. In Study 2, we examined additional measures of moral standing. We asked participants to rate objectified men and women on experience, moral patiency, and sensitivity to pain (K. Gray & Wegner, 2009). Objectified targets (especially men) were again denied moral patiency and the capacity for suffering.

Combined, these studies indicate that objectified persons are denied human traits and moral status. Our deeper understanding of the relationship between humanness attribution and moral concern has allowed empirical confirmation of the untested claim that the objectified are not viewed as fully human.

The perception of nonhuman animals is another domain in which we have recently examined how humanness relates to moral judgment. Although it might seem anomalous to refer to the "humanness" of nonhuman animals, denial of capacities and dispositions associated with being human can have significant implications for animals' perceived moral standing, just as denial of humanness can have morally problematic consequences for objectified humans. Exploitation of animals has typically been justified by claims that they lack some important characteristic that humans possess. Moral concern hinges on this critical component of humanness. Whether it was the lack of a soul (Aquinas), emotions (Descartes), or rationality (Kant), this missing piece meant that animals were neither moral agents nor patients. Although these arguments cannot withstand secular, philosophical scrutiny (e.g., Bentham & Browning, 1843; Singer, 1990), it is clear that human practices such as farming do routinely treat animals inhumanely. Even though the philosophical debate on the moral status of animals may have been fought and won, might people continue to deny animals the humanity needed to be considered moral patients? Stated otherwise, might animals be denied human attributes in a way that undermines their moral standing?

Broadly, people believe animals possess human nature but not human uniqueness attributes (Haslam et al., 2008; Loughnan & Haslam, 2007). By extension, animals should be seen as lacking inhibitive moral agency but possessing moral patiency. Denying moral agency to animals implies that we do not blame them for harmful acts, but retaining moral patiency implies that we see them as potential recipients of immoral actions (e.g., beating a dog is wrong). However, sometimes our actions towards animals—such as killing or factory farming—are clearly harmful. To help understand the role morality and humanity might play in the treatment of animals, we asked people to imagine or engage in meat eating and measured their perception of animals' humanness and moral status.

In Study 1, Bastian, Loughnan, and Haslam (2010) asked vegetarians and omnivores to rate the emotional experience (human nature attributes) and higher cognitive ability (human uniqueness attributes) of cows and sheep. Participants were told that the animal under consideration had either been bred for human consumption (food reminder) or simply lived on a farm (control). For vegetarian participants, food reminders had no effect on the attribution of mental states to the animals. By contrast, omnivores reminded that the animals were bred to become food rated the animals significantly lower in emotionality but not higher in cognition. This finding suggests that reminding people that animals are killed for human consumption triggers a denial of those traits that are linked to moral patiency.

In Study 2, Loughnan, Haslam, and Bastian (2010) examined the direct effect of eating meat on the attribution of emotionality and complex thought to meat animals. Meat-eating participants were randomly assigned to eat either nuts or beef jerky. In a second, supposedly unrelated task, they were asked to rate the mental states and moral status of a cow. Eating beef jerky significantly reduced moral concern for both cows in particular and animals in general and was accompanied by a general reduction in attribution of mental states to animals.

CONCLUSION

We intend the work described in this chapter to be a contribution to a moral psychology that recognizes the importance of perceived humanness. Most of the work emphasizes the moral implications of denying humanness to others, whether those others are members of particular groups, individuals perceived in particular ways (e.g., objectified), or even other species. Although we believe our humanness framework clarifies how various others are accorded diminished moral standing, the framework may also illuminate other issues germane to moral psychology. For example, if people see themselves as embodying human nature to a greater extent than others (Haslam et al., 2005), this might help explain why the self is often given an exceptional moral status, our own good deeds being seen as especially praiseworthy and our own moral worth as especially important. In short, our perspective may speak to the perceived moral standing of the self as much as that of others. It may also clarify cycles of immoral treatment and the ways in which victims and victimizers are both dehumanized (Bastian & Haslam, 2010; Kelman, 1976). Moral cognition appears to be tightly bound up with the perceived humanness of perceivers and targets, and as research continues to show the subtle ways in which people are denied humanness, it should help us to understand some of the psychological processes involved in moral and immoral conduct.

REFERENCES

Alicke, M. D. (2000). Culpable control and the psychology of blame. *Psychological Bulletin, 126,* 556–574. doi:10.1037/0033-2909.126.4.556

Bain, P., Park, J., Kwok, C., & Haslam, N. (2009). Attributing human uniqueness and human nature to cultural groups: Distinct forms of subtle dehumanization. *Group Processes & Intergroup Relations, 12,* 789–805. doi:10.1177/1368430209340415

Bain, P., Vaes, J., Haslam, N., Kashima, Y., & Guan, Y. (2010). *Folk psychologies of humanness: Beliefs about distinctive and core human characteristics in three countries.* Manuscript submitted for publication.

Bandura, A. (1999). Moral disengagement in the perpetration of inhumanities. *Personality and Social Psychology Review, 3,* 193–209. doi:10.1207/s15327957 pspr0303_3

Bandura, A., Underwood, B., & Fromson, M. E. (1975). Disinhibition of aggression through diffusion of responsibility and dehumanization of victims. *Journal of Research in Personality, 9,* 253–269. doi:10.1016/0092-6566(75)90001-X

Bastian, B., & Haslam, N. (2010). Excluded from humanity: Ostracism and dehumanization. *Journal of Experimental Social Psychology, 46,* 107–113. doi:10.1016/j.jesp.2009.06.022

Bastian, B., Laham, S. M., Wilson, S., Haslam, N., & Koval, P. (in press). Blaming, praising and protecting our humanity: The implications of everyday dehumanization for judgments of moral status. *British Journal of Social Psychology.*

Bastian, B., Loughnan, S., & Haslam, N. (2010). *Don't mind meat? The dementalization of animals used for human consumption.* Unpublished manuscript, University of Melbourne.

Bentham, J., & Browning, J. (1843). *The works of Jeremy Bentham.* London, England: Simpkin, Marshall, & Co.

Caprara, G. V., Steca, P., Zelli, A., & Capanna, C. (2005). A new scale for measuring adults' prosocialness. *European Journal of Psychological Assessment, 21,* 77–89. doi:10.1027/1015-5759.21.2.77

Castano, E., & Giner-Sorolla, R. (2006). Not quite human: Infrahumanization in response to collective responsibility for intergroup killing. *Journal of Personality and Social Psychology, 90,* 804–818. doi:10.1037/0022-3514.90.5.804

Chadwick, R. A., Bromgard, G., Bromgard, I., & Trafimow, D. (2006). An index of specific behaviors in the moral domain. *Behavior Research Methods, 38,* 692–697. doi:10.3758/BF03193902

Cikara, M., Eberhardt, J., & Fiske, S. (2011). From agents to objects: Sexist attitudes and neural responses to sexualized targets. *Journal of Cognitive Neuroscience, 23,* 540–551.

Cikara, M., Farnsworth, R. A., Harris, L. T., & Fiske, S. T. (2010). On the wrong side of the trolley track: Neural correlates of relative social valuation. *Social Cognitive and Affective Neuroscience, 5,* 404–413.

Deutsch, M. (1985). *Distributive justice: A social–psychological perspective.* New Haven, CT: Yale University Press.

Fredrickson, B., & Roberts, T. (1997). Objectification theory: Towards understanding women's lived experiences and mental health risks. *Psychology of Women Quarterly, 21,* 173–206. doi:10.1111/j.1471-6402.1997.tb00108.x

Frey, R. G. (1980). *Interest and rights: The case against animals.* Oxford, England: Clarendon Press.

Gray, H. M., Gray, K., & Wegner, D. M. (2007, February 2). Dimensions of mind perception. *Science, 315,* 619. doi:10.1126/science.1134475

Gray, K., & Wegner, D. (2009). Moral typecasting: Divergent perceptions of moral agents and moral patients. *Journal of Personality and Social Psychology, 96,* 505–520. doi:10.1037/a0013748

Haslam, N. (2006). Dehumanization: An integrative review. *Personality and Social Psychology Review, 10,* 252–264. doi:10.1207/s15327957pspr1003_4

Haslam, N., & Bain, P. (2007). Humanizing the self: Moderators of the attribution of lesser humanness to others. *Personality and Social Psychology Bulletin, 33,* 57–68. doi:10.1177/0146167206293191

Haslam, N., Bain, P., Douge, L., Lee, M., & Bastian, B. (2005). More human than you: Attributing humanness to self and others. *Journal of Personality and Social Psychology, 89,* 937–950. doi:10.1037/0022-3514.89.6.937

Haslam, N., Kashima, Y., Loughnan, S., Shi, J., & Suitner, C. (2008). Subhuman, inhuman, and superhuman: Contrasting humans with non-humans in three cultures. *Social Cognition, 26,* 248–258. doi:10.1521/soco.2008.26.2.248

Heflick, N., & Goldenberg, J. (2009). Objectifying Sarah Palin: Evidence that objectification causes women to be perceived as less competent and less fully human. *Journal of Experimental Social Psychology, 45,* 598–601. doi:10.1016/j.jesp.2009.02.008

Kant, I. (1980). *Lectures on ethics* (L. Infield, Trans.). Indianapolis, IN: Hackett. (Original work published 1888)

Kelman, H. C. (1976). Violence without restraint: Reflections on the dehumanization of victims and victimizers. In G. M. Kren & L. H. Rappoport (Eds.), *Varieties of psychohistory* (pp. 282–314). New York, NY: Springer.

Knobe, J. (2003). Intentional action in folk psychology: An experimental investigation. *Philosophical Psychology, 16,* 309–324. doi:10.1080/09515080307771

Laham, S. M. (2009a). [Ease of retrieval and the moral circle.] Unpublished data.

Laham, S. M. (2009b). Expanding the moral circle: Inclusion and exclusion mindsets and the circle of moral regard. *Journal of Experimental Social Psychology, 45,* 250–253. doi:10.1016/j.jesp.2008.08.012

Laham, S. M., & Haslam, N. (2009). [Humanness and the moral circle.] Unpublished data.

Leyens, J.-P., Rodriguez-Perez, A., Rodriguez-Torres, R., Gaunt, R., Paladino, M.-P., Vaes, J., & Demoulin, S. (2001). Psychological essentialism and the differential attribution of uniquely human emotions to ingroups and outgroups. *European Journal of Social Psychology, 31,* 395–411. doi:10.1002/ejsp.50

Loughnan, S., & Haslam, N. (2007). Animals and androids: Implicit associations between social categories and nonhumans. *Psychological Science, 18,* 116–121. doi:10.1111/j.1467-9280.2007.01858.x

Loughnan, S., Haslam, N., & Bastian, B. (2010). The role of meat consumption in the denial of moral status and mind to meat animals. *Appetite, 55,* 156–159. doi:10.1016/j.appet.2010.05.043

Loughnan, S., Haslam, N., Murnane, T., Vaes, J., Reynolds, C., & Suitner, C. (2010). Objectification leads to depersonalization: The denial of mind and moral concern to objectified others. *European Journal of Social Psychology*, *40*, 709–717.

Loughnan, S., Leidner, B., Doron, G., Haslam, N., Kashima, Y., Tong, J., & Yeung, V. (2010). Universal biases in self-perception: Better and more human than average. *British Journal of Social Psychology*, *49*, 627–636. doi:10.1348/014466610X487779

Lund, V., Mejdell, C. M., Röcklinsberg, H., Anthony, R., & Håstein, T. (2007). Expanding the moral circle: Farmed fish as objects of moral concern. *Diseases of Aquatic Organisms*, *75*, 109–118. doi:10.3354/dao075109

Nussbaum, M. (1995). Objectification. *Philosophy & Public Affairs*, *24*, 249–291. doi:10.1111/j.1088-4963.1995.tb00032.x

Opotow, S. (1990). Moral exclusion and injustice: An introduction. *Journal of Social Issues*, *46*, 1–20. doi:10.1111/j.1540-4560.1990.tb00268.x

Pizarro, D., Uhlmann, E., & Salovey, P. (2003). Asymmetry in judgments of moral blame and praise: The role of perceived metadesires. *Psychological Science*, *14*, 267–272. doi:10.1111/1467-9280.03433

Saminaden, A., Loughnan, S., & Haslam, N. (2010). Afterimages of savages: Implicit associations between "primitive" peoples, animals, and children. *British Journal of Social Psychology*, *49*, 91–105. doi:10.1348/014466609X415293

Schwarz, N. (2004). Metacognitive experiences in consumer judgment and decision making. *Journal of Consumer Psychology*, *14*, 332–348. doi:10.1207/s15327663jcp1404_2

Shaver, K. G. (1985). *The attribution of blame: Causality, responsibility, and blameworthiness*. New York, NY: Springer-Verlag.

Singer, P. (1981). *The expanding circle*. Oxford, England: Clarendon Press.

Singer, P. (1990). *Animal liberation* (2nd ed.). London, England: Jonathan Cape.

Staub, E. (1992). *The roots of evil: The origins of genocide and other group violence*. New York, NY: Cambridge University Press.

Wong, D. L., & Baker, C. (1988). Pain in children: Comparison of assessment scales. *Pediatric Nursing*, *14*, 9–17.

12

MORALITY ACROSS CULTURES: A VALUES PERSPECTIVE

NOGA SVERDLIK, SONIA ROCCAS, AND LILACH SAGIV

Morality, like art, means drawing a line someplace.

—Oscar Wilde

Theories of moral development and moral reasoning have long empha-sized universal principles that are common to all people in all societies. A growing body of research indicates, however, that universality in some aspects of morality is accompanied by important cultural differences in other aspects (see Miller, 2006, for a review). What is judged to be morally reprehensible in one culture may be judged as irrelevant to morality in another culture, and criteria that determine the severity of moral infractions depend on specific cultural contexts. Thus, considering Oscar Wilde's famous statement about morality, quoted above, morality is comparable to art not just because it necessitates "drawing a line someplace" but also because, like art, morality may consist of different lines or arrangements of lines that result in different images.

Recent advances in research on personal values can contribute to a deeper understanding of individual and cultural differences in moral outlooks. Like moral principles, *values* are conceptions of the desirable that guide the way people behave, evaluate other people and events, and explain choices and actions. Values reflect what people believe to be good or bad and what should or should not be done (Hitlin & Piliavin, 2004). Values, however, are not identical to moral principles: They are cognitive representations of basic motivations and broad personal goals. Therefore, they may refer to a broader spectrum of domains than is usually encompassed by moral principles in theories of morality.

In this chapter, we integrate insights derived from research on values and research on morality to better understand the motivational under-pinnings of individual and cultural differences in moral outlook. We discuss the commonalities and differences between values and moral principles. We then apply the values perspective to organize different models of morality. We review past research on cross-cultural differences in morality and show how values contribute to an understanding of these differences. Finally, we outline future directions for research integrating values and morality.

VALUES AND MORAL PRINCIPLES

Personal values are broad, socially desirable goals that vary in their importance and serve as guiding principles in people's lives. They are the combined products of socialization, unique personal experiences, and genetic heritage (Knafo et al., 2008; Schermer, Feather, Zhu, & Martin, 2008). People in a particular society share some important values, but they also vary considerably in their personal value hierarchies.

Values and moral principles are similar in important respects: Like moral principles, values are used as criteria to select, evaluate, and justify actions, people, and events (e.g., Cushman, Young, & Hauser, 2006; Roccas & Sagiv, 2009; Schwartz, 1992). Both values and moral principles transcend specific circumstances. Thus, for example, striving for success in life is pursuing a value, whereas seeking to obtain a high grade on an exam is a specific goal (Roccas, Sagiv, Schwartz, & Knafo, 2002). Similarly, not harming others is a moral principle, but avoiding hurting one's friend during a game is a specific goal. Like moral principles, values are inherently socially desirable: Most individuals in most societies agree that they are right, good, and worthy (Schwartz, 1992). Finally, multiple conflicting moral principles and multiple conflicting values may be relevant to a behavioral choice. Thus, one's choices sometimes entail resolving a conflict between important values (Schwartz, 1992; Tetlock, 1986) or moral principles (Miller & Bersoff, 1992).

Values and moral principles differ, however, in an important way: The morality domain is delimited. According to classical views of morality, a social infraction is judged to be a moral violation only if it infringes on an objective obligation, one that is independent of specific social consensus and personal preferences (e.g., Bersoff & Miller, 1993; Miller, Bersoff, & Harwood, 1990; Turiel, 1983; see Smetana, 2006, for a review). Thus, for example, murder is viewed as belonging to the moral domain because the judgment that it is wrong is independent of social consensus or personal preferences. Violating the dress code of one's school, however, may constitute a violation of a social norm; it might even be punishable, but it is not generally judged to be a moral violation. In contrast, personal values refer to any socially desirable broad motivational goal. Thus, whereas all moral principles are likely to be viewed as parts of the value domain, not all values are viewed as belonging to the moral domain (Schwartz, 2007a). This difference implies that values may serve as a broader construct that helps organize in the same theoretical framework moral principles along with other important mechanisms of social regulation, such as norms, conventions, and personal preferences.

Despite this apparent clarity of the classical definition of morality, there is growing evidence of cross-cultural and intracultural differences regarding what is included in the moral domain. Actions that are viewed as belonging to the moral domain in one culture may be viewed as belonging to the realm of social convention or personal choice in another culture. Even within a culture, there is often disagreement regarding what should be viewed as pertaining to the moral domain. Thus, for example, conservative Republicans have moral concerns that Democrats do not recognize as pertaining to the moral domain (Haidt & Graham, 2007). Such inter- and intracultural differences can lead to severe conflicts because morality is a core issue in people's self-definitions.

We propose that applying a values framework to studying moral principles will provide a unifying theoretical perspective for analyzing the spectrum of moral principles within and across cultures. For this purpose, we use Schwartz's (1992, 2009) value theory to organize moral principles and discuss their relationship to values.

Schwartz's (1992) value theory identifies 10 motivationally distinct types of values: hedonism, stimulation, self-direction, universalism, benevolence, tradition, conformity, security, power, and achievement. These values are structured in a circle according to their conflicts and compatibilities. The circle is organized by two basic dimensions: conservation versus openness and self-enhancement versus self-transcendence. Conservation values (tradition, conformity, security) emphasize self-restriction, order, and resistance to change. These values express motivation to avoid uncertainty, ambiguity, and instability. They conflict with openness-to-change values (self-direction, stimulation) that emphasize independent action and thought as well as readiness for new experience. The second dimension contrasts self-enhancement and self-transcendence values. Self-enhancement values emphasize enhancing one's own personal interests even at the expense of other people. They conflict with self-transcendence values (universalism, benevolence) that emphasize concern for others' welfare. Hedonism values share elements of both openness and self-enhancement. Schwartz's value theory has been tested in more than 270 samples from more than 70 countries using different measurement instruments (Davidov, Schmidt, & Schwartz, 2008; Schwartz, 2006; Schwartz & Sagiv, 1995; Spini, 2003).

Individuals from different cultures differ in their values. Thus, for example, individuals from Western European countries tend to attribute greater importance to benevolence and universalism and less importance to power values than people from many other countries. Individuals from East Asian and African countries tend to emphasize conformity and tradition more than people from many other countries (see Sagiv, Schwartz, & Arieli, 2011, for a review). In sum, Schwartz's theory of personal values presents the full spectrum of motivational guiding principles as well as the dynamic relationships of conflict and compatibility among them.

We next use this value theory to identify the motivations that are compatible with the different moral principles that have been discussed in past literature, as well as the motivations that conflict with each moral principle. Thus, by integrating theories of values with theories of morality, we move from describing how people and cultures differ in their moral outlook to investigating the motivational basis for these differences.

WHAT IS INCLUDED IN THE MORAL DOMAIN? DIFFERENT PERSPECTIVES AND MODELS

Defining the moral domain has been controversial in psychology; Table 12.1 summarizes the definitions reviewed in this section. The developmental analysis of morality (Kohlberg, 1969, 1981; Piaget, 1932/1965) followed the Western philosophical tradition of defining morality in terms of issues related to rights and justice. From a values perspective, this view of morality resonates with universalism values, which are values that emphasize concern for social justice and care for humanity and nature. The developmental perspective regards self-interest as belonging to the lowest level of morality. Thus, according to this view, attributing importance to self-enhancement values (power and achievement) should correlate negatively with moral development. In support of this view, Helkama et al. (2003) found that the higher the moral reasoning level of medical students, the more importance they placed on universalism values and the less importance they placed on self-enhancement values.

Gilligan (1982) proposed a "morality of care" as an alternative to Kohlberg's "morality of justice." This approach highlights the importance to moral judgments of care for close others and interdependence with them, an emphasis closely aligned with benevolence values. Gilligan's findings that women tend to use this moral ethic more than men are consistent with findings that women assign more importance to benevolence values than do men (Schwartz & Rubel, 2005).

222 SVERDLIK, ROCCAS, AND SAGIV

TABLE 12.1
Mapping Models of Morality and Values

Author	Social justice	Suffering of others	Area of concern		
			Group's norms and interests	Social order and hierarchical obligations	Physical and spiritual contagion
Kohlberg (1969)	Moral development (Stage 6)	Morality			
Gilligan (1982)		Morality of caring (equally developed as justice)			
Turiel (1983)	Morality	Morality	Community	Community	Divinity
Shweder et al. (1997)	Autonomy	Autonomy	Ingroup/loyalty	Authority/respect	Purity/sanctity
Haidt & Graham (2007)	Fairness/reciprocity	Harm/care	Security	Security	Tradition
Schwartz (1992)	Universalism	Universalism	Conformity	Conformity	
		Benevolence	Tradition	Tradition	
			Benevolence		

A more explicit content-based definition of morality was developed in the social–cognitive domain (e.g., Turiel, 1983). This perspective distinguishes the moral domain from two other domains: the conventional and the personal. Turiel (1983) defined the *moral domain* as consisting of principles that are universally applicable and obligatory and included in the moral domain issues of justice and care. The *conventional domain* is contextually relative and alterable and refers to norms, group interests, and relations to authorities. Finally, the *personal domain* concerns the welfare of oneself and one's private life. Thus, from a value perspective, the moral domain in Turiel's analysis includes universalism and benevolence values; the conventional domain includes conformity, tradition, and security values; and the personal domain includes the other half of the value circle: power, achievement, self-direction, stimulation, and hedonism.

Cultural psychologists and scholars with various relativistic perspectives questioned Turiel's (1983) conception of the moral domain (e.g., Miller, 2006). For example, analyses of interviews with Hindu Indians about norm violations led Shweder, Much, Mahapatra, and Park (1997) to develop a tripartite model of morality that includes ethics of autonomy, community, and divinity. The *ethic of autonomy* focuses on obligations based on an individual's worth and dignity. Moral violations are conceptualized in terms of harm, infringements of personal rights, and injustice. The *ethic of community* focuses on obligations toward the community one lives in. The basic moral obligation is to transcend one's self-interest for the sake of the community. Moral violations refer to lack of respect for the community's history, hierarchy, and collective interests. The *ethic of divinity* addresses issues of the divine and sacred and avoidance of moral impurity. Moral discourse focuses on issues of purity and pollution of the divine essence of the individual. Thoughts and actions that are deemed to be inconsistent with what is sacred and divine are viewed as moral violations.

Each of these moral codes resonates with some of the values identified by Schwartz (1992). Issues of the autonomy ethic (avoiding harm and injustice) are related to benevolence and universalism values. These values emphasize the welfare of others. People who emphasize these values attribute high importance to social justice and equality. They value helpfulness and kindness. Thus, unjust and harmful actions should evoke stronger condemnation the more one assigns importance to benevolence and universalism values (Roccas & McCauley, 2004).

The ethic of community shares with values of tradition, security, and conformity a concern for the consequences of one's actions for the community. These values emphasize the importance of social harmony and express a desire for adherence to social expectations and to the group's traditions and structure. Thus, actions denoting insolence and lack of respect for the community should evoke stronger condemnation the more one assigns importance to tradition, security, and conformity values (Roccas & McCauley, 2004). The community moral code is also compatible with benevolence values that express concern and care for ingroup members. Finally, the ethic of divinity is similar to the emphasis that people with traditional values place on faith and on abnegation of personal striving for the sake of religious imperatives.

Recently, Guerra (2009) developed a quantitative measure of the relevance of Shweder et al.'s (1997) three moral codes to the judgment of possible violations. She explored the relations of moral codes to the importance attributed to different values in two cultures: Brazil and the United Kingdom. For most values, relationships with the moral codes generalized across British and Brazilian students and were consistent with our reasoning regarding the compatibilities delineated above between moral codes and values.

Shweder and colleagues' (1997) theory inspired a search for finer distinctions among moral domains. Moral foundations theory (Haidt & Graham, 2007; see also Chapter 1, this volume) focuses on five moral systems: harm/care, fairness/reciprocity (both related to the ethic of autonomy), ingroup/loyalty, authority/respect (both related to the ethic of community), and purity/sanctity (related to the ethic of divinity). The harm/care foundation is expressed in sensitivity to suffering and disapproval of people who cause harm. The fairness/reciprocity foundation is expressed in sensitivity to injustice, inequality, and infringements of personal autonomy. The ingroup/loyalty foundation is expressed in a sense of duty toward one's ingroup. The authority/respect foundation leads to a concern for status and hierarchy and sensitivity to actions that challenge the accepted social stratification.

The finer distinctions embedded in Haidt and Graham's (2007) model should be reflected in the relationships with values. The harm/care foundation shares with fairness/reciprocity a concern for the welfare of others, which is reflected in benevolence and universalism values. The harm/care foundation, however, puts more emphasis on concern for close others, which is more compatible with benevolence than with universalism values, whereas the fairness/reciprocity foundation emphasizes general principles that are more compatible with universalism than with benevolence values. The ingroup/loyalty foundation shares with authority/respect a concern for the integrity of the community and its traditions, norms, and leadership, which is expressed in values of tradition, conformity, and security. The ingroup/loyalty foundation, however, has an additional aspect: concern for the welfare of community members, which is compatible with the emphasis of benevolence values on the welfare of people with whom one is in close contact.

In sum, analyzing the value basis of the various models of moral domains enables us to coherently organize the different models. Self-transcendence values (benevolence and universalism) are related to concerns about justice and harm, which are underscored in all of the models reviewed above. Conservation values (conformity and tradition) are related to concern about norms, social order, and purity, which are underscored in the more recent theories of morality.

Interestingly, all of the models of moral domains explicitly emphasize only half of the values circle—those values that focus on relationships with people and groups. Consistent with this analysis, preliminary findings from a recent study (Schwartz, 2007a) revealed that 70% to 80% of an adult Israeli sample labeled all or most of benevolence, universalism, conformity, tradition, and security values as moral values. In contrast, fewer than 20% labeled any of the power, achievement, hedonism, and stimulation values as moral, and fewer than 30% labeled more than one of the self-direction values as moral.

If only half of the values circle relates to morality, is the other half of the circle irrelevant to this domain? The other half consists mainly of openness to change and self-enhancement values. Openness to change values focus on independence of action and thought and on novelty, change, and excitement. The expression of these values is likely to be related to violations of norms and expectations. Thus, these values may be perceived as immoral to people who emphasize the moral foundations that Graham and Haidt (Chapter 1, this volume) call ingroup/loyalty, authority/respect, and purity/sanctity. Self-enhancement values focus on the importance of promoting self-interest even at others' expense. Behaviors associated with these values are likely to violate moral imperatives associated with issues of harm/care and fairness/reciprocity. This analysis suggests that the value circle includes prescriptive as well as proscriptive morality (Janoff-Bulman, Sheikh, & Hepp, 2009; see also Chapter 7, this volume). Whereas self-transcendence and conservation values focus on what one ought to do (respect authority, care for others), openness to change and self-enhancement values focus more on what one ought to avoid doing (caring about oneself, expressing one's individuality).

We investigated the associations between the five moral foundations and Schwartz's (1992) 10 value types in a sample of Israeli students ($N = 146$). As expected, harm/care and fairness/reciprocity correlated most positively with universalism values. In addition, harm/care—but not fairness/reciprocity—correlated positively with benevolence. Ingroup/loyalty and authority/respect correlated most positively with tradition and conformity values and most negatively with the opposing self-direction, stimulation, and hedonism values. In addition, the correlation of benevolence values was stronger for ingroup/loyalty than for authority/respect. Finally, as we reasoned, the pattern of associations with values of purity/sanctity was similar to the pattern found for authority/respect and ingroup/loyalty, but the correlation with tradition values was stronger.

VALUES AND CROSS-CULTURAL DIFFERENCES
IN MORAL OUTLOOKS

Shweder and colleagues' (1997) insight that culture affects the inclusiveness of the moral domain has received additional support in studies across a variety of cultures: Whereas issues of harm and fairness are judged to be part of the moral domain in all cultures, other issues, such as purity, loyalty to the ingroup, and respect for authority, are considered part of the moral domain in some cultural groups but not in others. Thus, when asked to consider the morality of specific actions, people from Western cultures apply mainly the ethic of autonomy, whereas people from non-Western societies usually apply all moral foundations (see Vasquez, Keltner, Ebenbach, & Banaszynski, 2001, for comparisons of Americans and Filipinos; Jensen, 1998, for Americans and Indians; Guerra & Giner-Sorolla, 2010, for Britons and Brazilians). These differences in the inclusiveness of the morality domain are consistent with differences in value patterns in those cultures: People from non-Western cultures attribute greater importance to tradition and conformity values than do people from Western cultures (Schwartz, 2007b).

Differences in the application of moral foundations are also found between cultural groups within a nation. For example, religiously conservative participants in the United States apply the divinity ethic more and the autonomy ethic less than religiously liberal people (e.g., Jensen, 1997). These differences are consistent with positive correlations between tradition values and religiosity (Roccas, 2005; Saroglu, Delpierre, & Dernelle, 2004; Schwartz & Huismans, 1995) and political conservatism (Barnea & Schwartz, 1998).

Similarly, in a study of moral condemnation, Haidt, Koller, and Dias (1993) showed that Americans from high socioeconomic backgrounds limit the moral domain to actions that directly harm others. In contrast, Americans from low socioeconomic backgrounds include in the moral domain actions that evoke disgust or show disrespect for community symbols. This pattern was replicated among Brazilians. The findings also revealed a cross-cultural difference such that the tendency to include in the moral domain actions that do not harm others directly was more apparent among Brazilians than among Americans. Values can help us understand these differences, too: Education consistently correlates negatively with the importance assigned to values of tradition, security, and conformity (Schwartz, 2005), the values that are most closely related to community and divinity moral principles. Thus, educated people attribute lower importance to values emphasizing adherence to social and religious expectations. Consistently, they do not see actions that conflict with these values as moral violations.

The universal emphasis on the ethic of autonomy highlights a paradox: Although people from all cultures believe that harming others is wrong, actions that can cause immense harm to others are sometimes applauded and considered to be moral. A blatant example is the wide support that military attacks sometimes evoke. We suggest that although the ethic of autonomy is considered to be part of the moral domain in all cultures, people and groups vary in the inclusiveness of the targets to which this ethic applies: In some cultural groups, concern about justice and protection from harm (i.e., the ethic of autonomy) applies to all people, whereas in others such concern applies mainly to ingroup members.

Integrating research on values with research on morality can help us understand why the application of the ethic of autonomy is not universal. Discussing the meaning of social justice and equality values, Schwartz (2007a) proposed that in some cultures people tend to understand these values as applying to all people, including outgroup members. In other cultures, however, people tend to understand these values as applying mainly to the ingroup. These findings suggest that cultures may differ in the inclusiveness of the targets to which the ethic of autonomy applies. Societies that view the individual as an integral part of the collective (i.e., societies in which conservation values are highly important; Schwartz, 2007b) encourage a narrower view of the application of the ethic of autonomy.

Another process that could explain why violations of the ethic of autonomy are sometimes perceived as morally justifiable lies in the relative importance of different moral principles. The more inclusive the moral domain, the more likely it is that one needs to prioritize conflicting actions that draw on different moral foundations. As research on the culture of honor exemplifies, in cultures where honor is highly important, harming a person who violated one's honor may be justifiable (e.g., Cohen, Nisbett, Bowdle, & Schwarz, 1996; Vandello & Cohen, 2003). Similarly, in cultures that foster a duty-based interpersonal moral code (e.g., Hindu Indians; Miller, 1994), principles of interpersonal responsibility may be prioritized over principles of justice (Miller & Bersoff, 1992). Thus, one can feel morally justified in harming others or in violating justice principles because actions that draw on the ethics of community or divinity can have priority over actions that draw on the ethics of autonomy. Considering the values that are important in different cultures, one can predict not only which moral foundations apply (see Table 12.1), but also which principle is likely to be preferred over others.

In sum, people who emphasize conservation values have an inclusive conception of the moral domain but a narrower application of the ethic of autonomy. They view the ethic of autonomy as applicable mainly to ingroup members. In contrast, people who emphasize values of openness hold a more inclusive view of the applicability of the ethic of autonomy but hold a narrower conception of the moral domain. They view the moral domain as consisting mainly of the ethic of autonomy.

INTEGRATING VALUES AND MORAL OUTLOOKS: FUTURE DIRECTIONS

The integration of the values and morality literatures has the potential of presenting further directions for research in cross-cultural contexts. In this section, we address two research directions. First, we suggest that by studying the relationship between the value of being moral and other values, we may learn how different cultures define who the moral person is. Then we suggest that by applying a values perspective, we may learn how different people manage their conflicts between multiple moral outlooks embedded in their multiple identities.

Who Is a Moral Person?

Cultures are likely to vary in their definitions of the "moral person" and the meaning they attribute to "being moral" depending on the inclusiveness of their moral domain. We suggest that being moral is a personal value, a stable broad goal that serves as a guiding principle in life. The meaning of this value could be inferred from its relations with other values (Schwartz, 1992). In social contexts in which morality is limited to issues of harm and justice, people who attribute high importance to being moral are likely to attribute high importance to values emphasizing concern for others. In contrast, in social contexts in which the domain of morality includes issues of divinity and community, a person who aspires to be moral will also attribute importance to values emphasizing adherence to group norms and religious imperatives.

In a recent study (Sverdlik, 2010), we exemplified this possible synergy between research on values and research on morality by comparing a sample of religious Israeli Jews ($n = 68$) with a sample of nonreligious Israeli Jews ($n = 132$). Respondents completed a values questionnaire to which we added an item labeled *being moral*. They rated the importance of all value items as guiding principles in their lives. As expected, in both groups, being a moral person was considered important by most respondents (Ms of 5.53 and 5.52 in the religious and secular groups, on a scale ranging from −1 to 7).

We inferred the meaning of being moral by considering its correlations with the 10 values. In both groups, being moral correlated positively with benevolence values that express concern and care for others. In addition, being moral correlated positively with tradition and negatively with universalism and self-direction values in the religious group. In the nonreligious group, it correlated positively with universalism and negatively with power and hedonism values. Thus, tradition values that express adherence to norms and authorities are associated with being moral in the conservative religious group, whereas universalism values that express acceptance and tolerance toward all human beings are associated with being moral in the secular sample.

Thus, although members of all groups in society are likely to agree that being a moral person is a positive aspiration, cultural groups vary in the meaning they attribute to being moral and in the values they associate with being a moral person. Such a difference may lead not only to different judgments and actions in specific situations but also to cross-cultural misunderstanding and miscommunication.

Multiple Identities and Multiple Moralities

The increased heterogeneity of societies (Putnam, 2007; Verkuyten, 2006) has been accompanied by a sharp increase in the number of people who belong simultaneously to groups that may differ in their values, norms, and moral outlooks. The multiple identities stemming from the varied groups to which people simultaneously belong form a complex puzzle of partially overlapping social identities (Benet-Martínez & Haritatos, 2005; Roccas & Brewer, 2002; Tadmor, Tetlock, & Peng, 2009). Immigrants who identify with their culture of origin as well as their host culture, people with strong religious convictions who work in a nonreligious professional environment, employees in multinational companies who identify with the organization as a whole as well as with their local subsidiary—all need to juggle multiple identities.

Multiple identities may lead to exposure to the moral outlooks of different cultural groups that may differ extensively in their views of right and wrong and of what is included in the moral domain. In this sense, people with multiple identities are fluent in multiple "languages" of morality. Thus, for example, an Asian American may be aware of the moral domains of both Asian and Western cultures. As discussed above, the different values emphasized in these two cultures may yield different views about moral domains. Some actions (e.g., harming another person) are likely to be viewed as moral violations in both cultures. Others may be seen as moral violations in one culture but not in the other (e.g., divinity violations may be seen as immoral in Asian cultures more than in the United States; limiting one's autonomy may be seen as a moral violation in the United States more than in Asian cultures).

How do people manage the compatibilities and conflicts between the multiple moral outlooks embedded in their multiple identities? Possibly, exposure to different views of morality will lead people to include more life domains in their moral universe. An Asian American may regard as immoral anything that is viewed as immoral in any of his or her cultural groups and may view more areas as part of the moral domain than would Asians or Americans. But exposure to different views of morality may have the opposite effect as well: A bicultural person may recognize that moral outlooks depend on the social and cultural context. Thus, exposure to multiple identities may lead to more tolerance of moral infractions.

We suggest that the way in which people integrate their multiple identities has a profound influence on their moral outlook. Multiple identities could lead to a more restricted or more inclusive representation of the moral universe depending on how people integrate their multiple identities into a coherent self-concept. When integrating multiple identities, one can form an exclusive and simple social identity in which there is a single ingroup identification based on the dominance of one identity over the other (e.g., an Asian American might identify with the Asian group only) or on the intersection of one's multiple ingroups (e.g., an Asian American might view as ingroup members only those who are both Asian and American). This representation of one's multiple identities is positively related to an emphasis on conservation values (Roccas & Brewer, 2002). Conversely, one can acknowledge and accept the distinctive aspects of each group and form an inclusive and complex social identity. The most complex social identity (merger) is represented when divergent group memberships are simultaneously recognized and included in their most inclusive form. In the example above, the person will view as ingroup members all Asians and all Americans (Roccas & Brewer, 2002). This representation of one's multiple identities is negatively related to emphasis on conservation values (Roccas & Brewer, 2002).

We reason that people with a complex social identity are aware of the differences in beliefs, values, and moral outlooks among their multiple ingroups. They are likely to be aware that issues considered to be immoral in one ingroup are considered to be a matter of personal choice in the other group. Thus, people with a complex representation of the interrelations among their multiple ingroups are more likely to accept the notion that people may act in different ways, all morally admissible. For them, membership in multiple ingroups may translate into a permissive moral outlook. In contrast, we reason that people with a simple social identity are likely to develop a sense of absolute morality. They are likely to view moral obligations and moral violations as universal and to regard behaviors that defy their moral outlook as ones that should not be accepted in any society.

CONCLUSION

In this chapter, we have sought to tie theories of morality to the psychology of values. Integrating insights from research on values and research on morality contributes to a better understanding of the motivational underpinnings of individual and cultural differences in moral outlook. Analyzing the value basis of moral domains enables us to coherently organize different theoretical models of morality. Taking values into consideration helped us tease apart the two types of inclusiveness that permeate theories and debates about morality: People who emphasize conservation values hold an inclusive conception of the moral domain but an exclusive view of the targets worthy of concern. In contrast, people who emphasize values of openness hold an inclusive view of the applicability of moral imperatives related to concern for others but an exclusive conceptualization of the moral domain.

REFERENCES

Barnea, M. F., & Schwartz, S. H. (1998). Values and voting. *Political Psychology, 19,* 17–40. doi:10.1111/0162-895X.00090

Benet-Martínez, V., & Haritatos, J. (2005). Bicultural identity integration (BII): Components and psychosocial antecedents. *Journal of Personality, 73,* 1015–1050. doi:10.1111/j.1467-6494.2005.00337.x

Bersoff, D. M., & Miller, J. G. (1993). Culture, context, and the development of moral accountability judgments. *Developmental Psychology, 29,* 664–676. doi:10.1037/0012-1649.29.4.664

Cohen, D., Nisbett, R., Bowdle, B., & Schwarz, N. (1996). Insult, aggression, and the southern culture of honor: An "experimental ethnography." *Journal of Personality and Social Psychology, 70,* 945–960. doi:10.1037/0022-3514.70.5.945

Cushman, F., Young, L., & Hauser, M. D. (2006). The role of conscious reasoning and intuition in moral judgments: Testing three principles of harm. *Psychological Science, 17,* 1082–1089. doi:10.1111/j.1467-9280.2006.01834.x

Davidov, E., Schmidt, P., & Schwartz, S. H. (2008). Bringing values back in: The adequacy of the European Social Survey to measure values in 20 countries. *Public Opinion Quarterly, 7,* 420–445. doi:10.1093/poq/nfn035

Gilligan, C. (1982). *In a different voice: Psychological theory and women's development.* Cambridge, MA: Harvard University Press.

Guerra, V. M. (2009). *Community, autonomy and divinity: Studying morality across cultures.* Unpublished doctoral dissertation, University of Kent, Canterbury, England.

Guerra, V. M., & Giner-Sorolla, R. (2010). The Community, Autonomy and Divinity Scale (CADS): A new tool for the cross-cultural study of morality. *Journal of Cross-Cultural Psychology, 41,* 35–50. doi:10.1177/0022022109348919

Haidt, J., & Graham, J. (2007). When morality opposes justice: Conservatives have moral intuitions that liberals may not recognize. *Social Justice Research, 20,* 98–116. doi:10.1007/s11211-007-0034-z

Haidt, J., Koller, S., & Dias, M. (1993). Affect, culture, and morality, or is it wrong to eat your dog? *Journal of Personality and Social Psychology, 65,* 613–628. doi:10.1037/0022-3514.65.4.613

Helkama, K., Uutela, A., Pohjanheimo, E., Salminen, S., Koponen, A., & Rantanen-Vantsi, L. (2003). Moral reasoning and values in medical school: A longitudinal study in Finland. *Scandinavian Journal of Educational Research, 47*, 399–411. doi:10.1080/00313830308589

Hitlin, S., & Piliavin, A. (2004). Values: Reviving a dormant concept. *Annual Review of Sociology, 30*, 359–393. doi:10.1146/annurev.soc.30.012703.110640

Janoff-Bulman, R., Sheikh, S., & Hepp, S. (2009). Proscriptive versus prescriptive morality: Two faces of moral regulation. *Journal of Personality and Social Psychology, 96*, 521–537. doi:10.1037/a0013779

Jensen, L. A. (1997). Culture wars: American moral divisions across the adult lifespan. *Journal of Adult Development, 4*, 107–121. doi:10.1007/BF02510084

Jensen, L. A. (1998). Moral divisions within countries between orthodoxy and progressivism: India and the United States. *Journal for the Scientific Study of Religion, 37*, 90–107. doi:10.2307/1388031

Knafo, A., Israel, S., Darvasi, A., Bachner-Melman, R., Uzefovsky, F., Cohen, L., . . . Ebstein, R. P. (2008). Individual differences in allocation of funds in the dictator game associated with length of the arginine vasopressin 1a receptor RS3 promoter region and correlation between RS3 length and hippocampal mRNA. *Genes, Brain & Behavior, 7*, 266–275. doi:10.1111/j.1601-183X.2007.00341.x

Kohlberg, L. (1969). Stage and sequence: The cognitive–developmental approach to socialization. In D. A. Goslin (Ed.), *Handbook of socialization theory and research* (pp. 347–480). Chicago, IL: Rand McNally.

Kohlberg, L. (1981). *The philosophy of moral development: Essays on moral development* (Vol. 1). San Francisco, CA: Harper & Row.

Miller, J. G. (1994). Cultural diversity in the morality of caring: Individually oriented versus duty-based interpersonal moral codes. *Cross-Cultural Research, 28*, 3–39. doi:10.1177/106939719402800101

Miller, J. G. (2006). Insights into moral development from cultural psychology. In M. Killen & J. Smetana (Eds.), *Handbook of moral development* (pp. 375–398). New York, NY: Erlbaum.

Miller, J. G., & Bersoff, D. M. (1992). Culture and moral judgment: How are conflicts between justice and interpersonal responsibilities resolved? *Journal of Personality and Social Psychology, 62*, 541–554. doi:10.1037/0022-3514.62.4.541

Miller, J. G., Bersoff, D. M., & Harwood, R. L. (1990). Perceptions of social responsibility in India and in the United States: Moral imperatives or personal decisions? *Journal of Personality and Social Personality, 58*, 33–47. doi:10.1037/0022-3514.58.1.33

Piaget, J. (1965). *The moral judgment of the child*. New York, NY: Free Press. (Original work published 1932)

Putnam, R. D. (2007). E pluribus unum: Diversity and community in the 21st century: The 2006 Johan Skytte Prize lecture. *Scandinavian Political Studies, 30*, 137–174. doi:10.1111/j.1467-9477.2007.00176.x

Roccas, S. (2005). Religion and value systems. *Journal of Social Issues, 61*, 747–759. doi:10.1111/j.1540-4560.2005.00430.x

Roccas, S., & Brewer, M. (2002). Social identity complexity. *Personality and Social Psychology Review, 6*, 88–106. doi:10.1207/S15327957PSPR0602_01

Roccas, S., & McCauley, C. (2004). Values and emotions in the relational models: What happens when relationship norms are violated? In N. Haslam (Ed.), *Relational models: Theories, advances, and prospects* (pp. 263–286). Mahwah, NJ: Erlbaum.

Roccas, S., & Sagiv, L. (2009). Personal values and behavior: Taking the cultural context into account. *Social and Personality Psychology Compass, 4*, 30–41. doi:10.1111/j.1751-9004.2009.00234.x

Roccas, S., Sagiv, L., Schwartz, S. H., & Knafo, A. (2002). The Big Five personality factors and personal values. *Personality and Social Psychology Bulletin, 28*, 789–801. doi:10.1177/0146167202289008

Sagiv, L., Schwartz, S. H., & Arieli, S. (2011). Personal values, national culture and organizations: Insights applying the Schwartz value framework. In N. N. Ashkanasy, C. Wilderom, & M. F. Peterson (Eds.), *The handbook of organizational culture and climate* (2nd ed., pp. 515–537). Newbury Park, CA: Sage.

Saroglu, V., Delpierre, V., & Dernelle, R. (2004). Values and religiosity: A meta-analysis of studies using Schwartz's model. *Personality and Individual Differences, 37*, 721–734. doi:10.1016/j.paid.2003.10.005

Schermer, J. A., Feather, N. T., Zhu, G., & Martin, N. G. (2008). Phenotypic, genetic, and environmental properties of the portrait values questionnaire. *Twin Research and Human Genetics, 5*, 531–537. doi:10.1375/twin.11.5.531

Schwartz, S. H. (1992). Universals in the content and structure of values: Theoretical advances and empirical tests in 20 countries. In M. P. Zanna (Ed.), *Advances in experimental social psychology* (Vol. 24, pp. 1–65). San Diego, CA: Academic Press.

Schwartz, S. H. (2005). Robustness and fruitfulness of a theory of universals in individual human values. In A. Tamayo & J. Porto (Eds.), *Valores e trabalho* [Values and work] (pp. 56–95). Brasilia, Brazil: Editora Universidade de Brasilia.

Schwartz, S. H. (2006). Les valeurs de base de la personne: Théorie, mesures et applications [Basic human values: Theory, measurement, and applications]. *Revue Française de Sociologie, 47*, 249–288.

Schwartz, S. H. (2007a). Universalism values and the inclusiveness of our moral universe. *Journal of Cross-Cultural Psychology, 38*, 711–728. doi:10.1177/0022022107308992

Schwartz, S. H. (2007b). Value orientations: Measurement, antecedents and consequences across nations. In R. Jowell, C. Roberts, R. Fitzgerald, & G. Eva (Eds.), *Measuring attitudes cross-nationally: Lessons from the European social survey* (pp. 161–193). London, England: Sage.

Schwartz, S. H. (2009). Basic values: How they motivate and inhibit prosocial behavior. In M. Mikulincer & P. R. Shaver (Eds.), *Prosocial motives, emotions, and behavior: The better angels of our nature* (pp. 221–241). Washington, DC: American Psychological Association.

Schwartz, S. H., & Huismans, S. (1995). Value priorities and religiosity in four Western religions. *Social Psychology Quarterly, 58*, 88–107. doi:10.2307/2787148

Schwartz, S. H., & Rubel, T. (2005). Sex differences in value priorities: Cross-cultural and multimethod studies. *Journal of Personality and Social Psychology, 89*, 1010–1028. doi:10.1037/0022-3514.89.6.1010

Schwartz, S. H., & Sagiv, L. (1995). Identifying culture specifics in the content and structure of values. *Journal of Cross-Cultural Psychology, 26*, 92–116. doi:10.1177/0022022195261007

Shweder, R. A., Much, N. C., Mahapatra, M., & Park, L. (1997). The "big three" of morality (autonomy, community, divinity) and the "big three" explanations of suffering. In A. M. Brandt & P. Rozin (Eds.), *Morality and health* (pp. 119–169). New York, NY: Routledge.

Smetana, J. G. (2006). Social domain theory: Consistencies and variations in children's moral and social judgments. In M. Killen & J. G. Smetana (Eds.), *Handbook of moral development* (pp. 119–153). Mahwah, NJ: Erlbaum.

Spini, D. (2003). Measurement equivalence of 10 value types from the Schwartz value survey across 21 countries. *Journal of Cross-Cultural Psychology, 34*, 3–23. doi:10.1177/0022022102239152

Sverdlik, N. (2010). *Religiosity and the value of being moral.* Manuscript in preparation.

Tadmor, C. T., Tetlock, P. E., & Peng, K. (2009). Biculturalism and integrative complexity: Testing the acculturation complexity model. *Journal of Cross-Cultural Psychology, 40*, 105–139. doi:10.1177/0022022108326279

Tetlock, P. E. (1986). A value pluralism model of ideological reasoning. *Journal of Personality and Social Psychology, 50*, 819–827. doi:10.1037/0022-3514.50.4.819

Turiel, E. (1983). *The development of social knowledge: Morality and convention.* Cambridge, England: Cambridge University Press.

Vandello, J. A., & Cohen, D. (2003). Male honor and female fidelity: Implicit cultural scripts that perpetuate domestic violence. *Journal of Personality and Social Psychology, 84*, 997–1010. doi:10.1037/0022-3514.84.5.997

Vasquez, K., Keltner, D., Ebenbach, D. H., & Banaszynski, T. L. (2001). Cultural variation and similarity in moral rhetorics: Voices from the Philippines and United States. *Journal of Cross-Cultural Psychology, 32*, 93–120. doi:10.1177/0022022101032001010

Verkuyten, M. (2006). Multicultural recognition and ethnic minority rights: A social identity perspective. *European Review of Social Psychology, 17*, 148–184. doi:10.1080/10463280600937418

III

DEVELOPMENTAL, PERSONALITY, AND CLINICAL ASPECTS

13

AUTONOMOUS MORAL MOTIVATION: CONSEQUENCES, SOCIALIZING ANTECEDENTS, AND THE UNIQUE ROLE OF INTEGRATED MORAL PRINCIPLES

AVI ASSOR

Philosophers hold vastly different views concerning what is moral. In this chapter, I adopt the view that human actions can be viewed as highly moral if they involve an attempt to take into account others' needs while paying a significant personal cost. This definition is closely related to the notion of altruistic behavior: for example, rescuing persecuted minorities at considerable personal risk or giving up significant personal gains when they are based on acts one views as immoral (see Chapters 15 and 21, this volume). I assume that one source of such moral actions is what in self-determination theory (SDT; Ryan & Deci, 2000) is called *autonomous moral motivation*, which, according to SDT, is qualitatively different from controlled moral motivation. The major goal of this chapter is to explain what autonomous moral motivation is and show that one specific type of moral motivation—integrated moral motivation—is a particularly important determinant of moral behavior.

The first part of the chapter focuses on the notion of autonomous morality and contrasts it with controlled morality. The concept of *autonomous morality* refers to moral motives that are experienced as volitional, based on truly valuing the moral act, and perceived as emanating from one's authentic self rather than from external or internal coercive forces. The concept of *controlled morality* refers to moral motivation and behavior that are not experienced as truly valuable or volitional and are driven only by internal or external pressures.

In SDT, autonomous and controlled moral motives are viewed as located at different points on a continuum. Therefore, the chapter begins with a description of this continuum, the place of the two moral constructs on this continuum, and their relations with other moral constructs. I then describe findings from programmatic research on socialization antecedents of autonomous morality. This is followed by a discussion of the importance of one kind of autonomous moral motivation: *integrated moral motivation*, which is the propensity to act morally because the act is experienced as reflecting one's core self, central values, and identity. I end the chapter with a presentation of the consequences of autonomous versus controlled motives for moral behavior, social relationships, and personal well-being. I propose that integrated moral motivation is a crucial determinant of highly moral behavior, a sense of autonomy, and personal well-being and that research on its socialization antecedents and outcomes is of special interest.

THE SDT MOTIVATION CONTINUUM AS APPLIED TO MORAL OR PROSOCIAL MOTIVATION

SDT posits five types of motives that can be placed along a continuum of perceived autonomy (Ryan & Deci, 2000). Table 13.1 presents the five motivation types in order of lesser to greater perceived autonomy. The least

TABLE 13.1
The Moral Motivation Continuum

Type of motivation (lesser to greater perceived autonomy)	Description
External motivation	Moral behavior is driven by physical threats or the offering or withdrawal of material rewards.
Introjected motivation	Moral behavior is driven by self-worth or social approval concerns (e.g., avoiding guilt or shame, striving to feel highly worthy).
Identified morality	Moral behavior is guided by an understanding of and identification with the value of the behavior.
Integrated motivation	Moral behavior is guided by the experience of the behavior as reflecting core aspects of one's authentic self and identity.
Intrinsic motivation	Moral behavior is energized by positive feelings such as satisfaction and enjoyment that are generated by the moral act itself.

autonomous form of motivation is termed *external*. Behavior motivated in this way is experienced as originating from external contingencies involving physical threats or the offering or withdrawal of material rewards. The behaviors are experienced as clearly nonautonomous, and they persist only when the contingencies are present. An example of an extrinsically motivated "moral" behavior is investing effort to help others because this might cause them to put one in a position to derive material benefits. Another example would be a Gestapo official who helped Jews to escape being transported to a death camp in the final stage of World War II because it might help him in postwar trials.

Next on the autonomy continuum is *introjected* moral motivation. The term *introjection* is derived from the Latin words *intro* and *jacere*, meaning "into" and "to throw." Introjection is thus a process in which people feel as if values or goals were inserted into them by figures whose approval and appreciation they need, without having the option of modifying or even examining the values or goals (e.g., Assor, Roth, & Deci, 2004). Under the influence of this kind of motivation, behavior is controlled by a wish to avoid feeling guilty, ashamed, or unworthy or by a striving to feel highly worthy. Such strivings are based on the approving or disapproving reactions of significant others.

Although in the case of introjected moral motivation the enactment of behavior is not dependent on specific external contingencies, it is still considered relatively controlled (rather than autonomous) because people feel they are acting because they must, not because they want to. The source of the coercion that was once external has been introjected and now resides inside, causing the person to feel controlled by internal contingencies that link self-esteem and social acceptance to the enactment of specific behaviors or demonstration of particular attributes (Assor et al., 2004; Assor, Vansteenkiste, & Kaplan, 2009). An example of an introjected moral behavior would be investing great effort (even risking one's own safety) to help others and thereby feel worthy of significant others' esteem or love.

In my view, strivings motivated by self-worth concerns do not necessarily signify introjected motivation. Only when the self-worth concerns are tied to an expected lack of others' approval or love are they clearly introjected. Consistent with this view, self-related feelings may also accompany an integrated moral motivation (to be discussed later). In this case, the feeling of being guilty or unworthy is tied to the perception that by acting immorally one has failed to realize values that are central to one's authentic self and identity. The notion of guilt as related to integrated motivation is close to the notion of existential guilt (May, 1983) and Fromm's (1947) humanistic conscience (see also Penner & Chircov, 2010).

The next step along the continuum is *identified* morality. It is considered relatively autonomous because the person who experiences it has accepted the value of the activity as his or her own. Identified motivation, although not purely autonomous, is said to result from identifying with the importance of the behavior vis-à-vis the person's own values and goals. The experience of autonomy connected with identified motivation can emerge also when the activity is not pleasant. This is because the motivation is based on an understanding of the value of the behavior and not on the pleasure it creates. An example of an identified moral behavior would be investing a great deal of effort or taking a significant risk to help another person because one thinks the person deserves to be helped.

An even more autonomous form of moral motivation is called *integrated*. In this type of motivation, goals and behaviors that are enacted are experienced as reflecting core aspects of one's authentic self and identity. This linkage with core self and identity does not occur in the case of identified motivation. As a result, integrated morality is experienced as more autonomous than identified motivation. To attain integrated morality, a person has to resolve inconsistencies or conflicts between important goals and practices. This can be accomplished by prioritizing goals and modifying practices so that they fit together and, most important, reflect one's authentic inclinations and self-chosen values.

In a modern or postmodern world characterized by moral relativism, conflicting moral and ideological views, and widespread anomie, the formation of integrated moral principles and motives is difficult because there are bound to be authorities and groups whose views evoke doubts about one's own values. Therefore, developing truly integrated moral values often requires a process of personal exploration and reflection, without which a person might lack confidence in the principles adopted (Assor, Cohen-Malayev, Kaplan, & Friedman, 2005; Aviram & Assor, 2010). An example of an integrated moral behavior would be investing a great deal of effort or resources or taking a major risk to help another person because one thinks and feels that helping others in need is a fundamental aspect of who one is, of one's core values, and of the identity one has formulated.

Another highly autonomous kind of moral motivation is termed *intrinsic*. In this case, moral actions are guided by intrinsic motives and are engaged in because they produce positive feelings such as interest, enjoyment, and satisfaction. Although integrated and intrinsic motives are similar in terms of the depth and intensity of the sense of autonomy they generate, intrinsic motivation, unlike integrated motivation, is not originally based on external sources and does not involve unpleasant feelings. Within SDT, the notion of intrinsic prosocial motivation received relatively little attention, and the first attempt to develop scales assessing prosocial motivation did not assess the intrinsic type (Ryan & Connell, 1989). I believe, however, that moral actions can be viewed as intrinsically motivated if they are energized by enjoyment or by satisfaction based on empathy (Batson, 2010; Eisenberg, Fabes, & Spinrad, 2006). In these cases, helping others causes one to feel better because the recipients of the help feel better. Because moral actions are often costly to the person who engages in them, intrinsic moral motivation based on positive feelings is not likely to be sufficient to cause a person to be highly moral in general. Still, even if intrinsic moral motivation is not likely to be the prime motivator of moral acts, it may combine with other kinds of moral motivation and thereby strengthen the likelihood that a person will act morally. For example, whereas the prime motivation for taking significant risks to help persecuted minorities might be the perception that this act reflects one's core values and identity (integrated motivation), the altruistic act might be based on empathic concern and the positive feelings one experiences when acting effectively and connecting meaningfully with other people.

It is important to distinguish between SDT-based moral motives and Kohlberg's (1984) stages of moral reasoning. One difference is that SDT refers to motivation rather than cognition and therefore should predict actual behavior better than Kohlberg's stages. Also, although people who have reached Kohlberg's highest level of moral judgment are likely to have integrated moral motives and principles, people may have integrated moral motives and principles without having reached Kohlberg's highest level of moral judgment. That is, they may act on values incorporated into their core self or identity without being able to rationalize their behavior at Kohlberg's highest level.

RESEARCH ON THE BENEFITS OF AUTONOMOUS MORAL MOTIVATION

There have been three attempts to develop scales to assess the various forms of moral motivation posited by SDT. The first two attempts to distinguish among the different SDT-based prosocial forms of motivation were made by Ryan and Connell (1989) and Gagne (2000). A third attempt was made by Assor, Kanat-Maymon, Feinberg, and Kaplan (2010). Studies based on these measures have shown that children and youths in both the United States and Israel are able to distinguish between external, introjected, identified, and intrinsic forms of prosocial motivation. Because integrated motivation is more likely to emerge fully in adolescence, it was not assessed in these studies, which focused mostly on children.

Two recent SDT-based investigations of prosocial motivation were based on a general indicator of autonomous motivation (an average score of identified, integrated, and intrinsic motives), which was contrasted with a global indicator of controlled motivation (Weinstein & Ryan, 2010) or a specific indicator of introjected motivation (Roth, 2008). Weinstein and Ryan (2010) conducted a diary study and three experiments investigating relations between autonomous and controlled (mostly introjected) prosocial motives and various kinds of prosocial behavior. They found that autonomous prosocial motivation predicted more sharing, generosity, and helping than did controlled motivation. Two experiments included, in addition to autonomous versus controlled motivation conditions, a third condition in which participants were given an opportunity to do the same task but the products were not presented as contributing to someone else's welfare or benefits (the no-help condition). As expected, relative to the no-help condition, autonomous motivation led to higher effort and productivity, whereas controlled motivation led to lower effort and productivity.

Also as expected, work partners felt less able to relate to participants who were not encouraged or pressured to help (no-help condition) than to participants whose help was autonomously motivated; moreover, work partners felt least related to participants whose help was driven by controlled motivation. Thus, it appears that autonomous help promotes the highest level of perceived relatedness in partners, whereas no help promotes a somewhat lower level of relatedness, and controlled help results in the lowest sense of relatedness in work partners. In addition, Weinstein and Ryan (2010) showed that in both helpers and help recipients, autonomous prosocial motivation was associated with higher levels of subjective well-being, positive affect, vitality, self-esteem, and sense of relatedness and with lower levels of negative affect compared with controlled motivation.

The study by Roth (2008) showed that introjected prosocial motivation predicted self-oriented helping, whereas autonomous motivation predicted other-oriented helping. *Self-oriented helping* was defined as helping in order to gain others' approval and appreciation (e.g., "When I'm helping another person, it is important for me to have others aware of it and for them to appreciate me for helping"). *Other-oriented helping* was defined as helping while focusing on the other's needs and inclinations ("When I'm helping another person, it is important for me to know how she/he would like to be helped").

Other SDT-based research has focused on one specific type of autonomous moral motivation, namely, identified motivation, and contrasted it with other specific types of controlled motivation (Assor et al., 2004; Gagne, 2000; Ryan & Connell, 1989). Together, these studies suggest that identified prosocial motivation predicts higher levels of moral judgment, empathy, and engagement in activities such as donating blood, volunteering for a nonprofit organization, and donating money to a charity. In addition, this form of motivation is associated with positive socioemotional indicators such as positive affect, vitality, psychological need satisfaction, and sense of relatedness to parents and teachers. In contrast, introjected moral motivation was not related to engaging in prosocial activities, was less predictive of empathy and sense of relatedness to parents, was associated with unstable, fluctuating self-esteem, and was not associated with positive socioemotional indicators. As expected, external prosocial motivation was not predictive of prosocial actions and was negatively related to empathic concern, psychological need satisfaction, and relatedness (Gagne, 2000; Ryan & Connell, 1989).

The stronger association of autonomous moral motivation with prosocial behavior and positive socioemotional functioning relative to controlled motivation suggests that it is important to socialize children in ways that promote autonomous prosocial motivation. Therefore, in the next section I turn to research conducted by our research group on socializing practices that promote autonomous rather than introjected prosocial motivation, judgment, and behavior. I focus specifically on introjected motivation rather than the more global construct of controlled motivation because although introjected motivation is a widespread motivator of prosocial behavior, its roots in socialization practices have not been sufficiently studied.

Socializing Practices That Promote Introjected Versus Autonomous Morality

In this section, I describe studies by my research group that focus on two socializing practices—conditional regard and autonomy support—as predictors of moral or prosocial motivation and behavior. The concept of *conditional regard* refers to parents' tendency to base their affection or esteem for their children on the children's acting in a helpful and considerate way toward others (Assor, Roth, & Deci, 2004). The construct of *autonomy support* refers to parental behaviors that are likely to enhance children's tendency to engage in behaviors or adopt goals because they understand and/or appreciate their value and not because of external or internal coercion. Our research on autonomy-supportive practices has focused mainly on four of these practices: taking the child's perspective, providing rationales for parentally expected behaviors, intrinsic value demonstration, and allowing criticism.

Studies Examining the Correlates of Conditional Regard

The first study focusing on parents' use of conditional regard to promote their offspring's internalization of prosocial values was conducted by Assor, Roth, and Deci (2004). They found that North American college students' perceptions that their mothers and fathers (separately) used conditional regard in the prosocial domain as a socialization technique were associated with a stressful introjected internalization of prosocial principles and motivation. In this study, introjected motivation was assessed in terms of the feeling that something inside oneself forces or compels one to be overly sensitive to others' needs and feelings and leads one to ignore his or her own needs. Later studies (e.g.,

Assor, Israeli, & Roth, 2007) showed that indicators of internal compulsion were closely related to the more traditional introjection measure developed by Ryan and Connell (1989; e.g., "I help others in order to avoid feeling bad about myself"). Assor et al. (2004) also found that conditional regard successfully predicted the frequency of students' reported helping behavior. However, these relations were fully mediated by introjected motivation. This finding is important because it suggests that the positive effect of parental conditional regard on offspring's prosocial behavior is attained at the cost of creating a great deal of internal pressure and conflict.

The second study focusing on the prosocial effects of conditional regard was conducted by Roth (2008). The hypothesis was that although parents' use of conditional regard might contribute to offspring's prosocial behavior, the emerging behavior would be self- rather than other oriented. Results supported this hypothesis. In addition, the relation between parents' use of conditional regard and self-oriented helping was mediated by introjected prosocial motivation. Roth's findings, like the results obtained by Weinstein and Ryan (2010), suggest that introjected prosocial motivation leads to a lower quality of help, namely, helping that is more self-oriented, is less effortful, and generates a relatively low level of feelings of relatedness in the help recipient.

The third study was conducted by Roth and Assor (2010a). It showed that parents' use of conditional regard to promote the suppression of negative emotions (fear and sadness) predicted offspring's tendency to suppress their negative emotions, which in turn was associated with poor ability to listen and respond empathically when one's romantic partner was in distress.

The fourth investigation that suggested negative effects of conditional regard on prosocial and moral behavior was conducted by Kanat-Maymon and Assor (2010). In two studies, they examined the relation between young adults' empathic responding and their perceptions of two maternal behaviors: control and responsiveness to distress. The concept of perceived *maternal control* refers to mothers' use of both conditional regard and more direct controlling methods to promote compliance with their expectations. Regression analyses in which both perceptions of maternal control and responsiveness to distress were entered as predictors revealed that perceived maternal control had unique negative associations with empathic support of a romantic partner (indicated by both self- and partner reports) and empathic concern for others in general. Perceived maternal control had a unique positive association with personal distress in response to needy others. These findings suggest that experiencing one's mother as providing conditional regard and as generally controlling is likely to interfere with one's empathic responding. Moreover, high levels of perceived maternal responsiveness do not cancel the negative effects of controlling parenting. This is consistent with findings obtained by other researchers (see Kanat Maymon & Assor, 2010, for a discussion).

The fifth study was conducted by Roth and Assor (2010b) and focused on kindergarten children and their parents. Unlike the studies already described, parents' conditional regard was assessed from their own reports rather than their offspring's reports. Another innovative feature of this new study was the distinction between positive and negative types of conditional regard. In *conditional positive regard*, parents provide more affection and esteem when children act in accordance with parents' expectations. In *conditional negative regard*, parents provide less affection when children act contrary to their expectations. It was found that parents' self-reported use of conditional positive regard to promote children's tendency to suppress feelings of sadness was negatively associated with recognition of sadness in pictured facial expressions and with responding empathically to others' sad feelings. This finding is of special interest because it suggests that even an ostensibly more benign form of parental control—conditional positive regard—has detrimental effects on the development of empathy.

The correlational nature of the studies I have reviewed does not allow me to draw causal inferences. Yet, together, these studies suggest that parents' use of conditional regard to promote prosocial behavior, to suppress negative emotions, or to promote general child compliance is likely to undermine the development of empathic, other-oriented, prosocial responses in children. These harmful effects appear to emerge even when more benign forms of conditional regard are used and may not be cancelled by other positive parental attributes. Thus, parents who strive to foster a prosocial orientation in their children should forgo or minimize the use of any kind of conditional regard as a major socialization practice.

Studies Examining Correlates of Autonomy Support

The first study examining the effects of autonomy support was conducted by Roth and Assor (2000). This study focused on a practice termed *intrinsic value demonstration*, which had received relatively little attention in SDT-based research. Intrinsic value demonstration involves parents demonstrating the intrinsic value of the behaviors they expect from their children by engaging in these behaviors themselves and by showing considerable satisfaction or calmness when engaging in these behaviors. Roth and Assor hypothesized that witnessing such demonstrations of the intrinsic value of the expected behaviors would enhance children's motivation to engage in them. Unlike regular modeling, the emphasis here is not only on the parents' actual behavior but also on their display of positive states of mind while engaging in it. Roth and Assor found that students' perceptions of their parents as demonstrating the intrinsic value of prosocial actions predicted stronger autonomous prosocial motivation, which in turn predicted engaging in prosocial behavior.

Beyond assessing the parental use of conditional regard parenting, Roth (2008) focused on two kinds of autonomy support: taking the child's perspective (e.g., trying to understand why the child is not sufficiently helpful to a friend in need) and providing a rationale (e.g., why one believes it is important to help others). College students' reports indicated that perceptions of autonomy-supportive parenting (indicated by both perspective taking and providing rationales for proffered advice) predicted more autonomous prosocial motivation and other-oriented helping. Moreover, autonomous motivation mediated the relations between perceptions of parental autonomy support and other-oriented helping. In a related study, Roth and Assor (2010a) found that parents' use of autonomy support to promote regulation of negative emotions (fear and sadness) contributed to offspring's capacity to tolerate negative emotions and explore the causes of such emotions (i.e., integrative regulation), which in turn contributed to their tendency to listen and respond empathically to a distressed romantic partner. As in Roth's (2008) study, autonomy support was operationalized as high scores on perceptions of parental perspective taking and providing rationales.

In a study of teachers and 12th-grade students in regular and democratic schools,[1] Weinstock, Assor, and Broide (2009) explored two aspects of autonomy support not investigated in previous studies of socialization and prosocial tendencies: providing choices and acceptance/encouragement of critical thinking. Students' level of moral judgment was assessed by their responses to various moral dilemmas, with high scores reflecting a more autonomous rather than heteronomous view of morality (i.e., the latter being morality that is bound by the letter of the law or norm and is not determined by one's sense of justice, personal principles, or consideration of intentions and circumstances). Students' perceptions of their teachers as encouraging critical thinking were positively associated with higher (more autonomous) levels of moral judgment. Results also showed that being a student in a democratic school (as opposed to a regular school) was associated with higher levels of moral judgment, and this association was mediated by students' perceptions of teachers as encouraging critical thinking. A possible implication is that programs of moral education in schools should explicitly include having teachers encourage students' use of critical thinking.

Overall, our studies suggest that although parents' use of conditional regard as a socializing practice can lead children to engage in some prosocial

---

[1]In Israel, there are public schools known as "democratic schools," in which teachers encourage their students to express their opinions regarding important class and school issues, including the content of the curriculum, methods of learning, and social relations within the class and the school. In addition, there are weekly school meetings in which students and teachers make binding decisions and rules following lengthy discussions. These schools also allow a great deal of student choice from a young age.

behavior, the children are likely to lack empathic sensitivity to needy others and to experience feelings of internal compulsion and stress. Our research also points to a clear alternative: using autonomy-supportive practices, such as taking the child's perspective; demonstrating the intrinsic value of the expected moral behaviors; providing rationales; and encouraging critical thinking and open discussion of moral expectations. Specifically, children and youths who perceive their parents or teachers as using these practices are likely to engage in more empathic, other-oriented prosocial behaviors and to exhibit higher (more autonomous) levels of moral judgment. Moreover, the children's and youths' engagement in prosocial behavior is accompanied by a sense of choice rather than pressure. Thus, it appears that parents and educators interested in promoting morality and well-being in children would do well to use autonomy-supportive practices.

THE IMPORTANCE OF INTEGRATED MORAL PRINCIPLES AND BEHAVIOR

The research reviewed so far has not clearly distinguished between different kinds of autonomous motivation, mostly because its major aim was to contrast autonomous with controlled motivation. However, now that the advantages of the global autonomous motivation category are clear, it is important to examine the unique correlates of different subtypes of autonomous motivation. In this section, I propose that the autonomous motivation subtype that is most important for engaging in highly moral, personally costly behavior is integrated motivation. In addition, I also propose that integrated moral motivation contributes to perceived autonomy and well-being.

Recall that in the case of integrated moral motivation, goals and behaviors are enacted because they are experienced as reflecting core aspects of one's authentic self and identity. Why is this motivation so crucial for highly moral actions? In my view, the anchoring of this motivation in one's core self and identity provides the strength to endure unpleasant personal costs. In contrast, the other kinds of autonomous motivation—intrinsic and identified—almost by definition cannot sustain highly unpleasant and difficult forms of action. Intrinsic motivation is based only on positive feelings, such as pleasure and interest, so it cannot serve as the prime mover of highly moral actions, which are often unpleasant and personally costly. As for identified motivation, moral actions that impose significant personal demands are not perceived as more central to one's self and identity than other more pleasant actions, and therefore these more difficult actions are not likely to be preferred and sustained.

There is empirical evidence for the view that integrated motivation is a crucial determinant of behaviors that are both highly moral and growth promoting. Gagne (2000) showed that identified prosocial motivation was a stronger predictor of engagement in prosocial activities, such as donating blood, psychological need satisfaction, and empathic concern, than intrinsic prosocial motivation. This is consistent with findings by Burton, Lydon, D'Alessandro, and Koestner (2006) showing that identified motivation is a better predictor of long-term academic performance than intrinsic motivation. According to Burton et al., identified motivation, which involves identifying with the value and importance of the goal, is necessary for developing and maintaining commitment to a goal. As a result, the extent to which individuals identify with their goals is predictive of their goal commitment and progress, even in the face of considerable adversity.

Consistent with these findings, we posit that, ideally, highly moral behavior should be based primarily on identified and integrated motivation. Perhaps even more than studying hard, engaging in highly moral actions entails considerable costs, and therefore it must be based on deep identification with moral goals (i.e., identified motivation) and a sense that costly moral actions express one's core values and identity (i.e., integrated motivation). So far, research has not directly examined the unique effects of integrated moral motivation. However, in the related domain of proenvironment behaviors, integrated motivation has been found to be the best predictor of engagement in effortful environmental behaviors, such as recycling and reusing materials (Pelletier, Tuson, Green-Demers, Noels, & Beaton, 1998).

The importance of integrated moral motivation is also supported by research based on other theoretical perspectives. For example, Piliavin, Grube, and Callero (2002) found that individuals who continued their volunteer activities from childhood to adulthood did so largely because they adopted prosocial values as a "component of the self" (p. 472). Research on people who are considered to be moral exemplars has also suggested the importance of integrated moral principles. For example, Colby and Damon (1992) reported that such people are clear about their goals and feel personally responsible for acting on their values. Moreover, their moral principles and goals were closely tied to their sense of self and identity. Similarly, Eisenberg et al. (2006) claimed that adolescents who view morality as central to their self-concept are particularly likely to be altruistic. And Hart, Atkins, and Ford (1998) demonstrated the importance of moral identity, which they described as commitment consistent with one's sense of self to lines of action that promote others' welfare.

Research on rescuers of Jews during World War II suggests a fairly complex picture of the motives underlying these deeply humanitarian acts, but it appears that many rescuers were motivated by integrated moral principles (see Chapter 21, this volume). For example, Monroe (2003) concluded that what drove many rescuers to take moral action was mainly the extent to which their moral values were integrated with their sense of self and identity.

According to Oliner and Oliner (1988), most rescuers explained their rescue actions as responses to challenges to their fundamental ethical principles (although the authors also said that rescuing was a product of many other factors as well). Fogelman (1994) used the term *moral rescuers* for rescuers whose concepts of right and wrong were integral parts of who they were and are.

OUTCOMES AND SOCIALIZING ANTECEDENTS OF INTEGRATED MORAL MOTIVATION

One tenet of SDT (Ryan & Deci, 2000) is that integrated motivation is associated with well-being and growth because of its autonomous nature. Consistent with this view, I would like to suggest that especially in Western societies, integrated moral motivation may be of special importance because it may be a particularly stable and satisfying source of a sense of autonomy, perhaps even more than having choices and not being externally controlled. This conception is based on the notion that the experience of autonomy can be defined in at least two ways: negatively, as "freedom from," and positively, as "freedom for" (Aviram & Assor, 2010; Berlin, 1969; Fromm, 1941).

In the case of "freedom from," the experience of autonomy is based on freedom from external coercion and the availability of choices. In the case of "freedom for," the experience of autonomy is based on feeling that one has a strong internal compass—authentic, meaningful values and goals that allow a degree of independence in making decisions and evaluating oneself. When integrated moral principles are absent, choice may become a burden (Fromm, 1941). A long philosophical tradition suggests that the availability of direction-specifying, reflection-based values is the essence of autonomy (Aviram & Assor, 2010). Moreover, integrated direction-specifying values may be especially important in postmodern Western societies in which clear guidelines regarding which actions are worthy rather than unworthy no longer exist, given moral relativism and the collapse of traditional moral and ideological authorities and norms. Under these conditions, reflection-based integrated moral principles may be a crucial source of perceived autonomy and therefore vitality.

Integrated prosocial values might be particularly important in the postmodern period because they can serve as a relatively solid foundation for people's identity. In an era in which many people find it difficult to construct a solid identity, prosocial values have clear functional psychosocial benefits (Weinstein & Ryan, 2010), are highly valued across cultures, and have an apparent evolutionary foundation.

The importance of integrated principles and motivation as a source of perceived autonomy, volition, and well-being is supported by research conducted by my research group (e.g., Assor, 2009, 2010, in press). Findings have shown that educational and informal contexts in which youths engage in free discussions and activities aimed at formulating integrated values and goals (i.e., personally meaningful choices and reflection-based goals and values) are perceived by them as autonomy supportive. Moreover, youths engaging in such activities report having a strong sense of volition and feeling happier and more alive as a result. Interestingly, similar findings were obtained in research on modern orthodox Jewish religious families who support open dialogue and reflection on religious principles. Youths growing up in these families reported having a higher level of integrated religious motivation and greater perceived autonomy, purpose, and well-being compared with youths in families that did not support reflection and dialogue concerning religious principles (Assor et al., 2005; Cohen-Malayev, 2008).

My research (Assor, 2009) has identified two autonomy-supportive practices that were underemphasized in SDT research. The first is educators' or parents' support of reflective values and goals examination, which includes discussions and activities that enable youths to examine the extent to which they see various goals and values as worthy and personally meaningful. Another practice that appears to promote the formation of integrated values is fostering inner-directed valuing processes. This construct has three components:

1. helping children resist social pressure, withstand confusion, and take their time before making serious decisions by legitimizing confusion and unpopular (authentic) stances;
2. encouraging children to examine their authentic values and goals when faced with a difficult decision or with external pressures; and
3. encouraging consideration of alternatives and relevant information before making a decision.

This practice differs from support of reflective values and goals examination in that it is used only when a child faces difficult decisions and social pressures. As such, it provides effective training in making authentic and rational decisions under stress.

I am aware that I have presented integrated moral motivation as a highly desirable attribute. But people who appear to be guided by integrated moral principles might be intolerant of others who do not share their views (see Chapter 19, this volume). Therefore, in parental and educational processes aimed at supporting the growth of integrated moral motivation, it is important to include extensive discussions of the value of tolerating different opinions.

Overall, the studies on integrated values by my research group suggest that such values have a salutary effect on the development of autonomy, sense of purpose, and vitality. Preliminary findings also suggest that the relatively under-emphasized socializing practices of fostering inner valuing and supporting reflective examination of values contribute to the emergence of integrated values. Future research on these processes and on ways to help parents and teachers foster the development of integrated values is warranted and is likely to bear important fruit for both individuals and their communities.

REFERENCES

Assor, A. (2009, April). *Two under-emphasized components of autonomy support: Fostering reflective value/goal formation and inner valuing.* Paper presented at the Convention of the American Educational Research Association, San Diego, CA.

Assor, A. (2010, May). *Two under-emphasized components of autonomy support: Supporting value examination and inner valuing.* Paper presented at the 4th International Conference on Self Determination Theory, Ghent, Belgium.

Assor, A. (in press). Allowing choice and nurturing an inner compass: Educational practices supporting students' need for autonomy. In S. L. Christenson, A. L. Reschly, & C. Wylie (Eds.), *The handbook of research on student engagement.* New York, NY: Springer Science.

Assor, A., Cohen-Malayev, M., Kaplan, A., & Friedman, D. (2005). Choosing to stay religious in a modern world: Socialization and exploration processes leading to an integrated internalization of religion among Israeli Jewish youth. *Advances in Motivation and Achievement, 14,* 105–150.

Assor, A., Israeli, M., & Roth, G. (2007, March–April). *The harmful costs of parental conditional regard.* Paper presented at the Biennial Meeting of the Society for Research in Child Development, Boston, MA.

Assor, A., Kanat-Maymon, Y., Feinberg, H., & Kaplan, H. (2010). *Distinguishing among different prosocial motivations.* Unpublished manuscript, Ben-Gurion University, Beer-Sheva, Israel.

Assor, A., Roth, G., & Deci, E. L. (2004). The emotional costs of perceived parental conditional regard: A self-determination theory analysis. *Journal of Personality, 72,* 47–89. doi:10.1111/j.0022-3506.2004.00256.x

Assor, A., Vansteenkiste, M., & Kaplan, A. (2009). Identified versus introjected-approach and introjected-avoidance motivations in school and in sports: The limited benefits of self-worth strivings. *Journal of Educational Psychology, 2,* 482–497. doi:10.1037/a0014236

Aviram, R., & Assor, A. (2010). In defense of personal autonomy as a fundamental educational aim in liberal democracies. *Oxford Review of Education, 36,* 111–126. doi:10.1080/03054981003593480

Batson, C. D. (2010). Evolutionary perspectives on prosocial behavior. In M. Mikulincer & P. R. Shaver (Eds.), *Prosocial motives, emotions, and behavior: The better angels of our nature* (pp. 15–34). Washington, DC: American Psychological Association. doi:10.1037/12061-001

Berlin, I. (1969). *Four essays on liberty*. Oxford, England: Oxford University Press.

Burton, K. D., Lydon, J. E., D'Alessandro, D. U., & Koestner, R. (2006). The differential effects of intrinsic and identified motivation on well-being and performance: Prospective, experimental, and implicit approaches to self-determination theory. *Journal of Personality and Social Psychology, 91,* 750–762. doi:10.1037/0022-3514.91.4.750

Cohen-Malayev, M. (2008). *Exploration and religious identity: The tension between religion and religiosity*. Doctoral dissertation, Ben-Gurion University, Beer-Sheva, Israel.

Colby, A., & Damon, W. (1992). *Some do care: Contemporary lives of moral commitment*. New York, NY: Free Press.

Eisenberg, N., Fabes, R. A., & Spinrad, T. L. (2006). Prosocial development. In R. M. Lerner, N. Eisenberg, & W. Damon (Eds.), *Handbook of child psychology: Vol. 3. Social, emotional, and personality development* (pp. 646–718). New York, NY: Wiley.

Fogelman, E. (1994). *Conscience and courage: Rescuers of Jews during the Holocaust*. New York, NY: Anchor Books.

Fromm, E. (1941). *Escape from freedom*. New York, NY: Rinehart & Co.

Fromm, E. (1947). *Man for himself: An inquiry into the psychology of ethics*. New York, NY: Rinehart & Co.

Gagne, M. (2000). *The role of autonomy support and autonomy orientation in the internalization of autonomous regulation of prosocial behavior*. Doctoral dissertation, University of Rochester, Rochester, NY.

Hart, D., Atkins, R., & Ford, D. (1998). Urban America as a context for the development of moral identity in adolescence. *Journal of Social Issues, 54,* 513–530. doi:10.1111/j.1540-4560.1998.tb01233.x

Kanat-Maymon, M., & Assor, A. (2010). Perceived maternal control and responsiveness to distress as predictors of young adults' empathic responses. *Personality and Social Psychology Bulletin, 36,* 33–46. doi:10.1177/0146167209347381

Kohlberg, L. (1984). *The psychology of moral development*. San Francisco, CA: Harper & Row.

May, R. (1983). *The discovery of being: Writings in existential psychology*. New York, NY: Norton.

Monroe, K. (2003). How identity and perspective constrain moral choice. *International Political Science Review, 24,* 405–425. doi:10.1177/01925121030244001

Oliner, P., & Oliner, S. (1988). *The altruistic personality: Rescuers of Jews in Nazi Europe*. New York, NY: Free Press.

Pelletier, L. G., Tuson, K., Green-Demers, I., Noels, K., & Beaton, A. (1998). Why are you doing things for the environment? The Motivation toward the Environment Scale. *Journal of Applied Social Psychology, 28,* 437–468. doi:10.1111/j.1559-1816.1998.tb01714.x

Penner, L., & Chircov, V. (2010, May). *Is introjected motivation always detrimental? An exploratory mixed-method investigation of the motivation for health-related behaviors.* Paper presented at the 4th International Conference on Self-Determination Theory, Ghent, Belgium.

Piliavin, J. A., Grube, J. A., & Callero, P. L. (2002). Role as resource for action in public service. *Journal of Social Issues, 58,* 469–485. doi:10.1111/0022-4537.t01-1-00027

Roth, G. (2008). Perceived parental conditional regard and autonomy support as predictors of young adults' self- versus other-oriented prosocial tendencies. *Journal of Personality, 76,* 513–533. doi:10.1111/j.1467-6494.2008.00494.x

Roth, G., & Assor, A. (2000, June). *The effect of conditional parental regard and intrinsic value demonstration on academic and prosocial motivation.* Paper presented at the Conference of the European Association for Learning and Instruction, Malmö, Sweden.

Roth, G., & Assor, A. (2010a). *The costs of parental pressure to express emotions: Conditional regard and autonomy support as predictors of emotion regulation and intimacy.* Manuscript submitted for publication.

Roth, G., & Assor, A. (2010b). Parental conditional regard as a predictor of deficiencies in young children's capacities to respond to sad feelings. *Infant and Child Development, 19,* 465–477.

Ryan, R. M., & Connell, J. P. (1989). Perceived locus of causality and internalization: Examining reasons for acting in two domains. *Journal of Personality and Social Psychology, 57,* 749–761. doi:10.1037/0022-3514.57.5.749

Ryan, R. M., & Deci, E. L. (2000). Self-determination theory and the facilitation of intrinsic motivation, social development, and well-being. *American Psychologist, 55,* 68–78. doi:10.1037/0003-066X.55.1.68

Weinstein, N., & Ryan, R. M. (2010). When helping helps: Autonomous motivation for prosocial behavior and its influence on well-being for the helper and recipient. *Journal of Personality and Social Psychology, 98,* 222–244. doi:10.1037/a0016984

Weinstock, M., Assor, A., & Broide, G. (2009). Schools as promoters of moral development: The essential role of teachers' encouragement of critical thinking. *Social Psychology of Education, 12,* 137–151. doi:10.1007/s11218-008-9068-9

14

AN ATTACHMENT PERSPECTIVE ON MORALITY: STRENGTHENING AUTHENTIC FORMS OF MORAL DECISION MAKING

PHILLIP R. SHAVER AND MARIO MIKULINCER

In recent years, attachment theory (Bowlby, 1973, 1980, 1982), which was originally designed to characterize infant–parent emotional bonding, has been applied first to the study of adolescent and adult romantic relationships (Hazan & Shaver, 1987) and then to the study of prosocial behavior and other-regarding virtues (Mikulincer & Shaver, 2007a). In this chapter, we expand our consideration of links between attachment patterns and prosocial motives into the realm of morality and propose that dispositional patterns of attachment can help us distinguish between authentic and inauthentic (defensive) moral choices (see Chapter 9, this volume, for a discussion of moral hypocrisy).

We begin by presenting our now familiar theoretical model of the activation and psychodynamics of the attachment behavioral system in adulthood (Mikulincer & Shaver, 2007a) and describe the intrapsychic and interpersonal manifestations of attachment security, anxiety, and avoidance. We then review studies showing (a) that the two major forms of attachment insecurity, anxiety and avoidance, interfere with and distort prosocial motives, emotions, and behavior and (b) that experimental enhancement of attachment security increases empathic concern, compassion, altruistic behavior, gratitude, and forgiveness. We then describe new studies that extend our previous findings into the realm of morality. Specifically, we show that attachment insecurities, especially attachment anxiety, encourage the use of moral choices to defend against threats to the self. We also show that experimentally enhanced security counteracts attachment-anxious individuals' defensive use of morality and allows them to make more authentically prosocial moral choices.

ATTACHMENT THEORY: BASIC CONCEPTS

In his classic trilogy on attachment, separation, and loss, Bowlby (1973, 1980, 1982) conceptualized what he called the *attachment behavioral system*—an innate psychobiological system that motivates human beings, from infancy through adulthood, to seek proximity to significant others (i.e., attachment figures) in times of need as a means of attaining safety and security. According to Bowlby (1982), the goal of the system is to attain a subjective sense of protection or security, which normally terminates the system's activation. The goal of attaining security is made salient by perceived threats and dangers, which drive people to seek actual or symbolic proximity to attachment figures (Bowlby, 1982). During infancy, attachment system activation includes nonverbal expressions of need and desire for proximity, as well as observable behavior aimed at restoring and maintaining actual proximity or contact (Ainsworth, Blehar, Waters, & Wall, 1978). In adulthood, however, attachment strategies do not necessarily involve actual proximity-seeking behavior, but they can be measured indirectly in the form of soothing, reassuring mental representations of past experiences with supportive attachment figures (Mikulincer & Shaver, 2004).

An abiding inner sense of attachment security (based on actual experiences) promotes a pervasive faith in other people's good will; a sense of being loved, esteemed, understood, and accepted by relationship partners; and optimistic beliefs about being able to handle frustration and distress. Bowlby (1988) considered attachment security to be a mainstay of mental health and social adjustment. A host of cross-sectional and longitudinal studies have supported his theoretical ideas (for reviews, see J. A. Feeney, 2008; and Mikulincer & Shaver, 2007a).

However, when attachment figures are not reliably available, responsive, and supportive, a sense of attachment security is not attained, negative working models of self and others are constructed, worries about self-protection and lovability are heightened, and strategies of affect regulation other than appropriate proximity seeking are adopted (defensive maneuvers that Cassidy & Kobak, 1988, called *secondary attachment strategies*). Attachment theorists (e.g., Cassidy & Kobak, 1988; Mikulincer & Shaver, 2007a) emphasize two such secondary strategies: hyperactivation and deactivation of the attachment system.

Hyperactivation is manifested in energetic attempts to attain greater proximity, support, and protection, combined with a lack of confidence that these benefits will be provided. Deactivation of the system involves inhibition of proximity-seeking tendencies, denial of attachment needs, maintenance of emotional and cognitive distance from others, and compulsive reliance on oneself as the only reliable source of safety and comfort.

When studying these secondary strategies during adolescence and adulthood, attachment researchers have focused on a person's *attachment style*—the chronic pattern of relational cognitions and behaviors that results from a particular history of attachment experiences (Fraley & Shaver, 2000). Initially, attachment research was based on Ainsworth et al.'s (1978) three-category typology of attachment patterns in infancy—secure, anxious, and avoidant— and on Hazan and Shaver's (1987) conceptualization of similar adult styles in the romantic relationship domain. Subsequent studies (e.g., reviewed and extended by Brennan, Clark, & Shaver, 1998) revealed, however, that attachment styles are more appropriately conceptualized as regions in a two-dimensional space. The first dimension, *avoidant attachment*, reflects the extent to which a person distrusts relationship partners' good will, deactivates his or her attachment system, and strives to maintain behavioral independence and emotional distance from partners. The second dimension, *anxious attachment*, reflects the degree to which a person worries that a partner will not be available in times of need and therefore hyperactivates efforts to gain a partner's attention and support. People who score low on both insecurity dimensions are said to be secure with respect to attachment, or *securely attached*. The two dimensions can be measured with reliable and valid self-report scales and are associated in theoretically predictable ways with mental health, adjustment, and relationship quality (Mikulincer & Shaver, 2007a).

ATTACHMENT INSECURITIES, CAREGIVING, AND PROSOCIAL BEHAVIOR

Beyond conceptualizing the attachment system, Bowlby (1982) proposed that human beings are innately equipped with another behavioral system aimed at providing nurturance (the *caregiving behavioral system*). Theoretically, the caregiving system evolved because providing care for dependent or injured individuals (e.g., infants, frightened or injured family members) increased inclusive fitness (Shaver, Mikulincer, & Shemesh-Iron, 2010). Its operation is most evident in parents' emotional and behavioral reactions to their offspring's signals of need or distress. We believe, however, like Batson (2010) and others, that this system is also the innate foundation of broader empathy, compassion, and prosocial behavior (Mikulincer & Shaver, 2007a).

According to Bowlby (1982), there is a dynamic interplay between the attachment system and the caregiving system: Activation of the attachment system can interfere with the caregiving system because potential caregivers may feel that obtaining safety and care for themselves is more urgent than providing care and support for others. At such times, people are likely to be so focused on their own vulnerability that they lack the mental resources needed to attend sensitively to others' needs. Only when a sense of attachment security is restored can most people perceive others to be not only potential sources of security and support but also worthy human beings who need and deserve comfort and support themselves.

Reasoning along these lines, attachment theorists (e.g., Kunce & Shaver, 1994; Mikulincer & Shaver, 2007a) have hypothesized that attachment security provides an important foundation for optimal caregiving. Moreover, being secure implies that a person has witnessed, experienced, and benefited from generous attachment figures' effective care, which gives them a model to follow when they occupy the caregiving role. According to theories of social learning and "assimilation" (e.g., Bretherton, 1985; Sroufe & Fleeson, 1986), we learn prosocial behavior from observing and experiencing our parents' (and other attachment figures') behavior. That is, a secure person comes to show genuine interest in others' welfare and a desire to help them by knowing what it is like to be cared for by considerate others (George & Solomon, 2008) and by modeling one's behavior on the observed behavior of one's own care providers.

Research shows, in line with attachment theory, that secure individuals are comfortable being intimate and interdependent with others (Hazan & Shaver, 1987), so it is relatively easy and nonthreatening for them to have other people approach them for help and express feelings of vulnerability and need. In addition, secure individuals' positive working models of others make it easier for them to construe others as deserving sympathy and support, and their positive models of self allow them to feel confident about their ability to respond to other people's needs while effectively regulating their own emotions. All of these qualities make it easier for secure people to act in a caring, prosocial, and moral manner toward others.

In contrast, individuals who score relatively high on measures of anxious or avoidant attachment are likely to have difficulty providing effective care (e.g., George & Solomon, 2008). Although people who suffer mainly from attachment anxiety may have some of the qualities needed for effective caregiving (e.g., willingness to experience and express emotions and comfort with physical closeness and psychological intimacy), their habitual focus on their own distress and unsatisfied attachment needs may draw important mental resources away from attending accurately and consistently to others' needs. Moreover, their strong desire for closeness and their need for approval may cause them to become intrusive or overly involved, blurring the distinction between another person's welfare and their own. Attachment anxiety can, in other words, lead to what Kunce and Shaver (1994), following Bowlby (1982), called *compulsive caregiving*.

Avoidant individuals' discomfort with closeness and negative working models of others may also interfere with optimal caregiving. Their discomfort with expressions of need and dependence may cause them to back away rather than get involved with someone who strongly expresses needs for comfort and closeness. As a result, avoidant individuals may attempt to detach themselves emotionally and physically from needy others, feel superior to those who are vulnerable or distressed, and experience disdainful pity rather than empathic concern.

We have examined associations between the dimensions of attachment insecurity, on the one hand, and prosocial feelings and behaviors, on the other. For example, Mikulincer et al. (2001) found that various methods of contextually heightening a person's sense of attachment security (using what we call *security priming* techniques; see Mikulincer & Shaver, 2007b)—methods such as subliminally presenting the names of the person's security-enhancing attachment figures or asking participants to visualize the face of such a figure or to think about a particular interaction with him or her—increased compassionate responses to other peoples' suffering. We also found that higher scores on avoidant attachment were negatively associated with empathic reactions to others' suffering. Higher scores on the anxiety dimension were associated with increased personal distress in response to another's suffering but not with empathic reactions. In another series of studies, Mikulincer et al. (2003) found that security priming increased the endorsement of two *self-transcendence values* (Schwartz, 2010), benevolence and universalism, which encourage prosocial behavior (see Chapter 12, this volume). In these studies, higher scores on the avoidance dimension were negatively associated with endorsement of these values.

Attachment insecurities are also negatively related to offering care to a mate. Individuals who score high on anxiety or avoidance are less sensitive to their romantic or marital partner's needs, report less cooperative caregiving, and offer less comfort and reassurance to their distressed partner in laboratory studies (e.g., Collins & Feeney, 2000; B. C. Feeney & Collins, 2001; Simpson, Rholes, & Nelligan, 1992). For example, Simpson et al. (1992) unobtrusively videotaped dating couples while the female partner waited to undergo a stressful procedure, finding that secure men recognized their partner's worries and provided more emotional support and more supportive comments if their partner showed higher levels of distress. In contrast, men who scored high on avoidance actually provided less support as their partner's distress increased.

Following this line of research, B. C. Feeney and Collins (2003) assessed motives for providing care to a romantic partner and found that secure adults tended to endorse more altruistic reasons for helping (e.g., helping out of concern for the partner needs). In contrast, avoidant adults reported more egoistic reasons for helping (e.g., to avoid a partner's negative reactions, to get something explicit in return). Moreover, they disliked coping with a partner's distress, lacked a sense of responsibility for their partner, and perceived the partner as too dependent. Attachment-anxious adults endorsed altruistic reasons for helping (helping because of concern for the partner), but they also reported helping in order to gain a partner's approval and increase the partner's relationship commitment. In addition, anxious people were reluctant to provide support for their partner's engagement in new and challenging activities and attributed this reluctance to worries that the partner's independent pursuits might damage the relationship.

In an attempt to examine attachment and caregiving dynamics in the wider social world, Gillath et al. (2005) examined associations between attachment insecurities, involvement in altruistic volunteer activities, and motives for volunteering. The findings were similar across the three countries we studied—the United States, Israel, and the Netherlands. Avoidant attachment was associated with engaging in fewer volunteer activities, devoting less time to such activities, and being less motivated by desires to express altruistic values and to learn about oneself and the world. Attachment anxiety was not generally related to engaging or not engaging in volunteer activities or to devoting more or less time to such activities, but it was associated with more egoistic reasons for volunteering (e.g., getting social approval and admiration, increasing one's sense of group belongingness).

In a series of laboratory experiments, Mikulincer, Shaver, Gillath, and Nitzberg, (2005, Studies 1 and 2) examined the actual decision to help or not to help a person in distress. Participants watched a confederate while she performed a series of aversive tasks. As the study progressed, the confederate became increasingly distressed, and the actual participant was given an opportunity to take her place, in effect sacrificing self for the welfare of another. Shortly before this scenario unfolded, participants were primed with either representations of attachment security (the name of a participant's security provider) or attachment-unrelated representations (the name of a familiar person who was not an attachment figure or the name of a mere acquaintance). This priming was conducted at either a subliminal or a supraliminal level in each of two studies. Both kinds of security priming increased participants' compassion and willingness to take the distressed person's place. Again, whereas avoidant attachment was associated with reduced expressions of compassion and willingness to help, anxious attachment was associated with increased personal distress but not necessarily with helping while witnessing another person's suffering.

Attachment insecurities are also associated with prosocial feelings of gratitude and forgiveness. Mikulincer, Shaver, and Slav (2006) found that avoidant attachment was associated with lower levels of dispositional gratitude and forgiveness and with a tendency to experience narcissistic threats and distrust while feeling grateful or forgiving. Although attachment anxiety was not significantly associated with dispositional gratitude or forgiveness, it was positively related to narcissistic threats and a sense of inferiority while feeling grateful or forgiving. In other words, anxious attachment was associated with more negative experiences of gratitude. We also found that the links between attachment insecurities and prosocial feelings of gratitude and forgiveness could be observed in daily reactions to specific partner behaviors in a sample of married couples. For both husbands and wives, avoidant but not anxious attachment predicted lower levels of daily gratitude and forgiveness toward one's partner across a 21-day study period. Interestingly, husbands' avoidant attachment interacted with daily perceptions of wives' behavior in determining daily gratitude. Whereas less avoidant husbands reported more gratitude on days when they perceived more positive spousal behavior, more avoidant husbands reported relatively low levels of gratitude even on days when they noticed their wife's positive behavior. In other words, a husband's avoidant orientation not only inhibited gratitude overall, it also interfered with feeling grateful for his wife's specific beneficial behavior on a particular day.

Overall, the reviewed findings indicate that attachment insecurities are related to reductions in or distortions of prosocial feelings and behavior. Avoidant attachment is related to lower levels of compassion, empathy, gratitude, forgiveness, and helping behavior even in interpersonal or relational contexts that might make these prosocial feelings and behavior seem natural. Anxious attachment has a more complex signature: It does not necessarily eliminate prosocial inclinations, but it sullies them with conflicting feelings and egoistic motives that may erode their expected beneficial effects on the welfare of other people.

ATTACHMENT INSECURITIES AND MORALITY

Here, we wish to extend our studies of attachment and prosocial inclinations into the realm of moral choices. As noted throughout this volume, there are many definitions and conceptions of morality: social prescriptions and principles concerning the distinction between right and wrong; intentions, choices, and behavior that are subject to (or judged according to) generally accepted moral norms of behavior; rational judgments and evaluations about the extent to which an action is right or wrong; and intuitions ("gut feelings") about the differences between right and wrong. For present purposes, we will accept Staub's (see Chapter 21) definition of morality as "principles, values, emotional orientations, and practices that maintain or promote human welfare." According to this definition, virtuous or good behavior is prosocial in nature and stems from an individual's genuine, or authentic, wish to benefit other people.

In a recent series of studies, Gillath, Sesko, Shaver, and Chun (2010) examined associations between attachment anxiety and avoidance, on the one hand, and various measures of authenticity (e.g., Kernis & Goldman, 2006) and honesty (e.g., Lee & Ashton, 2004), on the other. Attachment security was, as hypothesized, related to honesty and authenticity. Moreover, both conscious and unconscious security priming (compared with neutral priming) increased state authenticity and reduced dishonesty and cheating. Similar effects did not occur when positive mood priming, rather than attachment security priming methods, was used, indicating (in line with other studies reviewed by Mikulincer & Shaver, 2007b) that security priming is not just a form of elevated mood.

As explained in the previous section of this chapter, people who score high on attachment-related avoidance are less inclined than other people to embody other-regarding virtues or engage in prosocial behavior. Moreover, research has consistently shown that more avoidant people appraise others' traits and intentions negatively and tend to hold cynical and pessimistic views of human nature. They seem to be primarily focused on increasing their own personal resources while remaining independent and self-reliant (see Mikulincer & Shaver, 2007a, for a review). We therefore expect that more avoidant people will be less inclined to consider other people's welfare when making moral judgments and choices. That is, when facing situations in which the welfare of others is pitted against their own welfare, avoidant people will be less inclined to consider or base their decisions on moral principles and intuitions. Moreover, their personal identity and self-esteem can be expected to be less grounded in moral values and traits and based more on self-interest and a sense of agency and self-reliance.

Our previous research has shown that people who score high on attachment anxiety differ from those who score low, not in the extent to which they experience prosocial emotions or are inclined to behave in a prosocial manner but in the way they construe these experiences and inclinations. As explained earlier, whereas less anxious (i.e., more secure) individuals' prosocial states of mind include a blend of altruistic motives, positive feelings of love and kindness, and a positive outlook on others, the prosocial states of mind of more anxious individuals include a blend of these positive elements with narcissistic motives, personal distress, self-focused fears and worries, and a sometimes envious or hostile outlook on others. Thus, although anxious and secure people may score equally high on a measure of compassionate love, the secure person may feel real compassion for others in need and authentic concern for their suffering, whereas the anxious person may feel what he or she thinks is compassion but is actually colored by narcissistic propensities, such as wishing to be accepted and applauded, and by self-focused worries about rejection and abandonment.

In extrapolating previous findings to the realm of morality, we can expect that when anxious individuals are confronted with situations in which the welfare of other people is pitted against their own welfare, they will be inclined to make moral choices and behave according to moral principles and intuitions to the extent that this (a) promises to increase the social approval they receive as a result, (b) may compensate for their low or fragile self-esteem, or (c) may protect them from being rejected. They are likely to be less concerned with moral principles and intuitions and less likely to have ready mental access to moral cognitions and feelings when moral behavior is unlikely to provide any personal benefits.

Our ideas about the possible links between attachment anxiety and morality are influenced by Jordan and Monin's (2008; see also Chapter 9, this volume) observation that people sometimes use moral behavior as a defense against threats to the self. They found that people who completed a tedious task and then saw a confederate quit the same task (as compared with people in the same study who either completed the task without learning about other participants' behavior or saw a confederate quit without having done the task themselves) were more likely to view themselves as more moral than the person who refused to complete the task. This effect was eliminated if study participants engaged in self-affirmation, suggesting that moral self-elevation was less necessary when the self could be elevated in other ways (see Chapter 9, this volume).

We reasoned that this defensive use of morality might be more characteristic of people who score high on attachment anxiety compared with those who score low (and who are therefore more likely to operate according to genuine moral principles). In other words, we suspected that there are two different forms of morality: (1) *authentic morality*, manifested by relatively secure people and anchored in a genuine concern for others' welfare and (2) *defensive morality*, manifested by people who score high on attachment anxiety, have a shaky sense of self-worth, and use self-perceived moral behavior as a defense. According to this line of reasoning, we expected that increasing an anxious person's sense of security would move him or her toward a more authentic form of morality.

We conducted two as-yet unpublished studies testing the basic idea that attachment-anxious people sometimes make moral choices to defend against feelings of unworthiness or wounded self-esteem. There were two main hypotheses: First, we expected that threats to the self would increase the tendency of anxious individuals but not secure ones to make "moral" choices. Second, we predicted that security priming would reduce the tendency to engage in defensive forms of moral behavior and allow anxious individuals to be more authentically (i.e., less defensively) moral.

In the first study, we examined the effects of attachment anxiety and threats to the self on moral choices, expecting that more attachment-anxious participants would make more moral choices when their self-esteem was threatened than when it was not. We conducted a two-session laboratory study involving 60 Israeli university students (42 women and 18 men). In the first session, conducted during regular class time, participants completed the Experiences in Close Relationships (ECR) inventory (Brennan et al., 1998), a reliable and valid measure of attachment anxiety and avoidance. In the second session, conducted 2 weeks later by a different experimenter, participants individually performed four cognitive tasks while an ego threat—failure feedback—was imposed on a randomly selected half of them. In the threat condition, participants were presented with four unsolvable problems and told that they had failed them all. In the no-threat condition, participants were presented with the same four unsolvable problems but received no feedback concerning their performance. The cognitive tasks and manipulations were identical to ones used previously by Mikulincer (1998, Study 1).

Afterward, all participants received four scenarios in which they assessed moral choices that were adapted from Perugini and Leone's (2009) study. In each scenario, a moral choice was pitted against a financial loss (i.e., choosing the moral option meant losing money or forgoing potential economic gains). Two scenarios concerned investing in companies that make money from immoral activities, such as violent sports and prostitution. Two other scenarios concerned opportunities to break the law without suffering any consequences, such evading taxes on prize money or falsely reporting a large charitable donation.

The scenario dealing with prostitution, for example, was described as follows:

> Suppose a well-known newspaper has experienced a notable increase in earnings after beginning to publish explicit advertisements for paid sexual services. Most of the ads were paid for by organizations that control the illicit sex trade, mainly using young immigrant women as prostitutes. Since beginning to publish the sex ads, the newspaper company has become very profitable, and it is likely to become even more profitable in the future. Suppose you have some money to invest. Would you invest your money in the company that owns the newspaper?

The scenario dealing with a false report designed to help a car dealership evade taxes read as follows:

> You run an orphanage and have had a difficult time making ends meet. A car dealership offers you a new van worth $15,000 at no cost if you will falsely report to the government that the dealership donated a van worth $30,000. You really need the van, and it will give you an opportunity to make the children happy. Would you agree to take the van under these conditions?

Ratings were made on 7-point response scales ranging from 1 (*definitely not*) to 7 (*definitely yes*). The Cronbach's alpha for the four scenarios was .87, so we computed a single average score for each participant (after reversing scales so that higher scores indicated "moral" choices).

To examine the effects of threats to the self and of attachment anxiety and avoidance on moral choices, we conducted a two-step hierarchical regression analysis with participants' scores on the ECR anxiety and avoidance scales and ego threat as the predictor variables. In the first step, we entered ego threat, a dummy variable comparing the threat and no-threat conditions, as well as anxious and avoidant attachment Z scores, as a block to examine their unique main effects. In the second step, the 2-way interactions between threat to self and each of the attachment scores were entered as additional predictors.

Two main effects were significant: avoidant attachment, $\beta = -.37, p < .01$, and ego threat, $\beta = .26, p < .05$. Participants scoring higher on avoidant attachment were less likely to make moral choices, whereas those in the threat condition were more likely to make moral choices (than those in the no-threat condition). The regression analysis also yielded a significant interaction between attachment anxiety and threat, $\beta = .24, p < .05$. Examination of the interaction (using Aiken & West's, 1991, procedure) revealed that a threat to self produced more moral choices than no threat to self only when the score on anxious attachment was relatively high (+1 SD), $\beta = .50, p < .01$, not when it was relatively low (−1 SD), $\beta = .02$. Moreover, people who scored high on attachment anxiety were less inclined than those who scored low to make more moral choices in the no-threat condition, $\beta = -.37, p < .01$, but not in the ego threat condition, $\beta = .11$. Basically, the ego threat raised the more anxious individuals' level of morality to the level characteristic of the less anxious (i.e., more secure) individuals with or without a threat.

These results fit with Jordan and Monin's (2008) conclusion that a self-threat can sometimes cause people to make more moral choices, but the results also indicate that this kind of defensive morality is more characteristic of attachment-anxious people than of relatively secure people, who make moral choices with or without a threat. That is, relatively secure participants' moral choices were not influenced by threats to the self, suggesting that, for them, choosing the more moral of available options is a stable dispositional tendency. The findings also indicated that attachment-related avoidance is associated with less moral decisions when morality means forgoing a personal gain, and this relative lack of morality was unswayed by an ego threat. This finding fits with the results of previous studies we reviewed, suggesting that relatively avoidant people are more interested in gaining resources for themselves than in maintaining high moral standards.

In our second study, we examined the extent to which brief security priming provides an antidote to the defensive use of morality and helps attachment-anxious individuals make less defensive moral choices. To examine this issue, we conducted a two-session laboratory experiment involving 100 Israeli university students (71 women and 29 men). The procedure was based on the first study (described here), but it added security priming as an additional variable.

The first session was designed to assess participants' attachment patterns and acquire specific names of security-enhancing attachment figures and other familiar persons to be used as primes in the second session. In that first session, participants completed the ECR inventory and two computerized measures of the names of attachment figures and other familiar persons who were not attachment figures. The first of these two computerized measures was a Hebrew version of the WHOTO scale (Fraley & Davis, 1997), in which participants were asked to type into a Microsoft Excel worksheet the names of their security-enhancing attachment figures (although not described in those technical terms). The scale included six items, two of which addressed the proximity-maintenance function of attachment (e.g., "Who is the person you most like to spend time with?"), two of which addressed the safe-haven function (e.g., "Who is the person you would count on for advice?"), and two of which addressed the secure-base function (e.g., "Who is the person you can always count on?"). For each item, participants wrote the name of the person who best served the targeted attachment-related function. In the second measure, participants were asked to type into a separate Excel worksheet the names of their father, mother, brothers, sisters, best friend, current romantic partner, and grandparents, without making any reference to the attachment functions they did or did not serve. We assumed that because these people's names were not provided in the previous assessment as primary attachment figures, they probably did not meet the strict theoretical requirements for that role.

In the second session, conducted 2 weeks later by a different experimenter, participants performed a 30-trial computerized word relation task. During each of the trials, a participant was subliminally exposed (for 20 ms) to the name of his or her most security-enhancing attachment figure (based on the first session of the study) or the name of a familiar person who was not selected as an attachment figure. Following the priming procedure, participants in both priming conditions performed four cognitive tasks and were randomly divided into threat and no-threat conditions using the manipulations described above. In sum, participants were randomly divided into four experimental conditions (with 25 participants in each), according to a 2×2 factorial design defined by kind of priming (security, neutral) and presence of a threat to self (yes, no).

After they completed the four cognitive tasks, all participants were told that the experiment was over and that in exchange for participating they would be given one free lottery ticket for three prizes of NIS120 (about $30), to be drawn from the names of participants in the experiment. The experimenter explicitly and unambiguously said "one ticket." They were then sent to another room where they could collect one ticket from another research assistant. But in the other room, a research assistant gave each participant two lottery tickets (the moral temptation), providing them a greater chance of winning the lottery compared with the rest of the participants. If a participant returned the additional ticket, the experimenter apologized for the mistake. The dependent variable was whether a participant returned the additional undeserved lottery ticket (the moral choice) or not. Participants were partly debriefed and provided an e-mail contact for a full debriefing when the entire study was completed. The undeserved lottery ticket was kept by 58 participants (58% of the sample) and given back to the experimenter by 42 (42%).

To examine the extent to which security priming eliminated the difference in anxious individuals' moral choices between threat and no-threat conditions, we conducted a three-step hierarchical regression analysis with participants' scores on the ECR anxious and avoidant attachment scales, security priming (no, yes), and threat induction (no, yes) as the predictor variables. The dependent variable was each participant's decision to keep or return an undeserved ticket (no $= 0$, yes $= 1$). In the first step of the analysis, we entered security priming (a dummy variable comparing the security priming condition with the neutral priming condition), threat induction (a dummy variable comparing the threat and no-threat conditions), and anxious and avoidant attachment Z scores; these variables were entered as a block to examine their unique main effects. In the second step, the two-way interactions between security priming and threat induction, between security priming and each attachment score, and between threat and each attachment score were entered as additional predictors. In the third step, we added the three-way interactions: Security Priming $\times$ Threat $\times$ Anxious Attachment and Security Priming $\times$ Threat $\times$ Avoidant Attachment.

In line with the findings of the first study, the main effects for avoidant attachment, $\beta = -.42$, $p < .01$, and ego threat, $\beta = .22$, $p < .05$, and the interaction of ego threat and attachment anxiety, $\beta = .21$, $p < .05$, were significant.

Participants scoring higher on avoidance were less likely to return the undeserved lottery ticket, and a threat led to more moral choices (than when no threat was present) only when anxious attachment was relatively high (+1 SD), $\beta = .43, p < .01$, not when it was relatively low ($-1\ SD$), $\beta = .01$. However, the three-way interaction of threat, security priming, and attachment anxiety was also significant, $\beta = -.32, p < .01$. Examination of the interaction revealed that a threat led more anxiously attached people to return the additional lottery ticket only in the neutral priming condition, $\beta = .75, p < .01$, and not in the security priming condition, $\beta = .11$. After receiving security priming, neither threat nor attachment anxiety increased the tendency to return the additional lottery ticket, mainly because the level of moral choices was about the same as the level for less anxious, more secure individuals under all conditions. This suggests that the anxious participants were more genuinely moral under all conditions, when before they had been (presumably defensively) moral only when threatened. The fact that security priming led them to be as moral as nonanxious individuals even when there was no threat suggests that their usual reasons for being less moral than their secure counterparts had been temporarily erased.

Overall, the findings were in line with our predictions. A temporary increase in the sense of attachment security counteracted the tendency of attachment-anxious individuals to make moral choices only after receiving an ego threat. In other words, security priming eliminated the effects of attachment anxiety on moral choices, making it less necessary to use morality as a defense against viewing oneself as deficient. It is important to note that there was not a significant interaction between security priming and attachment-related avoidance, implying that avoidant people were less inclined to make moral choices even after being primed with what we intended to be security-enhancing individuals' names. Evidently their self-sufficiency and unsympathetic views of other people were well entrenched and did not respond, at least in the short run, to subliminal attempts to bolster their sense of security.

CONCLUDING REMARKS

A growing body of research indicates that attachment security is conducive to prosocial motives, emotion, and behavior and that more secure individuals are generally more authentic and honest in their dealings with other people. Even when people are relatively insecure with respect to attachment, they can sometimes become more considerate, helpful, and honest if their sense of security is temporarily augmented. Here, we have extended the existing research to include the defensive use of moral choices to bolster a threatened self-image. Whereas many previous studies had shown that attachment insecurities can erode prosocial and moral inclinations or dilute them with egoistic concerns, the two new studies described here indicate that attachment-anxious individuals sometimes make moral choices defensively, a motivational tendency that can be eliminated in the short run by a boost in felt security. In these new studies, attachment-related avoidance did not respond to security priming, suggesting that avoidant people's lack of sympathy for others and tendency to feather their own nests are deeply ingrained. This finding is interesting theoretically because previous security priming studies have shown that avoidant negativity toward outgroups and lack of concern for others' suffering can be mitigated by security priming. The studies reported here, which involved a more explicit and concrete opportunity to gain something for oneself, may have made it more difficult for security priming to overcome lack of concern for others. This is something that deserves to be examined further, and more systematically, in future studies.

REFERENCES

Aiken, L. S., & West, S. G. (1991). *Multiple regression: Testing and interpreting interactions*. Newbury Park, CA: Sage.

Ainsworth, M. D. S., Blehar, M. C., Waters, E., & Wall, S. (1978). *Patterns of attachment: Assessed in the Strange Situation and at home*. Hillsdale, NJ: Erlbaum.

Batson, C. D. (2010). Empathy-induced altruistic motivation. In M. Mikulincer & P. R. Shaver (Eds.), *Prosocial motives, emotions, and behavior: The better angels of our nature* (pp. 15–34). Washington, DC: American Psychological Association. doi:10.1037/12061-001

Bowlby, J. (1973). *Attachment and loss: Vol. 2. Separation: Anxiety and anger*. New York, NY: Basic Books.

Bowlby, J. (1980). *Attachment and loss: Vol. 3. Sadness and depression*. New York, NY: Basic Books.

Bowlby, J. (1982). *Attachment and loss: Vol. 1. Attachment* (2nd ed.). New York, NY: Basic Books. (Original work published 1969)

Bowlby, J. (1988). *A secure base: Clinical applications of attachment theory*. London, England: Routledge.

Brennan, K. A., Clark, C. L., & Shaver, P. R. (1998). Self-report measurement of adult attachment: An integrative overview. In J. A. Simpson & W. S. Rholes (Eds.), *Attachment theory and close relationships* (pp. 46–76). New York, NY: Guilford Press.

Bretherton, I. (1985). Attachment theory: Retrospect and prospect. In I. Bretherton & E. Waters (Eds.), Growing in attachment theory and research (pp. 3–35). *Monographs of the Society for Research in Child Development, 50*.

Cassidy, J., & Kobak, R. R. (1988). Avoidance and its relationship with other defensive processes. In J. Belsky & T. Nezworski (Eds.), *Clinical implications of attachment* (pp. 300–323). Hillsdale, NJ: Erlbaum.

Collins, N. L., & Feeney, B. C. (2000). A safe haven: An attachment theory perspective on support seeking and caregiving in intimate relationships. *Journal of Personality and Social Psychology, 78,* 1053–1073. doi:10.1037/0022-3514.78.6.1053

Feeney, B. C., & Collins, N. L. (2001). Predictors of caregiving in adult intimate relationships: An attachment theoretical perspective. *Journal of Personality and Social Psychology, 80,* 972–994. doi:10.1037/0022-3514.80.6.972

Feeney, B. C., & Collins, N. L. (2003). Motivations for caregiving in adult intimate relationships: Influences on caregiving behavior and relationship functioning. *Personality and Social Psychology Bulletin, 29,* 950–968. doi:10.1177/0146167203252807

Feeney, J. A. (2008). Adult romantic attachment: Developments in the study of couple relationships. In J. Cassidy & P. R. Shaver (Eds.), *Handbook of attachment: Theory, research, and clinical applications* (2nd ed., pp. 456–481). New York, NY: Guilford Press.

Fraley, R. C., & Davis, K. E. (1997). Attachment formation and transfer in young adults' close friendships and romantic relationships. *Personal Relationships, 4,* 131–144. doi:10.1111/j.1475-6811.1997.tb00135.x

Fraley, R. C., & Shaver, P. R. (2000). Adult romantic attachment: Theoretical developments, emerging controversies, and unanswered questions. *Review of General Psychology, 4,* 132–154. doi:10.1037/1089-2680.4.2.132

George, C., & Solomon, J. (2008). The caregiving system: A behavioral-system approach to parenting. In J. Cassidy & P. R. Shaver (Eds.), *Handbook of attachment: Theory, research, and clinical applications* (2nd ed., pp. 833–856). New York, NY: Guilford Press.

Gillath, O., Sesko, A. K., Shaver, P. R., & Chun, D. S. (2010). Attachment, authenticity, and honesty: Dispositional and experimentally induced security can reduce self- and other-deception. *Journal of Personality and Social Psychology, 98,* 841–855. doi:10.1037/a0019206

Gillath, O., Shaver, P. R., Mikulincer, M., Nitzberg, R. E., Erez, A., & van IJzendoorn, M. H. (2005). Attachment, caregiving, and volunteering: Placing volunteerism in an attachment-theoretical framework. *Personal Relationships, 12,* 425–446. doi:10.1111/j.1475-6811.2005.00124.x

Hazan, C., & Shaver, P. R. (1987). Romantic love conceptualized as an attachment process. *Journal of Personality and Social Psychology, 52,* 511–524. doi:10.1037/0022-3514.52.3.511

Jordan, A. H., & Monin, B. (2008). From sucker to saint: Moralization in response to self-threat. *Psychological Science, 19,* 809–815. doi:10.1111/j.1467-9280.2008.02161.x

Kernis, M. H., & Goldman, B. M. (2006). A multicomponent conceptualization of authenticity: Research and theory. In M. P. Zanna (Ed.), *Advances in experimental social psychology* (Vol. 38, pp. 284–357). San Diego, CA: Academic Press.

Kunce, L. J., & Shaver, P. R. (1994). An attachment-theoretical approach to caregiving in romantic relationships. In K. Bartholomew & D. Perlman (Eds.), *Advances in personal relationships* (Vol. 5, pp. 205–237). London, England: Kingsley.

Lee, K., & Ashton, M. C. (2004). Psychometric properties of the HEXACO Personality Inventory. *Multivariate Behavioral Research, 39,* 329–358. doi:10.1207/s15327906mbr3902_8

Mikulincer, M. (1998). Adult attachment style and affect regulation: Strategic variations in self-appraisals. *Journal of Personality and Social Psychology, 75,* 420–435. doi:10.1037/0022-3514.75.2.420

Mikulincer, M., Gillath, O., Halevy, V., Avihou, N., Avidan, S., & Eshkoli, N. (2001). Attachment theory and reactions to others' needs: Evidence that activation of the sense of attachment security promotes empathic responses. *Journal of Personality and Social Psychology, 81,* 1205–1224. doi:10.1037/0022-3514.81.6.1205

Mikulincer, M., Gillath, O., Sapir-Lavid, Y., Yaakobi, E., Arias, K., Tal-Aloni, L., & Bor, G. (2003). Attachment theory and concern for others' welfare: Evidence that activation of the sense of secure base promotes endorsement of self-transcendence values. *Basic and Applied Social Psychology, 25,* 299–312. doi:10.1207/S15324834BASP2504_4

Mikulincer, M., & Shaver, P. R. (2004). Security-based self-representations in adulthood: Contents and processes. In W. S. Rholes & J. A. Simpson (Eds.), *Adult attachment: Theory, research, and clinical implications* (pp. 159–195). New York, NY: Guilford Press.

Mikulincer, M., & Shaver, P. R. (2007a). *Attachment in adulthood: Structure, dynamics, and change.* New York, NY: Guilford Press.

Mikulincer, M., & Shaver, P. R. (2007b). Boosting attachment security to promote mental health, prosocial values, and inter-group tolerance. *Psychological Inquiry, 18,* 139–156.

Mikulincer, M., Shaver, P. R., Gillath, O., & Nitzberg, R. A. (2005). Attachment, caregiving, and altruism: Boosting attachment security increases compassion and helping. *Journal of Personality and Social Psychology, 89,* 817–839. doi:10.1037/0022-3514.89.5.817

Mikulincer, M., Shaver, P. R., & Slav, K. (2006). Attachment, mental representations of others, and interpersonal gratitude and forgiveness within romantic relationships. In M. Mikulincer & G. S. Goodman (Eds.), *Dynamics of romantic love* (pp. 190–215). New York, NY: Guilford Press.

Perugini, M., & Leone, L. (2009). Implicit self-concept and moral action. *Journal of Research in Personality, 43,* 747–754. doi:10.1016/j.jrp.2009.03.015

Schwartz, S. (2010). Basic values: How they motivate and inhibit prosocial behavior. In M. Mikulincer & P. R. Shaver (Eds.), *Prosocial motives, emotions, and behavior:*

The better angels of our nature (pp. 221–241). Washington, DC: American Psychological Association. doi:10.1037/12061-012

Shaver, P. R., Mikulincer, M., & Shemesh-Iron, M. (2010). A behavioral systems perspective on prosocial behavior. In M. Mikulincer & P. R. Shaver (Eds.), *Prosocial motives, emotions, and behavior: The better angels of our nature* (pp. 73–92). Washington, DC: American Psychological Association.

Simpson, J. A., Rholes, W. S., & Nelligan, J. S. (1992). Support seeking and support giving within couples in an anxiety-provoking situation: The role of attachment styles. *Journal of Personality and Social Psychology, 62*, 434–446. doi:10.1037/0022-3514.62.3.434

Sroufe, L., & Fleeson, J. (1986). Attachment and the construction of relationships. In W. Hartup & Z. Rubin (Eds.), *The nature and development of relationships* (pp. 51–71). Hillsdale, NJ: Erlbaum.

15

PARADIGM ASSUMPTIONS ABOUT MORAL BEHAVIOR: AN EMPIRICAL BATTLE ROYAL

LAWRENCE J. WALKER, JEREMY A. FRIMER, AND WILLIAM L. DUNLOP

The horrors of the Second World War blindsided social scientists, along with most everyone else on the planet. Faced with more than 60 million casualties, the use of nuclear weapons on civilian populations, and especially the Holocaust—all carried out by modern nations—the social sciences were vastly underequipped to explain, let alone suggest prophylaxes for, such atrocities. World War II demanded (and still demands) a credible psychological explanation and a lesson learned that will prevent a repeat. In response, social scientists grappled with the challenge of explaining both heinous behavior (by the likes of Hitler and Eichmann) and heroic behavior in defiance of authority (by the likes of Schindler and Bonhoeffer). Both dispositional and situational explanations came to the fore.

From a dispositionalist perspective, personality psychologists (e.g., Adorno, Frenkel-Brunswik, Levinson, & Sanford, 1950) advanced the notion of the authoritarian personality, which explained people's frequent complicity in the callous agendas of authoritarian regimes. In a somewhat similar vein, developmental psychologists (e.g., Kohlberg, 1964) advanced the possibility that immature moral reasoning explained these complicit behaviors, with developmentally advanced individuals more likely to challenge the dictates of authorities whose edicts were at variance with concern for human dignity.

In contrast, from a situationalist perspective, Arendt's (1963) commentary on Eichmann, the architect of the Holocaust, claimed that Eichmann (and most other Nazis) were not psychopathic monsters; instead, these perpetrators were ordinary people, caught in the wrong place and at the wrong time—yielding the "banality of evil" epithet. Early systematic evidence regarding the power of the situation was provided by Milgram's (1974) research demonstrating people's ready obedience to authorities who commanded harm to others and by Zimbardo's prison experiment (Zimbardo, Banks, Haney, & Jaffe, 1973) in which participants quickly embraced the malevolent roles to which they had been randomly assigned.

Differences between dispositionalism and situationalism are not superficial or trite. This distinction cuts to the heart of what we mean by morality, to our understanding of the processes that drive moral behavior, and to the implementation of preventive or corrective interventions. For example, the dispositionalist perspective prescribes the socialization of moral character in individuals, whereas the situationalist perspective calls for selecting and constructing contexts that bring out individuals' humanity.

The specific question we address in this chapter concerns the source of moral heroism. Is moral action set in motion primarily by situational factors operating on otherwise ordinary people, or do some aspects of individuals' character interact with opportunity to initiate and perpetuate a moral career? Later in this chapter, we put predictions emerging from these situationalist and dispositionalist perspectives "into the ring" and referee an empirical battle royal to see which of the various contenders contribute to our understanding of moral heroism. The research involves an examination of the psychological functioning of moral exemplars—people who have engaged in extraordinary moral action that has real-world significance—in comparison with that of ordinary people. Our intent in this chapter is to shed new light on the processes that give rise to moral heroism.

Before attending to this specific question about the sources of heroism, however, we undertake a wider angle examination of the relationship between moral psychology and the real-world problems it aims to explain. Moral psychology is fundamentally an applied discipline: Real-world social issues are the standard to which the discipline's methods and data ought to be held to account. To transform chaotic social problems into empirical questions, researchers, by necessity, impose a degree of order on a domain, yielding methodologies, measures, and research designs. This imposed order, and the paradigmatic assumptions it entails, also needs to be scrutinized relative to the gold standard of real-world social relevance. The assumptions we make in defining the parameters of the moral domain and in establishing how morality works have significant implications for the directives we derive for improving the human condition. How well these assumptions allow us to tap the moral psychological phenomena of interest is the question that frames the first part of this chapter, to which we now turn.

PARADIGM ASSUMPTIONS

As with all approaches to knowing, taken-for-granted assumptions underwrite the scientific method. These assumptions are in the very fabric of inquiry, often reflected in methodological approaches. Initially, such premises are often scrutinized and adopted on the basis of their intuitive appeal, but not all commonsense ideas turn out to have merit. Revisiting these assumptions in light of updated theory and evidence is crucial for scientific progress.

In this section, we take up this vital task by revisiting two paradigmatic assumptions that frame research on moral behavior: (a) that the laboratory provides a lens on the moral world and (b) that all people function according to the same psychological processes. Although our stance on these theses is critical, our intent is not to reject them unilaterally, but rather to move toward a more balanced synthesis. To forecast what will come after, we review a recent study of ours that illustrates some of the key points.

Assuming the Lab to Be a Lens on the Moral World

Motivated by an enormous social problem—the evils of the Third Reich—Milgram (1974) set out to test the possibility that the potential for evil is within all of us and can be exposed by the "right" situational presses. Part of the brilliance of Milgram's work was the control he exerted over situational forces, moving the setting from the European death camp to the American research lab while presumably holding the qualities and processes endemic to the pressure-to-obey phenomenon constant (albeit in a different degree), thereby establishing a valid analog. This move set up the first questionable paradigmatic assumption we wish to address—that laboratory research is sufficient to yield a veridical account of morality in the real world.

The lab analog experiment is uniquely efficacious in isolating variables and assessing causality. The problem, however, is that the qualitative differences between the social reality the lab is meant to simulate and the lab itself often draw the inquiry away from the phenomena of interest in significant ways. The norm for the lab-based researcher is merely to assume that one's setting has external validity, rather than to demonstrate it. We offer two reasons to doubt that a lab setting is good enough, standing alone. Laboratory experimentation is often limited by (a) the use of a single, overconstrained behavioral measure and (b) reliance on abstract vignettes removed from everyday experience. Each is discussed in turn.

The first concern revolves around reliance on one-off, peculiar, overly constrained (either/or) scenarios in lab settings to make inferences about patterns of behavior in the real world. Undergirding this method is the assumption that one-off behaviors extrapolate to real-world patterns of behavior in a simple, additive fashion and that the processes at play remain unchanged. Irrespective of how clever the behavioral test and how much ecological validity attends it, singular assessments of behavior cannot definitively tap a domain as complex and multifaceted as morality. In any given scenario, context is a stronger press than disposition in eliciting behavior (Fleeson, 2004). For this reason, relying on one-off behaviors as a portal to real life leads to a fundamental attribution error flipped on its head—an overestimation of the power of the situation on behavior. Drawing conclusions about individuals' functioning from a single assessment of behavior makes no more sense than making inferences from a single questionnaire item—each method is unreliable (Epstein, 1983).

Aiming to isolate phenomena, researchers are prone to devise somewhat peculiar and overly constrained assessments of moral functioning that are remote from everyday moral experience. Such assessments include Kohlberg's (1984) Heinz dilemma (stealing a miracle drug to save one's wife), Haidt's (2001) moral dumbfounding dilemma (having sex with one's sibling), Greene's (Greene, Sommerville, Nystrom, Darley, & Cohen, 2001) trolley dilemma (pushing a fat man off a bridge to save five other people from an out-of-control trolley), and Pizarro's (Pizarro, Uhlmann, & Bloom, 2003) causal deviance scenario (attempting to murder someone whose demise is caused instead by the would-be-victim's fluky heart attack).

These assessments place participants in an overly constrained situation, facing a dichotomous decision (e.g., push vs. don't push). Researchers deliberately disallow the alternatives that would otherwise come to mind for participants. But the tendency to accept dualisms (e.g., win/lose) as opposed to seeking higher, integrative forms of social interaction (e.g., win/win) is an important developmental difference (Perry, 1970). And although these assessments may isolate psychological processes, they do not remotely model the kinds of moral problems people more typically confront in everyday life. When this degree of abstraction is combined with a constrained response format, little insight regarding real-world moral functioning is likely to be gained. Our point is that only by aggregating responses across situations and sensitizing our methods to the ways in which individuals shape (e.g., select, explore, construe) the situations they face can a researcher capture a phenomenon in its real-world form.

As an example, Haidt (2001) attempted to show that affective intuition is what primarily drives moral judgment and that reasoning plays only an after-the-fact rationalizing and social persuasion role. To arrive at this conclusion, Haidt relied on an imaginatively concocted incest dilemma to which most respondents reacted by asserting that incest is wrong but without being able to provide a convincing reason for this judgment given the constraints of the scenario. The point Haidt was trying to make was not confined to this specific vignette, but was generalized to everyday sorts of moral scenarios. Incest is not, however, the sort of issue with which most people are faced. What, then, happens when individuals are faced with real dilemmas? Do they rely purely on intuitive processes or some interaction of intuitive and rational ones (Narvaez, 2008; see also Chapter 4, this volume)? Haidt's artificial methods distance his data from this very real question.

A gold nugget in Gilligan's (1982) critique of moral psychology was her skepticism concerning such constrained dilemmas and her advocacy for assessing moral judgment more naturalistically, tapping moral problems from individuals' own experience. For whatever reason, her advocacy has not gained much of a foothold in the field despite evidence indicating that reasoning about real-life moral conflicts better predicts everyday moral behavior than does reasoning about hypothetical dilemmas (Trevethan & Walker, 1989; Walker, Hennig, & Krettenauer, 2000). Perhaps the degree to which an individual is invested in a moral issue moderates the processes used to resolve it. This much is speculative; until researchers who explore moral functioning include realistic problems, speculative it will remain.

Assuming Homogeneity in the Face of Developmental Variability

Another paradigmatic assumption to which we draw attention asserts that people are psychologically "cut from the same cloth," uniformly operating by the same moral psychological processes. This assumption is manifest in the frequent reliance on a single kind of research participant (e.g., undergraduate students garnering course credit), a lack of consideration for individual differences, and a homogenizing "people" label. Diversity among people is ignored and sacrificed to error variance. But at what cost? A high one, we contend.

To illustrate what is lost when individual differences are ignored, we return to Milgram's (1974) paradigm-establishing obedience-to-authority studies. The received wisdom from these studies was a confirmation of the banality of evil view, a not-so-subtle nod to the power of the situation; dispositional differences were largely dismissed. In the classic manipulation, a majority of participants administered electrical shocks "to the limit." A common reading of this finding is that all participants responded similarly, with the difference between continuing the experiment and quitting being a matter of chance (left to the error variance bucket). But, as it turned out, those who shocked to the limit and those who quit were not all the same; interactions lingered in the mist.

In an important but rarely cited study, Kohlberg (1984; then Milgram's colleague at Yale University), interviewed some of Milgram's participants to assess their stage of moral reasoning. Developmental level was powerfully predictive of behavior—almost none of the lower stage participants (14%) quit the experiment, but almost all of the higher stage participants (83%) defied the authority. In the appendix to his book, Milgram (1974, p. 205) dismissed these data as being merely suggestive. On the contrary, Kohlberg's data entirely reverse the moral of the Milgram study, that evil is fundamentally banal. A conclusion that better represents the data holds that situational pressures can elicit evil only in some people.

In terms of which dispositions should we distinguish people? The answer depends on many factors, much beyond the scope of this chapter. But we do present a menu of dispositional courses worth considering. McAdams's (1995) personality template highlights multiple levels of personality, all of which should be assessed if we are to begin to (really) know a person. The typical assessment of personality is along the lines of dispositional traits (e.g., the Big Five); these are descriptive assessments of individuals' past behavior that tend to be relatively stable over the life course. But traits do not tap the intrapsychic processing that energizes and causes future behavior through motivation and the desire for a coherent sense of self (John & Robins, 1994; McAdams, 1992). To tap these causal aspects of personality, McAdams pointed to characteristic adaptations such as goal motivation and integrative life narratives that capture individuals' construction of identity and personal meaning. The argument here is to consider the various parts of individuals' uniqueness in an attempt to get to know the whole person.

Our preference (or paradigmatic assumption) on this matter is to focus not on just any individual differences, but on those that develop. We focus on development because of its conceptual and practical significance: It can inform an understanding of the sequence of development, define its endpoint (i.e., maturity), explicate the processes of acquisition, and specify optimal means of intervention in real-world settings. Failure to consider developmental level can contribute to fallacious inferences about moral functioning.

To illustrate, consider a hypothetical study of competitors in a winter Olympic event, such as snowboarding. If performing a study on efficacy in snowboarding with a sample composed solely of novices first trying their hand at this sport, the conclusions drawn regarding strategies and processes governing performance would lead to myopic conclusions about snowboarding (e.g., "Despite trying not to, just about everyone falls down"). Olympic athletes function differently from novices—both quantitatively (e.g., speed) and qualitatively (e.g., processing different kinds of information). Ignoring this difference and sampling at random would render a sample constituted almost entirely by novices and lead to the aforementioned bleak conclusions about "people" and the snowboarding domain.

For this story to become a proper analog to the moral domain, one needs to assume that (a) a particular moral function is difficult but adaptive to perform well, (b) people can change in their ability to perform that function, and (c) these changes tend to follow some developmental pattern. These points have been well argued and demonstrated for several aspects of moral functioning that develop (see Walker & Frimer, in press, for a review), but most demonstrably so for stage of moral reasoning, a variable that cleanly differentiated Milgram's shockers from his quitters. The take-home message is thus again modified to read "evil is banal for the developmentally immature."

This critique applies to developmentally homogenizing research both old and new. By not considering developmental level, many researchers arrive at skewed conclusions about moral functioning. Consider, for example, the implications of Haidt's (2001) conclusions about the phenomenon of moral dumbfounding. Do experts hold to a moral judgment even when reason dictates a change of tune? This is a highly consequential question; Rawls (1993), in his influential *Political Liberalism*, argued that a civil society requires citizens to be "reasonable" with their opinions, which includes a readiness to change one's position when good reasons so dictate. Bracketing the aforementioned limitations of Haidt's study, do we conclude from his demonstration that "people" rely primarily on intuition, or do we conclude that parents, teachers, and other societal leaders have educational work to do? Perhaps both.

As another example, Skitka and Morgan (2009) reported evidence regarding the apparent evils associated with steadfastly holding moral convictions. Colby and Damon (1992) argued that moral maturity entails not only certainty in conviction but also open-mindedness to differing ideas. Might Skitka and Morgan's findings highlight the woes of moralistic dogmatism (which may be a developmental stepping-stone)? We believe so. Our point is that research based solely on people of one developmental level will, at best, offer a constricted account of moral processing. Instead, we advocate considering developmental variables germane to the situation and choosing research designs that entail comparison across developmental levels. In sum, we contend that individual differences, particularly of the developmental kind, have much to contribute to our understanding of processes of moral functioning and that the frequent homogenization of people entails conceptual costs.

THE SOURCE OF MORAL HEROISM

Having examined paradigmatic assumptions underlying some of the methods of moral psychology, we now turn to a specific question—the source of moral heroism. The purpose of this exploration is to test competing claims regarding this important issue but, in so doing, also illustrate our key points about paradigmatic assumptions. Moral heroism is the rather neglected positive side of morality, a qualitatively different form of moral action than the resolution of circumscribed moral quandaries. The challenge of living a life of moral heroism is an underdetermined, supererogatory problem for which many options are available—achieving a morally exemplary life certainly does not reduce to resolving some kind of dualistic dilemma.

So what, then, drives the heroic deeds of moral heroes like Gandhi, Mother Teresa, and Oskar Schindler? To frame this question, we revisit the person versus situation debate. Is moral action fueled purely by potent life circumstances dealt to an "ordinary" person? Or does some aspect of the individual's personality react with an opportunity to ignite a moral career? The latter, interactional claim can further be broken down into differing perspectives on the nature of moral personality.

To summarize what is to come, we begin by setting up four competing predictions about the source of heroism. We then step outside the lab to assess the personalities of individuals who have lived by high moral codes. Our methodology entails a broadband assessment of psychological functioning, and our person-level analysis allows for the study of lives rather than being restricted to the study of variables. Because our moral exemplars will also be compared with ordinary people—in essence, experts versus novices—we have clear intimations of developmental variability. Finally, the predictions of Aristotle, Immanuel Kant, Owen Flanagan, and Philip Zimbardo will "get in the ring" and clash for the explanatory title, battle royal.

Situationalist Perspective

People who commit "moral failures" often externalize responsibility for their actions (Bandura, 2002), and those who engage in moral heroism similarly disavow praise. Do these claims capture the psychological reality of moral behavior? Are moral (and immoral) behaviors fundamentally banal? The *situationalist perspective* identifies the cause of moral behavior purely in features of the situation, denying any causal significance for dispositional factors.

Among psychologists, perhaps Zimbardo (2004, 2007) has been the most vocal and radical proponent of this perspective, arguing by analogy from the Stanford prison experiment (Zimbardo et al., 1973):

> The banality of evil is matched by the banality of heroism. Neither is the consequence of dispositional tendencies. . . . Both emerge in particular situations at particular times, when situational forces play a compelling role in moving individuals across the line from inaction to action. (Zimbardo, 2007, p. 275)

Philosophers have more typically aligned with the dispositionalist perspective on moral character, but recently some (Doris, 2002; Harman, 2009) have expressed sympathy with the situationalist perspective, contending that ethical theory can and should abandon the notion of moral personality but somehow retain the notions of agency and moral responsibility. Thus, the core empirical claim of the situationalist perspective denies the causal operation of dispositions in producing moral heroism and asserts the instigating role of situational factors.

Dispositionalist Perspective

The *dispositionalist perspective* emerges from ethical frameworks that identify the source of moral behavior in human character. Difficulty arises, however, when trying to identify theorists who advance the simplistic view that dispositions ubiquitously and solely cause moral behavior, without reference to the situation. The classic Aristotelian view and many so-called dispositional accounts are, in actuality, context sensitive, consisting of if–then conditionals. Dispositionalists agree among themselves on the causal role of virtue but diverge in their understanding of its nature. Whereas some define a single ideal type of moral personality—either entailing the embodiment of the full complement of virtues or focusing on a single superintending virtue—other theories advance a variety of moral personality types.

The Aristotelian tradition in moral philosophy (Aristotle, 350 BC/1962) characterizes the morally excellent person as possessing the full array of virtues. This view posits that the virtues entail a functional, psychological interdependence: A person cannot really possess any one cardinal virtue without also embodying the others. Although a timeworn view, it has also received contemporary endorsement (McDowell, 1979; Watson, 1984). Unpacking this view within the realm of the empirical, the claim is that moral heroes exhibit high functioning across the full gamut of virtues (i.e., morally relevant personality variables).

A different formulation of the dispositionalist perspective contends that the morally excellent person is guided by a single, general-purpose moral principle or algorithm (not the complete array of virtues). Enlightenment-era philosophers, in particular, held that some single superintending deliberative principle is not only necessary but sufficient for dictating the morally good life, solving moral problems, and compelling moral behavior. This zeitgeist sidelined a characterological basis for morality and championed a rationalistic one, as illustrated by Kant's (1785/2002) categorical imperative and Bentham's (1789/1970) utilitarian rule. This formulation is illustrated in contemporary moral psychology by Kohlberg's (1981) advocacy of the principle of justice as that superintending algorithm and Gilligan's (1982) popularization of the ethic of care. Regardless of which moral algorithm takes center stage, this formulation of the dispositionalist perspective implies an empirical claim of homogeneity among moral heroes, with their adaptive similarity defined by one superintending psychological function.

Although moral philosophers have typically been advocates of a singular moral archetype, more recently some (Flanagan, 1991) have embraced the notion of plurality in moral ideals. Thus, a third formulation of the dispositionalist perspective posits varieties of moral personality. Folk conceptions of moral functioning (Walker & Hennig, 2004) indicate that people attribute a range of psychological profiles to moral exemplars. And within moral psychology, theorists have argued for the existence of different ethical frameworks; for example, Shweder, Much, Mahapatra, and Park's (1997) ethics of autonomy, community, and divinity. Thus, the fundamental empirical claim of this perspective is that multifarious moral personalities are evident, each embodying a somewhat different and partial set of virtues.

THE EMPIRICAL BATTLE ROYAL

In a recent study (Walker, Frimer, & Dunlop, 2010), we tested competing claims about sources of moral behavior by assessing the psychological functioning of a sample of moral exemplars. Our 50 participants were recipients of a national award for their moral action through the Canadian honors system; half received an award for bravery in risking their lives to save others, and half received an award for long-term volunteer commitment in providing care, community service, or humanitarian relief. These are behaviors with real-world significance. One of the additional design features of this study was the inclusion of individually matched comparison participants drawn from the general community (ordinary people in contrast to developmentally advanced exemplars).

Rather than asking these participants to resolve hypothetical dilemmas, our method involved starting from their real-life experiences. To provide a comprehensive assessment of psychological functioning, we used measures at each level of personality description (including personality inventories and an extensive life-review interview), relying on McAdams's (1995, 2009) threefold taxonomy of dispositional traits, characteristic adaptations, and integrative life narratives. In our analyses, we tapped a total of 13 variables that had been implicated in previous research as being relevant to the topic at hand.

Variables assessed at the level of dispositional traits included the interpersonal circumplex dimensions of dominance and nurturance, as well as the conscientiousness, emotional stability, and openness to experience factors of the five factor model (Wiggins, 1995). At the level of characteristic adaptations, goal-oriented motivation was assessed by relational, generativity, and self-development strivings (Emmons, 1999). Structural–developmental variables also reflect the characteristic adaptations level and were assessed by stage of moral reasoning development (Colby & Kohlberg, 1987) and by epistemic development (Fowler, 1981). The third level of personality description, integrative narratives of the self, was assessed in the context of a life-review interview that was coded for motivational themes of agency and communion (McAdams, 1988), as well as for *redemption sequences* (McAdams, 2006), or the tendency to construe positive benefit out of some negative event.

A simple comparison of the personalities of exemplars versus comparison participants would allow us to differentially test the situationalist and dispositionalist perspectives. But to simultaneously test the claims of the three dispositionalist formulations, we allowed the exemplars to form clusters of like-natured individuals—to let exemplars of a feather flock together (so to speak). How many clusters would emerge? As a reminder, the situationalist perspective makes no predictions about the number of clusters but claims that members of each cluster would be indistinguishable from their matched nonexemplars. In contrast, the three dispositionalist accounts uniformly predict differences between exemplars and comparisons but differ in the number and nature of the clusters. The Aristotelian unity-of-the-virtues formulation predicts one cluster, exemplary on all variables; the Kantian single-algorithm formulation also predicts a single cluster, but exemplary on only one variable; and Flanagan's varieties formulation predicts multiple clusters, each with its respective signature personality profile.

Our analytic strategy was to conduct a (person-level) cluster analysis of the sample of moral exemplars, clustering in terms of all variables rendered by the broadband assessment of personality. A three-cluster solution was found to best fit the data, favoring the varieties perspective over the other two dispositional accounts. Note that the cluster procedure did not simply split the sample in terms of the nature of the award (brave vs. caring)—three, not two, clusters were found, and both brave and caring exemplars populated each of the clusters. Once the clusters were derived, we assessed which variables defined each cluster.

The first cluster was defined by themes of communion in life stories, goal motivation entailing relational and generativity strivings, and the trait of nurturance. Hence the label *communal* seemed appropriate for this cluster. About three quarters of the people in this cluster were caring exemplars.

The second cluster was defined quite differently: by the structural–developmental variables of epistemic development and moral reasoning, self-development strivings, and the trait of openness to experience. Emphasis on sophisticated, reflective judgment and concerns with self-development suggested the label *deliberative* for this cluster. This cluster was balanced in terms of caring and brave exemplars.

The third cluster had low scores on many personality variables relative to the other clusters (scoring lowest on most variables and highest on none). Across the broadband assessment of personality, this cluster was consistently unremarkable in comparison with other exemplars, and so the label *ordinary* seemed apt. About three quarters of the exemplars in this cluster were brave awardees.

With the varieties perspective outpredicting its dispositional perspective counterparts, we now turn to the dispositionalist versus situationalist claims. Once the exemplar clusters were identified, each cluster was then contrasted with its associated comparison participants to determine whether and in which ways each exemplar cluster might be exemplary (recall that the situationalist perspective predicts the null here). The exemplars in the communal and deliberative clusters scored higher than comparison participants on the personality variables that distinguished them from other clusters. Interestingly, exemplars in these clusters also scored higher than their comparison participants on several other personality variables, indicating that their personalities were anything but banal. The situationalist perspective does not predict the existence of these two clusters. In contrast, analyses indicated that the 13 personality variables collectively did not significantly discriminate the cluster of "ordinary" exemplars from their comparison participants at all, confirming the banality of this cluster.

TO THE VICTORS GO THE SPOILS

Our objective was to contrast four competing perspectives on the sources of moral behavior by examining the psychological functioning of real-world moral exemplars. Analyses discriminated three varieties of moral personality (communal, deliberative, and ordinary), buttressing two of these contenders.

Support for the dispositionalist perspective was garnered from the finding that two of the three exemplar clusters evidenced highly adaptive levels of certain aspects of personality. The communal and deliberative clusters were defined by different sets of personality variables—themes of social interdependence versus themes of thoughtful meaning making and personal growth, respectively—reflecting distinct moral ideals. This evidence undermines the notion that moral excellence can and should be evidenced by a single moral ideal, as claimed by two different formulations of the dispositionalist perspective. Although both clusters evidenced adaptive personality functioning on several variables in contrast to comparison participants, both patterns fell well short of the comprehensive array posited by the unity-of-the-virtues doctrine, and there was no evidence of a single superintending moral principle or virtue that was characteristic of moral exemplarity. Thus, we conclude that the notion of a "one size fits all" type of moral excellence does not accord with our data.

The finding of three moral personality types is consistent with the dispositionalist perspective in explaining moral behavior. However, the varieties perspective hardly predicted that one variety would be an empty set. By default, the existence of this ordinary cluster gives some credence to the situationalist perspective (Doris, 2002; Zimbardo, 2007).

Ultimately, the perspectives in contention here entailed causal predictions. How might we explore these causal predictions given the limitations of correlational data? On occasion, some extraordinary moral action can be evoked from ordinary people provided the right convergence of situational factors. But which heroic action might this be? Recall that the ordinary cluster was composed predominantly of brave exemplars who had engaged in one-off heroic rescues. In many emergencies, situational factors can be powerfully compelling, and dispositional factors may be less consequential for action. The single rescue of the brave awardees is similar (in number) to single behaviors assessed in lab settings. If only one-off behaviors (viz., bravery) had been considered in this study, an erroneous conclusion—one overattributing the source of moral action to the situation—would have ensued. Flawed conclusions about the source of moral behaviors may arise from paradigm assumptions espousing the observation of one-off behaviors.

In contrast, most of the exemplars in the other two clusters were caring awardees with long-term commitment to volunteer service. This type of enduring behavior requires considerable lifestyle change and continuity of purpose, the maintenance of which may entail a mature source of moral motivation. That is, ordinary people may be competent to enact a one-off moral behavior but less well-equipped for a "moral career."

Given the correlational nature of the data, however, a challenge can be mounted to the dispositionalist claim of a causal moral personality that is operative in the moral career. In our study's design, the psychological functioning of moral exemplars was assessed subsequent to their extraordinary moral behaviors and consequent recognition. A situationalist could contend that contextual factors were responsible for the moral behaviors (of those people in the communal and deliberative clusters) and that self-perception processes later created a personality description to match the behavior in retrospect, reformulating attitudes and personality to accord with self-perceived, past behavior. In this view, then, personality is analogous to a documentary without a causal mechanism for future behavior; in the competing dispositionalist perspective, the metaphor for personality would be an operator's manual wherein personality is functionally guiding behavior (see Walker & Frimer, 2007, for further discussion).

Although this challenge is plausible, the present data present difficulties for a usurping personality-as-documentary explanation. One is that self-perception processes are more likely instigated when internal cues are ambiguous in the face of relatively unimportant issues regarding the self (Baumeister, 1998). Aspects of moral character hardly qualify on that count. The second difficulty is that if people do indeed construe their personality to reflect behavioral manifestations, then differences between exemplar and comparison participants should be more pronounced on transparent, past-behavior-documenting types of personality (e.g., self-ratings on personality traits) than on more subtle, motivational assessments (e.g., structural–developmental and life-narrative interviews).

The present data do not conform to that pattern: Individuals in the communal and deliberative clusters evidenced the opposite pattern (with stronger effects on the interview measures than on the personality inventories), and individuals in the ordinary cluster did not differ from their comparison participants in self-ratings of personality traits at all. These findings suggest that the operative aspects of personality for moral behavior are located in the patterns of meaning making and identity that individuals construct in the context of life events rather than in decontextualized personality traits. Similar notions are posited by authors of other chapters in this volume: authentic morality based on attachment security (Chapter 14, this volume), integrated moral motivation (Chapter 13), and moral integrity (Chapter 9), among others.

That tentative conclusion is suggestive; the correlational nature of the present data do not readily allow for arbitrating between the documentary and operator's manual depictions of personality, particularly because in this case personality was assessed subsequent to engaging in significant moral behavior and receipt of public recognition for it. Because the sorts of personality implicated here are not readily manipulated, this empirical impasse warrants prospective longitudinal studies to identify personality precursors to long-term patterns of moral behavior.

Life narratives are about the individual in context, Person × Situation interactions encoded and internalized into self-defining stories. This Person × Situation encoding is illustrated by a serendipitous finding from an earlier analysis of this data set (Walker & Frimer, 2007), which revealed that caring exemplars were more likely to report suffering the death of a child than members of their matched comparison group. Usually, the death of a child causes self-focused despondency and anger, but it appears that these exemplars exhibited a distinctly different pattern, a kind of posttraumatic growth "on steroids" (see also Chapter 17, this volume). To address this question properly, both personality and situational data are needed; a limitation of the present study was the absence of direct assessments of situational pressures.

Our battle royal did not yield a single victor, but two—both situationalist and dispositionalist perspectives were vindicated in nuanced ways. The synthesis we endorse holds that a solitary focus on the situation or personality is misguided if one is interested in an accurate test of moral functioning. Fleeson (2004) similarly argued that both sides of the debate are right in some respects: The situationalist perspective is right about momentary behaviors; the dispositionalist perspective is right about behavioral trends. The typical dispositional focus of personality psychology can complement the situational focus of social psychology. However, the challenge for both disciplinary perspectives is to be more broadly based in their assessment of moral behavior rather than relying on one-off behavioral assessments in the lab or on descriptive trait inventories. Our proposal contends that lab experimentation should be balanced with real-world observation of socially significant affairs and that morally relevant aspects of personality should be tapped across all levels of personality description. Different methodologies should be mutually informative. Multiple lenses on the same phenomena contribute to a more comprehensive understanding, whereas divergent findings across methodologies harken our attention.

CONCLUSION

In this chapter, we refereed a battle royal between competing perspectives on the source of moral heroism. We will consider this exercise a triumph if our process and findings increase the field's focus on functional interactions between persons and situations, as well as encourage the careful scrutiny of paradigmatic assumptions.

REFERENCES

Adorno, T. W., Frenkel-Brunswik, E., Levinson, D. J., & Sanford, R. N. (1950). *The authoritarian personality*. New York, NY: Harper.

Arendt, H. (1963). *Eichmann in Jerusalem: A report on the banality of evil*. New York, NY: Viking.

Aristotle. (1962). *Nicomachean ethics* (M. Ostwald, Trans.). Indianapolis, IN: Bobbs-Merrill. (Original work published 350 BC)

Bandura, A. (2002). Selective moral disengagement in the exercise of moral agency. *Journal of Moral Education, 31*, 101–119. doi:10.1080/0305724022014322

Baumeister, R. F. (1998). The self. In D. T. Gilbert, S. T. Fiske, & G. Lindzey (Eds.), *Handbook of social psychology* (4th ed., Vol. 1, pp. 680–740). New York, NY: Oxford University Press.

Bentham, J. (1970). *An introduction to the principles of morals and legislation*. London, England: Athlone. (Original work published 1789)

Colby, A., & Damon, W. (1992). *Some do care: Contemporary lives of moral commitment*. New York, NY: Free Press.

Colby, A., & Kohlberg, L. (1987). *The measurement of moral judgment* (Vols. 1–2). New York, NY: Cambridge University Press.

Doris, J. M. (2002). *Lack of character: Personality and moral behavior*. Cambridge, England: Cambridge University Press.

Emmons, R. A. (1999). *The psychology of ultimate concerns: Motivation and spirituality in personality*. New York, NY: Guilford Press.

Epstein, S. (1983). Aggregation and beyond: Some basic issues on the prediction of behavior. *Journal of Personality, 51*, 360–392. doi:10.1111/j.1467-6494.1983.tb00338.x

Flanagan, O. (1991). *Varieties of moral personality: Ethics and psychological realism*. Cambridge, MA: Harvard University Press.

Fleeson, W. (2004). Moving personality beyond the person–situation debate: The challenge and the opportunity of within-person variability. *Current Directions in Psychological Science, 13*, 83–87. doi:10.1111/j.0963-7214.2004.00280.x

Fowler, J. W. (1981). *Stages of faith: The psychology of human development and the quest for meaning*. San Francisco, CA: Harper & Row.

Gilligan, C. (1982). *In a different voice: Psychological theory and women's development*. Cambridge, MA: Harvard University Press.

Greene, J. D., Sommerville, R. B., Nystrom, L. E., Darley, J. M., & Cohen, J. D. (2001, September 14). An fMRI investigation of emotional engagement in moral judgment. *Science, 293*, 2105–2108. doi:10.1126/science.1062872

Haidt, J. (2001). The emotional dog and its rational tail: A social intuitionist approach to moral judgment. *Psychological Review, 108*, 814–834. doi:10.1037/0033-295X.108.4.814

Harman, G. (2009). Skepticism about character traits. *The Journal of Ethics, 13*, 235–242. doi:10.1007/s10892-009-9050-6

John, O. P., & Robins, R. W. (1994). Traits and types, dynamics and development: No doors should be closed in the study of personality. *Psychological Inquiry, 5*, 137–142. doi:10.1207/s15327965pli0502_10

Kant, I. (2002). *Groundwork for the metaphysics of morals* (A. W. Wood, Trans.). New Haven, CT: Yale University Press. (Original work published 1785)

Kohlberg, L. (1964). Development of moral character and moral ideology. In M. L. Hoffman & L. Hoffman (Eds.), *Review of child development research* (Vol. 1, pp. 383–431). New York, NY: Russell Sage Foundation.

Kohlberg, L. (1981). *Essays on moral development: Vol. 1. The philosophy of moral development*. San Francisco, CA: Harper & Row.

Kohlberg, L. (1984). *Essays on moral development: Vol. 2. The psychology of moral development*. San Francisco, CA: Harper & Row.

McAdams, D. P. (1988). *Power, intimacy, and the life story: Personological inquiries into identity*. New York, NY: Guilford Press.

McAdams, D. P. (1992). The Five-Factor model in personality: A critical appraisal. *Journal of Personality, 60*, 329–361. doi:10.1111/j.1467-6494.1992.tb00976.x

McAdams, D. P. (1995). What do we know when we know a person? *Journal of Personality, 63*, 365–396. doi:10.1111/j.1467-6494.1995.tb00500.x

McAdams, D. P. (2006). *The redemptive self: Stories Americans live by*. New York, NY: Oxford University Press.

McAdams, D. P. (2009). The moral personality. In D. Narvaez & D. K. Lapsley (Eds.), *Personality, identity, and character: Explorations in moral psychology* (pp. 11–29). New York, NY: Cambridge University Press. doi:10.1017/CBO9780511627 125.002

McDowell, J. (1979). Virtue and reason. *The Monist, 62*, 331–350.

Milgram, S. (1974). *Obedience to authority: An experimental view*. New York, NY: Harper & Row.

Narvaez, D. (2008). The social-intuitionist model: Some counter-intuitions. In W. Sinnott-Armstrong (Ed.), *Moral psychology: Vol. 2. The cognitive science of morality: Intuition and diversity* (pp. 233–240). Cambridge, MA: MIT Press.

Perry, W. G. (1970). *Forms in intellectual and ethical development in the college years*. New York, NY: Holt, Rinehart and Winston.

Pizarro, D. A., Uhlmann, E., & Bloom, P. (2003). Causal deviance and the attribution of moral responsibility. *Journal of Experimental Social Psychology, 39*, 653–660. doi:10.1016/S0022-1031(03)00041-6

Rawls, J. (1993). *Political liberalism*. New York, NY: Columbia University Press.

Shweder, R. A., Much, N. C., Mahapatra, M., & Park, L. (1997). The "big three" of morality (autonomy, community, divinity) and the "big three" explanations of suffering. In A. Brandt & P. Rozin (Eds.), *Morality and health* (pp. 119–169). Florence, KY: Taylor & Francis/Routledge.

Skitka, L. J., & Morgan, G. S. (2009). The double-edged sword of a moral state of mind. In D. Narvaez & D. K. Lapsley (Eds.), *Personality, identity, and character: Explorations in moral psychology* (pp. 355–374). New York, NY: Cambridge University Press. doi:10.1017/CBO9780511627125.017

Trevethan, S. D., & Walker, L. J. (1989). Hypothetical versus real-life moral reasoning among psychopathic and delinquent youth. *Development and Psychopathology, 1*, 91–103. doi:10.1017/S0954579400000286

Walker, L. J., & Frimer, J. A. (2007). Moral personality of brave and caring exemplars. *Journal of Personality and Social Psychology, 93*, 845–860. doi:10.1037/0022-3514.93.5.845

Walker, L. J., & Frimer, J. A. (in press). The science of moral development. In M. K. Underwood & L. H. Rosen (Eds.), *Social development*. New York, NY: Guilford Press.

Walker, L. J., Frimer, J. A., & Dunlop, W. L. (2010). Varieties of moral personality: Beyond the banality of heroism. *Journal of Personality, 78*, 907–942. doi:10.1111/j.1467-6494.2010.00637.x

Walker, L. J., & Hennig, K. H. (2004). Differing conceptions of moral exemplarity: Just, brave, and caring. *Journal of Personality and Social Psychology, 86*, 629–647. doi:10.1037/0022-3514.86.4.629

Walker, L. J., Hennig, K. H., & Krettenauer, T. (2000). Parent and peer contexts for children's moral reasoning development. *Child Development, 71*, 1033–1048. doi:10.1111/1467-8624.00207

Watson, G. (1984). Virtues in excess. *Philosophical Studies, 46*, 57–74. doi:10.1007/BF00353491

Wiggins, J. S. (1995). *Interpersonal Adjective Scales: Professional manual.* Odessa, FL: Psychological Assessment Resources.

Zimbardo, P. G. (2004). A situationalist perspective on the psychology of evil: Understanding how good people are transformed into perpetrators. In A. G. Miller (Ed.), *The social psychology of good and evil* (pp. 21–50). New York, NY: Guilford Press.

Zimbardo, P. G. (2007). The banality of evil, the banality of heroism. In J. Brockman (Ed.), *What is your dangerous idea? Today's leading thinkers on the unthinkable* (pp. 275–276). New York, NY: Harper Perennial.

Zimbardo, P. G., Banks, W. C., Haney, C., & Jaffe, D. (1973, April 8). The mind is a formidable jailer: A Pirandellian prison. *The New York Times Magazine*, Section 6, pp. 38–46.

16

WHEN MORAL CONCERNS BECOME A PSYCHOLOGICAL DISORDER: THE CASE OF OBSESSIVE–COMPULSIVE DISORDER

GUY DORON, DAR SAR-EL, MARIO MIKULINCER,
AND MICHAEL KYRIOS

John, a 28-year-old man, steps into his psychologist's office and describes his problem:

> I find it very difficult to leave my apartment. I have thoughts that I might hit someone. I just can't stop thinking about it . . . it drives me crazy. I try to tell myself, "You never hit someone . . . except in high school, 15 years ago" and ask my parents whether they think I am that kind of a person. . . . They always say no. I also worry all the time that bad things will happen to my parents. That is why I have to do things in a certain way before I go to sleep or leave the house. I have to check the stove 33 times and make sure that I locked the doors and windows . . . three times each. I can't fall asleep if something goes wrong with my night routine, because something bad might happen.

John suffers from obsessive–compulsive disorder (OCD), an anxiety disorder that has been rated as a leading cause of disability by the World Health Organization (1996). His symptoms, like those of many others with this disorder, include morality-related worries, feelings, and cognitions such as perceived violation of moral standards, guilt, and inflated responsibility (Salkovskis, 1985; Steketee, Quay, & White, 1991). However, sensitivity to moral issues, by itself, is unlikely to lead to an emotional disorder. Many of us experience events or thoughts challenging our moral standards but are not flooded by negative self-evaluations, dysfunctional beliefs, and pathological preoccupations. In fact, for most people, such experiences would result in the activation of distress-regulation strategies that dissipate unwanted thoughts, reaffirm the challenged self, and restore emotional equanimity. In this chapter, we propose that dysfunctions of the attachment system, as manifested in heightened attachment anxiety, can disrupt the process of coping with morality-related concerns and therefore contribute to OCD. For people with high attachment anxiety, experiences challenging an important self-domain, such as morality, can increase the accessibility of "feared-self" cognitions (e.g., "I'm bad," "I'm immoral") and activate dysfunctional cognitive processes (e.g., an inflated sense of responsibility) that result in the development of obsessional preoccupations.

We begin this chapter with a brief description of OCD and current cognitive models of the disorder. We then describe the role of dysfunctional self-perceptions and *sensitive self-domains*—domains of the self that are extremely important for maintaining self-worth (Doron & Kyrios, 2005)—in OCD. Next, we review empirical findings linking attachment insecurities and obsessive–compulsive phenomena and propose a diathesis–stress model whereby experiences challenging sensitive self-domains, such as morality, and attachment insecurities interact to increase vulnerability to OCD. We then focus on morality as a particularly important self-domain in OCD and present new, previously unpublished findings showing that experiences in the morality domain can lead to OCD symptoms and that this effect is moderated by attachment anxiety.

OBSESSIVE–COMPULSIVE DISORDER

According to the *Diagnostic and Statistical Manual of Mental Disorders* (4th ed., rev.; *DSM–IV–R*; American Psychiatric Association, 2000), a diagnosis of OCD is appropriate when either, or both, obsessions or compulsions (a) are experienced at least at some stage as excessive, unreasonable, and inappropriate; (b) cause significant distress; and (c) are very time consuming or interfere with daily functions. *Obsessions* are unwanted and disturbing intrusive thoughts, images, or impulses. Obsessional themes include contamination fears, pathological doubt, a need for symmetry or order, body-related worries, and sexual or aggressive obsessions. *Compulsions* are deliberate, repetitive, and rigid behaviors or mental acts that people perform in response to their obsessions as a means of reducing distress or preventing some feared outcome from occurring. Common compulsive behaviors include repeated checking, washing, counting, reassurance seeking, ordering behaviors, and hoarding.

Although a wide range of etiological models have been proposed for OCD, cognitive–behavioral theories have been supported by a large body of empirical evidence and have led to the development of effective treatments (see Frost & Steketee, 2002, for a review). According to these theories, most people experience a range of intrusive phenomena that are similar in form and content to clinical obsessions (Rachman & de Silva, 1978), but individuals with OCD misinterpret such intrusions on the basis of dysfunctional beliefs (e.g., inflated responsibility, perfectionism, threat overestimation; Obsessive Compulsive Cognitions Working Group [OCCWG], 1997). Moreover, individuals with OCD tend to rely on ineffective strategies for managing intrusive thoughts and reducing anxiety (e.g., thought suppression, compulsive behavior) that paradoxically exacerbate the frequency and impact of intrusions and result in OCD (Clark & Beck, 2010; Salkovskis, 1985). For instance, John believed people should control their thoughts and was highly distressed by his inability to prevent the occurrence of intrusions inconsistent with his values and moral standards (e.g., hitting others). John also exhibited an inflated sense of responsibility and believed that by acting in a certain way (i.e., checking and counting) he could prevent bad things from occurring to close others. According to cognitive theories, these cognitive processes increase the reoccurrence of intrusive thoughts and exacerbate compulsive behaviors.

Although cognitive models have improved the understanding and treatment of OCD, recent findings suggest that a substantial proportion of individuals with OCD do not exhibit higher levels of dysfunctional beliefs than recorded in community samples (e.g., Taylor et al., 2006). Further, findings regarding the specificity of the dysfunctional beliefs related to OCD are equivocal (e.g., OCCWG, 2005; Tolin, Worhunsky, & Maltby, 2006). Cognitive theories have also been criticized for not sufficiently addressing the developmental and motivational bases of the disorder (Guidano & Liotti, 1983; O'Kearney, 2001). Moreover, although very effective with most clients, a substantial proportion of patients do not respond to cognitive–behavioral therapy (Fisher & Wells, 2005).

SELF-SENSITIVITY AND OCD

In response to these criticisms, Doron and colleagues (e.g., Doron & Kyrios, 2005; Doron, Kyrios, & Moulding, 2007; Doron, Kyrios, Moulding, Nedeljkovic, & Bhar, 2007) incorporated theories of the self within existing cognitive models of OCD. Specifically, they proposed that the transformation of intrusive thoughts into obsessions is moderated by the extent to which intrusive thoughts challenge core perceptions of the self. Indeed, Bhar and Kyrios (2007), Clark and Purdon (1993), and Rachman (1997) had already argued that the appraisal of an intrusive thought as challenging or inconsistent with one's sense of self (i.e., as ego dystonic) contributes to the formation of obsessions.

According to Doron and Kyrios (2005), because of sociocultural and developmental factors (e.g., parental acceptance contingent on competence in particular domains or ambivalent parenting characterized by rejection but camouflaged by an outward appearance of devotion; Guidano & Liotti, 1983), specific self-domains become extremely important for defining one's sense of self-worth (Doron & Kyrios, 2005, called these *sensitive self-domains*). As a result, perceived competence in these self-domains becomes crucial for maintaining self-worth (Harter, 1998), and people tend to be preoccupied with events that bear on their perceived competence in sensitive self-domains (e.g., Wolfe & Crocker, 2003). In OCD, sensitive self-domains include areas such as morality and job or school performance (Doron, Moulding, Kyrios, & Nedeljkovic, 2008).

Doron and Kyrios (2005) also proposed that thoughts or events that challenge sensitive self-domains (e.g., immoral thoughts or behaviors) damage a person's self-worth and activate attempts at repairing the damage and compensating for the perceived deficits. In the case of individuals with OCD, these coping responses may paradoxically further increase the occurrence of unwanted intrusions and the accessibility of feared-self cognitions (e.g., "I'm bad," "I'm immoral," "I'm unworthy"). In this way, for such individuals, common aversive experiences may activate overwhelmingly negative evaluations in sensitive self-domains (Doron et al., 2008). These processes, together with the activation of other dysfunctional thoughts (e.g., an inflated sense of responsibility, threat overestimation), are self-perpetuating and can result in the development of obsessions and compulsions.

THE MODERATING ROLE OF ATTACHMENT INSECURITIES

Although sensitive self-domains have been implicated in OCD (Doron et al., 2008), it is unlikely that every person experiencing an aversive event that challenges such self-domains will be flooded by negative self-evaluations, dysfunctional beliefs, and obsessions. Some individuals whose sensitive self-domains are challenged by failures and setbacks adaptively protect their self-images from unwanted intrusions and restore emotional equanimity. In fact, for most people, experiences challenging sensitive self-domains would result in the activation of distress-regulation strategies that can dissipate unwanted intrusions, reaffirm the challenged self, and restore emotional composure. The main question here concerns the psychological mechanisms that interfere with this adaptive regulatory process and foster the activation of feared-self cognitions and the cascade of dysfunctional beliefs that result in OCD symptoms.

In an attempt to respond to this question, Doron, Moulding, Kyrios, Nedeljkovic, and Mikulincer (2009) proposed that attachment insecurities can disrupt the process of coping with experiences that challenge sensitive self-domains and thereby contribute to OCD. According to attachment theory (Bowlby, 1973, 1982; Mikulincer & Shaver, 2007a; see also Chapter 14, this volume), interpersonal interactions with protective others (called *attachment figures* in the theory) are internalized in the form of mental representations of self and others (*internal working models*), which have an impact on close relationships, self-esteem, emotion regulation, and mental health throughout life. Interactions with attachment figures who are available and supportive in times of need foster the development of both a sense of attachment security and positive internal working models of the self and others. When attachment figures are rejecting or unavailable in times of need, attachment security is undermined, negative models of self and others are formed, and the likelihood of self-related doubts and emotional problems increases.

When testing this theory in studies of adolescents and adults, most researchers have focused on a person's attachment orientations—the systematic pattern of relational expectations, emotions, and behaviors that results from a particular attachment history (Mikulincer & Shaver, 2007a). Research, beginning with Ainsworth, Blehar, Waters, and Wall (1978) and continuing through recent studies by social and personality psychologists (reviewed by Mikulincer & Shaver, 2003, 2007a), indicates that attachment orientations are organized around two orthogonal dimensions: anxiety and avoidance (Brennan, Clark, & Shaver, 1998). The first dimension, *attachment anxiety*, reflects the degree to which a person worries that a partner will not be available or adequately responsive in times of need. The second dimension, *avoidance*, reflects the extent to which he or she distrusts relationship partners' goodwill and strives to maintain autonomy and emotional distance from them. People who score low on both dimensions are said to hold a stable sense of attachment security.

According to attachment theory, a sense of attachment security facilitates the process of coping with, and adjustment to, life's adversities and the restoration of emotional equanimity following aversive events (Mikulincer & Shaver, 2007a). Indeed, secure attachment (indicated by relatively low scores on attachment anxiety or avoidance) has been found to buffer the adverse emotional effects of stressful and traumatic events (see Florian, Mikulincer, & Hirschberger, 2002, for a review). Moreover, attachment security is associated with heightened perceptions of self-efficacy, constructive distress-regulation strategies, and maintenance of a stable sense of self-worth (e.g., Collins & Read, 1990; Mikulincer & Florian, 1998). During aversive events, securely attached individuals mobilize internal representations of supportive others or actual sources of support, which in turn sustain optimistic beliefs, constructive strategies for distress regulation, and mental health (Mikulincer & Shaver, 2003). Laboratory studies also indicate that experimental manipulations aimed at contextually heightening access to security-enhancing representations (i.e., security priming) restore emotional equanimity after distress-eliciting events and buffer posttraumatic dysfunctional cognitions (see Mikulincer & Shaver, 2007b, for a review).

According to Doron et al. (2009), the sense of attachment security may act, at least to some extent, as a protective shield against OCD-related processes, such as the activation of feared-self cognitions and dysfunctional beliefs following events that challenge sensitive self-domains. For people who have chronic or contextually heightened mental access to the sense of attachment security, these aversive experiences and the intrusion of unwanted thoughts result in the activation of effective distress-regulation strategies that dissipate the thoughts, reaffirm the challenged self, and restore well-being.

Conversely, attachment insecurities can impair the process of coping with experiences challenging sensitive self-domains and thereby increase the chances of OCD symptoms. Following these experiences, insecurely attached individuals may fail to find inner representations of security or external sources of support and so may experience a cascade of distress-exacerbating mental processes that can culminate in emotional disorders. For example, anxiously attached individuals tend to react to such failure by catastrophizing, exaggerating the negative consequences of the aversive experience, ruminating on negative events, and hyperactivating attachment-relevant fears and worries such as the fear of being abandoned because of one's "bad" self (Mikulincer & Shaver, 2003). Avoidant people tend to react to such aversive events by attempting to suppress distress-eliciting thoughts and negative self-representations. However, these defenses tend to collapse under an emotional or cognitive load (Mikulincer, Dolev, & Shaver, 2004), leaving the avoidant person flooded with unwanted thoughts, negative self-representations, and self-criticism. These kinds of thoughts and feelings tend to perpetuate threat overestimation; lead to overwhelming, uncontrollable distress; exacerbate unwanted thought intrusions and negative self-views; and thereby contribute to the development of obsessions.

SELF-SENSITIVITY, ATTACHMENT ANXIETY, AND OCD: EMPIRICAL EVIDENCE

There is growing evidence for the role of self-structures in the transformation of intrusive thoughts into OCD symptoms. For example, Rowa, Purdon, Summerfeldt, and Antony (2005) found that individuals with OCD rated more upsetting obsessions as more meaningful and contradictory of valued aspects of the self than less upsetting obsessions. Bhar and Kyrios (2007) found that individuals with OCD exhibited higher levels of self-ambivalence (i.e., worry and uncertainty about one's self-concept) than nonclinical controls, although they did not differ from individuals suffering from other anxiety disorders. Doron, Kyrios, and Moulding (2007) found that young adults who reported higher sensitivity to morality-related self-domains, social acceptability, and job or school competence (overvaluing a domain while feeling incompetent in that domain) were more likely to report OCD-related cognitions and symptoms. In another study, Doron et al. (2008) found that individuals with OCD reported higher levels of self-sensitivity in the domains of morality and job competence than individuals with other anxiety disorders.

There is also evidence supporting the involvement of attachment insecurities in vulnerability to OCD. First of all, both attachment anxiety and avoidance are associated with dysfunctional cognitive processes similar to those included in current cognitive models of OCD (OCCWG, 2005). For instance, attachment anxiety is associated with exaggerated threat appraisals (e.g., Mikulincer & Florian, 1998), perfectionism (e.g., Wei, Mallinckrodt, Russell, & Abraham, 2004), difficulties in suppressing unwanted thoughts (e.g., Mikulincer et al., 2004), rumination on these thoughts (e.g., Mikulincer & Florian, 1998), and self-devaluation in aversive situations (Mikulincer, 1998). Similarly, avoidant attachment is associated with setting high, unrealistic, and rigid personal standards of excellence (Mikulincer & Shaver, 2003, 2007a); self-criticism; maladaptive perfectionism; and intolerance of uncertainty, ambiguity, and personal weaknesses (Mikulincer & Shaver, 2007a). Moreover, avoidant people tend to overemphasize the importance of maintaining control over undesirable thoughts and suppressing thoughts of personal inadequacies and negative personal qualities (Mikulincer et al., 2004).

Recently, Doron et al. (2009) provided direct evidence for a link between attachment insecurities and OCD symptoms. Australian university students ($N = 467$) completed questionnaires assessing attachment orientations (Experiences in Close Relationships scales, or ECR; Brennan et al., 1998), OCD symptoms (Padua Inventory of Obsessive Compulsive Disorder Symptoms; Burns, Keortge, Formea, & Sternberger, 1996), OCD dysfunctional beliefs (Obsessive Beliefs Questionnaire; OCCWG, 2005), and depression symptoms (Beck Depression Inventory—II; Beck, Steer, & Brown, 1996). As expected, attachment insecurities, both anxiety and avoidance, predicted dysfunctional OCD-related beliefs and OCD symptoms. Moreover, the contribution of attachment anxiety and avoidance to OCD symptoms was fully mediated by OCD-related beliefs and remained significant even after statistically controlling for depression symptoms.

In two additional unpublished studies, Doron, Mikulincer, and Sar-El (2010) examined the extent to which experimentally induced access to security representations (security priming) weakens the link between dispositional attachment insecurities and OCD-related behavioral tendencies. As is common in OCD research, analogue nonclinical samples (Israeli university students) were used in these two studies. Previous studies have shown that, like clinical samples, nonclinical samples also report intrusive thoughts but with lesser frequency and less associated distress (Rachman & de Silva, 1978). Like individuals clinically diagnosed with OCD, nonclinical individuals also report engaging in compulsive behaviors in order to remove distress or prevent feared outcomes (e.g., Muris, Harald, & Clavan, 1997). More recently, taxometric studies (e.g., Haslam, Williams, Kyrios, McKay, & Taylor, 2005) have found that OCD symptoms and cognitions are best conceptualized in terms of dimensions rather than categories. These results support the appropriateness of studying OCD in nonclinical subjects.

In the first study ($N = 87$; Doron et al., 2010), we examined the effects of subliminal priming (for 22 ms) with names of people whom participants had nominated as sources of security (a procedure known as *security priming*) on OCD-related behavioral tendencies (compared with subliminal priming with names of mere acquaintances). OCD-related tendencies were measured by asking participants to rate distress, urge to act, and likelihood of acting in response to 10 hypothetical scenarios related to washing and checking (Menzies, Harris, Cumming, & Einstein, 2000; Moulding, Kyrios, & Doron, 2007). In the second study ($N = 90$; Doron et al., 2010), attachment security was supraliminally primed by asking participants to recall a security-enhancing experience (in the experimental group) or a shopping experience (in the control group). All participants then completed the OCD-relevant scenarios questionnaire. In both studies, participants also completed the ECR, which measures attachment orientations along the anxiety and avoidance dimensions.

Findings from the first study indicated that subliminal priming with security representations (compared with neutral priming) reduced distress and urge to act in response to OCD-related washing scenarios. However, this effect was significant only for participants who scored relatively high on attachment anxiety or avoidance. In other words, security priming weakened the link between attachment insecurities and OCD-related washing tendencies. This effect remained significant even after controlling for depression, general anxiety, and stress symptoms. Findings from the second study, however, revealed that supraliminal priming of attachment security was not significantly associated with participants' responses to the OCD-related scenarios and did not change the responses of insecure participants. Thus, it seems that only the bypassing of deliberate, controlled processes, as happened with the subliminal priming of attachment security, can counteract the cascade of mental processes related to obsessive–compulsive symptoms.

MORAL SENSITIVITY AND OCD

Morality is one of the sensitive self-domains most frequently involved in the development and maintenance of OCD. The idea that moral preoccupation is related to OCD has been a part of the mental health literature since the beginning of the 20th century. For example, Freud (1909/1987) suggested that persistent unwanted aggressive, horrific, or sexual thoughts accompanied by ritualistic behaviors are the result of unsuccessful defense mechanisms (characteristic of the anal-sadistic psychosexual developmental stage) against potential violations of moral standards. Individuals with OCD tend to suffer from unconscious conflicts between unacceptable, immoral sexual or aggressive impulses and the demands of the superego (moral conscience). They attempt to resolve this conflict by relying on undoing (i.e., defensively neutralizing unacceptable ideas by compulsive acts) and reaction formation (i.e., unconsciously developing attitudes and behaviors opposite to the unacceptable repressed impulses).

More recently, cognitive theories of OCD have also implicated morality concerns in the maintenance of OCD. For instance, Rachman and Hodgson (1980) argued that individuals with OCD are of "tender conscience," and Salkovskis, Shafran, Rachman, and Freeston (1999) suggested that individuals suffering from OCD exhibit "dedication to work and an acute sense of social obligation" (p. 1060). Salkovskis (1985) argued that an overinflated sense of *personal responsibility*, defined as the tendency to believe that one may be pivotally responsible for causing or failing to prevent harm to oneself or others, is one of the core beliefs leading to the transformation of common intrusive thoughts into obsessions. Beliefs about the importance of thoughts have also been suggested to have an important moral element, such as the belief that having a negative thought is as bad as performing a negative act (moral thought–action fusion; Shafran, Thordarson, & Rachman, 1996).

Research has also linked morality-relevant emotions such as guilt, shame, and disgust with obsessive–compulsive phenomena. For instance, stronger feelings of guilt and shame (i.e., negative emotional reactions to social or moral transgressions) have been associated with OCD, anxiety, and depression (see Tangney & Dearing, 2002, for a review). Disgust has been theoretically and empirically linked with OCD symptoms (Olatunji, Lohr, Sawchuk & Tolin, 2007; Rachman, 2004) and has been found to be provoked by violations of moral standards (e.g., Miller, 1997; Rozin, Haidt, & McCauley, 2000) and to elicit the need to physically cleanse oneself (Zhong & Liljenquist, 2006).

Finally, there are indications that obsessive–compulsive phenomena are associated with religious denomination and strength of religiosity (e.g., Sica, Novara, & Sanavio, 2002). Highly religious individuals exhibit OCD-related beliefs and symptoms with religious themes, such as praying or washing away one's sins (Abramowitz, Deacon, Woods, & Tolin, 2004; Rasmussen & Tsuang, 1986; Steketee et al., 1991).

More recently, research has provided evidence of the association between OCD and sensitivity in the morality self-domain (e.g., Doron et al., 2008). For example, Ferrier and Brewin (2005) reported that compared with individuals with clinical anxiety disorders as well as normal controls, individuals with OCD were more likely to draw negative moral inferences about themselves from their intrusive thoughts (e.g., perception of oneself as dangerous by virtue of being bad, immoral, or insane). However, Franklin, McNally, and Riemann (2009) failed to find an association between moral reasoning and OCD. Specifically, OCD patients and controls responded to a series of hypothetical moral dilemmas requiring them to choose one of two undesirable courses of action, both involving loss of life. No group difference was found in the choice of options and latencies to resolve the moral dilemmas. Hence, it is possible that the relationship between OCD symptoms and morality is not extended to moral reasoning but is limited to the emotional and self-relevant aspects of moral concerns. In an unpublished study, Ahern (2006) examined associations between OCD symptom severity, self-ambivalence, and the extent to which self-worth was contingent on morality in a nonclinical student cohort. Morality-contingent self-worth was positively related to OCD symptoms only when self-ambivalence, a marker of attachment insecurities, was high. Interestingly, contingent moral self-worth was negatively related to the severity of OCD symptoms when self-ambivalence was low. It is possible that when individuals are certain about themselves, they may be less sensitive to judgments about being immoral and, thus, less prone to OCD symptoms.

In a laboratory experiment, Doron and Sar-El (2010b) recently examined whether challenging self-perceptions of morality would lead to an increase in obsessive-like symptoms (checking, perfectionist behavior). Forty-five Israeli university students were invited to participate in a study examining the link between personality factors and performance on a computer graphics task. Before coming to the laboratory, all participants completed measures of OCD symptom severity (Obsessive–Compulsive Inventory; Foa et al., 2002) and depression, anxiety, and stress (Depression Anxiety Stress Scales; Lovibond & Lovibond, 1995) and 10 items tapping contingency of self-worth in the domains of morality and sports. Upon arrival at the laboratory, participants were randomly assigned to one of three conditions (morality, sports, neutral). In all conditions, participants were asked to reposition six objects (five textboxes and an arrow) such that their location and properties (i.e., thickness, width, and length) would be identical to a graph presented on the top half of the screen. That is, the objects on the bottom half of the screen were identical to the objects on the top half of the screen, but they had different properties and were all positioned at the bottom-left of the graph.

In the morality and sports conditions, the top graph consisted of a normal curve indicating a below average score (also marked as the 17th percentile) and three colored textboxes with the words *low level*, *high level*, and *you are here*. These textboxes were positioned such that the participant's low score was emphasized. In the morality condition, the words *your morality level* below the graph suggested that the graph described the participant's morality level. In a textbox on the right side of the graph, a comment indicated that "This graph shows your morality level." In the sports conditions, the word *morality* was replaced with the word *sports*. In the neutral condition, all text boxes included a combination of Xs and Ys. The main dependent variable was the time taken by participants to complete the task (indicator of perfectionistic checking behavior) and response to obsessive–compulsive-related scenarios.

Participants in the morality condition took significantly longer to complete the task than the other two groups (sports and neutral) and showed stronger distress in relation to contamination-related scenarios. These differences were still significant after controlling for depression, stress, and self-reported computer performance skills. Moreover, the time taken to complete the task in the morality condition was significantly and positively associated with both the severity of OCD symptoms reported before the laboratory session and the extent to which self-worth was contingent on the morality domain. These initial findings imply that an experience challenging one's self-perception as a moral person ("Your morality level is low") led to more contamination-related fears and perfectionistic checking behavior mainly among participants who overvalued the moral self-domain and tended to suffer from OCD symptoms.

In a second study, Doron and Sar-El (2010a) examined the hypothesized role of attachment insecurities in moderating the link between sensitivity of the morality self-domain and OCD symptoms. A community sample of 68 participants completed self-report measures of attachment anxiety and avoidance, OCD symptoms, depression, stress, and anxiety and reported on the frequency of morality-related daily hassles (e.g., ignoring a request for aid, violating a promise, acting in contradiction to one's own moral values). As expected, there was a positive association between morally challenging events and OCD symptoms. However, this association was significant only when participants scored relatively high on attachment anxiety or avoidance, not when the levels of attachment insecurities were low. These associations were significant even after controlling for depression, anxiety, and stress symptoms. The findings therefore strengthen our confidence concerning the protective shield provided by attachment security against the adverse effects of challenges in the morality self-domain on possible OCD.

CONCLUDING REMARKS

According to our model, some individuals perceive themselves as incompetent in domains that they view as extremely important for self-worth (i.e., sensitive self-domains), one of which may be the domain of morality. Experiences challenging such self-domains (e.g., failure to provide help to someone) may lead to an increase in unwanted mental intrusions by negative self-cognitions (e.g., "I'm bad," "I'm immoral") and to the development of obsessions. Attachment insecurities can exacerbate this cascade of unpleasant mental events by impairing adaptive coping. Conversely, attachment security may protect a person against the adverse effects of these experiences.

In this chapter, we reviewed both correlational and experimental findings that support the hypothesized roles of morality concerns and attachment insecurities in OCD. Taken together, the reviewed findings expand our understanding of the ways in which morality and attachment orientations are involved in the development and maintenance of OCD. Intrusions are more likely to activate dysfunctional beliefs and trigger OCD symptoms in insecurely attached individuals who are sensitive in the self-domain of morality.

Although consistent with our theoretical model, this new body of research has several limitations. First, most of it was conducted with nonclinical samples. Although nonclinical individuals experience OCD-related beliefs and symptoms, they may differ from clinical patients in the type and severity of symptoms and the resulting degree of impairment. Future research on the links between morality, attachment insecurities, and OCD symptoms should include clinical samples. Examining different clinical groups would facilitate the identification of specific factors associated with particular kinds of OCD symptoms. Second, the associations between sensitive self-domains and OCD have been found in cross-sectional correlational studies that do not allow conclusions about causal directions. Laboratory studies conducted with clinical and non-clinical samples should examine further whether dispositional attachment insecurities intensify the adverse effects of experimental inductions related to the moral domain. Such studies should also examine the extent to which experimentally induced security representations (security priming) buffer the adverse effects of dispositional attachment insecurities and morality-related experiences on OCD-related behavioral tendencies.

Despite these limitations, and pending further replication of the reviewed findings, particularly with clinical samples, our findings may have important implications for the cognitive understanding and treatment of OCD. We believe that OCD-related assessments and interventions focused on the morality self-domain and on attachment insecurities can improve outcomes. When dealing with individuals suffering from OCD, therapists should consider expanding their conceptualization of OCD to include the evaluation of a patient's sensitivity in the morality self-domain and his or her attachment working models (Doron & Moulding, 2009). Patients may, for example, have a rigid and limited perception of morality (e.g., believing they should be free of sexual urges before marriage), such that any urge or thought that challenges their moral standards leads to self-criticism, morbid rumination, and compulsions. When a client has this kind of limiting self-view, special emphasis should be placed on expanding his or her self-concept and conception of morality. This could be done by identifying and bolstering other self-domains, increasing the client's skills in other domains, or challenging the rigidity and boundaries of the moral domain (e.g., "What does being moral mean to you?" "What other behaviors [or beliefs, or attitudes] could be included in this domain?"). The contingency of self-worth in the morality domain could be explicitly explored, such that the client understands the relation between anxiety and perceptions of failure in that self-domain. This would help the clinician with case formulation, particularly understanding why specific mental intrusions lead to heightened emotional reactions or avoidance behavior.

In a similar way, attachment-based cognitive–behavioral therapy (Doron & Moulding, 2009) addresses issues regarding trust and heightened fear of abandonment and explores attachment-related internal models within the therapeutic context. It is common for OCD symptoms to be associated with strong attachment-related fears (e.g., experiencing horrific images of a partner having an accident followed by making repeated phone calls). In such cases, fear of abandonment can be addressed by challenging dysfunctional perceptions, exploring the relation between relationship fears and OCD, and devising behavioral experiments aimed at increasing tolerance for ordinary separations. This may reduce a client's tendency to interpret relationship experiences, including the therapeutic relationship, in frightening terms; improve therapeutic efficacy; and possibly reduce dropout and relapse rates compared with those for patients undergoing traditional cognitive–behavioral therapy.

REFERENCES

Abramowitz, J. S., Deacon, B. J., Woods, C. M., & Tolin, D. F. (2004). Association between protestant religiosity and obsessive-compulsive symptoms and cognitions. *Depression and Anxiety, 20*(2), 70–76. doi:10.1002/da.20021

Ahern, A. (2006). *Self-perceptions as a vulnerability to obsessive-compulsive disorder: Investigation into self-ambivalence and self-worth contingent upon high moral standards.*

Unpublished honors thesis, Swinburne University of Technology, Melbourne, Australia.

Ainsworth, M. D. S., Blehar, M. C., Waters, E., & Wall, S. (1978). *Patterns of attachment: Assessed in the strange situation and at home*. Hillsdale, NJ: Erlbaum.

American Psychiatric Association. (2000). *Diagnostic and statistical manual of mental disorders* (4th ed., text rev.). Washington, DC: Author.

Beck, A. T., Steer, R. A., & Brown, G. K. (1996). *Manual for the Beck Depression Inventory—II*. Unpublished manuscript, San Antonio, TX.

Bhar, S. S., & Kyrios, M. (2007). An investigation of self-ambivalence in obsessive-compulsive disorder. *Behaviour Research and Therapy, 45*, 1845–1857. doi:10.1016/j.brat.2007.02.005

Bowlby, J. (1973). *Attachment and loss: Vol. 2. Separation: Anxiety and anger*. New York, NY: Basic Books.

Bowlby, J. (1982). *Attachment and loss: Vol. 1. Attachment* (2nd ed.). New York, NY: Basic Books.

Brennan, K. A., Clark, C. L., & Shaver, P. R. (1998). Self-report measurement of adult attachment. In J. A. Simpson & W. S. Rholes (Eds.), *Attachment theory and close relationships* (pp. 46–76). New York, NY: Guilford Press.

Burns, G. L., Keortge, S. G., Formea, G. M., & Sternberger, L. G. (1996). Revision of the Padua Inventory of Obsessive Compulsive Disorder Symptoms: Distinctions between worry, obsessions, and compulsions. *Behaviour Research and Therapy, 34*, 163–173. doi:10.1016/0005-7967(95)00035-6

Clark, D. A., & Beck, A. T. (2010). *Cognitive therapy of anxiety disorders: Science and practice*. New York, NY: Guilford Press.

Clark, D. A., & Purdon, C. (1993). New perspectives for a cognitive theory of obsessions. *Australian Psychologist, 28*, 161–167. doi:10.1080/00050069308258896

Collins, N. L., & Read, S. J. (1990). Adult attachment, working models, and relationship quality in dating couples. *Journal of Personality and Social Psychology, 58*, 644–663. doi:10.1037/0022-3514.58.4.644

Doron, G., & Kyrios, M. (2005). Obsessive compulsive disorder: A review of possible specific internal representations within a broader cognitive theory. *Clinical Psychology Review, 25*, 415–432. doi:10.1016/j.cpr.2005.02.002

Doron, G., Kyrios, M., & Moulding, R. (2007). Sensitive domains of self-concept in obsessive-compulsive disorder (OCD): Further evidence for a multidimensional model of OCD. *Journal of Anxiety Disorders, 21*, 433–444. doi:10.1016/j.janxdis.2006.05.008

Doron, G., Kyrios, M., Moulding, R., Nedeljkovic, M., & Bhar, S. (2007). "We do not see things as they are, we see them as we are": A multidimensional world-view of obsessive compulsive disorder (OCD). *Journal of Cognitive Psychotherapy, 21*, 221–235. doi:10.1891/088983907781494555

Doron, G., Mikulincer, M., & Sar-El, D. (2010). *Effects of supraliminal vs. subliminal priming of attachment security on obsessive-compulsive phenomena*. Manuscript in preparation.

Doron, G., & Moulding, R. (2009). Cognitive behavioral treatment of obsessive compulsive disorder: A broader framework. *Israel Journal of Psychiatry, 46*, 257–264.

Doron, G., Moulding, R., Kyrios, M., & Nedeljkovic, M. (2008). Sensitivity of self beliefs in obsessive compulsive disorder (OCD). *Anxiety and Depression, 25*, 874–884. doi:10.1002/da.20369

Doron, G., Moulding, R., Kyrios, M., Nedeljkovic, M., & Mikulincer, M. (2009). Adult attachment insecurities are related to obsessive compulsive phenomena. *Journal of Social and Clinical Psychology, 28*, 1022–1049. doi:10.1521/jscp.2009.28.8.1022

Doron, G., & Sar-El, D. (2010a). *Attachment, obsessive compulsive phenomena and self sensitivity*. Manuscript in preparation.

Doron, G., & Sar-El, D. (2010b). *Morality sensitivity and obsessive compulsive phenomena: Evidence from an experimental manipulation of moral sensitivity*. Manuscript in preparation.

Ferrier, S., & Brewin, C. (2005). Feared identity and obsessive compulsive disorder. *Behaviour Research and Therapy, 43*, 1363–1374. doi:10.1016/j.brat.2004.10.005

Fisher, P. L., & Wells, A. (2005). How effective are cognitive and behavioral treatments for obsessive-compulsive disorder? A clinical significance analysis. *Behaviour Research and Therapy, 43*, 1543–1558. doi:10.1016/j.brat.2004.11.007

Florian, V., Mikulincer, M., & Hirschberger, G. (2002). The anxiety buffering function of close relationships: Evidence that relationship commitment acts as a terror management mechanism. *Journal of Personality and Social Psychology, 82*, 527–542. doi:10.1037/0022-3514.82.4.527

Foa, E. B., Huppert, J. D., Leiberg, S., Langner, R., Kichic, R., & Hajcak, G. (2002). The Obsessive-Compulsive Inventory: Development and validation of a short version. *Psychological Assessment, 14*, 485–495. doi:10.1037/1040-3590.14.4.485

Franklin, S. A., McNally, R. J., & Riemann, B. C. (2009). Moral reasoning in obsessive-compulsive disorder. *Journal of Anxiety Disorders, 23*, 575–577. doi:10.1016/j.janxdis.2008.11.005

Freud, S. (1987). Notes upon a case of obsessional neurosis ("the Rat Man"). In A. Richards (Ed.), *Case histories II: The "Rat Man," Schreber, the "Wolf Man," a case of female homosexuality* (Vol. 9, pp. 33–128). Harmondsworth, England: Penguin Books. (Original work published 1909)

Frost, R. O., & Steketee, G. (Eds.). (2002). *Cognitive approaches to obsessions and compulsions: Theory, assessment, and treatment*. Amsterdam, Netherlands: Pergamon/Elsevier.

Guidano, V. F., & Liotti, G. (1983). *Cognitive processes and emotional disorders*. New York, NY: Guilford Press.

Harter, S. (1998). The development of self-representations. In W. Damon & N. Eisenberg (Eds.), *Handbook of child psychology* (5th ed., Vol. 3, pp. 553–617). Hoboken, NJ: Wiley.

Haslam, N., Williams, B. J., Kyrios, M., McKay, D., & Taylor, S. (2005). Subtyping obsessive-compulsive disorder: A taxometric analysis. *Behavior Therapy, 36*, 381–391. doi:10.1016/S0005-7894(05)80120-0

Lovibond, P. F., & Lovibond, S. H. (1995). The structure of negative emotional states: Comparison of the Depression Anxiety Stress Scales (DASS) with the Beck Depression and Anxiety Inventories. *Behaviour Research and Therapy, 33,* 335–342. doi:10.1016/0005-7967(94)00075-U

Menzies, R. G., Harris, L. M., Cumming, S. R., & Einstein, D. A. (2000). The relationship between inflated personal responsibility and exaggerated danger expectancies in obsessive-compulsive concerns. *Behaviour Research and Therapy, 38,* 1029–1037. doi:10.1016/S0005-7967(99)00149-7

Mikulincer, M. (1998). Adult attachment style and affect regulation: Strategic variations in self-appraisals. *Journal of Personality and Social Psychology, 75,* 420–435. doi:10.1037/0022-3514.75.2.420

Mikulincer, M., Dolev, T., & Shaver, P. R. (2004). Attachment-related strategies during thought suppression: Ironic rebounds and vulnerable self-representations. *Journal of Personality and Social Psychology, 87,* 940–956. doi:10.1037/0022-3514.87.6.940

Mikulincer, M., & Florian, V. (1998). The relationship between adult attachment styles and emotional and cognitive reactions to stressful events. In J. A. Simpson & W. S. Rholes (Eds.), *Attachment theory and close relationships* (pp. 143–165). New York, NY: Guilford Press.

Mikulincer, M., & Shaver, P. R. (2003). The attachment behavioral system in adulthood: Activation, psychodynamics, and interpersonal processes. In M. P. Zanna (Ed.), *Advances in experimental social psychology* (Vol. 35, pp. 53–152). New York, NY: Academic Press.

Mikulincer, M., & Shaver, P. R. (2007a). *Attachment in adulthood: Structure, dynamics, and change.* New York, NY: Guilford Press.

Mikulincer, M., & Shaver, P. R. (2007b). Boosting attachment security to promote mental health, prosocial values, and inter-group tolerance. *Psychological Inquiry, 18,* 139–156.

Miller, W. I. (1997). *The anatomy of disgust.* Cambridge, MA: Harvard University Press.

Moulding, R., Kyrios, M., & Doron, G. (2007). Appraisals and obsessive-compulsive behaviours in specific situations: The relative influence of appraisals of control, responsibility and threat. *Behaviour Research and Therapy, 45,* 1693–1702. doi:10.1016/j.brat.2006.08.020

Muris, P., Harald, M., & Clavan, M. (1997). Abnormal and normal compulsions. *Behaviour Research and Therapy, 35,* 249–252. doi:10.1016/S0005-7967(96)00114-3

Obsessive Compulsive Cognitions Working Group. (1997). Cognitive assessment of obsessive-compulsive disorder. *Behaviour Research and Therapy, 35,* 667–681. doi:10.1016/S0005-7967(97)00017-X

Obsessive Compulsive Cognitions Working Group. (2005). Psychometric validation of the Obsessive Beliefs Questionnaire: Factor analyses and testing of a brief version. *Behaviour Research and Therapy, 43,* 1527–1542. doi:10.1016/j.brat.2004.07.010

O'Kearney, R. (2001). Motivation and emotions in the cognitive theory of obsessive-compulsive disorder: A reply to Salkovskis and Freeston. *Australian Journal of Psychology, 53*, 7–9. doi:10.1080/00049530108255114

Olatunji, B. O., Lohr, J. M., Sawchuk, C. N., & Tolin, D. F. (2007). Multimodal assessment of disgust in contamination-related obsessive-compulsive disorder. *Behaviour Research and Therapy, 45*, 263–276. doi:10.1016/j.brat.2006.03.004

Rachman, S. (1997). A cognitive theory of obsessions. *Behaviour Research and Therapy, 35*, 793–802.

Rachman, S. (2004). Fear of contamination. *Behaviour Research and Therapy, 42*, 1227–1255. doi:10.1016/j.brat.2003.10.009

Rachman, S., & de Silva, P. (1978). Abnormal and normal obsessions. *Behaviour Research and Therapy, 16*, 233–248. doi:10.1016/0005-7967(78)90022-0

Rachman, S., & Hodgson, R. J. (1980). *Obsessions and compulsions.* Englewood Cliffs, NJ: Prentice Hall.

Rasmussen, S. A., & Tsuang, M. T. (1986). Clinical characteristics and family history in DSM–III obsessive-compulsive disorder. *American Journal of Psychiatry, 143*, 317–322.

Rowa, K., Purdon, C., Summerfeldt, L. J., & Antony, M. (2005). Why are some obsessions more upsetting than others? *Behaviour Research and Therapy, 43*, 1453–1465. doi:10.1016/j.brat.2004.11.003

Rozin, P., Haidt, J., & McCauley, C. R. (2000). Disgust. In M. Lewis & J. M. Haviland-Jones (Eds.), *Handbook of emotions* (2nd ed., pp. 637–653). New York, NY: Guilford Press.

Salkovskis, P. M. (1985). Obsessional-compulsive problems: A cognitive–behavioral analysis. *Behaviour Research and Therapy, 23*, 571–583. doi:10.1016/0005-7967(85)90105-6

Salkovskis, P. M., Shafran, R., Rachman, S., & Freeston, M. H. (1999). Multiple pathways to inflated responsibility beliefs in obsessional problems: Possible origins and implications for therapy and research. *Behaviour Research and Therapy, 37*, 1055–1072. doi:10.1016/S0005-7967(99)00063-7

Shafran, R., Thordarson, D. S., & Rachman, S. (1996). Thought–action fusion in obsessive compulsive disorder. *Journal of Anxiety Disorders, 10*, 379–390. doi:10.1016/0887-6185(96)00018-7

Sica, C., Novara, C., & Sanavio, E. (2002). Religiousness and obsessive-compulsive cognitions and symptoms in an Italian population. *Behaviour Research and Therapy, 40*, 813–823. doi:10.1016/S0005-7967(01)00120-6

Steketee, G., Quay, S., & White, K. (1991). Religion and guilt in OCD patients. *Journal of Anxiety Disorders, 5*, 359–367. doi:10.1016/0887-6185(91)90035-R

Tangney, J., & Dearing, R. (2002). *Shame and guilt.* New York, NY: Guilford Press.

Taylor, S., Abramowitz, J. S., McKay, D., Calamari, J. E., Sookman, D., & Kyrios, M. (2006). Do dysfunctional beliefs play a role in all types of obsessive-compulsive disorder? *Journal of Anxiety Disorders, 20,* 85–97. doi:10.1016/j.janxdis.2004. 11.005

Tolin, D. F., Worhunsky, P., & Maltby, N. (2006). Are "obsessive" beliefs specific to OCD? A comparison across anxiety disorders. *Behaviour Research and Therapy, 44,* 469–480. doi:10.1016/j.brat.2005.03.007

Wei, M., Mallinckrodt, B., Russell, D. W., & Abraham, W. (2004). Maladaptive perfectionism as a mediator and moderator between adult attachment and depressive mood. *Journal of Counseling Psychology, 51,* 201–212. doi:10.1037/0022-0167.51.2.201

Wolfe, C., & Crocker, J. (2003). What does the self want? Contingencies of self-worth and goals. In S. J. Spencer, S. Fein, M. P. Zanna, & J. M. Olson (Eds.), *Motivated social perception* (pp. 147–170). Mahwah, NJ: Erlbaum.

World Health Organization. (1996). *Global burden of disease: A comprehensive assessment and morbidity from disease, injuries, and risk factors in 1990 and projected to 2020.* New York, NY: Author.

Zhong, C. B., & Liljenquist, K. (2006, September 8). Washing away your sins: Threatened morality and physical cleansing. *Science, 313,* 1451–1452. doi:10.1126/science.1130726

17

MORAL DIMENSIONS OF TRAUMA THERAPIES

LAURIE ANNE PEARLMAN

Psychotherapy is a unique social relationship, generally taking place over time between two (and at times among more) people. It "can be viewed as a form of specialized social interaction" (Doherty, 1995, p. 35). One important aim of psychotherapy is for individuals to explore their foundational beliefs and worldviews. In his outstanding slim volume *Soul Searching*, Doherty (1995) noted that "morality in psychotherapy . . . [is] a delicate blend of clarifying, exploring, thinking together, and occasionally challenging" (p. 186). Because psychotherapy relates to human welfare, every aspect of it has moral dimensions. Others have written about moral issues in psychotherapy more generally, but these issues have not been examined in depth as they relate to trauma therapies, which address the needs of clients who have been treated immorally, even brutally, by other people. (See Thompson, 1995, for a discussion of moral issues in trauma research and Chapter 21, this volume, for a discussion of warfare and genocide.)

In this chapter, I hope to increase morality researchers' and trauma therapists' awareness of the moral dimensions of clinical work. This consciousness may help guide decisions related to many aspects of treatment that therapists typically view from clinical and/or interpersonal perspectives. In the first part of the chapter, I address three issues that arise in psychotherapy with trauma survivors that have important moral dimensions. In the second part, I explore the therapist's possible moral transformation through working with people who have experienced violence or victimization. Many of these issues, while particularly relevant to trauma therapies, also apply to human relationships more generally and so may be of interest to social psychology researchers.

I define *morality* as a dynamic relationship with principles and virtues reflected in beliefs and behaviors that affect others' welfare. By *dynamic relationship*, I mean that our morality can be authentic only when we are constantly reviewing our values, our actions, our own and others' needs and feelings, and the situations in which the need to make moral choices exists. Morality comprises both cognitive and affective elements, as several chapters in this volume explain. Here, rather than adopting a relativistic stance, I wish to emphasize the developmental, relational context that should inform moral choices or judgments.

Moral attributes such as empathy, compassion, acceptance, tolerance, kindness or caring, integrity, honesty, reliability, mutuality, courage, respect, and generosity are the building blocks of moral principles. Thus, for example, the attribute of empathy underlies the principle that we should relate to therapy clients with open-mindedness, sensitivity, and respect. Elsewhere, a colleague and I have written about empathic connection as having two aspects: cognitive and affective (Pearlman & Saakvitne, 1995). This conception of empathy is consistent with that of Baron-Cohen (2005), who wrote, "Empathy is about spontaneously and naturally tuning into the other person's thoughts and feelings, whatever these might be" (p. 168). The cognitive aspect of empathy has to do with understanding the other's experience and perspective. The affective aspect concerns one person's appropriate attunement and emotional relation to another person's emotional states.

This ethical empathy principle (relating to clients with sensitivity and respect) in turn gives rise to behaviors that include the therapist's best efforts to attune his or her awareness and sensitivities to the survivor client's experiences of violence and victimization, to the client's current life situation, and to the complexities that interfere with efforts to process and integrate trauma while fulfilling daily obligations. Moral judgments flow from principles. To continue with the empathy example, a therapist might negatively judge a client's behavior when she, a mother, humiliates her child when the child has done something the client dislikes. But the therapist might also continue to seek a compassionate understanding of both the past and present circumstances that affect the client's parenting behavior and to find ways to guide the client toward more empathic and respectful treatment of her child.

MORAL ISSUES IN PSYCHOTHERAPY
WITH TRAUMA SURVIVORS

Given the large number of clients who have engaged in psychotherapy (approximately 30% of the U.S. population had been in psychotherapy when Doherty wrote about it in 1995), and given its potential to shape the way individuals relate to others, it seems important to reflect on its moral dimensions. In this section, I address the following aspects of trauma therapy in which moral concerns are central: managing frame and boundaries, helping the client move toward a greater sense of moral agency, and attending to countertransference and vicarious traumatization. I have chosen these three issues because they are particularly salient in trauma therapy and because their management has the potential to promote recovery or to cause harm.

Moral matters such as suffering, shame, guilt, justice, truthfulness, caring, and community, which can enter any relationship, are especially likely to emerge in psychotherapy, and they will likely emerge with greater intensity in therapy with people who have experienced early or severe violence, abuse, or neglect. This intensity is related to the affect regulation problems that many such "complex trauma" survivors endure. They often feel their emotions more intensely than those whose development has not been shaped by violence and victimization.

Managing Frame and Boundaries

The *frame and boundaries* of a psychotherapy relationship are a series of agreements that the therapist and client reach in their work together (Pearlman & Saakvitne, 1995). In every interpersonal relationship, we develop a frame and boundaries. In psychotherapy, these agreements influence how the therapy will be conducted, including treatment goals, frequency and duration of meetings, payment arrangements, the participation of third parties, therapist self-disclosure, confidentiality, forms of address, and so forth. These issues are extremely important because they define the relationship and facilitate (or hinder) treatment outcomes. In this section, I will not address the clinical, ethical, and legal perspectives on frame and boundary issues in trauma treatment because they have been addressed extensively elsewhere (e.g., Brown, 2008; Courtois, 2010; Pearlman & Saakvitne, 1995; Pope & Vasquez, 2001). I am interested here in examining the moral dimensions of frame and boundaries. I differentiate therapy-related *ethics* (a system of principles that govern appropriate behavior, usually codified by professional associations or administrative bodies) from *morals* (one's internal dynamic relationship with principles and affect governing therapy-related behavior).

The *frame* reflects the therapist's theory of change. For example, a cognitive–behavioral therapist might propose a time-limited therapy focusing on the client's current life circumstances, behaviors, and cognitive distortions. In this therapy, lengthy examination of the client's childhood history is not within the frame, because it is not relevant to the therapist's formulation of how change will come about.

Frame issues are crucial in therapies with survivors of interpersonal victimization because the harm they have endured likely occurred in the context of a violation of boundaries. Individuals who have experienced betrayals or abuse in important relationships are particularly sensitive to boundary violations. Often, someone has intruded on the survivor's body and his or her emotional, psychological, or spiritual space, privacy, or integrity. Adult survivors of childhood abuse and neglect often arrive in therapy with fear or suspicion about the therapist's interests, motives, and behaviors. This suspicion grows out of experience with others who were supposed to look out for the welfare of the individual but dramatically failed to do so and who also betrayed the client's trust and violated his or her boundaries. These violations most often involve a loss of control by the victim, resulting in helplessness, fear, guilt, and/or rage. It is not unusual for a survivor of childhood interpersonal violence or victimization to begin therapy prepared to protect himself or herself from the therapist. Early conversations about boundaries have the potential to alert the client that things will be different in this relationship: Boundaries are discussed, negotiated, and—if the therapist behaves competently and ethically—honored.

Helping the Client Evolve to Moral Agency

A therapy client who had experienced war-related trauma once told me his goal was to move from victim to victor. Initially, I was uncomfortable with the possibility that *victor* might mean *aggressor* to him. Fortunately, this was not the case. He was talking about being a positive actor in his life rather than the object of others' harmful actions. Doherty (1995) and Kottler (2010) both wrote about the therapist's role in encouraging clients to develop their moral perspective. This is initially delicate work with persons who have been subjugated to others' will and suffered as a result. The moral perspective of survivor clients initially may focus on themselves as the victim, the injustice of what was done to them, and their valid needs for acknowledgment and restoration. In time, with adequate empathy, compassion, and support, these clients can begin to broaden their perspective to include a greater understanding of the context of their victimization. This often allows them to become interested in understanding why the perpetrator engaged in harmful behavior and why the perpetrator chose them for abuse, neglect, or other forms of victimization.

In cases of child maltreatment, the therapist can eventually invite the client's opinions about the harm doer's motivation. What kind of child rearing did the harm doer experience? Where did he or she learn to use power over others in this way? This exploration is not intended to excuse the harm doer from responsibility. Instead, its goal is to help the survivor client integrate what happened into a broader context: What are the larger family history, social context, and cultural meaning of the harmful events, including the way others did (or did not) respond to the client's needs at the time?

Some (although not most) who have been the objects of aggression turn aggressively against others who are more vulnerable. For some abused children and adolescents, this takes the form of bullying or harming younger siblings, pets, or children for whom they babysit. This behavior may be understood in a variety of ways—for example, as modeling, attempting to assert control to compensate for the lack of control in other situations, discharging aggressive impulses, identifying with the aggressor, or reliving the traumatic experiences in a different role as a path to mastery. Whatever the reason, trauma therapists who work with survivor clients encounter a moral opportunity when the client reports or suggests that he or she may have harmed others. Doherty (1995) pointed to the value and challenges in helping the client explore his or her role as a potential agent of injustice rather than only as a victim. He asked, "When is it appropriate to introduce the discourse of justice and fairness in talking about client behavior that is morally, though not legally, suspect?" (p. 52). The answer, of course, depends in part on the strength of the therapeutic relationship and in part on the level of harm the client is inflicting on others. Harm against children and elders must be stopped and, in most states in the United States, must be reported as soon as the therapist is aware of it. Serious harm to anyone must also be stopped. But the therapist must use clinical acumen to ensure that it is the harmful behavior, and not the therapy, that the client brings to an end. Transparency on the therapist's part, combined with compassion for all parties, can provide a foundation for managing such difficult therapeutic challenges.

For example, upon learning that a client was engaging in harsh physical punishment of her son, one therapist opened a discourse about how challenging child rearing is, how demanding the client was finding the child, and whether this form of punishment was working. The therapist also said that he was concerned about the physical and emotional harm the punishment might be doing to the child and that he was certain the parent wanted what was best for the child as well as for the family. The conversation soon moved to an exploration of why the son's behavior might be worsening, whether there might be a more effective way to address his behavior problems, and the need to find another way to work with the child to ensure everyone's safety. The therapist explained to the client that he was legally obligated to report to the state instances of child abuse and that the type of punishment the mother was using might well meet the state's definition of abuse. This discussion opened many paths for the therapist and client to explore. The mother was distressed and surprised that the therapist thought the son might be experiencing harm or even abuse. Her initial fear and anger passed as the therapist helped her see the connection between her behavior and the harsh parenting she received as a child. She was stunned to realize that she was doing to her son what her own mother had done to her. The therapist invited the client to bring the son into the next session, which the mother did. This gave the therapist an opportunity to observe the dyad's interactions and to initiate a family therapy referral. This entire process extended over only three sessions. The longer term work included opportunities for the therapist and client to discuss what kind of parent and what kind of person she wanted to be: how she wanted to relate to others in her family, community, and society and how she wanted to view herself as a mother. Doherty (1995, pp. 49–54) also provided an extended example that serves as a lovely illustration of the process of inviting the client to examine his or her own role as a moral agent.

How can a trauma therapist help a client move toward moral agency? For many survivors of interpersonal victimization, action is fraught with challenges. The fear of punishment can be very strong in people who were victimized as children. Passivity is a well-known survival strategy for many, if not most, children who grow up in unpredictable or violent homes or communities. Being invisible and squashing one's own needs and feelings are ways children try to avoid harm. In adulthood, then, the difficulty of being an agent in one's own life is enormous. If action is to be based on empathy, compassion, and an accurate assessment of psychological needs, then the first step is for the client to have access to his or her emotional states. Developing this access can open up a deluge of unprocessed pain.

These vital survival strategies—emotional numbing, self-denial, inhibition—often result in deep resentment and rage. It takes a great deal of emotional work to suppress needs and feelings over time, and the result can be serious emotional, physical, and spiritual deprivation. The essential warming of a frozen emotional life is often accompanied by much pain, parallel to the experience of frostbitten hands or feet beginning to warm.

In addition to learning to experience, recognize, and tolerate feelings, the survivor must overcome the fear that expressing a need will be met with rejection or punishment. This process requires cognitive–behavioral intervention and the processing of affect, built on a solid foundation of connection with the therapist and social support that may need to be acquired and developed. (See Pearlman, Wortman, Feuer, Farber, & Rando, in press, for an approach to assisting trauma survivor clients in developing social support.) The work of building a therapeutic relationship, addressing disrupted cognitive schemas related to self and others, and processing trauma-related affect is described in numerous volumes written for therapists (e.g., Allen, 2001; Briere & Scott, 2006; Cloitre, Cohen, & Koenen, 2006; Courtois, 2010; Courtois & Ford, 2009; McCann & Pearlman, 1990a; Najavits, 2002; Pearlman & Courtois, 2005; Ross & Halpern, 2009; Saakvitne, Gamble, Pearlman, & Lev, 2000).

Trauma therapists who work with clients who have developed complex trauma adaptations are familiar with this work. What may be less familiar is conceptualizing it as moral work. What are the client's moral obligations to others? This conversation will be most productive when it builds on the empowerment of the client in his or her everyday life, as described above. What are the long-term consequences of the client's concerns and the resolution of these concerns, for both self and others? The culture of psychotherapy is one of self-focus. The field has adopted this orientation partly because of the self (rather than self-in-community) focus of contemporary Western culture. Thus, broadening the focus to include others, both those who are and those who are not in the client's "meaningful psychological environment" (Rotter, 1982), to include all living beings and the natural environment must be done with sensitivity to the client's capacity to expand his or her attention. This is a developmental process within the client and within the therapy relationship, one that may evolve once the survivor client feels that the therapist recognizes and validates accumulated pain.

People who have been harmed by others may have limited empathy with others' needs. Those with complex trauma adaptations (e.g., dissociation, affect dysregulation, somatization, identity problems, relationship problems; Courtois & Ford, 2009) may have grown up in survival-focused conditions, including childhood homes characterized by harsh or cold parenting, abuse, violence, or neglect or in urban or ethnopolitical conflict zones. For these people, the capacity to empathize with others and even to prioritize others' needs may be inadequately developed. (This is different from the people-pleasing or caretaking behavior that some survivors adopt in order to survive, which is typically based on fear of rather than empathy for others.) To become a victor, then, can be construed to mean becoming someone who lives a life informed by empathy for self and others, using compassion and understanding of the world as a basis for acting on behalf of both oneself and others, and contributing to a society in which violence and neglect are no longer tolerated.

Of course, self-focus is not limited to persons who have been traumatized. Those who have been wounded psychologically through inadequate understanding, acceptance, and compassion or other life injuries may also find it difficult to empathize with others whom they view as more fortunate. Groups that have been harmed, whether through scapegoating, discrimination, or violence, may not only find empathy difficult; they may actively harm others (Staub, 2010; see also Chapter 21, this volume).

Attending to Countertransference and Vicarious Traumatization

What are the trauma therapist's moral responsibilities? What constitutes "right action" on the part of a trauma therapist? When I asked two seasoned trauma therapists of my acquaintance these questions, each immediately responded that the trauma therapist's most important moral responsibility is to attend to his or her own needs and feelings in a way that precludes harming the client and instead promotes clinical goals. "Recognizing and confronting our own emotional reactions to our clients . . . is a special form of courage required of therapists more than of any other group of professionals" (Doherty, 1995, p. 157). Paralleling the client's feelings, the therapist's needs and feelings are also likely to be stronger in trauma therapy than in therapy with non-traumatized persons.

My colleagues and I have written extensively elsewhere about the professional and clinical management of countertransference (the therapist's responses to a particular client) and vicarious traumatization (the cumulative response to all of one's trauma survivor clients and their trauma material; McCann & Pearlman, 1990b; Pearlman & Caringi, 2009; Pearlman & Saakvitne, 1995; Saakvitne et al., 2000). Additional, excellent contributions to the literature on countertransference in trauma therapies include, for example, those by Dahlenberg (2000), Danieli (1984), Wilson and Lindy (1994), and Wilson and Thomas (2004). Here I add some reflections on the moral dimensions of this matter—the aspects of the therapist's reactions that affect others' welfare.

Neglecting the effect that trauma work has on the therapist can result in direct harm to clients. Pearlman and Saakvitne (1995) postulated that unaddressed vicarious trauma is a foundational element of sexual misconduct among trauma therapists. Various researchers have found that incest survivors are more likely than other therapy clients to become victims of therapist sexual misconduct (Armsworth, 1989; Broden & Agresti, 1998; Kluft, 1990; Pope, 1994; Pope & Bouhoutsos, 1986; Pope & Vetter, 1991; Somer & Saadon, 1999). This behavior may be related to unaddressed vicarious trauma. Short of this egregious outcome, therapists may harm clients in other ways. They may avoid trauma material, violate boundaries, fail to remember important therapy material, or otherwise mishandle treatment relationships (Dahlenberg, 2000; Pearlman & Saakvitne, 1995). Each of these behaviors has the potential to slow the client's recovery and/or to reinjure the client.

A lack of awareness of countertransference can lead a therapist to attribute feelings and dynamics to the client that in fact are the therapist's. This misguided ascription can pose an obstacle to progress in the therapy or create self-doubt and confusion in the client (Dahlenberg, 2000; Pearlman & Saakvitne, 1995). For example, early in one treatment, a therapist had a deeply negative reaction to an adult male client's account of sexual abuse that he experienced as a child. She felt repulsed by the details of the story and furious at the person who had harmed a vulnerable little boy. She was overwhelmed by these feelings and did not acknowledge them, perhaps wishing to protect the client or protect herself or simply being unable to figure out how to do so. The next week, the client canceled his session. The therapist felt regret as well as some relief that she would not have to sit with this man and feel these intense emotions again. The client decided not to return to this therapist because he was aware of her disgust and anger, and this reinforced the same feelings he held toward himself for being victimized for the past 30 years. Therapists, and people in general, may not process their reactions and may be unaware of their origins, depth, meanings, and ramifications. To act in an effective and moral way requires such awareness, one of the important demands on a therapist. Effective clinical work also requires self-awareness on the therapist's part.

Dahlenberg and Brown (2001) addressed ethical issues in the treatment of child crime victims. They noted that certain adaptations to childhood maltreatment, "such as sexual promiscuity or sexual acting out (Hartman, Burgess, & McCormack, 1987), suicidality (Bryant & Range, 1997), and disorders of attachment that lead to manipulative or dishonest behaviors on the part of child and adult clients (Briere, 1992)" may be "morally complex" (Dahlenberg & Brown, p. 21). These typical adaptations may present challenges to a therapist who finds them morally questionable, a stance that will inhibit the client's disclosure and thus the dyad's ability to explore, understand, and address these behaviors. Attempting to contextualize these behaviors, extending compassion, and suspending judgment until one can understand help therapists and people in all relationships connect to each other more effectively. This process is a moral demand of psychotherapy: to use one's reactions to promote the client's well-being.

A clinical guideline for using countertransference constructively is to notice or name it, process it in consultation with a colleague, and then use it to advance the therapy (Pearlman & Saakvitne, 1995; Saakvitne et al., 2000). We must consider the implications of our thoughts, feelings, and actions for the client. Our responses have implications for clients' view of themselves, as well as their own behavior toward themselves and others. Some of the ways therapists treat clients badly or immorally include engaging in sexual or social behavior with a client, disregarding the client's privacy or confidentiality (e.g., sharing details unnecessarily, even concerning clients who have given written consent), judging the client's behavior without understanding or helping the client understand the behavior in its context, refraining from addressing concerns related to the client's or his or her children's safety, or shaming or humiliating a client. Some of these behaviors are less subtle than others, and all can harm clients and perhaps cause them to harm others. These "therapeutic errors" can reduce clients' sense of self-worth, rob them of the ability to develop a potentially therapeutic trusting relationship with the therapist, reenact the betrayal they may have experienced in other relationships, or allow them to continue to engage in harmful behavior.

THE TRAUMA THERAPIST'S MORAL EVOLUTION

In addition to fostering clients' growth, trauma therapists also have an opportunity for moral growth and expansion as a result of their work. "Psychotherapy at its best . . . can be a profoundly humanizing experience that increases [therapists'] moral capacity" (Doherty, 1995, p. 19). This is particularly true for therapists working with trauma survivors who have undergone deep moral and spiritual violations. (I use the term *spirituality* to refer to an awareness of ephemeral aspects of existence. My colleague, Debra Neumann, and I developed this definition for use in unpublished interview research on spirituality in the early 1990s.) Despite the myth of neutrality (Kottler, 2010; London, 1986), all of us bring our own moral and spiritual perspectives to every encounter. In this section, I trace a possible moral developmental progression that a trauma therapist might experience in his or her work with traumatized clients.

A natural beginning response to learning about the terrible experiences of victimization endured by many clients is shock, which may be followed by disbelief, disgust, and/or great sorrow. Of course, these reactions temper over time. Without a personal trauma history (which many trauma therapists do have; see, e.g., Pearlman & Mac Ian, 1995, and Wilson & Thomas, 2004), a therapist's shock at deeds that harm doers commit is almost inevitable, and the shock can grow as the number of stories and their awful details mount. Although therapists typically have heard about child abuse, neglect, emotional victimization, and other harmful deeds perpetrated against children, there is something deeply disturbing about sitting with someone who is recounting such experiences in detail, coupled with a responsibility to help. Our hearts must be open to our clients' pain if we are to be effective, but an open heart is also open to injury. The open-hearted therapist is likely to feel some of the client's pain. The moral concomitant of this response is usually a judgment against the inflicters of the harm. Over time, this judgment may expand to include those who stood by passively when they might have prevented the harm, those who responded unhelpfully or harmfully, and a society in which such deeds, even today, are often accepted as an unfortunate but inevitable part of child rearing. This social acceptance of the victimization of children is evident in a thirst for violence that is partially sated through popular culture—movies, television shows, sports events, music that promotes violence—as well as our refusal in the United States to pay for adequate psychotherapy for abuse survivors.

Therapists working with survivors of interpersonal violence commonly develop feelings of personal vulnerability. Therapists who are parents often focus that vulnerability on the safety of their children. Many trauma therapists feel increased personal insecurity in the world, knowing that violence is often random and that they, too, could be harmed (assuming that this has not already happened in the therapist's life). These feelings are uncomfortable and can become intolerable. One quick-fix defense against these feelings is to blame the victim. This blaming can take subtle forms, such as thoughts about the victim having done something wrong or being in the wrong place at the time of the violence or the therapist being different from (and therefore less vulnerable than) the client (e.g., "She shouldn't have been walking alone in the park," "Child abuse happens only in chaotic families," "Between my tai chi training and my ability to remain calm under pressure, I could protect my child in any situation"). These thoughts may help the therapist manage his or her fears, but they also reflect negative judgments about survivors, who are in fact not responsible for the actions of the people who harmed them. Children growing up under threat often develop laser-sharp attunement in environments in which moods and meanings can change rapidly and dangerously. Thus, they are likely to sense victim blaming, however subtle, unconscious, unintentional, or well disguised. When this occurs, the client will not likely develop the trust in the therapist that is essential to engaging in treatment authentically and benefiting from it. This is a moral malfunction on the therapist's part, depriving a person who is suffering of services that might help him or her recover.

An alternative to victim blaming is to find other circumstances that might explain the victimization that have nothing to do with the client but serve to protect the therapist from imagining himself or herself as the victim of a random traumatic event such as an assault or natural disaster. Janoff-Bulman (1998) pointed out humans' reluctance to acknowledge the role of chance in extreme misfortune because doing so can open us to unmanageable fear of our own vulnerability.

Therapists may, consciously or not, use other defenses to protect themselves from this insecurity and the fear that accompanies it. These self-protective behaviors include, for example, tuning out when clients are talking about painful material, forgetting important things the client has said, missing or running late for appointments, not returning client phone calls, and so forth. Although none of these actions can categorically be termed a defense, any of them could serve that purpose. Clients with childhood trauma histories, who are already prone to feeling confused, guilty, responsible, inadequate, or even toxic, may feel this way even more as a result of defensively and unintentionally inconsiderate therapist behaviors. The therapist's defenses may suggest to clients that there was something they could or should have done or known that might have protected them from victimization. Or they may feel that the therapist is avoiding them because they are "too much," a common concern for people who grew up in homes where their needs were not met.

At the beginning of work with clients who have endured interpersonal violence or victimization, a therapist may feel angry about these violations. This anger may grow with each new report of selfishness, neglect, intentional harm, and cruelty. The therapist might express his or her anger at the perpetrators, disparage them in his or her speech, or paint them as bad, or even inhuman, people. In a consultation group for trauma therapists, after hearing the horrible details of childhood abuse that yet another client had reported to her therapist, one of the participants suggested, with mild sarcasm, that the group swap names of their clients' perpetrators and each participant hunt down and harm one of these despised individuals. This suggestion elicited an enthusiastic chorus of agreement, as well as uneasy laughter at their own frustration and sense of being overwhelmed arising from vicarious trauma: too many awful stories resulting in way too much pain, coupled with feelings of helplessness. The laughter also reflected some discomfort with even holding a fantasy of harming others, signaling to the therapists how much the work had changed them, as the subsequent discussion revealed.

Anger is very organizing and helps people move from feelings of vulnerability to feelings of strength. While this anger toward harm doers is often wholly justified, it can reduce them to one-dimensional figures and constrain the ability of both the therapist and the client to understand these individuals' complexities, including their motivations and history, and the social forces that surrounded the victimization. A less complex understanding (e.g., "he's bad") eliminates the client's potentially contextualizing his or her victimization, reducing the likelihood of eventually making sense of and integrating his or her experiences of harm. (See Chapters 20 and 21, this volume, for discussions of the causes and complexity of evil behavior.) This reaction also affects the ability of the therapist to help the client move from victim to moral agent, as discussed earlier. This sort of expanded understanding also applies in other sorts of interpersonal relationships. The more we understand each others' behaviors in context, the more likely we are to feel empowered to act on our own and others' behalf.

Vicarious trauma can itself result in moral judgments and consequent behaviors. Someone must be eliciting the bad feelings, the cynicism, the despair, and the emotional reactivity that the therapist is experiencing. Without the theoretical framework of vicarious trauma (constructivist self-development theory; McCann & Pearlman, 1990a; Pearlman, 2001; Pearlman & Saakvitne, 1995), one may attribute these difficulties to the wrong source. That source could be one's work setting and its leaders. In my experience leading workshops on vicarious traumatization, it is very common for participants who work in social service agencies to view the organization as the primary cause of their work-related stress and distress and the administrators as the enemy. Within a trauma-focused organization, the victim–perpetrator–bystander dynamic (Miller, 1994) is a highly available template for understanding group dynamics. Although the stressors of agency work should not be minimized, the extent to which administrators are demonized is often excessive. Social service agency administrators work under very challenging conditions of shrinking budgets, growing waiting lists, demanding boards or public overseers, and, yes, sometimes hostile staff. Disgruntled staff members have been known to engage in subtle or overt denigration and sabotage of administrators out of their own sense of victimization. I suggest that this is often a moral error, arising from a narrow focus on one's own experience (occluding that of the administrators) and from the need for a scapegoat.

How does the therapist respond to adult clients who acknowledge that they harmed someone more vulnerable as a child in an abusive context or in adulthood? When such information emerges in a therapy relationship in which the therapist has known only of the client's victimization, the therapist may experience a crisis. The therapist now needs to expand his or her view of the all-good, innocent victim to include behaviors that he or she judges as bad. The therapist may feel confused. One possibility is that the moral formulation shifts to "People who have been harmed by others are capable of doing harm." Alternatively, or eventually, his or her moral formulation may expand to "Everyone is capable of harming others." This latter stance, of course, includes potentially enormous growth, including "I am capable of harming others," which usually is modified to a tolerable concept by "under certain circumstances." This may feel morally repugnant or, more likely, narcissistically injurious. As it is not possible to live up to our ideals at all times, we must develop ways of comprehending our own lapses. Perhaps we can do so in a way that also broadens our compassion for others when they inevitably fail to meet our own or their own moral standards.

Clients can benefit from seeing their therapists struggle, and from struggling with them, with the desire for revenge and the wish for a more considered, compassionate, and complex way of understanding and responding to harm doers (for a discussion of this issue beyond the psychotherapy setting, see Pumla Gobodo-Madikizela's [2003] wonderful account of her interviews with Eugene De Kock, one of the masterminds of apartheid in South Africa). Those who engage in violence, abuse, and neglect are responsible for their actions and must be held accountable. At the same time, it is possible to understand such actions, and understanding does not imply accepting or forgiving them.

Some excellent examples exist of complex frameworks for understanding perpetrators of group (Staub, 2010) and individual (Athens, 1992) violence. Ervin Staub and I have worked in East Africa to promote understanding of harm doers through a public education project in the hopes of helping all parties recover psychologically and preventing future violence (Staub & Pearlman, 2006). Previous research on the effects of understanding on orientation to a formerly hostile group found positive results in a community group context (Staub, Pearlman, Gubin, & Hagengimana, 2005).

A next step in the therapist's moral development would be something like this: "Although harm doing is wrong, those who harm others deserve compassion and the opportunity to process, acknowledge, and make amends for their deeds." They must also engage in justice processes, taking responsibility for harm done.

A strong sense of right and wrong is often accompanied by clear lines between *us* and *them*. As moral judgments become more complex, this distinction begins to break down. In terms of the therapist's moral evolution, the next step is the discovery that there is no *them*. It requires the therapist to think carefully about the usual categories and to make discerning judgments about who or what is right or wrong, on the basis of a broader understanding of how wrong behavior comes about (see Chapters 20 and 21, this volume). As Kohlberg, Levine, and Hewer (1983) suggested, moral development involves an expanding circle of role taking, considering events from many perspectives. At the extreme, it might mean considering the perspectives of perpetrators.

Few people are capable of operating in the world with such a broadly inclusive morality. Exemplars are such figures as the Buddha, the Dalai Lama, Gandhi, Jesus, and Mohammed. The fact that these figures are exemplars underscores the rarity of the ability to live as if we all are *us*. This does not imply that there is no moral responsibility or that we are not to pass judgment on others. Although it is important to try to see the humanity in everyone and to comprehend people's actions, it is also essential to take a stand against harming others. This means that while we attempt to understand and empathize with everyone, we also act in the world rather than withdrawing from it. Certain actions are reprehensible, even if they are accepted within a culture or understandable in the context of people's lives. For example, harsh treatment of children is wrong because it dehumanizes and injures them.

Relinquishing *us* versus *them* invites a therapist to consider his or her own potential to harm others. This moral expansion of the therapist can result from actively struggling with the horrors of interpersonal violence. It can be viewed as a vicarious transformation arising from engaging with one's own vicarious traumatization.

CONCLUSION

This chapter has explored various moral dimensions of trauma therapies. Many of these processes are universal, applying to all human relations. We can all grow from our own and others' responses to life experiences. Given the power of trauma therapies to shape people's behavior toward others, it is valuable to consider these therapies from a moral perspective. Doing so may provide opportunities for greater growth in clients and therapists alike.

REFERENCES

Allen, J. (2001). *Traumatic relationships and serious mental disorders*. Chichester, England: Wiley.

Armsworth, M. W. (1989). Therapy of incest survivors: Abuse or support? *Child Abuse & Neglect, 13*, 549–562. doi:10.1016/0145-2134(89)90059-8

Athens, L. (1992). *The creation of dangerous violent criminals*. Champaign, IL: University of Illinois Press.

Baron-Cohen, S. (2005). Literally a total focus on the self? In T. E. Feinberg & J. P. Keenan (Eds.), *The lost self: Pathologies of the brain and identity* (pp. 166–180). New York, NY: Oxford University Press.

Briere, J. (1992). *Child abuse trauma*. Newbury Park, CA: Sage.

Briere, J., & Scott, C. (2006). *Principles of trauma therapy: A guide to symptoms, evaluation, and treatment*. Thousand Oaks, CA: Sage.

Broden, M. S., & Agresti, A. A. (1998). Responding to therapists' sexual abuse of adult incest survivors: Ethical and legal considerations. *Psychotherapy: Theory, Research, Practice, Training, 35*, 96–104. doi:10.1037/h0087812

Brown, L. (2008). *Cultural competence in trauma therapy: Beyond the flashback*. Washington, DC: American Psychological Association. doi:10.1037/11752-000

Bryant, S. L., & Range, L. (1997). Type and severity of child abuse and college students' lifetime suicidality. *Child Abuse & Neglect, 21*, 1169–1176. doi:10.1016/S0145-2134(97)00092-6

Cloitre, M., Cohen, L. R., & Koenen, K. C. (2006). *Treating survivors of childhood abuse: Psychotherapy for the interrupted life*. New York, NY: Guilford Press.

Courtois, C. (2010). *Healing the incest wound: Adult survivors in therapy* (2nd ed.). New York, NY: Norton.

Courtois, C. A., & Ford, J. D. (Eds.). (2009). *Treating complex traumatic stress disorders: An evidence-based guide*. New York, NY: Guilford Press.

Dahlenberg, C. (2000). *Countertransference and the treatment of trauma*. Washington, DC: American Psychological Association. doi:10.1037/10380-000

Dahlenberg, C., & Brown, L. (2001). Ethical issues. In M. Winterstein & S. R. Scribner (Eds.), *Mental health care for child crime victims: Standards of Care Task Force guidelines* (pp. 2.1–2.10). Sacramento, CA: State of California.

Danieli, Y. (1984). Psychotherapists' participation in the conspiracy of silence about the Holocaust. *Psychoanalytic Psychology, 1*, 23–42. doi:10.1037/0736-9735.1.1.23

Doherty, W. J. (1995). *Soul searching: Why psychotherapy must promote moral responsibility.* New York, NY: Basic Books.

Gobodo-Madikizela, P. (2003). *A human being died that night: A South African story of forgiveness.* Boston, MA: Houghton Mifflin.

Hartman, C. R., Burgess, A. W., & McCormack, A. (1987). Pathways and cycles of runaways: A model for understanding repetitive runaway behavior. *Hospital & Community Psychiatry, 38*, 292–299.

Janoff-Bulman, R. (1998). From terror to appreciation: Confronting chance after extreme misfortune. *Psychological Inquiry, 9*, 99–101. doi:10.1207/s15327965 pli0902_3

Kluft, R. P. (1990). Incest and subsequent revictimization: The case of therapist–patient sexual exploitation, with a description of the "sitting duck" syndrome. In R. P. Kluft (Ed.), *Incest-related syndromes of adult psychopathology* (pp. 263–287). Washington, DC: American Psychiatric Press.

Kohlberg, L., Levine C., & Hewer, A. (1983). *Moral stages: A current formulation and a response to critics.* Basel, NY: Karger.

Kottler, J. (2010). *On being a psychotherapist.* New York, NY: Wiley.

London, P. (1986). *The modes and morals of psychotherapy* (2nd ed.). New York, NY: Taylor & Francis.

McCann, I., & Pearlman, L. A. (1990a). *Psychological trauma and the adult survivor: Theory, therapy, and transformation.* New York, NY: Brunner/Mazel.

McCann, I. L., & Pearlman, L. A. (1990b). Vicarious traumatization: A framework for understanding the psychological effects of working with victims. *Journal of Traumatic Stress, 3*, 131–149. doi:10.1007/BF00975140

Miller, D. (1994). *Women who hurt themselves: A book of hope and understanding.* New York, NY: Basic Books.

Najavits, L. (2002). *Seeking safety: A treatment manual for PTSD and substance abuse.* New York, NY: Guilford Press.

Pearlman, L. A. (2001). Treatment of persons with complex PTSD and other trauma-related disorders of the self. In J. P. Wilson, M. D. Friedman, & J. D. Lindy (Eds.), *Treating psychological trauma and PTSD* (pp. 205–236). New York, NY: Guilford Press.

Pearlman, L. A., & Caringi, J. (2009). Living and working self-reflectively to address vicarious trauma. In C. A. Courtois & J. Ford (Eds.), *Treating complex traumatic stress disorders: An evidence-based guide* (pp. 202–224). New York, NY: Guilford Press.

Pearlman, L. A., & Courtois, C. A. (2005). Clinical applications of the attachment framework: Relational treatment of complex trauma. *Journal of Traumatic Stress, 18*, 449–460.

Pearlman, L. A., & Mac Ian, P. (1995). Vicarious traumatization: An empirical study of the effects of trauma work on trauma therapists. *Professional Psychology: Research and Practice, 26*, 558–565. doi:10.1037/0735-7028.26.6.558

Pearlman, L. A., & Saakvitne, K. W. (1995). *Trauma and the therapist: Countertransference and vicarious traumatization in psychotherapy with incest survivors.* New York, NY: Norton.

Pearlman, L. A., Wortman, C. B., Feuer, C. A., Farber, C. H., & Rando, T. A. (in press). *Traumatic bereavement: Treatment for survivors of sudden death.* New York, NY: Guilford Press.

Pope, K. S. (1994). *Sexual involvement with therapists: Patient assessment, subsequent therapy, forensics.* Washington, DC: American Psychological Association. doi:10.1037/10154-000

Pope, K. S., & Bouhoutsos, J. (1986). *Sexual intimacies between therapists and patients.* New York, NY: Praeger.

Pope, K. S., & Vasquez, M. (2001). *Ethics in psychotherapy and counseling: A practical guide* (2nd ed.). San Francisco, CA: Wiley.

Pope, K. S., & Vetter, V. A. (1991). Prior therapist–patient sexual involvement among patients seen by psychologists. *Psychotherapy: Theory, Research, Practice, Training, 28*, 429–438.

Ross, C., & Halpern, N. (2009). *Trauma model therapy: A treatment approach for trauma, dissociation, and complex comorbidity.* Richardson, TX: Manitou Communications.

Rotter, J. (1982). *The development and applications of social learning theory.* New York, NY: Praeger.

Saakvitne, K. W., Gamble, S. J., Pearlman, L. A., & Lev, B. T. (2000). *Risking connection: A training curriculum for working with survivors of childhood abuse.* Lutherville, MD: Sidran Foundation and Press.

Somer, E., & Saadon, M. (1999). Therapist–client sex: Clients' retrospective reports. *Professional Psychology: Research and Practice, 30*, 504–509. doi:10.1037/0735-7028.30.5.504

Staub, E. (2010). *Overcoming evil: Genocide, violent conflict, and terrorism.* New York, NY: Oxford University Press.

Staub, E., & Pearlman, L. A. (2006). Advancing healing and reconciliation. In L. Barbanel & R. J. Sternberg (Eds.), *Psychological interventions in times of crisis* (pp. 213–243). New York, NY: Springer.

Staub, E., Pearlman, L. A., Gubin, A., & Hagengimana, A. (2005). Healing, reconciliation, forgiving, and the prevention of violence after genocide or mass killing: An intervention and its experimental evaluation in Rwanda. *Journal of Social and Clinical Psychology, 24,* 297–334. doi:10.1521/jscp.24.3.297.65617

Thompson, B. (1995). Ethical dilemmas in trauma research. *American Sociologist, 26,* 54–69. doi:10.1007/BF02692027

Wilson, J. P., & Lindy, J. D. (Eds.). (1994). *Countertransference in the treatment of PTSD.* New York, NY: Guilford Press.

Wilson, J. P., & Thomas, R. B. (2004). *Empathy in the treatment of trauma and PTSD.* New York, NY: Brunner-Routledge.

IV

GOOD AND EVIL: MORALITY, CONFLICT, AND VIOLENCE

18

KILLING WITH A CLEAN CONSCIENCE: EXISTENTIAL ANGST AND THE PARADOX OF MORALITY

GILAD HIRSCHBERGER AND TOM PYSZCZYNSKI

Self-interest, or rather self-love, or egoism, has been more plausibly substituted as the basis of morality.

—Thomas Jefferson

Two thousand years ago, in the wake of the unsuccessful Bar Kochbah revolt against the Romans, a debate ensued between the disciples of two Jewish sages, Rabbi Akiva and Rabbi Ishmael. The students of Rabbi Akiva, a messianic ultranationalist who inspired the revolt against the Romans, interpreted their teacher's position to say that the laws and restrictions of the Bible pertain only to fellow Jews and not to interactions with non-Jews. Rabbi Ishmael, a universalist who advocated moderation and dialogue with the Romans, delivered a starkly different message to his disciples and contended that biblical law was intended for all people and that "Thou shalt not kill" applies to Jews and non-Jews alike (M. Arad, personal communication, February 2010).

This ancient debate reflects a conflict between competing conceptions of morality that persists today. To whom should moral consideration be extended? In most intergroup conflicts, each side views its opposition to the other as a morally righteous and religiously sanctioned response to the evils of the other side. Thus, the moral issues that arise in the context of clashes between groups often hark back to the ancient debate between Rabbis Akiva and Ishmael.

Our discussion in this chapter is intended to shed light on issues that have been debated by generations of theologians, moral philosophers, and social scientists. Do morals encourage people to transcend egotistical concerns and consider the condition of the "other," or do they serve the opposite function of glorifying one's self-image and group's status under the guise of benevolent concern? Do morals reflect context-dependent and relativistic prescriptions for human behavior or universal rules of human conduct? How can people commit acts, under the guise of moral righteousness, that most outsiders would view as immoral and even evil? How do the group-level and individual-level functions of moral behavior relate to each other?

In this chapter, we focus primarily on the role of moral concerns in intergroup conflicts and the potential of moral principles to both defuse and intensify conflicts between groups. Paradoxically, moral strivings often increase the viciousness of interactions between people with different group identities, partly because of the diverse moral principles cultures use to govern behavior. Although moral principles are typically thought of as promoting more humane and other-oriented behavior (see Chapter 21, this volume), they can also promote the defense of one's own group, which often includes vanquishing another group perceived as evil. To shed light on these issues, we use terror management theory (TMT; Greenberg, Pyszczynski, & Solomon, 1997) to explain how moral principles, which often promote group cohesion, are used by individuals in regulating themselves (e.g., Carver & Scheier, 1981). We suggest that moral behavior involves implicit calculations aimed at enabling an individual to maintain self-esteem by means of enhancing a moral self-image. This often entails sacrificing one set of moral values for another, which in many cases leads to a "righteous" crusade or jihad against another group.

TERROR MANAGEMENT THEORY

TMT contends that the uniquely human awareness of the inevitability of personal death generates the potential for overwhelming terror because it threatens the very basic desire to live. This potential for terror drives people to construct their reality in a way that infuses life with meaning, value, and hope of transcending death. Terror management research has demonstrated that investing in a cultural worldview and defending it against threats is an essential means of defending against existential terror. *Cultural worldviews* are symbolic, social constructions of reality that (a) imbue life with meaning and order and answer basic questions about existence; (b) establish standards of value that, if met, provide a sense of personal self-esteem and group value; and (c) give hope of life continuing after physical death, either literally in the form of an afterlife or symbolically in the form of contributions to something greater and more enduring than the physical self. Thus, to achieve psychological equanimity in the face of mortality, people need to feel that they are valuable contributors to a meaningful and important world as defined by their culture.

Because this protection from existential terror is provided by ideas, concepts, values, and symbols, the existence of others who share one's worldview lends credibility to it and increases its ability to protect one from anxiety. Problems arise, however, when one encounters people or ideas that threaten the validity of cherished beliefs about oneself and one's group, because this undermines the social consensus supporting one's worldview and self-esteem, thereby reducing the ability of these symbolic structures to quell anxiety.

To cope with the threat to emotional security posed by groups with different worldviews, people often try to convert others to their worldview (e.g., missionary work) or incorporate the nonthreatening aspects of a competing worldview into their own preexisting worldview (e.g., the recent increase in the popularity of Americanized Middle Eastern food). Another strategy is to derogate the adherents of competing worldviews (e.g., referring to Islam as an "evil religion") or to use violent means to defeat or completely annihilate those who pose a significant challenge to one's core beliefs. Although most wars and violent conflicts involve disputes over territory, resources, or other concrete issues, they also invariably involve a clash of worldviews. We argue that protecting oneself from existential fear motivates violent, aggressive responses when one's worldview is challenged. Perceiving a severe threat to core beliefs often allows a lifting of moral prohibitions against killing that exist in most cultures.

EMPIRICAL SUPPORT FOR TERROR MANAGEMENT THEORY

To date, more than 400 studies conducted in diverse cultures in at least 21 countries have provided convergent evidence for hypotheses derived from TMT (see Greenberg, Solomon, & Arndt, 2008, for a comprehensive review). Much of this evidence comes from studies showing that reminders of death (*mortality salience*) cause people to bolster their defense of their cultural worldview in an effort to defend self-esteem and maintain close social relationships.

Research has also implicated terror management processes in promoting violent solutions to political conflicts. Specifically, mortality salience has been found to prime (a) increased support among American conservatives for extreme military interventions in the "war on terror," including the use of nuclear and chemical weapons that would kill thousands of civilians (Pyszczynski et al., 2006, Study 1); (b) increased support among Iranian students for suicidal terrorism against Western targets (Pyszczynski et al., 2006, Study 2); (c) increased support among Israelis for a preemptive nuclear strike on Iran (Hirschberger, Pyszczynski, & Ein-Dor, 2009a); and (d) increased support among Israelis for violent retributions for acts of violence conducted against them, even if the acts of violence were deemed ineffective (Hirschberger, Pyszczynski, & Ein-Dor, 2009b). These studies suggest that in times of war and terrorist threat, when death-related concerns are likely to be more prominent than usual, and when hostility toward one's culture on the part of another group is rampant, people are especially likely to consider violent approaches to resolving conflicts.

This research implies that when increased protection from existential fear is needed because of increased salience of death and vulnerability, as is typically the case in times of war and conflict, people work especially hard to meet the standards prescribed by their cultural worldviews. But cultural worldviews and the standards they prescribe are complex and multifaceted. According to theories of self-regulation (Carver & Scheier, 1981), self-regulatory efforts are oriented toward meeting whichever of the many standards a person holds is most salient or mentally accessible at the time. From a terror management perspective, conflict and war highlight the need to defeat an opposing worldview while also perceiving one's own group as being more morally righteous. Because violence against another group is often at odds with values of compassion and with self-perceptions of moral superiority, managing conflicting moral motives may explain the many paradoxes that violent conflict entails.

Research has demonstrated that even in the context of violent political conflict, the influence of mortality salience on support for violent solutions to the conflict can be reduced by highlighting moral values that favor compassion (Rothschild, Abdollahi, & Pyszczynski, 2009) and shared humanity (Pyszczynski et al., 2010). For example, Pyszczynski et al. (2010) found that encouraging Americans, Palestinian citizens of Israel, and Israeli Jews to consider the shared global consequences of climate change blocked the usual support for violence following a mortality salience manipulation. These findings suggest that in addition to encouraging defense of one's worldview, which sometimes involves increased hostility toward outgroup members, reminders of death also encourage greater adherence to fundamental cultural values, which in most cases include sanctions against violence and encouragement of compassion. Although most people in modern cultures think of violence as immoral and peacemaking and compassion as moral, recent theories of moral behavior suggest that both forms of behavior can stem from striving for morality.

FUNDAMENTAL FOUNDATIONS OF MORALITY

Moral foundations theory (see Chapter 1, this volume) identifies five foundational themes that characterize the moral domain: harm/care, fairness/reciprocity, ingroup/loyalty, authority/respect, and purity/sanctity. From this perspective, gut-level moral intuitions are the primary causes of reactions to morally significant persons and situations, and they play an important role in instigating more abstract moral reasoning. Graham and Haidt argue in Chapter 1 of this volume that all human beings react emotionally, to a greater or lesser extent, to behavior and situations that impinge on all five of the moral foundations. They also argue that whereas political liberals are especially committed to the harm/care and fairness/reciprocity foundations, conservatives are roughly equally committed to all five, which means they place more emphasis than do liberals on ingroup/loyalty, authority/respect, and purity/sanctity.

Looking back at over 25 years of terror management research in light of Graham and Haidt's conceptualization suggests that moral concerns have been a primary focus of this research and are likely to be important sources of protection from existential anxiety. For instance, in the very first TMT study (Rosenblatt, Greenberg, Solomon, Pyszczynski, & Lyon, 1989), municipal court judges who were reminded of their own mortality recommended higher (i.e., more punitive) bonds for an alleged prostitute than did judges in the control condition, especially if the judges were morally opposed to prostitution. This finding indicates that mortality salience strengthens moral judgments based on Graham and Haidt's purity dimension. Research conducted by Goldenberg and her colleagues (e.g., Goldenberg et al., 2001) indicated that mortality salience increases feelings of disgust toward various bodily functions and sensations, further suggesting that death concerns amplify responses related to the moral purity dimension.

Research pertaining to the fairness dimension of morality has shown that mortality salience increases concerns with fairness, such as greater agreement with hate crime legislation (Lieberman, Arndt, Personius, & Cook, 2001, Study 1). But other research indicates that mortality salience leads to more blaming of innocent victims (Hirschberger, 2006). Thus, it appears that mortality salience does not necessarily lead people to support the fair treatment of others. Rather, it increases the motivation to believe in a just world and act in a manner that supports this belief—in some cases by showing compassion, and in other cases by setting it aside (Hirschberger, 2010).

Just as mortality salience does not indiscriminately increase the desire for fairness, it also does not uniformly increase the motivation to care for others. Research indicates that mortality salience increases prosocial responses only toward worldview-relevant causes (Jonas, Schimel, Greenberg, & Pyszczynski, 2002) and only when the prosocial cause is perceived as nonthreatening (Hirschberger, Ein-Dor, & Almakias, 2008). Thus, mortality salience increases other-oriented responses most clearly when they benefit one's own group, worldview, or self-esteem. When the prosocial cause is nonbeneficial or even threatening to oneself, death concerns often induce selfish, ethnocentric, or callous responses to the plight of others (Hirschberger, 2010).

Research also shows that death concerns influence responses to those high and low on social hierarchies corresponding to Graham and Haidt's authority dimension (see Chapter 1, this volume). For example, Landau, Solomon, et al. (2004) found that mortality salience led to increased support for President George W. Bush in the months after the September 11, 2001, terrorist attacks in the United States, and Cohen, Solomon, Maxfield, Pyszczynski, and Greenberg (2004) found that mortality salience increased support for a hypothetical charismatic leader over a merely competent one.

Perhaps the most thoroughly investigated influence of death concerns on morality is in the realm of intergroup relations. Numerous terror management studies have shown that mortality salience increases ingroup loyalty and outgroup rejection (for a review, see Greenberg et al., 2008). Recently, this research has been extended to the study of political conflict and to the morality-laden decisions people make when deciding how to deal with an adversarial group (e.g., Hirschberger & Pyszczynski, 2011).

Moral foundations theory seems particularly useful in understanding recent TMT findings related to political conflict, because ethical and moral dilemmas involve conflicts between different specific moral standards to which individuals are committed to varying degrees and between the welfare of the individual, the ingroup, and the outgroup (see Chapter 1, this volume). Because behavior is regulated on an individual level and is motivated by the death anxiety aroused when individuals feel they are falling short of their moral standards, these conflicts are usually resolved by doing whatever is most likely to enable one to view oneself as a moral person. In this sense, moral behavior often appears to be selfish or ethnocentric. This tendency is exacerbated by the importance that cultures and individuals place on morality over other dimensions of personal value (e.g., Baumeister, 1991; see also Chapter 20, this volume).

We suggest that moral values are imbued with such extreme significance because, in the vast majority of cultures, they are seen as having been directly delivered to humankind by a deity that can provide or refuse access to literal immortality. Cultures began to link moral behavior to one's fate after death very early in the history of religion (Wright, 2009). This contingency between moral behavior and one's fate after death was a powerful inducement to look beyond one's selfish concerns to the welfare of others, at least others in one's own group. If the absolute annihilation that death might entail is the ultimate fear, then the promise of continued life after death is the ultimate incentive for behavior that benefits the group. We suspect that the juxtaposition of a supernatural force with concerns about cleanliness, purity, and disgust might have been a human innovation that gained popularity, in part, because of the increased control it gave group leaders over members.

Cleanliness—in all of its meanings—is next to godliness! And human beings want to be as close to the gods as they can get. As Goldenberg et al. (2001) suggested, one of the primary means through which people deny their mortality is by distancing themselves from other animals, denying their own creatureliness, and imbuing their lives with a spiritual dimension. All three major Western religions subscribe to the belief that "God gave man dominion over all things" (Genesis 1:26). By construing human life as rooted in a spiritual realm, people distance themselves from and elevate themselves above everything that dies. We contend that this concordance of ingroup loyalty with maintaining purity plays a significant role in the moral processes that govern intractable intergroup conflicts.

MORALITY IN TIMES OF CONFLICT

Moral issues lie at the heart of virtually all intergroup conflicts. Although selfish and ethnocentric desires for resources, territory, and tangible goods are usually involved, at the center of the conflict is a disagreement about who has the greater right to these things, who deserves them, who has treated whom unfairly, and how the deity wants these resources to be distributed. Given the security that people acquire from viewing themselves as morally righteous, it is no surprise that all sides to conflicts construe themselves as righteously fighting against undeserving, unjust, evil usurpers of their rights, a fight in which the deity and all that is good are invested in their victory.

War and violent conflict diminish a person's ability to achieve a balance between his or her own interests and the needs of others because during conflicts the stakes are high and threat looms large. Consequently, the motivation to uphold a moral self sometimes leads people to construe a conflict in a way that enables them to maintain a moral self-image while engaging in behavior that violates even their most sacred values. Terror management concerns play a role in the processes of moral amplification, moral disengagement, and the maintenance of moral identity, all of which serve to justify acts of dubious morality.

Moral Amplification

Moral amplification refers to "the motivated separation and exaggeration of good and evil in the explanation of behavior" (Haidt & Algoe, 2004, p. 323). In times of war and elevated violence, moral amplification is a powerful justification mechanism because people are motivated to view conflict as a battle of light against darkness in which they and their group are guardians of the light.

This leads them to dismiss complex explanations that include a consideration of the grievances of the other side and to avoid considering ways that their own group may have contributed to the perpetuation of conflict. We contend that this need to perceive the other as the epitome of evil is driven not by an objective appraisal of the facts but by the existential benefits of ingroup loyalty and purity (see Chapters 1 and 3, this volume).

Research suggests that when death is salient, moral amplification increases. First, mortality salience increases the need for a structured, meaningful world and decreases tolerance for ambiguity (Landau, Johns, et al., 2004). Second, mortality salience is known to increase punishment meted out to legal and moral transgressors (Florian & Mikulincer, 1997; Rosenblatt et al., 1989) and to increase the need to believe in a just world (Hirschberger, 2006). These findings suggest that the perception of a structured and unambiguous world facilitates the exaggeration of differences between good and evil.

Recently, we collected data indicating that reminders of death and the Holocaust led Israeli Jews to perceive Israeli Arabs as having malevolent intentions toward them and toward the state of Israel (Hirschberger, Canetti, Pyszczynski, Kahn, & Gubler, 2010). When death was salient, Israeli Jews simplified the complex identity of Israeli Arabs, who are typically torn between their conflicting identities as Palestinians and Israelis (e.g., Kimhi, Canetti-Nisim, & Hirschberger, 2009) and preferred to perceive them in simple, clear-cut terms—as enemies of Israel. This process of moral amplification via social categorization may support discriminatory attitudes toward minority groups.

Moral Disengagement

Given the nearly universal moral injunctions against harming others, it may not be enough to amplify and exaggerate moral differences between *us* and *them*. Research conducted in the past 2 decades suggests that an additional mechanism, moral disengagement, often facilitates support for violent conduct. In the words of Bandura (1998),

> Self-sanction plays a central role in the regulation of inhumane conduct. . . . Self-sanctions can be disengaged by reconstruing conduct as serving moral purposes, by obscuring personal agency in detrimental activities, by disregarding or misrepresenting the injurious consequences of one's actions, or by blaming and dehumanizing the victim. (p. 161)

All of these activities help to justify transgressions against humane moral values (for a discussion of dehumanization, see Chapter 11, this volume).

In the context of war and terrorism, moral disengagement has been positively related to support for military attacks against Iraq and Yugoslavia (McAlister, 2001) and related to support for harsher punishment of the perpetrators of the 9/11 attacks (Aquino, Reed, Thau, & Freeman, 2007). In a large, representative U.S. sample studied at the time of the 9/11 attacks, moral disengagement completely mediated the influence of the attacks on support for immediate retaliatory strikes (McAlister, Bandura, & Owen, 2006). These findings can be viewed as a dramatic field demonstration of the influence of death reminders on support for retaliatory violence.

One of the central mechanisms of moral disengagement is *dehumanization*, which divests the victim of all human qualities (see Chapter 11, this volume). Research has shown that dehumanization of a target increases aggressiveness toward the target (Bandura, Barbaranelli, Caprara, Pastorelli, & Regalia, 2001) and that when a group is dehumanized, people do not feel obliged to apply moral standards to them (e.g., Bar-Tal, 1990). Studies of dehumanization using a subtle task examining the attribution of emotions to ingroup and outgroup members (referred to as *infrahumanization*) have shown that reminding people of killings conducted by their group led them to infrahumanize the victimized group (Castano & Giner-Sorolla, 2006).

Infrahumanization serves a central role in the TMT analysis of moral behavior not only because thoughts of death increase the derogation of worldview violators but also because the need to elevate oneself and one's group above animal creatureliness and to affirm one's unique, nonanimalistic humanity serves an important existential function (Goldenberg et al., 2001). In support of the role of these processes in infrahumanization, research has shown that mortality salience increased humanization of the ingroup in three studies conducted with people from three different cultures (Vaes, Heflick, & Goldenberg, 2010).

In a related vein, a provocative study indicated that the deaths of outgroup members who threaten one's worldview can serve a terror management function (Hayes, Schimel, & Williams, 2008). Christian participants read either a worldview-threatening news article about the Muslimization of Nazareth or a nonthreatening article. Half of the participants were informed at the end of the article that a large group of Muslims had died in a recent plane crash on their way to Nazareth. Results indicated that reading about the Muslimization of Nazareth increased the accessibility of death-related thoughts and the defense of participants' Christian worldview. However, these increases were not observed among participants who learned that many Muslims died in a plane crash. This finding suggests not only that mortality salience facilitates the use of lethal violence against outgroup members but also that the death of worldview violators can be soothing and reassuring. This disturbing finding may help to explain the bloodthirsty nature of much violent conflict.

However, there is also a more optimistic side to the TMT–infrahumanization link. Motyl, Hart, and Pyszczynski (2010) recently found that whereas mortality salience increased support for a preemptive strike on

Iran among Americans who are high in religious fundamentalism, when violence was *infrahumanized*—described as an animalistic behavior that humans share with other animals—mortality salience no longer increased support for violence. Thus, when participants were faced with the association between violence and animality, mortality salience led them to view violence as repugnant. This finding suggests that the same desire to view oneself as a transcendent spiritual being that sometimes increases violence toward an outgroup can also be used as an antidote to such violence.

If one way to reduce intergroup violence is by infrahumanizing violence, another way might be to humanize an adversarial outgroup. A series of studies conducted with Americans, Israeli Arabs, and Israeli Jews demonstrated that when people were induced to consider the shared humanity between their group and other groups, mortality salience decreased support of violence and increased support for peace and reconciliation between groups (Pyszczynski et al., 2010).

The Paradox of Moral Identity

Recent research documents a variety of ways in which the motivation to maintain a positive moral identity can lead to behavior that is callous or even harmful to others. *Moral identity* refers to the extent to which moral beliefs and values are either chronically present or contextually activated, and it has been shown to influence moral conduct. Because people are motivated to maintain self-consistency, those with a strong moral identity should be motivated to uphold moral values and behave as moral exemplars in order to maintain a positive self-image (Aquino, Freeman, Reed, Lim, & Felps, 2009).

Research generally supports this idea and indicates that priming moral identity increases intentions to behave in a prosocial manner (Aquino et al., 2009); it has also been shown to counter the effects of moral disengagement in response to war crimes committed by one's ingroup (Aquino et al., 2007). Thus, priming moral identity seems to promote ethical behavior.

However, recent research suggests that it may be premature to conclude that activating a person's moral identity always increases prosocial behavior. Because behaving ethically enhances moral identity, the motivation to behave ethically following a moral identity boost may actually be diminished because the need to view oneself as a moral person has already been satisfied. In this case, a strong sense of moral identity may ironically license unethical attitudes and behaviors (Mazar & Zhong, 2010). Research supports this contention and indicates that after participants acted in a gender-egalitarian manner and validated their moral identity, they subsequently displayed more gender-discriminatory behavior (see Chapter 9, this volume). In another study, reminding people of their humanitarian nature reduced charitable donations

(Sachdeva, Iliev, & Medin, 2009). Moreover, in a study of environmental values and behaviors (Mazar & Zhong, 2010), although mere exposure to "green" (i.e., environmentally friendly) products increased prosocial inclinations, purchasing green products had the ironic licensing effect of lowering prosocial behavior and inducing more cheating and stealing. This study revealed an important distinction between activating constructs related to moral issues, which may induce prosocial attitudes and behaviors, and engaging in actual moral behaviors, which may have the ironic effect of licensing subsequent conduct that ignores others' welfare.

The licensing effect of moral behavior seems particularly relevant to political conflict because the motivation to justify morally questionable behavior may be elevated. The tendency to morally amplify the righteousness of one's group and one's cause in times of conflict is likely to increase this licensing effect. In a series of studies, we examined whether mortality salience had different effects on the moral attitudes of Israeli political hawks and doves with regard to the conflict between Israel and the Palestinians and whether moral identity primes would moderate the effect. The research was conducted several months after the outbreak of violence between Israelis and Palestinians in 2009.

In the first study, we assessed the moderating effect of participants' political orientation on the impact of mortality salience on responses to a particularly salient moral dilemma—justifying civilian casualties. Participants were randomly assigned to a mortality-salience or pain-salience condition and read a vignette that described Palestinian civilian casualties during the conflict in Gaza. Results confirmed our expectations that right-wing, hawkish participants would respond to mortality salience with greater justification of civilian casualties, whereas those with a left-wing, dovish orientation exhibited the opposite effect.

In the next study, we examined whether priming moral identity moderates the impact of death reminders on moral attitudes. Because the moral dilemma in question pertained to the conduct of an entire group, and not that of a specific individual, we believed that group moral identity was especially relevant, and we therefore primed group moral identity. For similar reasons, we chose to prime a reminder of collective death—the Holocaust—instead of one's own death. Participants were first assigned to read a Talmudic passage that either characterized the Jewish people as a charitable and compassionate nation (moral condition) or a passage warning against displaying too much compassion and advising that showing compassion to the cruel is akin to being cruel to the compassionate (control condition). Then participants were assigned to either a Holocaust-salience or a control pain-salience condition and completed the measure of justifying civilian casualties that was used in Study 1.

Among participants who were not primed with moral identity, those with a right-wing orientation responded to the Holocaust prime by rating civilian casualties as more justified than those with a left-wing political orientation, replicating the findings of Study 1. However, much to our initial dismay, the moral identity primes increased justification of civilian casualties in the Holocaust-salience condition among left-wing participants, raising their justification level to equal that of right-wing participants. It appears that moral identity primes had a paradoxical effect on the resolution of moral dilemmas by reducing the discrepancy between participants' desire to view themselves as moral and the morally questionable attitude that Palestinian civilian casualties are acceptable. The fact that this effect was most pronounced among left-wing participants is consistent with other findings from this line of research indicating that such persons generally find civilian casualties less morally acceptable. Thus, when confronted with moral violations by their group, reading Talmudic passages that bolstered their sense of the morality of their group ironically may have facilitated shifting away from their typical moral stance of viewing civilian casualties as wrong.

To clarify the processes involved in this effect, we conducted another study in which we primed moral identity and examined whether moral disengagement would mediate the effects of mortality salience on the justification of civilian casualties during conflict. To extend the generality of our findings to individual moral identity, we used Aquino et al.'s (2007) individual moral identity manipulation. To get a clearer picture of the role of death concerns, we used a standard mortality salience manipulation rather than the manipulation of Holocaust salience, because the latter was likely to arouse a multitude of thoughts and feelings in our Israeli Jewish sample. In addition, we measured two facets of Bandura's (1998) conceptualization of moral disengagement—moral justification and advantageous comparison. The dependent variable was the same questions regarding the justification of civilian casualties used in the previous studies. Results indicated that mortality salience increased moral justification, advantageous comparison, and the justification of civilian casualties and that this occurred primarily in the moral identity condition, replicating the findings of Study 2. Moreover, the impact of mortality salience on the justification of civilian casualties was significantly mediated by moral justification. These results support our claim that the paradoxical influence of priming moral identity when death is salient involves processes of moral disengagement that facilitate the justification of morally objectionable conduct.

We suspected that one of the reasons that priming moral identity in our studies increased rather than decreased support for indiscriminate violence was that all of our studies referred to violent acts that had already been committed. Moral dilemmas regarding past events may be viewed by participants as counterfactual and as requiring pointless moral agonizing. Because history cannot be changed, people may be motivated to justify past group transgressions, especially when their moral identity has been boosted and their mortality is salient. Thus, we conducted a fourth study to determine whether similar facilitation of future violence by boosting one's moral identity would occur. We replicated the design of Study 3 and added an additional variable: Half of the participants were asked about the 2009 War on Gaza, which took place before the study was conducted, and the other half were asked to imagine a future violent outbreak between Israel and the Palestinians. We also measured feelings of shame and guilt following the reaction to the moral dilemma. We hypothesized that when mortality was salient and moral identity was not primed, left-wing Israelis would experience greater shame and guilt. However, when mortality was salient and moral identity was primed, we expected a reduction in shame and guilt among this group.

Results in the past-attack (Gaza War) conditions supported our predictions and replicated our previous findings. Mortality salience increased justification of civilian casualties among participants who were primed with moral identity. These findings indicate that processes of moral disengagement may be invoked retrospectively to justify a prior unethical act. In the future-violence condition, there were no significant effects of mortality salience or moral identity primes on support of civilian casualties. This suggests that elevating one's moral identity is less effective in justifying future indiscriminate violence.

Mortality salience and moral identity primes also affected shame and guilt. As expected, mortality salience increased feelings of shame and guilt for past violence when moral identity was not primed. However, moral identity primes reduced feelings of shame and guilt in the mortality-salience condition. This shows that moral disengagement facilitates violence by reducing self-conscious emotions reflecting discomfort with one's own actions or those of one's ingroup. In the future-violence condition we obtained the opposite response, indicating that mortality salience increased feelings of shame when moral identity was primed. This finding is in keeping with past research on moral identity primes (e.g., Aquino et al., 2007) showing that when people focused on possible future transgressions, priming moral identity inhibited support for immoral conduct.

According to Bandura (1998), most people develop personal standards of moral behavior that serve a self-regulatory role by promoting good behavior and inhibiting bad behavior. Behaving in ways that counter these standards results in self-censure and guilt feelings. Thus, individuals are likely to behave in ways that are consistent with their internal moral standards. The research described in this section indicates that past moral violations do not necessarily promote guilty, remorseful behavior. Sometimes people resolve the disparity between moral values and immoral conduct by rationalizing and justifying past transgressions to reduce the dissonance between values and behaviors.

This attempt to reconcile the discord between moral self-perceptions and immoral conduct by cognitively reconstructing the meaning and severity of the transgression has been labeled *moral hypocrisy* (e.g., Batson, Thompson, & Chen, 2002; see also Chapter 9, this volume). Moral hypocrisy occurs when people delude themselves into believing that serving their self-interest does not violate their moral principles. The more one is self-deceived in believing that one is moral despite behaviors that suggest otherwise, the more one seems sincere to others. Therefore, self-deception in the moral domain is adaptive and enables one to convince oneself and others of one's moral stature. Our findings are congruent with this definition of moral hypocrisy and indicate that moral hypocrisy is primarily observed in relation to past conduct.

CONCLUSION

The ongoing intractable conflict between Israel and the Palestinians concerns territorial disputes, differing historical perspectives, and clashing religious beliefs. We contend that underlying these momentous issues is an existential conflict over truth, identity, belongingness, and moral righteousness. Both Israelis and Palestinians view themselves as sitting on the edge of an existential abyss with no margin for error. Under such circumstances, when basic existence seems to be imperiled, ingroup unity and consensus are of utmost importance, dissent is akin to treason, and empathy toward the other side is seen as weakness and cowardice. Morals play an important role in the perpetuation of such conflicts and in conceptualizing conflict as an epic battle between good and evil. Unfortunately, it seems that to fight and kill fellow human beings it is necessary to abandon the basic morality of civilized life, and this requires profound mental adjustments. As English poet Wilfred Owen wrote from the trenches of World War I, "Merry it was to laugh there— / Where death becomes absurd and life absurder / For power was on us when we slashed bones bare / Not to feel sickness or remorse of murder."

We have shown in this chapter that existential concerns perpetuate and amplify justification of intergroup violence, but we contend that these same concerns may foster peaceful relations as well. At this moment in history, when "the true enemy is war itself," people may realize that peaceful attitudes are consistent with individual self-interest and with the moral values that justify and perpetuate these interests.

REFERENCES

Aquino, K., Freeman, D., Reed, A., II, Lim, V. K. G., & Felps, W. (2009). Testing a social–cognitive model of moral behavior: The interactive influence of situations and moral identity centrality. *Journal of Personality and Social Psychology, 97,* 123–141. doi:10.1037/a0015406

Aquino, K., Reed, A., II, Thau, S., & Freeman, D. (2007). A grotesque and dark beauty: How moral identity and mechanisms of moral disengagement influence cognitive and emotional reactions to war. *Journal of Experimental Social Psychology, 43,* 385–392. doi:10.1016/j.jesp.2006.05.013

Bandura, A. (1998). Mechanisms of moral disengagement. In W. Reich (Ed.), *Origins of terrorism* (pp. 161–191). Washington, DC: Woodrow Wilson Center Press.

Bandura, A., Barbaranelli, C., Caprara, G. V., Pastorelli, C., & Regalia, C. (2001). Sociocognitive self-regulatory mechanisms governing transgressive behavior. *Journal of Personality and Social Psychology, 80,* 125–135. doi:10.1037/0022-3514. 80.1.125

Bar-Tal, D. (1990). Causes and consequences of delegitimization: Models of conflict and ethnocentrism. *Journal of Social Issues, 46,* 65–81. doi:10.1111/j.1540-4560. 1990.tb00272.x

Batson, C. D., Thompson, E. R., & Chen, H. (2002). Moral hypocrisy: Addressing some alternatives. *Journal of Personality and Social Psychology, 83,* 330–339. doi:10.1037/ 0022-3514.83.2.330

Baumeister, R. (1991). *Meanings of life.* New York, NY: Guilford Press.

Carver, C. S., & Scheier, M. F. (1981). A control-systems approach to behavioral self-regulation. In L. Wheeler (Ed.), *Review of personality and social psychology* (Vol. 2, pp. 107–140). Beverly Hills, CA: Sage.

Castano, E., & Giner-Sorolla, R. (2006). Not quite human: Infrahumanization in response to collective responsibility for intergroup killing. *Journal of Personality and Social Psychology, 90,* 804–818. doi:10.1037/0022-3514.90.5.804

Cohen, F., Solomon, S., Maxfield, M., Pyszczynski, T., & Greenberg, J. (2004). Fatal attraction: The effects of mortality salience on evaluations of charismatic, task-oriented, and relationship-oriented leaders. *Psychological Science, 15,* 846–851. doi:10.1111/j.0956-7976.2004.00765.x

Florian, V., & Mikulincer, M. (1997). Fear of death and the judgment of social transgressions: A multidimensional of terror management theory. *Journal of Personality and Social Psychology, 73,* 369–380. doi:10.1037/0022-3514.73.2.369

Goldenberg, J. L., Pyszczynski, T., Greenberg, J., Solomon, S., Kluck, B., & Cornwell, R. (2001). I am not an animal: Mortality salience, disgust, and the denial of human creatureliness. *Journal of Experimental Psychology: General, 130,* 427–435. doi:10.1037/0096-3445.130.3.427

Greenberg, J., Pyszczynski, T., & Solomon, S. (1997). Terror management theory of self-esteem and social behavior: Empirical assessments and conceptual refinements. In M. P. Zanna (Ed.), *Advances in experimental social psychology* (Vol. 29, pp. 61–139). New York, NY: Academic Press.

Greenberg, J., Solomon, S., & Arndt, J. (2008). A basic but uniquely human motivation: Terror management. In J. Y. Shah & W. L. Gardner (Eds.), *Handbook of motivation science* (pp. 114–134). New York, NY: Guilford Press.

Haidt, J., & Algoe, S. (2004). Moral amplification and the emotions that attach us to saints and demons. In J. Greenberg, S. L. Koole, & T. Pyszczynski (Eds.),

Handbook of experimental existential psychology (pp. 322–335). New York, NY: Guilford Press.

Hayes, J., Schimel, J., & Williams, T. J. (2008). Fighting death with death: The buffering effects of learning that worldview violators have died. *Psychological Science, 19*, 501–507. doi:10.1111/j.1467-9280.2008.02115.x

Hirschberger, G. (2006). Terror management and attributions of blame to innocent victims: Reconciling compassionate and defensive responses. *Journal of Personality and Social Psychology, 91*, 832–844. doi:10.1037/0022-3514.91.5.832

Hirschberger, G. (2010). Compassionate callousness: A terror management perspective on prosocial behavior. In M. Mikulincer & P. R. Shaver (Eds.), *Prosocial motives, emotion, and behavior: The better angels of our nature* (pp. 201–219). Washington, DC: American Psychological Association.

Hirschberger, G., Canetti, D., Pyszczynski, T., Kahn, D., & Gubler, J. (2010). The commonalities and differences between group mortality and individual mortality: A terror management perspective on past victimization effects. Unpublished manuscript, Interdisciplinary Center Herzliya, Herzliya, Israel.

Hirschberger, G., Ein-Dor, T., & Almakias, S. (2008). The self-protective altruist: Terror management and the ambivalent nature of prosocial behavior. *Personality and Social Psychology Bulletin, 34*, 666–678. doi:10.1177/0146167207313933

Hirschberger, G., & Pyszczynski, T. (2011). An existential perspective on ethnopolitical violence. In P. R. Shaver & M. Mikulincer (Eds.), *Understanding and reducing aggression, violence, and their consequences* (pp. 297–314). Washington, DC: American Psychological Association.

Hirschberger, G., Pyszczynski, T., & Ein-Dor, T. (2009a). *An existential quest for justice: Mortality salience increases support for vindictive yet inefficient violent retributions.* Unpublished manuscript, Interdisciplinary Center Herzliya, Herzliya, Israel.

Hirschberger, G., Pyszczynski, T., & Ein-Dor, T. (2009b). Vulnerability and vigilance: Threat awareness and perceived adversary intent moderate the impact of mortality salience on intergroup violence. *Personality and Social Psychology Bulletin, 35*, 597–607. doi:10.1177/0146167208331093

Jonas, E., Schimel, J., Greenberg, J., & Pyszczynski, T. (2002). The Scrooge effect: Evidence that mortality salience increases prosocial attitudes and behavior. *Personality and Social Psychology Bulletin, 28*, 1342–1353. doi:10.1177/014616702236834

Kimhi, S., Canetti-Nisim, D., & Hirschberger, G. (2009). Terrorism in the eyes of the beholder: The impact of causal attributions on perceptions of violence. *Peace and Conflict, 15*, 75–95. doi:10.1080/10781910802589899

Landau, M. J., Johns, M., Greenberg, J., Pyszczynski, T., Solomon, S., & Martens, A. (2004). A function of form: Terror management and structuring of the social world. *Journal of Personality and Social Psychology, 87*, 190–210. doi:10.1037/0022-3514.87.2.190

Landau, M. J., Solomon, S., Greenberg, J., Cohen, F., Pyszczynski, T., Arndt, J., . . . Cook, A. (2004). Deliver us from evil: The effects of mortality salience and reminders of 9/11 on support for President George W. Bush. *Personality and Social Psychology Bulletin, 30,* 1136–1150. doi:10.1177/0146167204267988

Lieberman, J. D., Arndt, J., Personius, J., & Cook, A. (2001). Vicarious annihilation: The effect of mortality salience on perceptions of hate crimes. *Law and Human Behavior, 25,* 547–566. doi:10.1023/A:1012738706166

Mazar, N., & Zhong, C. B. (2010). Do green products make us better people? *Psychological Science, 21,* 494–498.

McAlister, A. L. (2001). Moral disengagement: Measurement and modification. *Journal of Peace Research, 38,* 87–99. doi:10.1177/0022343301038001005

McAlister, A. L., Bandura, A., Owen, S. V. (2006). Mechanisms of moral disengagement in support of military force: The impact of Sept. 11. *Journal of Social and Clinical Psychology, 25,* 141–165. doi:10.1521/jscp.2006.25.2.141

Motyl, M., Hart, J., & Pyszczynski, T. (2010). When animals attack: The effects of mortality salience, infrahumanization of violence, and authoritarianism on support for war. *Journal of Experimental Social Psychology, 46,* 200–203. doi:10.1016/j.jesp.2009.08.012

Pyszczynski, T., Abdollahi, A., Solomon, S., Greenberg, J., Cohen, F., & Weise, D. (2006). Mortality salience, martyrdom, and military might: The great Satan versus the axis of evil. *Personality and Social Psychology Bulletin, 32,* 525–537. doi:10.1177/0146167205282157

Pyszczynski, T., Motyl, M., Vail, K. E., III, Hirschberger, G., Rothschild, Z., & Arndt, J. (2010). *A collateral advantage of drawing attention to the problem of global warming: Increased support for peace-making and decreased support for war.* Unpublished manuscript, University of Colorado, Colorado Springs, CO.

Reed, A., II, & Aquino, K. (2003). Moral identity and the expanding circle of moral regard toward out-groups. *Journal of Personality and Social Psychology, 84,* 1270–1286. doi:10.1037/0022-3514.84.6.1270

Rosenblatt, A., Greenberg, J., Solomon, S., Pyszczynski, T., & Lyon, D. (1989). Evidence for terror management theory: I. The effects of mortality salience on reactions to those who violate or uphold cultural values. *Journal of Personality and Social Psychology, 57,* 681–690. doi:10.1037/0022-3514.57.4.681

Rothschild, Z. K., Abdollahi, A., & Pyszczynski, T. (2009). Does peace have a prayer? The effect of mortality salience, compassionate values, and religious fundamentalism on hostility toward ourgroups. *Journal of Experimental Social Psychology, 45,* 816–827. doi:10.1016/j.jesp.2009.05.016

Sachdeva, S., Iliev, R., & Medin, D. L. (2009). Sinning saints and saintly sinners: The paradox of moral self-regulation. *Psychological Science, 20,* 523–528. doi:10.1111/j.1467-9280.2009.02326.x

Vaes, J., Heflick, N. A., & Goldenberg, J. L. (2010). "We are people": In-group humanization as an existential defense. *Journal of Personality and Social Psychology, 98,* 750–760. doi:10.1037/a0017658

Wright, R. (2009). *The evolution of God.* New York, NY: Little, Brown.

19

MORAL CONVICTIONS AND MORAL COURAGE: COMMON DENOMINATORS OF GOOD AND EVIL

LINDA J. SKITKA

Moral courage is a rarer commodity than bravery in battle or great intelligence. Yet it is the one essential, vital quality for those who seek to change a world that yields most painfully to change.

—Robert F. Kennedy

We have no government armed with power capable of contending with human passions unbridled by morality.

—John Adams

On June 5, 1989, one day after the Chinese government's violent crackdown on the Tiananmen protests, a man placed himself directly in the path of a column of tanks that were approaching the square. He acted alone, holding nothing but one shopping bag in each hand. As the lead tank attempted to drive around him, the man calmly moved to continue to block the path of the tank, flapping the bags to signal his insistence that the tanks halt. After repeatedly trying to go around rather than run over the man, the lead tank stopped its engines, and the armored vehicles behind it seemed to follow suit. After some attempts at communication, the tanks restarted their engines apparently in anticipation of moving on, but the man jumped in front of the lead tank and continued his pattern of passively blocking the tank's movements. This showdown continued, and a crowd grew to watch with amazement as the dance between man and tank unfolded. Eventually two men (presumed to be secret service) emerged from the crowd and escorted the man away. Those close to the situation believe that the "Unknown Rebel" was likely executed in the

Thanks to Brad Lytle, G. Scott Morgan, Nicole Mayer, William McCready, and Daniel Wisneski for their comments on a previous version of this manuscript.

aftermath of the military crackdown on Tiananmen protesters; the Chinese government was never able to produce him after photos and videotape of the incident became public (Witty, 2009).

On the morning of May 31, 2009, Dr. George Tiller, a father of four and a grandfather of 10 children, was serving as an usher at Lutheran Reform Church in Wichita, Kansas. He was standing in the foyer of the church when he was approached by a man who raised a gun and shot Dr. Tiller once in the head, which instantly killed him. The assailant—Scott Roeder—threatened to shoot two other men who attempted to apprehend him at the scene, then got into his car and drove away. These witnesses later provided the police with the license plate number of the car Roeder was driving, and police apprehended him a couple of hours later. Dr. Tiller owned and operated one of the only abortion clinics in Kansas. Prolife political action groups had specifically targeted Dr. Tiller's clinic for protests and legal action, in part because his clinic provided late-term abortions when they were medically indicated. Roeder had previously posted anti-Tiller comments on various Internet sites; for example, one postdated September 3, 2007, placed on a site sponsored by Operation Rescue, claimed "Tiller is the concentration camp 'Mengele' of our day and needs to be stopped." Many prolife organizations condemned Roeder's behavior, but others (most notably the Army of God) embraced Roeder and even launched a "Scott Roeder: American Hero" website.[1]

Whether one agrees or disagrees with the positions, beliefs, or actions of the Unknown Rebel or Scott Roeder, each demonstrated moral courage—a willingness to personally stand up and stand out in defense of a principle, even when others were standing aside. In this chapter, I cover two topics related to the issue of moral courage. First, I challenge the accepted wisdom in social psychology that certain kinds of strong situations almost inevitably overwhelm people's motivation and willingness to take a stand in the name of their moral beliefs. Although there is evidence that people are inclined to obey authorities and conform to group norms, until recently few studies measured whether people are as likely to do so when their core moral convictions are at stake. Second, although some acts of moral courage are likely to be interpreted by observers as relatively unambiguous goods, I show that good and evil sometimes become less clear when acts of moral courage are related to actors' political, social, or cultural beliefs. The same behavior can be interpreted as good or evil depending on which side of the fence the perceiver happens to be on or which group the perceiver belongs to. Good and evil may therefore at times represent post hoc and subjective categorizations, not differences in the motivational foundations of the behavior being judged (A. G. Miller, 2004).

---

[1]http://www.armyofgod.com/POCScottRoederIndexPage.html

Before turning to evidence that challenges the view that strong situations overwhelm the capacity for moral courage and a discussion of the normative implications of this construct when attributing good versus evil, I first provide some theoretical and empirical background on the concept of moral courage and whether strong situations overwhelm the potential for its expression.

MORAL COURAGE

Moral courage is a willingness to take a stand in defense of principle or conviction, even when others do not (W. I. Miller, 2000). People who exhibit moral courage are often subject to a number of risks associated with taking a stand, including inconvenience, unpopularity, ostracism, disapproval, derision, and even harm to themselves or their kin. Although moral courage may have costs, it "does not back you fearfully into dangerous corners so much as draw you inexorably toward first principles. It is less about risks, hazards, obstacles, and [more] about values, virtues, standards, and rightness" (W. I. Miller, 2000, p. 36).

Several decades of work in social psychology reveal that strong situations seem to have the power to undermine or overwhelm people's moral courage. Strong situations can make even clearly normal, moral, and good people do what most would consider to be very bad things (see Zimbardo, 2005, for a review). Two of these situational constraints are reviewed next, along with some reasons for skepticism about whether they conclusively demonstrate the suppression of moral courage.

DO POWERFUL SITUATIONS OVERWHELM THE POTENTIAL FOR MORAL COURAGE?

Although one can certainly find other examples as well, two programs of research are among the most frequently cited as the strongest examples of the power of situational factors to shift people's behavior in general and to depart from moral norms in particular: Milgram's research on destructive obedience and Asch's and others' research on conformity. We turn to a brief review of this evidence next.

The Milgram Obedience Studies

One of the most convincing and famous demonstrations of the power of situations was a series of experiments on destructive obedience conducted by

Stanley Milgram (1974). In these studies, an authority figure commanded participants to inflict painful electric shocks on another person. More often than not, participants complied with the authority's commands and gave what they believed to be increasingly powerful shocks, even when the presumed victim protested that the shocks were not only uncomfortable but were aggravating a preexisting heart problem. Milgram (1974) interpreted the results of these studies in the following way:

> Ordinary people, simply doing their jobs, and without any particular hostility on their part, can become agents in a terrible destructive process. Moreover, even when the destructive effects of their work become patently clear, and they are asked to carry out actions incompatible with fundamental standards of morality, relatively few people have the resources needed to resist authority. (p. 6)

In summary, Milgram argued that people's overwhelming sense of obligation to obey authorities trumped their normal sense of conscience or morality, which would suggest that they should do no harm.

The view that people's personal moral standards become less relevant, or even functionally irrelevant, when they come into conflict with the commands or decisions of legitimate authorities, however, seems open to alternative explanations and conclusions. For example, Milgram did not establish whether his participants perceived the choice between defying and complying with the experimenter's requests as a trade-off between their personal morality and a duty to obey; rather, he assumed that his participants saw the situation in this light (see Doris, 1998, for a similar critique). Similarly, most studies that have examined people's willingness to accept negative decisions when they are made by legitimate or procedurally fair authorities do not measure whether perceivers have a moral stake in these situations rather than, for example, only a material stake in them. To know for certain whether people are willing to sacrifice their moral beliefs because of a duty or obligation to obey legitimate authorities, it seems necessary to know, first, what those moral beliefs are and, second, whether people see these beliefs as relevant to the situation at hand (an issue I return to shortly).

Conforming to the Group

Another famous demonstration of the power of the situation was a series of experiments conducted by Solomon Asch. In one version of the experiment, a naive participant showed up at the lab, only to discover that he was the last to arrive at the session. The other eight or 10 participants for that session had already arrived and were seated around a table (the other participants were actually working for the experimenter as confederates). Participants were told that the experiment was testing people's visual judgments and that their task was to say which of three different lines matched a standard. On some trials, all the other participants, one by one, claimed that an obviously incorrect line matched the standard. Surprisingly, more than half of the real participants went along with the majority on these trials, even though the majority of the group were clearly giving the wrong answer. These results led Asch (1955) to conclude that

> the tendency to conformity in our society is so strong that reasonably intelligent and well-meaning young people are willing to call white black. This is a matter of concern. It raises questions about our ways of education and the values that guide our conduct. (p. 34)

Asch had reasons for concern. For example, delinquent behavior is learned through exposure to delinquent companions, who can pressure new group members to conform to antisocial norms. Indeed, exposure to delinquent peers is the most powerful predictor of delinquent behavior (e.g., Warr, 1993). Nor are peer and situational influences on willingness to embrace asocial or illegal behavior limited to youths. For example, dozens of analyses have been conducted on what went wrong at Enron, an American energy company that once had spectacular profits and growth but is now known for one of the most stunning collapses in business history (Jenkins, 2003). Most analyses of what went wrong at Enron focus on its corporate culture, which was characterized by enormous pressure to conform to group norms (e.g., Tourish & Vatcha, 2005). Those who did not quickly get with the program were labeled "chumps" or "losers," or worse (e.g., they were summarily fired). Employees who wanted to survive in the company—and there were incredible financial incentives for them to want to do so—were essentially required to replace their preexisting beliefs and values with those of the group (Tourish & Vatcha, 2005). The outcome was an environment dominated by what has been described as *bounded choice* (Lalich, 2004), a context in which the expression of only a limited and tightly regulated repertoire of beliefs, behaviors, and emotions was permissible. There was little room for employees to focus on honesty or ethics when the corporate culture was consumed instead with generating unprecedented profits and growth.

Although it is clear that groups can have an incredible influence on whether and when people engage in immoral or unethical conduct, the notion that people consciously reject their moral compasses to conform to group norms in contexts like Enron is often based on inference rather than direct empirical tests. Putting the most Machiavellian extremes at Enron aside, the chances are that the majority of Enron professionals were at least initially unaware of the gradual accumulation of pressures on them to slant their conclusions, a process known as *moral seduction* (Moore, Tetlock, Tanlu, & Bazerman,

2006). Moreover, the ethics at Enron and elsewhere appear to have shifted in focus from what is morally right to what is technically legal (Moore & Loewenstein, 2004). Given what we know about motivated reasoning and self-serving biases in human cognition (Kunda, 1990), it is plausible that people at Enron psychologically managed to recode any possible moral breaches as something else entirely (e.g., behavior that was legally justified).

In summary, the notion that people reject their moral compasses in strong situations has often been inferred from various studies, but it is a question that until recently has seldom if ever been explicitly tested. Recent research suggests that when we directly measure whether people have a moral stake in a given situation, we find that they often muster the moral courage to resist pressures to obey legitimate authorities or follow the crowd.

MORAL CONVICTIONS AS BOUNDARY CONDITIONS ON THE POWER OF STRONG SITUATIONS

Many controversies involve advocates and opponents who see specific issues in terms of self-evident and fundamental truths about right and wrong. To support alternatives to what is "right," "moral," and "good" is to be absolutely "wrong" and "immoral," if not evil. Disagreements about issues that people view in a moral light seem to be closed to compromise—even in the face of pressure from authorities or peers to surrender one's position—because to do so would be to undermine first-order truths or conceptions of the good. More specifically, the strength of people's moral conviction about issues of the day should provide them with the moral courage to resist the usual pressures to obey legitimate authorities or to conform to group norms about those issues. Rationales for these specific predictions are outlined next.

Authority Independence

When people's moral convictions are at stake, they are more likely to believe that duties and rights follow from the greater moral purposes that underlie rules, procedures, and authority's dictates than from the rules, procedures, or authorities themselves (Kohlberg, 1976). Moral beliefs are not by definition antiestablishment or antiauthority, but neither are they dependent on establishment, convention, rules, or authorities. Instead, when people take a moral perspective, they focus more on their ideals and the way they believe things "ought" to or "should" be done than on a duty to comply with authorities.

Given that people often do not know the "right" approach to various decisions or conflicts, or exactly what they should do in novel situations like Milgram's (1974) experiments, they frequently rely on authorities, rules, or laws to provide guidance about appropriate ways to behave. However, when people do have strong moral convictions about what they should do or what outcomes authorities and institutions should deliver, they are more likely to have the moral courage to defy authorities, the rules, or the law. In short, the *authority independence hypothesis* predicts that when people have a personal moral stake in a given situation, they should be less concerned about complying with authorities or the law and more concerned about doing the right thing, even if it may be costly to do so.

Research with both children and adults is consistent with the prediction that people's moral convictions act as constraints on the power of authorities to constrain moral courage. For example, children say that hitting and stealing are wrong, even if a teacher says it is OK (e.g., Nucci & Turiel, 1978). Similarly, children endorse obedience to moral requests (e.g., to stop fighting) made by any person, including other children, but they endorse obedience to norms (e.g., seat assignments) only when a directive comes from legitimate authorities (Laupa, 1994). Moreover, these patterns of results replicate across a wide array of nationalities and religious groups and even when the religiously devout are confronted with counterfactuals about God's authority. For example, people continue to insist that killing would still be wrong even if God were to indicate it was OK (Nucci & Turiel, 1993).

The authority independence hypothesis has also been tested in the context of Americans' reactions to a recent U.S. Supreme Court ruling (*Gonzales v. Oregon*, 2006; Skitka, Bauman, & Lytle, 2009). The Court's task was to decide whether states have the power to legalize physician-assisted suicide. A nationally representative sample of adults was surveyed shortly before the Court heard arguments in the case, and then the same people were surveyed again after the Court made its ruling (the Court decided that states have the right to decide whether physician-assisted suicide is legal within their borders). Participants provided ratings of their support or opposition for physician-assisted suicide, the degree to which these attitudes were moral convictions,[2] and their predecision perceptions of the U.S. Supreme Court's legitimacy. The postruling survey included measures of decision fairness and acceptance, as well as postruling perceptions of the Court's legitimacy.

The authority independence hypothesis predicts that people would be more likely to accept the U.S. Supreme Court's ruling in this case if it was consistent with their morally vested support for legalizing physician-assisted

---

[2]Skitka, Bauman, and Lytle (2009) and Wisneski, Lytle, and Skitka (2009) operationalized moral convictions about physician-assisted suicide in terms of participants' responses to two items: "To what extent are your feelings about physician-assisted suicide a reflection of your core moral values and convictions?" and "To what extent are your feelings about physician-assisted suicide deeply connected to your beliefs about 'right' and 'wrong'?" Participants responded on a 5-point scale from *not at all* to *very much*. These items were strongly correlated, $r = .84$.

suicide. Conversely, people would be more likely to reject the decision as fair or final if their opposition to physician-assisted suicide was morally vested. Finally, this pattern of results should be equally likely regardless of whether people saw the Court as more or less legitimate before it made its ruling in this case and when controlling for whether their position on physician-assisted suicide was deeply connected to their personal religious beliefs. Results supported each of these hypotheses (Skitka et al., 2009). Similar results emerged in a variety of more controlled experiments (e.g., Bauman & Skitka, 2009; Skitka & Houston, 2001) and in other field studies of people's reactions to actual legal decisions (e.g., Skitka & Mullen, 2002).

Moreover, people's moral convictions about physician-assisted suicide not only predicted people's reactions to the Court's decision in the *Gonzales v. Oregon* case but also affected their preruling trust in the Court to get the question of physician-assisted suicide right in the first place (Wisneski, Lytle, & Skitka, 2009). Regardless of whether they supported or opposed physician-assisted suicide, those whose positions reflected strong moral convictions distrusted the Court to get the issue right. Moreover, this distrust reflected a quick and visceral response: Those with stronger moral convictions responded to the distrust item more quickly than those whose position on physician-assisted suicide reflected weak moral convictions (again, controlling for a number of alternative explanations, including attitude importance and religious conviction). In short, people not only react to decisions with which they morally disagree; they do not trust even legitimate authorities to make the right decision in the first place.

There is also behavioral support for the prediction that people reject authorities and the rule of law when outcomes violate their moral convictions. For example, Mullen and Nadler (2008) exposed people to legal decisions that supported, opposed, or were unrelated to their moral convictions. The experimenters distributed a pen with a postexposure questionnaire and asked participants to return the questionnaire and pen at end of the experimental session. Consistent with the prediction that decisions, rules, and laws that violate people's moral convictions erode the power of authorities and authority systems who decide these things, participants were more likely to steal the pen after exposure to a legal decision that was inconsistent rather than consistent with their personal moral convictions.

In summary, there is growing evidence that people make important distinctions between different judgmental and attitudinal domains and are much less likely to blindly follow authority's dictates when they are at odds with their personal moral convictions. Instead, even young children have the moral courage to defy legitimate authorities when authorities make decisions or requests that are directly at odds with their situationally relevant and activated moral beliefs. Similarly, adults feel no compulsion to accept even one of the most legitimate and trusted authorities in the United States (the U.S. Supreme Court) as having the final say about controversial issues of the day. In these cases, people are more likely to change their view of the Court than to change their minds about their fundamental beliefs about right and wrong (Skitka et al., 2009).

The Inoculation Hypothesis

That people usually conform to majority opinion in a group is well known (see Cialdini & Trost, 1998, for a review). The reason why people conform to group norms even when they individually have a contrary point of view stems in part from fears that going against group norms places one at risk for ridicule and disenfranchisement and in part from hopes that going along with the group will maintain or build acceptance and belonging (Asch, 1956). At other times, people conform because they are not confident about the right answer or the best way to behave, and they turn to peers for guidance and information (e.g., Deutsch & Gerard, 1955).

When people have strong moral convictions about a specific issue, however, they prefer to distance themselves from attitudinally dissimilar others' convictions (e.g., Haidt, Rosenberg, & Horn, 2003; Skitka, Bauman, & Sargis, 2005). They should therefore have little need to look to peers to discover the "right answer" in that attitude domain. In other words, when people have strong moral convictions about a given issue, they should be more resistant to majority influence because they have less need to be accepted by the group or to use consensus as a source of information.

In addition, because people experience moral convictions much like facts (wrong is wrong, right is right, end of story), there is little room for the group to provide informational influence. Finally, failing to defend a matter of perception (e.g., "Which line matches the standard?"), as people did in the classic Asch (1956) studies, has little cost in the form of shame, guilt, or moral inauthenticity to those who conform. In contrast, people are likely to experience a failure to defend their core moral convictions as a deep threat to their personal sense of moral authenticity. For these reasons, majority group influence, conformity, and other forms of social influence should be weaker for those with strong compared with weak moral convictions in the domains of attempted influence (the *inoculation hypothesis*).

Consistent with the inoculation hypothesis, strong moral convictions about a given issue do protect people from the usual pressures to capitulate to group norms or majority opinion. For example, Hornsey, Majkut, Terry, and McKimmie (2003) tested whether people would be more resistant to group norms when their attitudes had a moral dimension. Participants first indicated their support for or opposition to gay law reform and a number of other issues and then reported the degree to which their attitude about gay law reform reflected a moral conviction.[3] Participants were then told that the study in which they were participating was part of a much wider program of research that had been ongoing for some time. Using a procedure that has been established as inducing normative influence (White, Hogg, & Terry, 2002), participants (all of whom supported gay law reform to some degree) were presented with three graphs that presumably summarized the results of the last 3 years' worth of survey results. The graphs indicated that the student body was roughly evenly divided on two of the filler issues that participants had rated earlier but were very united in either their support of or opposition to the question of whether gay couples should be legally recognized. In the support condition, participants were told that, on average, 85% of the student body supported, 8% opposed, and 7% were undecided about whether gay couples should be legally recognized. In the oppose condition, participants learned that 85% of the student body opposed, 8% supported, and 7% were undecided about this issue. After being exposed to consensus information that they were either in the opinion minority or majority, participants rated their degree of willingness to engage in a variety of public actions (e.g., sign a letter to the editor, distribute information leaflets) or private behaviors (e.g., sign a petition, vote in a referendum) to support gay legal reform.

Consistent with the inoculation hypothesis that moral convictions buffer people from conformity pressure, strength of moral convictions emerged as a strong predictor of moral courage, operationalized as a stated willingness to engage in both public and private behavior in support of gay legal reform. More important for the argument being advanced here, however, is the fact that although degree of normative support (i.e., whether participants believed they were in the opinion minority or majority) affected whether those with weak moral convictions about legal reform were willing to engage in private acts of support (i.e., as normative support of their position increased, they were more willing to do private things to support the cause), degree of normative support had no effect on the willingness of those with strong moral convictions to do so. Rather, their willingness to sign a letter, for example, remained high (and higher than those with weak moral convictions) even when they were in the opinion minority.

Other results indicated that normative support or opposition did not significantly moderate the main effect of moral conviction on willingness to engage in public behavior in support of legal reforms. In other words, those with

---

[3]Hornsey, Majkut, Terry, and McKimmie (2003) used a three-item scale to assess moral conviction: (1) "To what extent do you feel your opinion is morally correct?" (2) "To what extent do you feel your position is based on strong personal principles?" and (3) "To what extent do you feel your position on gay law reform is a moral stance?" Responses were recorded using a 1–9 scale from *not at all* to *very much*; $\alpha = .73$.

stronger moral convictions were more likely to say they would engage in more public acts in support of the cause than were those with weaker moral convictions, regardless of whether they were in the opinion minority or majority. Moreover, these results emerged even when statistically controlling for plausible alternative explanations for the moral conviction effects, such as attitude extremity or strength (Hornsey et al., 2003; see also Hornsey, Smith, & Begg, 2007).

This initial research explored whether consensus affected people's decisions to take a stand in the name of their moral beliefs, with very promising results. However, it remained unclear whether self-reported intentions to voice one's opinion translated to actual behavior. Therefore, we recently tested whether strength of moral conviction predicted actual expression of one's opinion in the presence of a majority of one's peers who had a different opinion (Aramovich, Lytle, & Skitka, 2009). Hypotheses were tested in the context of recent public discussions about the permissibility of torture in interrogating suspected terrorists. Even though nearly every society and moral system condemns the use of torture, and despite recent outcries about Abu Ghraib, more than half of Americans say they support the use of torture when interrogating suspected terrorists. Perhaps more surprising, public support for the use of torture has been increasing rather than decreasing since 2005 (Sidoti, 2009).

To test whether people's moral convictions protect them from majority influence in the context of their positions about torture, we created a conformity paradigm inspired by Asch (1956) to measure participants' behavioral responses to a majority of peers who expressed a viewpoint opposed to that of the participants. More specifically, participants in this study provided their preexperimental positions on torture of suspected terrorists and the degree to which their attitude on the issue reflected a strong moral conviction (along with completing a number of attitude strength control measures) during a mass testing session at the beginning of the semester. (To reduce the specific salience of torture, the torture items were embedded in a longer questionnaire assessing attitudes toward a variety of issues.)

Several weeks later, participants who had indicated that they opposed the use of torture came into a laboratory for small-group sessions in which they sat at individual computer carrels. Participants were told that they were participating in a study to examine the effect of computer-mediated communication on a subsequent face-to-face small group discussion. They were also told that the goal of the in-person group discussion was to draft a short position statement summarizing the group's opinion about the use of torture. Prior to this discussion they would share their opinions with one another over the computer.

Participants met their fellow "group members" by sharing their initials, which were displayed to everyone in the "group" via a computer program. (All computerized feedback was in fact preprogrammed; although all participants thought they were interacting through their computer with other people in the room, they were actually receiving preprogrammed responses from the other group members.) Participants were instructed that they would, in a randomly determined order, share their opinions about the use of torture. In every case, however, the true participant was always selected to share his or her opinion last. Other group members' positions were displayed at 10- to 11-s intervals, and they respectively reported "strong support," "moderate support," or "slight support" of the use of torture against suspected terrorists (in that order). After viewing all four group members' opinions, participants shared their own opinion, at which point the experiment concluded (there was no subsequent face-to-face discussion).

Moral conviction associated with participants' opposition to the use of torture emerged as the strongest predictor of resistance to majority influence in this experiment, regardless of whether attitude change was measured continuously (degree of change from preexperimental positions) or nominally (i.e., changing sides from opposition to support of the use of torture). These results emerged even when controlling for attitude certainty and importance.

In summary, there is considerable evidence that people's moral convictions protect them not only from pressures to blindly obey or comply with authorities' commands and decisions but also from various other kinds of strong pressure to set aside their beliefs, including the pressure of majority group influence. Moral convictions demonstrably provide people with the moral courage and fortitude to "go it alone" if necessary and to defend their point of view, even when it is very lonely to stand up for what they are convinced is right.

REVISITING THE NORMATIVE IMPLICATIONS OF MORAL COURAGE

Heroism has been defined as the commitment to a noble purpose and the willingness to accept the consequences of fighting for that purpose (Franco & Zimbardo, 2006), a definition that seems quite consistent with what would count as an act rooted in moral courage. Moral courage and the capacity for heroism have typically been seen as basic goods—traits worth celebrating and encouraging as much as possible. Behaviors and actions that one person might interpret as acts of moral courage or heroism, however, seem to be profoundly influenced by whether those actions are consistent or inconsistent with the political, social, moral, or cultural views of the perceiver.

For example, although it is easy to see how a figure such as Oskar Schindler, who saved close to 1,200 Jews during the Second World War, might count as a hero, it is also not too difficult to imagine that he would have been seen as a traitor by the victors if Nazi Germany had won the war.

The men who flew airplanes into the World Trade Center and the Pentagon in 2001 undoubtedly believed that their actions and cause were noble, and they clearly accepted the ultimate personal cost of their actions. Few in the United States would say that these actions were moral or heroic, but more than 67% of respondents in a Gallup poll of nine Muslim countries did so (George, 2002).

In short, there seems to be a difficult, very fine, and subjective line between our definitions of who is to be counted as a hero and martyr and who is to be condemned as an evildoer and villain; both great good and great evil can be perpetrated in the name of noble and morally esteemed ends (see Chapters 18 and 20, this volume). As important as it is for social psychologists to study the psychological processes that lead to good and evil acts, it is equally important not to let our values about what counts as good or evil blind us to the possibility that others have an opposing but equally "moral" (by their standards) view. Without denying the reality of psychopathy and genuine evil, in many cases the people who perpetrate evil acts are motivated by beliefs that they feel are noble and morally inspired. Scott Roeder, for example, probably did not wake up on May 31, 2009, and say to himself, "Today is a good day to do evil." From all accounts, his position was, instead, "Today I'm going to rid the world of evil and save thousands of lives in the process."

Although some claim that the only way for people to overcome the usual self-sanctions against doing harm to others is to morally disengage and shut down normal moral self-regulatory functioning (Bandura, 1999), it seems more likely that people must be maximally morally engaged to reject the safety of "going along" and instead fight for their beliefs about right and wrong. Scott Roeder and the Unknown Rebel did not morally shut down; they morally revved up and found moral courage to do what they thought was right. That said, their actions may be judged as wrongheaded in the extreme. One's interpretation of their behavior as good or evil, brave or foolhardy, however, does not change the motivation that led them to take their respective stands. A complete psychological portrait of what leads to evil in the world, and not just to heroism, requires paying attention to the role that moral courage plays in motivating people to take a stand even when it means risking rejection of authorities and the rule of law, loss of the safety of normative support, censure and demonization by those with different views, and the possibility of jail or death.

It is therefore extremely important to study and understand the psychology of moral conviction and courage. As mentioned at the beginning of this chapter, Robert F. Kennedy argued that "moral courage . . . is the one essential, vital quality for those who seek to change a world that yields most painfully to change." Without moral courage, we would not see the advancement of women's literacy in Afghanistan, greater civil rights and economic growth among groups historically discriminated against in United States and elsewhere, or increased freedom from human rights violations in many parts of the world. Nor did many of the gains in these areas come without the price of blood. The American Civil War and the assassination of Martin Luther King, Jr., for example, were among the costs of the fight for civil rights.

Even if we come to the conclusion that great evil can spring from the same functional and motivational foundations as great good, we cannot afford to extinguish the human capacity for moral conviction and courage. What we need to do instead is come to a better understanding of the role of these motivations in human affairs and discover better ways to channel them toward a consensual conception of the good. A willingness to reject authorities, the rule of law, and even the influence of one's closest peers when one knows what is "right" may constitute the best of human nature if these actions are ultimately in the name of the greater good. Finding agreement on what constitutes the greater good, however, would seem to present a more difficult challenge than finding people willing to fight for it.

CONCLUSION

The power of the situation is not to be underestimated when trying to understand why people sometimes do horrible things. That said, the mantra that situations consistently overwhelm people's everyday commitments to their moral beliefs and convictions may be overstated. Few of the classic studies of the power of the situation directly tested the core hypothesis that morality was overwhelmed in the contexts studied. Because a great deal of blind obedience to authority was observed in Milgram's (1974) studies, for example, it was assumed that participants' moral convictions had been superseded. The analysis presented in this chapter does not undercut the conclusion that the majority of people in the Milgram (1974) studies complied, or that the majority of delinquents experience considerable peer pressure to engage in crime, or that Enron employees seemed to check their moral compasses at the door. It merely posits that participants' obedience, compliance, or conformity in these situations may have had nothing whatsoever to do with the suppression of active moral concerns.

At first pass, it may seem like very good news indeed to discover that people have the moral courage to resist destructive obedience or conformity to the group when their moral convictions are at stake. Our enthusiasm should be muted, however, because moral courage may not always come in flavors everyone finds palatable. It is all fine and good that people are willing to disregard legitimate authorities, cast off the shackles of law, and disregard peer opinion to do what they autonomously believe is right, moral, and good *if and when* their conception of what is right, moral, and good happens to be consistent with our own. One troubling aspect of moral convictions, however, is that they are associated not only with a greater willingness to reject the usual safeguards of civil societies (e.g., obeying authorities and the law, conforming to group norms), but also with an increased tolerance of violence and vigilantism to achieve preferred ends (e.g., Skitka & Houston, 2001).

The normative implications of these findings are therefore both reassuring and terrifying. Yes, moral conviction and associated moral courage act as a protection against obedience to potentially malevolent authorities or blind conformity to group norms. However, moral convictions also provide a motivational foundation and justification for violence and terrorism. History is replete with atrocities that were justified by invoking the highest principles and that were perpetrated upon victims who were equally convinced of their own moral superiority. Justice, the common welfare, universal ethics, and God have each been used to justify any variety of forms of oppression, murder, and genocide (Mischel & Mischel, 1976). Given that strong moral convictions are associated with accepting any means to achieve preferred ends, gaining more insight into the psychology of how and why moral convictions promote constructive, but potentially also quite destructive, forms of moral courage is a critical agenda for continued scientific investigation.

REFERENCES

Aramovich, N. P., Lytle, B. L., & Skitka, L. J. (2009, May). *We're not judging lines anymore: Moral mandates reduce conformity to the group.* Poster presented at the annual meeting of the Association for Psychological Science, San Francisco, CA.

Asch, S. E. (1955). Opinions and social pressure. *Scientific American, 19,* 31–35. doi:10.1038/scientificamerican1155-31

Asch, S. E. (1956). Studies of independence and conformity: A minority of one against a unanimous majority. *Psychological Monographs, 70,* 1–70.

Bandura, A. (1999). Moral disengagement in the perception of inhumanities. *Personality and Social Psychology Review, 3,* 193–209. doi:10.1207/s15327957pspr0303_3

Bauman, C. W., & Skitka, L. J. (2009). Moral conflict and procedural justice: Moral mandates as constraints to voice effects. *Australian Journal of Psychology, 61,* 40–49. doi:10.1080/00049530802607647

Cialdini, R. B., & Trost, M. R. (1998). Social influence: Social norms, conformity, and compliance. In D. T. Gilbert, S. T. Fiske, & G. Lindzey (Eds.), *The handbook of social psychology* (4th ed., pp. 151–192). New York, NY: Oxford University Press.

Deutsch, M., & Gerard, H. B. (1955). A study of normative and informational social influences upon individual judgment. *Journal of Abnormal and Social Psychology, 51,* 629–636. doi:10.1037/h0046408

Doris, J. M. (1998). Persons, situations, and virtue ethics. *Nous, 32*, 504–530. doi:10.1111/0029-4624.00136

Franco, Z., & Zimbardo, P. (2006). The banality of heroism. *Greater Good, 3*, 30–35.

George, L. (2002, March 3). Muslims skeptical on terror war. Retrieved from http://www.cnn.com/2002/WORLD/europe/03/03/gallup.reaction

Gonzales v. Oregon, 546 U.S. 243 (2006).

Haidt, J., Rosenberg, E., & Hom, H. (2003). Differentiating diversities: Moral diversity is not like other kinds. *Journal of Applied Social Psychology, 33*, 1–36. doi:10.1111/j.1559-1816.2003.tb02071.x

Hornsey, M. J., Majkut, L., Terry, D. J., & McKimmie, B. M. (2003). On being loud and proud: Non-conformity and counter-conformity to group norms. *British Journal of Social Psychology, 42*, 319–335. doi:10.1348/014466603322438189

Hornsey, M. J., Smith, J. R., & Begg, D. (2007). Effects of norms among those with moral conviction: Counter-conformity emerges on intentions but not behaviors. *Social Influence, 4*, 244–268. doi:10.1080/15534510701476500

Jenkins, R. (2003). Crisis of confidence in corporate America. *Mid-American Journal of Business, 18*, 5–7.

Kohlberg, L. (1976). Moral stages and moralization: The cognitive developmental approach. In T. Lickona (Ed.), *Moral development and behavior: Theory, research and social issues* (pp. 31–53). New York, NY: Holt, Rinehart, & Winston.

Kunda, Z. (1990). The case for motivated reasoning. *Psychological Bulletin, 108*, 480–498.

Lalich, J. (2004). *Bounded choice: True believers and charismatic cults*. Berkeley, CA: University of California Press.

Laupa, M. (1994). Who's in charge? Preschool children's concepts of authority. *Early Childhood Research Quarterly, 9*, 1–17. doi:10.1016/0885-2006(94)90026-4

Milgram, S. (1974). *Obedience to authority*. New York, NY: Harper & Row.

Miller, A. G. (2004). Introduction and overview. In A. G. Miller (Ed.), *The social psychology of good and evil* (pp. 1–20). New York, NY: Guilford Press.

Miller, W. I. (2000). *The mystery of courage*. Cambridge, MA: Harvard University Press.

Mischel, W., & Mischel, H. N. (1976). A cognitive–social learning approach to socialization and self-regulation. In T. Likona (Ed.), *Moral development and behavior: Theory, research, and social issues* (pp. 84–107). New York, NY: Holt, Rinehart, & Winston.

Moore, D. A., & Loewenstein, G. (2004). Self-interest, automaticity, and the psychology of conflict of interest. *Social Justice Research, 17*, 189–202. doi:10.1023/B:SORE.0000027409.88372.b4

Moore, D. A., Tetlock, P. E., Tanlu, L., & Bazerman, M. H. (2006). Conflicts of interest and the case of auditor independence: Moral seduction and strategic issue cycling. *Academy of Management Review, 31*, 10–29.

Mullen, E., & Nadler, J. (2008). Moral spillovers: The effect of moral violations on deviant behavior. *Journal of Experimental Social Psychology, 44*, 1239–1245. doi:10.1016/j.jesp.2008.04.001

Nucci, L., & Turiel, E. (1993). God's word, religious rules, and their relations to Christian and Jewish children's concepts of morality. *Child Development, 64,* 1475–1491. doi:10.2307/1131547

Nucci, L. P., & Turiel, E. (1978). Social interactions and the development of social concepts in pre-school children. *Child Development, 49,* 400–407. doi:10.2307/1128704

Sidoti, L. (2009, June 3). Poll: Half of Americans think torture is sometimes justified. *Huffington Post.* Retrieved from http://www.huffingtonpost.com/2009/06/03/poll-slight-majority-of-a_n_210700.html

Skitka, L. J., Bauman, C. W., & Lytle, B. L. (2009). The limits of legitimacy: Moral and religious convictions as constraints on deference to authority. *Journal of Personality and Social Psychology, 97,* 567–578. doi:10.1037/a0015998

Skitka, L. J., Bauman, C. W., & Sargis, E. G. (2005). Moral conviction: Another contributor to attitude strength or something more? *Journal of Personality and Social Psychology, 88,* 895–917. doi:10.1037/0022-3514.88.6.895

Skitka, L. J., & Houston, D. (2001). When due process is of no consequence: Moral mandates and presumed defendant guilt or innocence. *Social Justice Research, 14,* 305–326.

Skitka, L. J., & Mullen, E. (2002). Understanding judgments of fairness in a real-world political context: A test of the value protection model of justice reasoning. *Personality and Social Psychology Bulletin, 28,* 1419–1429. doi:10.1177/014616702236873

Tourish, D., & Vatcha, D. (2005). Charismatic leadership and corporate cultism at Enron: The elimination of dissent, the promotion of conformity, and organizational collapse. *Leadership, 1,* 455–480. doi:10.1177/1742715005057671

Warr, M. (1993). Age, peers, and delinquency. *Criminology, 31,* 17–40. doi:10.1111/j.1745-9125.1993.tb01120.x

White, K. M., Hogg, M. A., & Terry, D. J. (2002). Improving attitude–behavior correspondence through exposure to normative support from a salient ingroup. *Basic and Applied Social Psychology, 24,* 91–103.

Wisneski, D. C., Lytle, B. L., & Skitka, L. J. (2009). Gut reactions: Moral conviction, religiosity, and trust in authority. *Psychological Science, 20,* 1059–1063. doi:10.1111/j.1467-9280.2009.02406.x

Witty, P. (2009, June 3). Behind the scenes: Tank man of Tiananmen Square. *The New York Times.* Retrieved from http://lens.blogs.nytimes.com/2009/06/03/behind-the-scenes-tank-man-of-tiananmen/

Zimbardo, P. G. (2005). A situationist perspective on the psychology of evil: Understanding how good people are transformed into perpetrators. In A. G. Miller (Ed.), *The psychology of good and evil* (pp. 21–50). New York, NY: Guilford Press.

20

HUMAN EVIL: THE MYTH OF PURE EVIL AND THE TRUE CAUSES OF VIOLENCE

ROY F. BAUMEISTER

Why is there evil? This question has captured the interest of scholars of diverse specialties and backgrounds for centuries. The methods of answering it and the answers themselves have similarly reflected this diversity. My approach is that of a social scientist. The methods and research findings of social scientists can be brought to bear on what for others has been a legal, practical, theological, philosophical, or other kind of problem.

One obstacle for the social scientist is the conflict between the inherent immorality of the topic and the professional scientist's goal of unbiased neutrality. Social scientists are not supposed to let their values cloud their judgment, because doing so can impede the impartial search for truth. But can we view the crimes of Hitler and his minions with the same dispassionate and nonjudgmental attitude with which we observe the bar pressing of rats in a Skinner box?

When doing research for my book on evil (Baumeister, 1997), I was struck by how routinely other social scientists rushed to assert that this was not really a problem. To understand is not to forgive, they insisted. Yet I was not so sure. Indeed, my own work pointed toward different conclusions. In particular, as we understand the perpetrators' inner processes and attitudes, we come to see their crimes as considerably less heinous than how others judge them. Most people who commit evil acts do not themselves regard their actions as evil. Therefore, to understand their perspective is to understand the actions in a way that somehow diminishes their evilness. To be sure, as researchers and scientists our primary goal is to understand. Hence, we must perhaps accept that our approach will carry the moral risk of mitigating our condemnation of some of the worst things that human beings do.

The purpose of this chapter is to answer the question "Why is there evil?" from the perspective of psychological research. Because few people regard their own actions as evil, it is necessary to reformulate this question as, "Why do some people do things that other people consider to be evil?" This requires both an understanding of how people perceive evil and why people are motivated to perform certain kinds of actions. Hence, this chapter contains three sections. The first addresses the question of what evil is, including the gap between perception and reality. The second considers the root causes of such behavior. The third turns to the proximal causation, which ultimately may be more tractable than the root causes.

THE MYTH OF PURE EVIL

What is evil? Most people seem to think that intentionally harming someone who is innocent and undeserving of such treatment constitutes evil (e.g., see Chapters 1 and 21, this volume). Beyond harm, exploitation and oppression may be included in the definition. For some, this can include actions that have been explicitly prohibited by some presumably unassailable authority, such as religious divinities and those who speak for them.

As I said, however, most people whose acts are condemned as evil do not see their own actions as evil. For example, they may recognize that they harm or exploit someone but believe that the action is justified or that the victim deserved to be treated that way (for instructive examples, see Chapter 8, this volume). If we as social scientists restrict our focus to actions that everyone, including the perpetrator, agrees are evil, we will have almost nothing to study. It is therefore necessary to define evil as in the eye of the beholder, who may be victim or observer but is probably not the perpetrator. And this means that evil is defined in a way that is not strongly tethered to objective reality.

Let us begin with perception. To understand the perception of evil, it is useful to look at assorted sources, from comic books and second-rate movies to wartime propaganda and theological sources. When I did this, I found some impressive parallels and consistencies that held up across diverse representations. These I assembled into a composite that I labeled the *myth of pure evil*. Not every case necessarily shows all these characteristics, of course. But in general, they do go together more often than not.

Perceptions are important for more than simply providing a working definition or even as a straw man theory against which objective data can be assembled. The sense that there is evil in the world is widespread. If people perceive the actions of others through the lens of the myth of pure evil, then they are likely to assimilate actual cases and behaviors to it. Thus, the actions of perpetrators are likely to be misperceived to some degree. Indeed, from what we know about social psychology, it would be utterly shocking if victims and observers were to perceive the actions of evildoers in wholly impartial, unbiased, objective terms. The likely fact of these distortions already suggests, however, that the perpetrators of violent and exploitative actions may have a legitimate claim to having been misunderstood and unfairly condemned. For example, to their victims, terrorists are malignant evildoers who pointlessly attack and kill innocent people, but the terrorists themselves typically regard themselves as fighting for freedom, dignity, and other rights, and they may even perceive their victims as accomplices in oppression. That is not to say they are fully innocent of wrongdoing. But it suggests that it is very possible in the majority of cases that their actions were not as terrible as some of their accusers say. This is not a pleasant conclusion, but it is hard to dismiss.

The myth of pure evil may also be important for us as social scientists to understand for methodological reasons. We researchers are people, too, and come to the problem of evil with the same ideas, images, and prejudices that others in our cultures have. Our initial tendency is to view the perpetrators of evil through the lens of this myth and to assimilate their actions to it. In a revealing passage in *The Nazi Doctors,* psychiatrist Robert Jay Lifton (1986) remarked that when interviewing some of these men, he occasionally began to see the world and the events as the men themselves had seen them and then felt some sympathy toward them. At that point, Lifton said, he always pulled back and reminded himself that this person was an evil monster, not a decent human being like the rest of us.

Although I sympathize with Lifton's (1986) moral convictions, to me that point of pulling back is precisely where he failed as a social scientist. The example captures the dilemma I noted earlier—the conflict between scientific understanding of evil and moral judgment of it. To refuse to understand the perpetrators in their own terms is ultimately to abandon the project of scientific understanding in favor of moral condemnation. My preferred view is that if you want to understand, then you may have to set aside moral judgments. These people were, after all, people, not evil monsters. We may condemn them and their actions, and indeed we should, but perhaps we cannot do that precisely while we are trying to understand them scientifically. Refusing to recognize the humanity of the perpetrator is probably an insuperable obstacle to fully understanding the genesis of his or her violent acts.

The proper moral condemnation of evil should not be neglected either, however, lest the researchers lose some of their own humanity. When we are done trying to understand the doings of evil scientifically, it may be necessary to deliberately resume the appropriate moral pose and condemn these wrongful acts.

What, then, are the main features of the myth of pure evil? The first component, as I hinted earlier, is the intentional harming of another person. Evil as depicted in sources ranging from children's cartoons to wartime propaganda emphasizes harming others. It is, moreover, harm done deliberately and intentionally. It does not include harm that is designed to benefit the person, as a dentist or surgeon might drill or cut into someone's body.

Second, the perpetrators of evil are typically portrayed as enjoying the harm they inflict. Even Satan, the biblical epitome of evil, is sometimes depicted as a trickster who takes a sporting pleasure in bringing misfortune on his hapless victims. The link to reality is tenuous here. Victim accounts often emphasize that the perpetrators were laughing or smiling or that in some other way they derived pleasure from what they did. Perpetrators' accounts are far, far less likely to indicate enjoyment. The victims' insistence on perpetrator enjoyment may thus be to some extent an assimilation of perception to the myth. To perceive the perpetrators as human beings who reluctantly and with anguished inner struggles inflicted harm is to make them seem less evil, in comparison to perpetrators who cheerfully go about their actions and derive pleasure from them. In myth, at least, the latter prevail. Film actors who depict bad guys must usually master a wicked smile and laugh that they use when setting about their dastardly deeds.

Third, the victim is typically depicted in accounts of evil as innocent and good. In many homicides, for example, if the story is fully and objectively reconstructed, one sees a pattern of mutual, even escalating provocations. Yet in the myth, the victims bear no responsibility for what happened to them. There are certainly cases of wholly innocent victims, of course, but they are probably far less common than the myth suggests. And certainly relatively few of the killers regard their victims as wholly innocent and undeserving. (Just to be clear, none of this justifies or excuses killing a person. The point is simply that many killings represent an overreaction to perceived misbehavior or provocation by the victim, which is different from the popular myth that depicts them as unprovoked, gratuitous murder of wholly innocent victims.)

In writing up a series of experiments on how news depictions stoke fear of crime, Heath (1984) compared two different versions of an actual news event. Unknown assailants burst into the home of a suburban couple and viciously beat them, leaving the man in the hospital in serious condition. Nothing was stolen, and the assailants remained at large. Many news outlets reported the crime in precisely those terms, which understandably stimulated fear among readers and viewers that such random violence was occurring in their community. Meanwhile, other reports added that the male victim had recently been indicted on charges of promoting juvenile prostitution. Consumers who were exposed to that version of the story—which thus departed in a crucial manner from the myth of pure evil—were understandably less frightened by it. It is of course possible that the victim's prior activity of luring girls into sexual exploitation was entirely irrelevant to the attack on him, and so one could say that omitting those details was justifiable. But that seems unlikely. Random crimes against wholly innocent victims do occur, but probably not as often as the news coverage makes it seem.

Fourth, the perpetrators of evil are often seen as not like us. They are foreign or alien. Earlier I quoted Lifton's (1986) comment about refusing to consider the Nazi doctors as genuine human beings. This reflects the common desire to think that people like us could not possibly perpetrate horrific crimes. Dower's (1986) account of the Pacific theater of World War II emphasized that the mutual demonization by Americans and Japanese was facilitated because both sides could view their enemy as members of a different, depraved race.

A more humorous illustration of the principle that evil is done by foreign or alien beings was an observation by Hesse and Mack (1991) in their study of children's cartoons. They noted that the bad guys generally spoke English with foreign accents. Cartoon characters are not real, and the creators who depict them can make them speak any way they like. Speaking with foreign accents makes them harder to understand. What sense does it make for cartoon filmmakers to make their characters hard to understand? Giving them accents makes them seem foreign and different, hence scarier and less likely to be as moral as "we" are.

The fifth feature, which is probably less common and more prone to exception than the others, is that evil is usually presented as having always been that way. The bad guy in a typical film is not someone who was once good but gradually turned bad over time. Rather, bad guys were that way almost from the start. Satan was supposedly a good angel before time began, but he may always have had rebellious tendencies, and in any case he turned against God before the universe was created. Likewise, we do not ask what unfortunate experiences turned a well-meaning and basically decent Josef Stalin or Adolf Hitler or Pol Pot away from the pursuit of virtue, but rather we ask how such a deeply evil man could have gained the power necessary to put his hateful agenda into practice.

The sixth feature is an alternative to the first. Alongside intentional harm, a second meaning of evil is chaos. Everywhere in the world, most people strive to create a social order characterized by peace, harmony, and stability. Evil is precisely the loss or thwarting of that order. Many horror films begin by depicting happy families or loving couples enjoying a stable, well-ordered life and its legitimate pleasures because that sets up the contrast with the incomprehensible chaos that is about to intrude into their lives.

The final two features are again less universal than the others but nonetheless often found. These are that perpetrators of evil often have inordinate egotism and poor self-control. As I shall suggest, these qualities do bear a significant resemblance to the truth in many cases. Still, as with most myths, they tend to be overstated to the extent of caricature. To those of us who have studied actual perpetrators, it is wearyingly disappointing to see the bad guys in one film after another depicted as relentlessly confident and optimistic. They certainly have high self-esteem. Even when embarking on very risky ventures, they remain convinced of their superiority and of their chances of success. Meanwhile, their lack of self-control is most commonly evident in their proneness to rage and violence. In many movies the bad guys turn on each other when their evil project begins to be thwarted. Setbacks cause those in charge to beat, threaten, or even kill their followers. Have you ever watched an action film and wondered how the bad guys always manage to recruit such large groups of lackeys who are willing to die for them, especially because the punishment for any failure is often death, thus making such jobs an especially poor career choice?

Taken together, these features constitute what I call the myth of pure evil. It is not based on some grand knowledge about what motivates some individuals to perpetrate harm. It may be a product of culture, though I suspect that it will not differ greatly from one culture to another.

ROOT CAUSES OF EVIL

I turn now to the basic, fundamental causes of violence, oppression, exploitation, and cruelty. The myth of pure evil allows many writers to dispense with providing bad guys with realistic, comprehensible motives. Fictional and mythical bad guys were born bad, and they do bad things because they like doing them. With actual human beings, however, there are usually different motives and influences. In attempting to integrate a large and diverse literature, I eventually settled on four basic causes, or perhaps, to be precise, I should say three and a half. Hence, this section focuses on what actually causes violence, which will bear only some resemblance to the myth of pure evil.

The first and perhaps least interesting one to a psychologist is instrumentality. Evil acts are often merely a means to an end. People turn to violence as one means of getting what they want. What they want is typically not so different from what other people want. They want money, land, power, sex, and the like. They turn to violence in some cases because they cannot get what they want by more accepted, legitimate means. Terrorists, for example, are often motivated by the sense that the accepted, legitimate channels of social action, such as democratic voting or the legal system, will not respond to their grievances or give them what they want. Likewise, it is no accident that criminals tend to have relatively low intelligence because in a society that rewards intelligence in many fields, people who lack that trait find they have fewer options than others for obtaining money and other rewards. At the macro level, war and tyrannical oppression are typically the result of a government that thinks it cannot achieve its ends by less violent means.

Over and over, scholars who study various forms of instrumental violence tend to conclude that it is ineffective. In the long run, it usually is. Few criminals become rich and retire to a life of genteel ease and pleasure. Terrorists and assassins do not get the government they want. Wars harm both sides. Domestic abusers do not get the family life they seek. Even imperial colonialism, which is nowadays fashionably decried as a collective evil, was largely a failure. What doomed the 19th century's project of building colonies and empires was less a moral self-awakening than the fact that they did not pay. The short-lived scramble for African colonies, in particular, was motivated by the expectation that the continent's natural resources would enrich the colonial powers, but in fact money mainly flowed in the other direction, and the ongoing costs in money, effort, and sometimes blood became unsustainable, or at least not worth the bother.

Yet that is the long-term perspective. In the short run, violence can be effective. Moreover, as I said, many perpetrators of violence do not believe that they have any other way of getting what they want. And sometimes the initial results seem promising. If you are arguing with your spouse over what television show to watch, and you strike him or her with a frying pan, you may get to watch the show you prefer. Assassins and terrorists do get attention and disrupt the social systems of their enemies. Criminals do sometimes get money and other valuables.

Since writing my book about evil, I have come to look at things in more evolutionary terms, and my strong impression is that instrumental violence is in some respect a hangover from an earlier stage in evolution (Baumeister, 2005). As animals became social, they derived the undeniable benefits of social life, but they also encountered a new set of problems. These include social conflict: Some degree of conflict is probably inevitable in social life. A group hunt may yield delicious food, but the best parts cannot be shared equally by all, and so some method must be used to apportion them. In most animal social groups, aggressive prowess confers status and hence superior access to rewards. The reason the young and weak defer to the alpha male is not respect for tradition or the sacredness of authority, but the simple fact that if you try to take the food he wants, he will beat you up. In this view, intraspecies aggression emerged as an adaptation to social life because it was an effective means to resolve the conflicts that social life makes inevitable.

Aggression enabled the biggest and strongest to survive and hence reproduce better than their weaker rivals.

Human beings have developed culture as a biological strategy. The progress of culture has been to offer alternative, nonviolent means of resolving disputes and conflicts. We have money, courts of law, negotiation, compromise, and voting. Evidence has recently accumulated that the occurrence of interpersonal violence has been in long-term decline (e.g., ever smaller proportions of people die violent deaths at the hands of other people), even despite the horrors of the 20th century; Bloom, in Chapter 4 of this volume, discusses this in terms of the phenomenon of moral progress.

Aggression is thus evolutionarily obsolete. We have accepted better ways of resolving our conflicts. Yet we remain social animals underneath the cultural veneer, and sometimes people fall back on aggression to get their way. This may occur especially among people who feel that the avenues provided by their culture do not work for them.

The second root cause of evil and violence is threatened egotism. When I began my research on evil, I had heard the standard theory that violence is perpetrated by people with low self-esteem. Many authors have repeated this standard assertion (e.g., Anderson, 1994; Levin & McDevitt, 1993; Renzetti, 1992; Staub, 1989). As I searched for the source and evidence, however, it emerged that this was one of those things that everybody knew but nobody had really ever shown. Moreover, the facts repeatedly contradicted it. A large literature review concluded, instead, that perpetrators of violence typically had very favorable views of themselves, sometimes absurdly so (Baumeister, Smart, & Boden, 1996). Likewise, our laboratory experiments on aggression found no shred of support for the low self-esteem theory and instead repeatedly found that narcissists were more aggressive than other categories of people (e.g., Bushman & Baumeister, 1998). When one separates self-esteem from narcissism, the effect of self-esteem is either negligible or, if anything, the opposite of what might be expected. High self-esteem contributes to aggression by compounding the effects of narcissism.

Yet it would be wrong to conclude, simply, that high self-esteem causes violence or that high self-esteem is evil. A more precise formulation is that violence is perpetrated by a subset of people who think well of themselves, and indeed it mainly occurs when they believe that their favorable images of self have been threatened or attacked. In our laboratory studies, for example, narcissists who received praise were no more aggressive than other people. It was only when they were criticized that they lashed out—and then only at those who had criticized them. Aggression thus emerged as a strategy to rebut criticism and avoid a loss of esteem in the perpetrators' own or other people's eyes.

The idea that aggression rebuts criticism may seem counterintuitive. Beating up someone who insults your intelligence does not really prove that you are a genius. Yet it does somehow seem to allow the person to maintain a favorable view of self. If nothing else, it discourages further criticism. The function of aggression as a rebuttal to criticism may also have roots in our evolutionary past. In many species, alpha males defend their superior status by fighting off challengers. When the alpha male loses a fight, his status is diminished, and so the attacks on him really do amount to a kind of challenge to his high esteem and put it in jeopardy.

In humans, at least, threatened egotism is not limited to individuals. Violent, aggressive nations and other groups often show the same pattern of believing themselves to be superior to others and also believing that they do not get the respect to which they are entitled. The Iraqi invasion of Kuwait, which put in motion the events that still influence Middle Eastern politics today, was a good example: Iraq's leaders believed it to be a great power that did not receive the respect it deserved. Earlier belligerents showed similar patterns. Inside nations, also, the threatened egotism pattern can be found. Tyranny and government-sponsored violence are typically perpetrated by elites who believe in both their superiority and in the failure of others to accord them the respect they deserve.

The third root cause of evil is idealism. In some ways, this is the most disturbing and tragic of the causes because the perpetrators are motivated by the belief that they are doing something good. Idealists of both the left and the right have sometimes believed that their noble goals justify violent means. The worst body counts of the 20th century were perpetrated by people who believed that they were doing what was necessary to create a utopian society, whether this reflected a left-wing vision (as in the communist slaughters in China and the Soviet Union) or a right-wing one (as in the horrors perpetrated by Nazi Germany). Earlier centuries witnessed slaughters perpetrated in the name of religion as people killed to serve their gods.

To be sure, sometimes the idealism was a cover for baser motives, including instrumental ones. Some people used religious wars or persecutions to enrich themselves. Yet it is not reasonable to dismiss the sincere idealism of many of the perpetrators. In a large expedition such as the Crusades, there were some along for adventure and others hoping to get rich. But many honestly believed that they were doing God's work by fighting the infidels in order to reclaim sacred ground for what they thought was the true faith (e.g., Runciman, 1951–1954).

The fourth and final root cause of evil and violence is *sadism*, defined as sincere enjoyment from inflicting harm. Earlier I said that it may be most precise to refer to three and a half roots rather than four. Sadism would be the half. Trying to understand the truth about sadism was among the biggest challenges in researching my book on evil and formulating a theory. As I said, sadism shows up far more commonly in victim than perpetrator accounts (including accounts by perpetrators who admitted to seemingly much worse things), and it was tempting to dismiss it as a myth. Yet there did seem to be widely scattered signs that it does occur, at least sometimes. True, hardly any perpetrators who have written memoirs claim to have gotten pleasure from killing others. But some of them did say that they thought some of their colleagues and accomplices came to enjoy it. It is possible that some of them mistook bravado for sincere enjoyment (a mistake that victims in particular may often make). Carrying out violent acts against others is a difficult and often upsetting task, and one may try out various ways of coping with it. Milgram (1963), in describing his studies of obedience to authority, reported that some of his participants had fits of nervous laughter while obeying instructions to deliver electric shocks to an innocent and protesting victim. One may easily surmise that had real victims or even accomplices heard those participants laughing, they would have assumed that the perpetrators were laughing with joy.

Ultimately, however, I came to think the evidence for sadism was too strong to dismiss entirely. Some people really do seem to enjoy inflicting harm. My best way of explaining this relied on opponent process theory (Solomon & Corbit, 1974). In that view, harming another person is initially upsetting and produces an intensely negative reaction. This seems to be less a matter of moral scruples than of physical disgust. Most accounts of having inflicted violence note that the first time one killed or tortured someone was highly upsetting. This reaction then diminished over time.

Opponent process theory holds that the body maintains equilibrium (homeostasis) by instigating a second process to counteract any process that departs from the norm (Solomon & Corbit, 1974). Initially, this second process is slow and weak, but with repetition it gains in strength and may come to predominate. That is how people learn to enjoy bungee jumping or skydiving: The initial and deep natural terror of falling evokes the opponent process of euphoria, and over time and repeated trials the terror grows weaker and briefer while the euphoria becomes stronger and longer lasting. I suggest that the same sort of reaction happens with repeated acts of inflicting harm.

Why do only a few people become sadists? Here one must invoke guilt, I think. There is no moral objection to allowing oneself to learn to enjoy skydiving or bungee jumping, and indeed that enjoyment is the goal. But most decent and normal people will not allow themselves to acknowledge that they may get some pleasure from inflicting harm. Some people have fewer such scruples, however. They, too, I think, initially find it gross and disgusting to kill or maim someone, but over time, as the opponent process gets stronger, they accept it. Then it starts to become fun.

Studies of torturers provided useful evidence, although I must note as a social scientist that these studies are hardly ideal from a research design standpoint. Still, consider the question of what causes one of the failures of torture—when the torturers get carried away to the point at which they kill the victim or at least inflict such serious harm that the ostensible goal of interrogation is thwarted? Initially, I supposed that such excesses would mainly be perpetrated by young torturers, whereas the more experienced old hands would be able to maintain professional detachment and restraint. Yet the evidence suggested the opposite: Lethal excesses of torture were perpetrated more by the old hands than the rookies. This fits the opponent process theory. The novice torturer is still disturbed by the violence and is restrained by empathic identification with the victim and other factors. As experience increases, however, some (not all) of the torturers may feel less distress and more satisfaction, and so getting carried away becomes more likely.

Another possibility is that sadism is linked to psychopathy. Psychopaths lack empathic identification with others and therefore are perhaps less restrained than others by empathic distress. They may get feelings of self-efficacy from the signs of pain and suffering they elicit, and these may increase over time.

In any case, sadism is not entirely a root cause of evil. In most of these cases, the person begins perpetrating violence for some other reason, generally one of the other three I noted. One has to be engaged in harming others for a while in order to discover the pleasure. When it does happen, however, it begins to become independent of the other causes. At that point, the sadist enjoys harming for its own sake.

From the victim's perspective, these different root causes do make a difference. The instrumentally violent person can be bought off. If he wants your money, you can give it to him, and that in most cases reduces, ends, or avoids the harm that comes to you. Threatened egotism likewise produces violence that is a means to an end, and so victims can sometimes satisfy the perpetrator and terminate their suffering. If and when the perpetrator's egotism is satisfied, the attack may stop. In contrast, the victims of the idealists have fewer options because in many cases the idealists believe that their sacred goals require the victim's death. It is harder to compromise with an idealist than with an opportunist. And last, if the perpetrator is a sadist, the victim's lot is clearly the worst. There is not much chance to buy him off or appease him to reduce your suffering, especially if your suffering is precisely what is rewarding to him.

PROXIMAL CAUSE

I began my project by asking why there is evil. Yet when one recognizes how widespread the impulses toward violence are—compounded by all the moderators that social psychologists who study aggression have identified—

the fact of violence becomes less and less surprising. Instead, one begins to ask, why isn't there more evil than there is?

For example, social psychologists have shown that aggression is increased by one's being criticized or insulted, by hot temperatures, by seeing violence in the media, and by being frustrated (for reviews, see Baron & Richardson, 1993; Geen, 1990). Who among us has not experienced insulting criticism, or heat, or media violence, or frustration? Who indeed has not experienced these within the past week? In that context, the incidence of violence is surprisingly low.

The explanation of why there is not more evil than there already is can most likely be found in self-control. Many circumstances give rise to aggressive impulses, but people restrain themselves from acting on them. Humans are social animals, and as such, they have the same aggressive impulses that enabled their evolutionary predecessors to resolve disputes in their favor and thereby to survive and reproduce. Yet humans also have a capacity for self-regulation that is at least as strong as that of other social animals. Culture relies heavily on self-regulation because culture consists partly of a system with rules and standards, and it can function only if people alter their behavior to bring it into line with those rules and standards. More and more, that includes restraining violence, which is mostly disruptive to the smooth inner functioning of cultural systems.

Hence it is probably fair to say that the inner processes of most human beings include some degree of aggressive impulses that are restrained by self-control. The progress of culture in reducing violence and other forms of evil has depended in part on using people's capacity for self-regulation to restrain their aggressive impulses. The proximal cause of evil and violence in many cases, therefore, is a breakdown of these inner restraints. When things are going according to a culture's plan, individuals check their aggressive impulses. When those checks fail, the impulses lead to violent action.

Many causes of aggression and violence operate by interfering with self-regulation. Alcohol, for example, has been shown to impair self-regulation in almost every sphere that has been studied (Baumeister, Heatherton, & Tice, 1994), and alcohol is well established as a cause of violence (Bushman & Cooper, 1990). (Alcohol is neither a necessary nor a sufficient cause, to be sure. It is just a moderator, though it is a rather powerful moderator.) Intense emotion impairs self-regulation, and it, too, can undermine restraints against violent impulses.

In my view, the role of self-regulation in restraining violence has more than theoretical importance. If one considers the four root causes of evil, it is easy to become pessimistic. Those four will not be eradicated any time soon, and so the problem of evil may appear intractable. But preventing evil and reducing violence do not depend on eliminating the root causes. We can simply strengthen the restraints. If we improve self-control, we can indeed make the world a better place and reduce the quantity of evil. In other words, it may be overly optimistic to hope that violent impulses can be eliminated from human social life.

In recent centuries, many have founded utopian communities in the hope that people would live together in peace and harmony if only certain oppressive social conditions were eliminated. The belief was that we could get rid of aggression by changing society to eliminate its root causes. These experiments have failed over and over. Instead of eliminating the aggressive impulses, it may be more realistic to strengthen the inner restraints against them.

REFERENCES

Anderson, E. (1994). The code of the streets. *Atlantic Monthly, 273*(5), 81–94.

Baron, R. A., & Richardson, D. (1993). *Human aggression.* New York, NY: Plenum Press.

Baumeister, R. F. (1997). *Evil: Inside human violence and cruelty.* New York, NY: Freeman.

Baumeister, R. F. (2005). *The cultural animal: Human nature, meaning, and social life.* New York, NY: Oxford University Press.

Baumeister, R. F., Heatherton, T. F., & Tice, D. M. (1994). *Losing control: How and why people fail at self-regulation.* San Diego, CA: Academic Press.

Baumeister, R. F., Smart, L., & Boden, J. M. (1996). Relation of threatened egotism to violence and aggression: The dark side of high self-esteem. *Psychological Review, 103,* 5–33. doi:10.1037/0033-295X.103.1.5

Bushman, B. J., & Baumeister, R. F. (1998). Threatened egotism, narcissism, self-esteem, and direct and displaced aggression: Does self-love or self-hate lead to violence? *Journal of Personality and Social Psychology, 75,* 219–229. doi:10.1037/0022-3514.75.1.219

Bushman, B. J., & Cooper, H. M. (1990). Effects of alcohol on human aggression: An integrative research review. *Psychological Bulletin, 107,* 341–354. doi:10.1037/0033-2909.107.3.341

Dower, J. W. (1986). *War without mercy: Race and power in the Pacific war.* New York, NY: Pantheon.

Geen, R. G. (1990). *Human aggression.* Pacific Grove, CA: Brooks/Cole.

Heath, L. (1984). Impact of newspaper crime reports on fear of crime: Multimethodological investigation. *Journal of Personality and Social Psychology, 47,* 263–276. doi:10.1037/0022-3514.47.2.263

Hesse, P., & Mack, J. E. (1991). The world is a dangerous place: Images of the enemy on children's television. In R. Rieber (Ed.), *The psychology of war and peace: Images of the enemy* (pp. 131–153). New York, NY: Plenum Press.

Levin, J., & McDevitt, J. (1993). *Hate crimes: The rising tide of bigotry and bloodshed.* New York, NY: Plenum Press.

Lifton, R. J. (1986). *The Nazi doctors: Medical killing and the psychology of genocide.* New York, NY: Basic Books.

Milgram, S. (1963). Behavioral study of obedience. *Journal of Abnormal and Social Psychology, 67,* 371–378. doi:10.1037/h0040525

Renzetti, C. M. (1992). *Violent betrayal: Partner abuse in lesbian relationships.* Newbury Park, CA: Sage.

Runciman, S. (1951–1954). *A history of the Crusades* (Vols. 1–3). New York, NY: Cambridge University Press.

Solomon, R. L., & Corbit, J. D. (1974). An opponent-process theory of motivation: I. Temporal dynamics of affect. *Psychological Review, 81,* 119–145. doi:10.1037/h0036128

Staub, E. (1989). *The roots of evil: The origins of genocide and other group violence.* New York, NY, and Cambridge, England: Cambridge University Press.

21

PSYCHOLOGY AND MORALITY IN GENOCIDE AND VIOLENT CONFLICT: PERPETRATORS, PASSIVE BYSTANDERS, AND RESCUERS

ERVIN STAUB

In this chapter, I consider the roles of psychology and morality in genocide and in intense violence and mass killing. The starting point for both can be either difficult social conditions in a society or conflict between groups. But psychology and individual-level morality have central roles. Even though there are many societal, cultural, and institutional forces at work, the proximal influences leading to genocide or mass killing are psychological. As the participants undergo a grim evolution, progressing along a "continuum of destruction" (Staub, 1989), moved by psychological and social forces, moral principles and orientations can be subverted. As people respond to these forces, they may engage in profoundly immoral actions without even struggling with the immorality of their thoughts, feelings, and actions. How psychological forces can overwhelm or subvert moral principles and emotions is the primary focus of this chapter. I consider the psychology and morality of perpetrators, passive bystanders, and active bystanders who endanger themselves as they attempt to save lives.

I define *morality* as principles, values, emotional orientations, and practices that maintain or promote human welfare (see also Chapters 13 and 14, this volume, for similar definitions). With the increasing awareness of our interconnected existence and the increasing spirituality in the world, *human welfare* could be replaced with the *welfare of all beings*. Rather than a code of conduct in a particular society or group, moral principles and values and ways of relating to others—and the very essence of morality, human welfare (or the welfare of all beings)—are universal considerations. Ultimately, it is *actions* that are moral or immoral. Principles and values are moral or immoral to the extent that they guide behavior in a moral or immoral direction.

Traditionally, philosophers and moral psychologists such as Kohlberg (1976) have classified actions as moral or immoral as a function of a person's intentions or reasoning about them. But as I wrote in *Overcoming Evil* (Staub, 2010),

> this judgment cannot be based *only or primarily* on the intentions of actors, especially their stated intentions. They themselves may not know what internal psychological or outside forces lead them to their actions, and if they do, what they say may not express their motives but provide justifications for them. . . . [When people act violently,] they may incorrectly perceive the need for self-defense, or act with unnecessary violence in the name of self-defense. They may be guided by ideals and visions that aim to benefit their group or to improve the world, but have developed the belief that any means are acceptable to serve these ideals. (pp. 32–33)

Guided by these beliefs, they engage in harmful action against people who have not done or intended to do harm to them.

In light of these considerations, and of others spelled out later, such as the fact that individuals—and societies—change as a result of their own actions, I view judging actions as good and evil, or moral or immoral, as requiring a consideration of intentions, the nature of the acts, their probable consequences, their actual consequences, the degree of environmental pressure on a person to act, and even their effects on the actors' further behavior. It requires a consideration of universal principles (e.g., sanctity of life, justice) and the principles of utilitarianism, the greatest good for the greatest number (Staub, 2010; that both universal principles and utilitarianism need to be considered is also proposed by Ditto and Liu in Chapter 3, this volume).

I have referred to genocide as evil because it involves extreme destructiveness (Staub, 1989). By the above criteria, killing a whole group of people in genocide, which invariably includes killing people who have done no harm, such as young children—against whom no defense is required and against whom retaliation, if one considers that moral, is not appropriate—would always be judged immoral. Group conflict is, by itself, not immoral. Unfortunately, however, conflict between groups can resist resolution, become intractable and violent, and lead to violence reaching the level of mass killing, in which many people are killed indiscriminately.

My concern is not simply to judge genocide or extreme violence in group conflict as immoral. Both are outcomes of normal, ordinary psychological processes that come together to create extreme and immoral actions and outcomes. Both are *banal,* to use Hannah Arendt's (1963) term, not in her sense that they are not extraordinary, but in the sense that they are the outcomes of ordinary psychological and social processes. In this chapter, I consider the influences that lead to the evolution of such extreme violence and the nature of the evolution itself, including the influences and processes in the steps along a continuum of destruction that ends in the motivation for and the perpetration of genocide or extreme violence. I also consider choices made by actors—leaders and followers who are perpetrators, witnesses who become passive bystanders, and active bystanders who are rescuers.

Usually, discussions of morality focus on principles or codes of conduct. However, moral action can be the result either of principles, values, and related norms that dictate certain action or of emotional orientations such as caring about other people and empathizing or sympathizing with them. *Caring* means genuine concern for the welfare of others. It is an outgrowth of feelings of connection to other people and feelings of empathy or sympathy. Emotional orientations such as empathy, and moral principles such as justice or the sanctity of life, can lead to moral action or inhibit immoral action. For example, a person can help another whom he or she does not care about, guided by principles, as in the case of some anti-Semitic Christians who rescued Jews during the Holocaust. But some Christian rescuers were primarily motivated by empathic feelings for persecuted Jews (Oliner & Oliner, 1988). A person can also harm others on the basis of principles, such as punishment for wrongdoing or reciprocity, or refrain from harming others because of empathic feelings.

Moral or helpful actions are especially likely on the part of people who feel personal responsibility for the welfare of others. The responsibility to act can be the result of nonmoral influences. For example, conditions may focus responsibility on a person—this person being the only one present when someone needs help, or the one who has the expertise to act, or the one who is in a role that requires action (Latané & Darley, 1970; Staub, 1978). Or the feeling of responsibility can be inherent in the person (e.g., Staub, 2003, 2010). Feelings or the belief in one's responsibility for another's welfare seem to mediate between caring or empathy and moral principles, with elements of both. These same variables are likely to be important inhibitors of harmful behavior (Spielman & Staub, 2000).

To finish this brief introduction focused on morality, I quote again from *Overcoming Evil,* where I wrote,

> At the start, evil is the action, not the person or the group. But individuals and groups change as a result of their actions. Victims are increasingly

devalued, violence intensifies as it continues. Destructive actions can become increasingly normal and probable, a characteristic of a system, a group—or a person. In such cases, we can regard the society, group, or individual actors as evil. (Staub, 2010, p. 33)

We can use the word *evil* when actions create extreme harm; this is an extreme form of immorality. In an immoral society, where actions that harm people who have themselves done no harm have become normal, as under slavery in the United States or in Nazi Germany, for people to act morally they must deviate from the standards or codes of conduct of that society. A leadership group, much of a society (with the population as passive bystanders also implicated), or a small terrorist group can develop beliefs, values, and practices that normalize violence against all members of another group. In the next section, I present two theories of motivation and action and then apply these theories to understand the psychological forces that underlie violence and genocide while focusing on the motivational forces that determine the moral behavior of perpetrators, passive bystanders, and active bystanders.

TWO THEORIES OF MOTIVATION AND ACTION: BASIC NEEDS THEORY AND PERSONAL GOAL THEORY

In this section I briefly review two conceptions I have developed over time about what determines people's behavior, including their moral behavior— basic needs theory and personal goal theory. I then apply these conceptions to the understanding of genocide and violent conflict.

Basic needs theory assumes that all human beings share certain universal psychological needs. The needs I have focused on include security, feelings of effectiveness and control over important events, positive identity, positive connection to others, and comprehension of reality (and of one's own role in the world). Although all human beings possess these needs, their forms or manifestations and their intensity (as a function of the ease or difficulty of their fulfillment) vary with culture and with individual experience. This theory was inspired by Maslow's (1971) theory of human needs and by the usefulness of needs in understanding the origins of genocide and other mass violence (e.g., Staub, 1989, 2003, 2010). In contrast to Maslow, I assume that basic needs do not form a hierarchy. Instead, all are present from an early age. Only security, which includes both physical/material and psychological security, might be more important than the other needs.

When the constructive satisfaction of basic needs is blocked, people attempt to fulfill them in ways that are destructive, insofar as the satisfaction of one need interferes with the satisfaction of another or is harmful to other people. Fulfilling the need for competence and control by attempting to exercise control over all aspects of one's relationships with others is a destructive mode of need fulfillment, both because it frustrates others' desire for control and because it interferes with the development of positive relationships. Fulfilling the need for competence and positive identity by dominance and aggression is similarly a destructive mode of need satisfaction.

The second theory, personal goal theory, assumes that different needs, values, and motives—and the outcomes they point to that are important for people and that they want to reach—vary in importance among individuals. For each person, they can be arranged in a hierarchy, according to their importance for that person. However, the individual hierarchies of personal goals are not static. Conditions in the environment can activate needs lower in the hierarchy and raise their position, making them dominant over needs that are normally higher in the hierarchy. Working in one's office, parenting one's children, relaxing at the beach, facing some threat—each of these activates different motives or personal goals (e.g., Staub, 1978, 2010). Environmental activators can be temporary. But lasting environmental conditions can create persistent changes in the hierarchy. Moral values may be high in a person's "resting" hierarchy, but certain environmental conditions can make other motives, such as basic needs, dominant over them.

The connection between basic needs theory and personal goal theory is that some, although not all, personal goals develop out of basic needs. In the course of socialization and experience, needs can be satisfied in habitual ways. For one person, intellectual activity can fulfill the need for effectiveness, can be a basis for positive identity, and can even be a primary way to develop positive connections. For another person, empathic engagement with other people may serve the same needs. Although not all values, goals, or motives necessarily develop out of basic needs, many do, or at least they have significant connections to basic needs. For example, a strong commitment to the principle of justice may have independent roots in socialization and experience, but it helps to meet the need for comprehending reality and can serve other needs as well.

THE ORIGINS AND PROCESSES OF GENOCIDE
AND VIOLENT CONFLICT

In my conception, the primary starting points or instigators of mass violence are either difficult life conditions (e.g., economic problems, political disorganization, great and rapid social or life changes) or conflict between groups. As difficult life conditions persist, or as conflict remains unresolved and becomes intractable, threats and fears can intensify and lead to the intense frustration of basic human needs. Especially in the presence of certain characteristics of culture, and with the underlying problems requiring persistent effort to resolve, people attempt to address their intense psychological reactions in ways that turn one group against another or intensify conflict and hostility. Members of one group scapegoat—blame—some other group for life's problems or for starting or maintaining a conflict. They adopt or develop ideologies or visions of social arrangements and relationships between groups and individuals that promise a better future. But because these are visions of the future, not currently available and difficult to reach, people tend to identify enemies who, in their eyes, stand in the way. The group progressively turns against the scapegoat or ideological enemy. The conflict then intensifies (see Staub, 1989, 2003, 2010, in press, for elaboration of this conception).

This process, and the evolution of increasing hostility and violence, are more likely to occur in groups with certain characteristics. One of them is a history of devaluing another group; the devalued group is likely to become the scapegoat or ideological enemy. Another is the past victimization of the group and the resulting psychological woundedness. Aspects of woundedness include feelings of vulnerability and a view of the world as dangerous. This can lead to perceiving the need for self-defense when there is no real danger and engaging in unnecessary defensive violence (i.e., a degree of force greater than what is required for defense against the real danger) and/or in hostile or vengeful violence (Staub, 1998, 2010; Staub & Pearlman, 2006). Another cultural characteristic that makes group violence more likely is overly strong respect for authority, which leads to an exaggerated tendency to look to leaders for guidance and to follow and obey leaders. A monolithic culture, which limits the range of views that can be expressed and often excludes some group(s) from participation in public life, is another contributing cultural/societal characteristic. Still another is a history of dealing with conflict by engaging in violence. As in individuals, in groups both limited self-worth and a low group self-concept and a sense of superiority frustrated by social conditions can also contribute.

Another important process leading to genocide or intense violence in conflict is the evolution of increasing hostility and violence. As actions are taken against the other group or as already hostile actions intensify, individuals and the group change. People learn by doing and change as a result of their actions. They justify their harmful actions in at least two ways. First, they further devalue the other group. Progressively they exclude the members of the other group from the moral realm so that the usual moral considerations no longer apply to them (e.g., Fein, 1993; Opotow, 1990; Staub, 1989, 2010; see also Chapter 11, this volume). Second, they use as a justification the "higher" ideals of the ideology, the cause that the group is presumably serving—whether it is racial purity, nationalism, social equality, or something else. As the evolution progresses, many perpetrators, some earlier and some later, experience a reversal of morality. Killing the other now becomes the right, moral thing to do. The society also undergoes an evolution, with transformed or new institutions that serve the violence, such as offices of Jewish Affairs in Nazi Germany or paramilitary groups in many countries, and with evolving standards of conduct that allow such violence to occur. Other psychological processes, such as adaptation and habituation, and the reduction of cognitive dissonance—"If I harm these people, they must be bad"—also serve this evolution (see Chapter 8, this volume, for a similar analysis).

The behavior of bystanders plays a crucial role in allowing this evolution to unfold. Witnesses, or people who are in a position to know what is happening and to take action, tend to remain passive as their group turns against a subgroup of society and as that subgroup increasingly becomes a target of hostility and violence. Often they are more than passive and are, to various degrees, complicit. They go on with business as usual, fulfilling roles and functions that support the system and even serve the violence. Their passivity and, even more, their complicity affirm the perpetrators in what they are doing. *External bystanders*—nations, groups, and individuals outside a country moving toward increasing violence—are also often passive. The passivity of external bystanders has similar effects to that of internal bystanders. Although there has been an increase in the number of U.N. diplomatic and peacekeeping missions over the last 2 decades (Fein, 2007), passivity is still often characteristic of the response of the international community, as in Rwanda, Darfur, and the Democratic Republic of the Congo.

THE PSYCHOLOGY AND MORALITY OF LEADERS, FOLLOWERS, AND PERPETRATORS

Difficult life conditions and intense conflict have strong activating potential for certain goals in people's goal or need hierarchy. Normally, basic needs, or the goals that develop from them, if they are satisfied to a reasonable degree, need not be in a strong state of activation. When life is normal, security is not a primary consideration for most people. Although identity is always important, it can be maintained as part of work, human relations, and so on. Under normal conditions, people live by the understanding of reality they have developed. But the instigating conditions for violence are powerful activators of basic needs, and the goals related to them move to the top of people's motive hierarchy. For many people, these goals become more important than values and emotional orientations related to morality. For some others, these conditions activate already important goals and values that incline them to hostility and the desire to harm. Their inclinations are restricted or controlled by societal standards and norms, but they become fully activated under difficult life conditions or group conflict. One researcher who studied members of the Nazi SS called such people "sleepers" (Steiner, 1980); another, a conflict specialist, wrote about the person who acts as a "crystallizing agent" when he notices that people are "vulnerable to his blandishments" (Zartman, 1989, p. 11).

But even for many "ordinary" people, security, identity, connection to others, and a comprehension of reality and of their role in the scheme of things become dominant over values of justice or the welfare of people unrelated to them. Although most people view themselves as good, identity has many components that can be separated from each other. What "being a good person" means can be defined quite differently by different people and under different conditions. The role of identity also changes as people, finding it difficult to stand on their own, shift from an individual identity to a collective identity. This is consistent with social identity theory (see Straus, 2006, in relation to Rwanda; also Staub, 2010).

This is one of the important effects of difficult life conditions and group conflict. Being part of a group, whether ethnic, religious, or political in nature, helps fulfill needs for security, identity, connection, and effectiveness. But this also means that people shift from individual, personal values and goals to group values and goals. The welfare of the members of the group becomes important, with that of people outside the group disregarded. Moreover, because the group is likely to adopt or intensify ideologies in these difficult times, the ideological goals also become dominant, including their destructive aspect, identifying and turning against an ideological enemy (see Chapter 18, this volume, for a similar discussion).

In addition, in difficult times people turn to leaders who offer quick solutions to their problems. These leaders, as members of groups, are also affected by life conditions and group conflict. They are looking for the satisfaction of their own basic needs. They are also aware of the needs of potential or actual followers in difficult times or in violent conflict. Both life conditions and a culture that emphasizes respect for authority enhance the reliance on and need for guidance by leaders. Leaders also have an additional motive: to attract followers. These forces and motives lead them to promote scapegoating and develop a destructive ideology.

There is an unanswered question in my mind concerning the extent to which leaders respond to the shared needs of the group, including their own basic needs, and the extent to which they manipulate the group to gain influence. To what extent do they themselves go through the "normal," although destructive, processes I described, and to what extent do they instigate others while being aware of the untrue nature of their claims (e.g., that another group is responsible for their group's life problems)? Prominent communists who have been studied tended to be true believers and had great difficulty shifting away from their ideology even after the collapse of communism and in the face of evidence of the violent nature of communist systems (Hollander, 2006). It is likely that in addition to their genuine beliefs, both leaders and followers are influenced by other motives, such as the desire to advance their careers. This was true of members of the SS in Nazi Germany (Steiner, 1980). In terrorist groups, some members tend to advocate views that are consistent with those of the group, but more radical, in order to gain influence in the group (Staub, 2010).

The shift in the relative importance of moral versus nonmoral values and goals is accompanied by people replacing moral values (e.g., harm, fairness) with other values that are not inherently moral (i.e., have no inherent connection to human welfare) but that people often define as moral—for example, loyalty and respect for and obedience to authority (see Chapter 1, this volume). These are both important values in human organizations, but they become destructive when they become dominant over or replace other values, especially genuinely moral ones.

Devaluation is another way that morality is undermined in the evolution of hostility and violence toward a targeted group. Combined with a vision of justice that focuses on punishment, it can lead to harmful actions. Both the evidence of real-world events and research indicate that devaluation leads to harm doing. In cases of genocide and mass killing, the victims are greatly devalued (Staub, 1989, 2010). Bandura, Underwood, and Fromson (1975) showed that when people overhear derogatory comments about someone, they punish this person more; when they hear positive comments, they punish less. In the case of the Janjaweed, Arab horseman who attacked Black Africans in Darfur, survivors' reports indicated a relationship between shouting more derogatory comments in the course of their attack and the intensity of violent actions (Hagan & Rymond-Richmond, 2008).

Morality can take a punitive form: People who are bad—who are immoral, who want to harm us—deserve punishment. Justice is an important aspect of morality in every moral system, and punishment is an aspect of most moral systems. Just-world thinking (Lerner, 1980) is a kind of morality; it involves the belief that the world is a just place and its corollary, that to uphold a just world, people who are bad ought to be punished. A group and its members can move from punishing bad actions to punishing those they believe are likely to engage in bad actions and then those whose supposed nature is bad.

We might regard the devaluation of people—a negative judgment of an entire group that is frequently not based on the actual behavior of members of the group, and certainly not the behavior of all members—as inherently immoral. It is a cognitive–emotional orientation that diminishes people and is likely to lead to harmful actions. This would also mean that the justification of harmful actions against others by increased devaluation of them is also immoral. Alternatively, the harmful actions caused by devaluation are immoral.

A significant aspect of morality is good judgment, a correct or veridical assessment of events, including both what is happening and the meaning of what is happening. Classical Greek philosophers thought that prudence, or good judgment, was one of the major virtues. To be moral requires the ability to assess whether particular claims are true or false. It requires a critical consciousness—not accepting what leaders, the media, or other people say, or even what one's culture teaches, without examining it and judging it for oneself. This is, of course, profoundly demanding. Children simply absorb their culture. Socializers, parents and teachers, only rarely foster the tendency to critically evaluate what the culture teaches. But to be a moral person, one must ask about devaluation: Is what is being said about these people true? Is this view justified, and in the rare cases when it is, what is a reasonable course of action in relation to these people? A society advances morality when it prepares its citizens for such critical examination and good judgment. Critical examination, to be useful for moral purposes, also requires, of course, citizens who have developed moral values (see Chapter 13, this volume, for a similar discussion).

It is also important to consider the effects of past victimization leading to defensive (and occasionally hostile) violence. In this case, psychological woundedness can lead to defensive reactions to the world and can subvert moral inclinations. Both psychological woundedness in response to the experience of harm and such reactions to it are normal psychological processes. Sometimes, having been victimized becomes deeply embedded in a group's culture. It becomes a "chosen trauma" (Volkan, 1997) and a screen through which the world and events are seen (Staub, 2010). Cultural self-examination becomes important in order to see this screen and its destructive effects and to develop a more veridical and constructive way to view the world.

I have been discussing the ways societal conditions and characteristics, such as difficult life conditions and one group devaluing another, affect and shape many members of a group. Individuals can do something about how they respond to or deal with these forces. They can participate in or avoid scapegoating, accept or reject a destructive ideology. But there are also structural characteristics of a society that have elements of immorality and have the potential to lead to conflict and violence. A primary one is inequality between groups—in power, wealth, and access. The genocide scholar Helen Fein concluded in 1993, after analyzing many cases, that after 1945 this was the most important source of violence between groups. Inequality can lead to violence as the less powerful group demands greater equality and the powerful group responds with repression and violence or as the less powerful group immediately moves to violence. Inequitable relations are maintained not only because those with power want to maintain their power and privilege but also because they come to believe that they deserve and have a right to their power and privilege (Staub, 2010). A moral course requires shifting away from a social dominance orientation (Sidanius & Pratto, 1999) and system justification (Jost, Banaji, & Nosek, 2004). It requires a moral vision based on justice as equality, or at least reasonable forms of equity, in which the contributions of every society member are appropriately valued. It requires a society that concerns itself with the fulfillment of its members' material and psychological needs.

THE PSYCHOLOGY AND MORALITY OF PASSIVE BYSTANDERS

As I noted earlier, the passivity and complicity of bystanders encourage perpetrators of unjustified harmful actions. It also changes the bystanders themselves. Many processes contribute to passivity: diffusion of responsibility, pluralistic ignorance (people not knowing what others think and feel; Latané & Darley, 1970), the belief in the impossibility of one person making a difference, and the difficulty in organizing and joining with others in societies that are often autocratic (Staub, 2010). People can also rationalize their inaction when, as is often the case, the evolution toward violence moves at first with small steps. At each point, a person can think that this is something small and has limited significance. But as people remain passive, or go along as if everything were normal, they change. Just as followers who become perpetrators justify their actions, so people justify their passivity, primarily by devaluing victims. Just-world research has shown that observers of harm to a person are likely to devalue that person if they have reason to believe that the harm—and the suffering—will continue (Lerner & Simmons, 1966).

To oppose a societal process, people need to have moral motives that support action. But many of them have absorbed from their culture a negative view of the targeted group. It requires strong moral motives to oppose one's own group for the sake of devalued others. It also requires *moral courage*, the willingness and ability to act according to one's values in the face of opposition and potential harm to oneself (see Chapter 19, this volume, for a discussion of moral courage). Moreover, if people do not act early, devaluation and the costs of action can be joined by self-protective emotional distancing as inhibitors of action. Empathizing with people who are harmed and who suffer creates distress. Distancing oneself from them diminishes distress.

There are a number of potential mechanisms of distancing: minimizing each step and suspending judgment about the meaning of events, justifying harm done, adopting an observer perspective, or avoiding information about and attention to harmful action and the other's suffering. In research in which people were told either to take an observer orientation to what was happening to someone or to imagine what it is like for that person or imagine themselves in that situation, those with an observer orientation responded with less empathy (Aderman & Berkowitz, 1970; Stotland, 1969). In one of my studies in which participants witnessed a study confederate collapsing on the street, we observed that some passersby turned aside after a single glance and never looked back (Staub & Baer, 1974). In my conversation with Germans in 1987 who were teenagers or older during the 1930s, they talked about sitting around campfires and singing songs. They were so engaged with their own satisfying lives in the Nazi era that they did not notice the very public persecution of Jews (Staub, 1989, 2010). Preoccupation with their own lives thus is a further reason that people remain passive. As a result of these processes, even people who engage with what is happening to a victimized group are likely, in the course of the evolution of hostility and violence, to increasingly relinquish their responsibility for the welfare of the persecuted other. We can regard these processes as having negative moral consequences or as being inherently immoral. Over time, some bystanders join the perpetrators (Lifton, 1986).

Passivity has also been the most common response of external bystanders. Because nations have not historically regarded themselves as moral agents, and because leaders are preoccupied with many matters, it has been relatively easy for them to ignore the increasing danger in another place and eventually the violence against people in other countries. International conventions and laws are progressively changing legal and moral standards for the behavior of nations as bystanders, but actions consistent with these new international standards are changing much more slowly.

THE PSYCHOLOGY AND MORALITY OF RESCUERS

Groups differ, and the subversion of morality via ordinary psychological processes is more likely in some cultures than in others. Individuals differ, and the subversion of morality through the processes I have just described is more likely in some people than in others. Usually, in societies that move toward group violence there is a vanguard that initiates scapegoating and destructive ideological visions, although many members of the society often follow, and most others remain passive. There is usually little resistance. In cases of group conflict as well, there is often limited resistance to the increasing hostility toward the opponent in the conflict.

There is also limited acknowledgment afterward of harmful actions by one's own group. However, over time, there can be a change in "collective memories" and an acknowledgment of harm doing, which is important for reconciliation. For example, Israelis who were witnesses or who participated as soldiers or in other capacities in actions to expel Palestinians in 1948 did not speak out for many years. But after decades, and after the work of "new historians" (e.g., Morris, 2004) established that various efforts were made to expel

Palestinians, and after a shift toward a more critical orientation toward the government, some wrote memoirs in which they described witnessing or being involved in the expulsion. Not speaking earlier had to do both with loyalty to their group still engaged in the conflict and with government censorship (Nets-Zehngut, 2009).

Although there is usually little resistance in the course of the evolution of violence, as it becomes evident that the members of a persecuted group will be killed, some people endanger themselves to save lives (Staub, 1997). This has been found in most cases of genocide: during the Holocaust in countries in Nazi Europe (Oliner & Oliner, 1988; Tec, 1986), in Rwanda (Africa Rights, 2002), during the Armenian genocide, and elsewhere. Rescuers hide members of the designated victim group and/or help them move to a safe area. Such people have had socializing experiences of the kind that have been found to develop caring and altruism (Oliner & Oliner, 1988; see also Eisenberg, Fabes, & Spinrad, 2006; Staub, 1979, 1997, 2003). The resulting empathy and caring, including inclusive caring, and moral values lead these people to act. Some of them are "marginal" to their group in some way—for example, being of a minority religion, having one foreign parent, or having been somewhat unconventional (Tec, 1986). This presumably makes it easier for them to separate themselves from the group's increasing hostility toward the victims.

Rescuers endanger themselves, and often their families as well, as they help others. Their actions are heroic. They go beyond the requirements of ordinary morality. Their example shows that although the reactions that arise from instigating conditions and lead to mass violence are common, they are not inevitable. Even under circumstances that exert powerful influence, there is variation in how people respond. The prevention of genocide and other mass violence requires the strengthening of moral orientations and other personal dispositions that reduce the likelihood of violence. It requires creating societal systems that protect people and developing the joint capacity of systems and individuals to respond to instigating conditions in constructive ways.

CONCLUSIONS AND PREVENTION

Ordinary, normal psychological processes can subvert moral motives. These processes include the activation of pressing universal human needs and their shift to the top of people's hierarchy of values, motives, and goals; devaluation of the other and just-world thinking; the reactivation of past trauma; a social dominance orientation and the tendency to justify existing systems; and elevating nonmoral motives and punitive tendencies over moral values and motives. Some of these normal psychological processes can be regarded as inherently immoral. For many members of a group, these processes can diminish the relative importance of moral values and goals.

There is a profound conundrum here, in that the normal psychology of people living in difficult times, and in certain cultures, can start them on the road to extreme violence. The tendency to categorize, which includes the division of people into *us* and *them*, as well as the information that children and adults get from outside sources about other people—from parents and teachers, the culture and its literature and media, including generalizations about groups (stereotypes)—help us function in the world. But the present discussion suggests that living a moral life requires greater awareness—a critical consciousness—and the ability to evaluate the information one receives about groups targeted for violence and, at worst, genocide.

The present discussion suggests several lines of prevention. On the individual level, we can strengthen moral values and emotional orientations through socialization. Developing inclusive caring for other people beyond one's own group is an important protective element (Staub, 2005, 2010, in press). Inclusive caring makes it more likely that people expand the boundaries of their group and create broader group identities (Dovidio, Gaertner, & Saguy, 2009), and even an identity that includes all people as members of the human family. Another aspect of prevention is to develop the capacity for critical consciousness in general, and especially with regard to both external and internal processes that can subvert moral thinking, feeling, and action.

In my and my colleagues' work in Rwanda—in seminars and workshops with many groups ranging from facilitators working with community groups to national leaders and members of the media—we aimed to develop knowledge of the influences that lead to intergroup violence and to have people use this knowledge to develop an understanding of events, past and current, in their own society. Promoting understanding of the influences leading to violence, as well as avenues to prevention and reconciliation, was one of our primary efforts (Staub & Pearlman, 2006). We also promoted such knowledge and understanding in educational radio programs in Rwanda, Burundi, and the Congo (Staub, 2010, in press; Staub, Pearlman, & Bilali, 2010). Evaluation research showed that such training (Staub, Pearlman, Gubin, & Hagengimana, 2005) had strong positive effects, as did an educational radio drama in which the training concepts were embedded in a story about conflict between two neighboring villages (e.g., Staub & Pearlman, 2009; Staub, Pearlman, Weiss, & Hoek, in press). These included more positive attitudes on the part of Hutus and Tutsis toward each other, more empathy, a reduction in trauma symptoms, a greater willingness to speak one's mind, and more independence from authority (see Staub, 2010, for an overview).

Understanding the influences that lead to mass violence increases people's prudence and their ability to correctly assess the importance of events that can lead to increasing hostility and violence. It can make people aware of times when action is needed and lead them to resist or counteract influences that might lead to violence. It can lead to active bystandership in the service of promoting positive relations. Our training programs also brought about some healing of past wounds and greater openness of members of the two groups toward each other. This creates openness to reconciliation.

Preventive actions on the group level include helping people constructively meet basic needs in difficult times. Constructive ideologies, visions of social arrangements that benefit all groups in a society and to which everyone can contribute, and the creation of groups in which membership provides security, connection, and identity can prevent people from turning to destructive ideologies and violent movements (Staub, 2003, 2010).

As this suggests, prevention requires the creation of structures. Constructive groups are structures or institutions of society. Schools and workplaces can provide opportunities for significant positive contact between members of different groups, which helps them overcome devaluation and develop positive attitudes across group lines. Psychological changes seem necessary for generating the motivation to create positive societal structures, but these in turn are needed to maintain and further develop the attitudes and behavior that create harmonious, peaceful societies. It is essential to consider jointly the roots of immoral and moral behavior both in the psychology of individuals and groups and in the institutions and structures that people create and live within.

REFERENCES

Aderman, D., & Berkowitz, L. (1970). Observational set, empathy, and helping. *Journal of Personality and Social Psychology, 14*, 141–148. doi:10.1037/h0028770

Africa Rights. (2002). *Tribute to courage*. Kigali, Rwanda: Author.

Arendt, H. (1963). *Eichmann in Jerusalem: A report on the banality of evil*. New York, NY: Viking Press.

Bandura, A., Underwood, B., & Fromson, M. E. (1975). Disinhibition of aggression through diffusion of responsibility and dehumanization of victims. *Journal of Research in Personality, 9*, 253–269. doi:10.1016/0092-6566(75)90001-X

Dovidio, J. F., Gaertner, S. L., & Saguy, T. (2009). Commonality and the complexity of "we": Social attitudes and social change. *Personality and Social Psychology Review, 13*, 3–20. doi:10.1177/1088868308326751

Eisenberg, N., Fabes, R. A., Spinrad, T. L. (2006). Prosocial development. In W. Damon (Ed.), *Handbook of child psychology: Vol. 3. Social, emotional, and personality development* (5th ed., pp. 646–718). New York, NY: Wiley.

Fein, H. (1993). Accounting for genocide after 1945: Theories and some findings. *International Journal of Group Rights, 1*, 79–106. doi:10.1163/157181193X00013

Fein, H. (2007). *Human rights and wrongs: Slavery, terror, genocide.* Boulder, CO: Paradigm.

Hagan, J., & Rymond-Richmond, W. (2008). *Darfur and the crime of genocide.* New York, NY: Cambridge University Press.

Hollander, P. (2006). *The end of commitment: Intellectuals, revolutionaries, and political morality.* Chicago, IL: Ivan R. Dee.

Jost, J. T., Banaji, M. R., & Nosek, B. A. (2004). A decade of system justification theory: Accumulated evidence of conscious and unconscious bolstering of the status quo. *Political Psychology, 25,* 881–919. doi:10.1111/j.1467-9221.2004.00402.x

Kohlberg, L. (1976). Moral stages and moralization: The cognitive developmental approach. In T. Lickona (Ed.), *Moral development and behavior* (pp. 31–53). New York, NY: Holt.

Latané, B., & Darley, J. (1970). *The unresponsive bystander: Why doesn't he help?* New York, NY: Appleton-Crofts.

Lerner, M. (1980). *The belief in a just world: A fundamental delusion.* New York, NY: Plenum Press.

Lerner, M. J., & Simmons, C. H. (1966). Observers' reaction to the "innocent victim": Compassion or rejection? *Journal of Personality and Social Psychology, 4,* 203–210. doi:10.1037/h0023562

Lifton, R. J. (1986). *The Nazi doctors: Medical killing and the psychology of genocide.* New York, NY: Basic Books.

Maslow, A. H. (1971). *The farther reaches of human nature.* New York, NY: Viking.

Morris, B. (2004). *The birth of the Palestinian refugee problem revisited.* New York, NY: Cambridge University Press.

Nets-Zehngut, R. (2009). *Determinants of war veterans, documentary literature: The Israeli case regarding the 1948 Palestinian refugee problem.* Unpublished manuscript.

Oliner, S. B., & Oliner, P. (1988). *The altruistic personality: Rescuers of Jews in Nazi Europe.* New York, NY: Free Press.

Opotow, S. (1990). Moral exclusion and injustice. *Journal of Social Issues, 46,* 1–20. doi:10.1111/j.1540-4560.1990.tb00268.x

Sidanius, J., & Pratto, F. (1999). *Social dominance: An intergroup theory of social hierarchy and oppression.* New York, NY: Cambridge University Press.

Spielman, D., & Staub, E. (2000). Reducing boys' aggression: Learning to fulfill basic needs constructively. *Journal of Applied Developmental Psychology, 21,* 165–181. doi:10.1016/S0193-3973(99)00034-9

Staub, E. (1978). *Positive social behavior and morality: Personal and social influences* (Vol. 1). New York, NY: Academic Press.

Staub, E. (1979). *Positive social behavior and morality: Vol. 2. Socialization and development* New York, NY: Academic Press.

Staub, E. (1989). *The roots of evil: The origins of genocide and other group violence*. New York, NY: Cambridge University Press.

Staub, E. (1997). The psychology of rescue: Perpetrators, bystanders, and heroic helpers. In J. Michalczyk (Ed.), *Resisters, rescuers and refugees: Historical and ethical issues* (pp. 137–147). Kansas City, MO: Sheed and Ward.

Staub, E. (1998). Breaking the cycle of genocidal violence: Healing and reconciliation. In J. Harvey (Ed.), *Perspectives on loss* (pp. 231–238). Washington, DC: Taylor and Francis.

Staub, E. (2003). *The psychology of good and evil: Why children, adults, and groups help and harm others*. New York, NY: Cambridge University Press. doi:10.1017/CBO9780511615795

Staub, E. (2005). The roots of goodness: The fulfillment of basic human needs and the development of caring, helping and nonaggression, inclusive caring, moral courage, active bystandership, and altruism born of suffering. In G. Carlo & C. Edwards (Eds.), *Moral motivation through the life span: Theory, research, applications* (pp. 33–72). Lincoln, NE: University of Nebraska Press.

Staub, E. (2010). *Overcoming evil: Genocide, violent conflict, and terrorism*. New York, NY: Oxford University Press.

Staub, E. (Ed.). (in press). *The panorama of mass violence: Origins, prevention, and reconciliation*. New York, NY: Oxford University Press.

Staub, E., & Baer, R. S., Jr. (1974). Stimulus characteristics of a sufferer and difficulty of escape as determinants of helping. *Journal of Personality and Social Psychology, 30*, 279–284. doi:10.1037/h0036645

Staub, E., & Pearlman, L. A. (2006). Advancing healing and reconciliation. In L. Barbanel & R. Sternberg (Eds.), *Psychological interventions in times of crisis* (pp. 213–243). New York, NY: Springer-Verlag.

Staub, E., & Pearlman, L. A. (2009). Reducing intergroup prejudice and conflict: A commentary. *Journal of Personality and Social Psychology, 96*, 588–593. doi:10.1037/a0014045

Staub, E., Pearlman, L. A., & Bilali, R. (2010). Understanding the roots and impact of violence and psychological recovery as avenues to reconciliation after mass violence and intractable conflict: Applications to national leaders, journalists, community groups, public education through radio, and children. In G. Salomon & E. Cairns (Eds.), *Handbook of peace education* (pp. 269–285). New York, NY: Psychology Press.

Staub, E., Pearlman, L. A., Gubin, A., & Hagengimana, A. (2005). Healing, reconciliation, forgiving and the prevention of violence after genocide or mass killing: An intervention and its experimental evaluation in Rwanda. *Journal of Social and Clinical Psychology, 24*, 297–334. doi:10.1521/jscp.24.3.297.65617

Staub, E., Pearlman, L. A., Weiss, G., & Hoek, A. (in press). Public education through radio to prevent violence, promote trauma healing and reconciliation, and build peace in Rwanda and the Congo. In E. Staub (Ed.), *The panorama of mass violence: Origins, prevention and reconciliation*. New York, NY: Oxford University Press.

Steiner, J. M. (1980). The SS yesterday and today: A socio-psychological view. In J. Dimsdale (Ed.), *Survivors, victims, and perpetrators: Essays on the Nazi Holocaust* (pp. 405–457). New York, NY: Hemisphere.

Stotland, E. (1969). Exploratory studies in empathy. In L. Berkowitz (Ed.), *Advances in experimental social psychology* (pp. 271–313). New York, NY: Academic Press.

Straus, S. (2006). *The order of genocide: Race, power, and war in Rwanda*. Ithaca, NY: Cornell University Press.

Tec, N. (1986). *When light pierced the darkness: Christian rescuers of Jews in Nazi occupied Poland*. New York, NY: Oxford University Press.

Volkan, V. D. (1997). *Blood lines: From ethnic pride to ethnic terrorism*. New York, NY: Farrar, Straus, and Giroux.

Zartman, I. W. (1989). *Ripe for resolution: Conflict and intervention in Africa*. New York, NY: Oxford University Press.

V

SYNTHESIS

22

GOOD AND EVIL, PAST AND FUTURE, LABORATORY AND WORLD

ROY F. BAUMEISTER AND JESSE GRAHAM

Why is there evil? Why do people do immoral things? How do people judge whether an act is right or wrong? How does virtue emerge, even in difficult times? These questions have been addressed in the research on good and evil covered in this volume and at the Herzliya conference on which this book is based. The psychology of morality may have languished for a time, but it has recently entered an exciting phase full of new ideas and methods. The chapters in this volume capture much of that excitement, just as they cover many of these ideas and methods.

This concluding chapter reflects on the work presented at the conference as a window on this newly emerging science of morality. It seeks to glean some insights into where the field is, where it seems to be going, and what additional directions deserve consideration.

PERCEIVING VERSUS DOING EVIL

Since the dawn of history, people have agreed that there is evil in the world and that some of it comes about by human actions. But as observers in this volume, such as Staub (Chapter 21), Skitka (Chapter 19), and Baumeister

(Chapter 20), have emphasized, most people who do evil do not regard their own actions as evil. In comic books and other mythical imaginings, some people knowingly dedicate themselves to evil (e.g., Dr. Evil, The Brotherhood of Evil Mutants), but this is seldom true of the real people known to psychological science.

As Baumeister (1997) concluded, this split between perception and action changes the problem for the social scientist. The age-old question "Why is there evil?" becomes "Why do some people do things that other people perceive as evil?" As a result, research must grapple with two separate problems. One involves perception and judgment: How do people make moral judgments about right and wrong? The other involves the causation of evil: What makes people carry out violent, cruel, or otherwise immoral acts?

Happily (if that is the right word, at least in the context of scientific progress), researchers are at work on both problems, as evidenced in this volume. The topic of moral judgment is thriving, for example, in work by Cushman and Greene (Chapter 2), Bloom (Chapter 4), Eyal and Liberman (Chapter 10), and Pizarro and Tannenbaum (Chapter 5). Meanwhile, others have focused on the causation of violent and other immoral acts, including Staub (Chapter 21), Graham and Haidt (Chapter 1), and Hirschberger and Pyszczynski (Chapter 18), as well as in the large and continually expanding literature on aggression represented by the preceding year's conference and volume (Mikulincer & Shaver, 2010). In this chapter, we reflect on how this work has illuminated moral processes within and between individuals and within and between groups.

INTRAPSYCHIC PROCESSES: MORALITY IN ONE PERSON

Plenty of interesting work has focused on the inner processes associated with morality. Ditto and Liu (Chapter 3) explained that the distinction between factual beliefs and moral opinions is often blurred and even deliberately fudged, insofar as people selectively recruit facts that support their moral opinions. In light of their findings, the assumption that people first study the facts and then construct their moral judgments about them is highly unrealistic.

Indeed, the possibility that moral judgments are often made on an intuitive, emotional, and automatic basis (Haidt, 2001) has become central in current moral psychology. The role of moral reasoning is therefore in question. For decades, psychologists studied moral reasoning on the assumption that it guides and informs choices, but that is no longer tenable. Yet neither is it viable to dismiss moral reasoning entirely. The field is grappling with the problem of how the conscious processes of moral reasoning interact with the intuitive and emotional bases of moral judgments.

The foundations of intuitive moral judgments were explored and explicated by Graham and Haidt (Chapter 1), who proposed that there are five such foundations: harm/care, fairness/reciprocity, ingroup/loyalty, authority/respect, and purity/sanctity. Violations of these principles can elicit moral condemnation in people, but not all five are equally important to all people. Liberals tend to emphasize the first two, whereas all five are about equally important to conservatives. That helps explain why liberals and conservatives tend to see each other's judgments and actions as morally deficient while believing firmly in their own morality (see also Ditto & Liu, Chapter 3; Janoff-Bulman, Chapter 7; and Skitka, Chapter 19).

Individual differences in morality is a theme that echoed in many chapters. Walker, Frimer, and Dunlop (Chapter 15) compared people who received Canada's highest moral honors for heroism and compassion against a matched sample of ordinary people who did not win such awards. Three clusters of highly moral persons emerged. One was marked by strongly communal values of caring about others. A second was marked by a tendency to think and deliberate before taking action (which suggests that moral reasoning may inform some personalities and some action patterns after all). A third was remarkably ordinary, differing in no apparent way from morally average citizens. This last cluster contained many persons who had been recognized for single heroic actions. The implication is that single acts of heroism may emerge mainly from situations and isolated impulses rather than from a particularly outstanding or rare sort of character or personality.

Other traits that have productively attracted the attention of morality researchers include attachment style (Shaver & Mikulincer, Chapter 14) and obsessive–compulsive disorder, which is characterized in part by a preoccupation with one's own immoral thoughts and actions (Doron, Sar-El, Mikulincer, & Kyrios, Chapter 16). Cultural differences in both moral and nonmoral values were noted by Sverdlik, Roccas, and Sagiv (Chapter 12).

The topic of self-deception has been of perennial interest in psychology, and moral psychology has much to contribute. Scientists are studying how people rationalize immoral actions. People can cheat yet continue thinking of themselves as good, honest people, such as by mentally shuffling contexts. Sometimes they even find moral bases for dishonest actions. Ayal and Gino (Chapter 8) provided evidence of "altruistic cheating": People cheat more to benefit someone else than to benefit themselves, at least under certain circumstances. Thus, the assumption that cheating is born of pure self-interest is not tenable. Friendly communication among group members increased the extent to which people cheated for the benefit of other group members.

Some of the most creative methods and ideas on moral hypocrisy were provided by Monin and Merritt (Chapter 9). Hypocrisy and inconsistency are not entirely the same thing, though they overlap. In the "sucker-to-saint" effect (Jordan & Monin, 2008), people who have suffered some disadvantage or relative setback that constitutes a blow to their positive self-image can convert it into a positive source of moral credit by explaining it to themselves as a sign of their virtue: for example, "I failed to get ahead not because I'm a fool, but because I'm a good person who doesn't cheat or take shortcuts." In this light, moral outrage at others' actions might often be what H. G. Wells called "jealousy with a halo" (Wells, 1914, p. 299).

Moral actions have all sorts of effects on the individual. Pearlman (Chapter 17) noted that both perpetrators and victims can feel themselves outside the normal moral order as a result of the transgression. That is, perpetrators feel they have done something wrong, and victims infer there must be something immoral about them to cause them to have deserved what befell them. Meanwhile, Gray and Wegner (Chapter 6) reported that doing morally good—or, especially, morally bad—things can increase agentic feelings of personal strength and lead to better performance on feats of physical strength and endurance.

DYADIC PROCESSES: MORALITY BETWEEN INDIVIDUALS

Much of moral life is interpersonal and serves to regulate how two people treat each other. Gray and Wegner (Chapter 6) provided some impressive evidence that moral relations have an essentially dyadic structure. They termed the two roles *agent* and *patient*. The essence of moral action is that one person does something to another, such as when a hero helps a victim or a villain harms one. Reading moral meanings into nondyadic actions often involves inferring or constructing an agent, for example, when people infer that God must have intentionally caused some natural disaster.

The roles of victim and perpetrator are both essential to interpersonal harm, which nearly all of the chapter authors took as the point of departure for understanding morality (see especially Graham & Haidt, Chapter 1, on the various dichotomies of moral sacredness vs. evil). Baumeister (Chapter 20) contended that these two roles are powerfully motivating. He alluded to his earlier work in which participants wrote stories about transgressions from victim and perpetrator perspectives. Despite the fact that these stories were furnished by the same people on the same occasion, the stories had many systematic differences, such as time frame, accounting for perpetrator intention, victim responsibility, and degree of external causation. Immoral, violent, evil actions seem quite different according to whether one takes the victim's or the perpetrator's perspective.

Interpersonal contexts and meanings change the physical effects of moral actions. Gray and Wegner (Chapter 6) mentioned their remarkable findings that people's subjective experience of pain changes depending on interpersonal context, even though the objective physical stimulus is precisely the same. If the pain comes as a result of an intentional act by someone else—that is, if someone deliberately tries to hurt you—the subjective feeling is more intense than if the pain was accidentally caused by a person or was administered by a machine or computer. Moral meanings seep into physical reality. This echoes Ditto and Liu's (Chapter 3) point that moral meanings alter people's subjective relations to physical facts.

Indeed, the very purpose and function of moral judgments may be to assess the character of other people so as to inform how one relates to them in the future. Pizarro and Tannenbaum (Chapter 5) challenged the conventional wisdom that moral judgments are mainly evaluations of specific actions. True, people pass judgments about acts, but the purpose of these judgments is to build coherent and reliable understandings of the people who perform those acts. After all, once an act has occurred, there may be little pragmatic value to ruminating about it or evaluating it. But learning about what kind of person the actor is can be of great help in knowing whether to trust that person subsequently and whether to build a relationship or avoid that person henceforth.

The view of moral judgment as a means of attributing important character traits to others helps make sense of many seeming exceptions and complications in the moral judgment literature, as Pizarro and Tannenbaum (Chapter 5) explained. People judge not only the action and the intention, but also how the decision was made. Someone who does the right thing for the wrong reason or in the wrong manner is still condemned. For example, sometimes it is necessary to harm someone for the greater good, such as in the much-discussed trolley problem, but people are supposed to perform such acts with appropriate dismay, hesitation, and remorse.

The remarkable findings reported by Bloom (Chapter 4) suggest that people begin to form moral judgments of others quite early in life. Six-month-old babies can apparently distinguish between helpers and hurters, and they alter how they treat those agents accordingly. These processes escalate and become impressively sophisticated in the first years of life. Small children generally dislike broccoli, but some of them will eat broccoli to prevent it from being eaten by someone who wants it—if they think that person is immoral.

The dyadic nature of psychotherapy provided an entry point for a discussion of the moral dimensions of clinical work by Pearlman (Chapter 17), who carefully noted the link between having been victimized oneself and later becoming an immoral agent who victimizes others. And, of course, attachment theory is one of the most influential and successful theories in all of psychology about one-to-one relationships. Shaver and Mikulincer's groundbreaking work linking attachment styles to moral behavior is essential to a full understanding of morality in dyads; in Chapter 14 they explored ways to distinguish authentically moral behavior from superficially similar behavior motivated by efforts to improve one's self-image.

INTRAGROUP PROCESSES: MORALITY WITHIN SOCIAL GROUPS

It is appropriate and probably inevitable that much research examines morality in relation to one person's judgments or two people's interactions, but moral rules have developed mainly in the context of social groups. Morality enables groups of people to live together in peace and harmony. It deals with the conflicts that are an inevitable feature of social life. Most animals have only aggression to resolve such conflicts, but human culture uses moral rules and laws to resolve them (Baumeister, 2005). Indeed, Friedman (2002) proposed that laws and morals serve the same function, namely to restrain selfish and self-interested behavior so as to make harmonious social life in groups possible. The difference, according to Friedman, is that morality relies on long-term relationships that make people care about the opinions of others. As populations expand and social relations become more transient, people have to rely more and more on laws instead of morals. Even in modern big cities with millions of people, where the rule of law is essential for regulating many social interactions, people still use moral pressures to regulate interactions in the context of long-term relationships, such as within families and among friends.

This emphasis on restraining individual self-interest to make group life possible is echoed in the definition of morality offered by Graham and Haidt (Chapter 1). The five foundations of morality all seem aimed at regulating group life. To be sure, the two values emphasized by liberals (harm avoidance and fairness) could be understood in exclusively dyadic terms, though cultures certainly also benefit from them. But the three values recognized by conservatives (loyalty to ingroups, respect for authorities and traditions, and physical/spiritual purity) are fully realized only in larger social systems. One could speculate on that basis that liberals are more attuned to one-to-one interactions and the needs of individuals, whereas conservatives are more attuned to the functions and needs of larger social systems. This line of interpretation gains plausibility from Janoff-Bulman's (Chapter 7) finding that liberal morality is more often prescriptive (focused on what one should do) and conservative morality more often proscriptive (focused on what one should not do).

One might expect sociologists and anthropologists rather than psychologists to lead the way in explicating how morality functions in social systems. Still, the cultural perspective is evident in many of the contributions to this volume, including those by Skitka (Chapter 19); Hirshberger and Pyszczynski

(Chapter 18); Haslam, Bastian, Laham, and Loughnan (Chapter 11); Pizarro and Tannenbaum (Chapter 5); Bloom (Chapter 4); and especially Sverdlik et al. (Chapter 12).

INTERGROUP PROCESSES: MORALITY BETWEEN SOCIAL GROUPS

The Herzliya conference from which this book is derived took place in the Middle East, where intergroup relations have had a long and difficult history and where conflicts between groups remain at the forefront of most citizens' everyday awareness. Intergroup relations crept into many talks at the Herzliya conference and sometimes were central. In fact, "How would you apply these findings to the Israeli–Palestinian situation?" was a common focus of the conference's question-and-answer sessions (usually to the consternation of the speaker, who was expected to provide an answer worthy of King Solomon).

If morals are essentially located in the culture or social group, then relationships between groups are inherently problematic. One cannot assume that other groups share the same moral values and principles, although some thinkers (e.g., Staub, Chapter 21) have sought to establish universal moral principles in light of moral atrocities such as the Holocaust and other genocides. In times of conflict, moral obligations of loyalty to one's own group may easily conflict with impulses to treat members of other groups fairly and avoid harming them (Graham & Haidt, Chapter 1; and Haslam et al., Chapter 11).

Political conflicts occur between groups that are part of larger groups. Many speakers expressed prejudicial and even hostile attitudes toward people who belong to rival political groups within their country or ethnicity (with conservatives bearing the brunt of the hostility). Such comments reflect the struggles that even morality researchers have with the conflict between ideals of universal tolerance and fairness, on the one hand, and intergroup disagreements on the other. On a hopeful note, Skitka (Chapter 19) stated that although America's Republicans and Democrats disagree, they generally respect the American democratic process and generally abide by outcomes that they find disagreeable, such as election losses or U.S. Supreme Court rulings.

The many allusions to politics seemed unusual to us, especially in comparison with other psychological conferences. Political discourse has clearly become an important area for the application of theories and research in moral psychology. Just as conflict between individuals is inevitable in social life, so is conflict between groups. In both cases, limited resources and competing interests make conflict resolution difficult. In nature, aggression is almost the only means of establishing dominance and resolving such conflicts, but human culture permits discussion, negotiation, compromise, and other nonlethal means.

For that to happen, however, the parties must be able to present their case on some basis that both sides can agree on, and morality is one such basis. Without morality, political discourse may be little more than an assertion of one's own interests and preferences. At the same time, as many of the talks at the Herzliya conference showed, different intuitions about or emphases in moral values and convictions can sometimes exacerbate, rather than resolve, political and other intergroup conflicts (see Skitka, Chapter 19; Ditto & Liu, Chapter 3; Graham & Haidt, Chapter 1; and Janoff-Bulman, Chapter 7).

COGNITIVE AND EMOTIONAL PROCESSES

There is little sign in these pages of the Kohlbergian approach to moral reasoning that dominated the psychology of morality for decades. Yet that does not mean that cognition is absent. On the contrary, today's morality researchers are bringing to bear on their subject many of the new theories about social cognition. What may seem business as usual to some social psychologists is, for others, a new page in the study of morality.

Moral judgments are influenced by a broad assortment of cognitive processes. Priming people with one sort of idea influences how they think about what comes to them next. So their responses to moral dilemmas are swayed by whatever they were previously thinking about, as shown in studies by Ditto and Liu (Chapter 3) and Cushman and Greene (Chapter 2). Priming people with thoughts of death changes their moral judgments, often causing harsher judgments—yet sometimes boosting approval of violent acts on behalf of one's own group (Hirschberger & Pyszczynski, Chapter 18). Priming people with creativity makes them become more creative in rationalizing their own dishonest behavior (Ayal & Gino, Chapter 8).

Mental states influence judgments, too. Studies based on construal level theory show that thinking of things in higher level terms with long time spans produces different moral judgments from thinking of things in immediate, concrete terms (Eyal & Liberman, Chapter 10). This difference between abstract, high-level thoughts and concrete, low-level ones is reflected in moral emotions, such as whether guilt or shame is felt, and moral rules, such as whether actions are prescribed or proscribed (Janoff-Bulman, Chapter 7). This is another important response to Haidt's position that moral judgments depend on emotional intuitions more than cognitive responses. Although the power of initial affective responses is undeniable, cognition may come along later and play a decisive role.

In other words, moral judgment emerges from a complex interplay of emotional intuition and reasoning. This is a major theme of Bloom's (Chapter 4) contribution. He discusses how moral reactions are often driven by gut impulses and quick emotional responses, which can be discerned even in the first year of life. Yet with increasing maturity, sophisticated moral reasoning and information from narratives refine and inform these reactions. Bloom's notion of moral progress throughout history, characterized by long-term downward trends in violence and bigotry, suggests interactions between moral intuitions and reasoning at societal as well as individual levels of analysis. Monin and Merritt (Chapter 9) likewise stressed the interplay of affective and motivational forces with reasoning, as Ditto and Liu (Chapter 3) also did but in a different way. Cushman and Greene (Chapter 2) showed that even the principled moral reasoning of people with PhDs in ethical philosophy can be affected by philosophically irrelevant (but emotionally impactful) order manipulations of moral dilemmas. Assor (Chapter 13) discussed a continuum of moral motivations ranging from autonomous to controlled, and he highlighted the positive well-being and behavioral effects of an integrated form of moral motivation. Together, works such as these have helped move the field forward to a new paradigm. The long-dominant emphasis on abstract moral reasoning (the Kohlbergian tradition) was radically challenged by Haidt's emphasis on moral intuition. But instead of seeing these explanations as diametrically opposed, the new generation of morality researchers is groping for a way to understand how they complement each other.

NOTABLY MISSING

Morality is one of the fundamental dimensions of human social life. It would be unrealistic to expect any conference or volume to address all aspects of it. Still, it might be worth noting some important aspects of moral life that deserve more attention than they received in this compilation, excellent as it is.

Nearly all the speakers treated morality in terms of one person harming another. In some cases, that was the explicit and exclusive focus (e.g., Staub, Chapter 21), whereas in others, it was implicit. But it is not the only meaning of morality.

Sexual morality was almost never mentioned at the conference. Yet it is an important dimension of morality for most people. Moreover, it is one that may reflect principles and processes that are different from those of harm-based morality (Young & Saxe, in press). All known societies regulate sexual behavior to some extent, not least because societies and cultures must manage reproduction effectively in order to continue existing and to compete with their neighbors and rivals. Historically, military and economic competition between cultures has often been resolved in favor of the larger group, and so having more bodies is vital. Other factors also contribute to a culture's interest in controlling sexuality with moral rules, such as the jealousies, violent conflicts, scandals, diseases, and symbolic impurities associated with sexual misdeeds.

An anecdote may be relevant. When seeking to fly home after the conference, Graham was held up for a while by airport security personnel, who asked him many questions about what he was doing in Israel and eventually had him get out his laptop, open PowerPoint, and reiterate the gist of his conference presentation. When he got to the part about purity (with photos of S&M sex club patrons), they told him that as an American his views about morality differed from those of Israelis, particularly insofar as Israelis lacked the concern with sexual morality that Americans had (or so they opined). He concurred that cross-cultural differences were important and was soon on his way. Still, if the security officers were correct that sexual morality is of minor concern to Israelis relative to Americans and to members of many other cultures, there may be a valid cultural reason. Most cultures depend heavily on managing sex to sustain and increase their populations. Israel, however, has seen its population swell by immigration, and indeed many Israeli scholars at the conference noted how their society was still integrating the influx of more than a million Russian immigrants (over 10% of the population) in barely a decade. The massive immigration may explain the lesser preoccupation with moralizing sex. Although the United States also deals with high immigration rates, it is possible that American culture-war debates over sexual issues such as gay marriage may reflect unique cultural aspects of America's Puritan roots (Uhlmann, Poehlman, & Bargh, 2009).

Interpersonal harm is generally and everywhere the predominant meaning of evil. Baumeister (1997; see also Chapter 20, this volume) noted, however, that there has been a secondary meaning, which is chaos and disorder. Life is change—but nearly all living things yearn for stability, including a regular, harmonious, and predictable environment. The loss of this peaceful and predictable order is an important form of evil that moral psychology has largely neglected (see also Graham & Haidt, Chapter 1, Table 1.1, on different shared perceptions of evil based on different foundational concerns).

The links between morality and religion received brief mention here and there during the conference, but they have not received research attention commensurate with their historical and cross-cultural importance. For many people, morality is scarcely feasible without a foundation in religious values. The secular foundations of morality remain tentative and problematic, whereas for people with strong religious beliefs, morals obviously come from their god.

Pizarro and Tannenbaum (Chapter 5) made a powerful argument that evaluations of character are central to moral judgment, even though moral philosophers and moral psychologists have concentrated more on evaluations of acts. A similarly compelling (and potentially field-changing) argument has been put forth by neurophilosopher Patricia Churchland (in press). Although most studies of morality posit moral rules that are either broken or not, human morality may in fact be more reliant on prototypes: A current situation may be evaluated based on its general similarities to one or more moral prototypes, in the absence of any specific moral rule governing what should be done in that situation (Churchland, in press). The psychological differences between prototype-based and rule-based moral judgment processes seem a fertile ground for future morality research.

The grand perennial question of free will has recently emerged as a fascinating and controversial topic for psychological research. It, too, was not mentioned at the conference—an unfortunate omission, though it did get some lively informal discussion among the conference attendees. There are many definitions of free will, only some of which are scientifically viable and tractable. (Our use of the term is not intended to invoke any supernatural or noncausal meaning.) At a basic level, however, *free will* means that a person could do different things in a particular situation, and moral and legal codes are based on that assumption. When laypersons come to disbelieve in free will, they seem to abandon their moral sensitivity (e.g., Vohs & Schooler, 2008). The very purpose of morality is presumably to encourage people to use their powers of choice to perform one sort of action rather than another, and thus it essentially assumes that good and evil actions are both possible. Future research and theory about morality seems likely to be drawn into the free will debate and may make profound contributions to it.

Indeed, the possibility that a person could respond to a given situation in different ways is essential to the understanding of morality. The moral dilemmas studied by morality researchers (e.g., those described by Cushman & Greene, Chapter 2) typically rest on the assumption that more than one action is possible. One way to understand these developments is that as consciousness evolved to become social and gained the capacity to simulate non-present realities, it became able to imagine multiple alternative possibilities. Free will refers to the set of psychological capabilities that evolved to deal with such situations by implementing one set of outcomes rather than other, less desirable outcomes. These include self-control, rational choice, and intentional planning. All of these are highly relevant to both moral action (which often entails resisting temptations and antisocial impulses) and moral judgment (where assessments of intention may substantially affect moral judgments; see Pizarro & Tannenbaum, Chapter 5). Morality in particular tends to advocate prosocial actions that may require sacrificing selfish advantage.

By extending their purview to address such issues, morality researchers may make contact with such perennial themes in social psychology as choice and impulse control. If the conference talks are any indication, issues of conscious versus unconscious processes will also be central to such a development.

THE BOTTOM LINE

The psychology of morality may have languished as an uninspiring back-water for several decades, but that has changed dramatically in recent years. Psychologists will have to watch this area for exciting growth and development in the coming years. A deeper and more profound understanding of human morality is emerging. The chapters in this book are a sign of new developments and even greater things to come.

REFERENCES

Baumeister, R. F. (1997). *Evil: Inside human violence and cruelty*. New York, NY: Freeman.

Baumeister, R. F. (2005). *The cultural animal: Human nature, meaning, and social life*. New York, NY: Oxford University Press.

Churchland, P. (in press). *Brain-based values*. Princeton, NJ: Princeton University Press.

Friedman, L. M. (2002). *Law in America: A short history*. New York, NY: Random House.

Haidt, J. (2001). The emotional dog and its rational tail: A social intuitionist approach to moral judgment. *Psychological Review, 108*, 814–834. doi:10.1037/0033-295X.108.4.814

Jordan, A. H., & Monin, B. (2008). From sucker to saint: Moralization in response to self-threat. *Psychological Science, 19*, 809–815. doi:10.1111/j.1467-9280.2008.02161.x

Mikulincer, M., & Shaver, P. R. (Eds.). (2010). *Human aggression and violence: Causes, manifestations, and consequences*. Washington, DC: American Psychological Association.

Uhlmann, E. L., Poehlman, T. A., & Bargh, J. A. (2009). American moral exceptionalism. In J. T. Jost, A. C. Kay, & H. Thorisdottir (Eds.), *Social and psychological bases of ideology and system justification* (pp. 27–53). New York, NY: Oxford University Press. doi:10.1093/acprof:oso/9780195320916.003.002

Vohs, K. D., & Schooler, J. W. (2008). The value of believing in free will: Encouraging a belief in determinism increases cheating. *Psychological Science, 19*, 49–54. doi:10.1111/j.1467-9280.2008.02045.x

Young, L., & Saxe, R. (in press). When the thought counts less: Intent matters less for incest than assault. *Cognition*.

Wells, H. G. (1914). *The wife of Sir Isaac Harman*. New York, NY: Macmillan.

INDEX

Aristotelian tradition, 283
Aristotle, 71, 95, 110, 135, 282
Army of God, 350
Aronson, E., 170
Asch, S. E., 351, 352–353, 357, 359
Assessments, 277, 278–279
Assimilation, 260
Assor, A., 243, 245–248
Asymmetry, moral, 135–136
Atkins, R., 250
Attachment anxiety
    as attachment dimension, 259, 297
    dysfunctional cognitive processes
        with, 299
    and moral choices, 266–270
    in moral decision making, 264–266
    and obsessive–compulsive disorder,
        294, 298–301
    and prosocial behaviors, 260–263
Attachment avoidance
    as attachment dimension, 259, 297
    dysfunctional cognitive processes
        with, 299
    and moral choices, 267–270
    in moral decision making, 264
    and obsessive–compulsive disorder,
        298
    and prosocial behaviors, 260–263
Attachment-based cognitive–behav-
        ioral therapy, 305
Attachment behavioral system, 258
Attachment figures, 297
Attachment insecurity
    in attachment perspective, 259–270
    and aversive experiences, 298
    and forgiveness, 263
    and morality self-domain, 303–304
    in obsessive–compulsive disorder,
        296–300, 305
Attachment perspective, 257–271
    attachment insecurities in, 259–270
    caregiving in, 259–263
    morality in, 263–270
    prosocial behavior in, 259–263
    theoretical concepts in, 258–259
Attachment security
    in attachment theory, 258
    and authenticity, 264
    and aversive events, 297–298
    and caregiving behaviors, 260

and honesty, 264
and obsessive–compulsive disorder,
    300–301
in romantic relationships, 261–262
in self-transcendence values, 261
Attachment style, 259–262, 264
Attachment system, 260
Attachment theory, 260, 297–298
Attitudes Toward War subscale, 25
Attribution theory, 100
Authenticity, 264
Authentic morality, 265
Authoritarian personality, 275
Authority, 19, 386, 388
Authority figures
    destructive obedience to, 352
    and moral courage, 355
    resistance to, 354, 356–357
Authority independence, 354–357
Authority independence hypothesis,
    355–357
Authority/respect foundation, 82, 226
Autonomous moral motivation, 239–253
    benefits of, 243–249
    and controlled motivation, 243–245
    and integrated moral motivation,
        251–253
    and moral motivation, 239
    moral principles and behavior in,
        249–251
    and SDT motivation continuum,
        240–243
Autonomy
    domains of, 141
    ethic of, 224, 225, 227–228
    and freedom, 251
    in moral judgments, 227
Autonomy support
    correlates of, 247–249
    defined, 245
    in educational contexts, 252
    in self-determination theory,
        252–253
Aversive events, 297–298
Aversive experiences, 298
Avoidance motivation
    emotions in, 138–139
    in political conservatism, 140–143
    and proscriptive morality, 135–136
    as self-regulation, 133

Avoidant attachment. *See* Attachment
 avoidance
Awards, 403
Awareness, 318–319
Ayal, S., 156–158
Ayers, Bill, 22

Babies, 75–79
Bad faith, 173–174
Balance, moral, 177–178
Banal actions, 383
Banality of evil, 276, 279–281
Bandura, A., 208, 338, 342, 343, 389
Barkan, R., 161
Bar Kochbah revolt, 331
Baron, J., 14, 39, 59, 190
BAS (behavioral activation system),
 133, 135
Basic needs theory, 384–385
Bastian, B., 208, 215
Batson, C. D., 169, 171, 259
Bauman, C. W., 355n2
Baumeister, R. F., 17, 402
Baumrind, D., 139
Bazerman, M. H., 152
Beaman, A., 157–158
Becker, E., 132
Behavior(s). *See also* Moral behavior
 as adaptations to maltreatment,
  319
 altruistic, 239
 of caring, 5, 138, 383, 393
 constraints on, 4–5
 delinquent, 353
 environmentally harmful, 179
 everyday unethical, 149
 integration of moral principles with,
  249–251
 plans for, 193–196
 reframing of, 160–161
 sexual, 409–410
Behavioral activation system (BAS),
 133, 135
Behavioral inconsistency, 169–179
 and hypocrisy, 168–169
 moral hypocrisy as, 169–171
 moral hypocrisy without, 171–174
 and moral integrity, 179–180
 without hypocrisy, 174–179
 without moral hypocrisy, 171–174

Behavioral inhibition system (BIS),
 133, 135
Beirut Massacre, 64
Beliefs. *See also* Factual beliefs; Moral
 beliefs
 about negative thoughts, 301
 dysfunctional, 295
 in gods, 12–13
 moral circle of, 84–85
 threats to, 333
Benevolence, 22, 198, 226
Benson, S. M., 157
Bentham, J., 283
Benton, J., 154
Berlin, I., 11–12, 16, 17, 22, 26
Bhar, S. S., 295–296, 299
Bias
 in act-based approach, 98–99
 in character-based approach, 99
 in moral judgments, 97
 and moral naiveté, 64–65
 negativity, 135
 in social scientists, 367–368
Bicultural individuals, 230–231
BIS (behavioral inhibition system),
 133, 135
Björklund, F., 23, 191–192
Blame. *See also* Moral blame
 criteria for, 96
 defined, 94
 judgments of, 98–104
 and typecasting, 120–121
Blehar, M. C., 297
Bloom, P., 83, 96–97
Body equilibrium, 376
Bombings, 21
Boundaries
 ingroup–outgroup, 142–143
 of moral concern, 210–212
 in psychotherapy, 313–314
Bounded choice, 353
Bounded ethicality, 152
Bowlby, J., 258–260
Bravado, 376
Brewer, M., 100
Brewin, C., 302
Broide, G., 248
Brown, L., 319
The Buddha, 324
Burton, K. D., 250

Bush, George W., 336
Bystanders
    behavior of, 387
    external or passive, 387, 391–392
    in victim–perpetrator–bystander
        dynamic, 323

Callero, P. L., 250
Capital punishment, 58, 58n1
Care, morality of, 222
Caregiving, 259–263
Caregiving behavioral system,
    259–260
Caring, inclusive, 394
Caring behaviors. *See also* Harm/care
        foundation
    and cognitive approach, 5
    emotions in, 383
    prescriptive morality in, 138
    of rescuers, 393
Carlson, K. A., 176
Cartesian theater, 44
Carver, C. S., 133, 138
Categorical imperative, 283
Catholic Church, 155
Causal attribution, 37–40
Causal deviance scenario, 278
Causal direction
    assessment of, 277
    in deontological dissonance,
        60–61
    in moral heroism, 287
    in moral judgment, 83–84
    in objectification, 213
    in OCD studies, 304
Causation
    and intention, 96–97
    judgments of, 98
    in legal tradition, 41–42
    theories of, 42
Central values, 198
Chaiken, S., 194–196
Change, 177, 314
Chaos, 371–372, 410
Character-based approach
    accountability in, 100–101
    emotional callousness in, 101–102
    situational constraints in, 103
    to understanding blame, 97–99
    unintentional harm in, 100

Character evaluation
    as basis for moral blame, 97–99
    as function of moral judgments, 405
    in level of blame assigned, 104
    in moral blame, 91–93
Charitable giving, 154, 157
Cheating
    altruistic, 158, 403
    moral reminders about, 152–153
    ordinary, 150
Child crime victims, 319
Childhood maltreatment
    adaptations to, 319
    boundary violations with, 314
    passivity in survivors of, 316
    survivor perspective of, 315
    therapist response to, 319–322
Children, 115, 134–135
Choice
    autonomy in, 251
    bounded, 353
    different values applying to same, 198
    moral, 60–61, 266–270
    moral principles in, 185
Chomsky, Noam, 81, 82
"Chosen trauma," 390
Chow, R., 135, 173
Chun, D. S., 264
Churchland, P., 410–411
Cialdini, R. B., 159
Cikara, M., 213
Circle, moral, 84–85, 210–212
Circumstances, mitigating, 190–191
Clark, D. A., 295–296
Cleanliness, 336–337
Cleansing, moral, 153–157
Clinical samples, 304
CLT. *See* Construal level theory
Codes, moral, 224–225
Codes of conduct, 383
Cognition, cultural, 59
Cognitive–behavioral theories, 295
Cognitive–behavioral therapy, 305,
    316–317
Cognitive dissonance. *See also* Deonto-
        logical dissonance
    and ethical dissonance, 150–151
    with hypocrisy, 170–171
    with moral dilemmas, 56–57
Cognitive models, 299

Cognitive processes, 312, 408–409
Cognitive–rationalist approaches, 5–6
Cognitive restructuring, 343–344
Cognitive systems, 40–41
Cohen, A. B., 173–174
Cohen, F., 336
Cohen, G. L., 180
Cohen, J. D., 52
Colby, A., 250, 281
Collective memories, 392–393
Collins, N. L., 261–262
Colonialism, 373
Comic books, 402
Communism, 388–389
Community, ethic of, 224–225
Comparison, advantageous, 342–343
Comparisons, social, 158–161
Compass, moral, 353–354
Compassion, 73, 334
Compatibility principle, 193–194
Complexity, 34, 37–40
Compliance, 155
Compromise, 354
Compulsions, 294
Compulsive caregiving, 261
Concrete language, 135, 136
Conditional negative regard, 247
Conditional positive regard, 247
Conditional regard, 245–247
Conduct, codes of, 383
Confabulation, moral, 56–59
Confession, 155–157, 179
Conflict. *See also* Violent conflict
    aggression in, 373–374
    between groups, 382–383, 385–387
    moral, 55–56
    and morality, 406
Conformity
    cross-cultural differences in value
        of, 22
    to group opinion, 352–354
    and moral convictions, 357,
        359–360
    resistance to, 362–363
Connection, 388
Connell, J. P., 243, 246
Conscience, 131–144
    development of, 139
    in liberalism and conservatism,
        139–143

    and moral asymmetry, 135–136
    and moral regulation, 133–135
    and regulatory balance, 143–144
    and self-regulation, 133
    and shame vs. guilt, 136–139
Conscience and Corporate Culture
    (K. E. Goodpaster), 131
Conscience of a Conservative
    (B. M. Goldwater), 131
The Conscience of a Liberal
    (P. Krugman), 131
The Conscience of a Libertarian
    (W. A. Root), 131
Consciousness, 131, 241, 390, 394
Conscious processes, 411
Consensus, 359
Consequentialist approach
    cost–benefit analyses in, 54–55
    moral blame in, 95
    moral naiveté in, 64–65
    psychological distance in, 192
Consequentialist intuitions, 59–60,
    65–67
Conservation values
    autonomy in, 228
    basis for, 225–226
    defined, 221
    and multiple identities, 231
Conservatives Without Conscience
    (J. W. Dean), 131
Conservatism. *See* Political
    conservatism
Consistency, moral, 168–169
Construal level theory (CLT), 185–199
    basic assumptions of, 186–188
    behavioral inconsistency in, 178–179
    moral judgment in, 190–198
    moral principles and values in,
        188–189
Constructions, cultural, 74–75
Consumer evaluations, 196–197
Contact, 85
Contextual variables, 152–153
Control. *See also* Self-control
    judgments of, 98–104
    maternal, 246
    by religion, 336
Controlled morality, 239–240
Controlled motivation, 243–245
Conventional domain, 224

Human character, 283
Humanistic consciousness, 241
Humanity, shared, 203, 334, 340
Human nature, 205–206, 208, 210, 212, 214
Humanness, 203–215
    in dehumanization, 204–206
    as distant from creatureliness, 337
    innate moral endowment of, 72
    and interpersonal violence, 324
    and meat eating, 214–215
    in moral circle membership, 210–212
    and moral status, 206–210
    and objectification, 212–214
Human papillomavirus (HPV), 59
Human uniqueness, 205–208, 210, 212, 214
Human welfare, 381–382
Hume, David, 71, 76, 82, 83, 132
Humean theory, 83–85
Hurricane Katrina, 117
Hyperactivation, 258–259
Hypocrisy. *See* Moral hypocrisy

Idealism, 375
Idealistic evil, 18
Idealistic violence, 18, 25, 375, 377
Identification, 159–160
Identified morality, 241–242
Identified motivation, 249, 250
Identity(-ies). *See also* Social identities
    in adverse life conditions, 387–388
    and goals, 250
    moral, 340–344
    in moral behavior, 288
    multiple, 231
    social, 142
Ideological narratives, 16–22
Ideology(-ies)
    under adverse life conditions, 388–389
    in escalation of violence, 386–387
    in group conflict, 386
    in group violence, 392–393
    social influences vs., 195
IED (inclusion–exclusion discrepancy), 212
Iliev, R., 155
Immigrants, 230–231
Immigration, 410

Immoral actions, 382, 383
Immoral intrusive thoughts, 301
Imperial colonialism, 373
Impulsivity, 102, 103
Inbar, Y., 103
Incest, 35, 279, 318
Inclusion–exclusion discrepancy (IED), 212
Inclusive caring, 394
Inconsistency, moral, 168–169
Incontinence, 175
Indelible victim effect, 116
Independence, authority, 354–357
Individual level
    differences at, 279–281
    morality at, 229, 402–404
Industrial societies, 73
Inequality, 390–391
Infants, 75–79, 258
Infrahumanization, 204–205, 339–340
Ingroup/loyalty foundation
    as dimension of moral domain, 225, 226
    early competence in, 82
    ideological narratives with, 19–22
Ingroup–outgroup boundaries, 142–143
Ingroups
    double standard applied to, 171
    in ethic of autonomy, 228
    humanness of, 205
    identification with members of, 159–160
    loyalty to, 336
Inhibitive agency, 207, 208
Injunctive norms, 159, 160
Innate morality, 72
Innocence, 122, 370–371
Inoculation hypothesis, 357–360
Insecurity, 321–322
Insights, moral, 85
Instrumentality, 372
Instrumental violence, 372–374, 377
Integrated moral motivation, 240, 242, 249–251
Integrating values and moral outlooks, 229–231
Integrity, moral, 169
Intention(s)
    and causation, 96–97
    judgments of, 98–104

Moral principles, *continued*
  overwhelment of, 381
  of rescuers, 250–251
  as universals, 219
  in values perspective, 220–222
Moral psychology
  application of, 276–277
  intuitive processes in, 132
  sacredness in, 14–15
  as scientific field, 71
  studies of real-life moral conflict
    situations in, 279
Moral purification, 154
Moral realism, 52–53, 57
Moral reasoning
  deontological perspective on, 189
  global principles underlying, 189
  immature, 275
  in moral judgments, 83
  and moral motives, 243
  and obsessive–compulsive disorder,
    302
  rationalizations in, 34–35
  role of, 402
  stage theories of, 75
Moral regulation
  asymmetry between systems of,
    135–136
  and conscience, 133–135
  conscience as, 132
  imbalances in, 143–144
  moral licensing in, 155
  in politics, 140–143
Moral relativism, 242
Moral rescuers, 251
Moral responsibility
  in blame judgments, 94
  in factual causation, 41
  and mental capacity, 111–113
  in proximate causation, 42
  situational constraints in, 102–103
  of therapist, 318–320
Moral rules, 190, 192
Morals, 313
Moral seduction, 353–354
Moral sensitivity, 301–304
Moral standards, 352
Moral status, 206–210, 213
Moral superiority, 155
Moral systems, 14–15

Moral typecasting, 119–124
Moral universals, 72–75
Moral violations, 220–221
Morgan, G. S., 281
Mortality salience
  and infrahumanization, 340
  and moral amplification, 338
  and moral disengagement, 342–343
  and moral foundations theory,
    334–337
Mother Teresa, 120, 282
Motivated consequentialism, 59–60
Motivated reasoning, 5
Motivation
  for actions perceived as evil, 361
  approach vs. avoidance, 135–136
  for character evaluations, 92–93,
    97–98
  controlled, 243–245
  goals as, 252–253
  guilt as, 136–139
  identified, 249, 250
  for moral regulation, 133–135
  for prosocial behavior, 240–243
  shame as, 136–139
  for types of values, 221–222
Motivation and action theories, 384–385
Motives, ulterior, 173–174
Motyl, M., 339–340
Moulding, R., 297, 299
Moynihan, Patrick, 67
Much, N. C., 224, 284
Muentener, P., 42
Mullen, E., 356
Multiple identities, 230–231
Multiple moralities, 230–231
Murnane, T., 213
Murphy, S., 23
Murray, K. T., 134

Nadler, J., 356
Nagin, Ray, 117
Naiveté, 64–65
Naiveté, moral, 64–65
Narcissism, 374
Narratives
  ideological, 16–22
  as individual in context, 288
  sacred principles in, 19–22
National Alliance, 19–20

Proactive agency, 207–208
Production theory of causation, 42
Profanity, 13–14
Prohibitions, 142
Proscriptive morality
    in moral asymmetry, 135–136
    in moral regulation, 133–134
    in parenting, 139
    in political conservatism, 140–143
    shame in, 137–138
Prosocial behavior
    in attachment perspective, 259–263
    and attachment style, 260–261, 264
    identified motivation in, 250
    and intrinsic value demonstration,
        247–248
    and moral identity, 340–341
    and mortality salience, 335
    motivation for, 240–243
    and parenting style, 248–249
    in self-determination theory, 243–249
Protected values, 14, 59, 190
Protection, 142
Protestant ethic, 134
Prototype-based moral judgment, 411
Proximal causes, 377–379
Proximate causation, 41–43
Proximity, 41
Psychological distance
    and compassion, 73
    in construal level theory, 185–188
    in inoculation hypothesis, 357
    mechanisms of, 391–392
    and moral judgment, 192
    and moral principles, 189
    and persuasion, 196–197
    and values-based behavioral plans,
        193–196
    in values vs. mitigating circumstances,
        190–191
Psychological forces
    in genocide and violent conflict,
        381–384
    in moral blame, 93–98
    in victim blaming, 122–123
Psychological needs, 384–385
Psychological woundedness, 386, 390
Psychopathy, 377
Psychotherapy, 311, 313–320
Public schools, 248

Punishment
    capital, 58, 58n1
    in conscience development, 139
    deserved, 38
    fear of, 316
    as justice, 389
    moral intuitions about, 74, 78–79
Purdon, C., 295–296
Pure evil, 92, 368–372
Purification, moral, 154
Purity/sanctity foundation, 82, 226,
        335–337
Pyszczynski, T., 334, 336, 339–340

Qualitative approach, 19–22
Quantitative approach, 22–26

Rachman, S., 295–296, 301
Rage, 103
Random sampling, 280
Rashness, 103
Rational deliberation, 84, 85
Rationalistic approach, 5. See also
        Cognitive–rationalist approaches
Rationalistic theory of ethics, 5
Rationalizations, 34–35, 156
Rational person model, 6
Rational perspective, 52
Rawls, John, 81, 85, 281
Reaction formation, 301
Realism, moral, 52–53, 57
Reality, objective, 58n1, 367, 368
Reality, physical, 404–405
Real-life experiences
    in experimental methodology,
        284–286
    folk theories about, 43–44
    in laboratory settings, 278
    moral and factual beliefs in, 61–63
    moral psychology explanations for,
        276–277
Reasoning. See also Moral reasoning
    in cognitive approach, 5
    deliberative, 52
    motivated, 5
    in philosophical perspective, 34–37
Rebellion, 172–173
Reciprocity, 74. See also Fairness/
        reciprocity foundation
Reconciliation, 392–393

ABOUT THE EDITORS

Mario Mikulincer, PhD, is professor of psychology and dean of the New School of Psychology at the Interdisciplinary Center in Herzliya, Israel. He has published five books—*Human Helplessness: A Coping Perspective; Dynamics of Romantic Love: Attachment, Caregiving, and Sex; Attachment in Adulthood: Structure, Dynamics, and Change; Human Aggression and Violence: Causes, Manifestations, and Consequences;* and *Prosocial Motives, Emotions, and Behavior: The Better Angels of our Nature*—and over 280 scholarly journal articles and book chapters. Dr. Mikulincer's main research interests are attachment theory, terror management theory, personality processes in interpersonal relationships, coping with stress and trauma, grief-related processes, and prosocial motives and behavior. He is a member of the editorial boards of several scientific journals, including the *Journal of Personality and Social Psychology, Psychological Inquiry,* and *Personality and Social Psychology Review,* and he has served as associate editor of two journals, the *Journal of Personality and Social Psychology* and *Personal Relationships.* Recently, he was elected to serve as chief editor of the *Journal of Social and Personal Relationships.* He is a fellow of the Society for Personality and Social Psychology and the Association for Psychological Science. He received the EMET Prize in Social Science for his contributions to psychology and the

Berscheid–Hatfield Award for Distinguished Mid-Career Achievement from the International Association for Relationship Research.

Phillip R. Shaver, PhD, a social and personality psychologist, is Distinguished Professor of Psychology at the University of California, Davis. Before moving there, he served on the faculties of Columbia University, New York University, University of Denver, and State University of New York at Buffalo. He has coauthored and coedited numerous books, including *In Search of Intimacy; Measures of Personality and Social Psychological Attitudes; Measures of Political Attitudes; Handbook of Attachment: Theory, Research, and Clinical Applications; Attachment in Adulthood: Structure, Dynamics, and Change; Human Aggression and Violence: Causes, Manifestations, and Consequences;* and *Prosocial Motives, Emotions, and Behavior: The Better Angels of our Nature,* and he has published over 200 scholarly journal articles and book chapters. Dr. Shaver's research focuses on attachment, human motivation and emotion, close relationships, personality development, and the effects of meditation on behavior and the brain. He is a member of the editorial boards of *Attachment and Human Development, Personal Relationships,* the *Journal of Personality and Social Psychology,* and *Emotion,* and has served on grant review panels for the National Institutes of Health and the National Science Foundation. He has been executive officer of the Society of Experimental Social Psychology and is a fellow of both the American Psychological Association and the Association for Psychological Science. Dr. Shaver received a Distinguished Career Award and a Mentoring Award from the International Association for Relationship Research and has served as president of that organization.